MEDIEVAL ADAPTATION, SETTLEMENT AND ECONOMY OF A COASTAL WETLAND

THE EVIDENCE FROM AROUND LYDD, ROMNEY MARSH, KENT

MEDIEVAL ADAPTATION, SETTLEMENT AND ECONOMY OF A COASTAL WETLAND

THE EVIDENCE FROM AROUND LYDD, ROMNEY MARSH, KENT

by Luke Barber and Greg Priestley-Bell
with major contributions by Mark Gardiner and Sheila Sweetinburgh

Archaeology
South-East

University College London Field Archaeology Unit

for English Heritage

ENGLISH HERITAGE

OXBOW BOOKS

Published by
Oxbow Books, Oxford, UK

© Oxbow Books, Luke Barber, Greg Priestley-Bell
and the individual authors, 2008

ISBN 978-1-84217-240-7

This book is available direct from

Oxbow Books, Oxford, UK
(Phone: 01865-241249; Fax: 01865-794449)

and

The David Brown Book Company
PO Box 511, Oakville, CT 06779, USA
(Phone: 860-945-9329; Fax: 860-945-9468)

or from our website

www.oxbowbooks.com

*Front cover image: Reconstruction drawing of the 13th century landscape looking south-east
(Casper Johnson © UCLFAU)*

Printed and bound at Gomer Press
Llandysul, Wales

Contents

Acknowledgements

Thanks are due to Brett Gravel Ltd. for funding the excavations at Lydd Quarry and in particular Richard Hambley of Bretts for constant help throughout the project. ARC funded the fieldwork at Denge West and Caldicott Farm and particular thanks must go to Robin Lane for help throughout. English Heritage, through the Aggregates Levy Sustainability Fund (ALSF), funded the compilation of this monograph from all the different archive reports, as well as enabling historical research and scientific analysis on the pottery. Dr Helen Keeley, Chris Scull, Gareth Watkins and Karla Graham (English Heritage) are acknowledged for their help and advice throughout the ALSF stage of the work.

Continuing help and advice, particularly regarding the formulation of the excavation strategies, was given by Dr John Williams, Sally Howard and Wendy Rogers of Kent County Council. All Field Archaeology Unit staff are also owed thanks, especially for working so hard in some particularly unpleasant weather conditions: project managers Mark Gardiner, Chris Place, Tony Pollard and Ian Greig; the excavation directors: Ian Greig (Lydd 1), Greg Priestly-Bell (Lydd Stages 2 to 4 and 7–11 (part) and Denge West watching briefs), Jennifer Sawyer (Lydd 5/6), Casper Johnson (Lydd 11 (part)), Simon Stevens (Denge West field-walking), and all the excavators who are too numerous to mention, although special thanks must be given to Robert Beck. The help and interest of Jill Eddison is also gratefully appreciated.

Thanks are also due to all the specialists who have helped in studying the excavated material: David Atkinson, Tessa Machling, Chris Place, Pat Hinton, Ian Riddler, Rob Scaife, Rowena Gale, Louise Bashford, Elizabeth Somerville, Wendy Wood, Sue Browne, Deborah Jacques, Harry Kenward, Lucy Sibun, Sophie Seel, Adrian Tribe, Diana E. Friendship-Taylor. Thanks must also go to Jane Russell, Rob Gollar, Justin Russell and Fiona Griffin for producing the illustrations, and Casper Johnson for the reconstructions.

Sheila Sweetinburgh would like to thank Andrew Butcher, Spencer Dimmock, Gillian Draper and especially Mark Gardiner for allowing her to use material from their unpublished research. Dorothy Beck, Beryl Coatts and Anne Reeves similarly very generously gave of their time and expertise and she is extremely grateful for all their help. She should like to express her gratitude to Mary Dixon and Paul Cullen for permission to consult their unpublished doctoral work; and to Sally Elks similarly with regard to her MA dissertation. Some of the evidence used here on the fishing industry and on Christchurch Priory's marshland holdings was compiled as part of two projects funded by the Romney Marsh Research Trust, the latter under the direction of Andrew Butcher. Special thanks must also go to Dorothy Beck for organising the aerial photography at Lydd 1 and the late Graham Alleyne for undertaking it.

Luke Barber would particularly like to thank John Cotter, Duncan Brown and Alan Vince for help with some of the ceramics and John Cooper (Booth Museum of Natural History, Brighton) and Dr Bernard Worssam for help with identification of many of the stone types, Giles Guthrie of Maidstone Museum for help obtaining copyright for Fig. 3 and John Willson for comments regarding the original excavations at the Pioneer Pit.

Elizabeth Somerville would like to extend her thanks to Helen Crudgington and David Dunkin who did the initial identification and measuring of the shells from Lydd 1, and to John Bonnell for the initial identification and measuring of shells from Lydd 2 and 3.

Summary

Since 1991 excavations in advance of gravel extraction around Lydd on Romney Marsh have uncovered large areas of medieval landscape. Most of the work has been concentrated at Brett's Lydd Quarry, though ARC's quarries at Denge West and Caldicott Farm have also yielded important data.

Prior to reclamation the silted salt marsh appears to have been utilised for rough grazing. During the 12th century a system of drainage ditches was begun to improve the land, initially for pastoralism, but subsequently for arable cultivation. The construction of an earthen sea defence wall across the end of the initial ditch system later in the 12th century suggests either a response to increasing threats from flooding, or a greater emphasis on arable cultivation which could not tolerate even minor incursions of flooding. Judging by the dating from the different sites, the reclamation in the area appears to be somewhat piecemeal, though most ditch systems were in place by the end of the 13th century.

Following the establishment of the ditched field system and its associated trackways, more permanent occupation sites began to appear in the form of a number of small farmsteads and associated 'activity' areas. These appear to have been based on a mixed agricultural economy, though they were also supplemented by the exploitation of local natural resources. The sites to the south of Lydd, at Denge West, may have had a much greater reliance on fishing than those at Lydd Quarry, reflecting their closer proximity to the sea.

The density of settlement appears to drop off during the 14th century, possibly due, in part, to the great storms of the late 13th century. This decline rapidly increases at Lydd Quarry in the later 14th to 15th centuries, indicating depopulation of this area of the marsh at this time, probably in association with the increase in the use of the land for sheep. During this same period many of the field ditches were infilled to amalgamate smaller fields into larger ones. The settlement at Denge West, perhaps due to its slightly different economic basis, continued throughout this period, but it too was abandoned during the 16th century.

The excavations at the different sites have allowed an unprecedented opportunity to study the reclamation, occupation and economy of a large tract of marginal landscape through a considerable period of time.

Résumé

Depuis 1991, les travaux d'extraction de roche dans les environs du Romney Marsh, Lydd, ont mis à jour un vaste site médiéval. Cette découverte a mené à entreprendre des recherches plus approfondies. Les travaux ont été menés principalement dans les carrières de Brett, Lydd, bien que les carrières d'ARC à Denge West et Caldicott Farm aient également permis de rassembler d'importantes données.

Avant la mise en valeur de la région, le marais semble avoir été utilisé comme zone de pâturage. Au 12ème siècle, un système de drainage avait commencé à être introduit dans le but d'améliorer le terrain, pour l'élevage initialement, puis pour la culture des terres. Un rempart en terre, construit vers la fin du 12ème siècle, à l'extrémité des canaux de drainage d'origine, laisse supposer une mesure de protection contre les risques croissants d'inondation ou l'intention d'encourager la culture du terrain, et ainsi protéger les terres de la moindre crue. A en juger par la datation des différents sites, la mise en valeur du terrain semble avoir été plutôt parcellaire, cependant la plupart des canaux de drainage était en place à la fin du 13eme siècle.

Dans les champs, à la suite de la mise en place de ce réseau de drainage et de leurs routes adjacentes, ces sites commençaient à se peupler de manière plus permanente. On voit apparaitre un certain nombre de fermes et de zones d'activités similaires. Celles-ci semblent avoir survécu grâce à une activité agricole mixte, également soutenue par l'exploitation des ressources naturelles locales. Les sites au Sud de Denge West comptaient certainement d'avantage sur la pêche, comme le suggère la proximité des sites de la carrière de Lydd avec la mer.

Le nombre de villages semble avoir diminué au 14ème siècle. Ce phénomène a pu être causé, en partie, par les orages de la fin du 13ème siècle. Ce déclin s'est rapidement accéléré au 14ème et 15ème siècle dans les environs de la carrière de Lydd. A cette époque, on note un dépeuplement de la région marécageuse, probablement du fait de l'augmentation de l'utilisation du terrain pour l'élevage de moutons. Pendant cette même période, dans les champs, les canaux de drainage ont été comblés afin de former de plus grand espaces à partir des différentes parcelles de terrain. Le village de Denge West, quant à lui, était alors toujours habité, probablement car il reposait sur une activité économique différente. Pour autant, lui aussi a été abandonnée au 16ème siècle.

Les fouilles menées sur ces différents sites nous ont donné une opportunité sans précédent d'étudier le développement de la population, l'économie et la mise en valeur de vastes espaces précaires sur une période de temps considérable.

Zusammenfassung

Seit 1991 wurden in der Umgebung von Lydd on Romney Marsh bei der Kiesgewinnung in einem Steinbruch grosse Flächen von mittelalterlichen Landschaften zum Vorschein gebracht. Die meiste Arbeit hat am Steinbruch in Brett's Lydd Quarry stattgefunden und auch in West-Denge und in der Gegend von Caldicott Farm haben sich wichtige Funde ergeben.

Vor der Landgewinnung wurde die Wattmarsch zum Fettgrasen benutzt. Während des 12. Jahrhunderts wurde ein dichtes Netz von Gräben auf Anlandungsfeldern angelegt, anfänglich zum Weiden von Schafen, und später zum Ackerbau. Im späteren 12. Jahrhundert baute man sichere Seedeiche um das neue Ackerland. Das deutet auf eine erhöhte Ueberschwemmungsgefahr oder auf einen grösseren Bedarf von Ackerbau, bei dem keine Ueberschwemmungen in Kauf genommen werden konnten. Den Untersuchungen gemäss sieht man, dass dieses Neuland Stück für Stück zu verschiedenen Zeitpunkten erworben wurde, obwohl die meisten Gräben bis Ende des 13. Jahrhunderts angelegt worden waren.

Nach der Anlegung des Grabennetzsystems und deren angeschlossenen Kanälen, erschienen beständigere Landstrecken in Form von kleinen Bauernhöfen und Geschäftsunternehmen, die damit verbunden waren. Diese waren auf eine gemischte Agrarwirtschaft gegründet, obwohl sie auch zur Gewinnung von Naturbodenschätzen nutzbar gemacht wurden. Die Landflächen südlich von Lydd, in West Denge waren, bedingt durch ihre nähere Lage am Meer in grösserem Masse auf den Fischfang angewiesen, als diejenigen bei Lydd Quarry.

Es schien, dass während des 14. Jahrhunderts das Land weniger dicht besiedelt war, möglicherweise wegen der grossen Stürme gegen Ende des 13. Jahrhunderts. Der Rückgang beschleunigte sich schnell um den Steinbruch von Lydd Quarry am Ende des 14. und 15. Jahrhunderts. Das deutete auf eine Entvölkerung dieser Marschgegend zu diesem Zeitpunkt, wahrscheinlich im Zusammenhang mit der zunehmenden Nutzung des Landes zum Weiden von Schafen. Während derselben Zeit wurden viele der Kanäle wurden gefüllt um kleinere Weiden an grössere anzuschliessen. Die Siedlung im West-Dengegebiet wurde, wahrscheinlich wegen ihrer Sonderwirtschaftslage, während dieser ganzen Zeitspanne weitergeführt, aber auch diese wurde während des 16. Jahrhunderts aufgegeben.

Die Ausgrabungen auf den verschiedenen Landflächen bieten uns eine einmalige Gelegenheit diese Randlandschaft des Neulands und dessen Ansiedlung und Bewirtschaftung über eine längere Zeitspanne zu untersuchen und zu studieren.

List of Figures

List of Tables

Pottery

1. Medieval and post-medieval pottery assemblages from Lydd Quarry, excavation Phases 1–11
2. Site A (Lydd 10): Combined pottery assemblage from building post-holes
3. Site A (Lydd 10): Combined pottery assemblage from Ditches A19, A65, A67 and Drain A17
4. Site A (Lydd 10): Pottery assemblage from Pit A62, Fill A64
5. Site D (Lydd 1): Pottery from Context 151
6. Site H (Lydd 2): Pottery from Context 2400.
7. Site H (Lydd 2): Minimum number of vessels in Context 2400
8. Site G (Lydd 5/6): Pottery from Context 5120
9. Site G (Lydd 5/6): Pottery from Context 5092
10. Site G (Lydd 5/6): Pottery from Context 5359
11. Site G (Lydd 5/6): Pottery from Context 5066
12. Site Ja (Lydd 3): Pottery from Context 3017
13. Site Jb (Lydd 3): Pottery from Context 3318
14. Site Jb (Lydd 3): Pottery from Context 3329
15. Site Jb (Lydd 3): Pottery from Context 3180
16. Site Jb (Lydd 3): Minimum number of vessels in Context 3180
17. Site Jb (Lydd 3): Pottery from Context 3075
18. Site Jb (Lydd 3): Pottery from Context 3105
19. Lydd 5/6: Pottery from Context 5014
20. Site Lb (Lydd 5/6): Pottery from Context 5084
21. Site Jb (Lydd 3): Pottery from Context 3151
22. Lydd 5/6: Pottery from Context 5010
23. Site Lb (Lydd 5/6): Pottery from Context 5287
24. Site Lb (Lydd 5/6): Pottery from Context 5292
25. Lydd 5/6: Pottery from Context 5044
26. Site N (Lydd 5/6): Pottery from Context 5138
27. Denge West: No. of unstratified pottery sherds by period for Areas A–G
28. Denge West North: Pottery from Context 9
29. Denge West North: Pottery from Context 26
30. Denge West North: Pottery from Context 68
31. Denge West South: No. of pottery sherds by period for Fields A–D
32. Denge West South: No. of pottery sherds by period for watching brief
33. Caldicott Farm: Pottery from Context 9
34. Caldicott Farm: Pottery from Context 86

Metalwork

35. Characterisation of metalwork assemblage, by number, from Lydd Quarry (Excavation Phases 1 to 11)
36. Context 5138: quantification of nail types
37. Characterisation of Denge West North ironwork assemblage
38. Denge West North: nails in Contexts 68 and 69

Ceramic Building Material

39. Brick: the quantity of different fabrics in 15th to mid 16th century contexts at Lydd 5/6
40. Tile: the tile in different period contexts at Lydd 5/6
41. Tile in Ditch 5017, Fill 5018 (Lydd 5/6)
42. Denge West: Tile in Cut 67, Fill 68

Geological Material

43. Characterisation of geological material assemblage (worked and unworked) for Lydd Quarry
44. Characterisation of worked stone assemblage for Lydd Quarry

Bone

45. Percentages of butchered, gnawed and burnt bone fragments
46. Lydd Quarry: Quantification of assemblage by phase
47. Percentages of main food species by century
48. MNE: 12th century
49. MNE: 12th/13th century
50. MNE: 13th century
51. MNE: 14th century
52. MNE: 15th/16th century
53. Dental eruption: cattle
54. Dental eruption: sheep/pig

Insects

Marine Molluscs

Pollen, charcoal and wood

Seeds

Colour Figures

A section of colour plates appears at the back of the book.
Illustrations are prefixed with an asterisk "*" in the text (for example, *Fig. 8).

General Introduction

Romney Marsh is the largest coastal lowland on the south coast of England (Fig. 1). It is formed of several linked marshes: Romney Marsh proper forms the eastern portion of the whole, with the 'younger' Walland Marsh forming the majority of the western portion with Denge Marsh to the south. Despite the internal divisions, all three portions are collectively known as Romney Marsh. The area has had a long and complex natural history of formation and alteration (Green 1968), which has been the subject of much research in the recent past (Eddison and Green 1988, Eddison 1995, Eddison *et al.* 1998 and Eddison 2000).

It would appear the Marsh was initially created when a shingle barrier started to form in a north-east direction from the area of Hastings around 6,000 years ago. This created a tidal lagoon, with a mouth close to Hythe, in what had previously been a sandy bay open to the sea. Silting in the lagoon soon led to the establishment of mudflats which were colonised by plants and, after further silting, a developed salt-marsh environment with areas of vegetation interspersed with sinuous natural drainage channels. From about 4,800 BC freshwater marsh environments started to appear, firstly in the adjacent river valleys, but spreading out across the former salt-

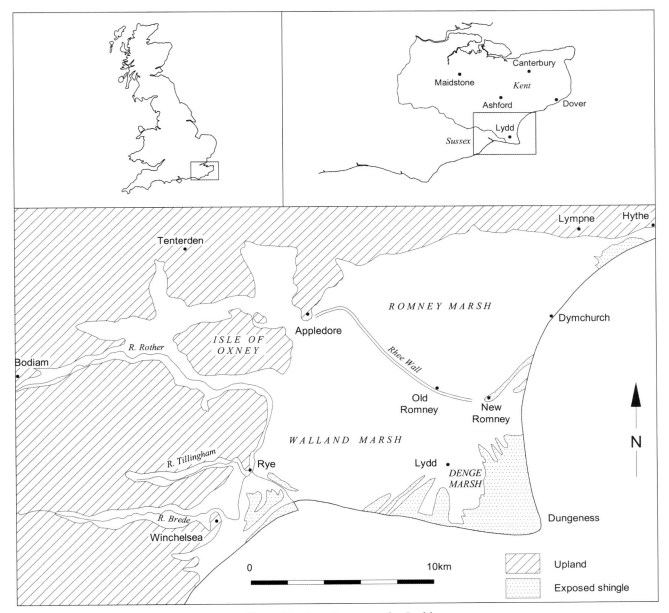

Fig. 1 Site location maps for Lydd

marsh (Long *et al*. 1998, Figs. 4.6 and 4.7). Within this freshwater marsh, peat deposits were being formed. By about 1,000 BC the sea began to slowly reclaim the area, once more depositing further sediments over the peat. As such, by the Roman period large areas of Romney Marsh proper consisted of a large tidal inlet once again and, following continued inundation, the area appears to have been abandoned by man in the 2nd to 3rd centuries AD. However, the process of silting within the lagoon recommenced establishing new areas of mud-flats, which again developed into salt-marsh, but this time the land continued to drain and offered good opportunities for the creation of valuable farmland by the early medieval period (Eddison 2000). The areas of younger sediments, representing the post-Roman deposition, are calcareous and usually at a slightly higher elevation than the earlier sediments, which tend to be decalcified. This has allowed the extent of the later lagoon to be mapped using the present-day topography and soils (Green 1968). Although much of the land is still fertile today, its longevity relies on the constant upkeep of the drainage system and the massive man-made earthen defence walls and natural shingle barriers that protect it from the sea. Its complex history of formation has given rise to a variable series of young geological deposits consisting of peats, clays, silts, sands and, particularly along its south-western edge, flint shingle ridges from barrier beach formation.

Although much research has been undertaken on the development of Romney Marsh, particularly with the encouragement and frequent funding from the Romney Marsh Research Trust (RMRT), until very recently this had primarily used the media of geomorphological, documentary and cartographic research. Comparatively little archaeological work had taken place on the marsh itself despite the rich potential of this resource. The few excavations that had taken place, such as those at Broomhill (Gardiner 1988), New Romney (Rigold 1964 and Willson 1987) and West Hythe (Cross 1997, Gardiner *et al*. 2001), had all been on a small scale. Important archaeological data had also been collected by a number of field-walking surveys. These included those at Old Romney (Gardiner 1994), the line of the proposed New Romney and Dymchurch bypass (Place 1993a, 1993b and 1994) and most importantly, the extensive survey undertaken by Anne Reeves on the Romney Marsh proper (Reeves 1995, 1996 and 1997). The latter studies were of particular interest in that they indicated the potential medieval settlement density on the marsh for the first time.

Archaeological work on the Marsh has increased dramatically since the implementation of PPG 16 in 1991. Most of the developer-funded work during the 1990s was undertaken by the University College London Field Archaeology Unit (UCLFAU) (trading as South Eastern Archaeological Services and subsequently Archaeology South-East). Since the late 1990s fieldwork on the Marsh has been undertaken by a number of other organisations,

though most of this has been confined to the towns of New Romney and Hythe. Fieldwork by UCLFAU at extraction sites such as Lydd Quarry (Fig. 1) (Greig and Gardiner 1996; Priestley-Bell 1999, 2002a, 2002b, 2003, 2004a), Denge West Quarry (Eddison 1992a; Priestley-Bell 1994, 1998 and this volume; Priestley-Bell and Gardiner 1994; Gardiner 1995a; Stevens 1996) and Caldicott Farm Quarry (Priestley-Bell 2004b and this volume) have for the first time provided large-scale excavations on open areas. Archaeological work on new road schemes, such as the Brookland Diversion (Eddison 1992b, Barber 1995a and b) and Stockbridge to Brenzett road (Greig 1992a; 1992b; 1992c; Greatorex 1993; 1994; Priestley-Bell 1995), have been complementary in providing the chance to examine linear transects across the marsh. Although some of the more recent excavations have been on early sites such as the Roman salt-workings at Scotney Court (Barber 1998a) and the important Saxon settlement at West Hythe (Gardiner *et al*. 2001), most, including those of Lydd Quarry, have dealt primarily with the medieval period: the majority of excavated sites dating to between the 12th and early 16th centuries.

These recent excavations and field-walking surveys have added greatly to the earlier small-scale works and have shown that the Marsh was exploited for its resources from at least the Early Bronze Age. More permanent seasonal occupation, primarily concerned with salt-production, appears to have been established by the Romano-British period. Such sites have been found from Dymchurch in the east to Scotney Court in the west (Eddison 2000). However, based on the current evidence, it is not until the onset of the medieval period that major alteration to the natural landscape appears to have begun. The marsh was reclaimed by a series of innings to provide new farmland and the opportunity for permanent settlement on this newly established fringe. The innings, which were certainly well under way during the early medieval period on Romney Marsh proper, were still being undertaken in the early post-medieval period on areas of Walland Marsh and overall provide an interesting insight into man's chronological encroachment onto an inhospitable natural landscape.

As developer-funded rescue work has been the mainstay of recent archaeological work, there is a somewhat haphazard distribution to the excavations. Despite this, the growing body of data from developer-funded work is such that it is proving quite capable of addressing important regional and national research themes. The developer-funded work on the marsh can be categorised into three groups:

i. Residential/commercial development – usually small-scale and set within the towns (particularly New Romney).

ii. Road building – usually medium-scale and providing linear transects across the landscape, sometimes close to existing villages/towns (particularly in the central marsh).

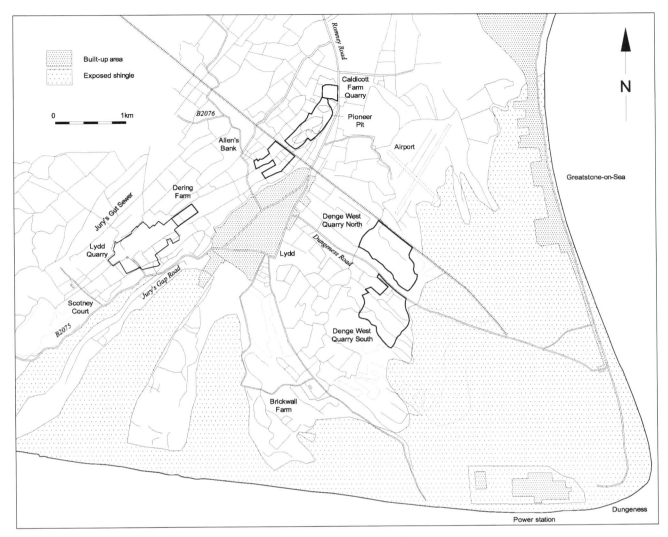

Fig. 2 Location map for investigated quarry sites:
Lydd, Caldicott and Denge Quarries, Dering Farm, Pioneer Pit and Allen's Bank

iii. Quarrying – usually large-scale, covering large tracts of open countryside (particularly around Rye, Lydd (Walland Marsh) and Denge Marsh where shingle predominates).

It is gravel extraction, however, that has provided by far the largest dataset for archaeology. By its very nature the extraction totally removes the archaeological (and related shallow geoarchaeological) deposits, changing the open flat landscape of reclamation into huge water-filled gravel pits.

Generally, but not exclusively, the archaeological deposits at all these sites have been adequately catered for within the remit of PPG 16. The best archaeological evidence has come from three aggregate sites situated around the town of Lydd (Lydd Quarry, Denge West Quarry and Caldicott Farm Quarry, Fig. 2). Other sites have also been investigated in this area on a smaller scale (Pioneer Pit, Allen's Bank and Dering Farm, Fig. 2), (Needham 1988, GSB Prospection 1998, John Samuels 1999 and Gardiner 1992). Considering that the town of

Lydd forms the centre point of this area it is unfortunate that to date only very limited archaeological work has been undertaken in the town itself, and that which has taken place has not located much of archaeological significance (Gardiner 1995b and Griffin 2002) despite the wealth of the extant buildings and documentary sources (Pearson 1995, Pearson *et al.* 1994 and Kent County Council 2003).

Of the three main quarry sites, by far the most extensive results have come from Brett Gravel Ltd's Lydd Quarry, where staged archaeological excavations, fully funded by Bretts, have been carried out in advance of extraction since 1991 by UCLFAU. The work here has revealed over 20 hectares of a buried medieval landscape of reclamation and occupation spanning the 12th to 16th centuries. A brief overview of the medieval evidence has already been published (Barber 1998b), though the current volume supersedes it. ARC's Caldicott Farm and Denge West Quarries have provided less coherent, but nevertheless crucially important, evidence of medieval and early post-medieval settlement to the north-east of the town and on Denge Marsh to the south. Funding for the fieldwork on these two sites was provided by ARC.

The funding for post-excavation analysis and publication of these sites has not been consistent and until the current volume all remained either unstudied or as unpublished reports/post-excavation assessments produced for the developer and held by UCLFAU and Kent County Council. The developer-funded archaeological work at Lydd Quarry was, and still is, undertaken in stages (Lydd 1, Lydd 2, *etc.*) each time the quarry expands. Financial provision had been made by Bretts for the post-excavation assessment and subsequent analysis of each stage of the work. This resulted in the production of twelve post-excavation assessment reports and eventually seven unpublished archive reports. Post-excavation funding at Denge West Quarry, being an old consent, was unlikely to be forthcoming, and that at Caldicott Farm was in the process of being agreed as late as 2003.

Even once analysis on the results from all the excavation phases at Lydd Quarry (and other close-by quarries) was complete, there was a need to combine and link all the stages of archaeological work together, and undertake some new targeted work. The latter revolved around documentary and cartographic research to compliment the archaeological data, and further research on the regional and national setting of the excavated dataset. These elements of additional work were undertaken by Dr Sheila Sweetinburgh and Dr Mark Gardiner respectively (see below). Most of this additional work was beyond the remit of developer-funding for any one particular site. As such, a project outline was submitted to English Heritage to raise the additional funding needed from the Aggregates Levy Sustainability Fund (ALSF). A full project design was subsequently commissioned which succeeded in securing the necessary ALSF funding (Barber 2002a).

Although archaeological work is still continuing at Lydd Quarry, the most recent phases (Lydds 12 to 14) suggest that new discoveries are likely to relate to both the prehistoric and Roman, rather than the medieval, periods. It was therefore considered an appropriate juncture to draw together the medieval evidence from these and other excavations in the vicinity to date. Work associated with the synthesis of the prehistoric and Romano-British remains may form the focus of a future publication.

The synthesis of data in the current volume has been linked as far as possible to one of three academic research themes. These are outlined below.

1. Reclamation and the Evolution of the Medieval Landscape

Firstly, the area is one of the larger later medieval landscapes to be exposed in southern England. Landscape evidence is usually studied from either earthworks or surviving features – including field patterns and relic woodlands. In the present case, it has been possible to strip the topsoil from very large areas to add the buried archaeological remains to the normal sources of evidence outlined above. This has enabled the study of the development of landscape in a way that is barely possible from surface features alone. It has allowed the determination of the age of features with greater precision and enables more certain conclusions to be drawn about the development of the landscape. There is one further aspect which is relevant here: marshland landscape is often studied as if its morphology is more or less frozen at the point of reclamation (Rippon 1996) and consequently the landscape is treated as if it has no, or little, time-depth. The Lydd area, perhaps uniquely, allows the development of a medieval marshland landscape to be studied over a period of centuries, during a time of considerable change as pastoralism increased.

2. Medieval Settlement Patterns

The second area of particular significance is the identification of a series of occupation sites and their enclosures. Work at Shapwick (Somerset) and, most recently, at the Whittlewood project in the East Midlands has shown the importance of looking, not only at villages, but also at patterns of dispersed settlement. The excavations at Lydd Quarry have shown how dispersed settlement existed alongside the nucleated market settlements on Romney Marsh. Excavation of an area of landscape containing dispersed settlement has revealed how the pattern of farmsteads changed and developed over a period of time. The excavation of dispersed settlements is particularly difficult due to the scale of work required to produce meaningful results. In this case it has been possible to work on sufficiently large areas to allow significant conclusions to be drawn. The excavations were less informative in providing information about the layout of buildings within farmsteads. The method of building used locally did not rely upon earth-fast footings in most instances, and it has been difficult to identify the location of buildings within their enclosures.

3. Medieval Rural Economy and Exploitation of Natural Resources

The final area to which the sites around Lydd have made a significant contribution to our wider understanding, is that of the rural economy. Advances in the historical studies of the rise of commercialism in medieval England have not been matched by a corresponding contribution by archaeology, even though the data are potentially available from excavation. Study of the artefacts and ecofacts from the farmsteads at the quarry sites allow broader statements to be made about production and consumption. These can be placed within the context of the nearby markets of Lydd, New Romney and Brookland (Gardiner 1998), and the regional centres of Winchelsea, Rye and Canterbury. The discovery of evidence for fishing is particular significant in light of the developing understanding of the importance of the practice to the rural economy (Fox 2001).

The fieldwork and post-excavation analysis of the UCLFAU investigated sites has been undertaken by a number of individuals. Greg Priestley-Bell has undertaken the majority of fieldwork. He has been responsible for that at Denge West North, Denge West South (part), Caldicott Farm and Lydds 2–4, 7–10 and Lydd 11, Phase 1 (part), Phases 2 and 3. Ian Greig directed the fieldwork at Lydd 1, Jennifer Sawyer at Lydd 5/6, Casper Johnson at Lydd 11, Phase 1 (part), and Mark Gardiner and Simon Stevens at Denge West South (part). Post-excavation analysis for the original 'archive' reports was equally mixed. Lydd 1 was undertaken by Mark Gardiner and Ian Greig, Denge West South field-walking by Simon Stevens, while all other analyses has been undertaken by Greg Priestley-Bell with Luke Barber. Project Managers have included Mark Gardiner (Lydd 1 and fieldwork for Lydds 2 and 3 and Denge West), Tony Pollard (fieldwork for Lydds 4 to 9 and Caldicott Farm) and Ian Greig (fieldwork for Lydds 10–14). Project Management of the post-excavation analysis for all phases, excluding Lydd 1, was undertaken by Luke Barber. The current volume has been compiled by Luke Barber using the 'archive' reports and results of new research and synthesis by various specialists.

Due to the different sources and authors of elements of the text, every effort has been made to blend the writing styles together within this monograph, though it is acknowledged that without completely re-writing all sections by an individual author (which was outside the remit of the ALSF funding) a seamless text is virtually impossible to achieve. Similarly, the wide time-span of the excavations, together with the different challenges encountered at the various sites, has led to a developing excavation and sampling strategy, which sometimes makes comparison of evidence between areas more difficult. The monograph has been laid out in what is considered to be a logical format (see contents) whereby the sites are described after the documentary section but before that on the finds. Interpretation relevant to a particular occupation site or section of field system is included with the basic stratigraphic description for that area, with detailed descriptions of soils or finds only being included where regarded as significant. A wider overall chronological discussion by research theme is included after the finds section. The final section sets the results in the wider setting of the Marsh and beyond.

The archive from Lydd, Caldicott Farm and Denge West Quarries is currently held by UCLFAU, but will hopefully be deposited in Folkestone Museum.

1

The Documentary Sources

by Sheila Sweetinburgh

ABSTRACT

Quarries, Manors and Sources

During the medieval period the land at Lydd Quarry primarily fell within the manor of Old Langport, which was held by the Archbishop of Canterbury. To the east was the land of Lydd manor, part of the archbishop's bailiwick of Aldington. Also within the quarry site were the lands of two other manors: Scotney and New Langport. By the 1440s the former was held by All Souls College, Oxford; the latter in lay hands. The lands of the other two quarries were under ecclesiastical jurisdiction. Caldicott was also in Old Langport manor and possibly Bilsington Priory's holding of Belgar, while Denge fell within Battle Abbey's Dengemarsh manor, part of the great manor of Wye.

Extant documentary sources for these manors vary tremendously from the very few scraps for New Langport to the relatively large archive for Dengemarsh. Furthermore, even though the sources are comparatively abundant, they are patchy and primarily cover the activities of the ecclesiastical institutions, not their tenant farmers. This is also true for the extensive collection of records from Canterbury Christchurch Priory, which also had extensive interests in the Romney Marshes. Consequently, the early 14th century taxation records for the Hundred of Newchurch are invaluable because they provide a window onto the farming practices of the peasantry.

Reclamation and Field Systems

Natural silting and the presence of shingle banks around Lydd allowed the land to be used for seasonal grazing during the late Anglo-Saxon period. Reclamation and permanent colonisation may have first occurred in the 11th century, such work being undertaken by peasant families as part of agreements with their institutional landlords. As a result, a number of embankments were constructed, with such features sometimes acting as property boundaries. Ditches were equally important; the aerial photographs of Caldicott and Lydd Quarries showing a pattern of small regular fields.

At Denge Quarry the field system generally followed the alignment of the shingle ridges and again the fields were often small. Reclamation here may have followed a similar chronology, but the absence of early manorial records means this cannot be verified. However, later records for Dengemarsh and those for Scotney highlight the need for constant vigilance against encroachment by the sea, the costs being borne by both the great ecclesiastical landlords and their tenant farmers.

Settlement Pattern

From at least the late Anglo-Saxon (8th to 10th century) period, the settlement at Lydd served a developing society based on agriculture, fishing and trading. In addition, there was a long-established seasonal fishing settlement of cabins at the Ness. For the local peasant farmers reclamation offered increasing opportunities, giving rise to a landscape characterised by numerous dispersed farmsteads, often clustered along trackways and embankments, close to sources of fresh water and/or on the periphery of the monastic farm. These farms were small (some no more than a few acres) and even these might comprise several plots scattered across one or more manors. Interestingly, the crises of the 14th century do not appear to have produced significant changes to this settlement pattern during the following century, but by the end of that century the first signs of change were evident. The rise of the butcher-grazier and the increasing importance of absentee lay landlords (though not a new phenomenon) led to a decline in the number of farmsteads across the Marshes during the 16th century.

The Local Economy

Lydd provided a valuable gateway for the local population of farmers, fishermen and other producers and traders. Farming and fishing were the primary industries, with salt and timber production also important, though the former had declined significantly by the later Middle Ages due to foreign competition. The latter too may have been hit by imports, though in this case from the Weald; the growing shortage of local wood by the 16th century a consequence, perhaps, of changing farming practices and the decline in the number of rural farmsteads (elm, in particular, was often grown close by). Like their landlords, the local peasantry appear to have adopted a mixed farming regime during most of the medieval period. Oats and wheat were the major cereals, the former grown principally for home consumption, the latter for the market. Sheep and pigs were ubiquitous, and in addition cattle and horses were fairly common.

The late 15th and early 16th centuries, however, brought significant changes, in part a product of the shift from direct farming to leasing of the demesne lands by the ecclesiastical landlords. Although arable farming did not disappear, the emphasis was on stock production, which in time led to the consolidation of holdings, the amalgamation of small plots of land, and the disappearance of some farmsteads. For a few local families this was a golden age of rising expectations, but for others it meant an increasing reliance on by-employment to survive. Fishing may have offered some opportunities, yet even for the well-established fishing families the industry was precarious and most combined such activities with other forms of employment. Thus for a significant minority in Lydd and its hinterland, the early modern period was a time of dearth as they sought to eke out a living, while others travelled north to seek a better life in the booming industrial towns of the Weald.

INTRODUCTION

By drawing on the documentary sources for the Romney Marshes, this section seeks to complement the archaeological report which forms the majority of this publication. For the pre-Conquest period, charters are valuable records, especially when they include boundary clauses, and compared to many places the survival of such materials for the Lydd area is relatively good. Documentary sources for the 12th and 13th centuries are similarly relatively abundant – the records being a product of the scattered ecclesiastical estates on the Romney Marshes. From the late 14th century these records become more plentiful, though the fullest series of materials for the medieval period date from the 15th century. Early modern ('post-medieval') sources are even better, both in quality and quantity, and where advantageous these have also been studied. Consequently, in seeking to piece together the history of reclamation, land use and rural settlement for the medieval countryside around the marshland town of Lydd, a wide range of archival materials have been used to compile this report. In part this was due to the fragmentary nature of the extant sources – documentary records for Lydd's hinterland being used alongside those covering Romney, Walland and Denge Marshes. Having employed a comparable approach, it seems advisable to provide a brief assessment of these primary sources to highlight their advantages and weaknesses before examining the results.

THE NATURE OF THE EVIDENCE

During the Middle Ages in the Romney Marsh region as a whole only a small proportion of the land was held by the laity, but locally such landlords might be important figures. Instead, ecclesiastical lords were the dominant landholders, including the Archbishop of Canterbury and the great monastic houses of Canterbury Christchurch Priory, St Augustine's Abbey at Canterbury and Battle Abbey (Brooks 1988, 90; Smith 1943, 172). Other religious establishments were also significant landlords, for example St Mary's Hospital, Dover, Bilsington Priory and Dover Priory. Small houses, like the Hospital of St Stephen and St Thomas at Romney, had estates locally, and in the late 15th century the foundation of several colleges at Oxford produced a wave of new institutional landlords in the Romney Marshes. One result of this ecclesiastical dominance is the relatively good survival of estate documentation, particularly from the 15th century onwards. However, this differs considerably among the various institutions, in part a reflection of their fate at the Dissolution. For example, the holdings of Christchurch Priory were primarily transferred to the Dean and Chapter at Canterbury, whereas those of St Mary's Hospital were sold off, but in some cases such estates remained largely intact in the hands of wealthy lay families.[1] As a result medieval documents sometimes survived; their preservation a matter of good fortune or the need to provide evidence of ownership. Similar estate records were presumably produced by lay holders of marshland manors, but such records are extremely limited, as they are for Kent generally.[2] Thus, the surviving materials primarily provide evidence about institutional estate management, not the peasantry.

The excavation sites under review here are located to the west, north and south-east of Lydd, of which the most important are the Lydd Quarry site at Burnthouse Wall (part of the manorial lands of Old Langport, with Scotney manor to the west and Lydd manor in the bailiwick of Aldington to the east); and Denge Quarry on Denge Marsh (part of Dengemarsh manor, the quarry abutting Denge Marsh sewer and the lands of Lydd manor). The holder of another, smaller quarry, Caldicott Farm to the north of Lydd, is more uncertain but the quarry site was apparently also part of the manor of Old Langport, though Bilsington Priory's estate at Belgar included land in this area. Consequently, the documentary sources that cover these sites or neighbouring areas are All Souls College records for Scotney, the archive of Battle Abbey for its manor of Dengemarsh, the archiepiscopal records for Aldington and its sub-manors of Old and New Langport, and the materials for Belgar. Each of these sources have been examined in the past. Gill Draper (1998, 113–28) continues to work on the All Souls archive, Mark Gardiner (1995c, 127–37; 1998, 129–45) and Spencer Dimmock (2001, 5–24) have used the Dengemarsh and Aldington records on several occasions, and Eleanor Vollens (1995, 118–26) has looked at salt-working at Belgar. Other manors in the area, especially those of Christchurch Priory, have also been studied by historians, including R.A.L. Smith (1943), Anthony Gross and Andrew Butcher (1995, 107–17) and Sheila Sweetinburgh (2000, 6–9). This essay draws on their published and unpublished work (see Bibliography) to demonstrate the nature of the various archives, and tries to answer a number of different, though related, questions regarding peasant society in the Lydd area.

Scotney and Bletching

During the 1440s All Souls College, Archbishop Chichele's foundation, acquired several holdings in Walland Marsh and Romney Marsh. These included the manor of Scotney (and Ocholt), and the associated lordship of Bletching, which were often grouped together, though the manor and lordship were farmed separately (Trice Martin 1877). The accounts for Bletching were the responsibility of the 'collector or beadle', who collected annually a small sum from the seigniorial court, and rents totalling £6 7s. 7.5d.[3] Scotney was leased out, the lessee paying over £56 per year in the 1450s, though this had fallen to £49 in 1504 (Draper 1998, 117). The college was responsible for the maintenance of the marsh and its sea defences, as well as repairs to the manorial buildings – items which were recorded annually in the rent rolls. Unfortunately, not all the rent rolls are extant for the period 1443–4 to *c.* 1500, but in each decade several successive rolls do survive (Evans 1997). Draft and neat copies for the same year are rare, but attached bills are more common, the fullest providing details about the sums spent on scouring named ditches, repairing sea walls and manorial buildings.[4] The earlier history of the area is far more difficult to ascertain, however, because the All Souls College archive contains very little information about previous landholders and none of the evidence pre-dates 1337. Thus any assessment of the development of reclamation around Lydd Quarry rests on late medieval evidence for the area and the use of comparable and earlier sources from elsewhere in the Romney Marshes (Smith 1943, 166–89). Ideas about farming practices are also predominantly reliant on these late medieval records, with the rent rolls indicating the importance of sheep farming, which appears to have replaced a more mixed agricultural regime.

Dengemarsh Manor

Dengemarsh manor was the shore member of the great royal manor of Wye when William I conferred it on Battle Abbey in the late 11th century (Searle 1974, 23). Comprising a large single block of land, with a few small parcels to the west in Broomhill parish, the manor was unlike many of its neighbours, which were made up of large numbers of widely scattered areas (Gardiner 1998, 131). Denge Marsh sewer marked its northern boundary; the manor stretching as far as the shingle foreland of Dungeness to the south and south-east. Within the abbey's cartularies there are several undated and 13th century references to Dengemarsh and neighbouring Broomhill, some recording gifts by the local peasantry to the abbey, and other land transactions (Searle 1974, 40 n. 18).[5] Further contemporary records concerning landholdings in Dengemarsh and Broomhill are held at The National Archives, the British Library and Lincoln's Inn. Such evidence provides information about land transactions, rents, tenants' names, agreements regarding customary duties (part of the customs of the marsh) relating to inning and maintaining sea defences, and an indication of the acreage which had been enclosed.[6] This good collection of documents, produced when the abbeys of Battle and Robertsbridge were seeking to extend their marshland holdings, has been used by Gardiner (1988, 117–19) in his assessment of 13th century settlement patterns in the Broomhill area.

The 14th and 15th century records for Dengemarsh are primarily rentals and court rolls, including views of frankpledge. Although rentals list names of abbey tenants and rents due (paid), only the *c.* 1432 rental provides details about the customary holdings or *tenementa* and their division among the named tenants. Numerous topographical features and field names were used to position the various holdings, but it has only been possible to locate a few, as the majority of these names are discarded from the 16th century onwards (Gardiner 1998, 131).[7] Consequently, it is often extremely difficult to relate topographically the lands particular individuals held and the lands of the different *tenementa*. Nevertheless, this rental does provide an important snap-shot concerning peasant landholding in the early 15th century, although it should be remembered that some tenants may have held land in other manors. Looking at the 15th century more generally, the absence of comparable later rentals is also a handicap because it is difficult to ascertain the chronology of accumulation of large holdings (over 100 acres) and the transition to capitalist farming. Even though complementary records do exist, the Dengemarsh manor court rolls series is far from complete and, unlike those from many midland and East Anglian manors, these rolls rarely list the acreage, location or rent of the land involved.

Belgar

Bilsington Priory's land at Belgar was part of the manor of Upper Bilsington, the land having been granted to the house by John Mansel at its foundation in 1253. In the priory's survey of its lands and rents, its Belgar tenants and their holdings (based on new measurements in 1381) were listed separately along with the total rent due in money, salt and herrings (Neilson 1928, 207–12). This survey and a cartulary (primarily records of 13th century grants) have been published, as has a memorandum entitled 'Evidence of the enclosure of salt-marsh at Belgar'. The latter covers the history of enclosure between *c.* 1090 and *c.* 1307, as well as a note of the prior's request to Edward II to enclose a salt marsh – a request that can be followed in the crown records (Neilson 1928, 212–14; CPR 1327–30, 14; 1334–38, 555). Such sources are useful indicators of the likely chronology of reclamation and enclosure of marshland in the Lydd area during the 12th and 13th centuries and, as Vollans (1995, 120–6) has also shown, provide insights concerning slightly later attempts to reclaim land when flooding had become a severe problem.

Other Lydd Holdings

The Aldington bailiwick of Lydd apparently comprised a single or small number of areas. These covered the town and a few adjoining fields to the north, and a considerable acreage to the south and south-west of Lydd. Bordering the bailiwick to the south and west were the lands of Battle Abbey. Compared to Dengemarsh, far fewer estate records have survived for Lydd and the neighbouring manor of Old Langport, but there are two detailed 16th century rentals (Old Langport dated 1552, Lydd 1556).[8] The Lydd rental indicates the boundaries of each plot and its topographical arrangement, making it easier to follow than the one for Old Langport, although some problems remain concerning the position of certain holdings. The inclusion of Lydd town is also valuable because it has been possible to map the houses and holdings of a few individuals (Gardiner 1998, 138–40). Regarding the Old Langport rental, Gardiner (1998, 131) has suggested that the writer used a record compiled about a generation earlier, providing the names of one or more previous tenants and occasionally further information about the holding. Yet certain difficulties remain, not least the relatively late date of both rentals, which means the landholding structure described had seen considerable changes during the preceding century, including the effects of the Henrician Reformation. The other manor in the area was New Langport, for which almost no documentary sources survive, the manor having passed from the Septvans to the Fettiplace family in the mid 15th century (Du Boulay 1966, 351–2; Gardiner 1994, 339–41).

Other Marsh Holdings

The documentary materials so far described are those thought to most closely relate topographically to the area of study. However, as a way of assessing more fully the history of reclamation, settlement and the economy of the designated sites, other collections were also examined. Christchurch Priory compiled detailed records of its manors of Appledore and Agney, and many of these documents survive. Agney was a small manor close to the southern end of the Rhee Wall, whereas the manor of Appledore comprised demesne land and over 900 tenanted acres in numerous, scattered blocks in the parishes of Appledore, Fairfield and Brookland. Although there are references to Appledore and Agney throughout

the priory's archive, for the purposes of this study the most useful collections are charters, mainly from the 13th century; bedels' rolls from the late 13th to the mid 14th century; Appledore court rolls for about a century from the 1380s; and a rental for the same manor dated 1503. Like the Broomhill charters, those for Appledore provide evidence about the strategies adopted by the institutional landlords to extend their holdings through the involvement of the peasantry in reclamation. The bedels' rolls, too, contain evidence about the maintenance of reclaimed land. Occasionally they also note the devastating effects of flooding – information that Gross and Butcher (1995, 107–17) used in their assessment of the priory's agricultural strategy in the late 13th century. Although the bedels' rolls can be used to ascertain this strategy, the specialist farming policy at Agney (particularly at Orgarswick) was probably not adopted by the local peasant farmers, who may instead have followed a mixed farming regime (Sweetinburgh 2000, 6–9). Evidence concerning peasant farming practices is extremely difficult to obtain, hence the taxation materials for the Hundred of Newchurch are an invaluable resource (Butcher and Gross 1991). The Appledore court rolls also provide some ideas about the peasant economy for the late Middle Ages, including the importance of by-employment for many households, especially for those living in or near urban centres (Sweetinburgh 2002, 150–2). In addition, rentals and scott lists produce evidence about landholders and occupiers, of which there are a number (of varying usefulness) for the period *c.* 1470 to 1550: the Walland Marsh scot assessment (1477), Appledore manor rental (1503), Dengemarsh rental (1538), Old Langport (1552), Lydd (1556).

Testamentary Records

As well as manorial documents, this study has employed probate materials, particularly the unusually large collection of wills from Lydd. Between 1400 and 1600 over 450 Lydd parishioners made wills – a far higher proportion of the local populace than in neighbouring parishes. Consequently, will-makers were not only members of the middling sort or leading citizens, but included labourers and other poorer people whose assets were sometimes very meagre. The wills of those from neighbouring parishes have also been examined for the 15th and early 16th centuries, allowing genealogical reconstruction of several families. Even though such sources pose considerable problems (not least the likelihood of pre-mortem transference of goods and land, and different inheritance strategies relating to the testator's age and life-cycle stage) they are still valuable indicators regarding ideas about landholding, land use and other household activities.

Lydd Civic Records

The interdependence of town and countryside in the medieval period meant that it was important to look

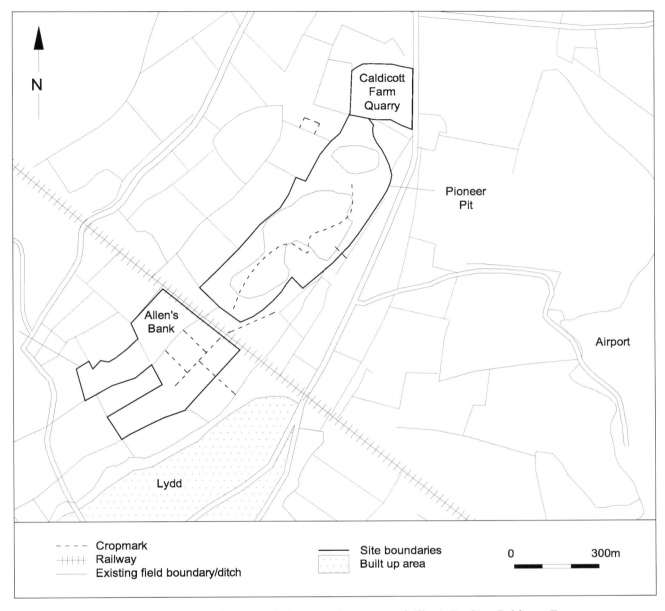

N

Caldicott
Farm
Quarry

Pioneer
Pit

Allen's
Bank

Airport

Lydd

- - - - Cropmark
++++ Railway
——— Existing field boundary/ditch

——— Site boundaries
·:·:· Built up area

0   300m

Fig. 4 Cropmarks noted on aerial photographs in area of Allen's Bank to Caldicott Farm

briefly at the civic records for Lydd, especially the chamberlains' accounts and the borough court books. The earliest accounts cover the year 1428–9, and thereafter the series is almost complete for the 15th and 16th centuries – the court books are much more limited, being confined to parts of certain years between 1507 and 1541. As well as naming the jurats for Dengemarsh, in addition to those for Lydd, the accounts also note matters such as gifts given to royal officials, members of the aristocracy, the Archbishop of Canterbury and other town officers; the payment of scots; town activities concerning Dungeness; the maintenance and provisioning of ships for royal service; and disputes among the townsmen and sometimes outsiders (Finn 1911). Such records are valuable, particularly when used in conjunction with

other sources, to provide ideas about the activities of certain occupational groups over time.

Other Documentary Sources

Three other types of documentary sources were employed: printed records, maps and aerial photographs. Crown records comprised the largest group of printed materials, yielding a variety of information about storm damage, landholding, reclamation, and other activities. Early maps, such as those by Thomas Gull and Matthew Poker (*Fig. 3), show relatively few details, but do indicate the position of certain features, such as roads, houses and walls, while the All Souls College maps of Scotney (1588/9) list the holders of adjacent fields. The large-scale Lydd tithe map of 1812–13 and the first

Fig. 5 Aerial photograph of Lydd Quarry prior to excavation (North to top of page)
© *Crown Copyright/MOD (1959) Reproduced with the permission of the Controller of Her Majesty's Stationery Office*

edition O.S. map produced useful information about field systems, and, as Gardiner (2002, 102–17) has demonstrated, when used in conjunction with Green's soil map of Romney Marsh and aerial photographs, can provide evidence about the landscape before the floods of the 13th century. The National Monuments Record office at Swindon holds a large collection of aerial photographs from the 1940s and 1950s, and those relevant to the study were consulted, as well as those at the Centre for Kentish Studies, Maidstone, and several more recent ones in private hands. Although some were difficult to interpret, some did appear to show the position of now lost pathways, field boundaries (ditches), buildings and other features, including waterways and creeks, for the quarry sites and surrounding areas. By far the most detail was noted on coverage of the excavated portion of Lydd Quarry (Figs. 4 & 5).

RECLAMATION AND FIELD SYSTEMS

Trying to piece together the progress of reclamation and colonisation in Romney Marsh has proven extremely difficult, although Green's (1968) work on the marsh soils was a major breakthrough. His distinction (and mapping) between the areas of 'decalcified' or old marshland (where over centuries the calcium has been predominantly leached away by natural drainage) and 'calcareous' or new marshland (subject to inundation in historic times) has been fundamental to our understanding of the development of the region. The former was available for colonisation during the early period of Roman occupation, though following environmental changes the old marshland suffered some inundation in the form of tidal creeks of the rivers Brede, Tillingham and Rother (Limen). The latter was subject to reclamation and enclosure from mid-Saxon to early modern times, generally westwards from Hythe to East Guldeford and the Wainway Channel. Nonetheless, recent research has highlighted points of contention, like the route of the Rother in the Saxon period, which has led to modifications and an increasing awareness of the complexity, chronologically and topographically, of the history of reclamation. This is important and demonstrates the significance of local studies using, where possible, documentary and archaeological resources. Unfortunately, the historical records for the Lydd area do not allow for a site-specific level of integration between the resources, but it has been possible to produce a limited analysis of reclamation using maps, photographs and documentary materials from further afield.

The Pre-Conquest Period

By the late Saxon period Romney Marsh proper (to the east of the Rhee Wall) was becoming increasingly available for agriculture as a result of natural silting and drainage (Brooks 1988, 98; Reeves 1995, 86–9). The area around Lydd seems to have developed in a similar way, with Green's map showing a substantial area of decalcified marsh to the north-west of a western shingle bank on which the town stood. To the south and east of Lydd was another massive shingle bank. Research has suggested that the shingle barrier stretched unbroken from Fairlight to Lydd, protecting what would become Walland Marsh (Rippon 2002, 93). Lydd's antiquity can be gauged from place-name evidence recorded in several pre-Conquest charters. Some local places-names, including Lydd, are Old English (Cullen 1997, 268–9). The earlier of the two charters, dated 741, refers to cattle grazing rights on or adjacent to the shingle bank to the south-west of Lydd – the land bounded by a marsh called *biscopes uuic* and a wood called *ripp* (Brooks 1988, 98–9; Birch 1885–99, no. 160, Sawyer 1968, no. 24). This grant from King Aethelberht to the monastery of Lyminge seemingly implies that grazing was freely available without the need to maintain any embankments or dykes. It may also indicate the seasonal movement of cattle and the likelihood of drove-ways between Lydd and Lyminge. Similarly, links between marsh and upland appear in the second charter involving Lydd, possibly also reflecting the situation in the 8th century. Brooks (1988, 99) considered that even though Offa's purported grant of 774 to Archbishop Jaenberht was probably written in the 10th century, the boundary clause was taken from an authentic charter (Birch 1885–99, no. 214, Sawyer 1968, no. 111). To the south of the three sulungs at Lydd was the king's land, *aduui*, called Denge Marsh, a phrase which suggests that this marsh was already part of the king's manor of Wye, and perhaps a source of seasonal grazing (Brooks 1988, 100; Cullen 1997, 270). The boundary clause also mentions *bleccing*, 'a place associated with Blecca' to the north-west (Cullen 1997, 270). The use of a personal name seems to indicate early colonisation, with Blecca and his family exploiting the decalcified marsh and the local waterway of Bletching Fleet, although whether they or the king (or their descendants) had actively engaged in ditching or embanking remains open to speculation. Yet Brooks (1988, 101–2) believes one of the boundaries in King Cenwulf's charter of 811 may be indicative of a linear boundary-dyke – an attempt to safeguard an area of marsh to the south-east of Appledore – but this too seems to be a 10th century version of possibly an earlier grant (Birch 1885–99, no. 335, Sawyer 1968, no. 168). Furthermore, the only pre-Conquest charter covering land in Walland Marsh (at Mistleham) makes no mention of such features, and recent analysis of both the documentary sources and archaeological findings points to embanking as being a 12th to 13th century development (Eddison and Draper 1997, 81–2; Sawyer 1968, no. 1623).[9]

Post-Conquest Marshland Management

Following William I's grant of Dengemarsh manor (as part of the manor of Wye) to Battle Abbey, almost all the land in Lydd parish was under ecclesiastical jurisdiction (Hasted 1799, vol. 8, 425–6). This situation was recorded in Domesday, where it was stated that Robert of Romney held Langport of the archbishop (it answered for one and-a-half sulungs), and Robert's overlord of two half-sulung holdings in Denge Marsh was the Bishop of Bayeux (Morgan 1983, entries 2, 43; 5, 177, 179). Elsewhere on the Marshes the presence of these institutional landlords had significant implications for the history of enclosure during the 12th and 13th centuries, and it seems likely that this was equally the case around Lydd. Eddison and Draper (1997, 82–3), in their study of reclamation of Walland Marsh, cite the 12th century agreements between several Christchurch priors and members of the Scadeway family acting collectively. Under these agreements, the Scadeway family agreed to enclose land at Mistleham from the sea and to defend it through the use of walls, and in exchange the family received rights to the land. This large-scale systematic colonisation produced a landscape dominated by 'a precise sub-rectangular pattern of drainage' where the main drain or Baldwin's Sewer bisected the piece of Christchurch land and, following a right-angle turn, formed the western boundary of the reclaimed area (Eddison and Draper 1997, 83).[10] Other records in the Christchurch archive show the south-westerly expansion of the enclosed area as further walls and ditches were constructed. Perhaps of particular interest with regard to Lydd Quarry is Eddison and Draper's (1997, 84) observation that Baldwin's sewer is on the seaward side of the embankment at Brookland church, implying that the area reclaimed was 'high' marsh, a long way from the sea and above high tide, with the embankment functioning as a property boundary rather than as a sea defence.

It is possible that similar agreements, involving groups of peasants and various archbishops or their chief tenants (Robert of Romney and his successors as holders of Langport manor), were employed for the area covered by the Caldicott/Lydd quarries. Such agreements would have given landlords and peasant families the opportunity to adopt a systematic approach, where straight walls and ditches were used to enclose and drain successive areas, gradually moving south-westwards parallel to the shingle barrier. Rippon (2002, 93) and Gardiner agree that the first of these walls in the Lydd Quarry area was the Midley/Gore Wall/Burnt House Wall, which enclosed an area that included Old Romney and Midley.[11] The embankment broadly followed a series of straight lines; the line dictated by what Gardiner calls 'arbitrary and locally determined elements'.[12] Thus Gore Wall/Burnt House Wall runs from Wheelsgate to Horsebones Bridge, where it turns a right-angle before running parallel to the shingle bank and then turning through another right-angle, finally ending at the shingle just to the north-west of a spring at Pigwell. Just to the west of this second turn is Jury's Gut Sewer, a substantial channel in the post-Conquest period that included the extensive creek relic of Bletching Fleet (recorded on some early maps as Broadwater Fleet in the New Langport rental, and still shown as marshy on the first edition O.S. map). This was a possible deterrent for those constructing the wall to continue any further westwards.[13] Alternatively, the fleet (or waterway) might denote a property boundary, possibly of Bleccing (see above pre-Conquest charter but linked to the manor of Scotney by the 13th century) because its eastern boundary in the 15th century (when All Souls College acquired the manor) followed the present line of Jury's Gut Sewer for a short distance.[14] Dating the wall is difficult from the documentary evidence, but it was probably constructed about the same time as Baldwin's sewer, or even slightly earlier, during the 11th or 12th century. For those constructing the embankment (counterparts of the Scadeway family and the men of Mistleham) it made sense to lay out their fields and ditches in a rectangular pattern, a strategy confirmed by the archaeological evidence at Caldicott and Lydd quarries (see below).

Tore Wall (enclosing the remaining part of Lydd Quarry) begins at Burnt House Wall and then runs parallel to the shingle on a course that is entirely determined by local topography, terminating at the 19th century county boundary. This connection between physical features or man-made structures (walls, ditches) and political or landholding boundaries, is significant in terms of many of the marsh manors.[15] For example, the ancient manor of Dengemarsh was bounded by Denge Marsh Sewer to the north and west, and Green Wall, the boundary between it and Belgar to the north-east. Such an arrangement was much less likely to hold true for later-formed manors. Clerk's map (1588/9) shows Tore Wall cutting across a number of fields belonging to the manor of Scotney, and on only two occasions did the wall form the manorial boundary.[16] Furthermore, the next wall did not enclose the manorial lands, but it was contiguous with a number of field boundaries. Both walls also apparently dammed several fleets – Widney Fleet ended at Tore Wall, and Ocholt Fleet and Horse Head Fleet at Sandy Land Wall. Dating the construction of Tore Wall is also extremely difficult, although a considerable acreage was enclosed at neighbouring Broomhill during the 12th or early 13th century, and contemporary reclamation of the area between Burnt House Wall and Tore Wall seems highly probable (Gardiner 1988, 114–15).

The pattern of small, regular fields found in the Caldicott and Lydd Quarry excavations (a reflection, perhaps, of the pressure on land from a rapidly growing population in the 12th and 13th centuries, mirroring the findings from the west of Mistleham on Walland Marsh) was apparently confirmed by aerial photography. Although there are certain problems associated with interpreting such evidence (not least the difficulty of seasonal differences among the various photographs and a range of altitudes) they seem to show that the major ditches/trackways ran south-west to north-east. This is clear for the Lydd Quarry area and the boundaries visible in the Pioneer Pit/Caldicott area today and prior to extraction. In addition, at Lydd Quarry the apparently infilled field ditches were numerous and clearly visible. However, in contrast to Lydd Quarry, very few earlier infilled ditches were noted on the aerial photographs for the Pioneer Pit/Allen's Bank sites (see below), though at least one sinuous natural channel was apparent in part of the former (Fig. 4), while the infilled field ditches at Allen's Bank may well be of post-medieval origin.[17]

The reclamation chronology of the tidal inlets at the Denge Quarry sites is impossible to ascertain from the Battle Abbey charters or the Dengemarsh court rolls, though it is possible to comment on the history of land use. In the 13th and early 14th centuries a mixed farming regime was apparently followed on the demesne land (mostly to the south of the quarry sites), but it is unclear whether this indicates Battle Abbey's willingness to upgrade the local marshland it had and was continuing to acquire (Searle 1974, 40, 148 n. 52, 150–1, 253).[18] Nonetheless, the abbey was spending some money on walls and ditches. In 1319–20 it spent 50s., which included work at Northlade (possibly part of the drainage system that would have covered the Denge Quarry sites) though some parts of the manor were still salt marsh.[19] Other indicative evidence of the state of the Denge Quarry site may be gleaned from an undated charter, in which the abbey did not include this area when it sought to claim any whales or porpoises that became stranded. This perhaps suggests that such events no longer occurred because what had been tidal inlets were now enclosed.[20] Yet none of this is direct evidence of reclamation at the excavation sites, and thus it seems advisable to look at documentary sources covering comparable areas such as Broomhill. In his discussion on the settlement of Broomhill, Gardiner, (1988, 114) following Searle (1980, 120–1), noted that initially Battle Abbey apparently saw the area in terms of its proximity to the abbey's manor of Dengemarsh. Any enclosure in the 12th century was the work of entrepreneurial, prosperous tenants, who sought the right to areas they inned at their own expense (Gardiner 1988, 114).[21] The second phase in the first half of the 13th century saw Battle Abbey and neighbouring Robertsbridge seeking agreements with groups of peasants, such as the men of Winchelsea, to enclose designated blocks of land between the tidal inlets and the sea.[22] Thereafter, the two abbeys engaged in further agreements to enclose and to divide up marshland areas around Broomhill, which meant that by the early 13th century Battle Abbey had well in excess of 1,350 acres in the area.[23] The men of Broomhill (the descendants of Doudeman who had been involved in the early reclamation) also held a considerable 600 acres (500 customary acres) in plots across the marshes. These plots had been sub-divided among the Broomhill men, leading to a proliferation of small units – a field system that may have mirrored conditions at Mistleham (Gardiner 1988, 117–18). However, whether such a strategy was employed at the Denge Quarry area remains unclear, and consequently the archaeological findings continue to provide the best evidence for the process of reclamation.

Equally problematic are the documentary sources for wall and ditch maintenance, due to the survival of only a few pre-Black Death Dengemarsh sergeant's accounts.[24] However, as at Broomhill, some enclosed marshland may have been subject to the type of agreements found among the Christchurch and Battle Abbey charters. Documentary evidence for the Lydd Quarry area is almost equally non-existent for this period, but assuming that the area had been reclaimed it seems likely that management of both areas was covered by the 1288–90 royal commission and ordinances, which included the marshes of Walland and Denge (Smith 1943, 168).[25] These initiatives were primarily in response to the catastrophic storms of 1288, but presumably drew on long-standing customary practices, described by Neilson (1928, 39–56) in her work on Bilsington Priory and its marsh holdings.

After the Great Storms

The extent of the damage caused by the period of the great storms (1250, 1252 and 1288) is difficult to quantify from the documentary materials alone. Matthew Paris provided a dramatic description of the effects of the inundation in 1250, and a later chronicle does the same for February 1288 when the sea was said to have burst through all the walls and covered nearly all the land from the great wall of Appledore towards the south and west as far as Winchelsea (Luard 1880, vol. 5, 176; Stubbs 1880, vol. 2, 293). These descriptions provide valuable indicators of scale, but cannot be used to map the actual areas affected. Nevertheless, some flooded areas can be located. On Christchurch Priory's manor of Ebony its rent from an area of pasture called the *Prioratus* fell dramatically in 1287–8 – the priory responding by spending £8 7s. on new walling and ditching that year to recover its pasture (Gross and Butcher 1995, 108–9). During the next two years expenditure on walling and ditching at the manor remained at a high level, and a new wall was also built on the priory's Appledore manor in 1293–4, costing £124.[26] Flooding also occurred in the Broomhill area but how far east this extended is difficult to gauge. Across Walland and Denge Marsh the process of reclaiming the flooded areas was a piecemeal operation. Some was recovered almost immediately, but during the early 14th century it is difficult to see a clear trend, with some areas successfully reclaimed while some landholders, such as Bilsington Priory, appear to have struggled (*CPR* 1334–8, 555). Conditions at Scotney in the mid 14th century are described in a commission of inquiry document, which noted the relationship between several guts. These included the old gut of Jury's Gut and a new one, and walls, such as Gore Wall and All Saints Wall, as well as the formation of a new piece of marsh called Southnewland. The account is confusing, but when used in conjunction with the field evidence it seems likely that the Lydd Quarry area was fresh marsh. However, according to an inquiry of 1365, inundation had occurred at Broomhill and at Ocholt (Ocholt at Scotney was sometimes called 'Little Ocholt' to distinguish it), and at lands belonging to Christchurch Priory, which it had acquired from the de Gestling family in the early 13th century (that is to the west of Kent Pen and Sandy Land Walls).[27] For the holders of neighbouring manors expenditure on sea defences was, therefore, seen as essential to safeguard their own holdings. For example, the few surviving bailiff's accounts for Scotney record sums of about £10 (including scots) spent annually.[28]

The early 15th century records for Scotney and Dengemarsh continue to show that landlords spent money on walling and ditching.[29] Later accounts do not survive for Dengemarsh but those for Scotney show heavy expenditure in certain years: in 1453–4 ditching cost 125s. and three years later over 57s. was spent on repairing the sea wall.[30] Disaster struck again in 1468–9, but the flooded demesne land may not have been close to

Lydd Quarry.[31] As noted earlier, the cost of maintaining the walls and ditches was not solely borne by landlords – all those who held land in the area were expected to pay scots. Those liable were listed when the land was periodically surveyed. Unfortunately it has not been possible to find a list where the areas of Lydd/Caldicott or Denge are identifiable, the former being just to the south of the Walland Marsh record dated 1477. Although such records, when used in conjunction with rentals and court rolls, may provide ideas about landholding, they are more difficult to interpret with regard to local field systems. The very small size of some tenant holdings recorded in the 1432 Dengemarsh rental (almost two-thirds of the tenants listed had less than five acres and often this was in several plots) may indicate the presence of small fields on at least part of the manor.[32] Some of these plots are known to have been in the same field and it is possible names such as 'Mychellysacre' denote an area within a field linked to the name of an early landholder. Nevertheless, fields called 'Fyfacres' and 'le Twelfacre' presumably indicate acreage, an hypothesis apparently confirmed by the Lydd tithe map. Furthermore, even though the Denge Quarry fields on the tithe map are far less regular in shape when compared to those for Lydd Quarry, they still demonstrate a general alignment with the shingle ridges – a pattern also seen on the aerial photographs.[33] Thus, in broad terms the documentary sources would seem to confirm the archaeological findings regarding the process of reclamation and the resultant field system.

SETTLEMENT PATTERN

Pre-Conquest Lydd

The parish of Lydd in layout, if not in scale, seems to resemble those of Romney Marsh proper rather than the parishes of Walland Marsh – the latter being characteristically long and narrow with the parish church near the eastern boundary. Although much larger at 12,000 acres, Lydd church and its associated settlement were situated near the centre of the parish. The antiquity of the Romney Marsh churches is attested by the inclusion of most of them in the *Domesday Monachorum*, and Lydd's similar pre-Conquest foundation might be inferred from its being under the minster church of Lyminge, a 7th century monastic house (Du Boulay 1966, 24). Another indicator of its early establishment is the timing of the town fair, held on the feast day of St Anacletus (26th April) at least until the 18th century, which Everitt (1986, 227 n. 5) thinks may denote the dedication of the parish church (later changed to All Saints). The choice of saint is unusual but in keeping with an early foundation because St Anacletus is traditionally thought to be a late 1st century martyr, having been bishop of Rome after St Peter and St Linus but before St Clement (Farmer 1978, 84). Moreover, as noted above, charter and place-name

evidence also points to Lydd's Anglo-Saxon ancestry; Cullen (1997, 269) believes the name Lydd may be a derivation of OE 'hlid' – a lid, a cover, a gate – suggesting access to marshland pasture. Apart from drovers and graziers, such an access point would in time probably attract others, and if King Offa's charter does describe an authentic grant, it is possible that certain 9th and 10th century archbishops would have seen the advantages of a settlement on their land at Lydd. In addition to providing a gateway to the pasture, Lydd may have been an early distribution point for waterborne trade from the sea, tidal creeks and waterways. Even though there is no indication when the 'old haven' (marked immediately to the west of Holmstone on 17th century maps of Denge Marsh) was operational, it may mark the position of an early harbour because by the 11th century shipping was using the lee (eastern) side of Dungeness (Gardiner 1996, 18). Thus, probably from at least the late Anglo-Saxon period, the settlement at Lydd seems to have served a developing society based on agriculture, fishing and trading.

Landholding and Settlement

Turning to the medieval period, field-walking on Romney Marsh proper has revealed a landscape of numerous dispersed farmsteads and small settlements grouped around a parish church. Reeves (1995, 89) discovered that during the Middle Ages as a whole, rural occupation sites averaged one for every fifteen acres of land, but there were significant changes over time. These sites were most numerous during the 'Early Medieval' period (1050–1250), after which there was a gradual decline until *c.* 1450, and then a much sharper fall. Moreover, this general settlement pattern was not uniform across the marsh. One important factor was the manorial (ecclesiastical and lay) structure – the proportion of demesne to tenant land, whether the land was scattered or consolidated – which meant that at Orgarswick, for example, the peasant occupation sites were clustered around the periphery of the monastic farm (Reeves 1995, 89). Another related factor was the pattern of landholding. Using the Hundred of Newchurch records for the early 14th century, Butcher (2000) found an extremely densely populated peasant society where many were dependent on a very small acreage – a pattern resembling Reeves' findings for the 'Early Medieval' period.

For the post-Black Death period, the late 14th and 15th century manorial records for Appledore and Dengemarsh suggest that a high proportion of the peasant farmers there held less than fifteen acres, frequently in numerous small plots, with some apparently holding particular pieces of land jointly. Where these farmers had their farmsteads is more difficult to ascertain, but of the 799 land transactions listed in the Appledore court rolls for the period 1403 to 1471, 187 (almost a quarter) included a messuage or tenement.[34] The size of the piece of land with the dwelling varied considerably, but in a rural society where many farmers held scattered plots of land, their farmsteads may not always have been on their largest holding. Instead other factors, such as the presence of fresh water, accessibility and the proximity of local markets, may have been equally significant. However, there are problems interpreting this evidence because it is extremely difficult to locate the Appledore farmsteads, which are often only identified as part of a named *tenementum* or area, such as Mistleham, and it is possible some dwellings were sub-leased. In addition, the views of frankpledge for the town of Appledore (whose population overlapped but was not the same as that for Appledore manor) indicate that some of those who were active in the local land market lived in or close to the town (Sweetinburgh 2002, 151). Many of these men were probably engaged in agriculture to a lesser or greater extent, but the nature of the evidence means that the incidence of such quasi-urban farmsteads cannot be quantified. The 1432 Dengemarsh rental appears to show a similar pattern. Half the tenants had a messuage on land encompassed by the manor. Presumably almost all the rest lived either in or close to Lydd (or Romney), or on their other rural holdings, although Johanna, the wife of William Edmond of Fordwich, and Herbert Finch, who had considerable interests across the region, probably lived off the marsh.[35] Absentee lay landholders were not a new phenomenon in the 15th century, and even though they seem to have been few numerically before *c.* 1500 and may have sub-rented their holdings, their presence would have affected local settlement patterns (see below under Local Economy). Of those who had Dengemarsh farmsteads in 1432, their total landholdings varied in size from under 5 acres to over 50 acres, but just over half had less than 5 acres, leading to an uneven density of messuages across the manor.

Infrastructure and Settlement

As Reeves (1995, 90) found, the occupation sites of Romney Marsh were not scattered randomly across the marshland but predominantly bordered trackways, paths and field gateways. This observation is important and might have been equally applicable for Walland Marsh and Denge Marsh, especially for those areas enclosed before the late Middle Ages. Unfortunately the few surviving documentary sources are difficult to interpret, and those for the pre-Black Death period are particularly problematic. However, the evidence for 13th century Mistleham may provide useful indicators about the Lydd Quarry/Caldicott area. Of those holding 35 acre plots from Christchurch Priory, not all of these men of Mistleham would have had their farmstead adjacent to Mistleham Lane, though many probably did (Eddison and Draper 1997, 83).

Evidence for this relationship between farmsteads and roads can also be found in the later sources. Even though the New Langport rental of 1393–4 is in poor condition and many of the entries are unclear, it seems a considerable proportion of the holdings abutted a

road or lane, and this also held true for the far fewer messuages.[36] Impressionistically, these findings appear to resemble those for the more detailed mid 16th century Old Langport rental, which means that the latter may provide a number of indicators about local settlement patterns, though presumably there had been significant changes by 1551.[37] The later rental mentions relatively few messuages and several of these had recently fallen down or been converted into barns, which is suggestive of a landscape in transition. Of the 200+ parcels of land listed, almost 60% were less than five acres and over 77% were no more than ten acres. This continuing pattern of small plots may indicate a landscape of small fields – the process of amalgamation into larger fields having started but not yet finished. Over 60% of all the plots were said to abut a street or lane, giving a picture of a manor criss-crossed by a series of trackways. These connected the farmsteads to the towns of New Romney, Lydd, and the shrinking settlement of Old Romney, as well as to the various embankments and waterways.[38] Therefore, examining the roads, walls and sewers together, it seems likely that the marsh was a landscape of small fields, and, by extension, that this had produced a settlement pattern dominated by numerous small farmsteads set alongside these features. The roads and walls were higher than the surrounding marsh, affording a degree of protection for adjacent messuages, with the roads also providing arteries of communication for the farmers, who must have spent a considerable part of their working lives travelling between their scattered landholdings. This relationship between roads (higher ground – shingle banks?) and farmsteads is also visible on the early maps, where four houses are shown adjoining a road which runs from Burnt House Wall to the outskirts of Lydd (one of the excavated trackways at Lydd Quarry) (*Fig. 3).[39] The exact position of these houses is difficult to pinpoint and although they may be later constructions, it seems likely that they occupy medieval sites – the few remaining occupation sites of a once densely populated area. Their survival is of interest and may denote the position of a trackway from Lydd's late medieval harbour, located at Wainway Gate and associated with Ocholt Fleet (in earlier times the waterway probably extended eastwards, possibly as far as the northern borders of Lydd town).[40] These houses were also in the vicinity of Pigwell, also marked on the early maps, suggesting the significance of fresh water supplies, as many of the water channels may have contained brackish water.

For those living and working on Denge Marsh such matters were equally vital for their existence. According to the 1432 Dengemarsh rental, about half of the messuages for which abutments were recorded bordered a road. The remainder (in descending order) abutted land, the demesne, and shingle; Roger Hykke's farmstead was at Pyperesford.[41] The earliest maps also indicate the provision of roads across the manor, the most important being the three roads from Lydd. The first ran eastwards to Stone End; the second to the 'cabons' (fishermen's cabins – seasonal living quarters and storage facilities) at the Ness via Cockerels Bridge; while the third ran south-east to Dengemarsh manor court before turning north, cutting across the road to the cabins and joining the Stone End road. To the west was a fourth road that linked South Brooks to the Wick. Many of the roadside messuages were probably to the north of Dengemarsh court, close to the place where the road to the cabins crossed the third road from Lydd. Some of the farmsteads thought to abut other land may also have been in this area, while some of those close to the shingle may have been in the vicinity of the cabins. Information included in the rental about previous holders of the messuages, and the absence of any references to decayed properties, may imply that the situation in 1432 was similar to that of the late 14th century (the generation before the current holders). This apparent stability over time has been discussed by Dimmock (1998, 172–6).[42] Thus, the likelihood of occupation sites at Denge Quarry was confirmed by the archaeological excavation, though exactly whose 15th century messuages they were is difficult to say, each being surrounded by its small plot of land. This settlement pattern of a dense concentration of farmsteads abutting roads was a consequence of still high population levels, and the farmers' and smallholders' need to be able to travel easily to their various holdings and to Lydd, for marketing and other purposes.

Settlement at the Ness

Some of those living in Lydd parish gained all or part of their livelihood from the sea, which had implications for the settlement pattern. The presence of the fishermen and mariners will be considered in more detail in the next sub-section, but it is worth noting here that there is evidence of a long-established seasonal settlement at the cabins near the Ness (Gardiner 1996, 18). In 1510 Thomas Inglott bequeathed his tenement (location unspecified), his two tenements at the Ness close to the chapel of St Mary and the neighbouring hall, three other tenements and half a tenement called a 'cabon' at the Ness to his wife for life.[43] The other half tenement or cabin was to pass to Thomas' partner, Adrian Dyne, another Lydd fisherman. Whether these included Thomas' principal house is unclear, but he did not mention any other property in his will. However, it does indicate that there were a number of tenements at the Ness, presumably for rent, and a chapel, where the fishermen (and their wives) resided during the various fishing seasons, selling the fish at Dungeness market.[44] In his study of the medieval fishing villages of South Devon, Fox (2001, 131) noted that fishermen farmers associated with what he called 'cellar settlements' (the fishermen were non-resident, solely using the cellars to store boats and tackle) had their farms and dwellings inland within a short distance of their cellars. The situation at Lydd seems slightly different, with the settlement at the Ness apparently a hybrid form between Fox's fishing village

and cellar settlement, although presumably most had their principal tenement in or close to the town, or possibly in the surrounding countryside.

THE LOCAL ECONOMY

Before the Conquest

A number of pre-Conquest charters shed some light on the early economy of Romney Marsh. Grazing was important, with cattle pastured near Holmstone to the south-west of Lydd, and pasture for 300 sheep at a place called *Rumining seta*, between Blackmanstone, Orgarswick and Dymchurch, which was given to the minster at Lyminge in 697 or 700 (Ward 1936, 20–7; Brooks 1988, 93. Birch 1885–99, no. 98; Sawyer 1968, no. 21). Moreover, the link between the manor of Wye and its sub-manor of Dengemarsh presumably meant that the latter provided grazing land for Wye in some form, possibly from the 8th century. The area known as the Wick may denote the importance of sheep farming, but interestingly, unlike the north Kent marshes, there seem to be few unnamed wicks in Dengemarsh, though the first edition O.S. map does show numerous sheep folds (Evans 1953, p. 144–5). Other activities during the Anglo-Saxon period included salt production and fishing – King Aethelberht II gave land for a saltern at *Sandtun*, West Hythe, to the monastic community at Lyminge, and a fishery with fishermen's houses has been tentatively identified as New Romney (Brooks 1988, 96, 98. Birch 1885–99, no. 148; Sawyer 1968, no. 23. Birch 1885–99, no. 160; Sawyer 1968, no. 24). The presence of a number of permanent settlements on the marsh, including Lydd, suggests that farming, fishing and wild fowling (no documentary evidence but a likely marshland pursuit) were not the only occupations, but the level of diversity of employment is difficult to establish for this period.

The Late 11th Century

Domesday paints a similar picture. There were ten salt houses and two fisheries at Bilsington, being the property of the Bishop of Bayeux, and in Langport Hundred Robert of Romney's holdings included a fishery worth 2*s*. (Morgan 1983, nos. 5, 175; 177; 179). Grazing was still important but at least some of the marsh (both demesne and tenant land) was under the plough, and at Lydd, as at Romney, the local inhabitants were earning part of their living from the sea. Like Dover and Sandwich, Romney was providing ship-service to the crown in 1086, and Lydd's development may have shadowed that of Romney (Morgan 1983, no. 5, 178). However, it is unclear what Dengemarsh contributed to Battle Abbey at this time because the Domesday entry lists Wye manor in its entirety (Morgan 1983, no. 6, 1).

Before the Black Death – Landlords and Tenant Farmers

Although documentary sources are more extensive for the 13th and 14th centuries, those for Dengemarsh, Langport and Aldington bailiwick (Lydd) are still severely limited. Consequently, it is useful to draw on those for Christchurch's manors of Appledore, Agney and Ebony, but it should be remembered that these records provide information about the economy from the perspective of the monastic houses, not the peasantry (Smith 1943, 128–65). For the peasant economy, occasional references to tenants in the manorial records may provide a few details, and there is a valuable series of early 14th century tax assessments covering Newchurch Hundred. When considering Lydd's hinterland, it is important to remember the inter-relationship between landlord and tenant, which means neither sector of the economy can be assessed in isolation, though for convenience each is described separately here.

During the 13th century Battle Abbey was engaged in a general policy of acquiring small pieces of land to extend and consolidate its estates, including plots on Denge Marsh. Some of these sellers were local prosperous townsmen (such as Simon le Fant of Lydd who had bought a substantial acreage in Denge Marsh before he quitclaimed his holdings to the abbey for sixty-three marks), while others were poor peasants on tiny holdings (Searle 1974, 150–1).[45] At about the same time, the abbey moved to a direct farming policy of its demesne lands and an inventory (as part of a charter, dated 1257) of the demesne livestock at Dengemarsh lists 10 oxen, 12 cows, 9 two year-old cattle and 13 yearlings (Searle 1974, 253 n. 16).[46] The sheep flock was said to comprise 132 sheep and 15 lambs, and there were 8 sucking pigs, 1 stot and a flock of swans. In addition to pasture, the arable land produced wheat, barley and beans. Continuing to follow a mixed farming strategy in the early 14th century, the abbey also grew oats and legumes: beans, peas and vetch, carting the corn back to Battle (Searle 1974, 453). These leguminous plants added fertility, particularly important where the soil was thin over the shingle, but the vetch also provided valuable fodder. In addition hemp was grown, with the sergeant spending 20*d.* on three and-a-half bushels of seed in 1319–20, and canvas produced locally from the crop. However, for the abbey, wool and meat were especially valuable marshland products. Even though the abbey's sheep flock experienced severe losses in 1319–20 (the end of a disastrous period nationwide), there were still 149 ewes and 86 wethers. The cow herd was similarly large, comprising 36 cows, 3 bulls and various young cattle; while the pig herd stood at 1 boar and 4 sows. Horses and oxen did the field work and there were several carthorses. The manorial buildings included the granges, a cow house, sheep fold and stable, and there was also a garden. Among the abbey's labour force at Dengemarsh were a number of specialists: three ploughmen, a cowman, a pigman, and two shepherds; and

a cheese maker was employed for the summer months. Other labour was provided by the *famuli*, some of whom may have lived at the manor. Other income came from renting out grazing land, the most lucrative of which was the pasture in the Common Brooks, contributing £12 10*s.* 1*d.* in 1319–20.[47]

A similar pattern of mixed farming was found for Christchurch's marshland manors where the long series of bedels' rolls from the 1270s to 1359–60 (though not continuous) showed the priory's response to the various disasters of the late 13th and early 14th centuries (Butcher and Gross 1995, 108–15).[48] As noted above, Christchurch was apparently able to rapidly overcome the problems created by the great storms, and seems similarly to have recovered from the agricultural disasters of the 1310s in the short term, but the general trend during the early 14th century was a slight decline in profitability. Nevertheless, wheat and oats continued to be grown, with yields of the latter significantly improved through practices such as marling (Smith 1943, 137–8). As a result, the acreage under wheat and oats remained broadly consistent over this period. At Agney wheat was the most important crop, whereas at Appledore the acreage under oats was often five times greater than that under wheat. Of the legumes, these were grown at both manors throughout the period, though the amount of vetch grown quadrupled between the 1310s and the 1340s at Appledore. This increase corresponds to the introduction of cows in 1339–40, the herd of twenty being farmed out for £5 per annum from the following year. Such a move away from direct farming was indicative of future trends. However, Christchurch was still prepared to spend considerable sums on manorial buildings and on walls and ditches, although, like other landlords, the priory appeared to expect the peasantry to bear an increasing proportion of the sea defence maintenance expenses (Butcher and Gross 1991).

Unlike their monastic landlords, peasants struggled, sometimes unsuccessfully, to recover from difficult years, and the records suggest that many experienced severe hardship. Although it is difficult to quantify the effect of partible inheritance on peasant society at Lydd, the division of the land belonging to the men of Broomhill through inheritance seems to have left some with small holdings when they sold the land or the rent to Battle Abbey (Gardiner 1988, 118). The accumulation of such holdings by the abbey allowed it to increase its tenant land as well as the demesne, leading to a decline in the proportion of peasant freeholders. However, certain prosperous townsmen and entrepreneurs among the peasantry were able to capitalise on the abbey's policy of increasing the tenant acreage, but many of these accumulated holdings were broken up following the death of their creators, producing a volatile land market (Butcher and Gross 1991). Such men might also rent pasture on Dengemarsh or from other marshland manors on an annual basis, allowing them greater flexibility to respond to changes in the market. They may also have rented kiddles or fish traps from the abbey, which were potentially profitable assets for both parties.[49] Consequently, in the difficult conditions of the early 14th century an ability to diversify was presumably extremely valuable, allowing more prosperous peasants to utilise family labour effectively and to spread risk.

It is possible to gain further insights into the peasant economy of this region from the early 14th century Newchurch Hundred taxation returns, and this summary uses an unpublished report by Butcher and Gross (1991).[50] Like the ecclesiastical landholders, the Newchurch peasantry employed a mixed farming strategy, though comparably on a very small scale. For example, three-quarters of those taxed owned sheep but over 80% of these flocks had less than twenty-one animals. Pigs were similarly ubiquitous, whereas cows, requiring a greater acreage, were only owned by 58% of taxpayers and most had a small herd. Interestingly, over 40% had horses, often including mares and foals, but there were few oxen, suggesting that, like the lords, the peasants used mixed teams or ploughed using horses. Although the tax returns only recorded crop surpluses, these seem to show that oats and wheat were the main cereals. Most peasants put a greater percentage of their holding down to oats, growing wheat for the market, perhaps. Again, like their landlords, a majority of the taxpayers grew beans and vetch for both human and animal consumption, and hemp was also favoured by a significant minority. Although the marshland conditions were ideal for growing hemp, the presence of this labour-intensive crop would seem to be indicative of the conditions of the early 14th century peasantry. Other household activities (not recorded in the tax returns) might similarly save a family from destitution or, for a few, aid their advancement, such as fishing or cutting turf for fuel.[51] In certain years, income from such sources might make the difference between failure and survival for some households, though it is unclear whether the status of the Romney Marsh peasantry before the Black Death was one of unremitting decline.

Salt Production

The importance of fishing to the local rural economy cannot be gauged from the surviving documentary records, but like wild-fowling and turf-cutting, fishing was presumably undertaken by both lords and peasants (see above). However, there is some evidence for the salt industry, at least for Belgar, though salt making was also carried out at other places in the Romney Marshes. Salt was produced at Belgar from at least the late 11th century until the late 14th century. In the 1090s it formed part of the demesne economy of Bilsington manor, but under William d'Albini's descendants and Bilsington Priory, which received Belgar at its foundation in 1252, salt production appears to have been undertaken by local tenants, who paid rent in salt, herrings and money. As Vollens (1995, 120–5) has charted, the balance between land for salt production and for agriculture (where this resulted from reclamation and parcellation) was dependent on a number of factors, including local topography, silting and other geomorphological processes, as well as on the price of salt, which shifted considerably over time.

Wood – Production and Use

Salt production may have been linked to the availability of wood for fuel, but timber was also required for buildings, boats, carts, sea defences and in the manufacture of many household and other items (Smith 1943, 175). Moreover, wood, in the form of hawthorn and other species, was needed for sea wall construction, and holly (OE 'holegn' – holly tree) provided valuable winter fodder on the Holmstone from at least the 8th century (Wallenberg 1934, 484; Birch 1885–99, no. 160; Sawyer 1968, no. 24).[52] Documentary references concerning timber or woodland are relatively scarce but, as Reeves (2004, 21–4) has shown, when used in conjunction with field walking can provide a picture of the distribution of various tree species across the marshes. Field names and charter evidence indicates the availability of wood and timber during the pre-Conquest period and it seems these materials continued to be available locally until the early 16th century. Such stocks may not, however, have been sufficient at times of heavy demand, whether for reclamation or building, which may explain the need for timber to be brought from Newenden and Sandwich in 1319–20.[53] Later references similarly imply that timber was shipped down onto the Romney Marshes from the Weald, and it was also imported into neighbouring Romney during the late Middle Ages (Murray 1945, xlvii).[54] This apparent trade in timber may indicate abundance in the Weald and on the uplands more generally, rather than scarcity on the Marshes, with the peasants on the archiepiscopal estate at Aldington expecting, among other duties, to carry timber and make hurdles, unlike their counterparts living on the marsh (Witney 2000, 212–20, 228–39).

Among the tree species and their uses noted by Reeves (2004, 23–4) are elm, oak and willow. Willow provided valuable windbreaks and might be used for fuel and for sea walls, leading to their widespread distribution across the Marshes (Beck 1995, 166). In contrast elm was grown close to farmsteads or in neighbouring hedgerows, with the timber being used in the production of agricultural implements, household goods and in the construction of buildings and sea walls.[55] Oak was far less common, being mostly confined to the north-east corner of Romney Marsh, which may explain the seemingly valuable nature of John Blakbourne's oak tree – a gift he bequeathed to his wife in his will in 1466.[56] This scarcity may in part explain the introduction of the holm oak onto the Marshes in the 16th century, thereby providing a local source of material for the maintenance of the Dymchurch Wall (Beck 1995, 165; 2004, 19). Also required for the construction and maintenance of sea walls were thorn bushes, their presence in such documentary sources as the 14th century Appledore bedels rolls, the 15th century Scotney records and later accounts for the Level of Romney Marsh, indicative of their value to the wall builders.[57] For example, it was considered vital that assessments should be made of the 'nomber of acres of frighte bushes old and new' within certain waterings on the Level of Romney Marsh and, furthermore, these thorn bushes were not to be felled under four years growth – a traditional management system that probably pertained across the whole marsh.[58]

The Late Middle Ages –
Landlords and Tenant Farmers

Documentary sources for the state of the late medieval economy at Lydd do shed some light on a number of subjects, including changes in the tenurial system and the land market, which had implications for land-use strategies by various social groups and institutions; the town's place in the rural economy; fishing, and other activities. Some of these substantial topics have been discussed at length elsewhere, and consequently this study will merely summarise, seeking to relate the information as closely as possible to the excavation sites.

Of the institutional landholders, Battle Abbey continued its policy of direct farming at Dengemarsh manor during the late 14th century, though sporadically it leased the whole manor – a strategy it used more frequently for its distant manors (Searle 1974, 258–60 n. 39). The first decades of the 15th century saw a continuation of this policy, but it seems to have ended in 1431 after which the manor was leased to farmers for longer periods (Dimmock 1998, 171). Whether the abbey's earlier policy of short-term leases had resulted in certain changes to the farming regime adopted on the demesne lands is unclear. Even though cereals and beans were still grown in 1429–30, the sheep had disappeared, leaving only the cattle and pigs. However, the demesne sheep pasture was apparently retained, being rented out to John Lucok, John Osebarn and Thomas Brogges for their own flocks.[59] Decayed rents were also causing the abbey severe difficulties, a problem it was similarly encountering on its other estates, and this too may have hastened the move away from direct farming to leasing the whole manor (Searle 1974, 258). Possibly the first of these 'new' lessees was John Bate whose son, Andrew, was the abbey's farmer in the 1460s (Dimmock 1998, 172). Dimmock (1998, 184–94), in his doctoral thesis, has used the activities of Andrew Bate as a case study of the rise of capitalist farmers in Lydd. Father and son were butcher-graziers and Andrew Bate was particularly notorious in the Lydd area for his heavy-handed approach towards the Dengemarsh tenants.[60] Threats and violence accompanied his enlargement of the demesne at the expense of his neighbours' holdings on Denge Marsh. Bate's successor, Thomas Robyn, used a different method to increase his holdings within the manor, with his activities in the land market resulting in an accumulation of a substantial consolidated acreage

that he was then able to pass on to his sons (Dimmock 1998, 108–9).[61] The next two abbey farmers were men in the same mould. Thomas Strogull took on the lease of Dengemarsh for thirty years in 1536 and the following year signed a similar agreement with the abbey for 'the tenement of Northlade', an area of newly enclosed marsh, which seems to have been 'added' to the demesne primarily through Andrew Bate's activities (Dimmock 1998, 181–2).[62] Strogull did not confine his interests to Denge Marsh because he was listed as holding over eighty-two acres in Old Langport, including Calcolte, in 1551, and in the same year he bequeathed his lease of Bletching (and that of Northlade) to his only son.[63] His successor at Dengemarsh, William Bocher, similarly held land in other lordships.[64] In addition to his principal tenement, he held a tenement and a close in Lydd High Street, another close by the churchyard, and, adjoining his barn to the east of the town, two further tenements and two closes together.[65]

The sources for Scotney manor (and to a much lesser extent the two Langport manors) provide a different narrative, but the end result was similar. Scotney (and Ocholt) had been the target of considerable outside interest since at least the mid 14th century. The area had been the subject of a boundary agreement between Sir William de Septvans and William Claptus (a citizen of London) and his wife in 1348, and another London citizen (John Gisors) had granted Scotney and Ocholt to a group of six men in 1369.[66] Thereafter these lands and appurtenances changed hands several times. Those showing an interest in the marsh included Henry, bishop of Wakefield, and John de Nevill, lord of Raby, though by the mid 1390s the holders were local leading townsmen and their prosperous rural neighbours.[67] However, the 15th century brought renewed interest from outsiders, London citizens and members of the minor aristocracy, possibly implying a return to land speculation.[68] A group of local men may have been similarly motivated when they accumulated substantial holdings, including Scotney manor, in the decades before 1440 for Archbishop Chichele's new Oxford college (Draper 1997, 7–8, 10).

During the late 14th century, the bailiffs at Scotney maintained a mixed farming regime, sowing wheat, barley, oats and the three types of legume. Yet, even at this stage greater emphasis may have been placed on the livestock because the cow herd numbered 65 in 1394–5, as well as 441 ewes and 5 sows, possibly enhancing its attraction, especially for outsiders.[69] At first the All Souls College lessees apparently adopted a similar strategy, except they expanded sheep numbers at the expense of the cow herd. Nevertheless, expenditure on the old barn and the great barn in 1457–8, and on the little barn three years later, seems to suggest that some arable farming was still practised, though sheep probably provided the lessee's prime source of income.[70] For the college too sheep were valuable assets, with All Souls expecting its lessees to maintain at least 800 ewes and 200 lambs at

Scotney, and the same numbers still required in the early 16th century (Draper 1998, 118).[71] However, in 1520, and again in 1536, the college may have had certain difficulties attracting prospective tenants, though this seems to have been a temporary inconvenience.[72]

During the 15th and early 16th century lessees such as Henry Alayn, John Pulton and Vincent Daniell were prosperous farmers (Daniell styled himself yeoman), having a number of holdings across the marsh and beyond.[73] Nonetheless, they also saw themselves as men of Lydd, serving as jurats and giving generously to the parish church. Indeed, Daniell wished priests and clerks to accompany his body from Scotney to Lydd after his death so that he could be buried with due ceremony before the altar of St James in his home church. Daniell's successors at Scotney, however, were not from Romney Marsh. Thomas Culpeper was a member of the east Kent gentry and John Philipp was a yeoman farmer and butcher from Tenterden.[74] In many ways these outsiders were very similar to their 14th century predecessors, the marshes offering them opportunities either as farmers or as landlords (through sub-leasing). Where they did differ was in their desire and ability to pass on these newly acquired lands to the next generation, which led to the establishment of a number of families from the yeomanry and lesser gentry who had considerable interests in the Romney Marshes over several generations (Draper 1998, 120–2).

For the 'middling' farmers (those lower in terms of status and wealth) this period brought mixed fortunes. Some seem to have allied themselves with entrepreneurs such as Thomas Strogull, while others found themselves the target of Andrew Bate's activities. These men sought to maintain their family's place in the rural community by adopting various strategies – buying and selling, marriage, inheritance, engaging in by-employment. Mixed farming may have remained the norm among this group, but some, especially those with relatives or other contacts in the meat trade, may have increasingly turned to livestock farming.[75] A few families seemed able to prosper under these conditions – possibly a testimony to their adaptability. In certain cases, however, their disappearance from the records was not a product of their farming ability, but rather an absence of heirs, although some families may have survived through the female line.[76]

Even survival might have been difficult for their poorer neighbours. Smallholders often only had a few scattered tiny plots, and many of these people (particularly from the 1520s) sought to abate their scot payments.[77] Most were presumably dependent on by-employment (as servants, labourers, artisans or fishermen) to increase their meagre income, but the records provide few details.[78]

Turning to the land market, Thomas Robyn (see above) was particularly active after he became the abbey's farmer of Dengemarsh, and he may have been equally acquisitive in the neighbouring manors. The lost court rolls make it impossible to follow all his transactions, but at the court held in February 1489, for example, he was due to pay relief for eleven pieces of land (over seventy acres in total) he had acquired, and in May of that year he was expected to pay for a further six purchases (over fifty acres).[79] This level of activity by individuals was apparently rare in the various Romney Marsh manorial courts before the last decades of the 15th century, and even where particular tenants did acquire a number of pieces of land it was usually done over a longer period of time. Furthermore, as the Appledore manor rolls demonstrate more clearly, such purchases were predominantly of small pieces of land and individuals were as likely to sell land as to buy it (Sweetinburgh 2002, 145–52). Consequently, among the local peasantry an individual's total holding probably rarely exceeded fifty acres, though any assessment of landholding is hampered by the nature of the documentary sources.[80] Another factor that presumably stopped the accumulation of large holdings by individuals was the frequency of group buying and selling, a process that often involved small plots. Yet such land was probably not farmed jointly, suggesting the prevalence of sub-letting, either to co-buyers or others. Thus, like the alterations in tenurial policy described above, the changing deployment of the land market by individuals had profound implications for land use on the marsh, and by extension for the rural economy more generally.

In summary, Denge Marsh and the southern part of Walland Marsh changed from a densely populated landscape, where there were almost as many farmers and smallholders in the early 15th century as there had been in the mid 14th century, to one which was home to relatively few people by the last decade of the 15th century. During the next fifty years this depopulation of the marshland continued. Throughout the later Middle Ages the majority of those holding land in the various manors around Lydd lived on their farmsteads, often close to trackways, or in Lydd itself, but by the mid 16th century the number of dwellings on the marsh had fallen dramatically. Lydd continued to provide housing for some, including those still working on the marsh, whereas others among the dispossessed (or those who had sold their holdings) had probably left for the Wealden towns, hoping to find work in the cloth and iron industries (Zell 1994, 116–17). Farming practice was also changing. Rather than mixed farming on both demesne and tenant land, which had characterised the Romney Marshes until the mid to late 15th century, men such as Andrew Bate were pasturing growing numbers of cattle and sheep on the demesne and other lands they held. In some areas this alteration had been accompanied by the amalgamation of previously small plots of land by the more prosperous farmers, allowing them to hold whole fields or much larger blocks within fields. This does not mean that the arable land had gone completely by the mid 16th century, but the balance had changed profoundly towards livestock production.

Lydd and its Hinterland

It is neither possible nor feasible to assess the rural economy without considering the town of Lydd. The demarcation between rural and urban society is an artificial construct with respect to medieval small town society. At its most basic, a number of those who counted themselves as farmers lived in the town, with most others having relatives and friends in Lydd. Those who lived on the Denge Quarry sites, and at Lydd Quarry/Caldicott, worshipped at All Saints parish church in the town, and it was to this church that they were brought for burial. Its structure and ornamentation was their collective business, and in addition certain individuals were prepared to commission expensive works and alterations to the fabric at their own expense.[81] Lydd was also a market place, used by Battle Abbey, as well as the local population, to both buy and sell goods. Agricultural produce was bought for direct consumption or for brewing or baking as a way of adding value. Similarly other raw materials might be purchased, leading to the local production of cloth, rope or other manufactured or part-manufactured goods.[82] The town similarly offered opportunities for by-employment, and the contacts and connections fostered between the town and its hinterland, and with other Cinque Ports, places in Kent and abroad, meant that the fortunes of Lydd were interwoven with those of the surrounding countryside. This symbiotic relationship has been studied by Dimmock (1998, 69–70) for the late medieval period and a single case study is used here to illustrate the interconnections between Lydd and Denge Marsh. Battle Abbey and the leading citizens of Lydd clashed over claims to the right of wreck off the coast of Dengemarsh manor, but the dispute really concerned the status of Dengemarsh. Although this disagreement probably began in the early 14th century, or even earlier, the battle for Dengemarsh started again in earnest in 1466, following the issuing of a charter that year which confirmed the Cinque Port franchises of Dengemarsh and Lydd, including the right of wreck.[83] The abbey apparently claimed that Dengemarsh had never legally been a corporate member of the Federation as a limb of Lydd, and thus its inclusion through the sending of four jurats to sit on the town council should cease. In 1477 the dispute was decided in the abbey's favour. However, this did not stop the town clerk, who had been extremely active on the town's behalf, from including Dengemarsh's representation in the custumal produced that year. This struggle for autonomy coincided with the Dengemarsh farmer's more aggressive policy towards his poorer neighbours. The coincidence was not lost on the supporters of the town's position, who understood that the loss of legal civic jurisdiction over Dengemarsh would have serious repercussions for their community.[84] Thus, for those living at the Denge Quarry site in the late 15th century, the abbey's desire to drive a wedge between them and Lydd was a serious development, and one which might have far-reaching implications for their livelihood.

Fishing

The impact of the fishing industry on the local economy over time is difficult to gauge, but for some families in the Lydd area it provided all or part of their income. The fishermen sold their fish at the market on the Ness, with those of Lydd allowed to sell most of their fish before the 'Westermen', who came annually to fish the coastal waters around Dungeness.[85] From the 1567 Muster roll and other sources Elks (1987, 125) has calculated that there were between twenty-one and thirty-six working fishermen of Lydd at any one time. Most, however, did not earn all their income from fishing and, though difficult to interpret, the testamentary evidence would seem to substantiate this (Sweetinburgh, forthcoming). There were considerable differences between the poorest and wealthiest fishing families, though most belonged to the prosperous 'middling sort'. However, there were a few fishermen, such as Robert Lawless, who were more affluent, and as a leading citizen of Lydd he was regularly elected as one of the twelve jurats.[86] Others were less fortunate – several fishermen or the widows of fishermen were listed among those in Lydd who were unable to pay the local taxes in the decades after 1520.[87] In part this stratification was a measure of the hierarchical nature of the industry. At the top there were the boat owners and masters, and at the bottom the one or two boys who served in the crew. Between them were the members of the boat's company, some of whom provided nets for the boat, thereby enhancing their share of the catch when it was divided. The large numbers of nets required by individual boats were made up of units of three nets (two nets in the eastern ports), called the 'mansfare' in the south coast ports, which was regarded as equivalent to a crewman's share of the catch (Dulley 1969, 48; Middleton-Stewart 1996, 73). Other differentiation included the masters who were not boat owners, while the boats themselves were often divided into boat shares; some owners at Dover held a sixteenth share in a single boat (Dixon 1992, 383).[88]

Some fishermen worked kiddles or fish traps, and those on Dengemarsh came under the jurisdiction of the abbey. Like other assets they were the subject of transactions in the manorial court, and in May 1432 the new holders of two halves were expected to pay relief of 16.5*d*. each. However, in December 1499 the relief payment of a different kiddle was only 2*s*., perhaps being a reflection of its less favourable position.[89] The testamentary evidence suggests that kiddles were often highly valued and, like land, might be sub-rented.[90] Nevertheless, like the other fishermen, those using kiddles may similarly have suffered during the second half of the 16th century, a time apparently marked by a general decline in the fortunes of the industry in the eastern ports (Dulley 1969, 55–61; Kowaleski 2000, 448–51).[91] National factors, such as changing demands for fish, as well as local conditions (problems associated with the French threat, periods of high mortality and harvest failure), meant that men from previously prosperous fishing families seem to have had relatively few assets at death. In part the state of the industry may explain the relatively high failure rate among those involved in fishing, but others factors (variable annual catches, losses at sea and prolonged storm periods) presumably contributed to the lack of stability (Sweetinburgh, forthcoming). There were a few families whose members remained fishermen throughout the period, though in some cases these men combined fishing with overseas and coastal trading, or other commercial, land-based activities.[92]

Other Activities

Such activities might involve the victualling trades, or crafts associated with leather or cloth, though in terms of scale, production levels of the latter were far below those of the Weald. As a result, those in the countryside around Lydd and at the coast became involved in trading networks that encompassed the local Romney Marsh and Wealden towns, Canterbury and London (Dimmock 1998, 33–6, 43–52).[93] In addition, during this period wild fowl, like fish, were often given as gifts to royal officials and others by the civic authorities at Lydd, the birds presumably having been trapped nearby, possibly on the remaining fleets to the north of the town.[94] However, salt panning had become far less significant locally by the late Middle Ages. Nine tenants paid part of their rent as white salt at New Langport in 1393–4, but the growing importance of Bay salt from the 15th century probably damaged the English coastal industry (Bridbury 1955, 76, 92–3). However, the illegal taking of goods from wrecks (and following incidents of piracy) remained popular, while the authorities sought to halt the practice in an area that remained difficult to control.[95] Thus the local rural economy, though primarily agricultural, did provide some opportunities with respect to by-employment for a few of the hard-pressed small-scale farmers and their urban counterparts. By the early 16th century, however, the profits of many of the local leading families were tied to the growing conversion of arable to pasture, although frequently they too might invest in a range of commercial ventures as a way of safeguarding their rural mansions or town houses for their sons and grandsons (Draper 1998, 121–2).

THE LYDD QUARRY AREA IN 1552
by Mark Gardiner

The area around Lydd is covered by a number of detailed surveys from the period 1470 to 1560, as Sweetinburgh has noted above. However, there are considerable problems in utilising the wealth of information from these records and, in particular, plotting that information on a map. One method is to show the information semi-schematically, incorporating our knowledge of the geography of the area. This avoids the problem of establishing the precise

location of each parcel. The area around Old Romney church which was described in the 1552 Old Langport survey was reconstructed in this manner in earlier work (Gardiner 1994, Fig. 6). This cannot entirely solve the difficulties of such surveys which contain ambiguities and apparent contradictions, but does allow the information to be displayed in a useful manner.

Most of the area covered by the Lydd Quarry excavations lay within the manor of Old Langport, and much of this can be reconstructed from the 1552 survey (Fig. 6).[96] Land to the east lay in Lydd manor, and that to the west in the manor of Scotney. To the north lay the manor of New Langport, which included some land falling within the excavated area. The two roads identified in excavation and shown on Poker's map of 1617 (*Fig. 3) can be readily recognised in the survey. The more northerly was described as a street leading between Hendeley's tenement and Goreswall, while that to the south is variously called the street between Smith's barn and Goreswall, or the street between Thomas Harlackinden's tenement and the church of Lydd. The position of Smith's barn is noted on the north side of the track. Harlackinden's house is also indicated and is shown on the 1588–9 map made for All Soul's College.[97] The position of the building has also been suggested by excavation (see Overall Discussion below) and the survey tends to support that identification. These two roads, together with the road from Lydd to Camber (along the line of the present road), Gores Wall itself and a short embankment across the north-east end of the Wicks near to Pigwell Farm called Pigwell Wall, provide fixed points which allow the land parcels to be located, if not precisely, then in general terms.

The only buildings in the area examined here, in addition to the house of Thomas Harlackinden and Smith's barn mentioned above, were two houses near Pigwell. One was held by Thomas Agas and lay in the manor of Old Langport near to the Lydd-Camber road. The second to the south-east was held by the heirs of Alan Epce and lay in the manor of Lydd. The surveys confirm that by the mid 16th century the landscape was sparsely settled, though with a greater number of buildings in and immediately around Lydd. They do not list the sites of earlier buildings, although that information was provided for by the Old Langport rental for the area around Old Romney (Gardiner 1994). It is, however, possible to infer something of the character of the earlier landscape. Thomas Harlackinden appears to have obtained, either by purchase or by inheritance, the land of Thomas Breges. Thomas was a substantial landholder in Langport vill in *c.* 1430, though it is uncertain whether his house lay on the same site as his successor.[98]

One further feature which evidently pre-dates the 16th century is the block of fields called Gensing. The name is derived from the place so-called in Hastings and presumably comes from a locative name of a former tenant. These fields may have formed a tenement, with the land being held by an earlier tenant in the manor.

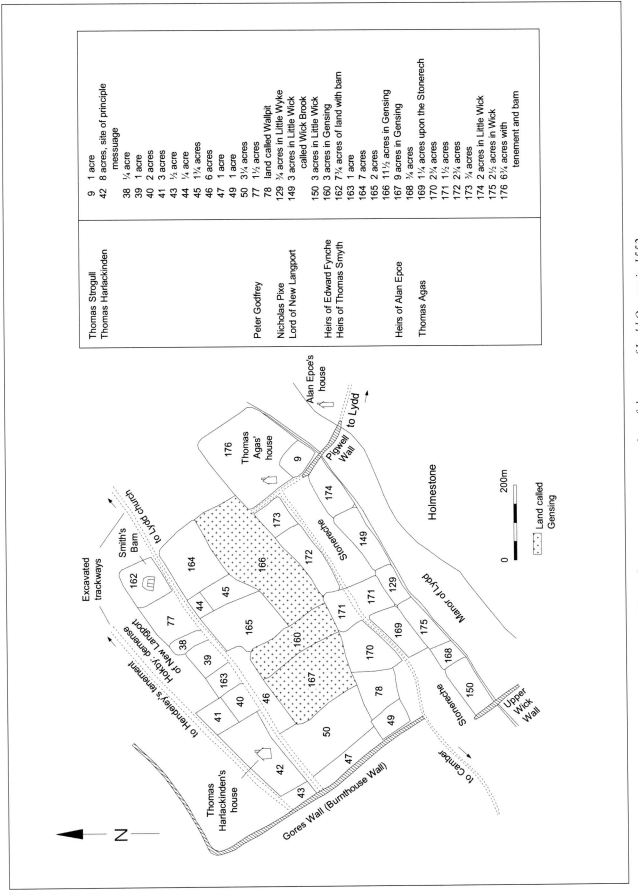

Thomas Strogull	9	1 acre
	42	8 acres, site of principle messuage
Thomas Harlackinden	38	¼ acre
	39	1 acre
	40	2 acres
	41	3 acres
	43	½ acre
	44	¼ acre
	45	1¾ acres
	46	6 acres
	47	1 acre
	49	1 acre
	50	3¼ acres
Peter Godfrey	77	1½ acres
	78	land called Wallpit
Nicholas Pixe	129	¾ acres in Little Wyke
Lord of New Langport	149	3 acres in Little Wick called Wick Brook
	150	3 acres in Little Wick
Heirs of Edward Fynche	160	3 acres in Gensing
Heirs of Thomas Smyth	162	7¾ acres of land with barn
	163	1 acre
	164	7 acres
	165	2 acres
	166	11½ acres in Gensing
Heirs of Alan Epce	167	9 acres in Gensing
	168	¾ acres
Thomas Agas	169	1¼ acres upon the Stonerech
	170	2¾ acres
	171	1½ acres
	172	2¾ acres
	173	¾ acres
	174	2 acres in Little Wick
	175	2½ acres in Wick
	176	6¾ acres with tenement and barn

Fig. 6 Semi-diagrammatic reconstruction of the area of Lydd Quarry in 1552

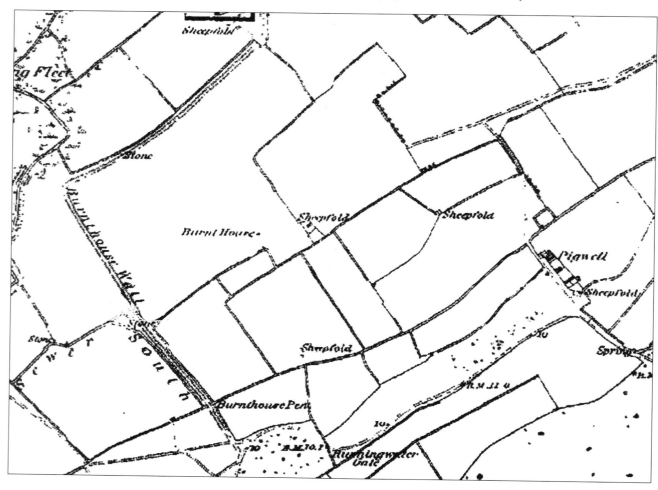

Fig. 7 First edition 6-inch Ordnance Survey map, dated 1877

The landscape described in 1552 was little different from that shown on the first edition 6-inch map of the 1880s (Fig. 7). A number of field boundaries had been removed, Harlackinden's house and Smith's barn had gone, but in other respects it was substantially the same.

Notes

1. The Lydd tithe apportionments show that the Earl of Thanet in the early 19th century held a significant part of Dengemarsh manor; The National Archives [TNA]: Lydd tithe apportionments [seen on microfilm]. Beryl Coatts kindly drew my attention to this.

2. One such document that has survived, albeit in a poor condition, is a rental dated 17 Richard II (1393–4) for Sir William Septvans' manor of New Langport; Centre for Kentish Studies [CKS]: U442/M72.

3. Though sixteen acres was leased separately from the lordship with limited success in the 1460s; Bodleian Library: MS dd All Souls c324.

4. In 1459–60, for example, 20*d*. was spent mending a 'shepeway' on the salt marsh to save the sheep; Bodleian Library: MS dd All Souls c323, 324.

5. East Sussex Records Office [ESRO]: XA3/19.

6. Although it does not record the acreage held by individual tenants, there is a printed early Dengemarsh rental (time of Edward I); *Custumals of Battle Abbey 1283–1312*, ed. S.R. Scargill–Bird, Camden Society, new series vol. 41 (London, 1887), 42–9, 50, 52.

7. The 19th century Lydd tithe apportionments designating most fields as 'Dengemarsh'; TNA: Lydd tithe apportionments [seen on microfilm].

8. CKS: U442/O34/5; U1043/M4.

9. Gardiner, pers. comm.

10. For similar agreements between Christchurch and local men regarding Appledore marsh; Canterbury Cathedral Archives and Library [CCAL]: DCc/Ch Ant A123–7.

11. Gardiner, pers. comm.

12. *Ibid.*

13. CKS: U442/M72. Scotney manor map dated 1588 and 89; Bodleian Library: All Souls CTM 226/64. Matthew Poker's map of 1617 (engraving by James Cole in 1737 of Poker's map); CKS: U1823 P2. Andrew, Drury and Herbert's map of 1768; copy in Canterbury Archaeological Trust library.

14. Scotney manor map dated 1588 and 89; Bodleian Library: All Souls CTM 226/64.

15. Gardiner, pers. comm.

16. Bodleian Library: All Souls KeS/13.

17. In particular: NMR, Swindon: RAF/543/328/F22/23/24; RAF/58/2724/F42/352/353; RAF/58/2937/F44/143/144; RAF/CPE/UK/1752; RAF/543/328; RAF/58/2937; OS/73182.

18. ESRO: XA 3/19.

19. In 1319–20 the abbey was renting pasture adjoining the salt marsh; TNA: SC 6/889/13. An area of land called salt marsh provided the abbey with 63*s*. 4*d*. in rent from two tenants in 1377–8; TNA: SC 6/890/1.

20. ESRO: XA 3/19.

21. *Curia Regis Rolls* John 8–10, 203. BL: Campbell Ch. XXV 7, 15.

22. Lincoln's Inn: Hale MS 87.

23. *Ibid.*

24. There are two, dated 1319–20 and 1336; TNA: SC 6/889/13, 14.

25. BL: Cott. MS Galba E iv, ff. 148–52.

26. CCAL: DCc/Bedels' Rolls, Appledore 6.

27. ESRO: RYE 57/4. Bodleian: MS dd All Souls c184/1. Gardiner, pers. comm.

28. Bodleian Library: MS dd All Souls c183/51a, b.

29. In 1429–30, 57*s*. was spent at Dengemarsh, and in 1446–7 slightly more, 62*s*., was used at Scotney; TNA: SC 6/890/7. Bodleian Library: MS dd All Souls c323.

30. Bodleian Library: MS dd All Souls c323, 321.8; 322.1.

31. Bodleian Library: MS dd All Souls c324.

32. One apparently much larger area was called 'Southmede', but tenants held small plots within it; TNA: E 315/56.

33. Photograph of Lydd town copy of the tithe map. NMR, Swindon: RAF/543/328/F22/23/24; RAF/58/2724/F42/352/353; RAF/58/2937/F44/143/144.

34. CCAL: U15 10/14–42.

35. TNA: E 315/56.

36. Of the *c*. 140 holdings just over 40% abutted a highway, for messuages the figure was over 50%; CKS: U442/M72.

37. CKS: U1043/M4.

38. More than half of the remaining plots were bounded by one of these embankments or watercourses, an indication of their local significance.

39. I should like to thank Beryl Coatts for drawing my attention to the likely significance of this trackway and its houses.

40. Kent County Council: Kent Towns Assessment. Goods are recorded as having been shipped up the Wainway Channel and then brought overland in carts to Lydd from a place known as Wainway Gate, but this was no longer possible by the late 16th century; East Kent Archives [EKA]: Ly/JQs1, ff 63–v. BL: E 134/17 Jas I Mich. 9.

41. TNA: E 315/56.

42. Though difficult to be certain, four of the messuages listed do not appear to be occupied; TNA: E315/56.

43. CKS: PRC 32/10, f. 113.

44. The market is occasionally recorded; TNA: SC6/1107/10.

45. ESRO: XA 3/19.

46. *Ibid.*

47. TNA: SC 6/889/13.

48. CCAL: DCc/Bedels' Rolls Appledore, 2–4, 6–40; Agney 1–49.

49. In 1319–20 Battle Abbey received 19*s*. 3*d*. from the rents; TNA: SC 6/889/13.

50. I should like to thank Andrew Butcher for allowing use of this report.

51. The important right to cut turf was retained by William son of Eilwin when he granted his lands at Broomhill to Robertsbridge Abbey; BL: Egerton Ch. 383.

52. Holly, after cutting and wilting, may have been used *in situ*, but during the later medieval period 'holme' was carried to Dengemarsh manor farm for the demesne livestock; TNA: SC 6/890/7.

53. CCAL: DCc/Bedels' Rolls Appledore, 21.

54. Timber was bought at Kingsnorth and Warehorne, including elms; EKA: S/D/FAc1. The bailiff at Denge paid for timber to be carried from the Wainway to the manor farm; TNA: SC 6/890/7. Timber was still being brought in to Lydd via the Wainway in the later 16th century; EKA: Ly/15/4/1/1/2.

55. Elm was used a great deal where contact with water occurred. This included water pipes, sea defences, harbour walls and supports (an extremely durable timber especially if kept constantly wet). Elm also has great resistance to splits, thus it was used in the making of cart hubs and other structural work; Maylam, pers. comm.

56. CKS: PRC 17/1, f. 215.

57. CCAL: DCc/Bedels' Rolls, Appledore 24. Bodleian Library: MS dd All Souls c324.

58. EKA: S/Rm/Z9; S/Rm/FAe 3. According to a Kent dialect dictionary, frith means a hedge, copse or coppice of sparse, scrubby woodland, which has little or no value as timber, a product of the soil's infertility; Major, A., *A New Dictionary of Kent Dialect* (Rainham, 1981), 38.

59. *Ibid.*

60. EKA: Ly/FAc 1, ff. 130, 181v.

61. CKS: 32/14, f. 140.

62. TNA: SC 6/Hen 8/3675.

63. CKS: U1043/M4. Though a large-scale sheep farmer, his will shows that he continued to grow cereals, so maintaining the mixed farming tradition of the marsh; CKS: PRC 32/24, f. 16.

64. TNA: C 66/1068. I should like to thank Beryl Coatts for bringing this document to my attention.

65. EKA: Ly/ZM1.

66. Bodleian Library: MS dd All Souls c182/2, 3.

67. Bodleian Library: MS dd All Souls c182/4, 7, 9, 12, 13.

68. Bodleian Library: MS dd All Souls c182/17, 20, 21, 23, 24, 27.

69. Bodleian Library: MS dd All Souls c183/b.

70. Bodleian Library: MS dd All Souls c323; c324.

71. Bodleian Library: MS dd All Souls c266/41.

72. In both of these years the lessee also received the use and profit of twenty marks, possibly as an incentive to take on the holding on the usual terms because the rent remained the same; Bodleian Library: MS dd All Souls c185/1, 2.

[73] In his will Henry Alayn mentioned his twenty acres in Woodchurch amongst other lands; CKS: PRC 32/2, f. 98. John Pulton left several cows to a number of people, and his lands and tenement in Lydd parish to his son Robert; CKS: PRC 32/2, f. 275. From the will evidence Vincent Daniell was far more prosperous than his predecessors, bequeathing 200 ewes, 10 cows, 6 seams of wheat and various other livestock and agricultural implements to his wife. Several others received a smaller number of livestock and his executors were to manage his Scotney lease for four years. Among his other lands and tenements was a tenement and land at Denge Marsh, sub-let to Thomas Browne, who was allowed to remain there until Vincent's nephew was twenty-four; CKS: PRC 32/13, f. 32.

[74] Bodleian Library: MS dd All Souls c227/5 (1); c228/6. I should like to thank Beryl Coatts for drawing my attention to these documents.

[75] Thomas Lucas (1501) had relatives in Halden, including his brother, who also seems to have been working as a butcher-grazier; CKS: PRC 32/7, f. 7. Thomas Holdernesse (1506) left 6 cows and other cattle, a bushel of hemp growing in the ground and a howe of hops, also growing to his wife. His son, Laurence, was to receive a cow, 12 ewes, a horse and a cart. Thomas apparently had at least 3 barns; CKS: PRC 32/8, f. 129.

[76] Thomas Edryk bought a number of small plots at Denge Marsh. Of his three sons Stephen seems to have been the most successful, and following his death the land was shared between his two sons. Thereafter the family disappear from the records, though their affinal connections with the Bate family meant Stephen's descendants remained in the area; CKS: PRC 32/9, f. 75. PRO: SC 2/180/61; 180/62; 180/63.

[77] For example, these people were listed for 1525–6, 1526–7, 1527–8 (that year there was a debate over keeping the fishermen's market at the Ness, see below), 1528–9, 1529–30; EKA: Ly/FAc2, 111, 124, 134, 137, 142, 153, 156.

[78] For men like Stephen Colyn, however, being deprived of a flew net to pay his scot in 1528 may have made him even more vulnerable; EKA: Ly/FAc 2, p. 250.

[79] TNA: SC 2/180/61.

[80] It is possible to use post-mortem land transfers in the manorial courts, but it seems likely some of these holdings were not passed on in their entirety, and the degree of pre-mortem land transference is not clear from the sources.

[81] John Breggys intended that from the sale of two of his barns and several pieces of land, his executors would organise the construction of a new glass window, with paintings of the life of St John the Baptist, in the chancel of St Nicholas in Lydd parish church; CKS: PRC 32/6, f. 24.

[82] The few surviving views of frankpledge for Langport include the town of Lydd in which are listed those who broke the assize of bread and ale, such as John Serlys and Stephen Harry who were fined on both counts in 1449–50; Lambeth Palace Library [LPL]: ED 136. Unfortunately the fragmentary nature of the records means it is impossible to see any trends in the number of people involved in these trades over time.

[83] *CPR* 1281–90, p. 347; *CChR* 1300–26, p. 220.

[84] In the chamberlains' accounts there is a copy of an Edward II charter granting the barons of Lydd and Ingemareys [Dengemarsh] the same liberties and privileges enjoyed by the barons of Romney and the other Cinque Ports; EKA: Ly/FAc 1, ff. 142v–3.

[85] A letter of 1528 refers to an earlier, unenforced statute of 10 Edward IV, where it was stated that no West Country fisherman not being a freeman of Lydd be allowed to sell his fish at the Stade market until the Lydd fishermen had sold the majority of their fish, subject to a penalty of 40s.; EKA: Ly/8/1/8. There were also strict regulations about renting the Ness cabins to these West Country fishermen; EKA: Ly/FAc 3, p. 177, 185, 187. Such men came from ports such as Sidmouth and Burport; EKA: Ly/FAc 3, p. 60.

[86] In 1570 he had 4 boats and at his death in 1584 he had £10 worth of herring nets (total value of the inventory £131 12s. 2d.); EKA: Ly/FAc 3, p. 185; CKS: PRC 21/6, f. 378v.

[87] Lists were regularly drawn up in the chamberlains' accounts; EKA: Ly/FAc 2, pp. 250, 251, 254, 253, 256.

[88] At his death Adrian Dyne, a successful fisherman, had 3 half boats shares in the John, the Michael and the James; CKS: PRC 32/12, f. 171.

[89] TNA: SC 2/180/60; 61.

[90] John Cheyney probably rented his two kiddles on Dengemarsh; TNA: SC 6/Hen 8/3675.

[91] The formation of a fishermen's fraternity at Lydd in 1571 may be indicative of problems in the industry; EKA: Ly/ZB 9.

[92] Many of the prolific Dyne family were fishermen in the 16th century, though some combined fishing with farming.

[93] For example, Bartholomew Shoushart, a fisherman of Lydd was involved in a debt case with a Dover merchant; EKA: Ly/CPp 9/1. William Weston of New Romney and William Sebrand of Lydd were in dispute over 30 yards of silk: EKA: Ly/CPp 2.

[94] In 1439–40 the town paid 2s. for 3 herons as gifts; EKA: Ly/FAc 1, f. 25v.

[95] The patent rolls record numerous complaints by merchants who felt they had been subject to piracy or had their goods plundered on the pretence that they had been taken from a wreck. Like the case in 1335 when £230 worth of merchandise and other goods were wrongfully taken from a ship returning to Spain from Flanders; CPR 1334–8, 144.

[96] CKS: U1043/M4.

[97] Bodleian Library: KeS/13.

[98] TNA: E 179/225/44.

2

The Archaeological Investigations

LYDD QUARRY

Site Location, Geology and Topography

The site of Lydd Quarry is located to the south-west of Lydd and is centred on TR 025 204 (Fig. 2). The geology of the site consists of silty clays overlying ridges of Dungeness shingle at an average elevation of 2.4m to 2.6m Above Ordnance Datum (AOD) (*Fig. 8). In general, where the approximate elevation of the local shingle outcrops exceeds 2.6m to 3.0m AOD, the crests of the ridges are exposed on the surface. Although the presence of surface shingle outcrops was plotted generally across the whole of Lydd Quarry (Fig. 9 overleaf), the detail of individual recording within the different areas varied depending on the amount of time and resources available. As a result the natural deposits in some areas were recorded in some detail (Fig. 9, Lydd 1 and 11) while other areas were only very roughly plotted (Fig. 9, Lydd 2 to 6). The underlying deposits were examined in more detail at Dering farm, at the north-eastern end of the quarry. Here, the lowest investigated unit within the troughs between the shingle ridges consisted of a blue-grey clay containing sparse roots and plant fragments. This was overlain by a thin peat about 250mm thick. In certain areas of the quarry fire-cracked flint has been located in the upper portions of the peat, suggesting its formation may have been contemporary with the Early Bronze Age activity on the adjacent shingle ridges (see below). Above the peat was a mid yellowish-brown silty clay. It was into the surface of this deposit that most of the medieval features were cut. A similarly coloured clay subsoil and topsoil lay above the medieval features to an average depth of 350–400mm. Although this natural stratigraphy was dominant across the quarry there were variations brought about by local factors such as the topography of the underlying deposits and subsequent truncation. In some areas Roman features were found cut into silt clay deposits, which had in turn been sealed by further fine sediments before the main mid yellowish-brown deposit was laid.

Prior to the onset of quarrying (*Fig. 8) the area consisted of a mixture of flat, mainly arable, fields divided by water-filled drainage ditches (Fig. 5). The only notable feature in the area was the upstanding earthwork of a medieval innings wall known as the Burnthouse Wall (formally Gores Wall). This earthen embankment, which is one of a number on the Marsh, runs along the north edge of the quarry side in a north-east to south-west orientation (Fig. 9). To the south-west it takes a right angle turn onto a north-west to south-east alignment and heads toward the barrier beach shingle to the south of the quarry on the MOD ranges. Although the quarry extends either side of this last leg of the earthen wall, the earthwork itself will be preserved in situ.

Archaeological Background

Prior to the start of groundworks virtually no previous archaeological discoveries had been made in the area of the proposed Lydd Quarry. Several Bronze Age axes had been found to the north-east during gravel extraction at the Pioneer Pit (Needham 1988) and Roman material, including extensive evidence of salt-working, had been investigated at both Pioneer Pit (Willson pers. comm.) and Scotney Court to the west (Philp and Willson 1984, and Barber 1998a). Further evidence of prehistoric and Roman activity was found during the UCLFAU excavations at Lydd Quarry. Although these are not covered in detail in the current report it is considered appropriate to briefly outline the main findings here. Bronze Age finds in the form of hearth sites, worked flint (including a barbed and tanged arrowhead from Lydd 1) and Beaker pottery (Lydd 4 and 11) has been found during work at the quarry. The material, which, where diagnostic, appears to be of Early Bronze Age date, is almost always associated with the north-east to south-west trending shingle ridges of the area, which presumably gave access for the prehistoric people to exploit the marshland resources during hunting trips (Gardiner and Greig 1996, Priestley-Bell 2003a and 2004a). Similar remains were found at Caldicott Farm Quarry to the north-east (Priestley-Bell 2004b).

There has been no evidence from the area or Lydd Quarry itself for any other activity until the Late Iron Age. An extensive salt-working site appears to have been established at this time, which has been investigated at Lydd 12 (to the south-west of Lydd 1) (Priestley-Bell in prep.). In addition a large creek appears to have been open in the area of Lydd 9 at this time. The location of the remains of two butchered whales in this infilled creek, as well as timbers and pottery adjacent to it, suggest this may have been used as an inlet to load/unload goods associated with the salt-working (Priestley-Bell 2004a). The pottery, along with radiocarbon dates from a timber post and one of the whales, confirms the Late Iron Age

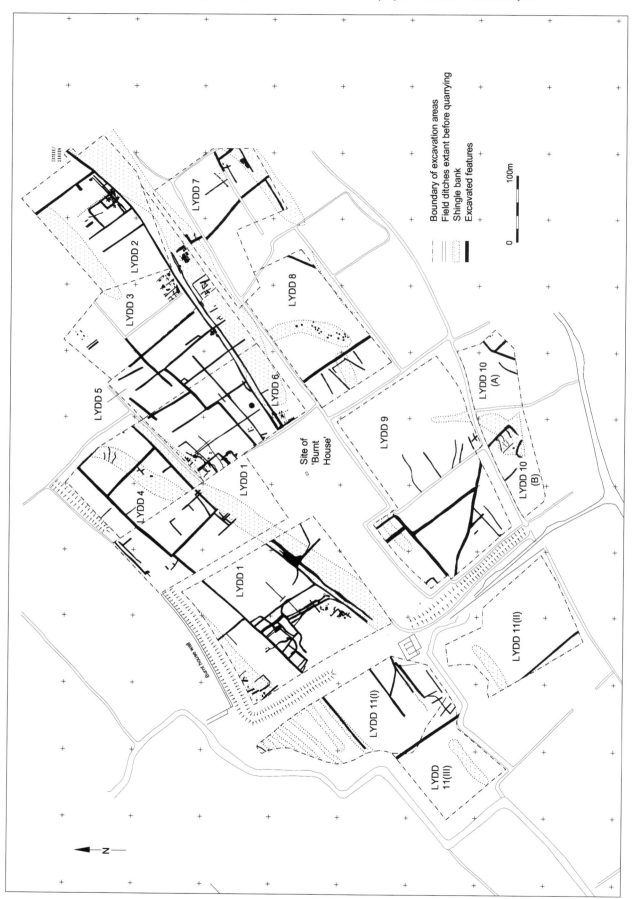

Fig. 9 Lydd Quarry, Parts 1–11. Plan of all archaeological features

date for this activity. The Late Iron Age salt-working activity at Lydd 12 continued into the early Roman period and numerous finds of Roman domestic waste have been found in other areas of the quarry, most notably at Lydd 1 (Area C), 4, 7 and 11 (Greig and Gardiner 1996, Priestley-Bell 2002b and 2004a). Most of these deposits appear to relate to the dumping of refuse into natural channels and/or the troughs between the shingle ridges during the 1st and 2nd centuries. However, at Lydd 1 a single urned cremation vessel was discovered together with an extensive layer containing Roman material interpreted as a possible flood deposit. The presence of this Roman activity in various parts of Lydd quarry, when taken with the evidence from Scotney Court to the west and Pioneer Pit to the north-east, show that the area saw quite extensive exploitation during the 1st and 2nd centuries, albeit on a probably seasonal basis. All these sites appear to have been situated on a relatively narrow spit of land with the sea to the south and a large tidal lagoon to the north. Cunliffe's original model for the occupation and economy of the marsh during the Roman period is still in agreement with the excavated evidence to date (Cunliffe 1988).

Some time after the early 3rd century the area at Lydd Quarry, with the exception of the tops of the shingle ridges, was buried by a deep layer of yellowish-brown silty clay. There was no evidence of any occupation between the latest material of the early 3rd century and the 12th century – the date of the earliest material recovered from ditches cutting the surface of the later deposits. Prior to the excavations at Lydd Quarry, evidence of medieval activity was confined to the historic fabric of the town of Lydd and occasional findspots of medieval pottery by local field-walkers.

Planning Background

As part of the principle of PPG 16 most new applications for extraction, including that for Lydd Quarry, had a condition attached to them by Kent County Council requiring archaeological work to be undertaken in advance of extraction. The archaeological strategy for this work at Lydd posed a problem in that the extent of the archaeological remains was such that total detailed study was not practical or economically viable. With this in mind an archaeological strategy for the recording of the site was jointly formulated by John Williams (County Archaeologist for Kent County Council) and Mark Gardiner (while Deputy Director for Archaeology South-East) during the initial excavations (Lydd 1). Emphasis was placed on obtaining the complete plan of the archaeological landscape. This was to be followed by selective sample excavations in order to ascertain the form, function, date and development of the ditched field system and its associated settlement sites. Full excavation of all archaeological features was deemed less important. The work at Lydd 1 enabled problems to be identified and the strategy to be refined for subsequent phases of work

at the quarry. One of the principle problems at Lydd 1 was controlling the on-site plant to achieve an acceptable stripped surface at the correct level without unnecessarily slowing down the speed of work. The agreed on-site work involves the monitoring of large areas of controlled topsoil stripping by 360 degree tracked excavators and 25 ton dumper trucks, followed by mapping of the features exposed using an Electronic Distance Meter (EDM). After consultation with Bretts and the County Archaeologist, selective excavation and further recording is then undertaken on key areas in an attempt to establish the date and development of the ditched field-system and its associated settlements. This approach has enabled the rapid and economic recovery of the plan of a large tract of medieval landscape. In certain areas, suspected of prehistoric and Roman remains, further archaeological monitoring is undertaken during the subsequent sub-soiling, when the yellow-brown silt clay into which the medieval features are cut is removed.

All stages of work at the site, together with its subsequent post-excavation analysis, have been fully funded by Brett Gravel Ltd.

Sequence of Work

Work at Lydd Quarry has been, and still is, undertaken in stages as the quarry expands, each being individually numbered (Fig. 9). The first stage of work was undertaken by UCLFAU in late 1991 in advance of the establishment of the new plant site and associated initial gravel extraction (Lydd 1). An initial watching brief was maintained during topsoil removal between late September and mid October. Areas A and B were stripped using a 360 degree tracked excavator. The planning consent provided for this work to be carried out at the normal industrial rate rather than to archaeological standards, though with the kind agreement of Bretts more control over stripping would be achieved in subsequent phases. During the course of work evidence for occupation and for an extensive ditch system was revealed.

The initial watching brief was followed by a programme of survey and excavation between mid October and mid December. Work was confined to Area B where the evidence was more extensive and better preserved. The relatively restricted resources available for such a large area permitted only limited sampling, particularly of the ditch system. The ditch system was surveyed using an Electronic Distance Meter (EDM) and theodolite, and most ditch intersections, together with some cross-sections, were excavated by hand to establish a chronology. In some of the later stages of work some ditch intersections were not excavated if the relationship was clear in plan after surface cleaning. Except in Area C, and indeed for many other areas of the ditch system in the quarry, no further cleaning of the surface was possible after the machine stripping. As such, the edges of the ditches could therefore generally be plotted to within 300mm or so, although there is no significant inaccuracy at the chosen scale.

Occupation evidence at Lydd 1 was found on the north-west and south-west of Area B, and in a small part of the north-east corner of Area A. The areas of occupation in Area B were excavated and planned to conventional archaeological standard using the same grid employed in the EDM survey. These more intensively studied sub-areas within Area B are referred to as C (Site E) and D (Site D) respectively (Fig. 10 opposite). The occupation evidence in Area A was recorded only during the watching brief. It was subsequently agreed that it should be left *in situ* and re-buried to preserve it.

During the course of excavation it was possible to have aerial photographs taken of the site (*Figs. 11 and 12). These clarified some aspects of the ditch system which could not be seen at ground level – principally two areas where the machining could not be taken down to a sufficient depth for archaeological purposes. This information was added to the EDM survey plot as accurately as possible.

In May 1995 the second stage of archaeological work began on the area designated for the first full-scale extraction (Lydd 2, Fig. 9) (Priestley-Bell 1999). The site of this excavation lay at an average elevation of 2.6m AOD, just to the north of an exposed shingle ridge that rose to 3.3m AOD. Unlike at Lydd 1, the topsoil stripping was now undertaken under more controlled conditions with the 360 degree excavator and two 25 ton dumper trucks being controlled more by an archaeologist who was in constant attendance.

The initial monitoring during stripping identified a ditch system and possible trackway with an apparently associated enclosed medieval occupation site (Site H) and activity area (Site I). The area of interest was cleaned to reveal the major features. A partial excavation of the ditch system was carried out, comprising the hand excavation of all ditch sections and intersections. Full excavation was limited to a 20 × 30m area, which appeared to be the focus of settlement activity.

Between October 1995 and June 1996 two further elements of work were undertaken creating the third stage of archaeological investigation at the quarry (Lydd 3) (Priestley-Bell 2002). Topsoil stripping and subsequent limited excavation revealed a continuation of the trackway identified in Lydd 2 together with further elements of the ditched field system. A smaller enclosed ditch system (Site C) and areas of 13th to 14th century activity were also located (Sites J and K).

In May 1996, a further watching brief was undertaken during the topsoil stripping of a new gravel extraction area (Lydd 4, Fig. 9). Significant Bronze Age and Romano-British remains were revealed, together with some further elements of the extensive medieval ditch/field system identified in previous work, as well as one activity area (Site B). Subsequent limited excavation in June of that year revealed a considerable amount of apparently *in situ* worked flint, including cores and scrapers of Bronze Age character, together with large quantities of fire-cracked flint. The prehistoric remains were stratified below a truncated Roman layer that contained predominantly very abraded late 1st to early 3rd century pottery. Study of the stratigraphy in the area suggested the potential for the survival of further prehistoric land surface near the crests of the higher gravel ridges. In view of this, and after consultation, a watching brief was held during the removal of subsoil in a selected area. This investigation produced additional large quantities of burnt and worked flint, together with a small quantity of pottery identified as Early Bronze Age in date. (Priestley-Bell 2002b).

In September 1996, a further watching brief, during continuing topsoil stripping in two adjacent areas, identified extensive medieval and early post-medieval remains. During October of that year a programme of limited excavation was carried out (Lydd 5/6, Fig. 9). The work identified an extensive area of the medieval field system together with a long section of integral trackway and a number of areas of medieval and early post-medieval activity (Sites G, L, M and N) (Priestley-Bell, 2003).

Between February and May 1997, an intermittent watching brief was held during further topsoil stripping in an area immediately to the south of Lydd 3. Evidence of prehistoric, Roman and medieval activity was uncovered. A limited excavation, Lydd 7 (Fig. 9), was carried out during May. Although no apparently associated features were identified, a small quantity of prehistoric worked flint was recovered from the exposed surface of the subsoil and the crest of a shingle ridge. An additional half-day's watching brief was maintained during the subsoiling along the margins of the shingle ridge from which the prehistoric material had been recovered. Again no features were identified, but further worked flint was recovered including two cores. Two areas of 2nd century Roman activity were represented by two pottery-rich layers and an associated ditch. In addition to a 13th century pit, further elements of the extensive medieval ditch system recorded in previous work were identified. Toward the end of May a watching brief was held during the topsoil stripping of a narrow salient (previously the quarry haul road) between the site of the Lydd 3 excavation and the northernmost section of Lydd 7. A short section of ditch containing 15th century pottery was uncovered. The excavation and consideration of this feature was included in Lydd 7.

Work at the quarry recommenced with topsoil stripping immediately to the west of Lydd 7 in October 1997 (Lydd 8). Two possibly medieval ditches were identified, together with part of a probably modern ditch system. Evidence for prehistoric activity on the site included two small hearths and significant quantities of burnt and worked flint. Following consultation with Brett and the County Archaeologist, a limited excavation was carried out in late November. Further quantities of worked flint, including cores and scrapers, were recovered from the surface of the principal south-west to north-east

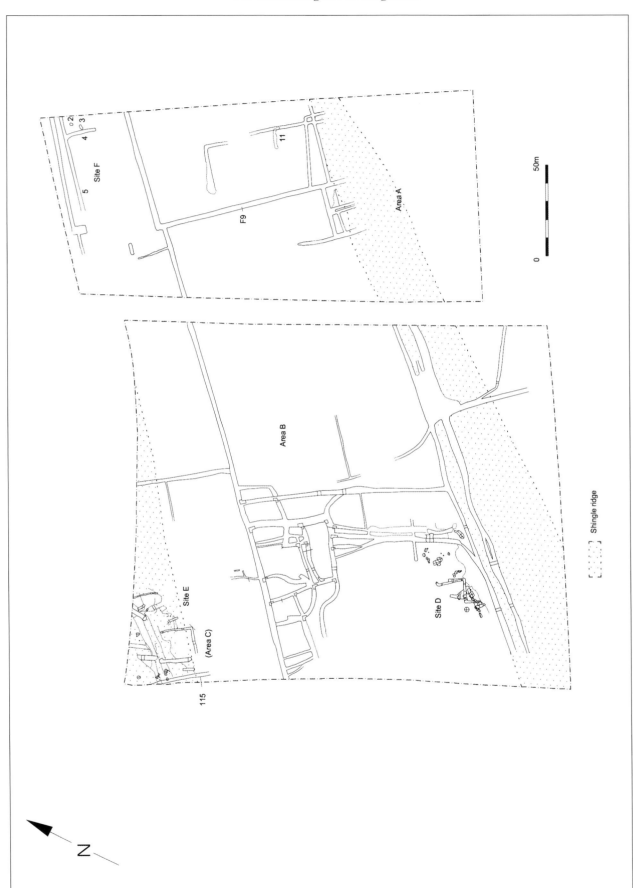

Fig. 10 Lydd Quarry 1. Plan of Areas A and B (incl. Sites D, E and F)

shingle ridge. An intermittent watching brief during the subsequent subsoiling and removal of overburden identified further concentrations of burnt and struck flint, together with a small probably prehistoric pit.

The monitoring of the Lydd 9 area was undertaken between June and early September 1998. The medieval field system was found to be absent in the eastern half of the area and only of limited extent to the west. Although a probably Late Iron Age timber feature and associated possible hard-standing were identified, no other *in situ* prehistoric remains were uncovered. In view of the low density of archaeological features and following consultation with Brett and the County Archaeologist, limited excavation was carried out concurrent with the watching brief. During the removal of the subsoil, a channel measuring between 30m to 80m wide and up to 7m deep was identified running east to west across the north of the site. A considerable quantity of whale bones, some showing clear signs of butchery, were recovered from the silty clays infilling the channel and from the surface of the underlying gravel.

In January and February 1999, a watching brief was maintained during further topsoil stripping in two fields immediately south-east of Lydd 9 (Lydd 10, Fig. 9). In the eastern field (defined by existing ditches) three possibly medieval ditches were identified, together with a probably medieval pit. In the western field a complex of six ditches and a large pit was identified, apparently associated with a medieval building (Site A). The building was excavated during late February and March 1999.

The first stage of work to the west of the Burnthouse Wall, known as Lydd 11 (*Fig. 11), was undertaken in three sub-phases (I–III) between October 1999 and August 2000. Phase I was undertaken in October 1999 when a watching brief was held during topsoil stripping and the cutting of a drainage ditch in the field immediately to the west of the present plant site (Lydd 1). A total of nine ditches and a gully of possibly medieval or later date were identified. One ditch was in alignment with Ditch D19, Lydd 1. In the northern corner of the site a 1st to 2nd century pottery rich Roman deposit was identified, together with a spread and a small ditch or channel of the same date. A limited excavation of this area (Lydd 11, Phase 1), in conjunction with specialist sedimentological analysis, was carried out between 24th and 29th November 1999. In June 2000, a further watching brief was held during topsoil stripping of a *c.* 120 × 120m area adjoining the south-west of Lydd 11, Phase I. An open rectilinear arrangement of three ditches was identified, together with the southward extension of a ditch found during Lydd 11, Phase I. In August of the same year further monitoring was undertaken during topsoil stripping immediately to the south of Phase I. Due to the proximity of high voltage power lines, the work was carried out using a box scraper and tractor. A single ditch of probably post-medieval or modern date was identified. Although no associated features were

identified, 53 pieces of worked flint of perhaps Bronze Age origin were recovered from the surface of a shingle ridge exposed during stripping. Recording and excavation (Lydd 11, Phase III) were carried out concurrently with the watching brief.

Throughout the various stages of archaeological work at the site, the timing of the subsequent stage was never known as the extraction timetable was dependent on many factors, including weather and depth of shingle. As a consequence each stage of work was treated as separate with independent sequences of context and level numbers, *etc.*, being used. The combination of the individual reports for the 11 stages into one report, as undertaken here, posed a problem for the description of the site and finds, due to the duplication of context numbers. As a result the context numbers from the different stages have been prefixed by a suitable number or letter so all can be discussed together without confusion. Context numbers for Lydd 1 are as they were originally (1, 2, 3, *etc.*), however, those from Lydd 2 have been prefixed by 2000 so Context 1 became 2001, 123 became 2123, *etc.* The same principle has been applied to Lydd 3 (3000s), Lydd 4 (4000s), Lydd 5/6 (5000s), Lydd 7 (7,000s), *etc.* The only variation to this rule is for Lydd 10 where context numbers are prefixed with 'A' and Lydd 11 where they are prefixed with 'B'. As such any Lydd Quarry context number quoted in this publication is easily ascribed to its stage and thus its area. It should be noted the archives for the different stages have not been so amended, though as the site codes change between stages there is no chance for mixing of archive material.

This part of the report will describe the ditched field system at Lydd first. The subject is tackled initially by area and then overall by phase. The occupation sites/activity areas within Lydd Quarry are subsequently described individually in chronological order. The findings from the other quarries are described after those from Lydd.

THE DITCH SYSTEM: OVERVIEW

With the exception of a single unstratified sherd of imported Pingsdorf pottery from the Rhineland, there is no evidence of activity in any of the areas examined at Lydd Quarry between the Roman period and the 12th century. Drainage of the area appears, on the current evidence, to have been undertaken during the 12th century. The ditches which compose the field system surround two converging trackways and most were cut into the surface of the silty clay, though some also cut the gravel ridges. It was clear from the outset that the ditches did not belong to a single period of medieval activity. They represent a superimposed network of various phases.

Lack of time precluded full investigation of the ditch system in most parts of the quarry. However, it is possible to establish from the morphology a basic division into a pattern of earlier, sometimes irregular ditches, and a later arrangement of generally straight ditches intersecting at approximately right angles and forming larger square or rectangular enclosures. While the later ditches appear to form one contemporary system, the relative chronology of the preceding ones is far from clear, mainly due to the incomplete nature of the excavations and the difficulty of interpreting the excavated data. It is clear that many ditches have a complex history. They may have been allowed to silt up, or even been filled in, and were later cleared out or re-cut, sometimes on different alignments.

Although there was a clear stratigraphic relationship at a number of the ditch intersections, many were unclear. Whether this is due to them being infilled contemporaneously, or the result of unclear stratigraphic relationships, is often difficult to ascertain. Although the stratigraphic relationship of the ditches provides a relative chronology, the evidence has been obscured by repeated cleaning and complete or partial recutting. The stratigraphy therefore is likely to reflect the relationships between the final stages of use of the ditches rather than provide a relative timetable for their inception. Where clearly defined relationships were identifiable, they are shown on the relevant figures – otherwise the relationships were indeterminate or appeared to be contemporary. Only limited information was provided by the individual morphology of the ditches.

The phasing suggested from the stratigraphic relationships and morphology can be supplemented by the ceramic evidence from the sections cut across the ditches. Three main periods of infilling are identified, the first from the later 12th to early 13th century, the second from the later 13th to early 14th century and the third from the 14th to 15th century. The pottery evidence needs to be considered rather carefully. The uppermost, sometimes the only, fills of all of these ditches may have been the product of deliberate backfilling, though this can rarely be shown from the nature of the fill. Certainly, the excavation of new ditches and the stopping up of old redundant ditches will have often necessitated backfilling. But equally, the top surviving fills of the ditches may have accumulated through silting within a water-filled drain. As such it should be borne in mind that the ceramic dating indicates the date the ditch went out of use (and thus can be removed from the next phase plan) but does not give any firm indication of when the ditch was first excavated or its length of use. Unfortunately pottery from the lower ditch fills was virtually absent. In addition there is further uncertainty about the ceramic dating.

Ditches would have been cleaned out regularly during their period of use, as they still are on the marsh, and this activity will often have totally removed the earlier deposits and any related artefacts and even changed the ditches' size and morphology beyond recognition. As such even pottery from the primary fills may not date the initial cutting of the ditches but their final recut, and even that relies on the few sherds that are present not being residual.

Another problem with the ceramic dating is the uneven chronological spread of the pottery at the site. As there appears to be less occupation activity at the site after the 13th century, and particularly after the 14th century (see below) there is significantly less ceramic material of these later dates at the site to be incorporated into the fills of the ditches. As such, a ditch infilled between the 14th and 16th century, is more likely to incorporate 13th century residual pottery from earlier settlement/manuring within its fill than pottery contemporaneous to its actual infilling. Exceptions to this are likely to be ditches adjacent to later settlement/activity areas, including the trackways. This problem is well highlighted at Lydd 2 with the apparent differential dates of infilling of the trackway Ditch 2006 in different areas (see below). Based on the ceramics, some sections suggest they were infilled in the 13th century, whereas others appear to have been receiving material as late as the 16th century, and indeed the track is still depicted on Poker's 17th century map. The uncertainty about the residuality of 13th century pottery in many of the ditches means that a certain amount of educated guesswork is needed to date the infilling of ditches, even when the fills have produced some pottery.

Due to these problems the dating of the ditch system presented below has been based on a mixture of the archaeological evidence, logic and educated guesswork. The most problematic task was the establishment of the extent of the first system of ditches as 12th century ditches which continued in use into the 13th to 15th centuries, as they could not be identified using either stratigraphic relationships or ceramic dating.

During the excavation the cuts of the features and their individual fills were assigned separate context numbers. However, for ease of reference principal ditches in this report are referred to by their cut context only prefixed by 'D', as D2005, D2006, *etc*. At Lydd 1 a number of excavated slots in different areas across the same ditch were allocated different cut numbers and as a result a ditch number was later assigned to cover all the cut numbers of one particular ditch across the site, D1, D2, *etc*. However, to avoid confusion cut numbers are also included in the text and on the plans. Some ditches may have been assigned different cut context numbers either side of intersections and are referred to by both numbers where applicable as D2013/2048, D98/134, *etc*. All other features are referred to by a brief description followed by their cut number, as in post-hole 2094 and pit 2102, *etc*.

Due to the size of the area investigated, the ditch system within each phase of archaeological work will be briefly described individually in order to give an insight into the contexts and stratigraphic relationships encountered in each area (Lydd parts 1 to 11). This has been done in three main sections, as the overall investigated system can be split into three areas based on the two converging trackways as follows:

- To the north of the northern trackway (investigated during Lydd parts 1, 4 and 11 (I and II)).
- Between the northern and southern trackways (investigated during Lydd parts 2, 3 and 5/6).
- To the south of the southern trackway (investigated during Lydd parts 7, 8, 9, 10 and 11 (III)).

Following this an overview of the whole system is put forward by phase. It should be noted that this overview has relied on morphology, stratigraphic relationships, ceramic dating and, to a point, educated guesswork/logic. As such the sequence may have errors but is considered to be on the whole representative of the evolution of the field system.

The System to the North of the Northern Trackway (Lydd 1, 4 and 11, Phases I and II)

Lydd 1 (Figs. 10, *11, *12, 13 and 23)

Parts of the ditch system were found in all areas investigated during this initial phase of archaeological work (Fig. 10, Areas A and B). The work was the first to study the ditch system at the quarry and therefore did so to a greater degree of detail than subsequent phases of work. Despite this the ditches in Area A were recorded only briefly during the watching brief, and have been plotted on Fig. 10 from a measured sketch produced at that time. None of the ditches in Area A were sectioned and the discussion below is confined to those ditches recorded and excavated in Area B (Fig. 13 opposite). The plan, however, shows that the ditches within the two areas do form parts of a single pattern.

Period 1a (natural channels – 12th century origin but most infilled 12th to early 13th century)

The sinuous courses of D1 and D2 suggest that these had a natural origin (Fig. 13). The line of D3, though not straight, meandered to a lesser extent than the others, and D4 is curved, but in a regular manner. Both D2 and D4 had short spur ditches, which were probably the stub ends of infilled natural channels. Ditch D4 was continued eastwards by a straight channel, D7, also probably dug at this early date, though certainly still in use into the following phase. Despite their irregular courses, all these ditches terminated at regular, straighter ditches, suggesting that they had been adapted for drainage purposes. The shape of the junction between D1 and D12, and particularly the shape of D12 to its south, suggests that the former natural line of D1 was adopted by the north-south ditch. There was no opportunity to clean the surface near to the ditches to identify possible traces of original channels.

It is very difficult to equate the various fills between excavated sections. It seems most likely that there is a sequence of silting and recutting. Some of the uppermost fills may have been formed by deliberate backfilling, though this is not certain. Ditch D1 illustrates the difficulties of interpreting these early ditches. At its western end, the cut (212) was 0.36m deep and contained one major fill (236), a dark brown silty clay, with a shallow upper fill (214), probably topsoil which had subsided into it (Fig. 23, Section (S) 1). The cut immediately to the east (164), however, shows clear evidence of two channels, one natural and one which was probably an artificial cut (Fig. 23, S2). There are possibly one or two further recuts at this point. Further east, cut 288 shows that D1, or more probably a recut of it, was later than D18 at that point, though it was shallower than 164 (Fig. 23, S3). The relationship between D1 and D17 was not clear. Ditch D16 (161) was quite clearly later than D1 (158) which suggests a complex arrangement at the junction of D1, D5 and D16.

The most likely interpretation is that the sinuous natural channel has been artificially straightened, leaving backfilled traces of its original course at the side of the new channel within D1, which would be earlier than D16 (161). Ditch 16 was straight, regular and undoubtedly man-made. It is likely that had the excavated trench been extended further north, a later artificial channel contemporary with, or later than, D16 would have been encountered in D1.

Period 1b (man-made ditches – mainly 12th century origin but most infilled late 12th to ?mid 13th century)

The morphology of other ditches is quite clearly artificial; if they did have any natural origin, all traces of this have been removed, effectively creating new cuts. Ditch D7 may in origin have been a natural channel connected to D2 and D4, but its course suggests that it must have been straightened.

It is possible to relate the fills in two excavated sections across Ditch D7 (Fig. 23, S4). The fills of 182 suggest an initial silting (187), probably largely derived from the newly cut sides, overlain by a deposit of black humic silt (186), suggestive of a slow accumulation of silt and organic debris in an open, water-filled ditch. The upper three fills are varying shades of yellowish-brown silty clay, and may have been formed either by deliberate back-filling or gradual silting. Fill 184 contained a high proportion of red burnt clay. Similar material was also found in relatively large quantities in fill 188 in the adjoining cut across D3 (Fig. 13, 189). A section cut across the junction of D7 and D9 showed a similar sequence (Fig. 23, S5). Fill 222 represented the primary silting and fill 202 was a dark humic soil equivalent to 186.

Ditch D17 and D16 may also belong to the earliest ditch system. However, D17 appears to have been infilled earlier in the 13th century than D16, based on the ceramics. The full length of D16 was difficult to trace because it was obscured by a considerable depth of overburden which could not be removed during topsoil stripping. Excavation of Area D, however, revealed a line of brownish gravel (549), which continued the line of

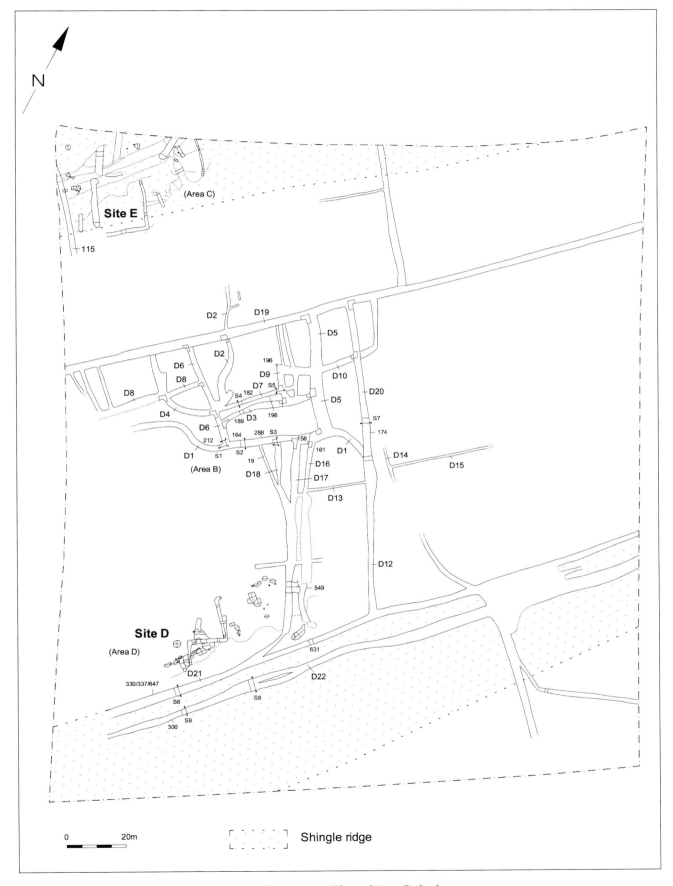

Fig. 13 Lydd Quarry 1. Plan of Area B ditch system

D16 (Fig. 13). Although not fully excavated, this gravel was evidently the truncated south end of D16. Ditch D17 turned towards the west at its southern end to join D21. The morphology suggests that D17 originally had a butt end, and was subsequently extended by a short, narrower length of ditch to link to D21. Although it was not possible to examine the junction of D17 and D21, it is suggested that the linking ditch is the same as the earliest cut (330) identified in the section excavated at the western end of D21 (Fig. 23, S6).

Ditches D21 and D22 demark the boundaries of a track or roadway, and were clearly open as part of the later ditch pattern, although a trackway along this shingle ridge was probably present from the earliest period of reclamation. The relationship, if any, between D16 and D21 did not survive the machining.

The pottery evidence broadly supports the morphological interpretation. The pottery from D1 to D6 suggests a late 12th or early to mid 13th century date for most of their infilling. D5 and D6 appear to have continued in use for a little longer, perhaps after being recut. D1, D2 and D4 were recognised as early features on the basis of their sinuous course. D3 and the parallel ditches D5 and D6 may be a development of the initial drainage pattern. They must have fed D19, which intercepts all the north-south drains, except D2 which it cuts. Unfortunately D19 did not produce any early pottery of note as it was clearly a key ditch in the drainage system which was cleaned out repeatedly.

Period 2 (elaboration of existing system – late 12th to mid 13th century origin but most infilled later 13th to early 14th century)

The ditch system was elaborated during this period and a number of the early ditches infilled. It is thought D17 was constructed, though this ditch has been tentatively linked to the early ditches on morphological grounds. Ditches D7, D8, D9 and D10 also appear to belong to this period. Most are east-west drains which linked the earlier north south drains D5 and D6. The infilling of these ditches, along with some of the Phase 1 surviving ditches, appears to have been during the mid to late 13th century, though some may have still been receiving material into the early 14th century.

Period 3 (14th to 15th century – most infilled by early 16th century)

The developed ditch system at Lydd 1 was the result of the simplification of the Phase 2 ditches to create much larger fields. The system at this time comprised D19, which could be traced from Area B to Area A, and the ditched trackway bounded by D21 and D22. The trackway presumably also ran across from Area B to A, but could not be traced in the east because of the depth of overburden. These east-west ditch lines were linked by probably new north-south ditches, D12 and D20 in Area B (Fig. 23, S7), though it is possible only D20 was new, as well as feature 9 in Area A (Fig. 10). It is not surprising that the pottery shows that many of these major ditches continued in use until the 15th or early 16th century. Ditch D12 and its continuation D20 had fills of that date. In addition, D16 persisted in use until this time. The stratigraphic record supports the dating. Drain D19, or later recuts of it, cut through the earlier features D2, D4 and D6, but remained open to D5 and D20. D5 presumably continued to act as a conduit for water from D16.

None of these later field boundaries showed any sign of having been recut. The fills of cut 174 (D20) may stand for others (Fig. 23, S7). The basal fills of the ditch, 172 and 173, were both silty, and greyish-brown and, although differentiated on excavation, are both likely to represent silting in the open ditch. The two upper fills, 170 and 171 were both yellowish-brown and more friable. Equivalent upper fills in other sections were recorded as either yellowish-brown or brown, and are generally homogenous with few inclusions. These deposits may represent either deliberate backfill with fresh material or an accumulation of material which rolled into a basically dry ditch. It should be remembered that all the ditch profiles recorded were truncated, most recently by the removal of topsoil. The farmer also reported that since his father took over the tenancy in the 1940s a certain amount of levelling and infilling had taken place.

The history of ditches D21 and D22, which demarcate the trackway, is more complicated. showing evidence of two or three recuttings (Fig. 13). The earliest cut of D21 appears to relate to the early ditch system, as has already been mentioned. Recut 647 (Fig. 23, S6) of the ditch can be equated with cut 631 further east (Fig. 13) and both clearly form part of the later field boundary system. The fills of 647 were recut (337), though there is not evidence of a corresponding recut in the section excavated further east.

The eastern section across D22 clearly showed three distinct cuts at a point where, on the surface, the ditch appeared to split briefly into two (Figs. 13 and 23, S8). A section to the west displayed one recut (300) and the position of fills 302 and 303, which are slumping from the sides, might suggest a second recut (Fig. 23, S9).

Although the final arrangement of the trackway as represented by D21 and D22 was clearly an integral part of the later system of field boundaries, the relationship of cut 330 and D17, discussed above, suggests that at least at the western end it was in place during the early phase of the ditch system. It was not possible to investigate fully the position further east. Section 631 (Fig. 13) suggests that there were no early ditches at that point, but at the eastern side of Area B the position, although obscured by material that could not be removed during machining, is less simple. For a short distance three distinct cuts were visible. It is possible that the trackway, which ran along the northern margin of a shingle ridge, was an early feature subsequently marked more formally by ditches.

Lydd 4 (Figs. 14 and 24)

Two ditches (Fig. 14, Contexts 4034 and 4041 and Fig. 24, S10), measuring 3.95m and 1.77m in width and 1.24m and 670mm in depth respectively, ran parallel *c.* 4m apart along the margin of a south-west to north-east shingle ridge. The larger (4034) had been extant prior to the onset of extraction, where it made up the southern boundary of a large field. Ditches 4034 and 4041 were traced for *c.* 100m (Ditch 4041 for *c.* 130m) and together almost certainly represented the boundaries of the track marked by D21 and D22 previously recorded at Lydd 1. Although only a small quantity of 13th to early 14th century pottery was recovered from Ditch 4041, evidence from Lydd 1 suggests that the trackway may have dated from the ?late 12th century and continued being maintained until at least the 15th or early 16th century. The longevity of the route is supported by cartographic evidence; this trackway is clearly identifiable on M. Poker's 1617 Map of Romney Marsh, on which it is shown as an established route between the present Westbroke House and the Burnthouse Wall (*Fig. 3). The boundary marking the southern side of the track had obviously been re-used to demarcate a ditched field boundary after the track had gone out of use, presumably at the time the northern boundary ditch (4041) had been infilled.

A small dendritic ditch (Fig. 14, Context 4005), consisting of a straight *c.* 15m section with two *c.* 5m branches, joined Ditch 4032 (see below); the ditch sections measured typically 2.20m in width and 400mm deep. A single sherd of 12th to early 13th century pottery was recovered from the sandy silt fill (4006), suggesting that Ditch 4005, along with two other undated spur ditches to the north-west and south, may have been a remnant of the earliest medieval drainage system.

The three remaining ditches are difficult to date precisely. Ditch 4028, which equates to D19 at Lydd 1, has already been shown to have probable early origins (Fig. 24, S11). However, the two ditches linking D4028 with D4041 (Ditches D4025 and D4032) are harder to be sure of. These ditches, which measure between 1.8 and 2.2m wide, appear to be contemporary with D4028 and 4041, or at least the latest recuts of them. As such it is equally possible that D4032 and 4025 were part of the original late 12th to early 13th century ditch system or were added as part of the more developed system in the later 13th or 14th centuries. Unfortunately too little pottery is present in their fills to be certain – D4025 yielded four sherds of early 13th century material while D4041 only yielded three 13th century sherds. Although this may indicate the infilling of the system in this area during the 13th century, the general field size and morphology suggests D4041, D4028, D4025 and D4032 may have remained as part of the developed field system which survived into the 14th and 15th centuries, and was thus contemporary with Period 3 at Lydd 1. Whatever the case D4028, D4041, D4025 and D4032 formed a large rectilinear field which measured *c.* 100 × 60m. A further area to the west (the large part of another field) measured 100m by at least 70m.

Lydd 11 (Phases I and II) (Fig. 15)

A number of ditches were identified during this phase of archaeological work. Unusually none of these features produced any datable finds and it has therefore been impossible to be certain of their date. However, based on the absence of artefacts, which are usually plentiful to the east of the Burnthouse Wall, combined with the fact that the general alignment of the ditches seems to correspond with those noted at Lydd 1, it would appear all the ditches probably relate to the earliest period of the ditch system.

Ditch B21 (Fig. 15 and Fig. 24, S12), measuring between 2.3 and 3.5m in width and 700mm deep, ran across the site for *c.* 100m. It contained a primary fill (B22) of light greenish-grey clay-like silt with 60% rounded flint pebbles, presumably marking rapid slumping of the gravel sides, and an upper fill (B23), of medium greenish-brown silt with 10% rounded flint pebbles. Although no independent dating evidence was recovered, Ditch B21 was probably the westerly continuation of D19 at Lydd 1 to the east and with an existing section of Jury's Gut Sewer to the west.

A further ditch (B35), measuring *c.* 3.6m in width and exceeding *c.* 1.1m in depth, contained a primary fill (B43) of medium grey silty clay with occasional rounded flint pebbles and an upper fill (B36) of medium greyish-orange silty clay. Ditch B35 ran at right angles to Ditch B21 and parallel to and *c.* 160m west of the Burnthouse Wall. It was apparent from a noticeable linear surface depression that Ditch B35 had at one time linked Jury's Gut Sewer with the Lydd Petty Sewer.

Ditch B8 (Fig. 15 and Fig. 24, S13), measuring *c.* 1.2m in width and 580mm deep, ran across the site for *c.* 85m parallel to, and *c.* 75m south of, Ditch B21. It contained a primary fill (B11) of light greyish-brown silt, a secondary fill (B10) of greyish-brown clay with occasional shell fragments and an upper fill (B9) of medium greyish-brown silty clay with occasional shell. Although not dissimilar to shallow spade-dug gullies found around the Severn Estuary, known as gripes (Rippon 1997, 52–3), the Lydd examples appear more substantial. A section of curving ditch (B2, Fig. 15), measuring *c.* 2.2m in width but only 230mm deep, ran for *c.* 55m from the south-eastern corner of the Phase 1 area to cut Ditch B8. Ditch B2 contained a primary fill (B4) of light orangey-brown silt with occasional marine shell and an upper fill (B3) of medium greyish-brown silty clay with occasional rounded flint pebbles and shell. Ditch B2 may be broadly contemporary with Ditch B8 or be a later drainage channel, possibly put in to create drainage for the possible trackway ditch B17.

The westerly extent of the trackway located at Lydd 1 (D21 and D22) was located within the Lydd 11 Phase I area. It was marked by two parallel ditches (B12 and B17, Fig.15 and Fig. 24, S14) *c.* 5m apart, measuring *c.*

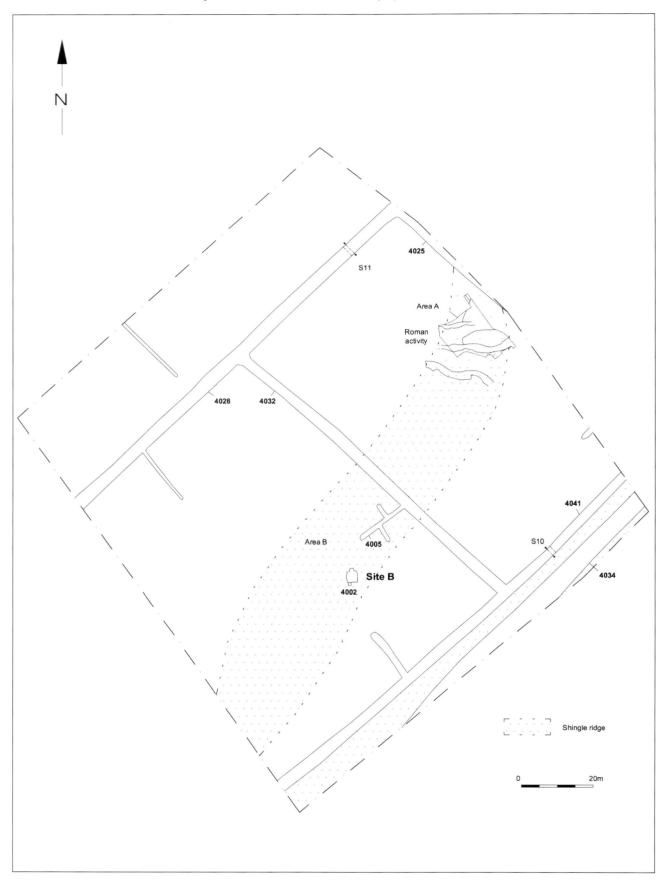

Fig. 14 Lydd Quarry 4. Plan of ditch system (showing Site B)

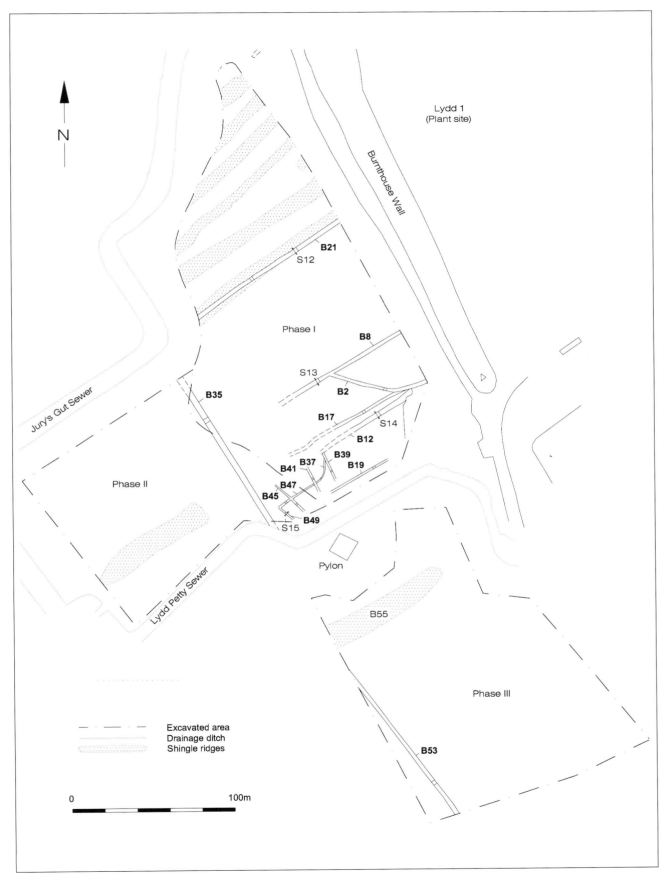

Fig. 15 Lydd Quarry 11. Plan of ditch system

2.6m and *c.* 2m in width and 630mm and 400mm deep respectively. They ran for up to 60m across the area parallel to Ditches B8 and B21, though both petered out to the west. Ditch B12 (Fig. 24, S14) contained a primary fill (B14) of greyish-brown silty clay with occasional rounded flint pebbles and an upper fill (B13) of similar type. Ditch B17 contained a fill (B18) of greyish-brown silty clay. Although it is probable this apparent track represents the northern track (Lydd 1 D21 and D22), it is to the west of the junction with the southern track (as in Lydd 2–6, see below) and could represent the latter or indeed the two tracks combined. Despite a metal detector survey of the track no metallic objects were located along the length of the trackway in Lydd 11.

Just to the south of the trackway was a series of small ditches. The earliest appeared to be a curving gully or small ditch (B37, Fig. 15) of probable natural origin, measuring 520mm in width and 100mm deep. It was cut by two small ditches (D39 and D41), *c.* 12m apart, measuring 1.5m and 1.6m in width and 210mm and 200mm deep respectively. B37 continued westward, where it was renumbered B47 and was found to turn sharply southward and shallow slightly (Ditch B49, Fig. 24, S15). A further ditch, B45, crossed B47 and appeared to be contemporary. All of the upper fills of these ditches were of a similar fine sandy silt and the lower fills were also similar to each other, being a stiff silt clay (B52). Although a little burnt clay was noted in Ditch B45 no datable material was recovered. As such the precise date of this group cannot be ascertained, though the adaptation of an apparently natural channel (B37) suggests a probable early origin. A further ditch (B19, Fig. 15), measuring between 0.8 and 1m in width and *c.* 400mm deep, ran broadly parallel to Ditch B12 and is probably related to the system of ditches B41 *et al.* However, it should be noted that the site of a former modern agricultural building lay *c.* 15m from the eastern end of B19 and it is possible this cluster relates to later activity.

The System Between the Northern and Southern Trackways (Lydd 2, 3 and 5/6)

Lydd 2 (Fig. 16)

Period 1 (12th to early 13th century)

Perhaps the earliest feature recorded in the Lydd 2 area consisted of a ditch (D2215, Fig. 16) of slightly sinuous character suggesting it may have originally been a salt-marsh creek or recut natural channel, probably predating the medieval field system. Although no ceramic dating evidence is available, this is supported to a limited extent by the stratigraphy. D2215 predated the apparently initial cut of the field boundary D2011, the infilling of which is dated to the 13th century.

Running through the central area of the investigated site were two sections of parallel double ditches, D2118

(Figs. 16 and 24, S16) and D2212 (Fig. 16) to the west and D2379 and D2381 (Fig. 16) to the east. The two sets were in alignment and may have been contiguous. Although the intervening section had been largely obscured by the later enclosure (see below), under certain soil conditions a possible continuation (2397) of D2212 was discernible between D2164 and D2134 (Fig. 42). This arrangement may have represented an earlier alignment of the trackway route later represented by D2006 (see below). There was a marked increase in elevation (0.4m on average) between the posited earlier route and that represented by the line of D2006, and it is possible that the proposed re-routing may have been necessitated by difficulties with rutting when not directly on the shingle. This contention is supported to a limited extent by the ceramic evidence which identifies D2118 as having been infilled during the 12th century; the earliest securely dated infilled ditch on the site. D2212, the parallel companion to D2118, produced 13th century pottery from the fill of a recut and seems to have been incorporated into the field system to form a small enclosure in the 13th century. No dating evidence was recovered from the primary fill of D2212.

There is no ceramic evidence that D2006 to the east and west of the earlier track alignment was of 12th century origin. However, repeated cleaning and recutting would have probably removed the primary fills along the entire length of D2006. If the proposed re-routing of the trackway is correct, it is likely that the part of D2006 which ran parallel to the earlier alignment was first established in the early 13th century soon after the disuse of D2118. The line of this southern trackway has been traced for over 500m along a prominent shingle ridge through the areas of Lydd 2 to 5/6 (see below). The track to the south-west of the Lydd 2 area is some 5m wide with flanking ditches on either side. However, as it passes through the Lydd 2 area it appeared to be bounded by only one ditch on its northern side (D2006). This is possibly the result of the slightly higher shingle in this area not requiring the establishment of a southern ditch or, more likely, it was not visible at the time of excavation. Had a second ditch existed, it would have been positioned within the edge of the now exposed shingle ridge. It has been observed during work both at Lydd and Denge West quarries that where the presence of ditches is suspected in the more elevated areas of exposed shingle, they are rarely visible on the surface but occasionally appear during the initial stages of industrial gravel extraction. The later history of the trackway as represented by D2006 is further discussed below.

No evidence for the earliest date of the field system ditches in the Lydd 2 area was forthcoming. Despite this, and based on evidence from Lydd 1, it seems likely that at least some of the ditches of the field system were excavated at an early date shortly after, or at the same time as, the establishment of the trackway. At present Ditches D2013/2048 and 2026 are considered logical candidates but both could equally have been initially excavated in the following century.

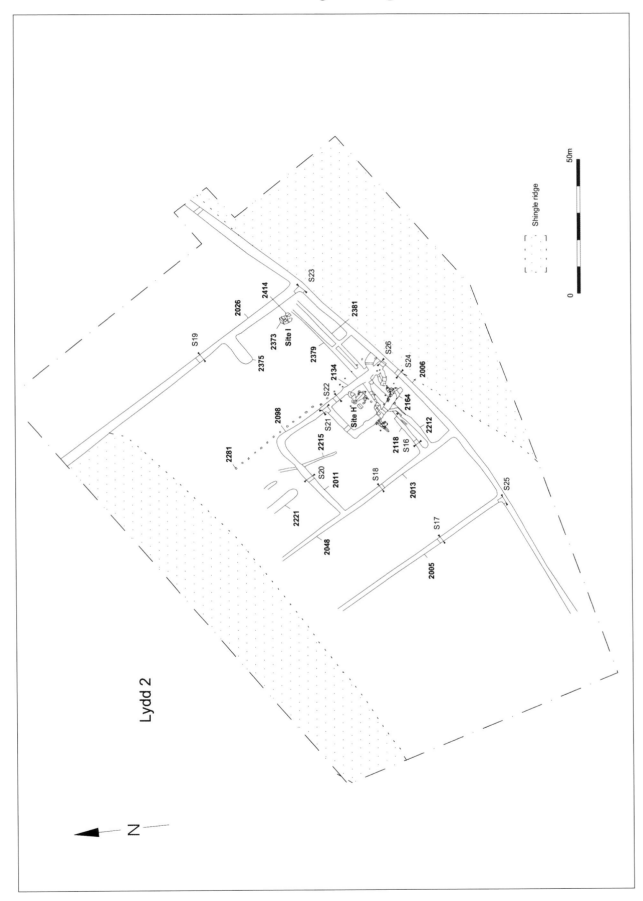

Fig. 16 Lydd Quarry 2. Plan of ditch system (showing Sites H and I)

Period 2 (13th century)

This appears to have been a period of more intense activity and the bulk of the field system was certainly established by this time. The trackway was certainly in use and was probably the access point for the serious reclamation/ consolidation in a similar way to the northern trackway at Lydd 1.

The initial imposition of a field system probably began with the cutting of drainage ditches D2005 (Fig. 24, S17), D2013/2048 (Fig. 24, S18) and D2026 (Fig. 24, S19) at right angles to the trackway ditch D2006. As has been noted above it is possible some of these may actually relate to the initial 12th century reclamation work, but this cannot be proven. A short spur, D2375 (Fig. 16), coming off D2026 at right angles produced later 13th to early 14th century pottery from its upper fill. This ditch probably became redundant when the later ditch system developed and thus the date of its infilling may be broadly contemporary with the establishment of the later field system.

It is likely that D2005, D2013/2048 and D2221 (Fig. 16) continued to the north-west but ceased to be visible on the surface where they met a rising body of semi-exposed shingle. The origin of the short section of the terminus of D2221 was unclear, although its infilling was contemporary with that of D2005 and D2013/2048. Ditches D2011 (Fig. 24, S20) and D2098/2134 (Fig. 24, S21 and 22) were perhaps slightly later additions, further sub-dividing the larger field formed by D2013/2048 and D2026. The establishment of this small field may have preceded or been contemporary with the emplacement of the settlement site and the cutting of the enclosure ditch D2096/2164. The development of the enclosure ditch is discussed below under the settlement section. Although there are few indications as to the relative and absolute chronology of the inception of the field ditches, with the exception of D2005 and D2026 which continued into the later period, there is considerable ceramic evidence for infilling of most ditches associated with the enclosure during the later 13th to early 14th centuries.

The profile of the last recut (2015) (Fig. 24, S18) of D2013/2048 north of its junction with D2118 was vertically sided with a flat base and contained a fill (2016) of silty clay with 60% gravel. The inherent instability of 90 degree sides indicated that the ditch was immediately infilled with shingle after recutting, thereby creating a French drain. Thus it seems that although the infilling of the ditch system may have reflected lower water levels or changes in boundaries or land use, a certain standard of drainage was still required to be maintained.

Period 3 (14th to 15th century)

The infilling of D2006 shows the trackway ditches were probably still open in this period, though the stratigraphic and artefactual data is somewhat mixed due to the problems of residuality and recutting. East of its junction with D2026 (Figs. 16 and *25, S23), pottery from the upper fill of D2006 (Context 2060) suggests an infilling date of the 13th to early 14th century. However, west of the junction with D2026 the infilling, according to the ceramics, apparently occurred in the early to middle 14th century (Context 2035, *Fig. 25, S24), while at its junction with D2005 (Figs. 16 and *25, S25), the lower and upper fills of D2006 producing 15th and 16th century pottery respectively (Contexts 2062–3). D2006 also appeared to cut the ditch of the settlement enclosure D2134 (see below and Figs. 16 and *25, S26), even though both must have been contemporary in use at one time. Indeed all the sections through D2006 showed the presence of varied discontinuous fills. This was perhaps as a result of localised recutting or minor realignments of the trackway. Thus the complexity of the stratigraphy of D2006 generally reflects the continued use of the trackway into the 16th century. Although D2006 was cut by D2026, and probably D2005, at their junctions, this reflects the relative chronology of their infilling rather than inception.

It is probable that by this period the only field ditches still functioning in this area were D2005 and D2026, both of which cut the fills of trackway Ditch 2006. D2026 was apparently incorporated into a larger rectilinear ditch system that evolved earlier and includes 'Lydd 3' ditches 3030 and 3130 (see below). This later system enclosed much larger fields, typically of approximately one hectare, and survived wholly or in part into the 16th century. The extended use of D2026 is supported by the presence of 15th to early 16th century pottery in its upper fill. In addition, the final profile of D2026 was considerably broader and deeper than the ditches that had become extinct during the earlier period (Fig. 24, S19).

Although D2006 produced 13th to early 14th century pottery at its junction with D2026, and 15th to mid 16th century pottery at the junction with D2005, the earlier material may have been residual. If this were the case, it is quite possible that the entire length of D2006 remained open into the 16th century. After the imposition of the later field system, D2006 seems to have served primarily as a boundary for the trackway rather than a functioning part of the drainage system. This may be due to D2006 being dug into the body of the shingle ridge in a position where a deeper, broader profile could not be maintained or where drainage was already sufficient.

The trackway appears to have continued in use throughout this period, with the ditches being finally infilled perhaps between the later 15th and mid 16th centuries. Whatever the case, evidence from Lydd 5/6, and indeed its depiction on Poker's map of 1617, show the track was in existence into the 17th century, though by this date the ditches may have all been infilled (*Fig. 3). By this time the track appears to have run from Dering Farm to the Burnthouse Wall and probably served the 'Burnt House', which is also depicted on the same map at the western end of the track.

Lydd 3 (Fig. 17)

Period 1 (12th to early 13th century)

The main southern trackway located to the north-east at Lydd 2 was identified running through the Lydd 3 area. It was represented by two parallel ditches (Fig. 17, Ditches 3150 and 3158) rather than a single northerly ditch as found at Lydd 2. Unsurprisingly the dating from these ditches showed them to have been infilled quite late (see below). However, Ditch 3148 ran for *c.* 13m parallel with D3150, and perhaps represented an earlier alignment of the ditch. Unfortunately 3148 did not produce any datable finds, though this in itself suggests an early date. As such it is considered probable this may be part of the original 12th century track which, as noted at Lydd 2 (Ditch 2118), was probably realigned in places during the 13th century.

To the south of the trackway was a ditch (D3364) which appeared to enclose an area of small ditches associated with mid 12th to early 13th century pottery (Site C). Although the exact function of this area is uncertain (see below) the early nature of the finds suggests it was probably in existence during Period 1. Unfortunately it has not proved possible to establish, even using circumstantial evidence, whether Ditches 3030, 3130 and 3368 had Period 1 origins.

Period 2 (13th century)

Due to the longevity of most of the field ditches in this area it is impossible to associate any of the main investigated ditches with the Period 2 'consolidation' works. However, D3030, 3130 and 3368 are likely to originally be of this period, if not the preceding one, but stayed in use into the next period. It is quite possible D3368 did not continue into the later period, however, due to the total lack of pottery from the ditch. This hypothesis is based solely on the observation that the later ditch system consists of larger fields and thus D3368 may not have been needed if 3030 stayed in use.

Period 3 (14th to 15th century)

Ditch 3130 was approximately 3.8m wide and contained a 3.1m wide recut (*Fig. 25, S27, Cut 3131). It joined the existing ditch (Fig. 17, D3030) at right angles. The map of the quarry prior to extraction shows D3130 to the north-east of the junction with D3030 to still be open. As such it must have been infilled quite recently. It is quite probable that the recut (3131) represents this later ditch with D3130 representing the medieval predecessor. Alternatively both D3130 and 3131 may be post-medieval recuts. Unfortunately, with the exception of a single small sherd of abraded medieval pottery from 3128, no pottery was recovered from either fill. Whatever the case, it is felt almost certain that this ditch is on the alignment of a 13th century ditch and to the east of D3030, continuing

until quite recently. Evidence from the main southern trackway ditches (D3150 and D3158) suggests infilling of these did not occur until at least the late 14th to 15th centuries, although it is known the trackway continued in use beyond this time. Fill 3151 produced a moderate sized assemblage of unabraded pottery of this date (*Fig. 25, S28). All these ditches as a whole can therefore be seen to be open and functioning into Period 3.

In Lydd 3 Area A, a pair of parallel ditches (Fig. 17, Ditches 3144 and 3146, *Fig. 25, S29 and 30) ran *c.* 3m apart and some 14m to the west of a postulated building/ activity area represented by post-holes 3134, 3138, 3142 and ?3132 (see Site K below). The westernmost of these two ditches may have represented a field boundary with the smaller eastern example (D3146) being added later to form a track. Ceramic evidence indicates that both D3144 and D3146 had probably been infilled in the 14th century. Ditches 3144 and 3146 roughly aligned with two similarly dated parallel ditches (D3006/3008 and D3010) identified in Area B (Site Ja, Fig. 45), and perhaps represent the north-eastern continuation of the same small trackway. If this were the case, the trackway would have provided access from the apparent focus of settlement at Site Ja/Jb to the activity area at Site K. The intervening section of the postulated trackway may have been removed by ploughing, or may have been too ephemeral to identify. It is likely that this trackway developed as a cross-over between the two principal north-east to south-west trackways across the site.

Lydd 5/6 (Fig. 18)

This part of the quarry contained the densest area of ditches associated with the field system, suggesting it to have perhaps been the focus of agricultural, or at least arable, activity. Although the majority of relationships between the different ditches was readily identifiable from their intersections without excavation, many produced ceramic dating which was at odds with the stratigraphic relationships. This is almost certainly due to residual pottery being incorporated in later infillings and has made allocating phases to the ditches very difficult. As such, educated guesswork has probably had to be used more on this part of the quarry than anywhere else. In the north-west of the Lydd 5/6 area lay a system of much smaller enclosures, measuring *c.* a quarter of a hectare, which probably represented the site of stock pens – perhaps sheep folds. These are discussed later under the section on occupation sites and activity areas (see Site G below).

Period 1 (12th to early 13th century)

The main southern trackway located to the north-east at Lydds 2 and 3 was identified running through the Lydd 5/6 area. As at Lydd 3 it was represented by two parallel ditches (Fig. 18, Ditches 5009 and 5011, *Fig. 25, S31 and S32 respectively) about 5m apart. In all about 500m of

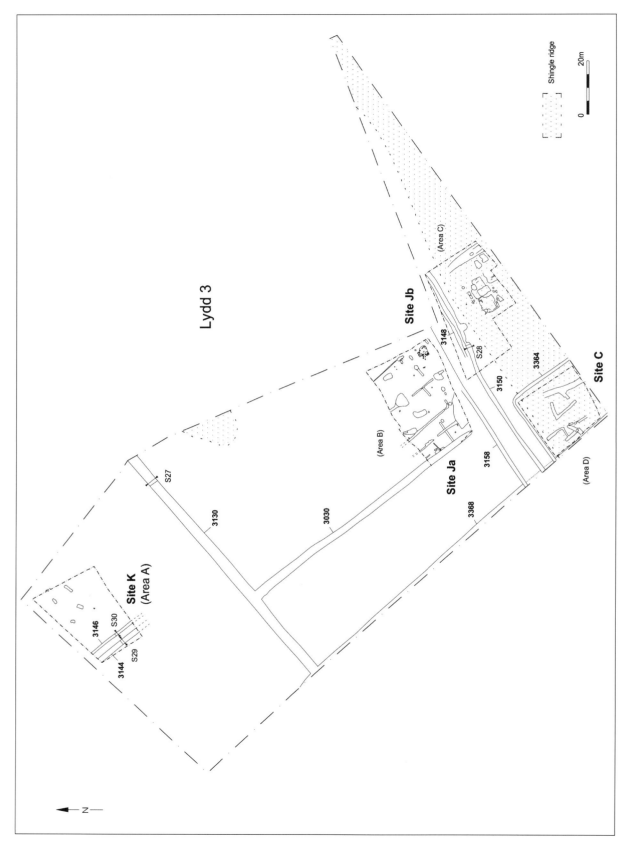

Fig. 17 Lydd Quarry 3. Plan of ditch system (showing Sites C, Ja, Jb and K)

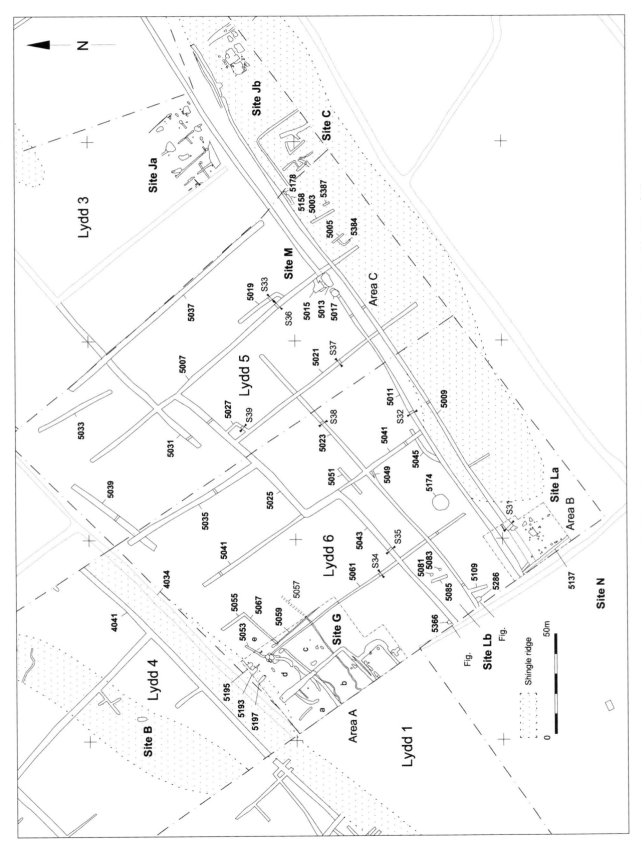

Fig. 18 Lydd Quarry 5/6. Plan of ditch system (showing Sites B, C, G, Ja, La, Lb, M and N)

this track has so far been exposed at the quarry. As before, the dating from these ditches showed them to have been infilled quite late (see below) with a variety of different fill types and cut profiles along their lengths. However, it is almost certain they formed part of the earliest route along the shingle ridge, which was used to gain access for reclamation. This suggestion is confirmed by a couple of areas of realigned ditch. Two short sections of shallow (truncated to 130mm deep) ditch (Fig. 18, D5158 and D5178), measuring at least 3.6m long and 1.8m long respectively and separated by a 1.1m wide interruption, ran parallel to and *c.* 1m south of D5009 in the extreme south-east area of Lydd 5. Both D5158 and D5178 produced 12th century pottery and it is likely that they represent an earlier alignment of trackway ditch 5009. This is supported by ceramic evidence from Lydd 2 which suggested that the trackway dated from at least the mid/late 12th century. The interruption between D5158 and D5178 was perhaps intended to provide access to an area of late 12th to early 13th century activity immediately to the east, previously identified in Lydd 3, Area D (Site C).

No field ditches definitely infilled in the 12th to very early 13th century were located in the Lydd 5/6 area. The earliest features may have been two 190mm deep sinuous probable natural drainage gullies (Figs. 18 and 39, 5057 and 5093) within Area A (see Site G below). Unfortunately neither produced any finds but both were cut by artificial ditches infilled during the early to later 13th century.

Several field ditches appear to have been infilled during the first three quarters of the 13th century. It is therefore reasonably certain that at least these were probably open during Period 1, though it is likely that a number of others were as well. Only three field ditches at Lydd 5/6, based on ceramics and stratigraphic relationships, can be shown to have been probably infilled at this early date: D5019 (*Fig. 25, S33), D5039 and possibly D5061 (*Fig. 25, S34). Ditch D5061 was traced for a distance of *c.* 115m. It cut the sinuous channel D5057 but was itself cut by Ditches D5023 and 5043 (*Fig. 25, S35). D5061 may have been initially established as a field boundary/drainage ditch, which subsequently also served as a boundary ditch for a secondary trackway (see below). However, due to the fact that the eastern trackway ditch (D5059) appears to have been infilled slightly later, it is possible that D5061, although of early origin, may have remained open throughout the 13th century (Period 2). D5019 was an L-shaped ditch, measuring 860mm wide (*Fig. 25, S33), which ran for *c.* 25m and was cut by D5007 (Figs. 18 and *26, S36). At the point sectioned, D5007 appeared to cut an earlier, deeper feature (5126) possibly representing a sump set within an earlier ditch cut on the same alignment. However, if D5019 was open at this early date then D5007 almost certainly was, as both appeared to form a narrow enclosure.

A *c.* 65m long, 1.5m wide, 0.48m deep, section of D5039 was located in the northern part of the area.

Unfortunately the full extent of this ditch could not be traced, though it was probably originally associated with D5007 and D5041, again suggesting both these ditches to be of probable early origin. D5039 was clearly cut by D5035.

Four undated ditches (Fig. 18, D5033, D5045, D5049 and D5051) were perhaps relics of the earliest ditch system: D5033 was a straight narrow ditch on a slightly different alignment to the majority of the field ditches; D5045 and D5051 were short sections of narrow ditch both cut by 14th century D5041; and D5049 was a short section of very narrow curving ditch.

Period 2 (13th century)

Due to the longevity of many of the field ditches in the Lydd 5/6 area it is impossible to associate any of the main investigated ditches with the Period 2 'consolidation' works with any degree of certainty, although most of the system was probably finally constructed at this time. Ditches infilled during the 14th century, if the ceramic dating is reliable, were almost certainly open during the 13th century, and many may have been excavated to consolidate the Period 1 works into workable sized fields.

The principle southern trackway, marked by D5009 and D5011, almost certainly continued in use with the ditches being cleaned out on a regular basis. This would explain the absence of any infill deposits of this date, although it should be noted that a number of 13th century coins were found in the ditches. These had almost certainly originated as casual losses along the track which became incorporated with the final infilling of the ditches. Although two ditches of the field system cross the trackway (D5007 and D5021), it is probable these were contemporary and simply needed to drain water from either side of the track. It is probable they were bridged by horizontal planking which left no trace in the archaeological record.

A possible subsidiary trackway, on the eastern edge of Area A, may have been established during this period by the addition of gully 5059, some 2m to the east of the presumably earlier and wider D5061. Gully 5059 consisted of a narrow cut which produced a small amount of 13th century pottery from its fill. This subsidiary trackway may have linked the medieval activity at Site G with the principal trackway (delineated by D5009 and D5011) *c.* 110m to the south. The postulated subsidiary trackway, defined by D5061 and gully 5059, met D5067 at a *c.* 4m wide interruption; D5067 (Fig. 18) continued to the east as D5055. Two pits (5075 and 5377) were located at the eastern terminus of D5067 and the western terminus of D5055, and possibly represented the position of a gate that would have controlled access across ditch 5067/5055 into an area of activity immediately to the north (Fig. 39).

Ditch termini 5193/5331 and 5197 (Figs. 18 and 39), together with a possible spur ditch (5195), lay *c.* 16m to the north of the postulated access-way, and perhaps represented the northern continuation of the subsidiary trackway. If this were the case, it is reasonable to assume that the subsidiary trackway had served as a cross-over between the two identified principal south-west to north-east routes. Another element of this pattern of communications has been tentatively identified in Lydd 3 (Fig. 17) where a postulated subsidiary trackway (delineated by D3006/D3008/D3002 and D3010/D3146) was similarly orientated (see above).

Ceramic evidence indicates that three field boundary/ drainage ditches (Fig. 18, D5021 (*Fig. 26, S37), D5023 (*Fig. 26, S38) and D5035), measuring between 1.3 and 1.8m wide and between 220 and 950mm deep, may have been infilled during the 14th century (though there is other evidence which suggests D5021 remained open – see below). A probably subsidiary drainage ditch (Fig. 18, D5387), measuring c. 8m long, also appears to have been infilled at broadly the same time. Three undated short narrow ditches (Fig. 18, D5003, D5005 and D5384) appeared to be perhaps inter-related elements of the same local subsidiary drainage system as D5387. D5085 and D5109 (Fig. 18) were two further ditches, one of which (5085) contained limited quantities of 14th century material whose full extent could not be traced, though both ditches were notable in that they were on a different alignment to the rest of the field system.

Although ceramic evidence suggests a 14th century infilling date for ditch 5041, the overall field layout perhaps argues against it, as it is likely that the northern part of D5007 with D5025 and D5041 remained open into at least the 15th century, enclosing a single rectangular field. This is supported to a degree by environmental evidence from fill 5123 of D5025. Analysis of the plant remains identified a particularly wide range of cereals, pulses and wild plant seeds, including the later free-threshing bread wheat as well as the earlier spelt wheat, perhaps as a result of the longevity of D5025. It was clear that although D5025 had originally been contemporary with D5041 it had remained in use (along with the later D5043 to the south-west) far longer, and later recuts of both D5025 and 5043 had cut the infilled D5041. Indeed part of D5041, which apparently linked D5025 and D5043, had been kept in use to link the two. A similar problem of establishing an infilling date is also encountered with D5021. At the junction of D5021 and D5025 was a small square enclosure marked out by D5027 (*Fig. 26, S39). The fills of the enclosure ditch consistently produced pottery indicating a 15th century infilling date. It is therefore highly probable that D5021 was not infilled during the 14th century, as without it the enclosure would not have been able to function. It is likely therefore that both D5021 and D5027 were established during Period 2 but continued in use into the 14th/15th centuries (Period 3). This would also explain why D5021 clearly cut D5023, which was actually probably infilled during the 14th century.

Period 3 (14th to 15th century)

Similar problems were encountered during the interpretation of ditches of this period to those in the earlier periods. Most ditches from Period 2, including the principle southern trackway, but with the probable exceptions of D5023 and D5035, continued in use. However, by this time it appears the enclosures in Area A (Site G) as well as the subsidiary trackway had also been infilled.

Although ceramic evidence suggests that D5025 was perhaps infilled during this period, again the pattern of land use argues against it, as it is an integral part of fields made up by 5007, 5011, 5021, 5025 and possibly part of 5041. This is supported to a degree by the presence of an activity area (see below under Site M), located either side of a south-eastern access into one of the fields. Ditch 5043 (*Fig. 25, S35) is likely to be the only new ditch actually excavated during this period, presumably replacing the earlier D5023.

Toward the end of Period 3, or perhaps just into the beginning of the 16th century, many of the field ditches appear to have been infilled. Ditches containing infilling of this date include D5007 and D5043.

Period 4a (early post-medieval – 16th to 17th century)

As with other parts of the quarry very few ditches appear to have been dug or infilled after the 15th to early 16th centuries. One of the notable exceptions to this are the ditches of the principle trackways. The northern ditch (D5011) of the southern principal trackway (see above) also delineated the southern boundary of adjacent fields. Ceramic evidence indicates that although the southern trackway ditch (D5009) had probably been infilled between 1475 and 1550, ditch 5011 was still open after 1550. The presence of worn Elizabethan coins from the track suggest usage into the 17th century. Two of the earlier ditch alignments were probably recut during this period, both being wide and straight (Fig. 18, D5031 and D5037).

Ditch 5137 (Figs. 18 and 50) was only partly exposed on the western edge of the excavation area. The presence of a significant number of tankards within the 17th to early 18th century pottery assemblage, together with a large quantity of clay pipe, perhaps suggests that the ditch had been used for the disposal of rubbish from an inn or tavern. Although it is very unlikely that such a sparsely populated area relatively close to Lydd town could have supported an inn, it is possible that a private dwelling may have incorporated a public room serving as a drinking parlour. This supposition is perhaps supported to a degree by circumstantial cartographic evidence which shows a large residence (Harlackinden's house, or the 'Burnt House') which lay a little to the west from at least the 16th century.

The System to the South of the Southern Trackway (Lydd 7–10 and 11, Phase III)

With the exception of the western half of Lydd 9 (Fig. 9, defined by an existing field), the rather fragmentary ditch/field system in Lydd Stages 7 to 10 and Lydd 11 Phase III, differed markedly to the system identified to the north of the southern trackway. The two areas (Lydd 8–10 and Lydd 2–6) were divided by a north-east trending principal shingle ridge with the former area closest to the barrier beach to the south.

With the possible exception of undated ditch D8006 (Fig. 20), and four very slightly meandering natural creeks (Fig. 21, 9010, 9012, 9014 and 9016), no medieval ditches were identified in Lydd 8 or the eastern half of Lydd 9, although some of the existing ditches may be based upon medieval features. It may be that these areas, lying in a trough between the barrier beach (the line of the present Camber Road broadly defines its landward edge) and a principal shingle ridge, were always too wet to be successfully drained and fully exploited. This supposition is perhaps supported by the exceptionally high density of later drainage features recorded in the western end of Lydd 8, together with the unprecedented complete absence of residual medieval or post-medieval material observed during topsoil stripping in that area. The presence of a former deep (in excess of 7m), broad silted-up channel (Fig. 21, 9074) running through the area may have represented such unfavourable underlying soil conditions that effective drainage would have been problematic.

At Lydd 7 (Fig. 19) and in the western half of Lydd 9 however, a system of square or rectangular fields became established as the ground rose with the development of further bodies of underlying shingle.

The western part of Lydd 10 (Fig. 22, Area B), was located on the edge of the main barrier beach, in an area with significantly better natural drainage. Consequently, the ditching here was of a specialised nature, predominantly associated with the site of a building (Site A). The presumed edge of a probable 13th century field system was revealed on the eastern edge of the eastern part of Lydd 10, and was represented by ditches A2, A8 and A12 (Fig. 22, Area A).

Period 1 (12th to early 13th century)

Very few ditches could be identified as being of early date in this area. Whether this is due to them being created later or as a result of later cleaning totally removing earlier material is uncertain, but the presence of some 12th to early 13th century features/finds in the area suggest some at least were early in origin. The two earliest identified ditches, dated by ceramics to the late 12th to early 13th century, were a probable field ditch (Fig. 19, D7031 (*Fig. 26, S40)) on the easternmost edge of the Lydd 7 area, and a narrow drainage ditch (DA19) (see occupation/activity sites below) on the southern edge of Lydd 10 (Fig. 22, Site A).

D7031 probably represented one side of a small field measuring *c.* 60 × 40m. The southern part of D7031 was cut into the edge of the shingle outcrop, a location that would have already provided relatively good natural drainage. The favourable position of this feature perhaps suggests that its prime function was as a barrier, which in turn would explain why it apparently had not been subject to the habitual cleaning and re-cutting widely seen elsewhere. It has already been postulated in previous work (Barber 1998 and see below) that initially agricultural activity in this marginal land would have been pastoral, and that consequently the earliest fields might have served as stock enclosures.

It is unsurprising that the earliest identified medieval features were located on the edge of the main barrier beach, as the crest of the shingle ridge would have offered another easy, if somewhat vulnerable, point of access to the area.

Period 2: 13th century

Ditches D7017, D7026 (*Fig. 26, S41), D7028 (*Fig. 26, S42), D7033 and D7036 (Fig. 19) were part of the same local ditch system as D7031 above and thus probably originated in the previous period. D7045/D7051 was cut by D7017 (Fig. 19) though its function is uncertain. D7026 was the second recut and D7040 the first recut of D7041 (*Fig. 26, S43). Although an 18th century lead token was recovered from the last recut D7026, there was no independent dating evidence available for the original cut (D7041) which may have been contemporary with D7031 above. The apparently open-ended shape of the enclosures, together with the presence of an interruption in an existing field ditch, perhaps suggests that this arrangement was intended to funnel stock through an access-way between fields. A large 13th century post-hole (Fig. 19, 7053) measuring 2.9 × 1.5m in the middle of the proposed access perhaps represented the site of a gate.

Ditch A12 (Fig. 22, Area A) (with recut A84) was located on the edge of the barrier beach, and together with associated undated ditch A2 perhaps formed the corners of two small fields or enclosures. Again, the improved natural drainage found in this location perhaps accounted for the apparent absence of cleaning or re-cutting of DA12.

Three broad ditches (Fig. 22, A58 (*Fig. 26, S44), A71 and A75), measuring 2.4m, 3.5m and 2.5m wide and 700mm, 530mm and 550mm deep respectively, together with the Lydd Petty Sewer immediately to the north, partially enclosed an area measuring *c.* 50 × 50m. Ditch A58 contained a recut (A85) measuring 1.2m wide and 360mm deep, and A75 contained a possible recut (A86) measuring 2.28m wide and 220mm deep. The fills (A72 and A80 respectively) of Ditches A71 and A75 produced 13th century pottery while mid 13th to mid 14th century pottery was recovered from the fill (A60) of Ditch A58. An ephemeral *c.* 2m long spur ditch (Fig. 22, Area A)

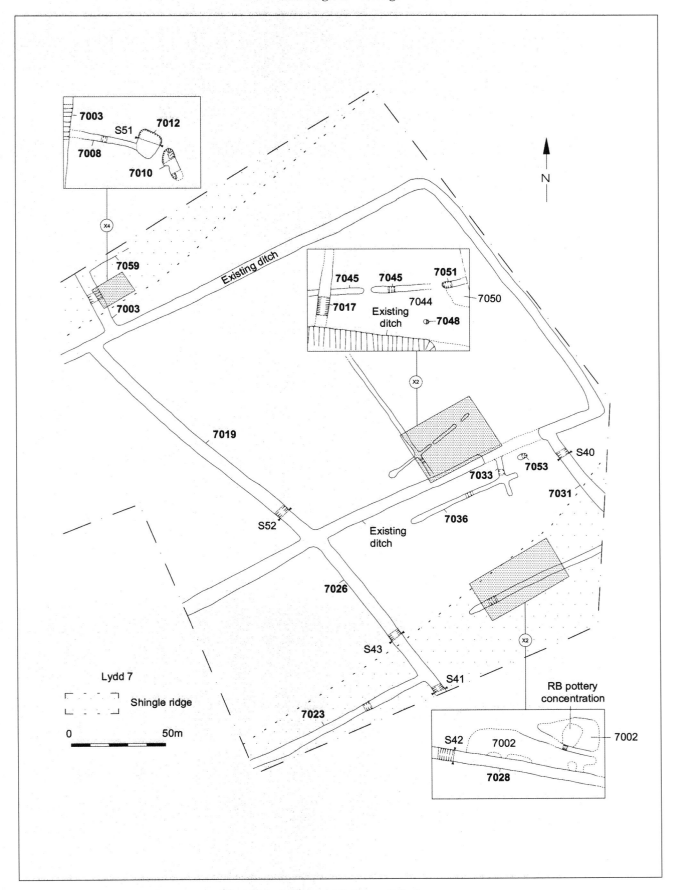

Fig. 19 Lydd Quarry 7. Plan of ditch system

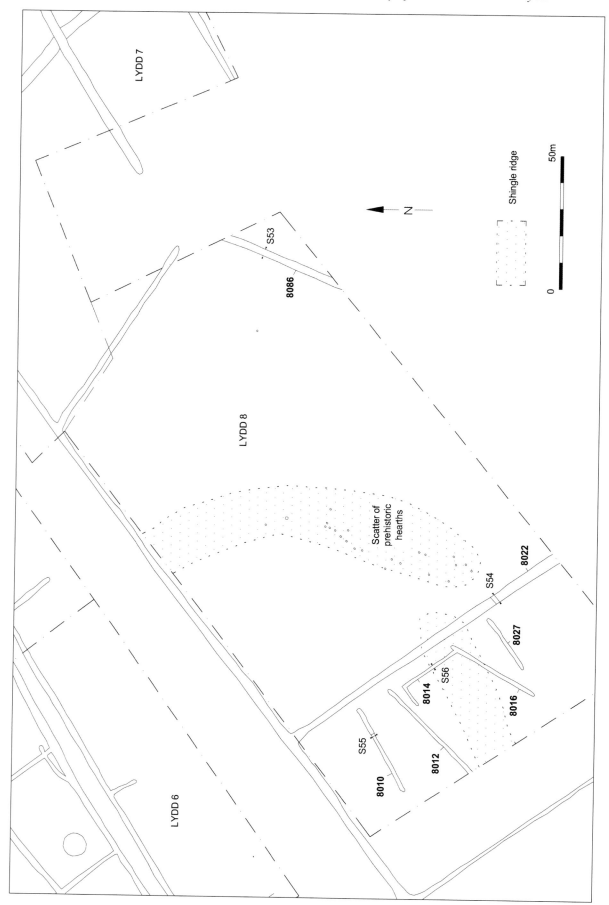

Fig. 20 Lydd Quarry 8. Plan of ditch system

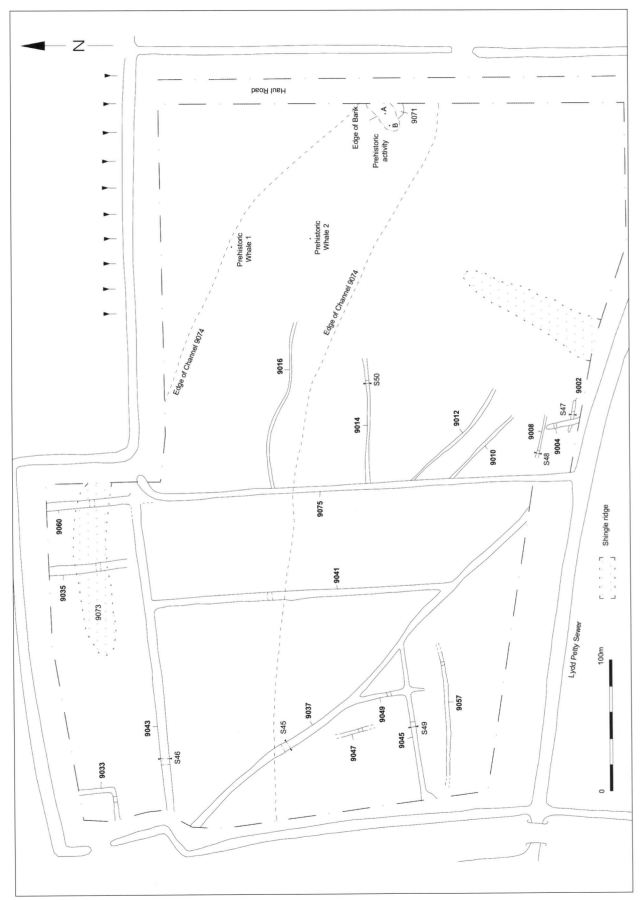

Fig. 21 Lydd Quarry 9. Plan of ditch system

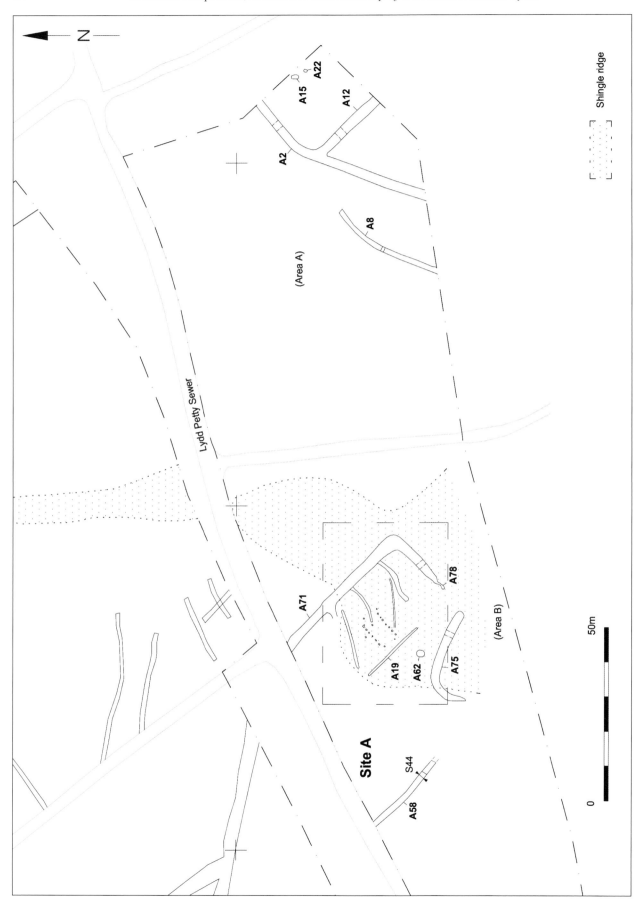

Fig. 22 Lydd Quarry 10. Plan of ditch system (showing Site A)

off A71 measured *c*. 1.5m wide and produced early 13th century pottery.

In the western part of Lydd 9, a probably natural or improved sinuous channel or creek (Fig. 21, 9037 (*Fig. 26, S45)) with a peaty primary fill (9038) had apparently been combined with a rectilinear system of three ditches (Fig. 21, D9035, D9041 and D9043 (*Fig. 26, S46)) to produce an enclosed area of fields. A single sherd of medieval, perhaps 14th century, pottery was recovered from the fill (9044) of D9043, while a small quantity of post-medieval material from D9037 suggested that it was one of the last ditches to be infilled. Both features are likely to originally have been of an earlier date. A short ditch (Fig. 21, 9004) with a terminal to the north-west had perhaps been a spur off a previous course of the present Lydd Petty Sewer. This feature cut one narrow ditch (Fig. 21, D9002, *Fig. 26, S47) and terminated just short of another (D9008, *Fig. 26, S48). Both contained 13th to 14th century pottery in their fills. These lay *c*. 8m apart and ran parallel for *c*. 12m beside the present Lydd Petty Sewer and in the same alignment. Although only short sections of these ditches were identified, they perhaps represented the route of a trackway.

A network of four slightly meandering/sinuous, probably natural or improved natural channels or creeks (Fig. 21, 9045 (*Fig. 26, S49), 9047, 9049 and 9057) with peaty primary fills (9046, 9048, 9050 and 9058 respectively) lay to the west, between D9037 and the Burnthouse Wall. Although there was no independent evidence, it is likely that channels 9045, 9047, 9049 and 9057 were infilled in the early part of this period after they were no longer required to aid drainage in this area.

Similarly D9041 was probably infilled later this period in order to create a larger field bounded by D9075 to the east, D9043 to the north and D9037 to the west. D9075 cut the western termini of four narrow, sinuous natural or improved creeks (Fig. 21, 9010, 9012, 9014 (*Fig. 27, S50) and 9016). This relationship of features suggests that the line of D9075 may have originally been broadly based on the line of a major creek with four subsidiary water courses draining into it.

The infilling of DA58 (Fig. 22) was perhaps associated with the last phase of use of a small local ditch system that related to the building at Site A (see below).

Period 3: 14th to 15th century

Ditch 7003 (Fig. 19) appeared to be the southern continuation of D3200, previously identified in Lydd 3. It was unusual in that it appeared to be cut through the full width of a principal shingle ridge (although a *c*. 5m wide strip could not be investigated because of the presence of a modern unmetalled road). Consequently the local drainage would have been relatively good. In view of this, it was likely that D7003's main function was as a barrier or perhaps to link the drainage systems to the north and south of the track. Although of a probably relatively early date originally, evidence from Lydd

3 suggested that D3200 began to be used for domestic rubbish disposal from some time in the 14th century until the early 15th century. The ceramic evidence from D7003 suggests infilling in the early to mid 15th century.

Ditch 7003 cut a 400mm wide gully or narrow ditch (Fig. 19, 7008) which terminated in a sub-rectangular pit (Fig. 19, 7012 (*Fig. 27, S51)) measuring approximately 1.3 × 1.4m; an elongate pit or short ditch (7010) immediately to the east pit 7012 measured 600mm × 1.3m. The fills (7011 and 7013 respectively) of pits 7010 and 7012 produced 14th century pottery. It is possible that the arrangement described above represented part of a small enclosure with an entranceway to the north-east.

Ditch 7059 (Fig. 19), or a recut of it, cut D7003 at right angles and may originally have been part of a localised ditch system associated with the buildings identified at Lydd 3, Site J. The slightly later date (possibly just into the 16th century) for the infilling of D7059 was perhaps due to its position near the crest of the shingle ridge; these higher areas would continue to be used for general access to the west, irrespective of the local pattern of settlement.

Ditch 9033 (Fig. 21) was perhaps the eastern corner of a small square enclosure, the western edge of which may have been represented by an existing ditch. If this were the case, the original enclosure would have measured *c*. 20 × 20m, with a western access opening onto the Burnthouse Wall. It is clear from Poker's map that an established track ran along the top of the Burnthouse Wall. It is therefore possible this postulated enclosure may represent an activity area or more probably, considering the low quantities of finds, a small stock enclosure beside this route.

Ditch 9043 was probably infilled in this period in order to create a larger field bounded to the east by D9060/9075, to the north by an existing ditch and to the south by D9037, or the Lydd Petty Sewer. A fragment of brick from D9037 suggests it may have remained open until quite late, though the overall field morphology would suggest the brick could be intrusive. Undated D9035 was also likely to have been infilled in this period, although it may have originally been an element of a small enclosure, with D9060 and the eastern part of D9043.

Period 4: (16th century or later)

Many, though not all, of the following ditches were undoubtedly of earlier origin, though this is impossible to prove.

Although D7019 (Figs. 19 and *27, S52) was undated by pottery, it did produce peg tile, suggesting that it may have been one of the last ditches to be infilled before the existing modern field system was established. The infilling of D7019 effectively created two large fields (*c*. two hectares each) from four small ones. D7023 was part of the same local field system as D7019 and produced early 19th century material. Although D7023 was only partly seen, it is likely that it too was infilled at a late date to create a larger field.

At Lydd 8, two broad ditches at either end of the site (Fig. 20, D8006 and D8022) (*Fig. 27, S53 and S54) may have been originally of medieval or later date. Both ditches were *c.* 3m wide and between 500 and 800mm deep. However, the presence of large quantities of modern rubbish and the complete absence of earlier material indicates that the ditches were probably infilled in the later 19th or 20th century.

Immediately to the west of D8022, five ditches of uniform character (Fig. 20, D8010) (*Fig. 27, S55), D8012, D8014 (*Fig. 27, S56), D8016 and D8027, measuring between 1.1m to 1.3m wide and between 200 and 250mm deep, formed a discrete system. All the ditches, with the possible exception of D8016, which may have deformed after cutting, were flat-bottomed with vertical sides. They contained a very similar grey silty fill with a minimum 60% shingle. Small quantities of brick, tile and 19th to 20th century pottery were recovered from the fills (8011, 8013 and 8017) of Ditches 8010, 8012 and 8016 respectively. It is unlikely that the vertical profile of the sides could have been maintained if the ditches had not been immediately infilled after cutting. This, together with the uniform shingle fill, suggests that this ditch system was designed as a network of French drains (*i.e.*, ditches deliberately infilled with shingle through which water may pass). The very straight edges of the features perhaps suggest that they had been mechanically excavated and were of late post-medieval/modern origin.

Only one ditch was recorded in the Lydd 11 (Phase III) area: Ditch B53 (Fig. 15), which measured 1.84m in width and 780mm deep. Although on the same alignment as Ditch B35 to the north the fill (B54) produced modern pottery and brick. Whether this ditch is a medieval one which has been kept open (or re-opened) in the post-medieval period, or whether it is of wholly post-medieval origin, is uncertain.

Discussion and Phasing of the Trackways and Field System

The excavations have revealed over 21 hectares of the medieval field system characterised by generally small fields of varying sizes demarcated by a system of drainage ditches. Three strands of evidence have been identified to help phase the system – morphology, ceramic dating and stratigraphy, and the limitations of each have been considered. Although the evidence of the three is generally in agreement, attention has been drawn to some areas of conflict. It is apparent that the evidence recovered both from the plan of the ditches and from the excavation is incomplete. The pattern of drainage ditches evolved over a considerable period of time, and many details have not survived and/or not been recovered. However, it is still considered crucial that the development of the overall field system is summarised here despite the highlighted

uncertainties over the phasing of some of its elements.

Running between the fields there is evidence for at least two diverging principle tracks, or droveways, each bounded by ditches. These appear to link up a number of occupation sites and activity areas (A–N), which are discussed further below. The exact origins and ultimate destinations of the tracks are at present unknown, but they appear to have enjoyed some longevity, being an integral part of all of the main periods of the field system. The trackways are up to 5m wide and, like the occupation sites, tend to be located on the shingle ridges of the area (Tooley 1995, 3). The northern track, first located at Lydd 1, ran between the Lydd 4 and 5/6 excavations. The northern boundary ditch of this track, located during Lydd 4 (Fig. 14, Ditch 4041), had been infilled during the medieval period. However, the southern boundary ditch was still open and formed part of an extant field boundary immediately prior to gravel extraction (Fig. 14, Ditch 4034), demonstrating how the extant system of ditches in the area has evolved from the medieval one.

No trace of any artificial surfacing was found on either trackway. This is unsurprising as the gravel would have provided a naturally well-drained hard surface. The use of metal detectors to survey the length of the southern trackway exposed in Lydd 5/6 (Fig. 18, Ditches 5009 and 5011) resulted in the location of numerous metalwork losses in the surface of the gravel. These have been extremely useful in dating the period of use of the southern trackway. A number of coins show the track to have been in use at least from the 13th century. The latest coins, consisting of worn Elizabethan issues, show usage at least until the early 17th century, which correlates with the depiction of both the northern and southern tracks on Poker's map of 1617 (*Fig. 3). Sporadic evidence from the flanking ditches (Fig. 16, Ditch 2006, see below) indicates that final infilling of these ditches, at least in places, did not take place until the 16th century. The trackways are therefore likely to have continued in use even after the flanking ditches were no longer extant. Evidence for other smaller subsidiary tracks was also recovered, though none of these appear to have survived into the 15th century.

The field system itself consisted of a patchwork of usually square or rectangular fields of varying sizes, roughly aligned with the shingle ridges in the area. This alignment suggests that drainage works within the low-lying finer-grained sediments were begun from the higher, better drained, shingle ridges. As a result the field boundaries would be set at right-angles to the ridges and link them up. The smallest fields, usually less than 0.4 hectares in extent, are similar in size to others noted on the marsh (Reeves 1996, 7; 1997, 65). Larger fields were also present but these were not usually more than a hectare in size. It has been suggested the small size of most of the medieval fields indicates their use for arable cultivation (Reeves 1996, 8); the larger fields in areas not suitable for cultivation were used for pasture (Rippon

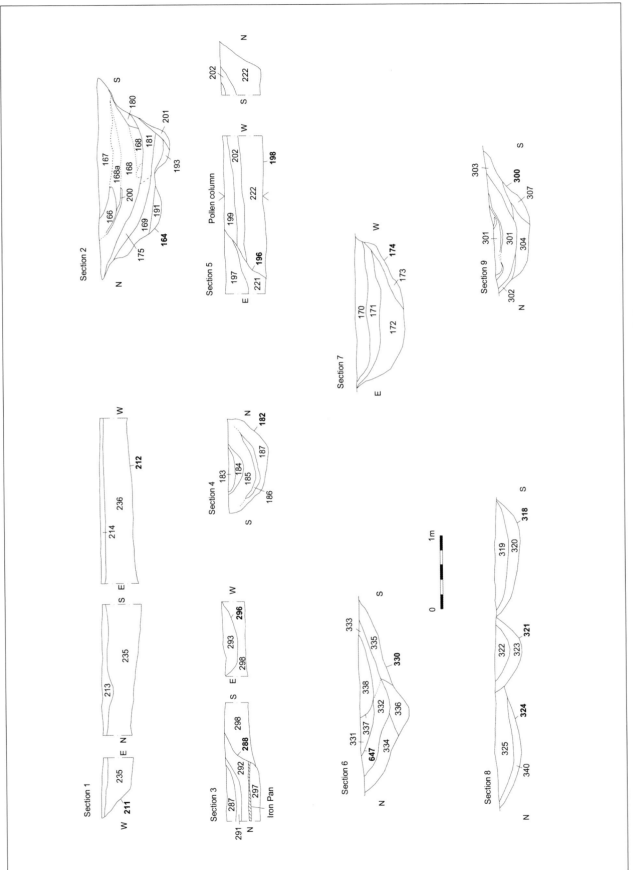

Fig. 23 Lydd Quarry, Ditch system: Sections 1–9

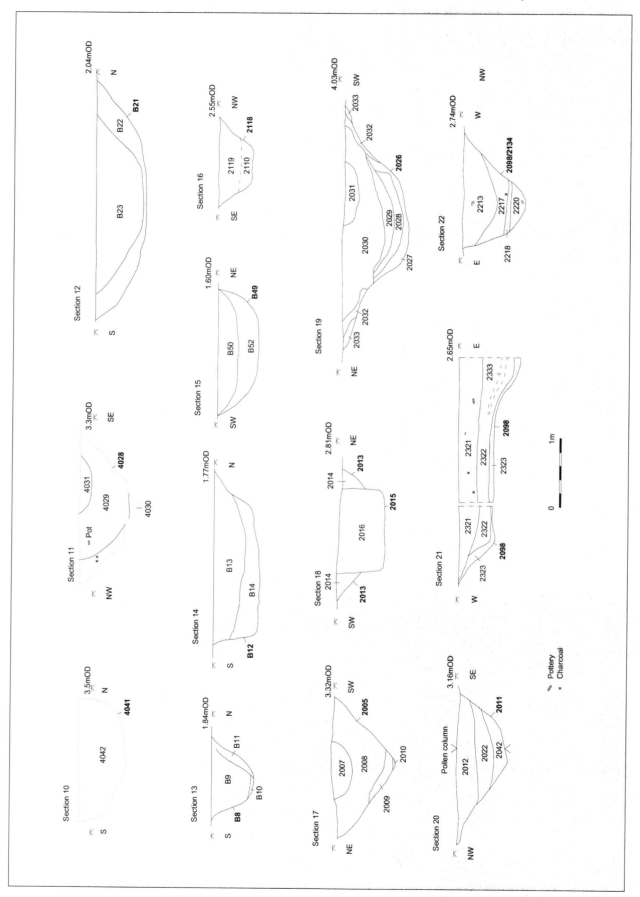

Fig. 24 Lydd Quarry, Ditch system: Sections 10–22

2001). The archaeological evidence from Lydd tends to confirm this, as in the later period, when pastoral farming is thought to be more dominant, and settlement sparse, there is a general trend toward larger fields (Period 3 – see below).

Medieval activity in the area appears to have started in the early 12th century. This is slightly earlier than the suggested onset of reclamation around Lydd suggested by Tatton-Brown (1988, 108) and certainly proves the area was occupied before the great storms of the later 13th century (Brooks 1988, 91; Waller *et al.* 1988, 6).

Period 1: 12th century to early 13th century (*Fig. 28)

The first phase of the ditch system has left very little archaeological trace, mainly due to the continual cleaning out of the ditches through time. However, in some areas the early ditches have been infilled during the later 12th or early 13th century with those ditches not being replaced, or cut on slightly different alignments. The isolated sections of ditches are found across the whole area of the quarry and demonstrate that the initial ditch system was far wider spread than the stratigraphic and artefactual evidence may suggest. It should also be borne in mind that during the initial reclamation and establishment of the ditched field system in this period there does not appear to have been any permanent occupation (see below) and thus artefactual material is scarce.

Perhaps the most archaeologically 'sterile' area for medieval artefacts was to the south-west of the Burnthouse Wall in the area of Lydd 11. In this area it is quite clear that a number of the ditches follow the line of those from the Lydd 1 area. For example, the main ditch D19 appears to run through (to become B21) as do the trackway ditches D21 and D22 (to become B17 and B12). These ditches are thought to be early features although the finds from within them to the east of the Burnthouse Wall suggest a late final infilling date. This late date is almost certainly a result of continual cleaning out of these ditches, although admittedly the flanking ditches of the trackway may have been added a while after the track along the shingle had been established. These ditches to the west of the Burnthouse Wall produced no finds, suggesting they were rapidly infilled after initial cutting, probably by natural processes – a point confirmed by the fill types. These ditches can therefore probably best be viewed as early examples cut during the early 12th century, but which were abandoned when the Burnthouse Wall was established to defend the reclaimed area to the east. It is interesting to note how the kink in the Jury's Gut Sewer lines up with the most westerly ditch at Lydd 11 (B35), suggesting that this part of the extant drain may also have originally been one of the earliest in the area. The exact extent of the earliest area of attempted reclamation in this area is uncertain. It could be argued that it was confined to B21, B35 and B17/B12. However, if this were the case the alignments of some of these ditches with the Jury's Gut Sewer would suggest the system did originally

extend further at this time or, and probably more likely, some of the earlier alignments were redug in the post-medieval period when reclamation extended to the west of the Burnthouse Wall.

At Lydd 1 a number of ditches were apparently infilled at this early date and thus can be assumed to be some of the first dug. Of interest is the use and adaptation of apparently natural channels such as D1–D4, together with other wholly artificial cuts (*i.e.*, probably D19, D17 and D7, and possibly D5 and D6, *etc.*). The failure to trace the full extent of these natural channels may be in part due to the nature of their fills or the lack of careful cleaning of extensive areas. The adoption of such channels has been demonstrated on Romney Marsh proper (Reeves 1996, 8), although they have been rarely found in subsequent stages of work to the east of Lydd 1. However, examples infilled during the Romano-British period were located at Lydd 4 (4005, Priestley-Bell 2003a) and a number probably infilled during the medieval period were noted at Lydd 2 (D2215), Lydd 5/6 (Fig. 18, Ditches 5053, 5057 and 5087) and Lydd 9 (D9010, 9012, 9014 and 9016). It must be assumed that there were a greater number of natural channels available for adaptation at Lydd 1, which may explain the somewhat unusually tight packing of ditches in this area. Similar relict channels may not have been available further to the east in such quantities.

The extent of the earliest ditch system to the south (Lydds 7–10) is uncertain. The morphology of the ditch system in this area is very different, probably due to the low-lying nature of the land and its proximity to the barrier beach. Only at the eastern edge of Lydd 7, the western edge of Lydd 9 and the southern edge of Lydd 10 is there any trace of a rectilinear ditch system. The fact that D7031 (Fig. 19) appears to have been infilled early suggests much of this system, at least at Lydd 7, may have originally belonged to this early period. As such, the other areas, as represented at Lydd 9 and 10, may also be of this date originally – a point perhaps strengthened by the presence of an early building at Lydd 10 (Site A). The area between the eastern edge of Lydd 7 and the western edge of Lydd 9 does not appear to have been incorporated in the early system. This is almost certainly due to its substantially marsh-like character, probably the result of the earlier in-filled prehistoric channel. This area would undoubtedly have been used for rough grazing.

The establishment of the trackways is likely to have occurred in this early period. Although there is no direct evidence from the northern trackway represented at Lydds 1 and 4, the southern trackway has given better evidence. Although most of the length of the southern trackway ditches remained in use throughout the track's life, and thus cleaning removed their earliest fills, one section of the track appears to potentially give the essential evidence of the earliest date of this feature. The early alignment of the southern track, as represented by D2118 and 2212 *et al.*, has given a 12th century date for its infilling, suggesting that the southern track was established, and flanked by ditches, in the 12th century. Further infilled early sections of track ditch at Lydd 3 (D3148) and Lydd 5/6 (D5158 and D5178) also suggests an early date. It is therefore quite possible that the northern track is of a similar date, though all traces had been removed by later usage, as had been the case for the newer alignment of the southern track.

The section removed from the Burnthouse Wall at Lydd 1 revealed two further parallel ditches (Fig. 10, 5 and un-numbered). Although unexcavated, due to their preservation *in situ*, it is tempting to speculate that these formed a third trackway along the northern edge of the investigated area, which was abandoned at the same time as the area in Lydd 11 when the Burnthouse Wall was built. If this were the case further earlier fields may have been laid out to the north – a point hinted at by the cartographic sources (see discussion below).

All in all the first period appears to be concerned with gaining a formal access to the area and establishing an extensive drainage system. This appears to have been closely followed by the establishment of a protective sea wall (then known as Gores Wall). This 'pioneering' period would have enabled a more reliable and longer grazing season as the area stabilised. This would be the initial step prior to the Period 2 works (*Fig. 28).

Period 2: 13th century (*Fig. 29 and cover illustration)

This period appears to represent a shift from the initial reclamation, or 'pioneering' work, to a programme of further consolidation, drainage and establishment of small fields, particularly between the trackways and probably for cultivation. Most of these ditches were probably dug initially during the late 12th to mid 13th centuries, at a time when relatively intensive settlement was occurring (see below). However, the ceramics suggest many of these ditches had been infilled by the end of the 13th or beginning of the 14th century, as the need for small fields decreased due to either a change in agricultural policy, land ownership, or simply improved ground conditions/ drainage.

The process of consolidation is seen in virtually all parts of the quarry. At Lydd 1, Ditches D7, D8 and D10 are probably established and the extension of D17 southward undertaken. Many of the earlier ditches would have continued in use: *i.e.*, D6, D19 and probably parts of D1 and D5. If the northern trackway had not had flanking ditches in the 12th century it is most probable that they were added in this period. These changes, together with the establishments of Sites D and E (*Fig. 29) suggest that a more organised system, less reliant on natural channels, was now in place.

At Lydd 2 most of the ditches were established by this date and it is probable the enclosure was added relatively quickly after the field system established. A similar picture is likely at Lydd 3 but the archaeological data to prove it is absent. At Lydd 5/6 many of the ditches forming the small regular field also probably date to this

period, and indeed many appear to have been infilled by the end of the century if the ceramic dating is reliable. A number of curious ditches forming small enclosed areas within fields are also apparent within the quarry, mainly in the Lydd 5/6 area (*e.g.*, Fig.18, Ditches, 5119 (Period 1) and 5027 (Period 2)). These do not appear to be associated with any occupation activity. As such they may either have been used for stock management or possibly for the production of thorn – a practice known of on the marsh (Reeves 1996, 11). In addition a set of small fields/large enclosures were established at Site G, probably for stock control or related work.

To the south of the southern trackway it is likely that either the earlier ditches were maintained and slightly elaborated or indeed, if they do not belong to the preceding period, the system was established during this period. Whatever the case, the field system in this area was confined to Lydd 10, the eastern edge of Lydd 7 and the western edge of Lydd 9, suggesting the area between was still not considered suitable for drainage.

There is no evidence of any activity to the west of the Burnthouse Wall (Lydd 11), suggesting that this area was still only used for grazing the open marshland.

Variation of the Ditch System in the three areas during the 13th century

It should be noted that the ditch system is generally most intensive in the trough between the two shingle ridges which carry the northern and southern trackways. All of the occupation sites are close to this area, suggesting it to be the heart of the system. Site D (at Lydd 1), lying just to the north of the northern trackway, is also close to an area of smaller fields to the north.

The areas of land to the north and south of these trackways is less well developed. To the north there is little sign of smaller fields, with the exception of the area of dense ditches at Lydd 1. Why this should vary from the rest of the area is uncertain, but may be due to the presence of a number of natural channels in this area allowing the establishment of smaller fields without too much labour.

To the south of the southern track the ditch system is very mixed. Large areas do not appear to have had ditches dug, and a number of sinuous natural channels are evident. Only in places are these signs of a more systematic rectilinear system, though a number of these may be of post-medieval date. It is probable that this area was not fully worked (particularly during the 13th century) for arable cultivation and it may have been utilised primarily for pastoralism.

Period 3: 14th to 15th century (*Fig. 30)

Period 3 of the ditch system witnesses the infilling of a number of the ditches (some of which were suitably silted by this time to perhaps not be functioning anymore) as well as the disappearance of all of the 13th century occupation/activity sites. The overall trend is towards the creation of larger regular fields. This process appears to begin in the 14th century but increases in the 15th to early 16th centuries. The process appears to have been a continuous one and it has not been possible to reliably divide the 14th from the 15th century system. This is perhaps due to depopulation and the increase in pastoralism over arable farming during this period. By the early 16th century the field system had stabilised, reaching its basic form for the next 300–400 years.

At Lydd 1 the Period 3 system, most of which was infilled by the early/mid 16th century is marked by the continued use of D19, D21 and D22 (trackway ditches), with the main linking ditch D12/D20. Other ditches appear to have still been kept open to aid drainage in certain areas. Further ditches running off D19 and D22 at right angles, are also probably of this date. This system of large fields appears to run all along the northern side of the northern trackway into the Lydd 4 area.

At Lydd 2 only D2005 and D2026 were probably still in use with the trackway. Most of the ditches at Lydd 3 were probably still in use, or infilled, during the latter part of this period. However, a few ditches (*i.e.*, D3030 and parts of D3130) survived into Periods 4a/b. At Lydd 5/6 the true form of the field system is difficult to discern with certainty at this time. A general transition from smaller to larger fields appears to be the trend (*e.g.*, the removal of D5035 to combine two fields). However, the date of infilling of some of the ditches tends to argue for the continuation of many of the earlier smaller fields (*e.g.*, whether D5021 and D5037 were infilled to combine two fields or remained open). This may indicate that this area, which always appears to have been the focus of the smaller fields, continued to undertake some arable cultivation. Whatever the case the obvious differences between this area and the fields to the north and south of the trackways noted in Period 2, are much less notable. This is also in part a result of further ditches being established to the south of the southern track in areas that had previously been open.

Period 4: (a) 16th to 17th century; (b) 18th to 20th century (*Fig. 31)

By the beginning of this period virtually all the above mentioned ditches had been infilled and the field system had more or less reached its final form, which continued through until the start of extraction at the site in the late 20th century. As such, the extant ditch system prior to quarrying was basically fossilised after the infilling of elements of the medieval system in the 14th to early 16th century. This clearly demonstrates that the modern field systems of the area are the end result of a complex chronological development which has its roots firmly in the 12th century.

Although some of the earlier medieval ditches had been kept open, very few were infilled, or indeed newly cut, during this period. Although the period has been divided into two, so little evidence relating to the field system was located at the site for this period in general that it is grouped under one heading. It should be noted however, that *Fig. 31, which has utilised cartographic as well as archaeological sources, relates to the Period 4b system.

Infilling appears to have sporadically occurred on some ditches throughout this period but is always rare. For example Ditch 5137, at Lydd 5, appears to have received its final fill in the early 18th century, though it is probable that the ditch was already well silted by this date. The evidence from Lydd 7 and 8 suggests some of this final infilling occurred as late as the 19th or early 20th century.

Only very few ditches were being dug during this period. These include a separate series of probable French drains at Lydd 8 (vertical sided ditches deliberately infilled with shingle to allow water perculation). Based on the limited archaeological evidence it is suspected that the majority of the field system to the west of the Burnthouse Wall, including B53, was a post-medieval establishment, in places utilising the line of earlier abandoned medieval ditches. This system was of generally larger fields and included the Jury's Gut Sewer and Lydd Petty Sewer. Since its establishment a number of the ditches have been infilled, often in relatively recent times (*i.e.*, Ditch B53 and possibly B35).

In general, ditches over 3m wide tend to belong to the latest phases of ditch cutting. Re-cutting of earlier medieval ditch lines has often increased the width of these drains. Presumably broad ditches were not only more efficient but provided an effective barrier for stock without the need for additional barriers. Many elements of this late medieval field system, albeit in a modified and recut state, still survive today.

Ditch Systems in the Surrounding Area

Photographic sources, held by the National Monuments Record, Kent County Council and the Romney Marsh Research Trust, were consulted in an attempt to trace the excavated ditch system at Lydd Quarry north-eastward toward Caldicott Farm (Sweetinburgh this volume and Fig. 4). Unfortunately the area of most clarity was that excavated at Lydd Quarry (Fig. 5), where the converging trackways can clearly be seen prior to topsoiling. It is not surprising that cropmarks are far clearer on the shingle ridges than the fine silty deposits between. Aerial photographs to the north-east, particularly around Pioneer Pit (prior to extraction), did not prove to be anywhere near as clear. This is almost certainly due in part to the time of year/vegetation/crop growth of most of the crops, but may also relate to the nature of the underlying subsoil. However, the lack of clear cropmarks suggests the medieval field system may not have continued through the area, although it should be noted that a number of the ditches known from excavation at Lydd Quarry and Caldicott Farm do not show up on the same photographs. Further images under favourable conditions, or excavation, will be needed to clarify the exact nature and date of the system in this area.

Activity Areas and Occupation Sites

The excavations at Lydd Quarry uncovered a number of sites where features and finds were concentrated together within the ditched field system. These occurred both close to the two trackways as well as in the fields some distance from them. These sites are notable in their variety of form and therefore presumably function. Add to this the chronological spread of the sites and truncation of features, including perhaps the total removal of some shallow features, and the interpretation of these sites becomes problematic. It is clear that not all concentrations of features and/or finds represent the sites of buildings, and indeed not all buildings appear to represent occupation sites. The labelling of all such sites as domestic occupation sites is clearly incorrect and the distinction has not only considered quantities of finds and features (including types of features) but location within the field system. Bearing these dangers in mind, this section will outline all the excavated sites at Lydd Quarry by general period rather than by function. The latter is considered and suggestions put forward for each site. Although grouped chronologically it should be noted that they are grouped under their main period of activity; most sites have a few features which are either earlier or later than the main period of activity. These features have been kept with the main description of the site to show the continuity through time and avoid disjointing the narrative.

Period 1: The Earliest Sites (probably late 12th to early 13th century)

Site A (Lydd 10, Area B): Building and Enclosure (Figs. 22 and 32)

This site was represented by a post-hole building, set on a slightly higher area of shingle, within a 'loosely' constructed enclosure.

The Enclosure

An arrangement of three ditches, A19 (Fig. 32 and Fig. 33, S57), A65 (Fig. 32 and Fig. 33, S58) and A67 (Fig. 32 and Fig. 33, S59), averaging 0.5m, 1.85m and 0.95m wide and 100mm, 450mm and 370mm deep respectively, appeared to form an enclosure with Ditch A71. Ditch A65, which may have modified a natural sinuous channel, contained a recut (A87) measuring 1.23m wide and 220mm deep and formed the southern side of

the enclosure. On the north side, it is uncertain if A67 linked up to D A71, although a small spur from the latter ditch (A69), which could not be traced with certainty, may have represented an earlier alignment of A67. Late 12th century pottery was recovered from the fill (A21) of Ditch A19, mid to late 13th century pottery from the fill (A79) of D A65, and early 13th century pottery from the fill (A66) of recut A87 (Fig. 32 and Fig. 33, S58). The fact that A71 cut A65 and A17 (see below), suggests that although this ditch originally formed the east side of the enclosure it remained in use as a field/drainage ditch (and was thus regularly cleaned out) after the building and enclosure had gone out of use.

The Building

Within the described enclosure lay an arrangement of 15 post-holes, (Fig. 32, A26, A28 (Fig. 33, S60), A30 (Fig. 33, S61), A32, A34, A36, A38 (Fig. 33, S62), A40 (Fig. 33, S63), A42, A44, A46 (Fig. 33, S64), A48, A50, A52 and A54)) measuring between 280 and 500mm in diameter and between 40 and 170mm in depth. The post-holes formed a *c.* 8.5 × 5.5m rectangle, facing end-on into the prevailing winds. No evidence of post-holes was found along the north-east facing end and only two were found along the south-western end. Pottery dating from the late 12th to early 13th century was recovered from the fills (A33, A35, A37, A43, A45, A47, A51 and A55) of eight of the post-holes (A32, A34, A36, A42, A46, A50 and A54 respectively). A further probably associated post-hole (A56, Fig. 33, S65), lay *c.* 1.5m from the posited north wall. Late 12th to early 13th century pottery was recovered from the fill (A57) of post-hole A56. A significant quantity of daub from the fills of the post-holes indicated that the structure was probably enclosed by wattle and daub walls, and the absence of tile suggests a thatched or turf roof.

A narrow sinuous ditch (Fig. 32, A17 (Fig. 33, S24)), possibly originally of natural origin, ran from within the building to Ditch A71. The fill (A18) produced 13th century pottery. Ditch A17 would have provided drainage from the north-eastern end of the building. To the south a further probable drain, measuring 450mm wide by 80mm deep (Ditch A73), could have taken water off the south wall drip line (no drip lines were identified during the excavation however).

To the west of the building enclosure was a large circular pit (Fig. 32, A62 (Fig. 33, S67)), measuring 2.57m in diameter and 330mm deep. The upper and lower fills (A63 and A64 respectively) produced late 12th to early 13th century pottery. Two further isolated pits were found to the east in Area A of Lydd 10 (Fig. 22, Contexts A15 and A22), one of which produced a single sherd of 13th century pottery. The precise function of these isolated pits is uncertain, but none produced large quantities of domestic waste. However, the lower fill of A62 produced just over 40 pot sherds, suggesting some domestic activity in the vicinity of the building.

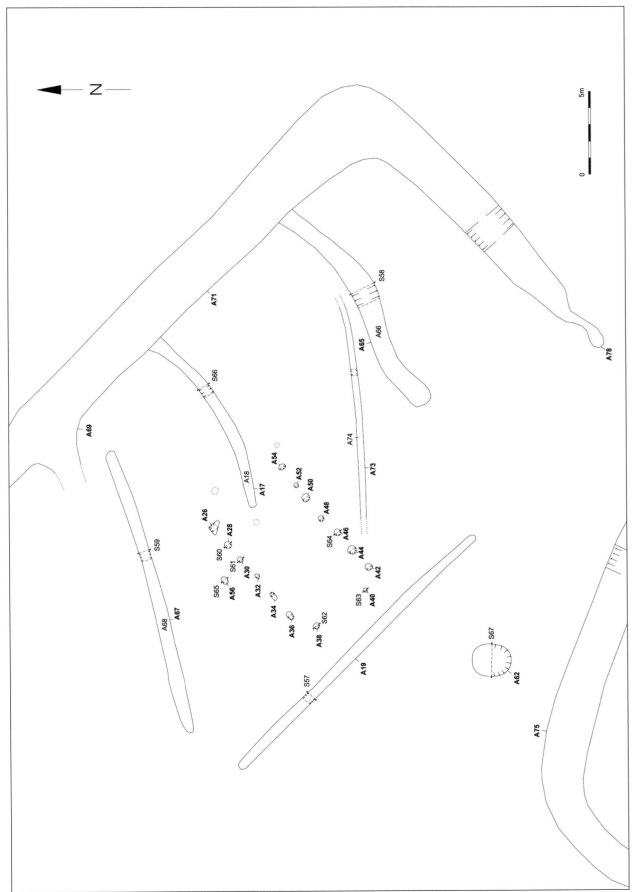

Fig. 32 Lydd Quarry, Plan of Site A (Lydd 10, Area B)

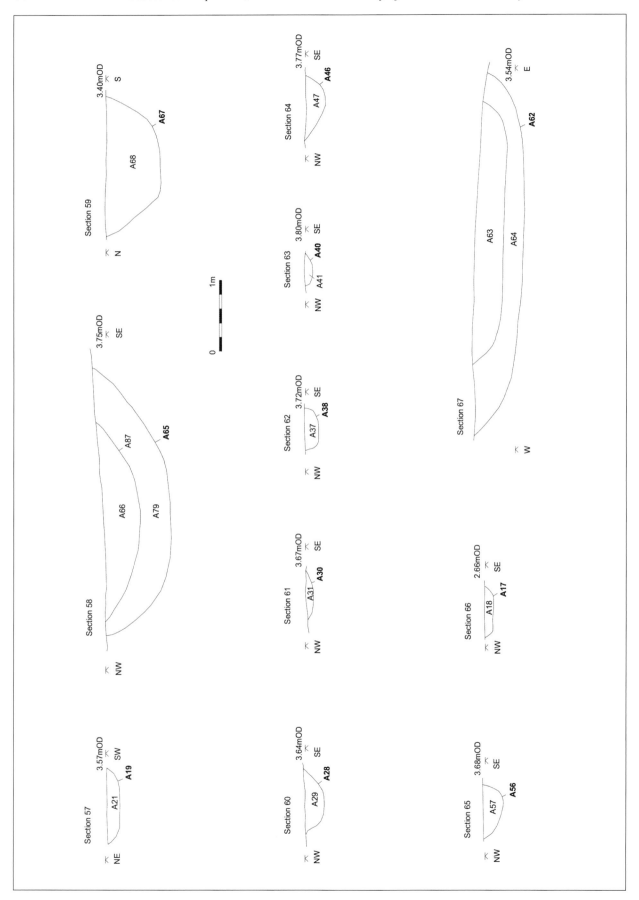

Fig. 33 Lydd Quarry, Site A (Lydd 10, Area B): Sections 57–67

Interpretation of the Building
by Mark Gardiner and Greg Priestley-Bell

Based on the ceramics, the building was probably constructed in the late 12th or at the very beginning of the 13th century, at the end of the initial 'pioneering' period in which the main ditch system was established. The building form belongs to a small group of excavated structures from the end of the 'middle medieval tradition' (Gardiner and Murray in prep.). The tradition of construction is characterised by the use of close-set, earth-fast paired timbers along the side walls and shallower timbers along the end walls. In this case, evidence for only two post-settings were found for the end-walls, but this may reflect the heavily truncated nature of the archaeology rather than demonstrating an open-ended structure. It is quite possible that there were other shallow posts along the end-walls which have not survived. It is, however, rather unusual that the two posts on the south-west wall survive towards the corners; usually the most deeply cut post is found in the centre of the end-wall.

The general pattern of the building is clear. It had posts paired across its width and there is some evidence that they alternated with timbers of larger and smaller scantling. Thus, A32 and A48 have smaller post-settings and A30 and A50 have larger ones. Only post hole A28 is larger than we might expect. It is, however, notable that A28, and the adjoining post A26, are more deeply set than the others, suggesting that there was some need to reinforce the north-east corner. The corresponding post hole for A42 does not appear to have survived on the north-west wall.

The other significant feature of the building is that two of the post-settings on the north-west wall (A34 and A36) were more elongated than the others. This is a common feature of middle medieval buildings where such posts flank the main door. The door posts were often rectangular in section and commonly larger than others to support the extra weight of the door. They are paired with two large, round posts on the opposite side (A44, A46) marking the corresponding door posts on the other side of the cross-entry. The difference in post shape implies that the main entrance to the building may have been from the north-west, while the door on the opposite side was built with timbers used in the round. That interpretation is supported by Ditches A19 and A67, which suggest that the entrance to the enclosure may have been to the north-west.

Buildings with alternate large and small posts seem to belong to the decades around 1200 and the best parallel is Boreham Airfield (Essex) where a structure of similar pattern (Building 98) is recorded but the feature is not discussed (Clarke 2003, Fig. 8). The main difference between the building at Site A and that at Boreham is the latter used posts set in a trench. It is probable that these buildings stand at the end of the tradition of 'common-post construction' in which all the posts, except the

door posts, were of equal scantling. The emergence of principal posts which support the weight of the roof and studs which support the wall is one of the features marking the start of the late medieval tradition of timber building. At Lydd, it is pleasing that the typological date which can be attributed to the building and that obtained from the pottery are so closely in agreement. We can interpret the building on the assumption that the larger post-settings took the weight-bearing principal posts, although the smaller post-settings may also have had a residual structural function at this date. The building would therefore appear to have two bays to the north-east of the possible cross-entry, a single entrance bay and a bay to the south-west.

The function of the building is problematic and two suggestions can be put forward. The position and width of the entrance, together with the building style, suggest that it may have been domestic with a hall to the north-east and a service end on the opposite side of the cross-entry (Gardiner 2000a). However, the nature of agricultural buildings constructed at this time is uncertain and it is quite possible they employed similar construction techniques. The presence of only one possible 'rubbish' pit (A62) and the relatively low level of domestic refuse associated with the site, suggests that either the building was short-lived or its function may have been agricultural, perhaps as a shelter used for animals and fodder to begin with (grazing the newly reclaimed land, but particularly the area to the south of the southern trackway which was not enclosed to such a degree). This proposition is supported by the results of the analysis of the plant remains from the lower fill (A64) of pit A62. Fill A64 produced a wide range of species including cereals, beans, vetches, grasses, rushes and sedges. This particular combination of plants would only normally be found together where animals were fed and housed. Cereals, beans and vetches could have been used for fodder, while the grasses, rushes and sedges would have provided hay and litter. A significant proportion of the grass seeds may have derived from the dung of hay fed animals. In any case, the presence of carbonised cereals suggest the building may have been used at some point to store crops, though some of the material, together with the small quantity of pottery, may have derived from food preparation by stock hands, from the builders of the structure, or indeed from its use as a domestic structure over a short period of time. There is no real evidence to suggest that the structure survived beyond the early to mid 13th century.

Site B (Lydd 4): Possible Shepherd's Hut (Figs. 14 and 34)

This site was represented by a shallow sub-rectangular cut/depression (4002) measuring *c*. 3.4 × 4m, situated within a large rectilinear field to the north of the northern trackway at Lydd 4 (Figs. 14 and 34). Two shallow deposits (4003 and 4004), measuring between 100 and 130mm in depth, lay within Context 4002 and contained significant quantities of fragmentary charcoal, fired clay and pottery (Fig. 34, S68) suggesting some domestic activity. A slight extension on the northern side could mark the site of an entrance. It is felt possible that the feature may have represented the floor (or area worn by use) of a small building probably with a temporary agricultural/ domestic function. As such, it could represent a hut for a shepherd and thus be performing a similar task to the later 18th and 19th century looker's huts on the marsh (Reeves and Eve 1998). The small assemblage of pottery from this feature is all of late 12th to early 13th century date and suggests that it may have been utilised prior to or during the construction/early use of the surrounding field system. This suggestion is strengthened by the different orientation of the structure when compared to the surrounding ditches.

Site C (Lydd 3, Area D): Small Enclosures (Figs. 18 and 35)

An irregular arrangement of narrow, shallow ditches (Figs. 17 and 35): D3351, D3353, D3355, D3359 (Fig. 35, S69) and D3362 (Fig. 35, S70)) was enclosed to the north and east by Ditch 3364, to the south by Ditch 3366 and to the west by an existing ditch (D3368). Ditch 3366 was seen just in the baulk of the machine stripped area and was unexcavated. The enclosed area measured *c.* 20 × 20m. A soakaway (3357) (Fig. 35, S71), measuring *c.* 700mm × 1.3m, was located at the junction of Ditches 3351, 3353 and 3355, and had been dug down to the surface of the underlying gravel.

Animal bone (including fish and shell) was recovered from D3351, D3353, D3355 and D3359, while 12th to early 13th century pottery was recovered from D3351, D3353, D3359 and Soakaway 3357. This close correlation between the features strongly suggests that they represented inter-related elements of a specialised activity area in which water management/drainage played an important part. The exact activities carried out here are uncertain, though there was clearly some food preparation/consumption occurring. It is possible the ditches represent some form of sheep fold but this cannot be proven.

Period 2: The Main Period of Occupation (13th century, possibly to early 14th century)

Site D (Lydd 1, Area D): Occupation Site (Figs. 13 and 36)

A concentration of pits, post-holes and ditches were identified towards the south-west of Lydd 1, adjacent to the northern side of the northern trackway. The relative chronology of these features is not certain, though the stratigraphic evidence suggests a change of use at the west, where several pits are cut by later ditches. This part of the area is described first, followed by the features to the east. The underlying shingle rose sharply to the south at this point toward the trackway, and the features on this side of Site D, which did not generally penetrate

the shingle, were extremely truncated by both machining and ploughing.

A complex of intercutting pits are the earliest features that may be recognised from the stratigraphic sequence. It was not possible to identify individual pits from the surface before excavation, and it was only possible to quarter-section the pit group due to lack of time; the full shape of some pits was not therefore established. Three cuts were identified, 615, 618 and 630, which together formed a large, irregular rectangular shape, together with Pit 558 which projected to the east. Pit 558 may have been part of the cut 618 (Figs. 36 and 38, S72), though the ratio of length to width would have been rather greater than other pits on the site. The only fill (617) of cut 615 was apparently formed from silting and had relatively few finds, though it should be stressed that this cut was largely unexcavated. The fills of 618 and 630 by contrast contained considerable amounts of organic material, including burnt clay and charcoal flecks, though there was no evidence of burning *in situ*.

A shallow trench, 557/604, cut Pit 558, though it did not cut the adjoining Pit 618. This supports the interpretation that 558 and 618 are different contexts. The relationship of the trench to the pit complex described above is therefore not certain. The trench was definitely cut by Pit 556 to the east and Ditch 559 to the west. Only 2.5m of this trench was therefore traced. Its function is not known, but it is notable that it runs parallel to the long axes of Pits 554, 556 and 558 and may be associated with a shallow, silted-up gully 560, of which only 40mm depth survived.

Pit 556 was cut by Pit 554 which was similar in form but slightly larger, measuring approximately 4.4 × 2.4m. The lowest fill of 556 was a thin layer of black silty material containing much burnt clay, though there was no evidence of burning *in situ*. The upper fills contained an extremely large amount of shell, and the feature is likely to have been simply a regularly shaped 'rubbish' pit (Fig. 38, S73). Pit 554 may have been two separate features; the section suggests fill 579 belongs to a later feature than the other fills. This may be the reason for the slightly enlarged western end visible in plan (Fig. 36). The lower fills contained burnt clay and large amounts of shell, indicating use for rubbish disposal. A small hole (555) adjacent to the south side of 554 has no obvious function.

Pit 588 was probably similar in shape, but was truncated by Ditch 563 to the south, and only limited excavation was possible. It was not possible to ascertain its relationship to Ditch 573, and they both shared a common upper fill (574), which was likely to have been topsoil material filling a slight depression created by the two features (Fig. 38, S74). Its upper fill, 589, may have been backfill or silting, but its lower fill (652, not shown on section) was unusual as it was a sloping layer of gravel. The origin of this is not known; it appears to have been deposited from one side, sloping down from east to

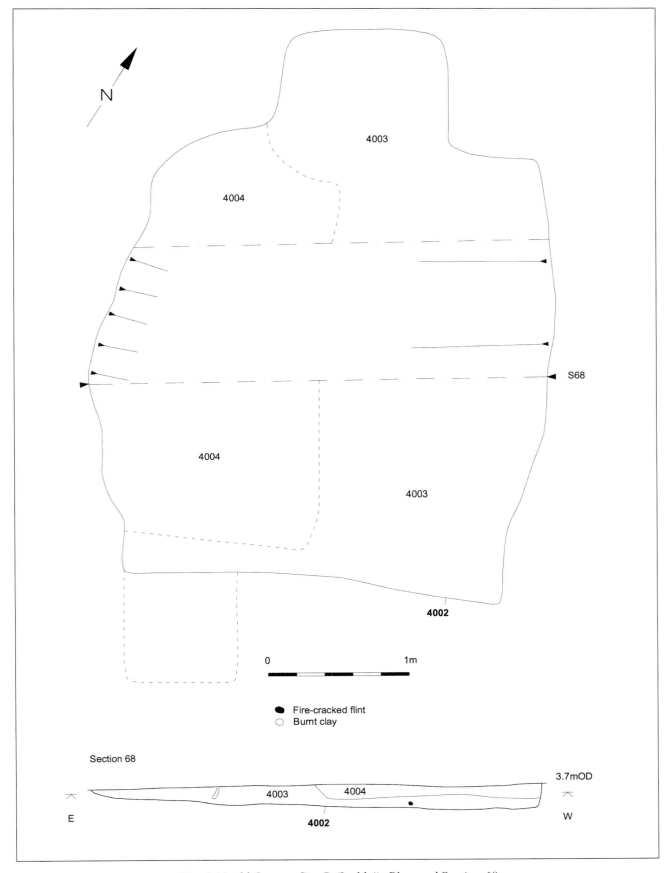

Fig. 34 Lydd Quarry, Site B (Lydd 4). Plan and Section 68

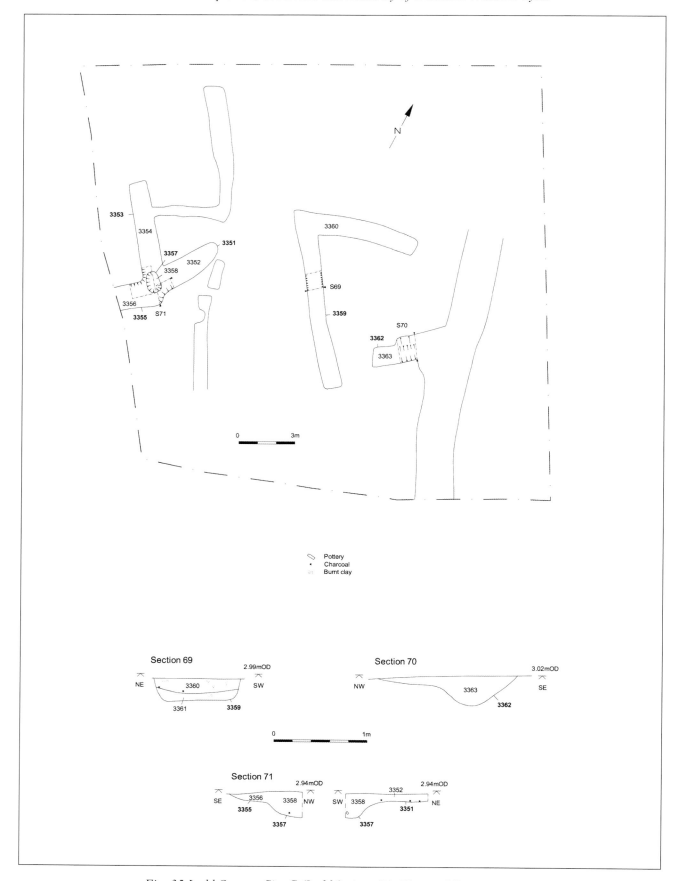

Fig. 35 Lydd Quarry, Site C (Lydd 3, Area D). Plan and Sections 69–71

west and partially filling the feature. Similar fills were also found in 573, 506 and 549, and are discussed further below. Pit 588 did not contain the quantity of rubbish of the other pits mentioned above.

A small pit (634) cut the pit complex (615, *etc.*) in the south-west corner. It was slightly elliptical, 1.35m across the long axis at the top, and was smaller than the majority of features interpreted as 'rubbish' pits. It was, however, cut into gravel for most of its depth, whereas all the other 'rubbish' pits had been cut down as far as the gravel but not into it, perhaps suggesting it initially had some other function. The base fill (638), which had a horizontal upper surface, suggests an initial partial backfilling, followed by periodic deposition of rubbish, including considerable amounts of shell (Fig. 38, S75).

Cut 634 may be associated with Cut 622 which appeared to be a post-robbing hole. The eastern projection may have been produced by excavating on one side of a post to loosen it and enable it to be fully removed. The fill of 622 contained burnt clay and charcoal. The function of the shallow projection to the west, 635, is not clear. It is notable that 622 and 634 had similar basal diameters (approximately 0.45m) and similar base levels (1.27 and 1.34m AOD respectively). Both 622 and 634 would, have contained quite substantial posts.

To the west of the pit complex (615, *etc.*) lay a group of small holes which may have been structural. Feature 606 was a rectangular, flat-bottomed post-hole. Approximately 1m to the south were three cuts: 611, 626 and 625. The latter two were associated with shallow depressions 613 and 624, and are separated by a distance of 1.2m. Features 626 and 611 were 2.4m apart. Although no hole was identified between the latter pair, the fact that they are separated by exactly twice the distance of the former pair suggests they have a specific relationship. The function of the two shallow depressions is obscure. Hole 611 cuts depression 612. The relationships between holes 625 and 626, and depression 624 were indistinct, although the latter appeared to be earlier. The base levels of holes 611, 625 and 626 vary only from 1.46 to 1.53m AOD, and their diameters are comparable. These features may have supported a structure, but it was impossible to identify its nature, or indeed if there was more than one structure.

One feature that was recorded may suggest permanent, or at least frequent, occupation in this area of the site. Pit 598 was slightly elliptical, with its axes measuring 1.9m and 2.5m, but may have been intended to be circular. It contained few finds and the lower fill suggests silting in an open cut. Its upper fill, which was quite stony, appeared to be deliberately backfilled. The base was very irregular (Fig. 38, S76). This pit was clearly not dug for rubbish, but may have been an abandoned, and perhaps uncompleted, well or cistern.

The pits were cut across by ditches. The earliest ditch had a terminal to the north, became very shallow and was completely truncated at the south where it met the rising shingle bank. The ditch was investigated at several points: sections 530 (Fig. 38, S77), 545, 559 and 584. It did not physically join feature 573, which, although it could not be investigated in detail, appeared to be a short length of ditch with terminals at both ends. Its position suggests that the two may have been related.

Later, the section of ditch numbered 584 was filled in and recut with two terminals, 563 and 586, to create an entrance (Figs. 36 and 38, S78). The position of this entrance relative to feature 573 suggests that it is unlikely that the two were in use at the same time. Subsequently, the eastern arm was extended and recut on a slightly different alignment (Cuts 531, 535, 550 and 568). The relationship between the two was both clear in section (Fig. 38, S77) and could be seen in plan at the southern end of the recut. The recut had a distinct terminal at the north end, but attenuated on the rising gradient at the south.

The recorded ditches do not form complete enclosures. Close inspection of the surface of the site considerably beyond their ends failed to reveal any continuations or related ditches.

The eastern part of Site D contained groups of pits. There were few stratigraphic relationships and it is not therefore clear which were contemporary. Immediately to the east of the ditches was a group of three pits and a small hole approximately 0.5m across (529), lying just to the south. Two of the pits (527 and 528) were sub-rounded. Pit 526 contained various thin fills representing successive depositions of rubbish, some burnt. The two other pits had a single fill of less definite origin; probably silting and organic rubbish.

A further group of sub-rounded pits lay to the north of the area. Rubbish was dumped in 477 and 510 and was covered by more mixed material. Pits 502, 503 and 504 had a single fill, probably formed by rubbish accumulation. Between these two pit groups were two larger rectangular pits, 490 and 506, one of which had one projecting corner. The earlier (490) had a slightly irregular base and had been used for rubbish disposal, including large amounts of shell and charcoal (Fig. 38, S79). The lowest fill (532) was greenish in colour, and may suggest that the feature was originally a cess pit. That fill contained patches of redeposited natural, and it may be that the shape of the southern edge of the pit was caused by the partial collapse of the side. Pit 506 had only two fills, the lower of which was a deep layer of gravel, sloping down from south to north. The upper could have been the result of silting or backfill. There was no evidence of rubbish deposition or any other use. The shape of the pit suggests it was cut to avoid encroaching upon the earlier pit to its south.

It is notable that two of the pit groups were associated with pairs of small holes set 1.3 and 1.5m apart. It is possible that the pits were originally within fenced areas and the pairs of holes represented deeper gateposts. The remains of the shallower fence posts may have been removed in machining.

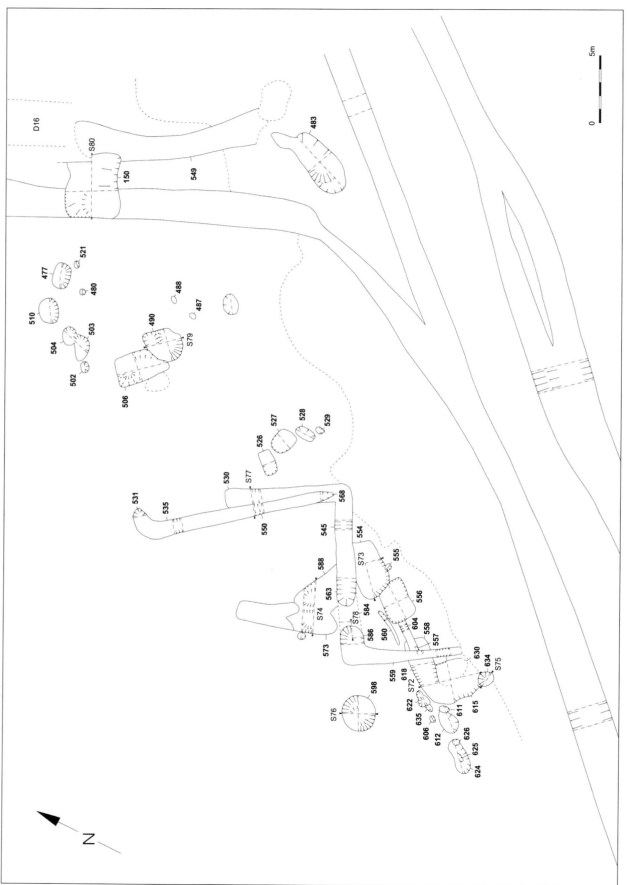

Fig. 36 Lydd Quarry, Plan of Site D (Lydd 1, Area D)

A complex of pits (150) lay on the east of Site D. It cut ditch D17 (Fill 513), but was in turn cut by D16 (Fills 496, 549, Fig. 38, S80). Fills 151, 152, 482 and 515 appear to belong to one pit. Fill 525 may also be part of that cut. The fills contained extremely large amounts of shell and pottery. The other fills belong to different cuts, but under the conditions of excavation it was not possible to distinguish them adequately.

A large elliptical pit (483) was situated at the south-eastern extremity of Site D. In addition to pottery and bone, the fill contained fragments of burnt clay. It is unlikely to be a 'rubbish' pit because of its location, which necessitated cutting deeply into the shingle. Only one quadrant was excavated. The upper fill is most likely to be part of the overlying soil that has subsided into a slight depression around the top of the cut. The function of the pit is not certain. It had no physical relationship with any of the ditches. The original function of the multitude of pits on this site, as well as other occupation sites at the quarry, is uncertain. Although many contain domestic refuse it is likely the majority of such waste would have been spread on the fields during manuring. As such, the pits may have been originally dug for another purpose (*e.g.*, temporary water storage or clay extraction for daub) but then infilled with whatever was to hand for convenience.

Some features were noted to the east of ditch D16, but were particularly difficult to identify as this part of the site was low-lying and partially flooded. No features were apparent between the north of Site D and the ditches excavated to the north, nor to the west.

The ditches and pit groups at Site D probably mark the location of a domestic settlement/farmsteads. Limited structural evidence was recovered in the area reflecting the degree of truncation to the archaeology, however, the site is located on or near to the free-draining shingle where the ground would have been drier.

No traces of buildings were found. If they were ground-set posts, the traces did not survive machining. If they were of sill beam construction, then they equally may have been removed by machining or earlier ploughing. The pottery from this site is virtually exclusively of the 13th century and as such there is a degree of residuality in features which may be from later in the century. However, a scattering of the features contain some possible 14th century material, usually in their upper fills (*i.e.*, 522 in Cut 490). This material may relate to the final occupation of Site D or later material infilling undulations left by the earlier occupation. Whatever the case, there is no definite evidence of occupation continuing into the 14th century for any length of time.

Site E (Lydd 1, Area C): 'Activity Area' (Figs. 13 and 37)

This area was found to have a very variable substrate of clays, silts, sands and gravels, as well as containing archaeological remains of two periods. The Roman activity (including an urned cremation burial) within this area is described elsewhere (Greig and Gardiner 1996), with the remainder of features apparently dating from the 13th century. Evidence for the medieval activity at this site is mainly indirect; no evidence of any structure was found, though medieval ditch terminals and small enclosures containing rubbish deposits were recorded. There was, however, one slightly irregular truncated pit (347), which probably represented a 'rubbish' pit. The fill contained considerable amounts of shell and charcoal, suggesting that it had been used for food waste.

Other features may be considered under two categories: ditches, and miscellaneous holes or pits of uncertain function. A north-south ditch with a rounded terminal at its southern end (412) appeared to form an enclosure with ditch (399/406/439) (Fig. 38, S81). The enclosure measured 16 × 14.2m. It probably had an entrance at its south-west corner, though this is not certain due to truncation of the western end of Ditch 406 by machining. Another highly truncated context (435) may be the remains of the lowest fill of the north side of the enclosure. Certainly, Ditch 412, although partially removed in machining, appeared to turn to the east at its northern end. Another ditch to the north of the possible enclosure (370, Fig. 38, S82) had been truncated at both ends. It is likely to have originally intersected with the north side of the enclosure, though the junction had not survived. A further ditch (652) was identified to the east of Ditch 370 as a surface indication at a very late stage in the excavation, but was not sectioned.

Only the fill at the very bottom of each cut survived. Ditch 370 had been recut once, and the later fill (388) was difficult to distinguish from 371 and was likely to be of similar origin (Fig. 38, S82). Ditch 412 contained a single fill which may have accumulated through silting. The fills of Ditch 399/406/439 indicate initial silting, followed by a deposition of domestic rubbish, including large quantities of shell. The shell appears to occur throughout the ditch, but there were occasional concentrations, such as that in fill 400, sectioned by Cut 399 (Fig. 38, S81). It is not clear whether the rubbish was present as part of a deliberate backfilling of the ditch, or merely casual disposal.

To the east of the enclosure were two further ditches, both with terminals at their southern ends. Ditch 402, which was of similar width to the south and east sides of the enclosure, was so truncated that little can be said about it. The second ditch (378) was comparable in width to 370 and 412, though of a greater surviving depth. Its lowest fill (390) was apparently accumulated through silting. The profile of the cut (Fig. 38, S83) suggests that the two upper fills represent a recut. Fill 379 was darker and stonier. It contained a high density of pottery and may be deliberate backfill.

A further ditch (115) was located towards the western side during the initial watching brief, and planned during the EDM survey (Fig. 10 only). It was extremely shallow and, before it could be excavated and recorded, was

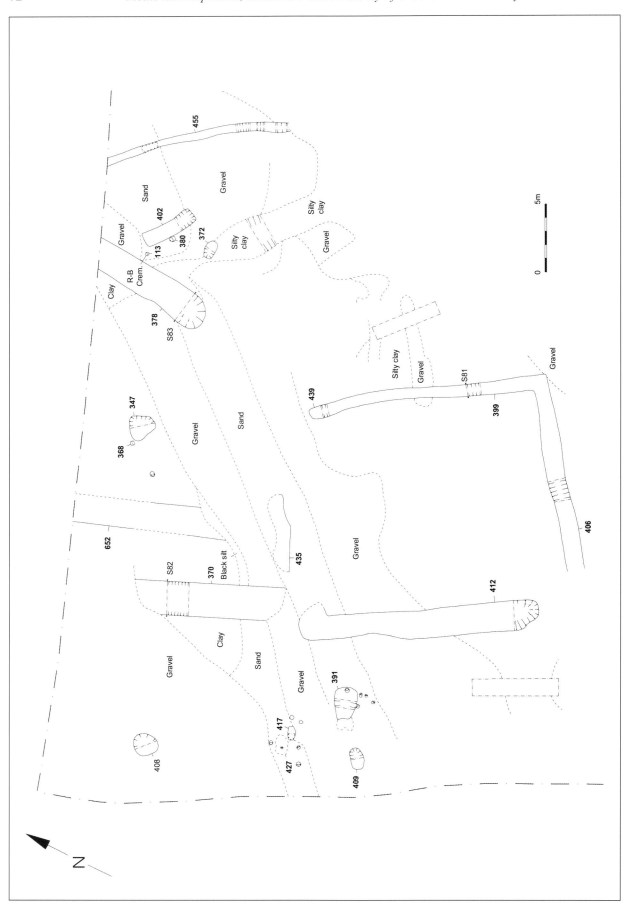

Fig. 37 Lydd Quarry, Plan of Site E (Lydd 1, Area C)

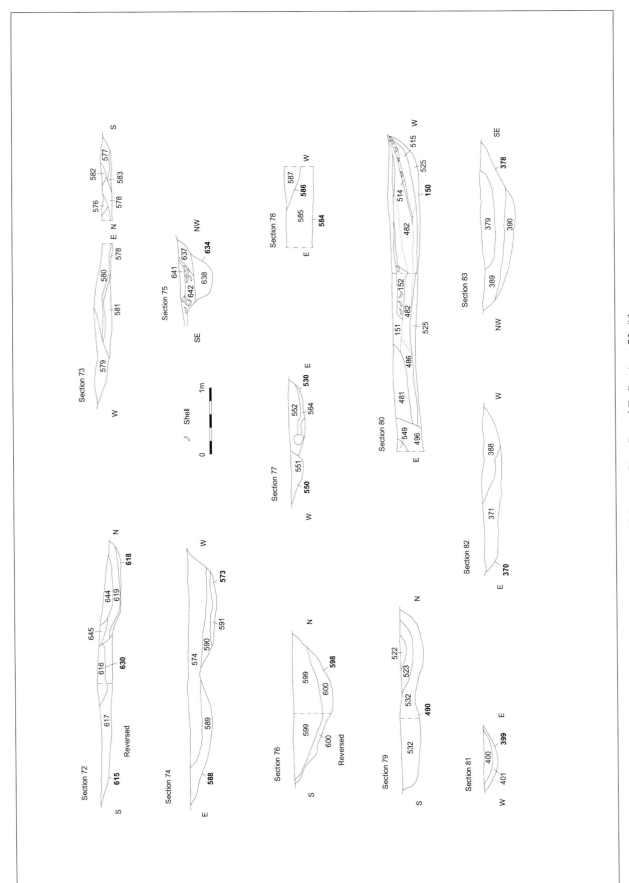

Fig. 38 Lydd Quarry, Sites D and E: Sections 72–83

destroyed partly by the second machining of Area C, and obscured by the final grading of the adjacent topsoil storage bank.

Towards the western edge of the area were a group of features consisting of pits, possible pits and small holes. Pits 409 and 417 contained dark brown silty fills with charcoal and burnt clay fragments. Feature 427 was an ill-defined area of darker sand which may represent the truncated remains of, or staining from, a third pit. The nature of feature 391 was not clear. It was extremely truncated, and its edges, particularly at the west, were not readily identifiable. It may have been a pit or the extremely truncated base of a ditch, for it was noted on excavation that it may have continued westwards and possibly turned south.

Close to these pits were numerous small holes, some of which cut the pits. Some of these appeared to be stake holes, V-shaped in profile, while others were more rounded. The proximity of the holes to the pits may suggest that they were related. Two isolated small holes (368 and 380) lay to the north of the excavated area. Although both were found adjacent to other features, they do not appear to be related to them. A shallow scoop (372) may be a natural depression rather than a humanly-dug feature.

With the exception of the small enclosure, it is not possible to discern a meaningful pattern in the ditches in this area, because of their extreme truncation. Ditches with terminals were also found in Area D (Site D), but although Site E contained only one probable 'rubbish' pit, many more were discovered in Site D (see above). There were similar deposits of rubbish in the ditch fills in both areas. It seems likely, therefore, that occupation debris was deposited at Site E, but permanent domestic occupation did not occur. It is therefore possible that Site E represents an enclosure used for collecting/stockpiling both animal and domestic waste prior to manuring. Human activity may have simply related to temporary periods when agricultural work was being undertaken at the site.

Site F (Lydd 1, Area A): 'Activity Area' (Fig. 10 only)

Area A was the smaller of the two areas investigated during the Lydd 1 works (Fig. 10). Archaeological features were found in the extreme north-east corner of the area, but they were not excavated and the plan was recorded only with a measured sketch. The area was to be preserved *in situ*. Two pits (Contexts 2 and 3), a ditch terminal (Context 4) and two ditches (Context 5) were located, though it is possible that further features may have been found if the surface had been cleaned to archaeological standards after machining. Ditch 5 and its northerly neighbour ran along the alignment of the Burnthouse Wall in a gap in the earthwork which was present prior to the commencement of quarry works at the site but, according to the historic maps, was not there in

1908. The approximate locations of the recorded features in Area A are shown on Figure 10. Pit 2 was elliptical, measuring 0.75 × 1.8m, with a dark brown silty clay fill. Pit 3 was rectangular with rounded edges, measuring 3.0 × 1.1m, and had a dark greyish silty fill with burnt red material at one end. It may have comprised two inter-cutting pits. Ditch 4 had a definite terminal to the south and formed a short branch from Ditch 5. The few sherds of pottery recovered from the surface of these features mainly date from the mid 13th to later 14th centuries, though some 19th to 20th century material was also present.

The two parallel ditches below the line of the Burnthouse Wall may originally have been marking out a 12th century trackway which was abandoned when the wall was constructed. Alternatively, they may represent later features of 20th century date, used to control stock access through the newly made gap in the wall. The presence of 13th to 14th century pottery in the surface of these features could be taken to either represent evidence of perhaps a medieval repair to the wall or to simply represent residual material. The pits in this area are, however, thought to represent an area of 'activity', though whether they relate to repair works to the wall or some other activity is uncertain. Further excavation would be needed in this area, and indeed the wall itself, to clarify the stratigraphic sequence.

Site G (Lydd 5/6, Area A): 'Activity Area'/Occupation Site (Figs. 18 and 39)

This site was in the most north-westerly corner of Lydd 5/6, and associated features were spread across a large area (Area A on Fig. 18). The earliest feature at Site G consisted of a narrow, probable drainage ditch (Fig. 39, D5087), the infill of which (5088) contained mid 12th to early 13th century pottery. Although this was the only ditch identified from this period, it is likely that other contemporary drainage features would have existed which were subsequently re-used and incorporated into the later ditch system.

By the mid 13th century, a system of small ditched enclosures (see below) had probably been established by the cutting of at least five ditches (D5061, D5067, D5089 (*Fig. 40, S84), D5103/5199 (*Fig. 40, S85) and D5324).

Possible Site of Stock Pens (a, b, c, d and e)

Four roughly rectangular adjoining enclosures (Figs. 18 and 39: *a, b, c* and *d*) of similar dimensions, perhaps representing stock pens, lay immediately to the north of the site of a possible structure (see below). A further probable enclosure (*e*) lay immediately to the east.

a) An area measuring *c.* 20 × 19m was enclosed on three sides by ditches: D5089 to the east, D5324 to the south and an existing ditch (D4034–Lydd 4) to the north. It is likely that an existing ditch, recorded immediately to the west of Lydd 5/6, Area B, had originally extended to the north, and would have formed the western side of the enclosure. Within the enclosure lay two ditch termini (5091 (*Fig. 40, S86) and 5191), probably infilled in the 13th century, together with a perhaps 12th to 13th century ditch terminus (5087) and undated ditch terminus (5119) of possible natural origin. The layout of the features perhaps indicates that they were intended to drain the central area of the enclosure. The character of the small enclosure suggests that it represented the site of a stock pen for cattle or sheep. Only one additional feature lay within the postulated pen; a single small post-hole (5189).

b) An area measuring *c.* 22 × 18m was enclosed on three sides: by D5324 to the north, D5089 to the east and D5103 to the south. Again, it is likely that an existing ditch, recorded immediately to the west of Area B, had originally extended to the north, and would have formed the western side of the enclosure. Two possibly associated post-holes (5101 and 5293) lay within this second postulated stock pen.

c) An area measuring 19 × 18m was enclosed on three sides by ditches: D5061 to the east, D5067 to the north and D5089 to the west. Five features were enclosed: three probable post-holes (5099, 5182 and 5184) (Fig. 39) producing late 13th to 14th century pottery, and two undated, possibly associated, post/stake-holes (5186 and 5211). Although the positioning of the five post-holes (5099 *et al.*,) did not immediately suggest the layout of a fence, they perhaps represented the southern side of the third stock pen.

d) An area measuring *c.* 18 × 22m was enclosed to the south by D5067, to the west by D5089, to the north by an existing ditch (D4034–Lydd 4) and to the east by ditch terminal 5193/5331 and the terminal of D5061. Ceramic evidence suggests that during the 13th century the pen had fallen out of use and that the area was subsequently used for rubbish disposal until the early 14th century (see below). A pit (5350) at the junction of ditches D5067, D5089 and D5324 may have acted as a sump or soakaway, or may have represented the cleaning of a silt trap.

e) A contiguous possible enclosure of similar dimensions was probably contemporary with enclosure *d*, which it adjoined. It was defined by ditch terminus 5055 and the northern terminus of D5061 to the west, by D4034–Lydd 4 and perhaps D5331 to the north and D5055 to the south and east (Fig. 18 only).

Possible Site of Structure (Fig. 39)

Ditch 5199 (*Fig. 40, S85) produced 13th century pottery and was perhaps a realignment of the field boundary ditch 5103. A contemporary L-shaped ditch (Figs. 39 and *40, S87, D5121) adjoined D5199, thereby forming a probable enclosure measuring at least 14 × 12m. Although the western end of the postulated enclosure would have lain beyond the edge of the excavated area, it is likely that an existing ditch, recorded immediately to the west of Lydd

5/6, Area B, had originally extended northwards, and would have formed the western side of the enclosure. An alignment of three possible post-holes (5105, 5115 and 5117) lay within the enclosure immediately to the south of D5199. Post-holes 5105 and 5117 had both been recut (5298 and 5339 respectively). All the fills (5106, 5118, 5299 and 5340) produced 13th century pottery, together with burnt clay, charcoal and small quantities of slag and shell. Post-hole 5115 did not produce any independent dating evidence but contained a large quantity of cockle shell, suggesting this feature may have been a pit for the disposal of food refuse (*Fig. 41). An undated small post-hole (5201) lay *c.* 500mm south of post-hole 5117. Three additional, probably associated, post-holes (5203, 5205 and 5207), with diameters between 700 and 1500mm, lay to the south and east. While post-hole 5207 contained 13th century pottery, post-holes 5201, 5203 and 5025 produced 13th to early 14th century material.

This arrangement of seven post-holes (5105 *et al.*) within an enclosing rectangular ditch probably represents the site of a structure measuring at least 10 × 12m. The exact nature of this structure is uncertain, but it could represent a domestic dwelling or perhaps a shelter shed for livestock and/or agricultural workers dealing with animals in the enclosures mentioned above. The lack of domestic 'rubbish' pits in the immediate vicinity, as found at the Lydd 1 and 2 occupation sites (Sites D and H, see above and below), suggests the latter explanation may be more likely. Alternatively the post-holes could simply represent a fenced enclosure.

Two further probable post-holes (5101 dated by pottery to the 13th to early 14th century, and 5293 undated) lay immediately to the north of D5103 and were perhaps associated with the possible structure. An additional feature (5209), with fill 5210, lay just to the south of D5121 and perhaps represented a small pit or post-hole.

Rubbish Disposal Area

Approximately 6m to the north of the subsidiary trackway/ access-way lay a group of four intercutting pits (Fig. 39: 5341, 5347, 5357 (*Fig. 40, S88) and 5363 (*Fig. 40, S89)) within a shallow spread of charcoal-rich silty clay (5063). The predominantly silty clay fills produced a large quantity of domestic waste including 13th to early 14th century pottery, bone, shell, charcoal and ash. Pits 5341 *et al.* were probably rubbish pits; Pit 5357 in particular showed evidence of at least eight separate depositional events. Two sinuous ditches (D5053 and D5065) and perhaps ditch spur D5334 appeared to have been intended to drain the area, perhaps utilising earlier natural channels. A possibly associated shallow elongated pit (5364) lay 1m west of Pit 5341. Two post-holes (5069 and 5071) approximately 1.5m to the east of spread 5063, produced late 13th to 14th century pottery and perhaps represented part of a fence or screen.

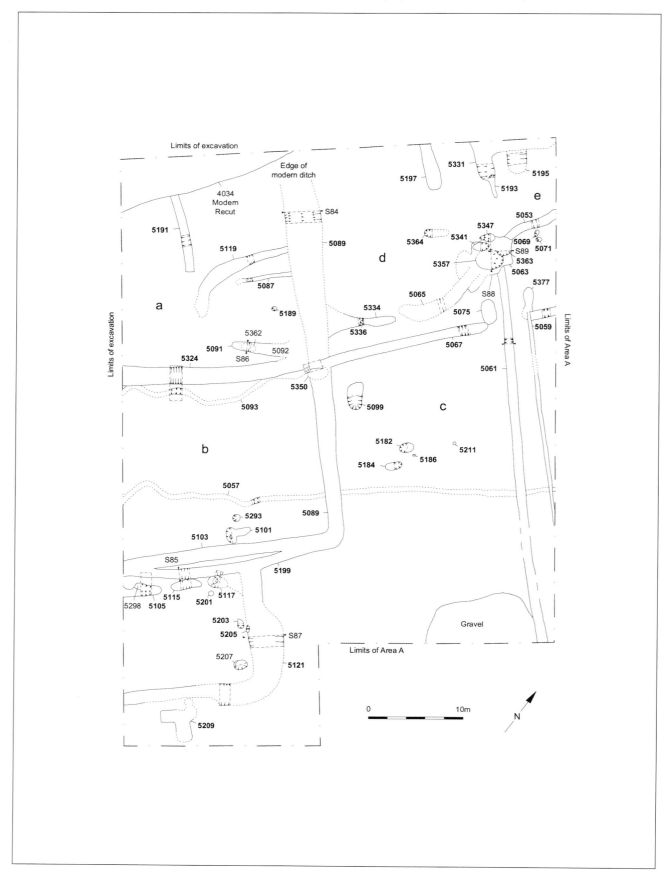

Fig. 39 Lydd Quarry, Plan of Site G (Lydd 5/6, Area A)

The finds evidence and the overall layout of the features suggest that when the postulated former stock pen (see *d* above) went out of use, it became a facility for the disposal of domestic refuse – predominantly food waste and the burnt debris from hearths. If this were the case, it is possible that the refuse was the result of periodic occupation/utilisation of the probable structure to the south-west.

Site H (Lydd 2): Enclosed Occupation Site (Figs. 16, 42, 43 and *44)

The excavations at Lydd 2 concentrated on a single enclosed occupation site set adjacent to the north side of the southern trackway.

The Enclosure Ditches

The enclosure was formed by a rectangular arrangement of ditches: D2164 (Fig. 43, S90), D2096 (Fig. 43, S91) and D2134/2098 (Fig. 24, S22) with a section of the trackway ditch, D2006, forming the southern side. It had been built over the probable 12th century alignment of the southern trackway at this point. In total an area some 24 × 12m (internally) was enclosed, though this was sub-divided into two unequal areas. A curving 5m length of ditch (D2186, Fig. 42) at the south-eastern corner of the enclosure was cut by D2006 and D2134. Indeed, D2134 was itself cut by D2006 (and subsequent recuts) demonstrating the maintenance of the trackway ditch after that of the enclosure had been infilled (Fig. 43, S26). The overall pattern of ditches around the enclosure perhaps suggests that the small field formed by D2013, D2011 and D2098/2134 (Fig. 16) was already in place when the enclosure was added as an internal subdivision.

Although there is ample ceramic evidence for the later 13th century infilling date of most of the ditches, there are few indications as to the relative chronology of the initial establishment of the settlement site. Many of the enclosure ditches did not contain pottery in their lowest fills. Nevertheless it is reasonably certain that, for a period in the 13th century, the active function of the enclosure and the field system were contemporary.

While the infilling dates of the enclosure ditches are broadly similar, there is evidence to suggest that during the final phase of settlement, possibly as late as the early 14th century, the site was no longer enclosed to the north and west by D2096. The upper fills of both the northern and western sections of D2096 produced 13th century pottery. Two pits or recuts (2399 and 2194) within the southern terminus of D2164 contained a dump of domestic refuse (2400) which included a substantial quantity of 13th to early 14th century pottery (Fig. 43, S92) and pottery of a similar date was recovered from a spur ditch (D2336, Fig. 42) off D2164. The stratigraphy of the junction of D2096 and D2098 was not particularly clear, though what evidence there was, combined with the ceramics from the two ditches, indicated that D2098

was probably recut after the infilling of D2096 (Fig. 24, S21). Thus it seems that D2096 and D2164 may have been allowed to silt up/infill when no longer required, possibly enabling the occupation to spread westward while still maintaining D2098 and D2011 as boundaries. Alternatively the redundancy of D2096 might be due to its replacement by a hedge, or it could reflect a change in land use or lower water levels. Whatever the case, the fact that the enclosure ditch was infilled during the 13th to early 14th centuries suggests that although the settlement may be considered closed in the initial phases of occupation, by the later period it was probably an open settlement.

Features Within the Enclosure (Fig. 42)

Generally the excavated features associated with Site H did not produce large groups of pottery, though most features contained small assemblages which helped rough spot dating. The ceramics are often not closely datable in their own right, particularly considering the large proportion of bodysherds in the overall assemblage. As such, this has not allowed close sub-phasing of the developing internal settlement morphology.

Pit Group with Hearth

An approximately 7 × 8m area beside D2134 contained a group of nine pits: 2102 (Fig. 43, S93), 2104 (Fig. 43, S94), 2106 (Fig. 43, S95), 2112, 2140 (Fig. 43, S95), 2144, 2148, 2152 and 2327, with 12 possibly associated post-holes and two slots (see below). With the exception of 2106, all the pits measured around 1.9m long, 0.9m wide and with a maximum depth of 320mm. Pit 2106 measured 2 × 1.9m with a depth of 570mm. The fills were predominantly sandy or silty clay containing 5–10% rounded flint pebbles. With the exception of 2102, all the pits produced pottery spanning the 13th century with a few sherds possibly as late as the early 14th century. In addition to the ceramic material, all the pits without exception contained significant quantities of charcoal (5–10%), burnt clay (5–10%), bone and shell. Pits 2102 and 2104 were stratigraphically discrete while 2152 was cut by 2112 and both were cut in turn by 2327; 2140 was cut by 2106.

A sub-circular bowl-shaped hearth (2366, not illustrated), measuring 1120 × 1160mm, was identified within the upper fill (2107) of Pit 2106 (Fig. 42). The hearth was represented by a 50mm thick compact layer (2302) of blackish red fired clay with 10% charcoal fragments within Cut 2366, from which no dating evidence was recovered. However, pottery dating from the 13th century was recovered from above and below 2302. It is possible that the hearth had originally been located in this position to take advantage of the slight depression formed by the settlement of the fill of 2106.

This group of features therefore, appears to have been a succession of 'rubbish' pits within a specialised

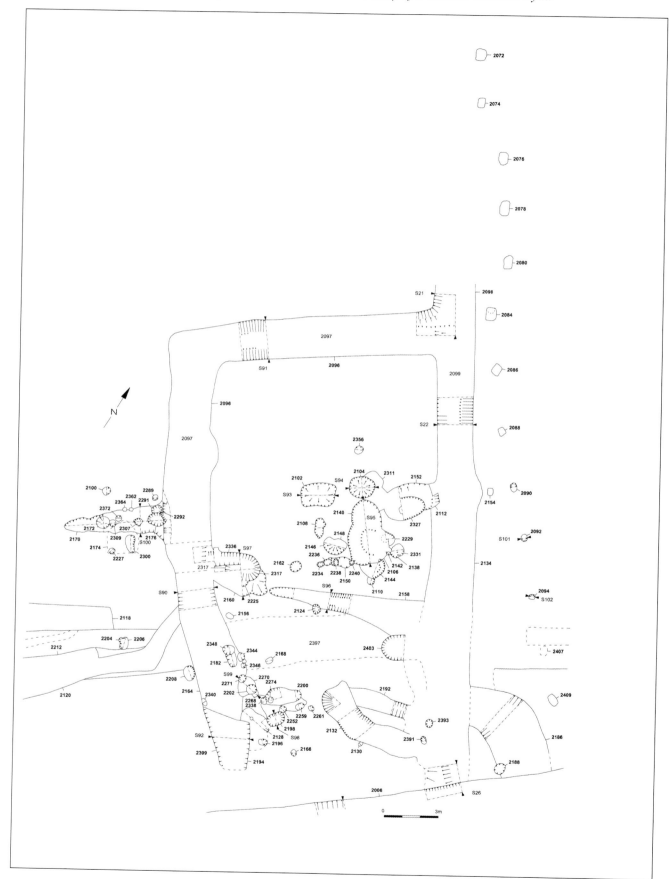

Fig. 42 Lydd Quarry, Plan of Site H (Lydd 2)

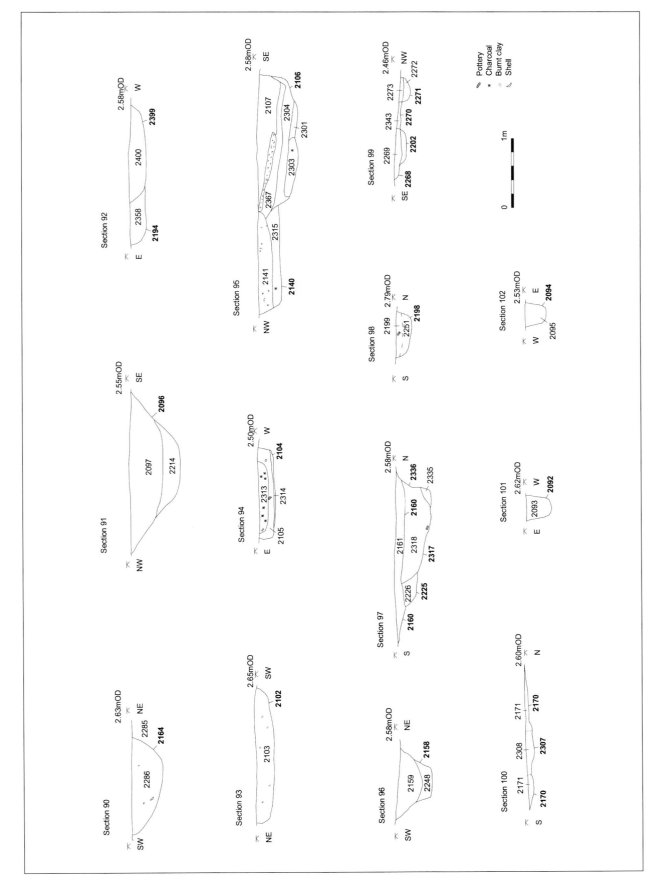

Fig. 43 Lydd Quarry, Site H: Sections 90–102

area that continued in use through much of the life of the settlement. However, at some time, probably in the later 13th century, the last of the pits were infilled and there was a change of use of the area represented by the establishment of a hearth.

Post-holes Adjacent to Pit Group

A series of eight post-holes (2138, 2142, 2162, 2234, 2236, 2238, 2240 and 2331) ran south-west to north-east along the southern edge of the pit group (2102 *et al.*). Three post-holes, 2236, 2238 and 2240 were cut into the fill (2151) of a slot (2150) in the same alignment. Pottery of the 13th century was recovered from 2142, 2150, 2238 and 2240. The arrangement of 2138 *et al.*, perhaps omitting 2162, may represent the line or lines of a fence or screen either associated with the pit group or the hearth (2366) and dividing this area from the southern part of the enclosure.

Four further post-holes lay in the immediate vicinity of the pit group: 2110 to the south, 2356 to the north and 2146 and 2351 to the west. Post-hole 2351 was cut into the fill (2109) of a slot (2108). 13th century pottery was recovered from 2108, 2110 and 2351. Although the relationship between these post-holes and the pit group is unclear, slot 2108 was aligned at right angles with the western end of slot 2150 and may represent a position of the northern return of the posited fence-line (2138 *et al.*).

Probable Site of Building

With the exception of post-hole 2356, the northernmost 10 × 5m of the enclosure was devoid of features, and it is in this area that a dwelling house is likely to have been situated. Although the absence of construction features and internal hearth may be due to ploughing, cut features survive immediately to the south, suggesting that the building is likely to have been constructed on sill-beams or post-pads. Quantities of sandstone recovered from various contexts may represent displaced sill-beam walling and post-pad material.

Internal Division

An 8m long spur ditch (2158, Figs. 42 and 43, S96) came off the western side of D2134 approximately at right angles. A second spur (2225) with two possible recuts or associated pits (2160, Figs. 42 and 43, S97) and 2317 and measuring approximately 2m in length, came off the eastern side of D2096 to terminate within 500mm of the terminus of 2158. Ditches 2158 and 2225, and features 2160 and 2317 produced 13th to early 14th century pottery. Although adverse soil conditions in the south-east of the enclosure made recognition of the stratigraphic relationship between fine grained deposits problematic, it appeared that D2158 was cut by a recut of D2134. D2158 and D2225 seem to have been intended to sub-divide the enclosure while maintaining a narrow access-way between their termini. It is possible that the 8 × 3m area between D2158, D2225 and D2132/D2192 may have served as a temporary stock pen. The possible recuts (2160 and 2317) of 2225 and post-hole 2162 may represent the position of a barrier to control access. D2158 and the post-holes 2138 *et al.* were of a comparable extent and broadly in the same alignment, suggesting that one had been intended to replace or augment the other. As the stratigraphy indicated that D2134 was open after the infilling of D2158, it is possible that the post-hole alignment (D2138 *et al.*) post-dated the active function of D2158. A single undated, possibly associated, post-hole (2124) (Fig. 42) did cut the southern edge of D2158.

Entranceway

Two spur ditches (2132 and 2192) measuring approximately 5m and 4m in length respectively, came off the western side of D2134 near its junction with D2006. Ditch 2132, with roughly the same alignment as 2158, terminated 3m from the eastern edge of D2164. A slot (2200) and adjoining cuts (2266 and 2338) came off the eastern side of D2164 at right angles, and terminated within one metre of the terminus of 2132. This arrangement suggests that it may have been intended to form the basis of a partial barrier, perhaps to restrict access to the interior of the enclosure, or to exclude or enclose stock. Although the stratigraphic relationship between D2132 and D2192 remains unclear, their infilling seems to have been contemporary with that of D2134. Pottery dated to the early 13th to early 14th centuries was recovered from D2132 and post-holes 2198 (Fig. 43, S98), 2252, 2261 and 2274, while D2192 produced slightly later material from the mid 13th to early 14th centuries.

The roughly east to west series of five post-holes (2198, 2252, 2261, 2274 and 2338), two of which (2274 and 2338) were cut into 2200, may represent the position of a gate, or a succession of gates or movable barriers. A small pit (2128) cutting D2164 may have been associated with this entranceway. The cut of D2164 attenuated as it approached D2006, and it is possible that post-holes 2196, 2202, 2338 and perhaps 2208 were contemporary with the open phase of D2164, and possibly represent a short fence that augmented the barrier function of the shallow terminus of D2164.

A further group of six post-holes: 2202 (Fig. 43, S99), 2268, 2271, 2344, 2346 and 2348 and slot 2182 were cut into the upper fill (2165) of D2164 roughly at right angles to post-hole line 2198 *et al.* Pottery from the late 13th to possibly early 14th centuries, was recovered from 2182, 2202, 2271, 2344 and 2348. This series of post-holes may represent the line of a fence that replaced D2164 as a barrier after the terminus of the ditch was infilled around the middle of the 13th century.

A line of four small post-holes (2130, 2166, 2391 and 2393) ran approximately three metres north of and parallel to D2006. Post-hole 2391 produced 13th century pottery and was cut into the fill of 2132, while 2393 was cut into the upper fill of D2134. This alignment may represent the position of a fence that replaced 2132 after its infilling.

Features Outside the Enclosure (Fig. 42)

Possible Hearth and Associated Post-holes

Immediately to the west of D2096/2164 lay a shallow linear depression (2170, Fig. 43, S100) containing significant quantities of burnt clay, shell, bone and charcoal, together with 13th century pottery. Eight post-holes (2172, 2289, 2291, 2307, 2309, 2362, 2364 and 2372) and a small pit (2176) cut 2170. Pottery from the 13th century was recovered from 2176 and 2307, while 2172, 2309 and 2362 produced material from the 13th to early 14th centuries. The enclosure ditch D2096 cut 2176, which in turn cut 2291. Four further, possibly associated, features lay adjacent to 2170: two post-holes (2100 and 2227), a depression (2300) and a spread of burnt clay (2174).

This apparently discrete group of features seems to represent an area of perhaps specialised activity associated with food preparation or cooking. The spread of burnt clay (2174) and the large quantities of burnt material recovered from 2170 may indicate the presence of a hearth truncated by weathering or ploughing. Although no south-eastern corner post-hole was identified, the arrangement of 2172 *et al.* together with 2100 and 2227 could represent the position of a structure, or the succession of light structures enclosing a 3 × 3m area. The postulated structure seems to have been contemporary with a period when D2096 was open and may have been positioned on the edge of the ditch to allow drainage. No immediately adjacent features were identified cut into the upper fill of D2096 and it is likely that this area was no longer in use when D2096 was infilled in the late 13th century.

Post-hole Line

An alignment of 21 post-holes (2068, 2070, 2072, 2074, 2076 2078, 2080, 2084, 2086, 2088, 2090, 2092 (Fig. 43, S101), 2094 (Fig. 43, S102), 2114, 2116, 2275, 2279, 2281, 2287, 2407 and 2409: Figs. 16 and 42) ran between 1 and 3m to the east of, and roughly parallel to, the eastern edge of the enclosure (D2098/2134). The post-holes were at approximate 3m intervals and were predominantly sub-rectangular, measuring approximately 400–500 × 500–700mm. All the post-holes, with the exception of 2409 which is cut into the fill of D2381, were cut into natural.

The northernmost post-hole (2281, Fig. 16) was one of the largest, measuring 500 × 680mm and had a slot in its western edge, perhaps indicating the presence of a support post. This suggests that the fence may have turned at this point, continuing south-west parallel to D2011. If this were the case, it is possible that the fence was erected to augment or replace the barrier function of D2098/2134 and D2011 after these ditches silted up or were infilled. Pottery of the 14th century together with possibly residual 13th century material was recovered from the fills of four of the post-holes (2070, 2114, 2275 and 2281). The weight of evidence suggests therefore that the fence-line may be contemporary with the last phase of settlement at Site H in the late 13th/early 14th century. No mid 14th to 15th century material was recovered from the site despite the surrounding field system and trackway continuing in use during this period.

Site I (Lydd 2): 'Activity Area' (Fig. 16 only)

Two metres to the west of D2026, a contiguous group of shallow cuts (2373, 2414 and 2416 within 2373) formed a discrete sub-rectangular area measuring approximately 3.3 × 4.6m. A significant quantity of apparently weathered burnt clay was recorded in 2373, while 2414 and 2416 produced 13th century and mid 13th to early 14th century pottery respectively. The nature of the features, together with the large unabraded sherds of conjoining pottery recovered from 2414, suggest that the feature is unlikely to have been the remains of a simple midden for manuring. Although no structural features were identified, it is possible that the sub-rectangular area formed by 2373, 2414 and 2416 represents a weathered activity area, maybe associated with a small structure broadly contemporary with the occupation site (Site H) to the west.

Site Ja (Lydd 3, Area B: part): 'Activity Area' (Figs. 17 and 45)

Although Area B at Lydd 3 mainly contained features relating to the 14th century occupation site (Site Jb – see below) it also contained some evidence of activity in the 13th century. Although the 13th century features may have related to activity at Site C (Lydd 3 Area D) they appear to just post-date Site C. As such, the 13th century features at Lydd 3, Area B, have been treated as a separate 'activity' area and called Site Ja.

Two probably intercutting pits (3054 and 3056) and Pit 3058 (*Fig. 48, S103) produced significant quantities of pottery and shell, together with animal bone, charcoal and iron, and were probably 'rubbish' pits. An undated post-hole (3052) may have been associated with Pit 3056. To the west, two probable pits (3044 and 3046), cut by a recut of Ditch 3030, contained significant quantities of shell, together with pottery and animal bone. A short gully (3040) containing pottery and shell, and two undated gullies (3042 and 3048) were probably associated with Pits 3044 and 3046. Before D3030 was recut, it seems likely that gully 3042 may have drained into it, and Pits 3044 and 3046 may have been located on the ditch edge. If this were the case, this group of features perhaps represented a specialised area for the processing of food, where waste water could carry refuse directly into the ditch.

Although ceramic evidence suggests that subsidiary trackway ditches D3006 and D3010 had probably been infilled in the 14th century, the trackway may easily have been in use, and the defining ditches open, during the 13th century. In view of this, Pits/Post-holes 3016, 3064, 3066 and 3224 may represent the position of a barrier to facilitate the driving of stock onto the trackway or droveway. Undated features 3012, 3014 and 3210 may have been part of this structure. Gully 3090 and intercutting pit 3088, along with undated gullies 3070, 3072 and 3215, may represent the subdivision of the area, perhaps into stock pens. Probably 13th century post-holes 3026 and 3242 and undated post-hole 3206 may be further elements of the postulated stock pens.

Period 3 (early): 14th century Occupation and Activity

Site Jb (Lydd 3, Area B (part) and Area C): Occupation Site (Figs. 17, 45, 46 and *47)

Area B: to north of southern track (Fig. 45)

A small hearth (3124) measuring *c.* 1.1m in diameter was located in the south-east corner of the area (*Fig. 48, S104). It consisted of a partial *in situ* single course brick lining containing a charcoal rich fill (3125) that produced 14th to 15th century pottery. Additional bricks and brick fragments in the immediate area, apparently displaced by ploughing, suggested that the hearth may have originally been fully lined. The hearth lay within a shallow depression (3122), perhaps representing a worn floor into which an arrangement of ten probably associated post-holes (3222, 3252, 3254, 3256, 3260, 3264, 3266, 3268, 3270 and 3272) had been cut. Ceramic evidence indicated that at least one of the post-holes (3254) was contemporary with Hearth 3124. An additional arrangement of four post-holes (3246 (*Fig. 48, S105), 3248, 3250 and 3262) lay *c.* 1.5m to the north-west of Hearth 3124, and two pits or large post-holes (3118 and 3126) and three post-holes (3100, 3102 and 3120, *Fig. 48, S106) lay within 5m. Pottery dating from the 14th to early 15th century from Pits/Post-holes 3118, 3120, 3126 and 3250 suggested that they were broadly contemporary with Hearth 3214.

In view of the relatively substantial nature of Hearth 3214, it is unlikely that it was constructed for occasional use. If it had been intended for at least seasonal use, it could not have functioned without a sheltering structure of some sort. It is likely therefore that many or all of the nearby post-holes/pits represented such a structure. If this were the case, the arrangement of post-hole groups 3222 *et al.*, 3246 *et al.*, and Post-hole 3120 would suggest that the enclosing structure might have measured *c.* 5 × 5m.

Alternatively, if Pits 3118 and 3126 represented elements of the structure it would have measured *c.* 8 × 5m, though surface sill beams could also have been incorporated. Although there is no direct evidence as to the function of the possible structure, it was perhaps a workshop or small shelter.

Two shallow pits (3114 and 3116) partially enclosing a group of stake holes (3670) lay *c.* 8m to the north of Hearth 3124. This arrangement probably represented a small specialised working area. A large pit (3104) measuring *c.* 3.5 × 2m, produced a significant amount of pottery, bone and shell, and was probably a domestic 'rubbish' pit. Two post-holes (3108 and 3110) of unknown function lay between Pits 3114 and 3116, and Pit 3104.

A large pit (3074), measuring 5 × 4.3m with a depth of 1.37m, had been dug down to the steeply shelving edge of an underlying shingle ridge (Figs. 45 and *48, S107). A section of oak plank 1.2m long, 300mm wide and 40mm thick, with a dowel hole and tooling marks was uncovered at the base of the pit within the primary fill (3336). The plank was positioned against the gravel on the eastern edge of the pit so as to suggest that it had been intended to act as shuttering to stabilise the gravel slope. If this had been the case, and if the water table had originally been above the base of the pit, an open well would have been formed by groundwater flowing in through the exposed gravel. A section of wooden stake that may have originally supported the plank was recovered from the secondary fill (3259). Fragments of a lathe-turned wooden bowl were also recovered. Ditch 3076, the terminal of which was cut by Pit 3074, would have acted as an overflow channel for the postulated open well.

To the west lay the probable secondary trackway identified to the north on the western side of Site K (Lydd 3, Area A) (see below). Within Area B the track was demarcated by two gullies placed some 5m apart (Ditches 3006, 3008 (*Fig. 48, S108 and S109) and 3010 (*Fig. 48, S110)). Although they appear to have been infilled during the 14th century, this was probably only done after a period of use, presumably including recutting on a number of occasions. As such, the trackway probably had its origins in the 13th century. The shallow and narrow nature of the flanking ditches would not have provided much of a barrier for stock, even accounting for truncation through later ploughing. It is therefore likely that either a hedge or hurdles were employed to contain stock. A *c.* 8m section of ditch (3036) and a small pit (3060) possibly represented the position of a barrier to limit access to the trackway defined by D3006/D3008 and D3010. However, if this was the case these features may not have stayed in use for long, as Ditch 3006 (or probably a recut of it) cut D3036.

A large, perhaps natural, depression (Fig. 45, 3020) measuring at least 12 × 4m and with a maximum depth of 580mm, ran under the southern baulk of the machine

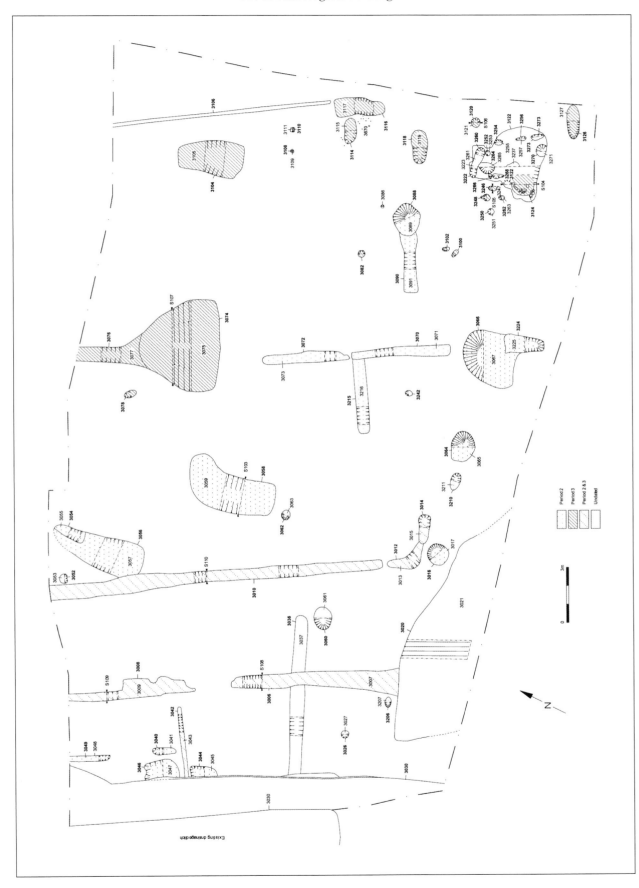

stripped area. Significant quantities of domestic refuse from fills 3021 and 3238, including 14th century pottery, bone and shell, indicated that the area had been used for rubbish disposal. However, the scale of the feature perhaps suggests its original function may have been that of a pond used after the trackway had gone out of use.

Two 14th century post-holes (3062 and 3078) and four undated post-holes (3082, 3086, 3108 and 3110) were not obviously associated with any other features. An undated straight narrow gully (3106) on the eastern edge of the area was likely to have been modern.

Area C (Fig. 46)

A spread of gravel (3294, Figs. 46 [opposite] and *47) measuring *c.* 5.5 × 6.5m, partially overlay two sandy silt deposits (3312 and 3321) within a broad shallow cut (3311) (*Fig. 48, S111). Three shallow lobate pits (3292, 3323 and 3344) with fills (3293, 3324 and 3340/3343 respectively) were located around the western and northern edges of feature 3311. A small post-hole (3290) lay below fill 3293. A large quantity of 14th century pottery, together with bone, shell, charcoal and iron, was recovered from deposits 3293, 3312, 3321, 3324, 3340 and 3343. Some 1.5m to the east was a second shallow cut (3308), measuring *c.* 5.5 × 7m, which contained a pottery-rich spread (3180) (*Fig. 48, S112). Eight apparently contemporary post-holes (3174, 3176, 3178, 3278, 3283, 3304, 3306 and 3332) lay immediately to the north of Spreads 3294 and 3180 in a roughly linear arrangement. A small isolated post-hole (3346) lay a little further to the north. Six additional post-holes (3156, 3160, 3184, 3186, 3276 and 3281) and a pit (3164) lay immediately to the south.

The above arrangement of features, considered as a whole, suggests the plan of a building containing two rooms. If this were the case, the dimensions of the rooms would be represented by the extent of Spreads 3180 and 3294. It follows therefore, that the 1.5m wide 'finds-barren' area between Spreads 3180 and 3294 could have been a through passage. Alternatively, a smaller, roughly 6m square structure with a gravel floor (3294) may have had an adjacent compound or working area (3180). This second hypothesis is thought less likely but is partially supported by the presence of three large shallow pits (3286 (*Fig. 48, S113), 3317, and 3327) apparently contemporary with and within Spread 3180. All these pits produced large quantities of domestic refuse, including 14th century pottery, bone and shell, and it seems unlikely that 'rubbish' pits would be dug within an enclosed structure unless they were dug after this part of the building had gone out of use.

Approximately 6m to the south-east lay a gravel spread (3199), measuring approximately 2 × 3m, within a shallow cut (3198, Figs. 46 and *48, S114). Approximately 1.5m to the north was a further depression (3196) of similar dimensions containing fills 3197 and 3310. A significant quantity of 14th to early 15th century pottery, together

with bone and shell, was recovered from fill 3110. Notwithstanding the difference in scale, the morphology of features 3180 and 3294 compared with features 3197 and 3199 was very similar. Accordingly, features 3197 and 3199 may represent sub-divisions of the floor of a small ancillary structure measuring *c.* 5 × 3m, while a 'finds-barren' area between Spread 3199 and feature 3196 may represent a through passage. Ceramic evidence from Spread 3199 suggests that the proposed structure was contemporary with the possible building defined by Spread 3294 to the west. A postulated cess-pit or sump (3348) lay *c.* 3m to the east, and it is possible that the ancillary structure may have been associated with it (see below).

The small steep-sided pit (3348), approximately 1m in diameter, had been cut into the base of Ditch 3200 through to the underlying gravel. Large quantities of domestic refuse, predominantly pottery and animal bone, were recovered from fills 3201 and 3350 of D3200. This suggests that at sometime in the 14th century D3200 began to be used for rubbish disposal. Pit 3348 contained a large quantity of well-preserved wood, predominantly oak with some alder, including five vertical stakes approximately 30mm in diameter. The stakes had been placed around the edge of the pit and appeared to have supported two 300–400mm long partially displaced sections of radially split wood. Further sections of wood with a diameter of approximately 20mm were horizontally braced against the vertical stakes along two sides of the pit.

The wooden structure in its entirety seems to have been intended to maintain access to the pit and prevent slumping. It is therefore possible that the feature represents the site of a cess-pit or sump; the disposal of large quantities of domestic refuse in the immediate area suggests the feature was not a well for domestic consumption of water. Pottery from this feature suggests it was infilled in the late 14th to 15th century.

A large pit or ditch terminal (3192/3297), measuring at least 5m wide, ran under the southern baulk of the machine stripped area. The significant quantity of domestic refuse from fills 3193 and 3300, including 14th to early 15th century pottery, bone and shell, suggests that the area was used for rubbish disposal.

Site K (Lydd 3, Area A): 'Activity Area' (Figs. 17 and 49)

To the east of the subsidiary trackway marked by Ditches 3144 and 3146 was an arrangement of three roughly rectangular large post-holes (Fig. 49, 3134 (S115), 3138 and 3142) and an ephemeral feature (3132). These perhaps represented the site of an agricultural building or stock pen measuring *c.* 10 × 6m. Ceramic evidence suggests that the possible structure was likely to be of 14th century date. A smaller post-hole (3140) of similar date immediately to the east, and a small ephemeral feature (3136) to the south, were perhaps associated with the structure.

Fig. 46 Lydd Quarry, Plan of Site Jb (southern part) (Lydd 3, Area C)

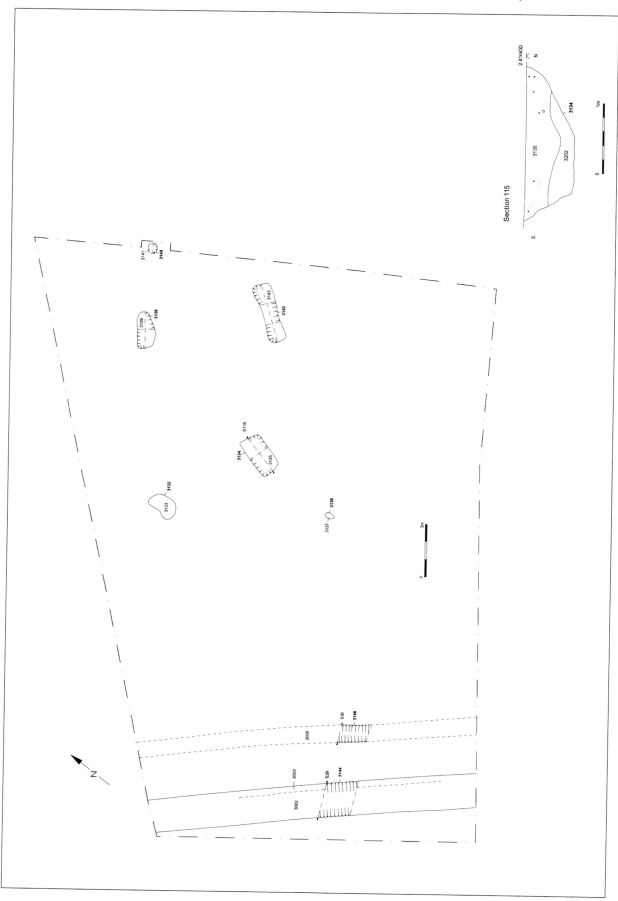

Fig. 49 Lydd Quarry, Plan of Site K and Section 115 (Lydd 3, Area A)

Period 3 (late): 15th to early 16th century

Only two sites at Lydd Quarry fall within this period, though their exact function is uncertain. Although it is possible Site La represents a domestic occupation site, it could easily represent an activity area (perhaps a satellite of the Burnt House) which may have its origins at this time.

Site La (Lydd 5/6, Area B): 'Activity Area' or Occupation Site (Figs. 18 and 50)

Approximately 10m to the east of Ditch 5137 lay a shallow, sub-rectangular cut filled with charcoal-rich silty clay (5151/5152, Figs. 50 and *54, S116) that possibly represented a worn floor. The postulated floor measured *c.* 3 × 3.5m and contained a little tile, shell and two small sherds of mid 15th to mid 16th century pottery. A pit (*Fig. 54, S116: 5155) with an adjoining small gully (5153) lay within 5151. A spread of twenty-nine probably contemporary post-holes (5148, 5155, 5163, 5165, 5167, 5180, 5213, 5215, 5216, 5217, 5218, 5220, 5222, 5232, 5234, 5236, 5238, 5240, 5242, 5244, 5250, 5252, 5254, 5256, 5260, 5262, 5264, 5266 and 5268) were grouped around 5151. The overall arrangement of the features may indicate the site of a small building, perhaps a shepherd's hut, measuring *c.* 4 × 5m, within a *c.* 8 × 12m compound. Two discrete groups of intercutting post-holes (5155, 5170, 5216, 5217 and 5165, 5167, 5213, 5215) *c.* 2m apart, lay on the eastern end of the feature group and perhaps represented an entranceway. However, a sheep wash is shown immediately to the south on 19th to early 20th century OS maps (Fig. 7) and some of the post-holes could be out-lying features relating to this. However, no 19th century finds were located in any of the features in Area B, suggesting the sheepwash features did not extend this far north. Whatever the case, the quantity of 15th to 16th century finds from Area B clearly show the presence of some domestic activity at that date.

A short section of undated narrow ditch (D5282) lay between (and was cut by) trackway ditches D5009 and D5011. D5282 was perhaps a relic of an earlier ditch system. An undated post-hole (5161) was cut into the fill (5010) of D5009.

Site Lb (Lydd 5/6, to north of Area B): 'Activity Areas' (Figs. 18, 51 and 52)

A number of isolated features were discovered to the north of Site La, which appear to relate to 15th to early 16th century occupation in the area. These are discussed below.

Two sub-rectangular pits (Fig. 18, 5081 and 5083) lay between the parallel Ditches 5023 and 5043 and produced significant quantities of 15th to mid 16th century pottery, brick, tile, bone and shell. These isolated features were likely to have been 'rubbish' pits associated with contemporary activity (5151 *et al.*) identified *c.* 40m to the south at Site La or to the west at the Burnt House.

A clay-lined pit (Figs. 18 and 51, 5286) contained the well-preserved lower section of a barrel (5291) constructed of oak staves and held together by inner and outer ash hoops, perhaps with external ash withies. Its fill (5292, Fig. 51, S117) of greenish-grey silty clay produced the remains of a wooden lathe-turned alder bowl and parts of leather shoes dated to the late 15th century, together with quantities of 15th to early 16th century pottery, bone and shell. Pottery of a similar date was recovered from the backfill from around the outside of the barrel (Contexts 5290 and 5287). The general nature of the feature and its fill suggest that it may have originally functioned as a cess-pit, perhaps within a privy. If this were the case, it would almost certainly have been associated with a nearby dwelling, perhaps located at Site La *c.* 35m to the south, or more probably Harlackinden's house to the south-west. The presence of a possible sandstone capping stone and significant quantities of brick, sandstone fragments and gravel within 5292 may be the result of intentional back-filling and closure when the feature fell into disuse.

To the north were the remains of a pit, approximately 1m square and 450mm deep (Fig. 52, 5366). This contained the remains of an oak timber lining (5376) apparently intended to prevent slumping; the feature was probably the remains of a well – a suggestion borne out by the insect remains found within it (see below). The dating from the different fills gave a wide range showing the feature to have been in use for some time. The earliest material was recovered from 5368, which appeared to be packing associated with the well's construction (Fig. 52, S118). Twelve sherds of later 15th century pottery from this context were recovered, suggesting the feature to be originally of late medieval date. Unfortunately no datable finds were recovered from 5371, which may have been a deliberately placed gravel base. The fills above this level produced mixed assemblages of finds, though most were apparently of much later date suggesting the well had remained in use, being cleaned out from time to time, until the 18th century. The basal line of fill 5370 represented the final clean out. Although the pottery from 5370 is of late 15th century date, and thus possibly intrusive from 5368, the presence of part of an 18th century leather shoe from its surface suggests that it may be of considerably later date. An organic fill (5369) contained the *in situ* remains of a localised stand of reeds that may have colonised the feature during the first phase of its disuse. Analysis of the plant remains also identified moss and aquatic flora, indicating prolonged wet conditions within the feature. The upper fill (5367) of the feature produced more pieces of the leather shoe found in 5370, suggesting some mixing of deposits when the final deliberate rubble infill (5367) was added. A little residual medieval pottery, as well as an 18th century sherd, were also found in this context. It is therefore possible that this feature was also used by Harlackinden's House (later the 'Burnt House')

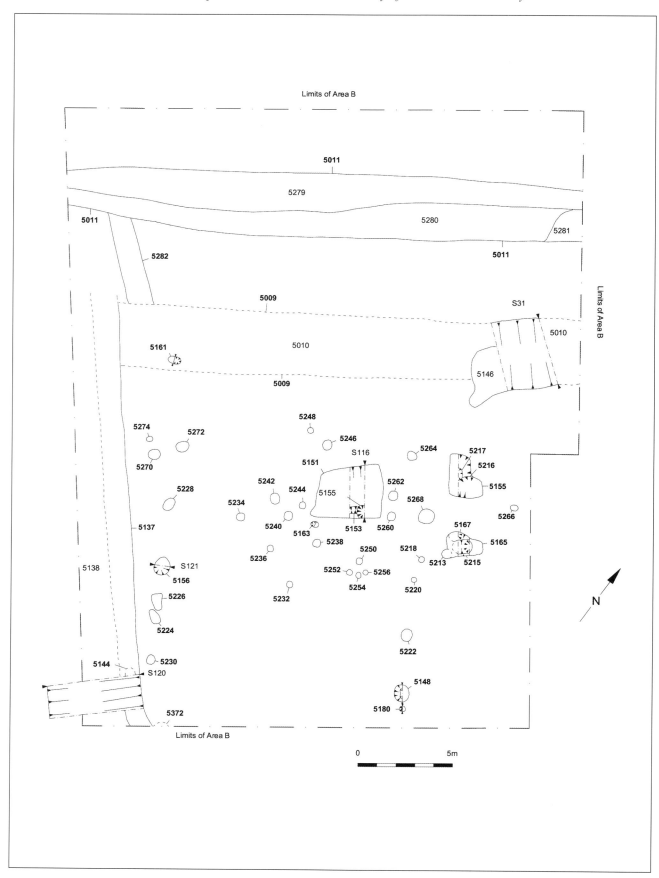

Fig. 50 Lydd Quarry, Plan of Site La (Lydd 5/6, Area B)

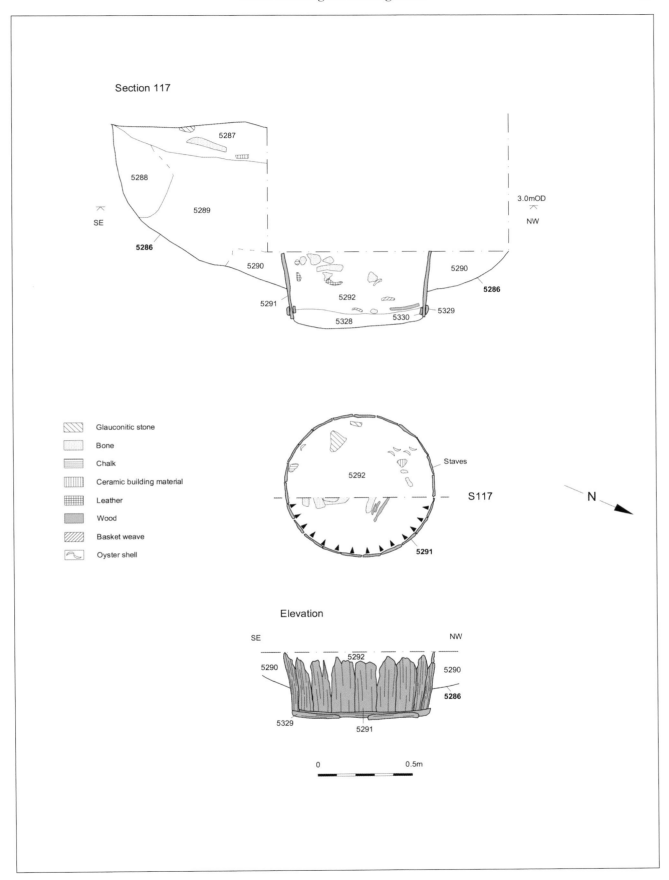

Fig. 51 Lydd Quarry, Site Lb, part and Section 117 (Lydd 5/6, north of Area B)

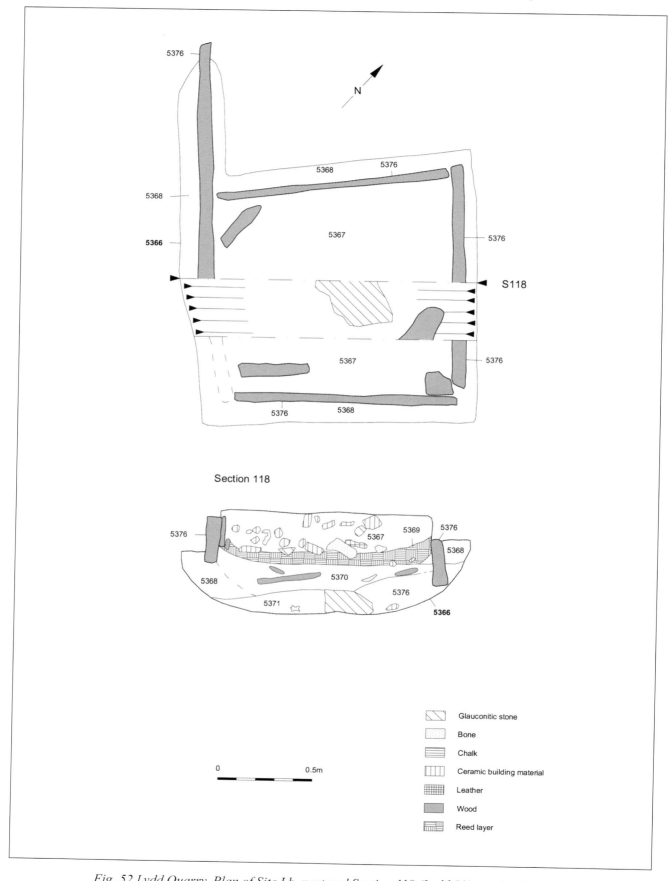

Fig. 52 Lydd Quarry, Plan of Site Lb, part and Section 118 (Lydd 5/6, north of Area B)

which is depicted on Poker's map of 1617 as lying a little to the west of this feature (*Fig. 3).

Site M (Lydd 5/6, Area C): 'Activity Area' (Figs. 18 and 53)

Three sub-rectangular shallow features (5013, 5015 (*Fig. 54, S119) and 5017) measuring approximately 6 × 4m, 7 × 4m, and 3 × 2.5m respectively, lay immediately west of Ditch 5007. The fills (5014, 5016 and 5018) of cuts 5013, 5015 and 5017 respectively produced late 14th to late 15th century pottery, brick, tile and sandstone fragments. Ceramic evidence suggests that Ditch 5007 was open during this period, in which case feature 5015 would have drained into it along an adjoining spur ditch (also 5015). Features 5013 and 5017 lay on the line of D5011 either side of an apparent interruption. Stratigraphic and ceramic evidence from other sections of D5011 indicate that it was still open after 1550, suggesting that the interruption in D5011 represented a well established access from the trackway to fields immediately to the north. Many such access-ways must have existed, probably in the form of small timber bridges, but have left no trace on the archaeological record.

The arrangement of features 5013 and 5015 is difficult to interpret. It is possible to suggest that they represent the floors of two sections within a single building/ shelter (perhaps a looker's hut), while the *c.* 1.3m wide corridor between them was perhaps a through passage. Alternatively, a smaller structure may have been located beside an associated yard or working area. A permanent access-way across a principal trackway ditch must have been a focus of local activity and it is unsurprising that features were established there. All three features are not dissimilar to Context 5151 in Area B (Site La).

Period 4: Continued Decline (Post 16th century)

Although no true 'sites' of this period have been excavated in the quarry so far, at least one concentration of finds suggests nearby domestic occupation.

Site N (Lydd 5/6 Ditch 5137 assemblage and Harlackinden's house/Burnt House) (Figs. *30 and 50)

The presence of 18th century material in the probable well (5366) has already been mentioned above. In addition to that material the upper fill of D5137 (*Fig. 54, S120, Fill 5138) produced a large late 17th to early 18th century finds assemblage dominated by pottery and clay pipes. A significant number of tankards were identified within the assemblage, suggesting that the ditch had been used for the disposal of rubbish from an inn or tavern. It is quite possible the 'Burnt House' (*Fig. 30) was the source of this material (see below).

A rough line of eight post-holes (Fig. 50: 5156 (*Fig. 54, S121), 5224, 5226, 5228, 5230, 5270, 5272 and 5274), lay *c.* 1m east of Ditch 5137. Unfortunately only one (5156) of these post-holes produced dating evidence. The alignment of post-holes 5156 *et al.* was broadly

parallel to D5137 and was probably a fence-line put in to reinforce the boundary. An ephemeral post-hole (5144) cut into the eastern edge of fill 5143 of D5137, as well as one of the main post-holes in the line, produced mid 15th to early 16th century pottery. However, this material could easily be residual from Site La immediately to the east. It is therefore quite possible that the fence-line is of 17th to 18th century date. An ephemeral pit (5372) in the excavation edge produced pottery ranging in date from the 14th to 17th centuries.

The activity in and around Lydd 5/6, Area B, does not appear to relate to an occupation site actually within the excavated area. However, as with the late Period 3 sites at La and Lb, it strongly indicates such a site in the near vicinity. Cartographic sources clearly show that a little to the west of this point, under the eastern portion of the current plant site, stood a building of some substance. It is quite probable that this building had its origins in the late medieval period, or at least the 16th century. This building is clearly depicted on a map by Thomas Clerke of Scotney Manor, dated 1589 (All Souls College KeS/12). This shows it to have been a three-storey structure with two central chimneys labelled as 'Harlackendens House', a wealthy man who also owned much of the land to the east and west of Gores (later re-named 'Burnthouse') Wall subjected to the archaeological investigation. As late as the early 20th century a small building, labelled 'Burnt House', is marked on maps at approximately this point, though its small size and close proximity to a sheepwash suggest this structure to be a looker's hut (*Fig. 31). The finds from 5137/8 would suggest that the original house, which also appears to be depicted on Poker's map of 1617 (*Fig. 3) and Hasted's map of around the 1790s, may have survived at least until the end of the 18th century, by which time it may have been used, at least in part, as an inn. Such a building is more likely to have been destroyed by fire and is therefore likely to be the source of the name change of the adjacent wall and the later, probably agricultural, building on or close to the site. It is interesting to note that the wall is still labelled 'Gores Wall' on Hasted's 1790s map, but is called 'Burnthouse Wall' by the time of the 1812 Tithe map.

The latest excavated feature at the site consisted of a sub-circular bowl-shaped cut (Fig. 18, 5174) to the north-east of Lydd 5/6, Area B (Site La). The feature was approximately 10m in diameter and in excess of 690mm in depth (it was not bottomed). The few finds recovered from the fills (5175, 5176 and 5177) included a modern enamelled tin cup. Although it appears that the feature was intentionally back-filled in recent times, it perhaps represented the site of a long-established pond. Alternatively, given that the area has been habitually used during the 20th century for military purposes, and the cup was similar to those issued to troops around the time of the Great War, feature 5174 may be a backfilled shell crater.

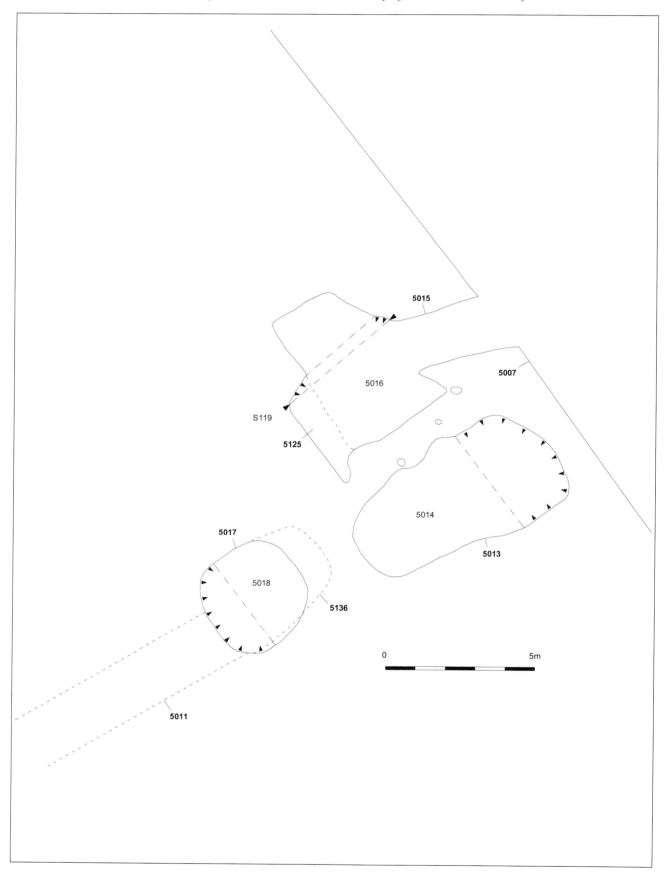

Fig. 53 Lydd Quarry, Plan of Site M (Lydd 5/6, east of Area B)

SAMPLE EXCAVATIONS AT DERING FARM, LYDD

Text extracted from a preliminary report
by Mark Gardiner (Gardiner 1992)

Introduction

Dering Farm lies at the north-east end of Lydd Quarry (Fig. 2) in an area of proposed gravel extraction. During January 1992 Brett Gravel Ltd. made available a mechanical excavator for three days to allow sample excavations within the land of the proposed Lydd Quarry called Area 1. No archaeological finds were previously known from the site, though the findings to the south-west at the plant site (Lydd 1) suggested the Dering Farm site to hold some potential for containing remains of interest. However, the presence of gravel at the surface over part of the site suggested that truncation of any archaeological remains may have been severe.

The area sampled by machine was limited by the gravel ridge which runs north-east to south-west across the site, and by land of ecological interest lying to the south-east of this. Work was therefore concentrated on the north-west where commercial boreholes suggested the basal gravel dived beneath later sediments (Fig. 55).

The site was sampled by cutting sub-parallel trenches 0.8m wide at 50m intervals using a toothless bucket. The trenches, lettered A to G, were dug from the north-western boundary of the field in a line until the shingle was reached. The trenches were excavated about 0.4m deep so that any features cut into the underlying subsoil could be clearly identified.

Some earthworks were noted within the field. These were identified as ditches or collapsed field drains. One ditch was recorded running parallel to (and at the foot of) the shingle ridge (Fig. 55). A circular mound was noted and sectioned by machine (Trench H) but the presence of a rusty tin beneath its make-up showed it to be modern. Though there was no evidence of recent ploughing, the tops of some features including gravel-filled land drains had been clearly truncated and spread by plough action. Evidence of deep (?steam) ploughing was noted in the section across Trench A where some plough furrows filled with topsoil were clearly identifiable in the layer below the topsoil (Context 9, subsoil, Fig. 56, section).

The Palaeogeographic Record

At the north-western ends of Trenches A and D deeper cuts were made to record the stratigraphy. Due to the ingress of water and the instability of the trench sides no measured sections were drawn. The sequence recorded in both trenches were similar to one another. In addition it bore a marked similarity to the general stratigraphy noted in the low-lying land between the shingle ridges in the main Lydd Quarry to the south-west. At the base of the trench lay a thick deposit of blue-grey clay, containing sparse roots and plant fragments. This was overlain by a thin peat about 250mm thick, on top of which was a mid brown silty clay and similarly-coloured clay, above which lay the topsoil.

At the south-eastern end of Trench E, this sequence was investigated in greater detail. The sequence overlying the basal shingle was similar to that described, except that an upper deposit of shingle had been thrown over the peat from the shingle ridge to the south-west. There was also some evidence that the peat had been disturbed.

At the north-west end of Trench F a further deposit of shingle was recorded. This seems to be the small 'island' of shingle mapped by the Soil Survey (Green 1968) at about this point. A second trench was excavated at right angles to Trench F and showed that the level of the shingle fell sharply to the west and that the foot of the shingle was overlain by peat.

Shingle on the top of the ridge at the north-west of Trench F, and shingle exposed at the south-east of Trench D at the foot of the main shingle ridge, both showed that the surface flint had been calcined by burning. No evidence of briquetage was found; however, the burning could relate to earlier prehistoric hearths which were found later to the south-west at the main quarry (Priestley-Bell 2003a and 2004a).

Medieval Ditches

Trench A ran nearly parallel to (and along the top of) a medieval ditch. The full extent of the ditch was not determined, though a machine-cut section showed that it had been recut twice (Figs. 55 and 56, Contexts 3 and 5). The first fill (6) of the second recut comprised shingle set in a matrix of dark brown silty clay, which seems to have been dumped to infill the ditch. The purpose of this is uncertain. Pottery of late 13th or early 14th century date (and a whetstone) were recovered from the uppermost fill (7).

Three ditches were recorded running at right angles to Trench F (shown on Fig. 55 by dashed lines). There was insufficient time to examine these fully and the sections were recorded only by means of measured sketches. Medieval pottery was recovered from one context. All the ditches are tentatively ascribed to the medieval period, though they were not located in the adjacent trenches E and G. Presumably they relate to the same ditch system excavated in the main quarry to the south-west.

Possible Site of Building

A shingle-filled, roughly rectangular feature between 300 and 390mm thick was recorded in Trench B. To determine its extent a trench was cut by machine at right angles and across the main trench. The feature had vertical edges and had been cut from at least the level of the base of the

Fig. 55 Dering Farm. Site Plan

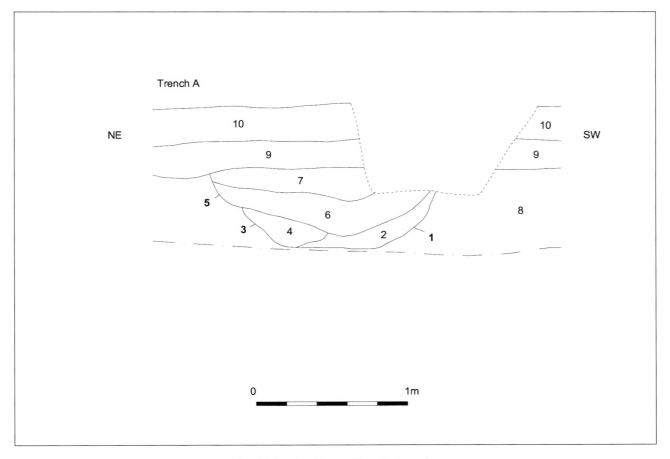

Fig. 56 Dering Farm. Trench A section

topsoil. It measured approximately 4.4m along its north-south axis and 4.2m east-west. A single sherd of medieval pottery was found within the gravel, though this provides inadequate dating evidence.

The shingle-filled feature is tentatively interpreted as the base for a building. Similar shingle 'floors' were subsequently excavated at the main quarry (Lydd 3, Site Jb) where they have been dated to the 14th century. In addition, Anne Reeves has noted elsewhere on Romney Marsh that scatters of shingle are often found in association with post-medieval pottery and has interpreted these as the sites of settlements. It seems possible that the shingle might have been used to provide a dry base within buildings and for their sole plates.

Discussion

The deposits recorded in the excavated trenches allow a preliminary interpretation to be offered for this, and indeed other, areas of the quarry. Dering Farm lies upon a broad shingle ridge, which may be traced over a distance of nearly 8kms, from Jury's Gut coastguard station in the south-west, to nearly as far as Belgar in the north-east (Green 1968, map). The exact date of formation of this feature has yet to be established. The Soil Survey records

a number of short recurves on the north-west side of the shingle ridge, and the isolated shingle 'island' discovered in the north part of Trench F may be a similar formation.

Subsequently, a lagoon appears to have formed in the depression behind the shingle ridge at Dering Farm. In due course this became sufficiently shallow to allow the formation of a peat from ?Phragmites reeds. The shingle ridge was liable to be overtopped by surges from the south-east, which threw shingle into the peat swamp and disturbed the peat, as recorded in Trench E. Evidence of similar surges driving shingle inland were recorded in Scotney Court Pit (Barber 1998a) and were clearly dated by association with archaeological material there to about the 1st century AD.

The human exploitation of this environment during the prehistoric and early Roman period appears to be primarily concerned with the exploitation of marshland resources, including summer grazing and salt production (Cunliffe 1988 and Priestley-Bell in prep). It may be speculated that the areas of burnt flint on the shingle 'island', and on the flank of the shingle bank seen in Trench D, are evidence of temporary camps situated on well drained land and exploiting the resources of the surrounding wetland.

The sections at the new plant site for Lydd Quarry (Lydd 1), at the Scotney Court quarry (Barber 1998a) and at Dering Farm, have all shown an upper mid brown sediment (Fig. 56, Section, Context 8). It has yet to be demonstrated that these deposits are synchronous, but they indicate a period, or periods, before the 12th century when the water level rose and sediment was deposited.

The limited scale of the archaeological work at Dering Farm does not allow any detailed comment to be made on the medieval activity. However, it ably demonstrates that the field system exposed in the main Lydd Quarry excavations to the west extended this far during at least the 13th to 14th centuries, and further domestic occupation and activity sites may be expected in the area.

EXCAVATIONS AT CALDICOTT FARM

Introduction

This 3 hectare site is situated to the north of Lydd, close to Caldicott Farm, and is bounded to the east by Romney Road, to the north by Castilore Farm land, and to the south by the former Pioneer gravel pit (Fig. 2). The geology of the site consists of silty clays overlying ridges of Dungeness shingle. A consent for minerals extraction was granted by Kent County Council. However, due to the archaeologically sensitive nature of the area, Kent County Council attached a condition to this consent in order to ensure that any archaeological remains were adequately recorded prior to destruction.

The initial stage of archaeological investigations was to consist of a watching brief during the removal of topsoil and overburden prior to gravel extraction. ARC Southern commissioned Archaeology South-East (a division of the University College London Field Archaeology Unit) to undertake this work. The watching brief was carried out in accordance with a Specification provided by the Heritage Conservation Group, Kent County Council. The archaeological strategy for the recording of the site was the same as was formulated by John Williams (County Archaeologist for Kent) and Mark Gardiner (former Deputy Director for Archaeology South-East) during the initial excavations (Stage 1) at Lydd Quarry.

The watching brief identified a probably medieval ditch system, together with significant quantities of worked flint and possibly associated hearths. After consultation with ARC and the County Archaeologist, a limited excavation was carried out on selected areas. The on-site work was undertaken during June 1998.

Excavation Results (Fig. 57)

Similar problems were encountered with dating/phasing the excavated ditch system to those already discussed for Lydd Quarry. The stratigraphy is therefore likely to reflect the relationships between the final stages of use of the ditches, rather than provide a relative timetable for their inception.

During the excavation the cuts of the features and their individual fills were assigned separate context numbers. However, for ease of reference principal ditches are referred to by their cut context only, prefixed by 'D', as in D34, D52, *etc.*

The earliest activity on the site was represented by four small probably Bronze Age pits and a section of possible ditch or creek, together with many spreads of fire-cracked flint and three scatters of worked flint. In addition, some Romano-British material was also located, though both these periods are described in detail elsewhere and are not considered further here (Priestley-Bell 2004b).

The Ditch/Field System

Two short sections of narrow ditch (D8, Figs. 57 and 58, S1 and D85, Figs. 57 and 58, S2) 1.4m and 1.9m wide, contained fills 9 and 86 respectively. Both produced large quantities of late 11th to 12th century pottery. In addition, quantities of burnt clay and charcoal were present in Fill 9, and bone and burnt clay in Fill 86. An undated shallow ditch (D17) measuring 2.2m wide with a pebble fill (18) lay *c.* 6m to the north-east of D8 (Fig. 58, S3). Although the south-western terminus of D17 was not identified, the alignment of D8 and D17 suggested that they may have lain either side of an entrance.

While D8 was isolated from other features, D85 was cut by D45 (see below). The location and alignment of D8 and D85 suggests that they represent remnants of an earlier field system (or more probably the initial field system) established along the edge of the principle shingle ridge. The position of D8 and D85 close to Romney Road, and the significant quantities of domestic refuse in their fills, might indicate an association with settlement along the road line. The pottery could either derive from small farmsteads adjacent to the road, or be derived from midden or dung heaps collected for manuring and set back from the road.

Six ditches (Figs. 57 and 58: D2, S4; D4, S5; D34, S6; D45, S7; D52, S8; and D77, S9) formed a broadly rectilinear field system that extended across the western lower-lying half of the site. The location and morphology of undated ditches D4 and D45 (East) suggests that they were perhaps further surviving elements of the earlier ditch/field system represented by D8 and D85. An earlier ditch (104) on the same alignment as D2, was only seen in the section just to the west of D2 (Fig. 58, S4). Although it could not be traced on the surface further to the south, the morphology of D104 suggested that it was a further element of the earliest ditch system.

Ceramic and stratigraphic evidence indicates that D52 was infilled by the late 13th to 14th century, while D2 remained open well into the 14th century. The small quantities of 19th century material from the upper fills (3 and 47) of D2 and D45 respectively, and from the fill (5) of D4, may have been intrusive or perhaps suggested that

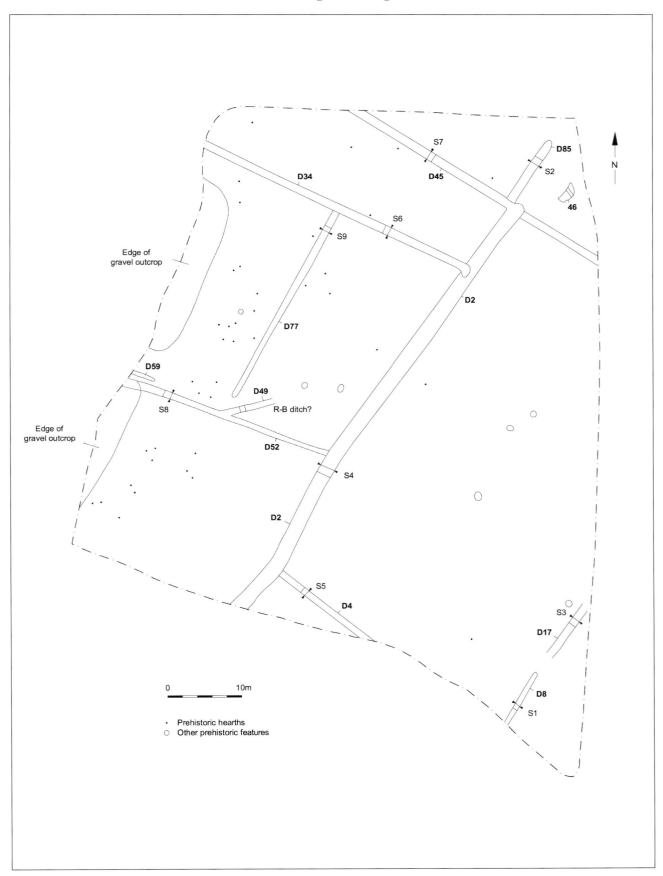

Fig. 57 Caldicott Farm. Site Plan

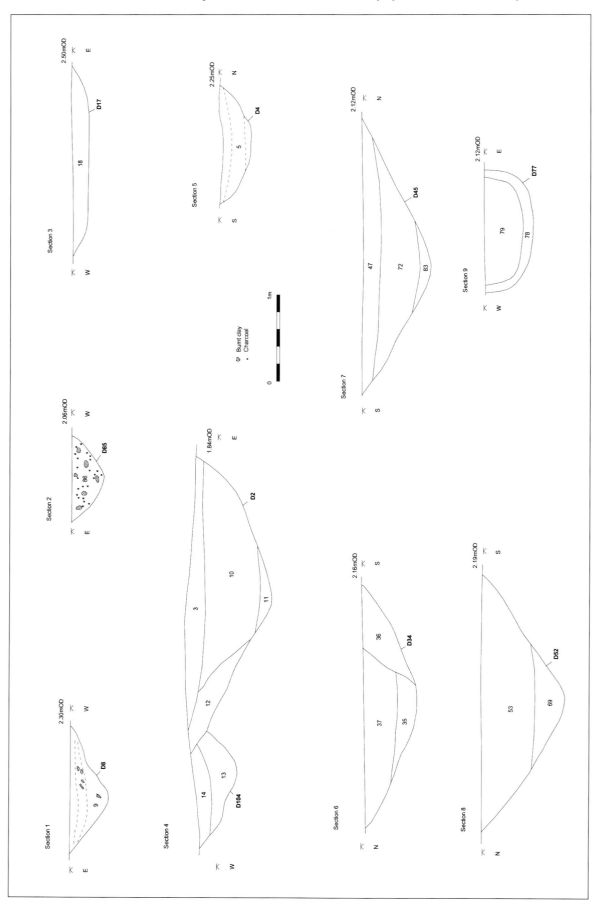

Fig. 58 Caldicott Farm. Ditch sections S1–9

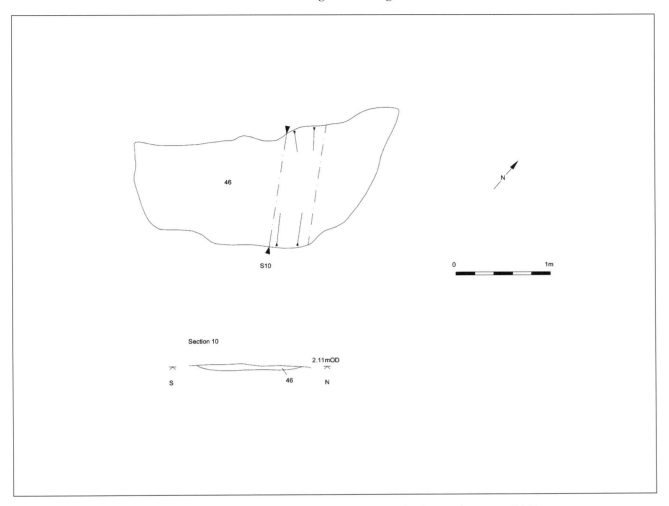

Fig. 59 Caldicott Farm. Activity Area. Context 46: plan and section (S10)

these ditches had remained as earthworks until modern times. However, the primary silting (11) in D2 produced 14th century pottery, perhaps indicating the date that it was last substantially cleaned.

'In plan' machining, following recording, revealed that undated ditch D77 was infilled before D34. It was also clear that the junction of undated ditch D34 and D2 had been cleaned/recut in such a way as to allow D34 to receive a flow from D2 (comparative levelling across the site indicated that D34 drained to the west and D2 drained to the north). Although D2 was partly silted at the time of the cleaning/recutting of the junction, it was obviously still active. Similarly, examination of the junction of D45 (west) with D2 showed that the final cleaning/recut of both ditches had apparently occurred at the same time. It is therefore very likely that D34 and D45 (west) were dependent upon a flow from D2 to prevent silting, and would have become redundant broadly at the same time as D2.

Thus, by the end of the 12th century the earlier (perhaps 11th century) system of shorter narrow ditches seems to have been superseded by a rectilinear system.

This system in turn was probably partly infilled by the late 13th to 14th century, effectively doubling field size from approximately 30 × 60m–60 × 120m. By the end of the 14th century, all the ditches on the site had probably been infilled. This pattern of development is similar to that noted at Lydd Quarry to the south-west.

The Activity Area? (Fig. 59)

An approximately 3 × 6m spread (Context 46, S10) of very dark blackish-grey clay-like silt containing 30% charcoal and 10% burnt clay, produced large quantities of late 11th to 12th century pottery. Although no associated features were identified, Spread 46 must represent the result of a specific activity – possibly a surface midden used for the collection of refuse prior to manuring. Alternatively, the feature may represent the worn floor of a small agricultural building. If this is the case then it is likely to have been a shepherd's hut, however, although not dissimilar to Site B at Lydd Quarry, the present structure is notably smaller.

Conclusions

The first evidence of activity at the site after the Roman period is in the 11th century. At this time a field system appears to have been established in the area of the quarry. At least two ditches are definitely of this early date (Ditches D8 and D85), though it is probable that at least four others were established at the same time (D4, D17, D45 (east) and D104). These ditches were probably primarily intended as boundaries that would have enclosed a single rectangular field measuring *c*. 35 × 60m. This is supported by the complete absence of ditches between D2 (/D104), D4, D45 (east), D8 and D17. As almost all the present site occupies a principal shingle ridge, it is unlikely that any significant form of reclamation would have been necessary; such an area would therefore be among the first to be exploited for agricultural use. Whether this early system extended further west is uncertain due to the later cleaning out of the ditches west of D2.

Considering the field's size, the presence of ditched boundaries and the relatively broad access-way between the apparent termini of ditches D8 and D17, it is likely that the field was intended as a stock enclosure. Despite this, environmental evidence has demonstrated that cereals, predominantly bread wheat with some oats and barley, were probably being cultivated in the vicinity from at least the late 11th century, though some may have been used as fodder.

Ditch D85 was probably an element of an adjacent field immediately to the north – perhaps a second stock enclosure. The probably 11th to 12th century activity area (46) was located in the corner of this second field and perhaps represented a shepherd's (looker's) hut. It is unsurprising that the earliest medieval agricultural activity should occur not only on an area of outcropping gravel, but immediately beside a principal route – the present Romney Road. The clear link between the establishment of all weather routes and the initiation of agricultural activity has already been identified during work at Lydd Quarry.

Ceramic evidence indicates that by the end of the 12th century ditches D8 and D85 had been infilled and the activity area (46) abandoned. Ditches D4, D17 and D45 (east) were also perhaps infilled during this period, while ditch D104 was recut and enlarged to form D2. Although there was no supporting independent evidence, ditches D34, D45, D52 and D77 were probably initially cut in the 13th century, if they do not represent recuts of earlier ditches. The smaller size of the fields in this area suggests that they may have been used for mixed agriculture. It is likely that by the mid 14th century D52 had been infilled, probably together with D77. Ditches D2 and D45 (west) almost certainly continued to be cleaned during this period. At some time after the last cleaning of D2, ditch D34 and its junction with D2 was cleaned/recut. By the end of the 14th century D2, D34 and D45 (west) had been infilled. As at Lydd Quarry the trend towards larger fields was probably the result of both economic and demographic factors.

ARCHAEOLOGICAL DISCOVERIES FROM PIONEER PIT AND ALLEN'S BANK

Between the sites at Lydd Quarry/Dering Farm and Caldicott Farm, two further areas have been subjected to archaeological investigation. Both sites are due north of the town and were/are potentially important to the study of the medieval landscape in that they cover a large area between the more extensively excavated sites described in this volume.

Pioneer Pit was the first site to be investigated archaeologically (Fig. 2 only), though this only occurred well after gravel extraction had commenced. Initially five Bronze Age axe heads were located in 1985 (Needham 1988). Further extraction in 1986 (at TR 0480 2185) encountered a large Romano-British site, some of which was excavated by the Kent Archaeological Rescue Unit from the edge of the water-filled gravel pit (Kent County Council SMR). Despite this no medieval features or finds were made during any of the archaeological works (John Willson, pers. comm., 2003). Although most of the area was not archaeologically monitored, and that which was monitored was under far from ideal conditions, the absence of medieval finds is odd, particularly when considering the finds at Caldicott Farm immediately to the north.

The site at Allen's Bank is proposed for extraction by Bretts, but this has yet to begin. The archaeological works at this site have consisted of an initial geophysical survey, including some basic aerial photographic work (GSP Prospection 1998), followed by a targeted stage 1 trial trench evaluation (John Samuels Consultants 1999). Although the aerial photographs suggested the presence of two small enclosures, the geophysical survey only located one on the ground. However, a dense area of occupation was detected on the southern of two shingle ridges across the site. The occupation seemed to be associated with a number of often curvilinear ditches, some of which appear to form circular/oval enclosures and pits. The morphology of the features appears to suggest a prehistoric or Roman, rather than medieval, date. It is also interesting to note that the ditches do not line up with the north-east/south-west trending ridges usually associated with the medieval field systems to the north-east and south-west. Above these features were a number of linear anomalies, originally thought to be the result of ridge and furrow, but subsequently believed to represent variations in the shingle ridges themselves. With the exception of a couple of natural palaeochannels, the western two thirds of the site produced no signs of any other features of archaeological interest.

The subsequent evaluation tended to confirm the findings of the geophysics in that nothing of archaeological interest was located in the western two thirds of the area, though admittedly only 10 trial trenches were employed across the whole 17 hectare site. The eastern part of the site, where the bulk of the archaeological activity was shown by the geophysics, was not trenched, however, the closest trenches to this area confirmed this activity was probably of Romano-British date. An enclosure to the south of the site was also located but produced no finds. The evaluation failed to locate any proven medieval features or finds (though the southern enclosure could be of this date). Even considering the small sample size given by the trenches, this is odd. In addition the lack of traces of a rectilinear field system in the geophysics results reinforces this negative evidence. As such, the current evidence from Allen's Bank suggests an extensive medieval field system, with associated settlements, was not developed in this area. This echoes the findings from the Pioneer Pit to the north and the general lack of crop-marks in this area on the aerial photographs. It would therefore appear that much of this area was unsuitable (or considered too much work) to reclaim during the medieval period, though some grazing may have taken place. However, it should be remembered that these observations are based on a small sample area of data recovered under poor working conditions, and more extensive stripping at the Allen's Bank site may yet reveal medieval activity.

DENGE WEST QUARRY

Introduction

In 1993 ARC Southern received planning permission from Kent County Council for the extraction of sand and gravel from the area known as Denge West. The consent area was divided into two by the Dungeness Road, with Denge West North lying on the north-east side and Denge West South on the south-west (Fig. 2). Mineral extraction was limited to the fingers of shingle which ran north-west to south-east across the area. Before work commenced at Denge West quarry only very limited investigation had been undertaken in the vicinity. At that time, probably the most important results were those gathered during a watching brief and subsequent excavations by South Eastern Archaeological Services between September and December 1991 on the Brett Gravel plant site at Lydd Quarry (Phase 1). The intensive medieval usage of the marshland is now well recorded, particularly from the earthwork survey and field-walking undertaken by Anne Reeves on the north-east of Romney Marsh (Reeves 1995, 1996 and 1997). Reeves also identified a considerable number of pottery sherds dating from 1250–1400/1450 adjacent to, and south-west of, Boulder Wall Farm in the area of Denge West South (correspondence to Kent County Council). Four occupation areas were identified.

In 1992 ARC commissioned a desk-based report from Jill Eddison of the Romney Marsh Research Trust to identify areas of archaeological and geomorphological interest (Eddison 1992a). Subsequently a geological assessment was undertaken for ARC and the Romney Marsh Research Trust by Dr Andrew Plater (1993) of Liverpool University. The results of both studies may be briefly summarised here.

The gravel complex of Dungeness was laid down during the last 5000 years, growing out eastwards from the old cliff line. However, Denge West quarry includes ridges of a much more recent date that have formed behind the ness structure of Dungeness. At Denge West, north-west trending shingle ridges were laid down upon fine-grained sediments, while the spaces between the ridges were eventually infilled by further fine-grained sediments, possibly as late as the Middle Ages.

Sedimentological investigations have suggested that the lower fine-grain sediments were laid down in a uniform and widespread phase of deposition, probably in a lower marsh or inter-tidal mudflat environment. The shingle ridges were emplaced in a much higher energy environment. The shingle continued to be reworked as the upper fine-grain sediments were laid down, producing feather edges of shingle within the upper laminated facies. These upper fine deposits may have formed through inter-tidal sedimentation in a back-barrier environment when the area remained open on the north and north-west to the sea. Balls of peat are found within this deposit, but are clearly redeposited. There is evidence of diachroneity in the stratigraphy of Denge West; the deposits to the north-east are later than those to the south-west. As the ness developed to the south with the consequent movement of the shingle foreland, the interface between the shingle and marsh moved eastwards. A detailed chronology of these processes has not yet been established.

Documentary evidence indicates that Denge Marsh was certainly occupied in the 10th century and probably as early as the 8th century. The main features of interest within the area of the quarry were the sites of medieval settlement, two routeways and a pattern of drainage ditches. The latter divided the area of finer grained sediment into smaller rectangular closes, which are similar to earthwork features which have been recorded elsewhere on Romney Marsh (Reeves 1997).

Methodology

Denge West North (Fig. 60)

An examination of the site in January 1994 suggested that there were significant differences between Denge West North and other areas previously examined, such as Lydd Quarry. Land-use is determined by the presence of shingle ridges, which have little soil cover and are almost uncultivatable. The study of aerial photographs had revealed a ditch system on the finer-grained sediments between the shingle ridges. It was hypothesised that the likely position of settlements would have been on, or very close to, the shingle ridges where the land was driest.

A specification for the archaeological work was prepared by Kent County Council for Denge West

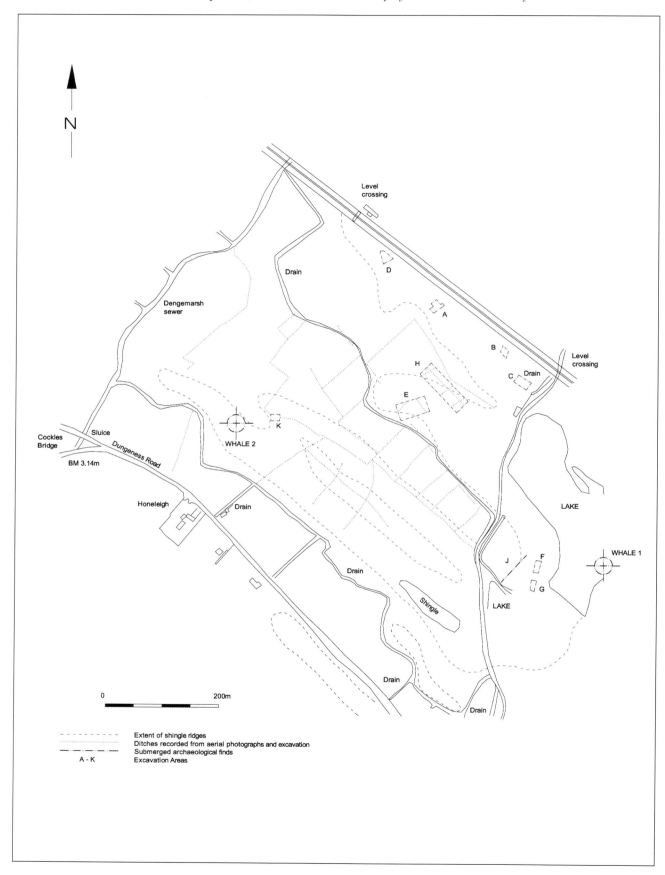

Fig. 60 Denge West North. Site plan showing investigated areas A–K and whales

North (Phases 1 to 4), but this was modified to respond to the working methods and to allow full recording or preservation *in situ* of the archaeological remains. The methods to be adopted during the gravel extraction process were agreed in April 1994 after discussion between KCC, ARC and SEAS.

The aims of the fieldwork were defined as 'to locate and record any Saxon and medieval occupations and field boundaries such as may be present' in Denge West North and 'to aid further understanding of the historical relationships between the higher/drier and lower/wetter areas'.

The main archaeological response to the gravel extraction was a watching brief during the removal of the minerals. Limited excavation was also undertaken. The fieldwork began on 1st June 1994 and continued intermittently until mid May 1995.

The gravel was extracted by (1) stripping the margins of the shingle ridge of topsoil using a D6 Bulldozer. (2) The area designated for the storage of topsoil and subsoil was stripped of topsoil using a D6 Bulldozer. (3) Topsoil from the stripped margins of the shingle ridge was removed to the adjacent storage area using a 360 degree excavator and dump trucks. (4) The 'top beach' – that part of the shingle ridge above the water table – was excavated and removed to the processing plant using a 360 and dump trucks. (5) Test holes were excavated and backfilled using a 360 to ascertain the depth of gravel where there was some uncertainty. These allowed a useful insight into the localised stratigraphy.

Stages 1 and 2 were fully monitored. The topsoil was examined for finds and the subsoil for archaeological features. Where features required to be more fully exposed, or where large quantities of spoil hindered excavation, ARC kindly allowed the use of a bulldozer to remove soil. Stage 3 was monitored only in the areas that had previously produced significant quantities of finds in the disturbed topsoil. Only those parts of the top beach immediately adjacent to the areas producing finds and/or features were examined during Stage 4. During Stage 5 the exposed sections were recorded and the excavated material from the test hole was examined prior to back-filling. The extraction of gravel from below the water-table was not monitored, but staff at the quarry kept a careful note of any finds. Even when finds were located below the water-table it was not possible to establish their context with great certainty.

ARC made available plant to clean up areas where archaeological remains had been found or were suspected. Two interim reports on this work were produced (Priestley-Bell 1994; Priestley-Bell and Gardiner 1994).

Denge West South (Fig. 61)

A review of the results of the archaeological work was held in July 1995 following the completion of the work at Denge West North. It was agreed with Kent County Council, as the planning authority, that the extraction work at Denge West South should be preceded by more detailed archaeological survey work.

As a result a pre-extraction survey was undertaken during July and August 1995 (Gardiner 1995a). This consisted of four elements: a walk-over and rapid field-walking survey of the area of gravel extraction; a trial use of geophysical survey in selected areas to determine the best method and its effectiveness; an aerial survey and plot of aerial photographs; and an assessment of the documentary and cartographic potential of the area of Denge West South.

The field-walking and walk-over surveys produced negative results at this time due to land-use; no areas within the proposed quarry were available for field-walking, and any earthworks in most areas were screened by tall crop growth. A systematic programme of field-walking was duly planned for when the land became available. The geophysical survey, undertaken by Stratascan, examined two areas, one of which proved unsuitable for survey due to the nature of the gravel substrate. The magnetometer revealed only two weak anomalies, one of which was also visible on the ground as a band of greener vegetation. The resistivity survey revealed more features, but was limited by the presence of the sub-surface shingle on the south-west side which produced very high resistance. A series of parallel lines were identified, which were interpreted as modern land drains, and a curved line of high resistance was also detected. Full details of the survey are housed with the archive.

Aerial photographs were taken by Air Photo Services of Cambridge on 19th July and revealed a series of ditches showing as cropmarks. The results have been digitally plotted (Fig. 61) and the evidence of that flight has been augmented by two aerial photographs held by the RSPB Bird Sanctuary at Denge Marsh. The results of the 1995 aerial photographic work are held in the archive and may be briefly summarised. Four main feature types were identified on the aerial photographs: crop-marked ditches, possible ditches, relic stream channels (distinguished by their irregular courses and less well-defined edges), and possible building foundations. Other features which were also picked up from the examination of photographs were the gravel ridges themselves, possible areas of quarrying, and areas of waterlogged deeper soil.

The purpose of the assessment of the documentary evidence was to determine the quality of the surviving material, its location and its potential for more detailed investigation. Full details of this work are housed with the archive, however, the documentary work in the current volume (Sweetinburgh, see section 1) supersedes this earlier work.

After a meeting with KCC in October 1995 it was decided to undertake a systematic field-walking survey of the area once the land became available, in an attempt to locate settlement sites. Pottery in a number of locations within the site had already been reported by Anne Reeves (letter dated 7th August 1992 to KCC) and the results

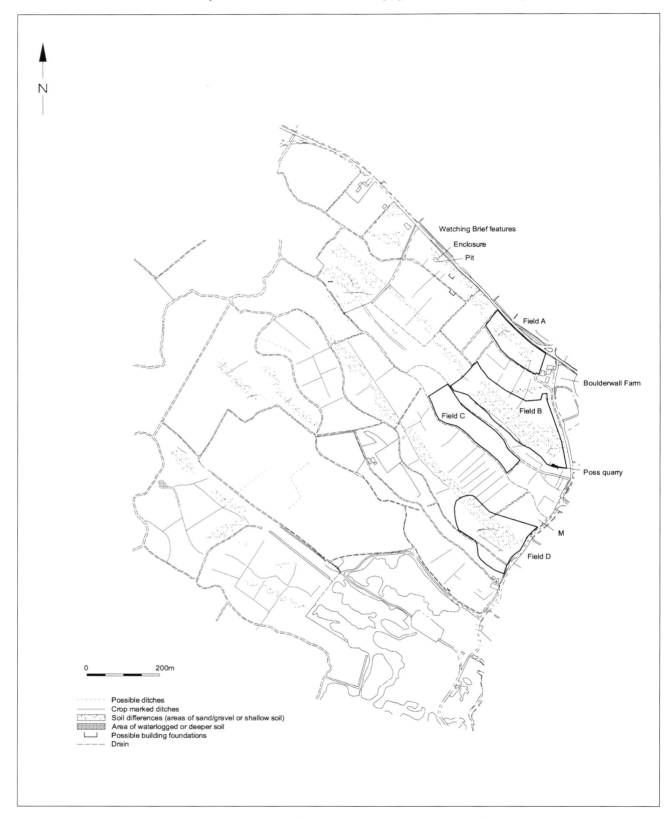

*Fig. 61 Denge West South. Site plan showing investigated areas
(Field-walking Fields A–D and watching brief discoveries)*

of the August survey suggested more archaeological remains were to be expected. The systematic survey was undertaken in four fields/part fields, selected on the basis of the earlier work (Fig. 61, Fields/Areas A–D). The survey was undertaken during February 1996 (Stevens 1996). Each field was divided into 20 × 10m areas based on the National Grid. The areas were then individually numbered and prefixed with the field letter (A–D). Each area was walked in four transects at 2m intervals with all visible artefacts being collected. The full results are housed with the archive, but the key findings are integrated below and four of the key plot-outs are shown in Figs. 64 and 65.

The two main concentrations of archaeological material noted by the field-walking survey (Fields A and B) were subsequently avoided by the gravel extraction and thus the sites preserved *in situ*. The remainder of the area at Denge West South was subjected to an intermittent watching brief. A Specification for this work was provided by KCC. The watching brief, which was maintained during 1997, located little of archaeological interest (Priestley-Bell 1998). However, two concentrations of material were located: Area M in Field D and a findspot to the north of Field A (Fig. 61). The latter proved the most important as it included archaeological features as well as finds. These features were preserved *in situ* with the kind co-operation of ARC. A later watching brief close to Boulderwall Farm yielded no finds (Griffin 1999).

The post-excavation analysis on both Denge West North and South, together with the additional historical research, was funded by an ALSF grant awarded by English Heritage in January 2003. ARC funded all fieldwork elements of the project.

Results

The character and usefulness of the archaeological remains uncovered at Denge West quarry is very varied, ranging from unstratified concentrations of artefacts from the topsoil with no associated features, to stratified pottery assemblage within a well-defined feature. In view of this, more weight has been given to direct evidence, while unsupported indirect evidence has been treated with caution.

In addition to the 'Early Discoveries' described below, a number of areas of archaeological interest were located during the watching brief at Denge West North. These were numbered Areas A to K. Letter I was not allocated. The location of the areas of interest are shown on Fig. 60. More remains were undoubtedly present but the location and excavation of features on the shingle proved very difficult, particularly when no/low quantities of finds were involved. Other features identifiable from aerial photographs have also been indicated on the plan.

Early Discoveries at Denge West North

The Whales

In 1994 during gravel extraction, the fragmented skull of a whale (Whale 1, Fig. 60) was recovered from within a well-defined unit of black sandy silt that lay below the clast-supported beach gravels. Tree trunks and smaller fragments of wood, detrital peat and occasional disarticulated mammal bones are habitually recovered from the same stratum (Ken Cooke pers. comm.). In 1995, a further significant quantity of whale remains, probably from a single individual (Whale 2, Fig. 60), was recovered from the same stratigraphic context as Whale 1. The earlier geomorphological work (Plater 1993) has identified this stratum as representing an inter-tidal flat, initially formed by sediment from the Romney Marsh catchment. Analysis of the Whale 1 remains, and subsequent comparison with the Whale 2 remains, indicated that both individuals probably belonged to the species northern or southern Right Whale (*Eubalaena glacialis* or *E. australis* respectively) (Gardiner *et al.*, 1998). Whale 1 and Whale 2 remains bore cut marks indicating that both animals had been systematically de-fleshed, probably with an edged, heavy metal implement.

Bones from the two whales were submitted for radiocarbon dating and both produced very similar calibrated dates falling between the mid 9th and mid 11th centuries (Gardiner *et al.*, 1998). In conclusion, the whales described here were probably either stranded in the shallows of the inter-tidal zone, or washed ashore as carcasses. Whichever the case, the butchery marks on both individuals were probably the result of opportunistic exploitation by the local population. This is the first unequivocal archaeological evidence for the exploitation of whale meat in Anglo-Saxon England.

Area D: Waterlogged Wood

A quantity of water-logged wood was exposed during the excavation of a test hole by a mechanical excavator (Fig. 60, D). Three fragments of the wood showed evidence of human wood-working, which included radially-splitting and axe (or adze) shaped pieces. The height of the water-table makes it difficult to give an accurate depth for the deposit from which the waterlogged material originated. However, the driver of the mechanical excavator estimated the deposit to be between 1 and 2m below the water table (between 2.5 and 3.5m below ground surface). From the material still adhering to the wood fragments, they seem to have come from a mid grey sandy silt with occasional peaty layers containing plant and humic material. The sediment description and the estimated depth fit very closely with that given for a deposit encountered in Borehole D11AD (Plater 1993, 32). Plater proposes that

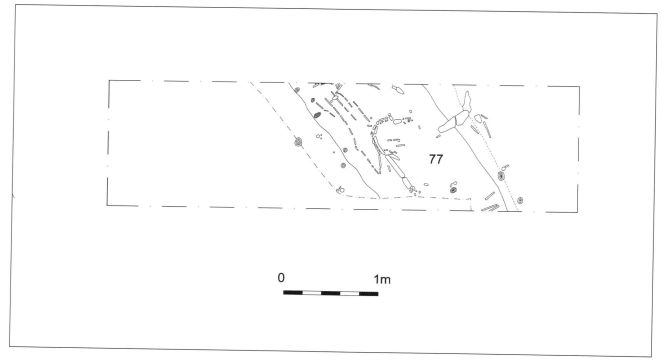

Fig. 62 Denge West North: plan of Area J – Fish trap

the deposit described in Borehole DM11AD was laid down in an inter-tidal environment, and even though the deposit producing the wood in Area D may not be contemporaneous, the mechanics of deposition may have been similar.

Area J: Fish Trap? (Figs. 60 and 62)

A linear wooden structure was found during mechanical excavation of a test hole to determine the depths of the gravel deposits. The structure comprised large quantities of wood laid parallel between timber uprights. It was traced by hand augering for a distance of more than 60m. The structure ran between two shingle ridges and seems to have enclosed a triangular area of low-lying ground. It may have been built as a trap for fish which entered the area during periods of high tide and were caught behind it as the tide receded. It seems less likely that it was a trackway, as the gravel ridge immediately to the south would have provided a convenient crossing point. This feature was preserved *in situ* with the co-operation of ARC.

The Field System (Denge West North and South)

All ditches relating to the field system and features associated with the contemporary occupation were cut into both the shingle ridges and the finer grained sediments between the ridges. As the earliest of these features is likely to be of early 13th century date, the shingle and subsequent fine grained deposits must have been in place by this date.

Sources of Evidence

Evidence for the morphology, and to a lesser degree the evolution, of the ditched field system has been gathered from three principal sources: aerial photography, archaeological mapping and excavation.

Aerial photographs were taken by Air Photo Services of Cambridge and the results digitally plotted onto a base map (Figs. 60 and 61). The AP survey identified a pattern of ditches showing as cropmarks. The evidence gathered from that flight has been augmented by two aerial photographs held by the RSPB Bird Sanctuary at Denge Marsh. Archaeological mapping of ditches revealed after topsoil stripping has added further elements of the ditch system identified in aerial photographs. Sample excavation by the cutting of ditch sections has produced limited dating evidence for the infilling of some of the field ditches.

Chronology and Morphology

The earliest activity in the area was likely to have been the establishment of permanent routes, and it is unsurprising that the first identified agricultural activity was located immediately beside one of these routes; in this case, Areas E and H at Denge North lay close to the modern footpath to the level crossing that represents the route of the ancient track. Based on the infilling dates indicated by ceramics, the earliest ditches at Denge North probably date from the early 13th century. Similarly at Denge South, concentrations of 13th century pottery were located beside ancient routes. These tracks may have initially been established as access to the shore for fishermen, or may have been droveways that served a regime of pastoral transhumance.

The small rectilinear ditch system recorded in Areas E and H probably represented part of the earliest field system, and comprised at least six ditches typically enclosing fields measuring *c.* 60 × 40m. A further ditch in Area A was probably part of the same system. Natural and modified creeks were likely to have been the first elements of the earliest field system; this is best illustrated in the aerial photographs of the south-west area of Denge South. The fields were generally orientated with their long axis at right angles to the line of the principal shingle ridges that here trend south-westwards; the crests of the ridges probably provided all-weather access to the plots. Perhaps unexpectedly, the ditches were cut deeply into the shingle ridges, with many crossing the ridges entirely. This perhaps indicates that the barrier function of the ditches was at least as important as drainage, suggesting that the plots were used for stock as well as arable farming.

Some of the small fields immediately to the south-east of Area E were of similar dimensions and orientation, and were perhaps further elements of the earliest ditch system. At Denge South, although the field sizes were more varied, the general pattern was similar and the absence of many of these ditches on 19th century maps suggests that they are probably medieval in origin, though their exact infilling date is uncertain. At Denge North ceramic evidence suggests that many elements of this system had been infilled by the late 13th century. It is therefore likely that by the early 14th century the smaller fields had been filled in to form a larger rectilinear system in the same orientation, but typically measuring *c.* 100 × 70m. The later field system was likely to have survived into the 15th century, but had probably fallen into disuse by the mid 16th century. This change in land use perhaps reflects a local reversion to pastoralism, or may be part of the more general pattern of landscape evolution that has been identified at Lydd Quarry.

The Occupation Sites/Activity Areas

Denge West North (Fig. 60)

Area A

Within Area A the sites of two possible buildings were found. The first building was indicated by four post-holes (Contexts 14, 16, 35 and 37) which formed a right-angle, probably representing the corner of a building. Context 9 may be associated with the postulated structure and perhaps represented the cut of a shingle filled feature which served as the building floor. A second building was perhaps indicated by a dark-finds rich layer within the shingle ridge (26, 29), although this might be interpreted as the site of a midden. A large quantity of associated pottery was recovered, dating from the 13th to mid 16th centuries.

Area B

The topsoil produced quantities of unstratified pottery dating from the 14th to mid 16th centuries. Other unstratified finds included building material, tile, bone, shell, bronze, iron and a fragment of stone mortar. No features were identified either within the topsoil or in the subsoil, although the density of the spread of material suggests an associated occupation site or activity area, possibly for the collection of refuse for manuring.

Area C

The topsoil produced quantities of unstratified pottery dating from the 14th to mid 16th centuries. Other finds included building material, tile, bone, and shell. Although further stripping was carried out under archaeological supervision by a D6 bulldozer, no archaeological features were identified either within the topsoil or in the subsoil.

A building, perhaps associated with a sheepfold recorded nearby, is recalled as having stood on or near Area C as late as 40 years ago (pers. comm. Mr. Ken Cooke). It is therefore possible that some part of the unstratified material collected originated from the site of this building. Alternatively, the area is immediately beside a track that is shown on Poker's 1617 map of Romney Marsh as an established east-west route; the material collected may therefore represent a midden associated with settlement or activity alongside this ancient roadway.

Area E

Two short ditches were recorded and sectioned in three places. A considerable quantity of pottery dating from the 13th to mid 16th centuries was recovered from one of the sections, together with a small quantity of 17th century material. The ditches appeared to be elements of a rectilinear field system identified from aerial photographs.

Area F (Fig. 63)

A concentration of 15th to mid 16th century pottery was recorded on the south-east side of the extraction area, together with a small quantity of 13th, 14th and 17th century material. A concentration of metal artefacts and building material, together with an L-shaped slot (Context 72) suggested that this was the site of a structure. Features in the area were very difficult to define and ARC Ltd. made available a JCB 3CX fitted with a ditching bucket. Further clearance of the area by the JCB did not improve the definition of the features. A section was cut across the spread of material (Context 68) and a limited further spread (Context 69) investigated. Limited excavation was undertaken recording two post-holes (Contexts 73 and 75) and surface finds were collected.

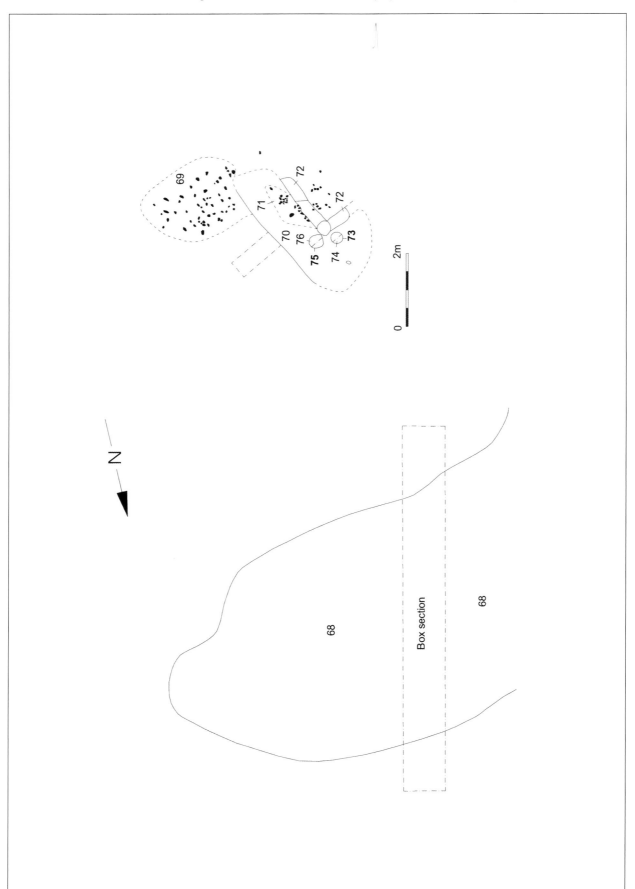

Fig. 63 Denge West North: plan of Area F

Area G

A significant quantity of finds dating predominantly to the 18th and 19th centuries were recovered from the topsoil before and during stripping. A small quantity of 14th, 15th and 16th century material was also present. It is possible that this area represented the site of a midden.

Chronology and Morphology

With the exception of the whale bones and deeply buried timber features, no 12th century or earlier remains were recorded. Although an overview of the ceramic evidence from Denge North quarry might therefore suggest that the area was first settled in the 13th century, in Areas E and H (Fig. 60) later 13th century pottery was associated with the last phases of disuse of a number of drainage/field ditches. It is therefore possible that some elements of the ditch system were already in place at the beginning of the 13th century, and perhaps seasonal agricultural exploitation of the area was underway. If this were the case, some or all of the unstratified and disassociated concentrations of artefacts and ecofacts may represent the sites of dung heaps or middens. Alternatively, the concentrations of material may be directly associated with occupation; four post-holes and associated features identified in Area A may represent the site of a small 13th century building.

Whichever the case, it seems likely that semi-permanent or permanent settlement did not take place until the 13th century. Once Areas A and E became utilised, they continued to be used through to the mid 16th century. However, after the 13th century infilling of the ditch system in Area H, activity in the immediate area appears to have ceased. Areas B and C did not become utilised until the 14th century, continuing in use until the mid 16th century, and perhaps represent a shift in activity from Area H. Although Area F was perhaps the site of low level activity in the 13th and 14th centuries, its period of most intense use was in the 15th and early 16th centuries when it may have been a domestic occupation site. Area G produced some of the latest material, and probably saw its main utilisation in the 18th and 19th centuries. A more detailed consideration of the dating is given in the pottery report.

Denge West South (Fig. 61)

The work at Denge West South uncovered fewer archaeological remains due to the detailed pre-extraction survey and field-walking programme allowing the most sensitive areas to be left *in situ*.

Field-walking Survey (Figs. 64 and 65)

The field-walking uncovered two notable concentrations of pottery and ceramic building material. The largest consisted of a spread of late 14th to early 16th century material adjacent to the Dungeness Road, to the north of Boulderwall Farm (Field A). To the south, adjacent

to a track, a further concentration of finds was made (Field B) dating to the 15th and 16th centuries. Both of these apparent occupation sites corresponded with areas highlighted during the pre-extraction survey; both were avoided by gravel extraction operations and as a result were preserved *in situ*. A general scatter of pottery from manuring was located across the whole area.

Watching Brief

A *c.* 15 × 10m ditched enclosure was recorded to the north-west of Field A of the field-walking survey. A 2m wide interruption located at the centre of its north-eastern side was likely to have been the entrance, facing the present Dungeness Road. An apparently associated 'rubbish' pit produced 14th to mid 16th century pottery. Although no structural elements were identified within the enclosure, it is likely that it was the site of a small building, perhaps a dwelling; possible foundations were noted close by on the aerial photographs (Fig. 61). The enclosure was preserved *in situ* with the kind co-operation of ARC. A small scatter of pottery was also recovered from the northern part of Field D (Area M).

Chronology and Morphology

The pottery from Denge West South would suggest manuring of fields, but not occupation, was taking place during the 13th century at least in Fields A, B and D. During the 14th century, probably around the middle of the century, the first occupation may have started in Field A. Some earlier outlying activity in the northern part of Field D may relate to small scale temporary activity, perhaps associated with harvesting or looking after animals. Subsequently, in the 15th and first half of the 16th centuries, the settlement in Field A intensified and expanded, with a further activity area/occupation site being established in Field B. The small enclosure identified during the watching brief to the north of Field A dated to the same period. Settlement appears to have continued at a less intense rate in both Fields A and B until perhaps the early to mid 17th century, by which time the investigated fields were once again subjected to only manuring, probably from Boulderwall Farm.

Discussion

Many of the features located related to a ditched field system which had been previously noted running across the 'troughs' between the shingle ridges on aerial photographs. This field system had initially been composed of small rectangular fields which had later been infilled to create larger fields. Although the evidence is slight, it is likely that elements of the field system were in place by the early 13th century. Ceramic evidence from Area H suggests that the earlier ditched field system was infilled by the late 13th century. A similar pattern of evolution has been noted at Lydd Quarry.

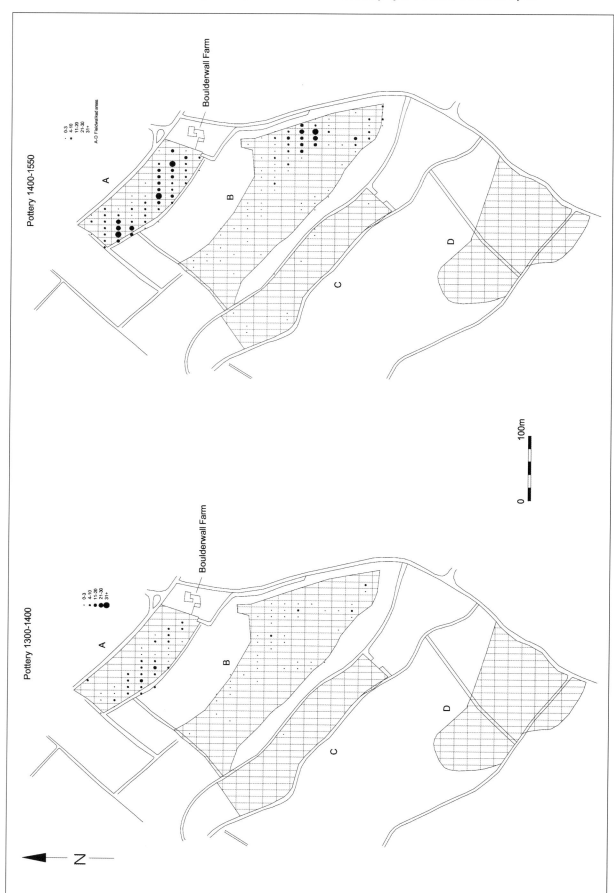

Fig. 64 Denge West South: Field-walking plots for 14th and 15th to mid 16th century pottery

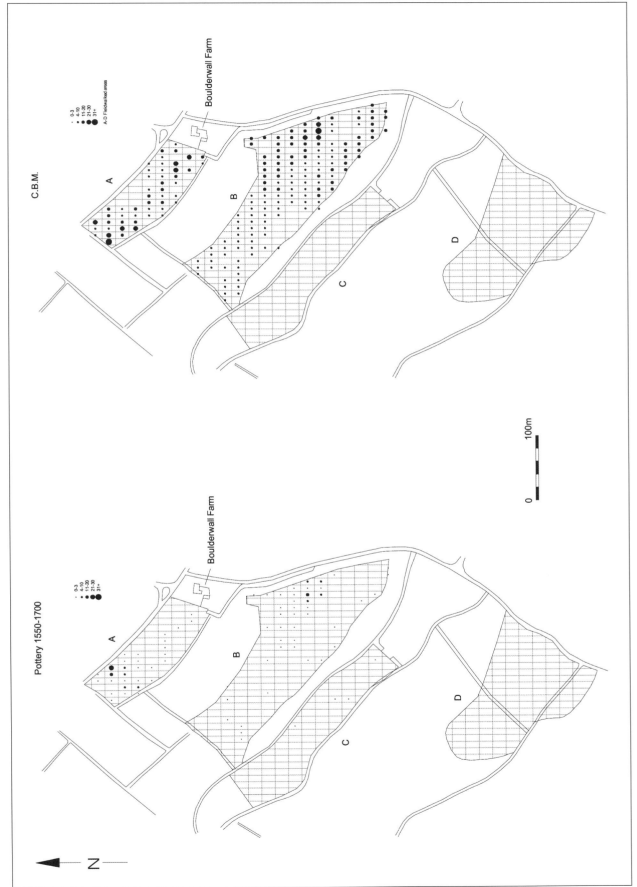

Fig. 65 Denge West South: Field-walking plots for post-medieval pottery and ceramic building materials

Two areas of possible settlement were identified at Denge North (Areas A and F) along with other areas of activity (*i.e.*, Area E). Area A seemed to have been relatively long-lived, beginning in the 13th century and continuing into the 15th century, apparently surviving the late 13th century demise of the ditched field system in nearby Area H. This perhaps suggests that the settlement/activity at Area A was not, or only partly, dependent upon agriculture. It is therefore possible that the settlement at Area A was associated with a small fishing community. Alternatively, the activity at Area A may have supplemented the diet by undertaking a mixed agricultural regime on the small area of better soil around it.

The main period of settlement at Area F seems to have been from the 15th to mid 16th centuries. Although the occupation of this area may have been associated with agriculture, finds evidence perhaps suggests that fishing and the collection of shellfish may have been more important. A large quantity of shells were recovered, together with fish hooks, a possible harpoon blade and large nails and clench bolts, possibly from boats (see metalwork report below). Green postulates that the aforementioned marine inlet would still have been open at this time, indicating that there would have been easy access to a shoreline during the settlement period Area F. The occupation at Area F may therefore represent a settlement shift from Area A by the postulated small fishing community. Such communities are known to have existed on the Dungeness Foreland from documentary sources (Gardiner 1996).

At Denge South, although there is evidence of low level agricultural activity in the 13th century, semi-permanent or permanent occupation does not appear to begin until the 14th century.

It is significant that four of the probable settlement sites (Area F (Denge North) and Fields A and B and the enclosure (Denge South)) and three artefact concentrations (Areas B, C and G (Denge North)) all lie beside two long-lived routeways: Field A and the nearby enclosure lie beside the modern Dungeness Road, while Areas B, C, F and G and Field B lie beside what is now

a footpath running south-westwards from Boulderwall Farm and north-eastwards over a level crossing.

These two principal routeways, together with a third (the modern Dengemarsh Road), can all be readily identified on Poker's 1617 map and also on an unnamed Elizabethan map at the British Library (Bendall 1995). Dungeness Road was called Ness Lane in the 17th and 18th centuries. The *c.* 1810 analysis suggests that there were probably a number of farms on this road, and two possible settlement sites were identified in the aerial survey near to Dungeness Road (Gardiner 1995a). The footpath separated the area called Outlands to the south-east from arable and pasture to the north-east. It too ran between a series of farmsteads. Dengemarsh Road linked Hart's Farm and Brickwall Farm and passed close to Dengemarsh Court Farm. The course of these roads was in part constrained by ditches and bridges, but elsewhere the tithe (parish) map suggests that they passed through fields without a well defined course. The roads were unmetalled and used the underlying shingle for their surface.

It therefore seems likely that all-weather routes were established before any semi-permanent or permanent occupation. This general pattern of settlement has already been recognised at Lydd Quarry, where a significant number of settlement sites have been identified as having been established beside pre-existing routeways. The presence of an existing route would be particularly important if the settlement was dependent upon agriculture, where stock and wheeled vehicles might require regular access.

However, permanent routes would not have been so important to the postulated small fishing community represented at Area A, *c.* 250m north-west of the footpath. Thus, the first activity at Denge North was probably associated with fishing, perhaps beginning in the late 12th century, but almost certainly underway by the early 13th century. The probably seasonal track to the shoreline represented by the modern footpath eventually became established as a permanent route, opening up the area to agriculture and semi-permanent or permanent occupation.

3

The Finds and Environmental Material

THE POTTERY *by Luke Barber*

Introduction

The excavations at Lydd, Denge West and Caldicott Farm Quarries have been the first medieval rural domestic sites to be excavated on the Marsh. The pottery from these sites is therefore important as it gives the first insight into the range of products present and thus an indication of trade and distribution in this apparently isolated area. The vast majority of the pottery covered by this analysis originates from the various phases of excavation undertaken at Lydd Quarry. As a result the pottery from this site was used to create the fabric series for the area, which was subsequently complemented by the assemblages from the other two quarries. The majority of this report concentrates on the Lydd assemblage, but overviews on the material from Denge West and Caldicott Farm are also given in their own sections within this report (see below).

Lydd Quarry

The Character of the Assemblage

The various phases of excavations at the quarry produced markedly differently sized assemblages. These, excluding the prehistoric and Romano-British sherds, are characterised in Table 1.

Although some phases of excavation produced prehistoric (Lydd 4 and 11) and Roman (Lydds 1, 2, 4, 7, 9 and 11) sherds, sometimes residual in medieval contexts, these are detailed in the archive reports and are not considered further here (Barber 1996a, Gibson 2002, Lyne 2002 and Lyne 2004). As can be seen from Table 1 the assemblages from the different phases are very variable in size, but they also contain a variable chronological range.

Fieldwork Phase	Total number of sherds	Total weight of sherds (grams)	Total number of contexts with pottery	Largest single context group
1	3,626	50.7kg	199	604/11,622g Context 151 – 13th century
2	4,177	33.8kg	133	520/6,620g Context 2400 – 13th century
3	3,142	28kg	102	937/9,846g Context 3180 – 14th century
4	40	282g	4	32/177g Context 4003 – early 13th century
5/6	2,270	29.1kg	110	244/5,672g Context 5138 – early 18th century
7	139	1.4kg	17	54/528g
8	20	1.2kg	7	-
9	63	360g	8	32/156g
10	216	2.3kg	22	46/548g
11	3	12g	1	3/12g
Total	13,696	147.2kg	603	-

Table 1. Medieval and post-medieval pottery assemblages from Lydd Quarry, Excavation Phases 1–11

Lydd 1 and 2

At Lydd 1 and 2 the majority of material was of 13th century date, though 12th, 14th, 15th and 16th century material was also present in small quantities. Most contexts only produced small amounts of pottery, often not enough to trust the spot-date with certainty, given the possible high degree of residuality, particularly in the field ditches. For example, at Lydd 1, of the 199 contexts containing pottery only 38 produced over 15 sherds and of those only five produced over 100 sherds. Similarly, at Lydd 2, of the 133 contexts containing pottery only 33 produced assemblages of 15 or more sherds and of those only seven contained more than 100 sherds.

Lydd 3

As with Lydds 1 and 2, most contexts only produced small quantities of pottery; only 26 contexts contained over 20 sherds and of these only eight produced assemblages of 100 or more sherds. The ceramics from this phase of the excavations are predominantly of the 14th century (*c.* 1300–75/1400) (Areas A, B and C). However, a number of small groups are present, which appear to relate to both earlier and later activity. In Area D (Site C) mid 12th to early 13th century material appears to dominate (*c.* 1125–1225), while later 13th century material (*c.* 1250–1300/1325) was located on the western side of Area B (Site Ja). Some 15th to very early 16th century material (*c.* 1375/1400–1500/1525) was also recovered from Areas B and C (Site Jb), though this may relate to the disposal of refuse from another site by this date.

Lydd 4

The assemblage from Lydd 4, although mainly of Roman date, contained a small quantity of medieval material. This was present in very small groups from both ditches and other cut features. The majority (32 sherds) were from a layer within the 'building' at Site B (Context 4003), though no rim or other diagnostic sherds are present.

Lydd 5/6

The assemblage from Lydd 5/6 is mixed, both in condition and date. Individual context groups are generally small; of the 110 contexts containing pottery only 27 contexts contain over 20 sherds and of these only four produced assemblages of 100 or more sherds. The ceramics from this phase of the excavations cover a much wider chronological range than those from the Lydd 2 and 3 assemblages. The pottery from Site G (Area A) is generally earlier and seems to be dominated by material of the 13th (and to a lesser extent) early 14th centuries (*c.* 1225–1300/1325). However, the majority of material from Site L (Area B), together with a number of assemblages from the infilling of ditches in the vicinity, are of 15th to early 16th century date. With the exception of Context 3151 from Lydd 3, this was the first time reasonable amounts of 15th century material had been

recovered from the quarry. There was only one very small early (12th century) group, however, the Phase 5/6 excavations did produced the first large group of true post-medieval pottery from the quarry – Context 5138, though this was an isolated assemblage. Only very few sherds of Romano-British pottery were recovered from this phase of excavations, all of which were residual.

Lydd 7

The Lydd 7 medieval pottery assemblage (together with the Romano-British assemblage) was analysed in full by Kathryn Blythe as part of an MA dissertation, and briefly re-examined for the current report by the present author. A copy of Blythe's dissertation report, together with thin section slides of some of the fabrics, is housed with the archive (Blythe 1998). The assemblage from this phase comes predominantly from ditch fills associated with the field system. The material, although generally being of a small average sherd size, is relatively unabraded. The assemblage spans the late 12th to early 16th centuries, though the majority relates to the 13th and 14th centuries. No large groups are present in the assemblage.

Lydd 8

The small assemblage of 20 sherds from this phase consisted entirely of 19th to 20th century material (transfer-printed wares and brown glazed earthenwares), which was discarded at the time of assessment.

Lydd 9

The 63 sherds from this phase are all of a generally small size and most show signs of abrasion. With the exception of a single post-medieval sherd, the assemblage is confined to the 13th and 14th centuries. All of the material relates to the infilling of medieval field ditches. The largest assemblage is of 14th century date but is dominated by small abraded sherds (Context 9034, Ditch 9033).

Lydd 10

The 216 sherds of pottery from this phase are of more interest in that most are associated with the excavated structure at Site A. The majority of the assemblage from this area is dated to between the late 12th and early 13th centuries (14 out of 22 contexts) and is discussed under the 12th to early 13th century pottery groups. Only three context groups can definitely be shown to contain material of mid 13th to mid 14th century date. One of these (A79, terminal of Ditch A78) produced an assemblage of 35 sherds, including an F3h Rye jug with an internal white slip on the interior of its rim/neck.

Lydd 11

The three medieval sherds from this phase of excavations all came from Context B44. All are small F2b sherds and could be intrusive. The presence of these sherds to the west of the Burnthouse Wall is interesting. However, the total absence of other medieval material in this area suggests these sherds may have derived from 13th century consolidation or repair work on the wall, or have been transported by post-medieval activity rather than relating to medieval agricultural activity to the west of it.

The pottery is generally in good condition and comes from closed contexts, both ditch and pit fills. Intrusive and residual material is surprisingly rare among the majority of assemblages, although where present it is usually the residual element which is the easier to isolate with certainty. Some groups are more mixed but generally these have not been studied in detail and are omitted from the current report.

Background to Analysis

The analysis of the Lydd pottery has been an intermittent but on-going project since 1991. The pottery from each stage has added to the growing body of data for the site, and dating and interpretations have changed as more material is collected. This has resulted in unpublished pottery archive reports for each stage of work, some of which are already out of date (Gingell 1996, Barber 1999a, Barber 2002b, Lyne 2002, Barber 2003a, Barber 2004a). These reports needed both reviewing and combining/re-ordering to allow proper publication of the results. This latter stage of work was made possible by the ALSF funding and has resulted in the present combined report. The work entailed re-spot dating of the Lydd 1 and 2 material, time to combine the existing reports into one and some additional works such as the petrological/chemical analysis on selected fabrics.

The overall objective of the present report is to give the most up to date account on the current thoughts on the fabric chronology for the site, and indeed Romney Marsh as a whole. As such, it is hoped that it will act as a platform to extend and refine our knowledge of the medieval and post-medieval pottery of the Marsh. It is hoped that recent excavations in the town of New Romney will test and refine the chronology presented below. The specific aims of the current report included the dating of individual contexts and indeed the occupation of the site as a whole. Other aims were to include the establishment, as far as possible, of the sources and quality of the pottery in order to assess the site's market contacts and status and show the range of forms present.

Methodology

The medieval pottery was divided into fabric groups based on a visual examination of tempering, inclusions and manufacturing technique. Each fabric was subsequently fully quantified by sherd count and weight for the larger, or more interesting, contexts. This information was recorded on pottery summary sheets which are housed with the archive. A quantification based on EVEs was not undertaken due to the small size of the majority of the groups (only 24.1 EVEs were present for the whole of the Lydd 1 assemblage). However, estimates of minimum number of vessels were undertaken for some of the larger assemblages (*i.e.*, Context 3180). Complete details of all the pottery, along with suggested dates for each context, are housed in the archive. The present report concentrates on establishing the range of fabrics and forms present and the general implications of the pottery to the site as a whole.

The Fabric Groups

The excavations at Lydd Quarry, as well as Denge West and Caldicott Farm, have enabled a fairly comprehensive fabric series to be established for this area of Romney Marsh. Different phases of excavations at Lydd Quarry have furnished the sequence with chronologically different, though often overlapping, fabric sequences. For example, although Lydd 1 and 2 produced mainly 13th century material, Lydd 3 produced mainly 14th century assemblages and Lydd 5/6 produced a mixture of 13th, 15th/early 16th, and the first significant post-medieval (late 17th/early 18th), assemblages. In addition, a number of new fabrics from Caldicott Farm have helped to provide more of the earlier fabrics. As a result the excavations have now provided an extensive fabric series covering the late 11th/12th centuries through to the mid 16th century with an isolated insight into the fabrics of the late 17th/early 18th century. Future work may hopefully strengthen the weaker areas of the series (*e.g.*, the late 11th to 12th centuries) and fill in gaps elsewhere (*e.g.*, the early/mid 16th to late 17th centuries).

The fabric series is based on that established for the Lydd 2 excavations (Barber 1999), which itself was created with reference to that from Lydd 1 (Gingell 1996). The Lydd 2 series was amended and expanded after the Lydd 3, 5/6 and 7–11 fieldwork and the Denge West and Caldicott Farm excavations (Barber 2002b, 2003, 2004a, see this volume and 2004b respectively). Although some re-ordering and re-numbering of the fabric series has been undertaken for this final report, this has been kept to a minimum in order to maintain consistency with the archive and previous reports.

The ALSF work has allowed the medieval fabric series to be compared with that of the Canterbury Archaeological Trust (CAT), particularly for the local wares, in an attempt to refine dating and help correlate the two sequences. CAT reference numbers and comments (by John Cotter) are shown in brackets under each fabric. It became clear that although there was a fairly good correlation between the two, the Lydd sequence had subdivided the Transitional wares to a greater extent than had been done in Canterbury, and indeed the reverse was true of some of the medieval sandy fabrics. The correlation was not undertaken for the post-medieval series, as division of the redwares was based on different criteria. In addition, the imported material within the sequence was commented on by Duncan Brown, whose comments are now included below.

The problem of sourcing the F2b sand and shell tempered, as well as the F3h Rye-type wares, was addressed using petrological (thin section) and chemical (ICPS) analysis by Alan Vince, utilising facilities at Royal Holloway College London (Vince 2003). Sherds from the kiln sites at Rye and Potter's Corner, Ashford (the latter housed at Maidstone Museum) were selected for this analysis. The main findings of this study have been incorporated within the relevant fabric section below, and the full report is housed with the archive.

Fabric 1. Flint tempered wares

This group of wares varies in the amount of flint present in the fabric, ranging from sparse to abundant. Many of the fabrics in this group are also tempered with sand and shell in varying quantities. (This group equates with the Stage 1 Fabrics F2A to F2C: Gingell 1996). These wares have proven relatively rare at Lydd Quarry, but where they do appear they are often in association with the coarse sand F3a. Several small assemblages were present at Lydd 1, 2, 3 (Area D) and 5/6 (Area A).

Fabric 1a

Abundant sub-rounded to sub-angular flint grits to 1mm. The colour of the flints ranges from white, through grey to dull red. There is virtually no sand in the fabric, and shell appears in some sherds only very rarely. Colours are variable but grey cores predominate. Surfaces and margins range from black to buff. The fabric is medium fired with a hackly fracture and rough surfaces. This is the only flint-tempered fabric from Lydd Quarry present at Caldicott Farm suggesting an early date. (CAT fabric EM33 'pimply' – dated at Dover to 1150–1250).

Forms recognised include undecorated cooking pots with simple everted/flaring rims.

Suggested date range at Lydd: 12th century.

Cat. Nos. – none

Fabric 1b

Moderate sub-rounded to sub-angular flint grits to 1.5mm. The colour of the flint ranges from white, through greys to dull reds and browns. There is no sand in the fabric, but shell inclusions, which are not normally more than 1mm across, are more common than in Fabric 1a. Even so, shell inclusions are rare. Colours are usually light brown throughout, although some sherds have darker brown surfaces. A medium to hard-fired fabric with rough breaks and generally smooth surfaces. (CAT fabric EM33 'pimply' – dated at Dover to 1150–1250).

Recognised forms include cooking pots and storage vessels. Occasionally these have thumbed vertical strips.

Suggested date range at Lydd: mid 12th century to early 13th century.

Cat. No. 17

Fabric 1c

Moderate to abundant rounded to sub-angular flint grits to 1.5mm. The grit colours vary from white, through grey to dull reds and browns and black. The fabric is also tempered with sparse to abundant medium sand and contains very rare to sparse shell inclusions to 2mm. Colours are very variable; cores are usually light to dark grey although some light brown/dull red examples are present. Surfaces range from light grey to black but are medium-fired with a rough break and rough surfaces. (CAT fabric EM33 'normal' – dated at Dover to 1150–1250).

Recognised forms include undecorated cooking pots.

Suggested date range at Lydd: 12th century.

Cat. Nos. 1–7, 9–10 and 70

Fabric 1d

Sparse sub-rounded to angular flint grits to 1mm. Grit colours range from white, through grey, to black with occasional dull brown examples. The fabric is also tempered with moderate to abundant medium sand and contains rare to very rare shell inclusions to 2mm. Colours are variable and range from grey to orange cores and grey to black or orange surfaces. A medium to hard-fired fabric with rough break and surfaces. (CAT fabric: similar to EM29 and EM34).

Recognised forms include cooking pots and, very occasionally, jugs. The latter sometimes have a patchy dull external green or dull yellow glaze. Some internal patchy glaze (yellow) is apparent on some cooking pot bases.

Suggested date range at Lydd: later 12th to 13th century.

Cat. No. 13

Fabric 1e

Very sparse to sparse sub-rounded to sub-angular flint grits to 1mm. Grit colours range from white, through grey, to black, but also include a number of dull brown examples.

The fabric is also tempered with moderate medium sand and contains rare to occasional shell inclusions to 2mm. Core colours range through various shades of grey to orange. Surface colours range form dull reds and browns to black. A medium-fired fabric with rough breaks and surfaces. This fabric appears to develop into, or is related to, F1g. (CAT fabric: EM33 and EM29 mix, dated 13th to early 14th century).

Recognised forms consist of cooking pots and bowls.

Suggested date range at Lydd: this fabric, which is very close to F1g and which may be the fore-runner of F4f, is thought to span the late 12th/early 13th to early 14th centuries. In East Sussex wares containing flint grits are known to continue into the 14th century.

Cat. Nos. 11–12

Fabric 1f

Rare to sparse sub-rounded to sub-angular flint grits to 0.75mm. Grit colours range from light grey to occasionally dark brown. The fabric is also tempered with moderate fine to medium sand and sparse chalk inclusions to 1mm. Core colour is a dark grey with dark grey inner surfaces and light grey outer surfaces. A medium to hard-fired fabric with rough break and surfaces. (CAT fabric: No match, though closest to EM33/29 mix).

Recognised forms include simple everted rim cooking pots.

Suggested date range at Lydd: *c*. late 11th century to 12th century.

Cat. Nos. – none

Fabric 1g

Medium to coarse moderate to abundant sand temper with very sparse to sparse dull orange iron oxides/grog to 1mm; very sparse shell (voids) to 2mm and very sparse to sparse black and brown semi-angular flint grits to 1.5mm. Usually grey cores and dull orange surfaces. A medium fired fabric. A few sherds were originally grouped with Fabric 2f during the Lydd 2 analysis (Context 2400). However, it is clear from the small, but significant, assemblage from the Lydd 5/6 excavations that this should be treated as a separate variant, though related, fabric group distinguished by its flint inclusions. (CAT fabric: EM29, dated mid 12th to 13th century).

Recognised forms include bowls, often with burnt exteriors and sometimes with patchy internal green glaze.

Forms are very similar to those noted in Fabric 2f.

Suggested date range at Lydd: *c*. 1200–1300.

Cat. Nos. 15 and 71

Fabric 1h

Abundant sub-angular flint grits to 1.5mm. The colour of the flints ranges from white, to grey to dull red and black. Sparse fine sand but no shell. Colours are variable but grey cores predominate. Surfaces and margins range from blacks and greys to dull brown oranges. The fabric is medium fired with hackly fracture and very rough surfaces. Only found at Caldicott Farm: this fabric has not yet been identified at Lydd Quarry. (CAT fabric EM41, examples found at Folkestone).

Suggested date range at Caldicott Farm: 11th to 12th century.

Recognised forms consist of unglazed cooking pots.

Cat. Nos. Caldicott Fm. 1–3

Fabric 1i

Sparse to moderate sub-angular flint (white, grey, brown) to 2mm (most to 1mm); sparse sub-rounded chalk and red brown iron oxides to 3mm and moderate fine sand. Colours vary from black to dull orange brown throughout. A low to medium fired fabric, distinctly sandy to the touch, with a hackly break. Only found at Caldicott Farm: this fabric has not yet been identified at Lydd Quarry. (CAT fabric: similar to EM32, dated late 11th to 12th century).

Suggested date range at Caldicott Farm: 11th to 12th century.

Recognised forms consist of cooking pot (bodysherds only).

Cat. Nos. – none

Fabric 2. Shell tempered wares

This group of wares is dominated by the sand and shell fabrics, with only one true shell tempered ware (F2a) being present. Although there appears to be a decline in the quantity of shell used through time (*i.e.*, F2b to F2d) there are a number of variations of fabric which do not fit this general trend. The shell tempered wares in Kent have proven both common and problematic, particularly when their source is considered (Cotter

2002). Although the only kiln site so far excavated is that at Potter's Corner, Ashford (Grove 1952), where fossil shell, possibly derived from the Hythe Beds (no Tertiary sources for fossil shell are known of in the area), was utilised, other sources for production must have existed. Many of these appear to have utilised 'modern' coastal shell deposits for tempering (Cotter 2002). Although very difficult to distinguish between, the Lydd material is thought, on balance, to probably represent coastal shell rather than fossil shell, and a production source on the Marsh is considered probable. Nevertheless, its similarity to Potter's Corner products means this source cannot be totally ruled out for some of the Lydd material (Vince 2003).

The shell tempered wares, principally F2b, dominated the Stage 1 (where they were originally numbered Fabric 1) and 2 excavations at Lydd Quarry, but were relatively rare in the Lydd 3 assemblage with the exception of the western half of Area B (Site Ja). They were present in the Lydd 5/6 assemblage but only in select areas – predominantly Area A (Site G). Although well represented at Denge West, they are surprisingly absent from the Caldicott Farm assemblage. The wares, again namely F2b, totally dominate the 13th century features at Lydd and Denge Quarries, but only appear in the 14th century features as generally small abraded residual sherds. As such, it seems likely that the shell tempered wares did not equally share the market with the sand tempered wares for long, and that production of shell tempered wares may well have ceased by the beginning of the 14th century or, probably more likely, toward the end of the 13th century. It is tempting to speculate that the sudden decrease in these wares may be a result of the great storms of the late 13th centuries, which may have severely hit any coastal industry (assuming the material is of coastal origin) allowing the sand tempered products from more upland industries, such as Rye, to flood the market. All the fabrics listed below were present at the Stage 1 and 2 excavations, though only 2b, 2d and 2e were recognised in the Phase 3 assemblage. The Phase 5/6 assemblage is dominated by the main type – Fabric 2b, though a little of the later Fabric 2d is also present.

Fabric 2a

Abundant fossil shell to 4mm, some of which has burnt out leaving voids. No sand is present in this fabric. Core and surface colours range from dark grey/black to dull orange. A low-fired fabric with soft, slightly smooth surface and very irregular breaks. Thick-walled vessels (*i.e.*, to 11mm) predominate. A rare fabric at Lydd, but interestingly, also located at Caldicott Farm. (CAT fabric EM2, dated mid 11th to mid 12th century).

Recognised forms consists of bowls.

Suggested date range at Lydd: *c*. 11th to 12th century?

(possibly earlier). This early date range is reinforced by the presence of this fabric in Context 86 at Caldicott Farm.

Cat. Nos. – none

Fabric 2b

Moderate medium sand and moderate to abundant shell to 3mm (sometimes burnt out). Some sherds have estuarine gastropods visible. Very rare grog/iron oxide inclusions to *c*. 2mm are present on some sherds. Core colours are usually various shades of grey with dull orange or orange brown surfaces. Grey and black surfaces are also present in some quantity. A medium to hard-fired fabric with slightly irregular break and rough sandy surfaces. Some wiping is present on some sherd surfaces. Decoration is rare but usually consists of incised lines. Thumbed strips are occasionally present. (CAT fabric: EM M5, dated late 12th to 13th century. Ashford Potter's Corner type, including coastal shell types – a sub-type of EM3).

This group is enigmatic in that although in appearance it is very similar to products from the Potter's Corner kiln at Ashford, the presence of the estuarine gastropods (*Hydrobia Ulvae*) and 'fresh' cockle in some sherds suggests a coastal production, probably around New Romney. The petrological and chemical analysis carried out on F2b sherds in comparison with kiln material from Potter's Corner showed both to be distinct from other shell tempered wares from the South-East, but very similar to each other. As such, some Lydd F2b material *could* be from Ashford. However, chemical analysis showed subtle differences, suggesting a source other than Ashford for the Lydd material was probable (Vince 2003).

Recognised forms include cooking pots, bowls, occasionally jugs (unglazed) and skillets. A full range of forms is shown in the catalogue where 62 vessels in this fabric are illustrated.

Suggested date range at Lydd: 13th century.

Cat. Nos. 18–34, 36–9, 41–6, 48, 50–1, 54–64, 67, 73–87, 91–4 and 99

Fabric 2c

Sparse to moderate shell to 3mm and moderate to abundant coarse sand. The fabric also contains very rare rounded quartz inclusions to 1mm. Colours usually consist of grey cores and dull brown to dark grey surfaces. A medium-fired fabric with irregular break and rough surfaces and probably related to F2e. (CAT fabric: EM3/EM M5 mixed, dated late 12th to mid 13th century).

Recognised forms include cooking pots and skillets.

Suggested date range at Lydd: *c.* late 12th to late 13th century.

Cat. Nos. 16 and 65

Fabric 2d

Rare to sparse shell to 3mm and moderate to abundant fine to medium sand. Some sherds exhibit very rare grog/iron inclusions to 2mm. This is undoubtedly a finer version of F2b, presumably partly demonstrating a chronological development. Colours are as Fabric 2b. The fabric is medium to hard-fired with slightly irregular breaks and slightly rough surfaces. (CAT fabric: EM M5).

Recognised forms include cooking pots and bowls.

Suggested date range at Lydd: mid 13th century to late 13th/early 14th century.

Cat. Nos. 52, 88 and 98

Fabric 2e

Rare to occasional shell to 3mm and moderate to abundant medium to coarse sand. The fabric also contains occasional sub-rounded clear to pinkish quartz grains to *c.* 2mm and is undoubtedly related to F2c. Colours are very variable and range from greys to browns and blacks as well as dull orange to off-white. A medium-fired fabric with rough break and surfaces. Although this fabric overlaps with F2b it appears to generally predate it, or at least does not continue into the second half of the 13th century. (CAT fabric: no parallel, though similar to EM31, dated 12th to mid 13th century).

Recognised forms include cooking pots.

Suggested date range at Lydd: late 12th to early/mid 13th century.

Cat. Nos. – none

Fabric 2f

Sparse to moderate shell to 3mm and moderate to abundant medium sand. This fabric is divided from F2b due to the presence of occasional to sparse grog inclusions to *c.* 2mm. Undoubtedly related to Fabric 1g, but without the flint. Colours are as Fabric 2b. A medium-fired fabric with irregular break and rough surfaces. (CAT fabric: included with EM M5).

Recognised forms include cooking pots.

Suggested date range at Lydd: 13th century.

Cat. Nos. 49 and 66

Fabric 3. Sand tempered wares

The sand tempered wares have a wide chronological range and the fabric groups tend to be 'loose-fitting'. Elements of this group generally appear to totally replace the shell-tempered wares relatively quickly at the end of the 13th or beginning of the 14th century. However, it should be noted that sand tempered wares appear alongside the shell tempered wares in 13th century contexts, albeit never in large quantities. At least two groups (3a and 3ai), based on rim forms, appear to be considerably earlier (late 11th to 12th century) than the rest. Fabric 3ai was only located at Caldicott Farm. The F3a sherds at Lydd are never present in any quantity and are usually found in 12th century contexts associated with the flint tempered wares (*i.e.*, Lydd 3, Area D). All the sand tempered wares noted during the Lydd 1 and 2 excavations were represented in the Lydd 3 assemblage, including an additional fabric group (3e) not yet seen at the site. Although well represented at Lydd 3, far fewer sherds are represented in the Lydd 2 and 5/6 assemblages. This fabric group equates with the Stage 1 excavation's Fabric 4.

Fabric 3a

Moderate to abundant coarse sand. Some sherds have very rare sub-rounded flint (brown) and quartz (clear to milky) to *c.* 3mm. Colours usually consist of grey cores with grey to black surfaces. A few sherds are oxidised giving light dull orange surfaces. A medium-fired fabric with rough break and surfaces. Some of the sherds within this group appear to be Canterbury products. (CAT fabric: sherds from both EM1 and EM45 are present in F3a, the latter dated to between the 12th and 13th centuries).

Recognised forms consist of shallow bowls/dishes and cooking pots with flaring rims.

Suggested date range at Lydd: early 12th to early 13th century.

Cat. Nos. 8 and 40; Caldicott Farm 4 & 5

Fabric 3a(i)

Moderate to abundant medium to coarse sand with sparse dull red grog/clay inclusions to *c.* 3–4mm. Colours are variable. Cores tend to be mid grey to brown orange while surfaces are usually dull brown orange. Some internal surfaces are dark grey, but an oxidised finish appears to have been the potter's aim. A medium-fired fabric with hackly/rough break and notably rough surfaces. Sherds tend to be thick-walled and less well finished when compared to F3a sherds. This fabric, which is perhaps the earliest of the Group 3 fabrics, was only recognised at Caldicott Farm. (CAT fabric: EM1, dated mid 11th to early 13th century and possibly deriving from Canterbury).

Recognised forms include cooking pots with early flaring rims. No decoration was noted. This fabric has mixed linkages. Based on inclusions this fabric sits most comfortably with F4a, though it is notably coarser. However, the presence of this fabric in Context 9 at Caldicott Farm, together with the early cooking pot rim forms, places it considerably earlier than F4a, which does not appear in any quantity before the mid/late 13th century. The fabric also has many similarities with the coarse sand tempered fabric F3a, and as the two appear to be chronologically similar F3a(i) is perhaps best viewed as a variant of F3a.

Suggested date range at Caldicott Farm: later 11th to early 13th.

Cat. No. Caldicott Farm, 6

Fabric 3b

Moderate to abundant medium sand. Some sherds have very rare inclusions of shell or iron oxides to *c.* 2mm. Colours are very variable: cores are usually grey although some dull orange examples are present; surface colours range from light dull orange to dull brown and from light grey to black. A medium to hard-fired fabric with slightly rough break and rough sandy surfaces. It is probable that these wares, which are likely to be locally produced, though perhaps not on the Marsh itself, filled the gap in the market caused by the decline in shell tempered wares at the end of the 13th century. This group is essentially the same fabric type that occurs alongside the shell tempered wares in small quantities during the 13th century. (CAT fabric: sherds from both EM1 and EM40B are present in F3b, the latter dated to the late 12th to 14th centuries).

Recognised forms include cooking pots, storage vessels?, bowls and jugs. Decoration is limited but where present usually consists of incised lines. Jugs, although rare at the Phase 1 and 2 excavations, are more common in the Phase 3 assemblage and are frequently decorated with a patchy dull green external glaze. Glaze on cooking pots is not common and is limited to interior bases. Some applied thumbed strips are present on coarseware forms, and two sherds from Phase 3 Context 3180 have white painted decoration.

Suggested date range at Lydd: 13th to mid/late 14th century, but more dominant in 14th century assemblages at Lydd.

Cat. Nos. 35, 47, 68–9, 89, 100, 105–6 and 116–19

Fabric 3c

Sparse to moderate fine to medium sand. Some sherds have very rare inclusions of iron oxide to 1mm. Colours are usually light dull orange/buff to dull red throughout, although some grey cores are present. A medium-fired fabric with smooth to slightly rough break and slightly rough surfaces. It is possible that some sherds within this group are from the Rye industry. This group is relatively well represented at Lydd 3 but not at Lydd 5/6. (CAT fabric: M40CS (Ashford/Wealden), dated mid 13th to mid 14th centuries).

Recognised forms include jugs, bowls and cooking pots. Jugs are the more frequent form and are often decorated with incised lines (horizontal and vertical), occasionally with applied thumbed strips and are frequently externally glazed. One sherd from Lydd 3 Context 3180 has white painted decoration under the glaze. Glaze is either patchy or even and is usually dull, or occasionally apple, green. Cooking pots, though much rarer, occasionally have a patchy glaze on their interior base.

Suggested date range at Lydd: mid 13th to 14th century, but more common in 14th century assemblages.

Cat. Nos. 101–2, 112 and 120

Fabric 3d

Moderate medium sand with very occasional black ashy stains (from organic material) and iron oxides to *c.* 1mm. Colours usually consist of light grey cores with light to mid grey surfaces. Very rarely the outer surfaces are fired to a light dull orange pink. A medium-fired fabric with slightly rough break and surfaces. Some of this fabric group may fall under the F3f group. Little of this somewhat indistinct fabric (it tends to merge with groups 3c and 3f) was located at Lydd 3 and none at Lydd 5/6. Some could be from the west Sussex area. (CAT fabric: no parallel though similar to M40BR).

Recognised forms consist of jugs. All examples show some external glazing. This is usually green and varies from sparse and patchy to a more extensive thick covering.

Suggested date range at Lydd: late 13th to 14th century.

Cat. Nos. – none

Fabric 3e

Moderate fine sand with very occasional dark grey or brown iron oxide inclusions to 1mm. Some sherds have very rare voids to 1mm where shell has burnt out. Cores and surfaces are consistently light to dark grey and the fabric is moderately fired and uniform in appearance. This fabric has only been recognised at Lydd 3, suggesting it is not of 13th century origin. The closest parallel is that of the predominantly 14th century East Sussex fabric known as 'Winchelsea Black', although it is not dissimilar to other fine textured greywares made in the Brede valley (Barton 1979) and indeed the Limpsfield area of Surrey (Prendergast 1974). Rigold (1964, fabric b) ascribed similar wares at New Romney to this Kent-Surrey border source. However, considering the geographical location of Lydd Quarry, a Winchelsea source is considered more likely. The current fabric would correlate with the sparse shell variety of Winchelsea Black ware. Its presence at Lydd Quarry during the 14th century is not surprising considering the quantity of East Sussex Rye-type material at the site (see below). (CAT fabric: M38a (similar to Limpsfield)).

Recognised forms consist of plain unglazed, but well finished, cooking pots, bowls and jugs. Sooting is apparent on the bases of some cooking pots.

Suggested date range at Lydd: 14th century.

Cat. Nos. 113, 121–3

Fabric 3f (formally W. Sussex-type)

Moderate to abundant medium (to coarse) sand with rare to sparse dull brown and black iron oxide pellets to 1mm. Colours usually consist of mid to dark grey throughout, though some sherds have cream coloured surfaces. A distinctly high-fired fabric with hackly break and rough surfaces.

The source of this very distinctive fabric is not known, though it is not thought to be Rye. This group of wares has some characteristics of the rather wide and ill-defined 'West Sussex Ware' which has been described in detail elsewhere (Barton 1979). However, many of these wares are difficult to identify with certainty, as similar fabrics were produced in other areas. Some coarser variants of West Sussex Ware are even similar to Normandy Glazed Ware (Vince and Jenner 1991, 109). (CAT fabric: M 40BR, coarse variant).

Recognised forms consist of decorated jugs. Vessels always have a thick external glaze, usually green yellow or dull green, often black flecked due to the iron oxides in the fabric. Applied triangular strips, often painted white or brown

Suggested date range at Lydd: 13th to 14th century.

Cat. Nos. 96–7

Fabric 3g (formally Surrey-type whiteware)

Sparse to moderate ill-sorted fine (to medium) sand. A well fired fabric with off-white to cream cores and surfaces. Although very similar to Kingston material in the Surrey Whiteware group (Pearce and Vince 1988), the fabric is not an exact match and the source of these wares must remain uncertain. Similar wares, also tentatively ascribed to the Surrey industry, have been found in Hastings (Barber 1993a: Fabric E) and a Wealden source is quite possible. (CAT fabric: M 53).

Recognised forms consist of glazed jugs, all with thick external patchy dark green glaze.

Suggested date range at Lydd: late 13th to 14th century.

Cat. Nos. – none

Fabric 3h (Rye-type ware)

The wares of this industry have been described in detail elsewhere (Barton 1979). Only eleven diagnostic sherds of this industry were located during the Lydd 1 excavations and only one at Lydd 2. However, Rye-type wares were plentiful in the 14th century assemblages from Lydd 3. Far less of this material was present in the Lydd 5/6 assemblage, but this is probably mainly due to the pottery being predominantly of 13th or 15th/early 16th century date.

This group contains two main fabric variations, though chemical analysis has shown that they probably derive from the same clay source (Vince 2003). The dominant is a medium to hard-fired fabric containing moderate fine to medium sand with sparse grey or dull red iron oxide inclusions to 1mm. Core colours are usually light grey or sometimes the more typical brick red. Surface colours vary from dull pale orange through to brick red. Cooking pots, bowls, storage vessels and jugs are all represented. The latter are usually externally glazed with a dull green, often patchy glaze, sometimes over bands of oblique incised decoration. A number of the cooking pots have a mottled green glaze on their interior base. Larger cooking pots/storage jars with applied thumbed strips and green glaze on their interior base are also present, some of which show signs of external sooting.

The second fabric group is less typical of Rye products and consists of a medium fired fabric tempered with sparse to moderate fine to medium sand with occasional dull red/brown iron ore inclusions to 0.5mm. This fabric, which appears exclusively in jugs, is a light reddish orange to orange pink throughout. Virtually all jugs in this fabric are externally glazed with dull mottled green glaze. Decoration includes applied and stamped white clay roundels and simple 'raspberry' stamps pushed out from the interior.

This group represents products from the Rye industry. This is confirmed by both the general fabric, form and decorative traits of the pieces, as well as petrological and chemical analysis (Vince 2003). The scientific study has, however, highlighted the variability of fabrics in both the Rye kiln products, as well as Lydd F3h sherds. However, the full extent of the Rye pottery industry is not yet known and more kilns undoubtedly await discovery around the town. Some of these may be 'outlying' workshops exploiting different clay/sand outcrops, though all producing stylistically similar wares. The presence of a number of sherds of grey sand tempered ware (Fabric 4e) of probable East Sussex origin tends to confirm the eastward movement of pottery onto the Marsh at this time. 'Pale buff' sandy ware from New Romney, frequently from jugs, some with Rye-type decoration, has also been ascribed to the Rye industry (Rigold 1964, fabric c). Based on the current evidence therefore, it would appear that with the decline of the local shell tempered wares at the end of the 13th century the Rye industry, which was probably at its largest in the 14th century, managed to corner a large part of the market on the Marsh at this time, particularly, but not exclusively, with jugs. If less diagnostic Rye products are present within Fabric Groups 3b and 3c, then this industry may have been the leading supplier at this time. Similarly, if a number of the later fabric groups (*i.e.*, 4h and 4e) are also heavily derived from this source, it suggests that Rye dominated the market in this area into the 16th century. Further analysis work, particularly on large assemblages on the Marsh and at Rye, will be needed to test this theory. (CAT Fabric M13).

Suggested date range at Lydd: late 13th/14th to early 15th century.

Cat. Nos. 110–11 and 128–34

Fabric 3i: Scarborough-type ware

Although only a few sherds of this ware were located at Lydd Quarry, it appears in most of the investigated areas. Five sherds (34g) of Scarborough Phase II ware were recovered from Lydd 1; two (7g) from Lydd 2; one from Lydd 3; and two from Lydd 5/6. This fabric has been described elsewhere (Farmer 1979). The sherds, which are all from well-made and glazed jugs, are decorated in a number of ways. The majority have applied strips and pellets under a thick even dark green glaze. Less common are sherds decorated with applied pellets of red clay arranged in vertical or horizontal lines with a clear/yellowish glaze applied over (glazing the pellets to brown and the pot body to a dark yellow orange). This type of decoration copies the Rouen jugs of the 13th century and may even have been an attempt to copy the London-Ware imitations of Rouen pottery. There are very few sherds of Scarborough ware with this

type of decoration and these sherds represent the most southerly examples to date (Farmer 1979). The Lydd 5/6 excavations produced the remains of a horizontal handle from an aquamanile. The other sherd from Lydd 5/6 is in a lower fired fabric tempered with sparse fine sand with sparse dull red iron oxide inclusions to 0.5mm. The body of this jug is a pale pinkish orange throughout. Externally the sherd is decorated with applied red clay pellets/slip under a clear glaze giving rise to brown pellets against a dull brown yellow main body (Context 5335). It is not inconceivable that this sherd is a Rye copy. (CAT Fabric M11a – Scarborough Fabric 1).

Suggested date range at Lydd: 13th to mid 14th century.

Cat. Nos. 95 and 104

Fabric 4. Sand and 'Grog/Iron Oxide' Tempered and Transitional Wares

This overall group of fabrics (originally labelled fabric 3 at Lydd 1) shows a chronological progression from the medieval into the post-medieval periods. Analysis of the Lydd 3 and 5/6 assemblages suggests the Transitional wares (4e–4p), which are predominantly higher-fired sand tempered wares, should be divided from the overall Fabric 4 group as they may easily have developed from the sand tempered and Rye-type wares rather than the sand and 'grog/iron oxide' tempered wares. However, the boundaries are blurred and it is probable that the sand and 'grog/iron oxide' tempered wares, particularly Fabric 4d, played an important role in the development of the Transitional wares, particularly the true earthenwares of the 16th century. For this reason all are retained under the general Fabric 4 grouping at present.

Analysis of the current assemblage highlighted the tendency for fabric groups, which were sometimes isolated due to firing rather than inclusions, to merge into each other. This was particularly problematic with the higher-fired Rye-type wares and Groups 4e and 4h, and at present it is strongly suspected that at least some vessels in Groups 4e and 4h are from the late Rye industry and represent a gradual evolution in forms and firing from the second half of the 14th century. Further analysis will be needed on 15th to 16th century material from the quarry, and indeed contemporary kiln sites in and around Rye, to determine to what extent these wares can be grouped.

All fabric groups under Fabric 4 were present at the Lydd 1 and 2 excavations, with the exception of groups 4f to 4i, which were first recognised during analysis of the Lydd 3 assemblage. All these fabrics were far more common in the Lydd 3 assemblage than those from the earlier phases, indicating their chronological development. The Lydd 5/6 assemblage, being later still, has added further fabrics to the series (4j to 4p), some of which appear to have continued in use into the 17th century. As these are similar to, and clearly related to, the sequence of 'Transitional wares' they have been included for the moment under the Fabric 4 group rather than the post-medieval series.

Sand and 'Grog/Iron Oxides'

Fabric 4a

Moderate to abundant medium sand with sparse to moderate dull red grog/iron oxide inclusions to *c*. 1mm. Some sherds have very rare inclusions of sub-rounded milky quartz to 2mm. Core and surface colours vary. Cores are either grey or dull orange while surfaces are usually dull orange to red. A medium-fired fabric with slightly rough break and surfaces. (CAT fabric: M40B/M40BR, dated late 12th to 14th centuries).

Recognised forms include cooking pots, bowls and jugs. Decoration is rare but usually consists of incised lines, although some thumbed strips are present on cooking pots/storage vessels and thumbed bases on jugs are relatively common. Some dull green external patchy (dull green to orange brown) glaze is apparent on the jugs, however, the cooking pots rarely have glaze. When apparent it always exists as a patchy covering on the interior base.

Suggested date range at Lydd: mid 13th to mid 14th century.

Cat. Nos. 53, 90, 107, 124–6

Fabric 4b

Moderate to abundant medium sand with sparse to moderate dull red grog/iron oxide (to 1mm). Rare sub-angular white flint (to 1mm) inclusions are also present in all sherds. Colours are as Fabric 4a. (CAT fabric: a mix of EM29 (dated early 12th to 13th century) and M45A (dated mid 13th to mid 15th century)).

Recognised forms consist of cooking pots and bowls. Decoration is rare but incised lines are used occasionally and some external spots of glaze are apparent on a few sherds.

Suggested date range at Lydd: later 13th to mid 14th century.

Cat. No. 108

Fabric 4c

Sparse fine sand with rare to occasional dull red grog/iron oxide to 1mm. Some sherds have very rare iron oxide inclusions to *c*. 2mm. Core colours are usually light grey with dull orange surfaces. A low-fired fabric with smooth break and surfaces. Always a rare fabric at Lydd Quarry. (CAT fabric: no parallel).

Recognised forms consist of cooking pots and jugs. Decoration consists of incised lines. Some internal dull green glaze is apparent on some sherds, as are applied thumbed strips.

Suggested date range at Lydd: mid 13th to 14th century.

Cat. No. 127

Transitional Wares

Fabric 4d

Rare to sparse fine sand with rare to occasional dull red grog to 1mm. Core colours range from light grey to orange. Surfaces are usually light orange to dull red. A hard-fired fine fabric with smooth break and surfaces. The surfaces, particularly around the bases, often show signs of wiping and/or knife trimming. This appears to be a late medieval forerunner to the early post-medieval earthenwares. (CAT fabric: LM 32, dated mid 15th to mid 16th century).

Recognised forms consist of cooking pots/jars and jugs/pitchers (including bunghole pitchers). The latter frequently have thumbed bases. Decoration is sparse. Some glaze is present. This is usually internal, particularly on the base of the vessels. Glaze colour is usually pale yellow or light brown.

Suggested date range at Lydd: late 14th to mid 16th century, but most common in 15th century.

Cat. No. 136

Fabric 4e

Moderate to abundant medium sand. Some sherds have very rare inclusions of sub-rounded quartz and dark grey iron oxides to 1mm. Core colours vary from grey to orange, while surface colours vary from light orange to dull red (most common) to dark grey. A noticeably hard-fired 'ringing' fabric with rough break and surface. This fabric group tends to merge with Group 4h and to a lesser extent with the higher-fired Rye-type wares. (CAT fabric: M10/M10R, dated mid 14th to mid 16th century).

Recognised forms include cooking pots, jugs/pitchers, bowls/dishes, bottles/flasks and storage vessels. Decoration is minimal: one pitcher from 3180 (Lydd 3) had incised lines around its neck and a few other vessels have occasional spots of glaze.

Suggested date range at Lydd: early 15th to mid 16th century.

Cat. Nos. 135, 137 and 143–5

Fabric 4f

Moderate fine sand with sparse sub-angular white, grey and brown flint inclusions to 2mm and occasionally voids to 1mm where shell has burnt out. A high-fired fabric similar to 4d with light to mid grey cores and dull orange surfaces. This is a distinctive but rare fabric noted at Lydd 3 and is almost certainly a variant of 4d. (CAT fabric: no parallel).

Recognised forms include cooking pots/jars. No decorated or glazed pieces were noted.

Suggested date range at Lydd: late 14th to 15th century.

Cat. Nos. – none

Fabric 4g

Sparse fine sand with rare grey iron oxide inclusions to 1mm and very rare sub-angular grey and brown flint and voids where calcareous material (shell/chalk?) has burnt out. A high-fired fabric similar to 4f but with a noticeably smoother surface. It is quite probable this fabric, which is close to being a true post-medieval earthenware, developed from 4d. Core colours are grey with dull orange surfaces. A very rare fabric which may have been intrusive in Context 3180 at Lydd 3. (CAT fabric: no parallel).

Recognised forms include cooking pots/jars. No decoration was noted, though one vessel had a patchy internal green glaze.

Suggested date range at Lydd: mid 15th to mid 16th century.

Cat. No. 146

Fabric 4h

Moderate fine to medium sand frequently with grey iron oxide inclusions to 1mm which sometimes create grey streaks on the surface. A high-fired fabric which tends to merge with the higher-fired Rye-types and Group 4e. It is quite possible this group marks the transition of mid/late 14th century Rye products to true 'Transitional' wares, though Rye may be one of a number of sources for the material. Core colours are usually light to mid grey, though some are dull orange. Surfaces range from buff,

through dull orange to orange red. (CAT fabric: LM 32, dated mid 15th to mid 16th century).

Recognised forms include cooking pots, bowls and jugs/pitchers. With the exception of a few vessels with white painted slip lines, no decoration is present, however, splashes and spots of clear glaze were noted on some vessels, while others have a thin and patchy clear or green internal glaze on base and sides. Strap handles are usually deeply slashed, though some smaller examples are stabbed.

Suggested date range at Lydd: late 14th/early 15th to early 16th century.

Cat. Nos. 114, 138–42, 147, 149–50, 154–6 and Denge West 1–2

Fabric 4i

Sparse fine to medium sand with very rare grey iron oxide inclusions to 1mm, rare sub-angular white, grey and black flint to 1.5mm. Some vessels have rare chalk inclusions to 2mm. A high-fired fabric similar to 4f but with noticeably less flint and coarser sand. It is quite probable this fabric is a variant of 4d. Core colours are grey with dull orange surfaces. (CAT fabric: M45A (Rye/Wealden), dated mid 13th to mid 15th century).

Recognised forms include cooking pots/storage jars. No decoration or glaze was noted.

Suggested date range at Lydd: mid 14th to 15th/early 16th century.

Cat. Nos. 109 and 115

Fabric 4j

Sparse fine sand with moderate dull orange or grey iron oxide inclusions to 2mm and occasional voids from lost iron oxide/?chalk pellets. A medium to high-fired fabric similar to 4i but with noticeably larger iron oxides. It is quite probable this somewhat rough fabric developed from F4a. Core colours are grey or dull orange with dull orange surfaces. (CAT fabric: M10R part, dated mid 14th to mid 16th century).

Recognised forms include cooking pots/storage jars and bunghole pitchers. No decoration has been noted, though some vessels have a good internal dull brown/green glaze on their bases.

Suggested date range at Lydd: 15th to early 16th century.

Cat. Nos. 151–3 and Denge West 3–6

Fabric 4k

Rare very fine sand with very occasional orange brown iron oxide inclusions to 0.5mm. A true medium-fired earthenware with virtually no sign of a tempering agent. Core colours can either be grey, or more usually the sherds are pale orange or dull red throughout, occasionally with slightly reduced surfaces. Similar to Fabric 4d, but a later, somewhat ill-defined, Tudor fabric. (CAT fabric: mainly PM2).

Recognised forms include cooking pots/storage jars and lid-seated pipkins. No decoration was noted, though occasionally vessels have a thin internal or external patchy brown glaze or, more frequently, occasional spots of glaze.

Suggested date range at Lydd: late 15th/early 16th to early 17th century.

Cat. Nos. 159–60

Fabric 4l

Rare very fine sand with very rare grey or dull brown iron oxide inclusions to 1mm. A high-fired true earthenware fabric, noticeably fine with smooth, often wiped, almost leathery, surfaces. It is quite probable this fabric is a progression from 4d, 4e or 4h. Core colours are grey with dull orange surfaces. (CAT fabric: PM2, a refinement of LM 32, dated early 16th to mid 17th century).

Recognised forms include cooking pots/storage jars. No decoration or glaze was noted.

Suggested date range at Lydd: late 15th/early 16th to early 17th century.

Cat. Nos. 157–8 and Denge West 7

Fabric 4m

Rare very fine sand with very rare grey or dull brown iron oxide inclusions to 1mm and very rare chalk inclusions to 2mm. A high-fired true earthenware fabric, noticeably fine with smooth surfaces. This fabric is virtually identical to 4l but is divided from it due to the presence of the chalk inclusions. Colours are dull orange throughout. (CAT fabric: PM 64, dated early 16th to 17th century).

Recognised forms include cooking pots/storage jars. No decoration or glaze was noted.

Suggested date range at Lydd: late 15th/early 16th to early 17th century.

Cat. No. 161

Fabric 4n

Sparse to moderate medium sand with occasional grey or dull brown iron oxide inclusions to 1mm. A very high-fired 'ringing' sandy fabric, noticeably rough to the touch and with reduced outer surface. Core colours are grey or dull orange, margins are usually present (either grey or dull orange). Outer surfaces are always mid to dark grey, with inner surfaces being either grey, brown or dull orange. (CAT fabric: M10R, dated mid 14th to mid 16th century).

Recognised forms include cooking pots/storage jars. Little decoration or glaze was noted. However, where glaze is present it is usually thin and patchy and on the exterior of the vessel. A couple of sherds exhibit white painted decoration.

Suggested date range at Lydd: mid 15th to 16th century. Some sherds may run into the 17th century.

Cat. Nos. Denge West 8

Fabric 4o

No tempering agent is visible in this fabric, though sparse calcareous inclusions to 0.75mm are present. A very high-fired 'ringing' fabric, noticeably smooth to the touch and with reduced outer surface. Core colours are usually brick red, dull blue grey or orange. Outer surfaces are usually light to mid/dark grey, though at least one buff brown example was noted in Context 5044. (CAT fabric: PM 64 reduced, dated early 16th to 17th century).

Recognised forms include cooking pots/storage jars and pitchers (represented by strap handles with heavy thumb imprints at lower end with junction of body. No decoration or glaze was noted.

Suggested date range at Lydd: very late 15th/early 16th to later 16th/early 17th century. Some sherds may run later into the 17th century.

Cat. Nos. Denge West 9–10

Fabric 4p

No tempering agent is visible in this fabric, though sparse dull brown iron oxide inclusions to 0.50mm are present in most sherds together with streaks of white clay in some. Fired to such a high temperature that vessels are really a 'proto-stoneware'. Smooth to the touch and usually thin-walled (less than 5mm). Core colours are usually brick red or dull purple. Outer surfaces range from dull orange/brick red to dull purple. (CAT fabric: PM 2 high-fired), dated early 16th to mid 17th century).

Recognised forms include cooking pots/storage jars. No decoration or glaze was noted.

Suggested date range at Lydd: very late 15th/early 16th to later 16th century.

Cat. Nos. – none

Fabric 5

Fabric 5a

Abundant semi-angular dull red/purple iron oxides to 2mm, sometimes reduced to black. Some rare fine to medium sand is also present. Colours usually consist of grey cores and grey to dull orange surfaces. A medium-fired fabric with irregular break and rough surfaces. The source of this very distinctive fabric is not known. Only present in the Lydd 1 and 2 assemblages. (CAT fabric: no parallel).

Recognised forms include cooking pots. No decoration has been noted.

Suggested date range at Lydd: 13th century.

Cat. Nos. – none

Medieval Imports

Imp. 1: Saintonge

Very fine silty fabric with no visible inclusions. Colours range from off-white to buff (often through staining). A medium-fired fabric with smooth break and smooth powdery surface. Heavy throwing marks are often visible on the interior. Saintonge. Both green glaze and polychrome jugs are present but only in low numbers. (CAT Fabric RM22g). All five imported sherds (43g) from the Lydd 1 excavations were in this fabric group, while at Lydd 2 all the sherds in this fabric were from a single jug with splayed base from Context 2415 (Cut 2414).

Suggested date range at Lydd: mid 13th to mid/late 14th century.

Cat. No. 103

Imp. 2 Seine Valley type whiteware

Sparse very fine sand. An off-white fabric with good thick external dark green glaze. Medium fired with slightly rough break and surfaces. Only jugs are present. French (possibly Seine Valley area of France). Present at Lydd 2 (3 sherds weighing 6g), (CAT Fabric ?EM40a or M19g).

Suggested date range at Lydd: mid 13th to mid/late 14th century.

Cat. Nos. – none

Imp. 3 Normandy Gritty Redware variant

Sparse fine sand with sparse grog/iron oxide pieces to 1mm and rare to sparse sub-angular/semi-rounded white quartz inclusions to 4mm. Colours range from brick red to buff. A medium-fired fabric with hackly fracture and slightly rough surfaces. Sherds appear to be from heavy vessels of unknown function. An orange external patchy glaze is present. Small quantities of this fabric were present at Caen in 12th century to 14th century contexts (Leenhardt 1983, 57) as well as at Pevensey (Lyne 1999) where, although most were residual, one sherd appeared in a 12th century context. North French Gritty Ware is considered most likely, though it could be an early Saintonge Redware. Most of the sherds in this group are from 12th century contexts at Lydd 2. No sherds in this fabric are present in the Lydd 3 or 5/6 assemblages. (CAT Fabric EM15). Forms are uncertain though three-handled pitchers are the most likely type.

Suggested date range at Lydd: 12th century.

Cat. No. 14

Imp. 4 Rouen type

Very sparse silt to very fine sand. A medium-fired white fabric with straight break and smooth surfaces. Jugs only. External clear/light green glaze with over patches of brown red slip/paint. Present at Lydd 2. (CAT fabric ?M19P). Developed Rouen.

North French?/Rouen. Mid/late 13th to 14th century.

Cat. Nos. – none

Imp. 5 Siegburg stoneware

Siegburg Stoneware. This fine light grey stoneware from the Rhineland is described in detail elsewhere (Hurst *et al.* 1986). (CAT Fabric LM7).

Suggested date range at Lydd: 15th century.

Cat. No. 148

Imp. 6 Aardenberg-type ware (Low Countries Highly Decorated Redware)

Two sherds from the Lydd 5/6 assemblage belong to this group. Both are in well-fired fine sand tempered wheel-thrown bodysherds from jugs (possibly the same jug). The fabric is brick red throughout with very rare dull red grog/iron oxide and mica inclusions to 0.5mm. The exterior surface is covered with a thick white slip under a good even apple green glaze. In places further red clay slip has been applied over the white, which then glazes to a dark dull green-brown (Context 5100). Aardenburg-type ware. (CAT Fabric M14).

Suggested date range at Lydd: late 13th to 14th century.

Cat. Nos. – none

Imp. 7 Pingsdorf

A single sherd of this ware was found unstratified at Lydd 1. The fabric is cream-white/buff, hard-fired with a coarse texture due to the presence of large, though not common, sand grains (Jennings 1981, 29). The sherd is decorated with red painted curving lines. This sherd is of importance as it is potentially the earliest from the site, though it could have been old when dropped. The sherd exhibits fresh breaks. (CAT Fabric EM10 RP).

Suggested date range at Lydd: mid 11th to 12th century.

Cat. Nos. – none

Imp. 8 Merida-type Ware (formally Fabric 4q)

Moderate fine sand tempering with very rare white irregular quartz inclusions to 1.5mm and sparse mica inclusions to 0.75mm. A medium-fired fabric with a noticeably sugary/granular texture. Core colours are pale orange to light pink. Outer surfaces are buff to pale orange. A very rare fabric, only noted in Context 5084. Pale Iberian red micaceous ware (Merida type) from Portugal. Although the ware appears in Britain in the late 13th century it is far more common in the 15th century and runs into the post-medieval period. (closest CAT fabric: M 22?).

Only bodysherds were noted (Context 5084) and it was not possible to recognise form, though normally flasks and costrels are the most common. No decoration or glaze was noted.

Suggested date range at Lydd: mid/late 15th to early 16th century to later 16th century.

Cat. Nos. – none

Post-Medieval Fabrics

Although some of the Transitional fabrics in Group 4 extend into the post-medieval period, a separate, though linked, post-medieval fabrics series has been established using the assemblage from Lydd 5/6. This has allowed the extension of the pottery series at the quarry from the late medieval/transitional period to the beginning of the 18th century. The early post-medieval wares have close links with the Transitional wares of the preceding period and display a general trend in changing fabrics and technologies. Lines cannot, and perhaps should not, be drawn between the later 15th to mid 16th century wares. However, for ease of analysis some division needs to be made at present. The true 'post-medieval' fabrics are briefly described below, using their common name wherever known.

Fabric PM1a – Hard-fired earthenware with sparse metallic glaze

Rare very fine sand with very rare grey or dull brown iron oxide inclusions to 1mm. A high-fired true earthenware fabric, noticeably fine with smooth surfaces. It is probable this fabric is a progression from 4l and 4m. Core colours are dull orange with mid brown to dark grey reduced surfaces.

Recognised forms include cooking pots/storage jars. No decoration is evident, though all vessels have a patchy, and frequently thin, internal purple brown 'metallic' glaze.

Suggested date range at Lydd: mid 16th to 17th century.

Cat. Nos. 162 and 163

Fabric PM1b – Hard-fired earthenware moderate iron oxides and metallic glaze

A hard-fired earthenware with some fine sand and moderate grey or dull brown iron oxides to 1.5mm. Similar to PM1a and c, but coarser due to the presence of the iron oxide inclusions. Core colours are dull orange with mid grey or dull orange margins and mid grey exterior surface.

Recognised forms include cooking pots/storage jars. No decoration is evident, though all vessels have a thin, internal purple brown 'metallic' glaze.

Suggested date range at Lydd: mid 16th to 17th century.

Cat. Nos. – none

Fabric PM1c – Medium to Hard-fired earthenware with even metallic glaze

A lower fired version of PM1a and a probable, though overlapping, development from it. Rare very fine sand with very rare grey or dull brown iron oxide inclusions to 1mm. A medium-fired true earthenware fabric, noticeably fine with smooth surfaces. Core colours are dull orange with dull orange or dark grey reduced outer surfaces.

Recognised forms include cooking pots/storage jars. No decoration is evident, though all vessels have a good even (varying from thin to thick) internal purple brown 'metallic' glaze.

Suggested date range at Lydd: mid/late 16th to 17th century.

Cat. Nos. 164–72

Fabric PM1d – Hard-fired earthenware with thick even 'glittering' metallic glaze

A medium to high-fired earthenware with no visible inclusions. Generally thinner walled vessels and a better finish mark this group apart from PM1b, suggesting this was used for tablewares rather than kitchen wares. Colours are either dull orange or dark grey throughout.

Recognised forms include bowls and tankards. Some cordons are present on the straight-sided tankard. All vessels have a good thick dark brown 'glittering' metallic glaze, either internally (on bowls) or all over (on tankards).

Suggested date range at Lydd: mid 16th to 17th century.

Cat. Nos. – none

Fabric PM2a – Medium to hard-fired earthenware with brown green glaze

A medium to high-fired earthenware with very occasional red brown iron oxide inclusions. Colours are dull orange throughout. Some vessels have been knife trimmed externally near the base.

Recognised forms include deep bowls/plates and storage jars. Some thick horizontal lines are impressed into the body of some closed. All vessels have a good thick brown green glaze, frequently crazed on internal, and sometimes external, surfaces.

Suggested date range at Lydd: mid 16th to 17th century.

Cat. No. 173

Fabric PM2b – Medium to hard-fired earthenware with dull green glaze

A medium to high-fired earthenware with very occasional

grey or red brown iron oxide inclusions. Colours are dull orange or mid grey, though surfaces are usually dull to mid orange. Some vessels have been knife trimmed externally near the base.

Recognised forms include deep bowls and storage jars. All vessels have a good thick dull green glaze, frequently with sparse black iron oxide flecks, on internal surfaces. Glaze occasionally on rims and spots and splashes on exteriors.

Suggested date range at Lydd: mid 16th to 17th century.

Cat. No. 174

Fabric PM2c – Medium-fired earthenware with dark dull brown green glaze

A medium-fired earthenware with occasional to sparse grey or red brown iron oxide inclusions to 1.5mm. Colours are dull orange throughout, though frequently with reduced surfaces. Some vessels have been knife trimmed externally near the base.

Recognised forms include jars. All vessels have a good thick dull brown green glaze, frequently with sparse black iron oxide flecks, on internal surfaces. Glaze occasionally on rims and spots and splashes on exteriors.

Suggested date range at Lydd: late 16th to 17th century.

Cat. No. 175

Fabric PM3a – Medium to hard-fired earthenware with thin and patchy red brown glaze

Rare very fine sand with rare to occasional grey or dull brown iron oxide inclusions to 1mm. A true earthenware fabric, noticeably fine with smooth surfaces. Colours are dull orange throughout. Similar to F2b.

Recognised forms include storage jars. No decoration is evident, though all vessels have a patchy, and frequently thin, internal, and occasionally external, red brown glaze.

Suggested date range at Lydd: 16th to 17th century.

Cat. Nos. 176–7

Fabric PM3b – Medium-fired earthenware with thin red brown glaze

Medium-fired earthenware with rare to occasional grey or dull brown iron oxide inclusions to 0.5mm. Colours are dull orange throughout.

Recognised forms include storage jars, bowls and plates. No decoration is evident, though all vessels have thin, but even, internal, and occasionally external, red brown glaze with sparse iron oxide flecking. A probable local chronological development from PM3a. No Dutch material is present from the site, though this group comes closest to matching the fabrics.

Suggested date range at Lydd: mid 16th to 17th century.

Cat. Nos. 178–81

Fabric PM3c – Medium-fired earthenware with thick red brown iron-flecked glaze

Medium-fired earthenware with sparse to moderate grey or dull brown iron oxide inclusions to 1.5mm. Colours are dull orange throughout.

Recognised forms include storage jars, bowls and plates. No decoration is evident though all vessels have a thick and even internal, and occasionally external, red brown to brown glaze with frequent iron oxide flecking. A probable chronological development from PM3b as the wares become finer and better made.

Suggested date range at Lydd: late 16th to early 18th century.

Cat. Nos. 182–5

Fabric PM3d – Medium-fired coarse earthenware with red brown glaze

Medium-fired earthenware with moderate grey or dull brown/orange iron oxide/clay pellet inclusions to 4mm. Colours are usually dull orange throughout, though some light grey cores are present.

Recognised forms include large storage jars only. No decoration is evident, though all vessels have an even, internal red brown glaze with sparse to moderate iron oxide flecking. A coarseware variant of F3c.

Suggested date range at Lydd: late 16th to early 18th century.

Cat. Nos. – none

Fabric PM4a – Trailed Slipware

Medium-fired earthenware with rare to occasional grey or dull brown iron oxide inclusions to 0.5mm. Colours are dull orange throughout.

Recognised forms include plates. Decoration consists of parallel bands of white slip glazed yellow under the clear glaze, against a light red brown glazed body with sparse iron oxide flecking. Probably related to Fabrics 3b and 3c.

Suggested date range at Lydd: 17th century.

Cat. Nos. – none

Fabric PM5a – Fine unglazed whiteware: Beauvais-type

A very fine untempered white fabric with a tendency to fracture in a slightly laminar way and surface prone to spalling. Rare dull orange iron oxide inclusions to 1mm. Off-white throughout. Although similar to late Saintonge products there appears to be too little mica in the fabric. This, in combination with some smears of red slip, suggests the fabric to be from Beauvais rather than Saintonge whitewares.

Recognised forms include ?storage jars. Only one vessel noted in 5138 – a closed form with horizontal incised lines on exterior. No glaze evident, though knife trimming towards the base and heavy throwing marks are apparent.

Suggested date range at Lydd: 16th to mid 17th century.

Cat. Nos. – none

Fabric PM5b – Green-glazed Whiteware: Borderware

Off-white to pinkish earthenware with good even bright green glaze. Forms include a Borderware comb-decorated plate (Pearce 1992) and chamber-pot. The latter, with its more pinkish fabric, may be a 'Wealden' product imitating Borderware.

Suggested date range at Lydd: mid/late 16th to 17th century.

Cat. No. 186

Fabric PM5c – Yellow-glazed Whiteware: Borderware

Off-white to pinkish earthenware with good even yellow glaze. Forms include open and closed vessels. As with PM5b most are likely to be from the Borderware industry (Pearce 1992) though a few more pinkish examples may be 'Wealden' copies.

Suggested date range at Lydd: mid/late 16th to 17th century.

Cat. No. 187

Fabric PM5d – Brown-glazed Whiteware: Borderware?

Off-white to pinkish earthenware with good even brown glaze with dark brown streaks. Forms include open and closed vessels. Probably all Borderware (Pearce 1992), though some may be 'Wealden' copies.
Suggested date range at Lydd: mid/late 16th to 17th century.

Cat. Nos. – none

Fabric PM6 – Tin-glazed Earthenwares

A range of tin-glazed earthenwares are now known from the quarry. These all appear to be of English manufacture but have been divided to help classification:

a) Plain white. Forms include ointment pots and bowls.

Cat. Nos. 188–92

b) Mottled purple. Forms include cups?

Cat. No. 193

c) White with crude coloured decoration (blue, yellow, green). Some early types with lead glaze on exterior. Forms consist of plates.

Cat. Nos. – none

d) Blue tinged with more refined coloured decoration (dark blue bordered by black lines). Forms consist of bottles and plates.

Cat. No. 194

Fabric PM7 – German Stonewares

a) Raeren – Strangely, no definite Raeren products have yet been identified at Lydd Quarry, though they were present at Denge West.

b) Colonge/Frechen. Forms consist of Bellarmine bottles. A date range of 1550 to 1700 is suggested for the material at Lydd.

Cat. Nos. 195–7

c) Westerwald. (Cobalt blue decoration). Forms include chamber pots and tankards. A mid 17th to early 18th century date is suggested at the quarry.

Cat. Nos. 198–200

Fabric PM8 – English Stoneware

a) London. Forms include straight-sided tankards and bulbous tavern pots. Dated later 17th to early 18th at Lydd.

Cat. Nos. 201–3

b) London/?Staffordshire. No definite forms but straight-sided tankards are probable. This type of stoneware dates to between the late 17th and early 18th centuries (Jennings 1981, 219).

The Pottery Groups

Relatively few assemblages from Lydd Quarry were deemed appropriate for detailed fabric quantification. Those that were are detailed below. These contexts were selected primarily on criteria such as assemblage size, date, and number of rim-sherds present. The overall aim of the selected analysis was to attempt to outline the chronological development of ceramics at the site, and wider area, and to identify any notable chronological shift in the ratio of fabric groups which may help to establish a relative sequence for the 12th to early 16th century material. Detailed study of forms was not undertaken due to the limited range represented by the relatively small amount of rim-sherds in the assemblages. However, all main forms, where possible, are reproduced in the illustrated catalogue.

12th to early 13th century

Although the excavations at Lydd Quarry have produced a wide scatter of 12th to early 13th century pottery, it is never present in large quantities. As such, small groups, often with very few feature sherds, have had to be used to outline the earliest medieval fabrics and forms so far discovered at the site. Perhaps the earliest confirmed piece is the single unstratified Pingsdorf sherd from Lydd 1. Although this would suggest maybe 10th or 11th century activity, it may simply be the loss of a traveller passing through or an old pot still in use in the 12th century. The first groups of pottery would appear to relate to 12th century activity, though their small size does not suggest permanent domestic occupation. As such, the material may represent refuse discarded by people engaged in establishing the ditch system. The assemblage from Site A is more interesting in that it relates to a structure and appears to represent a transitional period between the 12th century flint tempered wares and the development of the sand and shell tempered wares of the 13th century.

Fill 287 (Ditch 288: D1) (Lydd 1)

This small assemblage was the largest 12th century group from the Lydd 1 excavations. It consists of 57

Fabric	No. of sherds	% by number	Weight (grams)	% by weight
1a	1	4	2g	1.6
1c	1	4	14g	11.0
1d	1	4	8g	6.3
1e	1	4	10g	7.9
1g	2	8	5g	3.9
2b	6	24	40g	31.5
2c	7	28	28g	22
2e	5	20	19g	15
3a	1	4	1g	0.8
Total	25	100	127g	100

Table 2: Site A (Lydd 10) Combined pottery assemblage from building post-holes

sherds of which 56 are in variations of F1c and only one, almost certainly intrusive, in F2b. The F1c sherds, which include eight rim-sherds and four base-sherds, are from a minimum of six different cooking pots. A mid to late 12th century date is suggested for this group.

Catalogue Nos. (Fig. 66)

1. Cooking pot with thickened sharply out-turned rim. F1c.
2. Cooking pot with simple out-turned rim. F1c.
3. Cooking pot with everted rim. F1c.
4. Cooking pot with narrow mouth and simple rim. F1c.
5. Necked cooking pot or bowl with thickened rim. F1c.

Other Lydd 1 material

A small number of other diagnostic 12th century sherds were present across the site. A selection is listed below (Fig. 66).

6. Cooking pot with thickened sharply out-turned rim. F1c. (Fill 168. Ditch 164: D1)
7. Necked cooking pot with thickened rim. F1c. (Fill 181. Ditch 164 recut: D1)
8. Shallow bowl with indented rim. F3a. (Fill 202. Ditch 198: D7)
9. Cooking pot with curving out-turned rim. F1c. (Fill 327. Ditch 313: D6)
10. Cooking pot with slightly thickened gently everted rim. F1c. (Fill 327. Ditch 313: D6)

Contexts 2119 and 2210 (Lydd 2: Ditch 2118)

Context 2119 (Upper fill of Ditch 2118) and Context 2210 (lower fill of the same ditch) produced the only reasonable group of this period from Lydd 2 (55 and 37 sherds respectively). All the sherds are in flint tempered fabrics (1c–1e) and combined represent seven different vessels. Most appear to be cooking pots with everted or flaring rims. Both contexts contain sherds of Imp. 3 (three sherds from 2119 and one from 2210).

(Fill 2119: Ditch 2118) (Fig. 66)

11. Cooking pot with simple everted rim.
    Fabric 1e.
    A similar rim form from New Romney (Willson 1987, 209, No. 21) has been dated to the 12th century.
12. Bowl or cooking pot with thickened out-turned rim
    Fabric 1e.

(Fill 2210: Ditch 2118) (Fig. 66)

13. Cooking pot with flaring rim.
    Fabric 1d.
14. Heavy bowl? with simple rim and glazing.
    Fabric Imp. 3.

Lydd 10 assemblage

The assemblage associated with the building can be divided into two: that directly relating to the structure by being incorporated into post-holes, and that associated with it (in the drain and enclosing ditches). None of these features independently produced enough pottery to analyse in any detail. However, when combined, although still small, the assemblages become a little more useful.

The Post-holes

Nine post-holes relating to the building produced pottery (Contexts A33, A35, A37, A43, A45, A47, A51, A55 and A57). The largest assemblage from a single post-hole is from A46 (Fill A47) which produced five sherds. When combined the post-holes provide a meagre assemblage of 25 sherds; too small for meaningful analysis but enough to characterise the fabrics present and thus the date of the structure (Table 2).

The fabric percentages based on sherd count and weight only correlate generally, however, this is an unsurprising result of the very small size of the sherds involved and the overall assemblage size. Of interest is the presence of flint tempered wares in low quantities (F1a–F1g) together with much higher quantities of the coarser shell and sand

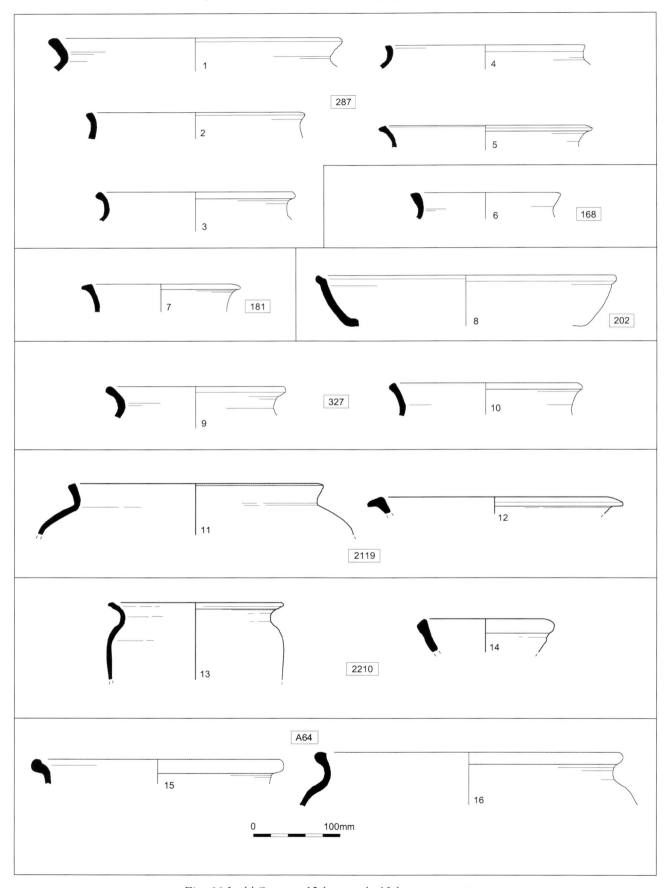

Fig. 66 Lydd Quarry: 12th to early 13th century pottery

Fabric	No. of sherds	% by number	Weight (grams)	% by weight
1c	6	15	72g	18.8
2b	5	12.5	16g	4.2
2c	1	2.5	4g	1.0
2e	28	70	290g	76.0
Total	40	100	382g	100

Table 3: Site A (Lydd 10) Combined pottery assemblage from Ditches A19, A65, A67 and Drain A17

Fabric	No. of sherds	% by number	Weight (grams)	% by weight
1e	1	2.2	10g	1.8
1g	22	47.9	194g	35.8
2c	20	43.4	304g	56.1
2d	2	4.3	24g	4.4
3a	1	2.2	10g	1.8
Total	46	100	542g	99.9

Table 4: Site A (Lydd 10) Pottery assemblage from Pit A62, Fill A64

tempered wares F2c and F2e. Normally at the quarry the finer shell and sand tempered wares (F2b) totally dominate the assemblages (see below) and it is rare for them to be less common than the F2c and F2e sherds. This, combined with the presence of flint tempered wares suggests the assemblage is relatively early, at a time when the flint tempered wares were being replaced by the shell and sand tempered wares, but before the more refined shell and sand tempered wares had developed. A date in the early 13th century is suggested for this assemblage. This would be in keeping with the rounded club-like cooking pot rim (probably from the same vessel) in Post-holes A44 and A46. A similar example, from Pit A62 (Fill A64) is illustrated in Fig. 66, No. 16. Where discernible, all the pottery from the post-holes consists of cooking pots. Whether this material entered the post-holes at the time of the building's construction, repair or demolition is difficult to be certain of. However, the presence of burnt daub in a number of the post-hole fills suggests one of the latter two possibilities. If this is the case the building may originally be of late 12th century date but was repaired or dismantled in the early 13th century. The general lack of later 13th century refuse in the immediate area may hint at the latter suggestion, though this cannot be proven.

The Enclosing Ditches

A number of associated ditches were located close to the building. Ditch A19 (Fill A21), Ditch A65 (Fill A66) and Ditch A67 (Fill A68) appear to form an enclosure around the building, while Ditch A17 (Fill A18) forms a drain running out from its eastern end. Similarly to the post-holes these features produced only small assemblages of pottery; the largest (31 sherds weighing 300g) came from the drain A17. When combined the assemblages offer the opportunity to compare the fabric composition with the combined assemblage from the post-holes.

Once again, the small size of the assemblage means the ratio of different fabrics by number of sherds and weight do not correlate well. The assemblage is somewhat biased due to the presence of a number of sherds from one cooking pot in F2e from Drain A17. Despite this, the presence of flint tempered wares together with F2c and F2e is similar to the fabric types seen from the post-holes. Fabric 2b is present but again, does not dominate the assemblage. As such, it would appear that the infilling of the ditches and drain occurred in the early part of the 13th century.

Pit A62

The largest group from the Phase 10 excavations was located in Pit A62 (Fill A64), just to the west of the enclosure containing the building (46 sherds weighing 542g).

The composition of the fabrics within this group is similar to those from the building and the surrounding ditches, suggesting it to be a contemporary feature of early 13th century date. With the exception of the F3a sherds, which are from a green glazed jug with an applied strip, all the material is from cooking pots. The bulk of the assemblage is made up of pieces from two pots. These account for all the sherds in Fabrics F1g and F2c. Both these pots show extensive signs of burning, some of which is post-breakage.

Fabric	No. of sherds	% by number	Weight (grams)	% by weight
F1b	16	2.6	692g	6.0
F2b	570	94.4	10,750g	92.5
F3b	15	2.5	150g	1.3
F4d	3	0.5	30g	0.3
Total	604	100	11,622g	100.1

Table 5: Site D (Lydd 1). Pottery from Context 151

Catalogue Nos. (Fig. 66)

15. Cooking pot with out-turned thickened rim. Fabric F1g.
16. Cooking pot with thickened club rim. Blackening on rim. Fabric F2c.
    An identical rim form, though in F2b, was located in post-holes A44 and A46.

In addition to the material from Fill A64, the upper fill (A63) produced a single sherd of the rare shell tempered fabric F2a.

13th century

The majority of the excavated assemblages from Lydd Quarry are of 13th century date. The pottery appears to relate to permanent domestic settlement, which seems to have been quite dense at this time. The assemblages are usually totally dominated by the sand and shell tempered wares, principally F2b, though low quantities of sand tempered wares are usually present.

Fill 151 (Pit 150 upper fill) (Lydd 1, Site D)

The assemblage is totally dominated by F2b sherds, though a few finer examples are present which mark the beginning of the transition to the F2d fabric thought to develop in the later part of the 13th century. The F2b sherds in the current assemblage consist of 454 (4,929g) bodysherds, 62 (1,788g) base sherds, 53 (3,968g) rim sherds and a single wide strap handle (65g). Cooking pots and bowls with sagging bases dominate the F2b assemblage. A small amount of F1b material is present, though all appears to be from the same cooking pot/ storage jar with applied thumbed strips. It is quite probable this was an old vessel when broken. The few sand tempered F3b sherds are from a minimum of three different vessels and include a bowl, cooking pot and jug. Whether this material is intrusive is uncertain, though the small abraded nature of the sherds would suggest this to be the case, as does the presence of some definitely intrusive F4d pitcher material. Many of the F2b forms can be closely paralleled with the Potter's Corner material (Grove 1952). A deposition date of around 1225–75 is suggested for the group.

Catalogue Nos. (Fig. 67)

NB. All F2b sherds have grey to dull orange cores and dull orange to orange brown surfaces.

17. Cooking pot/storage jar with out-turned squared rim and vertical applied thumbed strips. F1b.
18. Cooking pot with squared rim. F2b.
19. Cooking pot with triangular rim. F2b.
20. Cooking pot with out-turned thickened rim. F2b.
21. Cooking pot with out-turned thickened rim. F2b.
22. Cooking pot with out-turned thickened bead rim. F2b.
23. Cooking pot with out-turned thickened beaded rim. F2b.
24. Necked cooking pot with down-turned rim. F2b.
25. Necked cooking pot with simple horizontal rim. F2b.
26. Necked cooking pot with down-turned rim. F2b.
27. Cooking pot with simple bead rim. F2b.
28. Cooking pot with squared horizontal rim. F2b.
29. Cooking pot/large bowl with thickened triangular rim. F2b.
30. Bowl with rectangular down-turned rim. F2b.
31. Necked bowl with down-turned rim. F2b.
32. Necked bowl with down-turned rim. F2b.
33. Bowl with out-turned tapering rim. F2b.
34. Necked bowl with out-turned triangular rim. F2b.
35. Bowl with out-turned thickened rim. F3b.
36. Wide strap handle with central stabbing, possibly from a curfew. F2b.

Fill 152 (Pit 150 below 151) (Lydd 1, Site D)

This assemblage is again totally dominated by F2b sherds (or slight variations of); of 383 (6,308g) sherds, 378 (6,188g) are F2b with the remainder being probably residual 12th century F1d sherds. The assemblage is similar to that in 151 and indeed there are a number of cross-joins between the two. Cooking pots and bowls dominate the group, though at least two F2b jugs are present and the probable remains of a curfew (consisting of 4–5 sherds). The jugs are typically spartan in decoration with a little rilling and incised line decoration but no glaze. All in all, 16 different cooking pots are represented, six different bowls and two jugs. The form and fabric composition is virtually identical to that from 151, suggesting a similar deposition date. The absence of sand tempered F3 sherds suggests those in 151 may be intrusive. A few new rim types were noted.

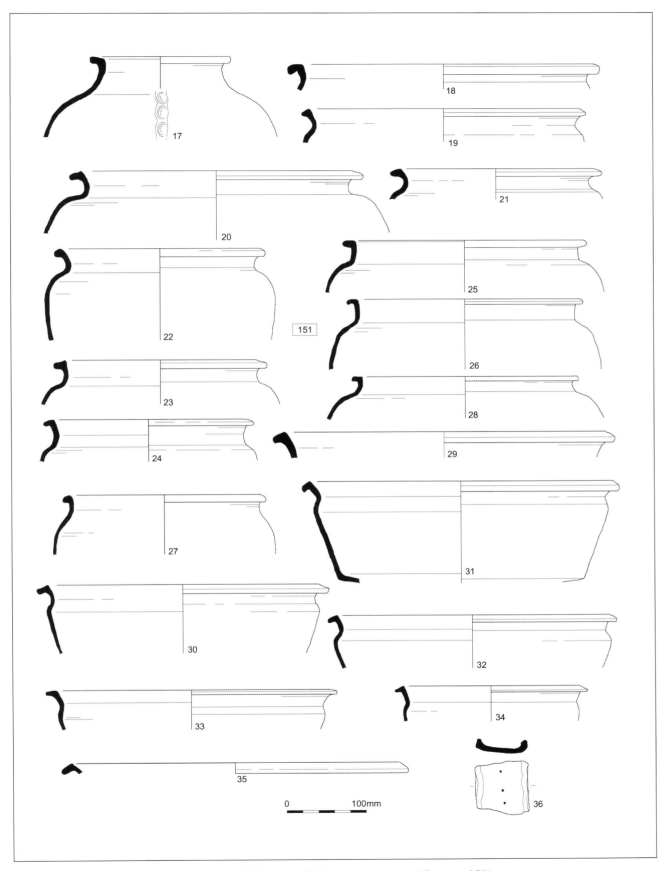

Fig. 67 Lydd Quarry: 13th century pottery (Context 151)

Fabric	No. of sherds	% by number	Weight	% by weight
F1d	16	3.1	130g	2.0
F1e	1	0.2	5g	0.1
F2a	2	0.4	5g	0.1
F2b	374	71.9	5,125g	77.4
F2d	47	9.0	350g	5.3
F2e	6	1.2	30g	0.6
F2f	18	3.4	425g	6.4
F3a	17	3.3	115g	1.7
F3b	12	2.3	105g	1.6
F4a	24	4.6	315g	4.8
F5a	1	0.2	5g	0.1
Roman	2	0.4	10g	0.1
Total	520	100	6,620g	100

Table 6: Site H (Lydd 2) Pottery from Context 2400

Catalogue Nos. (Fig. 68)

NB. All F2b sherds have grey to dull orange cores and dull orange to orange brown surfaces.

37. Cooking pot with out-turned thickened rim. Decorated with rough thumb indentations around shoulder. F2b.
38. Cooking pot with thickened out-turned rim. F2b.
39. Jug with simple out-turned rim, stabbed rod handle and incised line decoration. F2b.

Fill 481 (Pit 150 below 152) (Lydd 1, Site D)

This assemblage is again totally dominated by F2b sherds, though a few possible F2d sherds are also present indicating a slightly later date than that for 151/2: of 192 sherds seven were in F2d, one is in F3a and the remainder in F2b. The latter consists of a minimum of 16 vessels: 11 cooking pots, four bowls and one jug. The latter includes cross-joining sherds with Fill 152. A few new rim types were noted.

Catalogue Nos. (Fig. 68)

40. Cooking pot with squared rim. F3a. Possibly residual.
41. Jug with horizontal rilling on body. F2b.

Fill 482 (Pit 150 below 181) (Lydd 1, Site D)

This assemblage is similar in make-up to the others in Pit 150 and is dominated by F2b sherds. The quantities involved are nine F1b sherds (possibly from the same vessel as in Fill 151), 90 F2b sherds and one F3b sherd.

Catalogue Nos. (Fig. 68)

42. Cooking pot with simple out-turned rim. F2b.
43. Cooking pot with simple out-turned rim. F2b.
44. Cooking pot with out-turned triangular rim. F2b.
45. Cooking pot/storage jar with simple out-turned rim and horizontal applied thumbed strip on shoulder. F2b.
46. Cooking pot with slightly under-cut out-turned rim. F2b.
47. Cooking pot with simple out-turned triangular rim. F3b.

Fill 486 (Pit 150 below 482) (Lydd 1, Site D)

This assemblage is again dominated by F2b sherds. The F2b sherds represent a minimum of 12 different vessels consisting of nine cooking pots and three bowls. The quantities involved are one F1b sherd (possibly from the same vessel as in Fill 151), 242 F2b sherds and 20 F2d sherds. As such, it is likely that Fills 151, 152, 482 and 486 were deposited within a very short space of time, though some of the cross-joining sherds may be the result of mixing of deposits during excavation.

Catalogue No. (Fig. 68)

48. Cooking pot with out-turned triangular rim. F2b.

Fill 2400 (Cut/recut 2399 in enclosure ditch terminal 2194) (Lydd 2, Site H)

Context 2400 produced the largest single assemblage from Site H (Lydd 2). This group is dominated by Fabric group 2b which makes up 77.4% of the assemblage by weight (Table 6). Indeed, taking the shell tempered

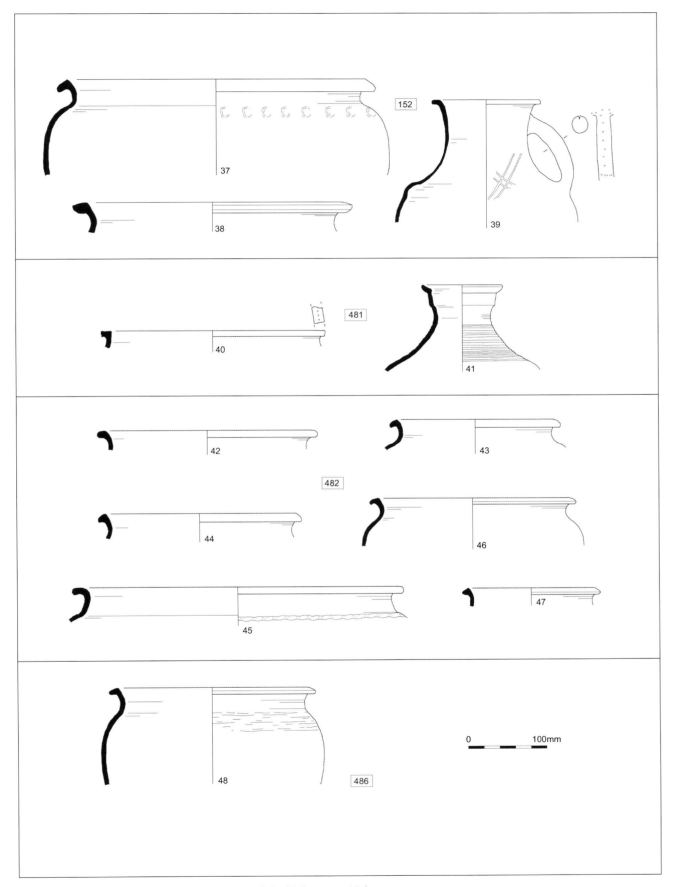

Fig. 68 Lydd Quarry: 13th century pottery

Fabric	Minimum Number of Vessels			
	Cooking Pots	Bowls	Jugs	Uncertain
1d	2	-	1	-
1e	-	-	-	1
2a	-	-	-	1
2b	13	4	2	-
2d	2	-	-	-
2e	-	-	-	1
2f	-	1	-	-
3a	1	-	1	-
3b	-	-	-	1
4a	1	-	-	-
5a	-	-	-	1

Table 7: Site H (Lydd 2): Minimum number of vessels in Context 2400

fabrics as a whole (F2a to F2f) they account for 89.8%, a figure similar to that from the Site D groups. The low quantities of flint tempered sherds (Group 1) suggests these are probably residual sherds or the last remnants of older vessels still in use. The presence of sand tempered (Group 3) and sand and 'grog' tempered (Group 4) wares tends to strengthen the theory regarding the F1 sherds and suggest a date between the mid 13th and early 14th centuries. It is interesting to note that despite being a large assemblage there are no imported sherds, though a few were found at Site H. This is typical of the 13th century Lydd assemblages. Unfortunately the lack of imported pottery, together with no associated diagnostic metalwork, makes precise dating of the ceramic groups problematic. It can be seen that although the Site D and H assemblages have many overlapping forms, a number of new forms are present in the Site H assemblage, suggesting an overlapping, but perhaps slightly later, chronology.

The exact number of vessels represented in this group is difficult to assess. Despite there being 43 rim-sherds in the group, it is apparent that far fewer vessels are present. These are summarised in Table 7.

The dominance of cooking pots, followed by bowls, demonstrates the general trend at the Lydd Quarry sites during this period. The lack of jugs is notable and those that are present, with the exception of a few imports, are usually crude until at least the 14th century when finer vessels appear.

Catalogue Nos. (Fig. 69)

49. Wide mouthed cooking pot or bowl with out-turned club rim. Fabric 2f. External sooting.
50. Cooking pot with thickened out-turned rim. Fabric 2b.
51. Cooking pot with distinct neck and hammer-headed rim. Fabric 2b.
52. Cooking pot with out-turned triangular rim. Fabric 2d. External sooting.

53. Cooking pot with out-turned thickened rim with internal bead. Fabric 4a. A similar vessel was located in New Romney (Willson 1987, 206, No. 4) where it was dated to the first half of the 13th century.
54. Cooking pot with out-turned rim with internal bead. Fabric 2b.
55. Cooking pot with simple out-turned rim. Fabric 2b. External sooting.
56. Cooking pot with thickened squared out-turned rim. Fabric 2b.
57. Cooking pot or bowl with rolled-over rim. Fabric 2b.
58. Cooking pot with thick rim with internal bead. Fabric 2b.
59. Cooking pot with simple out-turned rim. Fabric 2b.
60. Large deep bowl with triangular sectioned rim. Fabric 2b.
61. Large deep bowl with thickened out-turned rim. Incised wavy line on rim. Fabric 2b.
62. Bowl with internal lid-seating. Fabric 2b.
63. Jug with simple out-turned rim and crude stabbed strap handle. Fabric 2b.
64. Jug with simple rim with thickened collar. Fabric 2b.
65. Bunghole or handle probably from a skillet. Fabric 2c.

Fill 2358 (Enclosure ditch terminal 2194) (Lydd 2, Site H)

Context 2358 (Cut 2194, Fig. 43, S92) also contained a large group of pottery (339 sherds). The suggested date for this context is slightly earlier, but heavily overlaps, that suggested for Context 2400. However, the presence of cross-joining sherds and similar fabric compositions within the groups indicates that recut 2399 (containing Fill 2400) was of a similar date to the cut containing 2358 (Context 2194) and may even have been dug specifically for rubbish disposal.

Catalogue Nos. (Fig. 70)

66. Jug with short neck and simple rim. Fabric 2f.
67. Cooking pot with distinct neck and hammer-headed rim. Fabric 2b.

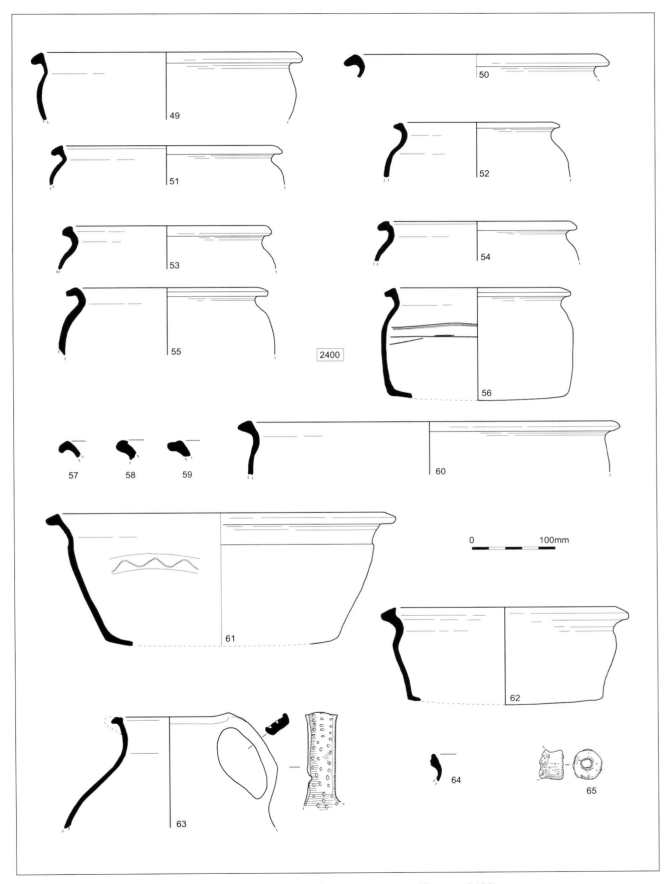

Fig. 69 Lydd Quarry: 13th century pottery (Context 2400)

Fabric	Number	% by number	Weight	% by weight
1c	1	4.5	48g	12.1
1g	4	18.2	206g	51.8
2b	17	77.1	144g	36.2
Total	22	99.8	398g	100.1

Table 8: Site G. Lydd 5/6: Pottery from Context 5120

Fabric	Number	% by number	Weight	% by weight
1d	8	8.2	80g	5.6
2b	79	81.4	1,236g	86.0
2f	2	2.1	66g	4.6
3b	6	6.2	28g	1.9
4a	2	2.1	28g	1.9
Total	97	100	1,438g	100

Table 9: (Lydd 5/6) Pottery from Context 5092

Fill 2376 (Ditch 2375) (Lydd 2, Site H)

Catalogue No. (Fig. 70)

68. Skillet handle with irregular stabbing on upper surface. Fabric 3b.

Fill 7032 (Ditch 7031) (Lydd 7)

The largest group from the Lydd 7 excavations is that from Context 7032 (54 sherds weighing 528g) which contains a somewhat mixed assemblage of late 12th to 13th century material. This assemblage contains mainly cooking pots in Fabrics F1b, F2b, F2d and F2e, but also contains very low quantities of F3b and F3c jugs. The sherds in F1b are probably from one vessel and it probably represents an old pot of the late 12th century, potentially in use towards the middle of the 13th century. This assemblage contains one sherd of particular interest.

Catalogue No. (Fig. 70)

69. An unglazed jug handle with zoomorphic decoration in Fabric F3b. The well-fired handle is mid grey and depicts a dragon by the use of applied clay and incised line decoration. Although no parallels have been found despite extensive searches it is most probably a mid 13th century Rye product (Blythe 1999).

Fill 5120 (Ditch 5119: Site G, Lydd 5/6, Area A)

This ditch is dominated by unabraded shell tempered wares (F2b) but also contains a representative spread of sand/shell and flint-tempered material, indicating its earlier date compared with the bulk of occupation in the immediate vicinity.

A deposition date spanning *c.* 1200–75 is suggested for this context.

Catalogue Nos. (Fig. 70)

70. Jug with upright rim with collar. Unglazed. Fabric 1c.
71. Bowl with down-turned rim. Fabric 1g.
72. Large bowl with down-turned rim. Exterior surfaces sooted. Fabric 1g.
73. Cooking pot with thickened out-turned rim. Sooting on exterior of rim. Fabric 2b.
74. Cooking pot with simple out-turned rim. Fabric 2b.

Fill 5092 (Ditch 5091): Site G, Lydd 5/6, Area A)

This small ditch is dominated by unabraded shell tempered wares (F2b) indicating its earlier date compared with the bulk of occupation in the immediate vicinity. A minimum of ten F2b cooking pots are represented, together with a single unglazed jug. The F1d sherds are all from the same vessel, which was probably somewhat old at the time of deposition.

A deposition date spanning *c.* 1225–1300 is suggested for this context.

Catalogue Nos. (Fig. 70)

75. Cooking pot with out-turned bead rim. Fabric 2b.
76. Cooking pot with rolled over rim. Fabric 2b.
77. Cooking pot with thickened out-turned rim. Fabric 2b.
78. Cooking pot with out-turned squared rim. Fabric 2b.
79. Cooking pot with thickened triangular out-turned rim. Fabric 2b.
80. Cooking pot with everted down-turned rim. Fabric 2b.
81. Jug with simple rim and pulled spout. Unglazed. Fabric 2b.

Fill 5359 (Pit 5357: Site G, Lydd 5/6, Area A)

This group is interesting in that it appears to show the beginning of the transition away from the shell tempered

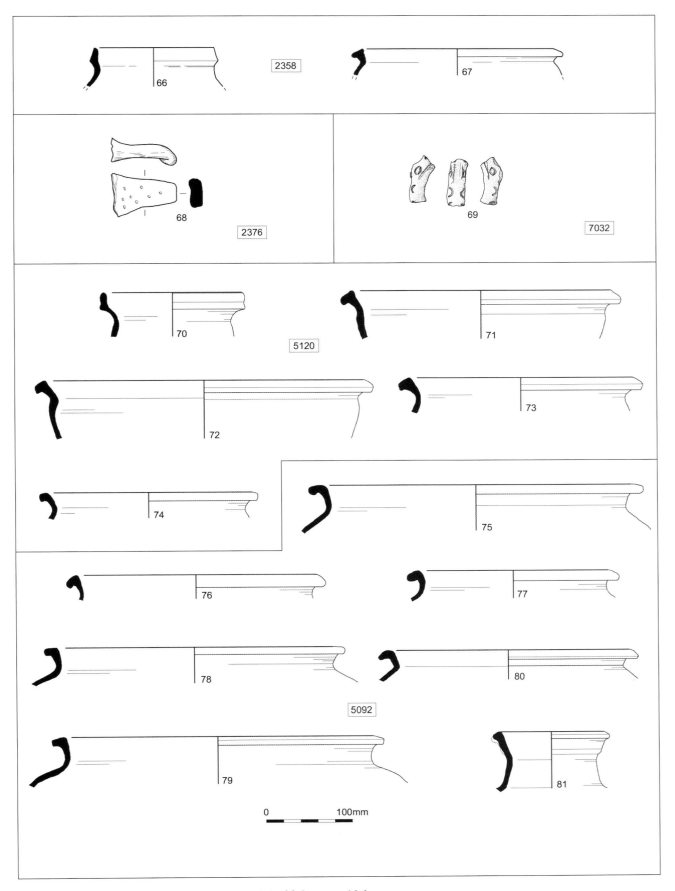

Fig. 70 Lydd Quarry: 13th century pottery

Fabric	Number	% by number	Weight	% by weight
2b	42	48.8	1,100g	57.5
2d	17	19.8	338g	17.7
2f	9	10.5	130g	6.8
3b	10	11.6	144g	7.5
4a	7	8.1	170g	8.9
Imp. 6 (Aardenberg)	1	1.2	30g	1.6
Total	86	100	1,912	100

Table 10: Site G (Lydd 5/6) Pottery from Context 5359

Fabric	Number	% by number	Weight	% by weight
1g	2	1.2	10g	0.6
2b	114	70.1	1,104g	70.9
3b	8	5.0	54g	3.5
3f	17	10.6	134g	8.6
3i (Scarborough)	3	1.9	154g	9.9
4e	11	6.8	74g	4.7
Roman	6	3.7	28g	1.8
Total	161	99.3	1,558g	100

Table 11: Site G (Lydd 5/6) Pottery from Context 5066

to the purely sand tempered wares. Although the shell tempered wares still dominate the assemblage (the combined shell tempered wares in this assemblage total 79.1% by number), there is a marked reduction in the percentage of the F2b fabric with an increase in the finer, and later, F2d fabric. This suggestion of a slightly later date is confirmed by the presence of sandy wares (F3b) in significant quantities, as well as the appearance of F4a sherds. This suggests that the deposition date was probably more toward the end of the 13th century. A deposition date spanning *c.* 1250–1300 is suggested for this context.

By far the majority of the assemblage consists of coarseware vessels, many of which show sooting on the exterior surfaces. Minimum number of identified vessels for the main fabric groups is as follows: F2b – seven cooking pots and two bowls; F2d – one bowl; F3b – one cooking pot, one bowl and one jug; F4a – one bowl. Only two jugs are represented in the assemblage: a glazed body sherd in F3b and a small bodysherd of probable Aardenberg-type ware (Imp. 6) with white slip under a green glaze. The majority of the assemblage from this context suggests it was derived from a close-by kitchen area.

Catalogue Nos. (Fig. 71)

82. Cooking pot with slightly down-turned square rim. External sooting on rim. Fabric 2b.
83. Cooking pot with thickened out-turned squared rim. Fabric 2b.
84. Cooking pot with thin horizontal rim. Exterior surface sooted. Fabric 2b.
85. Cooking pot with expanded rolled over rim. Exterior surface sooted. Fabric 2b.
86. Cooking pot/bowl with thickened out-turned rim. Fabric 2b.
87. Shallow bowl with thickened out-turned rim. Exterior surface sooted. Fabric 2b.
88. Large bowl with undercut down-turned rim. Fabric 2d.
89. Large bowl with down-turned rim. Some horizontal incised lines on exterior surface. Fabric 3b.
90. Bowl with undercut down-turned rim. Exterior surface sooted. Fabric 4a.

Fill 5066 (Ditch 5065 upper fill: Site G. Lydd 5/6, Area A)

This group is dominated again by F2b sherds. These consist of at least three cooking pots, one bowl, one pipkin and one unglazed jug decorated with incised lines. The single sherd of F1g cooking pot is probably residual along with the earlier Roman sandy greyware (four sherds) and South Gaulish Samian (two sherds). The presence of several sherds from a jug with thumbed base in fabric 4e suggest that there may well be intrusive material in this context. This is slightly problematic as this leaves doubt as to whether the F3b sherds are contemporary with the F2b material or are indeed also intrusive.

Of interest is the higher representation of jugs in the assemblage. At least one F3b jug is represented, one F4e jug (intrusive), a carinated F3f jug and a F3i Scarborough aquamanile. The F3f and F3i Scarborough products are of

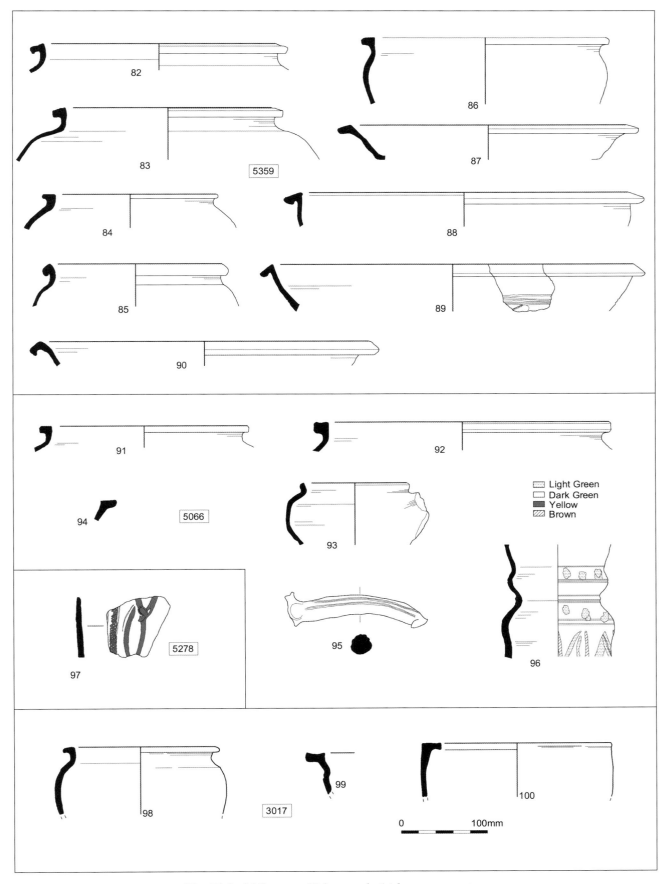

Fig. 71 Lydd Quarry: 13th to early 14th century pottery

Fabric	Number	% by number	Weight	% by weight
2b	74	64.3	1,038g	60.3
2d	3	2.6	76g	4.4
3b	25	21.7	524g	30.4
3c	12	10.4	78g	4.5
4a	1	0.9	4g	0.2
Total	115	99.9	1,720g	99.8

Table 12: Site Ja (Lydd 3) Pottery from Context 3017

interest as they are unusual in an assemblage otherwise dominated by local ceramics of generally utilitarian nature during the 13th century. However, French products and several Aardenberg-type sherds have been located by the current excavations. As such, it should be seen that the occupants were able to obtain higher quality wares if they so needed, desired and indeed could afford them.

A deposition date spanning *c.* 1250–1325 is suggested for this context.

Catalogue Nos. (Fig. 71)

91. Cooking pot with out-turned squared rim. Fabric 2b.
92. Large cooking pot with out-turned square rim. Exterior surface and rim sooted. Fabric 2b.
93. Pipkin with simple everted rim. Scar of handle remaining showing stab marks. Exterior surface sooted toward base. Fabric 2b.
94. Bowl with simple out-turned rim. Some sooting on rim. Fabric 2b.
95. Aquamanile handle. The horizontal rod handle has five prominent ribs on its upper surface and deep impressed thumb marks at junction with rim. Good thick even all over dark green glaze. F3i Scarborough Ware.
96. Decorated bodysherd from a carinated jug in mid grey, quite hard-fired sandy fabric (with some black iron-oxide?) inclusions. Externally decorated with a repeating pattern of low white and brown applied oblique clay strips glazed light green and brown. Higher up the vessel there are two rows of roughly applied white clay dots. The whole decoration is under a thin olive green glaze with brown mottles. Fabric 3f.

Context 5278 (Layer between 5065 and 5334, Site G, Lydd 5/6, Area A)

A single sherd of interest in that it is very similar in manufacture and decorative traits to No. 96. The close proximity of this context to 5066 suggests it is possible both sherds are from the same highly decorated vessel.

Catalogue No. (Fig. 71)

97. Decorated bodysherd from a jug in a mid grey quite hard-fired sandy fabric. Decorated with low applied strips of white clay (glazed yellow), some of which

are rouletted, possibly an attempt at copying a Rouen jug. The whole exterior is covered with a thin dull olive glaze. Fabric 3f.

Fill 3017 (Pit 3016: Site Ja, Lydd 3, Area B)

This pit is one of the few found during the Lydd 3 excavations which was dominated by unabraded shell tempered wares (F2b and 2d), indicating its earlier date compared with the bulk of occupation in the immediate vicinity.

However, the relative large quantity of sand tempered wares (3b), along with the presence of a jug with thumbed base in Fabric 3c, suggest the context may have still been receiving material into the 14th century. It is interesting to note that the sand tempered ware 3b, in contrast to the shell tempered wares (2b and 2d), constitute a larger percentage of the group when quantified by weight. This suggests that the shell tempered wares are generally represented by sherds of a smaller average size, possibly due to secondary breakage, hinting at their suspected earlier (*i.e.*, later 13th century) origin. Fabric 3c is over-represented by sherd count due to the generally fine nature of the vessels in this fabric fragmenting into smaller sherds. A deposition date spanning *c.* 1275–1325 is suggested for this context.

Catalogue Nos. (Fig. 71)

98. Cooking pot with slight neck and out-turned rim. Fabric 2d.
99. Large bowl with out-turned hollowed rim. Exterior sooting. Fabric 2b.
100. Cooking pot/storage vessel? with inturned simple rim. Fabric 3b.

14th century

Relatively few assemblages of this date were recovered from Lydd Quarry, and those that are present are virtually all from Site Jb (Lydd 3, Areas B and C). This strongly suggests that domestic settlement was not as widespread as it had been in the preceding century. However, Site Jb did produce enough 14th century pottery, sometimes in quite large groups, to allow a comparison to be made with the fabric and forms of the 13th century. As such,

Fabric	Number	% by number	Weight	% by weight
2b	3	1.2	12g	0.4
3b	134	55.6	1,234g	41.7
3c	14	5.8	96g	3.2
3e	2	0.8	30g	1.0
3h (Rye)	31	12.9	580g	19.6
4a	30	12.4	708g	24.0
4b	5	2.1	74g	2.5
4c	1	0.4	8g	0.3
4d	4	1.7	58g	2.0
4h	1	0.4	4g	0.1
4i	13	5.4	142g	4.8
Imp.2	3	1.2	8g	0.3
Total	241	99.9	2,954g	99.9

Table 13: Site Jb (Lydd 3) Pottery from Context 3318

the overall aim of the selected analysis on the 14th century groups was to attempt to identify any notable chronological shift in the ratio of fabric groups which may help establish a relative sequence for the 14th century material. The dramatic decrease, or virtual absence, of the shell tempered wares is acutely apparent in this century. Detailed study of forms was not undertaken due to the limited range represented by the relatively small amount of rim-sherds in the assemblages. However, all main forms, where possible, are reproduced in the illustrated catalogue.

Fill 3343 (Cut 3344: Site Jb, Lydd 3, Area C)

This context, which only produced a small assemblage of pottery, appears to have a deposition date between *c.* 1325 and 1400. Although too small to study the fabric ratios, the following drawable sherds were present.

Catalogue Nos. (Fig. 72)

101. Small bowl with simple out-turned rim. Spots of internal clear glaze. Fabric 3c.
102. Cooking pot with thin squared out-turned rim. Fabric 3c.
103. Not Illustrated. Strap handle from a Saintonge Polychrome jug. Imp. 1.
104. Rod handle with ribbing of anterior surface from a jug. Thick even green glaze. F3i Scarborough Ware.

Fill 3318 (Pit 3317 upper fill: Site Jb, Lydd 3, Area C)

This group shows what is currently believed to be the typical make-up of fabrics in the mid 14th century, though there may be a little blurring from residual and intrusive sherds. The general ratios are not dissimilar to those of Context 3180 (see below) though this context is the likely source of intrusive/residual pottery within Context 3318 and indeed the fill stratigraphically below (Context 3329). Based on the fabric percentages this pit may be

slightly earlier than 3180, however, some discrepancies in the groups suggest some mixing of pottery has occurred between 3317/3329 and 3180 and as such it is impossible to ascertain if there is any significant chronological difference between these contexts. A deposition range of *c.* 1325 to 1400 is probable, but 1325 to 1375 thought likely.

The medium fired sand tempered wares (*i.e.*, 3b) and F3h Rye-type products dominate, with only a little residual shell tempered ware being represented. The lower percentage of F3h Rye-type wares and Fabric 4d sherds in 3118, compared to 3180, suggest this context may have been deposited slightly earlier than 3180. However, the sand and 'grog' tempered wares (*i.e.*, Fabric 4a) are over-represented in Context 3118 due to the presence of a number of sherds from a badly fragmented bowl (comparison of percentages of F4a in 3180, 3118 and 3329 shows no patterning), and warns of the dangers of relying on fabric ratios alone for chronological ordering. The higher-fired fabrics (particularly 4d, 4h, 4i) are present in relatively low quantities and may represent their first introduction or, more likely, mixing with material from 3180. This is particularly the case when one considers the high percentage of F4h and F4i sherds in the lower fill of this pit (3329 – see below).

Catalogue Nos. (Fig. 72)

105. Bowl with thin squared out-turned stabbed rim. Slight rilling on exterior. Fabric 3b.
106. Bowl with out-turned hollowed rim. Some external sooting. Fabric 3b.
107. Bowl with thin out-turned, slightly beaded rim with thumbed and stabbed upper surface. Applied thumbed strips on vessel exterior. Fabric 4a.
108. Bowl with out-turned rounded and thickened rim and slight internal bead. Incised wavy line decoration of upper surface of rim. Fabric 4b.

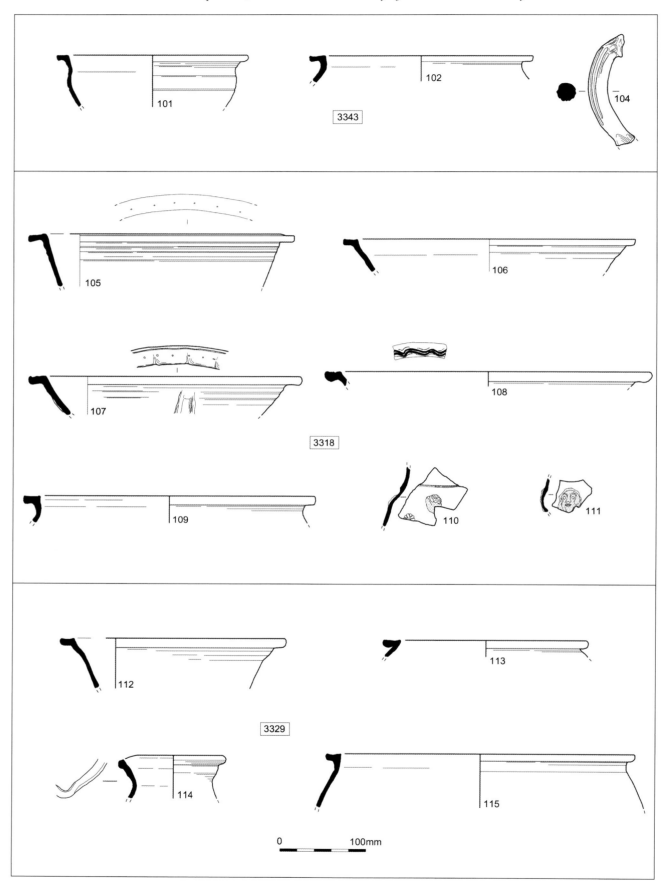

Fig. 72 Lydd Quarry: 14th century pottery

Fabric	Number	% by number	Weight	% by weight
1e	1	1.0	10g	0.7
2b	3	2.9	32g	2.2
2e	1	1.0	8g	0.6
3b	42	40.4	294g	20.2
3c	4	3.8	104g	7.2
3e	1	1.0	24g	1.7
F3g (Surrey)	2	1.9	22g	1.5
3h (Rye)	11	10.6	138g	9.5
4a	2	1.9	22g	1.5
4d	1	1.0	10g	0.7
4h	23	22.1	588g	40.4
4i	11	10.6	198g	13.6
Imp. 1	2	1.9	4g	0.3
Total	104	100.1	1,454g	100.1

Table 14: Site Jb (Lydd 3): Pottery from Context 3329

Fabric	Number	% by number	Weight	% by weight
2b	8	0.9	38g	0.4
3b	362	38.6	2,736g	27.8
3c	62	6.6	426g	4.3
3e	51	5.4	484g	4.9
3h (Rye)	213	22.7	3,524g	35.8
4a	113	12.1	1,492g	15.2
4b	15	1.6	146g	1.5
4c	1	0.1	34g	0.3
4d	58	6.2	490g	5.0
4e/h	19	2.0	240g	2.4
4f	20	2.1	192g	2.0
4g	2	0.2	18g	0.2
Imp 1	13	1.4	26g	0.3
Total	937	99.9	9,846g	100.1

Table 15: Site Jb (Lydd 3): Pottery from Context 3180

109. Cooking pot with out-turned squared rim. Fabric 4i.
110. Decorated jug bodysherd. Decorated with applied pellets of dark brown and white firing clay, which have then been stamped with a trefoil cross design by exerting pressure with a finger from the pot's interior. The whole exterior of the vessel is covered with a good even dull green glaze with black iron ore speckles. F3h Rye-type.
111. Decorated jug bodysherd. Decorated with an applied pellet of white-firing clay which has then been stamped with an anthropomorphic design by exerting pressure with a finger from the pot's interior. The main body of the jug has a good even light green glaze. The applied stamped pellet is covered with clear glaze giving it a yellow colour. F3h Rye type.

Fill 3329 (Pit 3317, middle fill: Site Jb, Lydd 3, Area C)

As discussed above, although this assemblage has similar fabric ratios to 3318, there are some significant anomalies which do not appear to make chronological sense (*i.e.*, the high percentages of Fabrics 4h and 4i), based on the suspected chronology of the deposit, and it is highly likely that there has been some mixing of sherds with 3180.

Fabric	Minimum number of vessels (based on rims, handles and jug bodysherds)					
	Cooking Pots	Storage Jars	Bowls	Jugs/ Pitchers	Skillets	Uncertain
2b	-	-	-	-	-	1
3b	5	-	4	5	-	-
3c	-	-	-	4	-	2
3e	2	-	-	1	-	-
3h (Rye)	-	2	2	4	-	-
4a	5	-	2	2	1	-
4b	-	-	-	-	-	1
4c	1	-	-	-	-	-
4d	1	-	1	2	-	-
4e/h	-	-	-	2	-	-
4f	2	-	-	-	-	-
4g	1	-	-	-	-	-
Imp 1	-	-	-	3	-	-
Total	17	2	9	23	1	4

Table 16: Site Jb (Lydd 3) Minimum number of vessels in Context 3180 by general form

This assemblage shows an interesting pattern in that the average sherd size of the sandy fabric F3b appears to be small (when comparing the percentage by sherd count and weight) and indeed these sherds are frequently abraded, suggesting a degree of residuality. The later fabrics show a reversal of this trend (*i.e.*, F4h), suggesting these vessels, represented by the larger sherds, have no residual element among them. Such a theory will need large isolated assemblages, with no residual/intrusive material, to test its accuracy. A deposition date similar to the upper fill 3318 is suggested (*i.e.*, *c.* 1325–1400) although 1325–75 is quite possible.

Catalogue Nos. (Fig. 72)

112. Bowl with out-turned slightly hollowed rim. External sooting. Fabric 3c.
113. Cooking pot with thickened, wide, flat-topped out-turned rim. Fabric 3e.
114. Pitcher/jug with thickened rim and simple pulled spout. External spots of green glaze. Fabric 4h.
115. Large cooking pot/storage vessel with thin out-turned square rim. Fabric 4i.

Fill 3180 (Cut 3308: Site Jb, Lydd 3, Area C)

Context 3180 produced the largest single assemblage from Site Jb (Table 15).

The fabric breakdown for this context suggests it also dates to a period post-dating the shell tempered wares (those present are residual) when the sand tempered fabrics dominated the market. Both the medium fired sand tempered wares and the better produced F3h Rye-type products dominate the assemblage at this time, although the sand and 'grog' tempered Fabric 4a is also well represented. The later harder-fired fabrics are present in small quantities (F4d, F4e/h, *etc.*), and it is probable they represent the first appearance of these new wares,

some of which at least probably originated from Rye. The difficulty dividing Fabrics 4e and 4h was particularly problematic in this context and as a result they have been grouped together in this instance. The definite F4e sherds are thought to possibly be intrusive, although their exact start date is still uncertain. A deposition date of *c.* 1325/50–1375/1400 is suggested for this context though some elements suggest that a date into the early 15th century is possible. As noted in earlier assemblages, some fabrics are represented by generally smaller sherds which tends to increase their overall percentage within the group when sherd count is used for the quantification medium. This is expected when dealing with finewares (*i.e.*, Fabrics 3c and Imp. 1) which, due to their very nature tend to break into numerous small sherds and are frequently over-represented by sherd count (but under-represented by weight). However, a similar discrepancy is noted with the medium fired sand tempered ware (F3b). This cannot be down to the fabric alone as the wares are fairly robust and unlikely to break into generally smaller pieces than the higher-fired sherds such as the F3h Rye-type wares. It is therefore considered probable that there is an earlier 14th century residual element in this assemblage, represented by at least a proportion of these medium fired sand tempered wares. The F3h Rye-type products are the dominant fabric type if sherd weight is used and this correlates well with the frequently large unabraded nature of these vessels. However, the presence of a number of very large sherds from two F3h Rye-type storage vessels/cooking pots in this group may be distorting the percentage of this fabric group in the assemblage.

The exact number of vessels represented in Context 3180 is difficult to assess. Despite there being 74 rim-sherds in the group, it is apparent that far fewer vessels are present. A breakdown of basic forms is given in Table 16.

Fabric	Number	% by number	Weight	% by weight
2b	2	1.7	26g	3.4
2d	1	0.8	10g	1.3
3b	14	11.7	108g	14.0
3c	14	11.7	48g	6.2
3d	2	1.7	6g	0.7
3e	1	0.8	4g	0.5
4a	3	2.5	46g	5.9
4d	79	65.8	488g	63.0
4e	3	2.5	34g	4.4
3i (Scarborough)	1	0.8	6g	0.8
Total	120	100	776g	100.2

Table 17: Site Jb (Lydd 3) Pottery from Context 3075

The coarsewares are unsurprisingly dominated by cooking pots, though bowls are more common than in the 13th century deposits at Lydd 2. However, the presence of external sooting on many of these bowls suggests they were also used for cooking. This trend, which currently appears most noticeably at Lydd 3, is understandable considering the easier access (*i.e.*, for stirring and ladling out food) afforded by their wide aperture. The dominance of jugs is in extreme contrast to the 13th century deposits at Lydd 1 and 2. However, this apparent dominance is not just the result of an actual increase in the use of jugs at the settlements in the 14th century, but also due to these 14th century vessels being far more easy to recognise in the assemblages. The 13th century jugs located at the quarry so far are mainly unglazed, undecorated shell tempered types. With these vessels rim-sherds or handles are needed to recognise them; bodysherds cannot usually be distinguished from cooking pots. The fact that most of the 14th century jugs are of a higher standard, and frequently show signs of external glaze, enables even their bodysherds to be identified with ease. It should therefore be considered that the above figures do not so much overestimate jugs but underestimate the minimum number of coarseware vessels present.

Catalogue Nos. (Fig. 73)

116. Cooking pot with slightly hollowed out-turned rim. Fabric 3b.
117. Bowl with squared rim. Internal spots of clear glaze. Fabric 3b.
118. Bowl with thickened rounded out-turned rim and pronounced neck. Heavy external sooting and applied thumbed strips. Fabric 3b.
119. Small bowl with thickened rim, extended internally. Stabbing around exterior. Fabric 3b.
120. Jug with everted rim and horizontal applied and thumbed decorative strip around base of neck. Dull light green glaze with brown iron oxide mottles on neck interior and over all exterior surface. Fabric 3c.
121. Cooking pot with flat-topped rim and thickened neck. Fabric 3e.
122. Cooking pot with wide out-turned rim. Fabric 3e.

123. Jug with thickened rim. Fabric 3e.
124. Bowl? with simple inverted rim. Fabric 4a.
125. Cooking pot with flat-topped rim and thickened neck. Fabric 4a.
126. Cooking pot with out-turned rim with stabbing on upper surface. Fabric 4a.
127. Cooking pot with thin wide out-turned rim and external applied thumbed strips. Fabric 4c.
128. Cooking pot/storage jar with thin squared out-turned rim and external applied thumbed strips. F3h Rye-type.
129. Storage jar with slightly hollowed out-turned rim. F3h Rye-type.
130. Cooking pot with flaring, internally beaded, rim. Slight external sooting. F3h Rye-type.
131. Shallow bowl with flat-topped, slightly hooked rim. Interior base glazed dull green. F3h Rye-type.
132. Decorated jug sherd. Applied pellets of clay which have been stamped with a roundel design. Depressions on the interior show finger pressure was used from this side to push the pot's body into the stamp. The stamps appear to be slipped dark brown and white alternately, with the whole exterior being covered by a thin dull green glaze. F3h Rye-type.
133. Decorated jug sherd. Applied pellets of white-firing clay have been stamped with a roundel design. Depressions on the interior show finger pressure was used from this side to push the pot's body into the stamp. The exterior of the jug is glazed dull brown/green with dark iron oxide mottles. The stamped applied pellets are covered with a clear glaze so they stay white in contrast to the body of the pot. F3h Rye-type.
134. Decorated jug sherd. Decorated with 'raspberry' stamps directly onto the vessel wall. Deep depressions on the interior show finger pressure was used from this side to push the pot's body into the stamp. The stamps, as with the rest of the jug's exterior, has a good even bright light and dark green mottled glaze. F3h Rye-type.
135. Pitcher with thickened rim and deeply slashed strap handle. Fabric 4e.

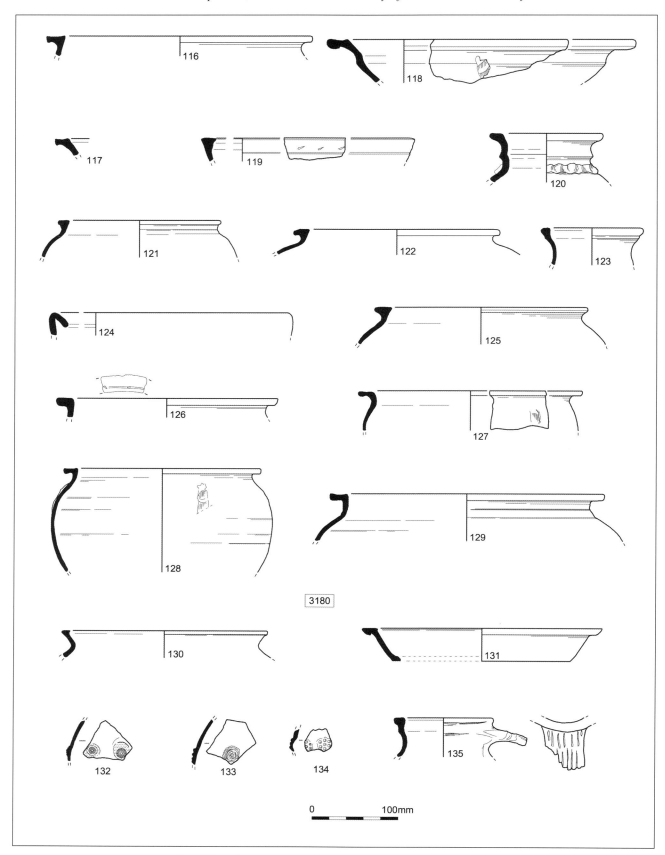

Fig. 73 Lydd Quarry: 14th century pottery (Context 3180)

Fabric	Number	% by number	Weight	% by weight
2b	4	3.4	18g	3.2
3b	3	2.6	12g	2.2
3c	38	32.8	110g	19.9
3d	2	1.7	6g	1.1
3e	3	2.6	14g	2.5
3h (Rye)	7	6.0	28g	5.1
4a	8	6.9	66g	11.9
4d	31	26.7	158g	28.5
4e	18	15.5	130g	23.5
4f	2	1.7	12g	2.2
Total	116	99.9	554g	100.1

Table 18: (Site Jb) Pottery from Context 3105

Fabric	Number	% by number	Weight	% by weight
3b	3	2.8	20g	2.3
3c	1	0.9	8g	0.9
4a	4	3.7	42g	4.9
4d	18	16.5	112g	12.8
4e	2	1.8	14g	1.6
4h	79	72.5	670g	76.3
4n	2	1.8	12g	1.4
Total	109	100	878g	100.2

Table 19: (Lydd 5/6) Pottery from Context 5014

15th to early/mid 16th century

The transition from the later 14th century into the 15th century is difficult to characterise due to the gradual nature in which the changes occurred. Some of the higher-fired wares, appearing from the mid 14th century, develop and merge into the 'ringing' utilitarian wares of the 15th century. As such, some of the groups listed below may be of late 14th century date, though all have been placed in an 'approximate' chronology. Pottery of the late 14th to 15th centuries was recovered from the latest features at Site Jb (Lydd 3, Areas B and C), as well as at various places at Lydd 5/6 (Sites L and M).

Fill 3075 (Pit 3074: Site Jb, Lydd 3, Area B)

This is an unusual make-up of fabrics within a context group. The shell tempered wares (2b and 2d) are undoubtedly residual in this deposit, a point confirmed by the small abraded nature of the sherds. The presence of a number of sherds from a bunghole pitcher in Fabric 4d account for the majority of the assemblage and tend to create an imbalance. A date of *c.* 1375–1475 is suggested for deposition. No vessels have been illustrated.

Fill 3105 (Pit 3104: Site Jb, Lydd 3, Area B)

The patterning of this assemblage is similar to that from Context 3075, suggesting both were deposited at around the same time. It is interesting to note that the latest fabric (4e) is represented better by weight rather than sherd count, again hinting at larger sherds and less re-working. However, it should be noted that the hard-fired fabrics (4d and 4e) in this group were particularly difficult to assign to fabric groups due to 'merging' of group characteristics. It is also interesting to note the difference between the percentage of sand tempered Fabric 3b when sherd count and weight are compared. As seen with the shell tempered fabrics in Context 3017, the smaller sherd size suggested by these figures may suggest that the vessels in this fabric within the pit had been around for a while (indeed some may be residual), whereas the newer harder-fired fabrics derive from freshly broken vessels (*i.e.*, compare the sherd number and weight ratio percentages of Fabric 4e). A deposition date between *c.* 1350 and 1475 is suggested, though it is felt a 1375 to 1475 range is more likely.

Fabric	Number	% by number	Weight	% by weight
3b	4	3.1	16g	1.5
F3g (?Surrey)	1	0.8	6g	0.6
3h (Rye)	2	1.6	14g	1.3
4d	4	3.1	44g	4.1
4h	47	36.4	382g	35.6
4j	13	10.1	110g	10.3
4k	26	20.2	212g	19.8
4l	25	19.4	206g	19.2
4n	6	4.7	72g	6.7
Imp 8	1	0.8	10g	0.9
Total	129	100.2	1,072g	100

Table 20: Site Lb (Lydd 5/6) Pottery from Context 5084

Catalogue Nos. (Fig. 74)

136. Cooking pot with out-turned squared rim. Fabric 4d.
137. Jug/pitcher with thickened rim. Thin splashed external brown glaze. Fabric 4e.

Fill 3349 (Cess Pit/Sump 3348: Site Jb, Lydd 3, Area B)

This context produced a very small assemblage of pottery, suggesting a deposition date of between 1375 and 1475. The assemblage was not large enough to warrant detailed study, however, the presence of a painted sherd is of some interest as these have been rare at the site.

Catalogue No.

138. Not Illustrated. Decorated bodysherd from a jug/pitcher. Decorated with painted vertical and oblique lines of white slip. Fabric 4h.

Fill 5014 (Ditch ? 5013: Lydd 5/6, Site M, wider field system)

The small quantities and abraded nature of the F3b and F3c sherds within this group suggest they are residual, as is, probably, the F4a material. Putting these aside the group is dominated by Transitional wares. Fabric 4h dominates and is represented by pitchers and cooking pots/jars, one of which is decorated with white slip painting.

The assemblage is typically utilitarian and a deposition date of *c.* 1400–75 is suggested for this context.

Catalogue Nos. (Fig. 74)

139. Large pitcher with thickened grooved rim. Occasional spots of clear glaze on exterior surface. Fabric 4h.
140. Pitcher with simple rim. No glaze. Fabric 4h.
141. Pitcher with flaring rim. Sparse exterior thin brown glaze. Fabric 4h.

Fill 5123 (lower fill of sump in Ditch 5007: Lydd 5/6, wider field system)

This context contains a lid-seated jar in Fabric 4h, which complements the pitchers from 5014. Of interest is the presence of a further example of white slip painted decoration (on an undiagnostic bodysherd). A date range between 1425 and 1525 is suggested for this context based on the ceramics. However, leatherwork from this context offers a much tighter date range of deposition (1490–1510).

Catalogue No. (Fig. 74)

142. Lid-seated jar with everted rim. Exterior surface unglazed, though interior has splashes of clear/greenish thin glaze. Fabric 4h.

Fill 5084 (Pit 5083: Lydd 5/6, between Ditches 5023 and 5043 – Site Lb wider ditch system)

This assemblage has a little residual 14th century material (represented by the F3b, F3g ?Surrey and F3h Rye fabrics). It is possible that the four jar bodysherds in F4d were from an older vessel or are also residual.

The dominant group is again Fabric 4h, but F4k and F4l are also well represented. Vessels appear to be limited to plain cooking pots/jars and pitchers, although a tripod pipkin is present in F4k. A deposition date of *c.* 1425–1525/50 is suggested for this context.

Fill 3151 (Trackway Ditch 3150: upper fill: Site Jb, Lydd 3, Area C)

This assemblage, although consisting of less than 100 sherds, was fully quantified, as it represented the chronologically latest pottery group (*c.* 1450–1525) from Site Jb. However, its position within the trackway ditch, and the lack of any settlement features of comparable date at Site Jb, suggest this deposit was dumped in the ditch after the settlement was abandoned. The hard-fired Transitional wares (*i.e.*, 4e and 4h) totally dominate the assemblage, and new forms such as bottles/flasks and open wares begin to appear with these fabrics, most noticeably F4e.

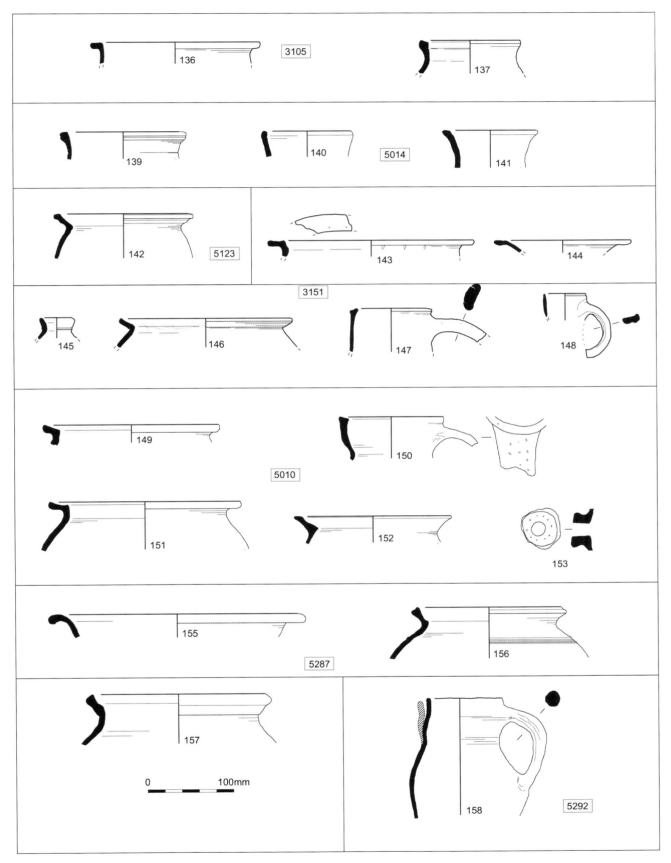

Fig. 74 Lydd Quarry: 15th to early/mid 16th century pottery

Fabric	Number	% by number	Weight	% by weight
3b	4	6.6	56g	6.9
3c	1	1.6	2g	0.2
4a	1	1.6	10g	1.2
4e	13	21.3	246g	30.1
4h	37	60.7	406g	49.8
4g	2	3.3	30g	3.7
4i	2	3.3	28g	3.4
Imp. 5 (Siegburg)	1	1.6	38g	4.7
Total	61	100	816g	100

Table 21: Site Jb (Lydd3) Pottery from Context 3151

Fabric	Number	% by number	Weight	% by weight
1e	1	1.2	10g	0.8
2b	2	2.4	8g	0.6
3h (Rye)	5	6.1	44g	3.4
4b	1	1.2	2g	0.2
4d	10	12.2	52g	4.0
4h	38	46.3	650g	50.6
4j	23	28.0	484g	37.7
Imp. 5 Siegburg	2	2.4	34g	2.6
Total	82	99.8	1,284g	99.9

Table 22: (Lydd 5/6) Pottery from Context 5010

Catalogue Nos. (Fig. 74)

143. Cooking pot/bowl with out-turned, slightly hollowed, rim with stabbing on upper surface. Fabric 4e.
144. Small shallow bowl/dish with slightly thickened everted rim. Fabric 4e.
145. Bottle/flask with simple rim. Fabric 4e.
146. Cooking pot/jar with simple sharply everted rim. Patchy, but thick, dull green glaze on internal rim. Fabric 4g.
147. Jug with triangular rim and oval-sectioned stabbed handle. Patchy external dull green glaze. Fabric 4h.
148. Narrow-necked jug with simple rim and small strap handle. Siegburg stoneware (Imp. 5).

Fill 5010 (Ditch 5009: Lydd 5/6, south ditch of southern trackway: wider field system)

The assemblage from the upper fill of this ditch in the Lydd 5/6 area shows quite a range of fabrics, mainly due to the presence of residual material. This is easily singled out as material in Fabrics 1e, 2b, 4b and 3h Rye products. Three residual coins are also present from this context, together with two worn and intrusive Elizabethan issues. The assemblage is dominated by F4h and F4j, though significant quantities of F4d are also present. Only pitchers and cooking pots/jars are present, all of which are undecorated. The two sherds of Siegburg stoneware represent the beginning of German imports to the area, and it is interesting to note that more were found further to the east at Lydd 3 in the same ditch (see above 3151). A date of *c.* 1425/50–1525 is suggested for this context's deposition.

The lower fill of this ditch (5146), dated *c.* 1400–1500, contained only two sherds: an F4e bodysherd and a rim from an F4h pitcher.

Catalogue Nos. (Fig. 74)

149. Cooking pot with out-turned slightly thickened rim. Fabric 4h.
150. Pitcher with crudely stabbed strap handle and simple rim. No glaze. Fabric 4h.
151. Cooking pot with out-turned hollowed rim. Fabric 4j.
152. Cooking pot/jar with everted rim with lid-seating. Fabric 4j.
153. Bunghole from a pitcher with stabbing around round aperture. Patches of light brown red external glaze. Fabric 4j.

Fills 5287 and 5292 (Pit 5286: Site Lb: Lydd 5/6, south side of Ditch 23: wider field system)

This feature contained a complex sequence of fills, most of which unfortunately produced no, or very little, pottery. Slightly larger assemblages were recovered from only two contexts.

Fabric	Number	% by number	Weight	% by weight
4a	1	1.7	20g	1.4
4d	7	11.9	122g	8.4
4h	30	50.8	860g	59.1
4i	1	1.7	8g	0.5
4j	5	8.5	78g	5.4
4k	2	3.4	60g	4.1
4l	5	8.5	176g	12.1
4n	6	10.2	102g	7.0
4o	1	1.7	24g	1.6
4p	1	1.7	6g	0.4
Total	59	100.1	1,456g	100

Table 23: Site Jb (Lydd 5/6) Pottery from Context 5287

Fabric	Number	Weight
4e	2	16g
4h	4	150g
4j	2	28g
4l	1	664g
4n	1	10g
4o	2	14g
Total	12	882g

Table 24: Pottery from Context 5292

The first of these contexts is 5287. Although a small group, there appears to be no residual material with the one exception of a single sherd from an F4a jug. The group is again dominated by pitchers and cooking pots/jars in F4h. A pipkin foot in F4k is also present. A deposition date of *c.* 1475–1525 is suggested for this context. It should be noted that there is a conjoining 4h base sherd with Context 5292.

Catalogue Nos. (Fig. 74)

154. Not Illustrated. Pitcher with wide stabbed strap handle. Very similar to Cat. No. 150. No glaze. Fabric 4h.
155. Jar or bowl with wide rolled over flaring rim. Splashes and patches of thin apple green glaze internally. Fabric 4h.
156. Jar with everted rim and lid seating. No glaze. Three lightly incised horizontal lines on exterior surface. Fabric 4h.
157. Jar with out-turned/everted rim and lid seating. (surfaces quite badly flaked). Spots of metallic brown glaze on interior surface. Fabric 4l.

This assemblage is too small for meaningful quantification, and the percentages would be totally distorted by the presence of the large part of the F4l jug. A deposition date of *c.* 1425/50–1525 is suggested for this context's deposition. This date can be considerably tightened by the leatherwork which suggests a date range of 1490–1500. It should be noted that there is a conjoining 4h base sherd with Context 5287.

Catalogue No. (Fig. 74)

158. Jug with simple pulled spout and crude rod handle. Buff core with brown orange surfaces. Knife trimming to lower exterior surface. The jug is asymmetrical in plan. Fabric 4l.

Fill 5044 (Ditch 5043: Site Lb area, Lydd 5/6, wider field system)

This assemblage has a small 13th and 14th century residual element marked by the F2b, F3c, F4a and F3h Rye sherds. It is possible, but far from certain, that the F4d and F4e sherds are also residual in this context. The assemblage is again dominated by F4h sherds, which represent a range of plain jars, pitchers and bowls.

The single sherd of German stoneware could either be intrusive or an early import for this area. The sherd has been ascribed a Cologne rather than Frechen source. A deposition date of *c.* 1475–1550 is suggested for this context.

Fabric	Number	% by number	Weight	% by weight
2b	12	9.2	138g	10.3
3c	2	1.5	50g	3.7
3h (Rye)	2	1.5	10g	0.7
4a	2	1.5	10g	0.7
4d	12	9.2	104g	7.7
4e	5	3.8	60g	4.5
4g	3	2.3	38g	2.8
4h	45	34.6	402g	29.9
4j	6	4.6	70g	5.2
4l	10	7.7	218g	16.2
4n	12	9.2	64g	4.6
4o	16	12.3	152g	11.3
4p	2	1.5	16g	1.2
Colonge PM7b	1	0.8	14g	1.0
Total	130	99.7	1,346g	99.8

Table 25: (Lydd 5/6) Pottery from Context 5044

Fabric	Number	% by number	Weight	% by weight
4h	1	0.4	4g	0.1
4k	4	1.6	142g	2.5
4l	3	1.2	42g	0.7
4m	3	1.2	58g	1.0
4n	2	0.8	16g	0.3
PM 1a	13	5.3	258g	4.5
PM 1b	1	0.4	15g	0.3
PM 1c	37	15.2	702g	12.4
PM 1d	2	0.8	35g	0.6
PM 2a	9	3.7	140g	2.5
PM 2b	8	3.3	300g	5.3
PM 2c	10	4.1	250g	4.4
PM 3a	22	9.0	456g	8.0
PM 3b	16	6.6	560g	9.9
PM 3c	21	8.6	678g	12.0
PM 3d	12	4.9	726g	12.8
PM 4a	1	0.4	2g	0.04
PM 5a	1	0.4	92g	1.6
PM 5b	4	1.6	134g	2.4
PM 5c	4	1.6	74g	1.3
PM 5d	1	0.4	34g	0.6
PM 6a	28	11.5	216g	3.8
PM 6b	1	0.4	2g	0.04
PM 6c	7	2.9	48g	0.8
PM 6d	8	3.3	116g	2.0
PM 7b	6	2.5	206g	3.6
PM 7c	9	3.7	230g	4.1
PM 8a	8	3.3	134g	2.4
PM 8b	2	0.8	2g	0.04
Total	244	99.9	5,672g	100.02

Table 26: Site N (Lydd 5/6) Pottery from Context 5138

Later Post-medieval

With the exception of a few isolated stray sherds, the only post 16th century group material comes from a single large group, though more may be expected closer to the 'Burnt House' (Site N).

Fill 5138 (Ditch 5137: related to Site N, Lydd 5/6, Area B)

This context, although only sampled by excavation, produced the largest group from the Phase 5/6 excavations and the latest group from the quarry to date. As such, all drawable rims from this assemblage have been included in the catalogue. A relatively small amount of residual pottery is present, as marked by the F4h, F4k, F4l, F4m and F4n sherds, though it is possible that some of these vessels may have survived long enough to still have been in 17th century assemblages. This is particularly the case with the F4m jar and F4k pipkin and bunghole pitcher, which may be late vessels anyway. More assemblages of this date will be needed to establish the longevity of these wares.

The assemblage is dominated by lead glazed coarsewares (PM1–3) though there is a wide diversity of both local, regional and imported wares. The local earthenwares are glazed both green and red/brown and show a wide range of firing temperatures, suggesting that the group contains vessels from a relatively wide chronological range. A range of domestic wares, dominated by jars, but including jugs/pitchers, pipkins and bowls, is represented. Other wares from further afield include a few examples of Borderware and Wealden whitewares (PM5) including a chamber pot, a range of tin-glazed earthenwares (PM6) and both German and English stonewares (PM7 and PM8). The German stoneware consists of Frechen Bellarmines of 17th century date and Westerwald tankards of later 17th to early 18th century date. It is interesting to note that the English stoneware, both from London (PM8a) and ?Staffordshire (PM8b), is only represented by tankards or tavern pots. This, combined with the quantity of clay pipes from this context, suggests the assemblage as a whole may not be totally 'domestic' in nature. It is possible it represents a mixture of both waste from a tavern *and* domestic occupation. A deposition date of *c.* 1675–1720 is suggested for this context based on the ceramics alone. However, the large assemblage of clay pipes helps tie the deposition date down to *c.* 1710. This is interesting considering the high percentage of pottery within the assemblage which appears to be of early to mid 17th century date.

Catalogue Nos. (Figs. 75 and 76)

159. Pipkin with lid seating. Unglazed. Fabric 4k.
160. Thumbed bunghole from a pitcher. Fabric 4k.
161. Jar with reeded rim. Unglazed. Fabric 4m.
162. Jar/pipkin. Exterior spots of glaze. Interior surface is a dark orange brown with sparse thin slightly metallic glaze. No. 163 may be the handle from this vessel. Fabric PM 1a.
163. Pipkin handle with deep thumb-mark at junction with body of vessel. Interior surface of vessel has a thin metallic purple glaze. May be the handle to vessel No. 162. Fabric PM 1a.
164. Tubular spout with splashes and patches of green brown metallic glaze. Fabric PM 1c.
165. Large bowl/jar with flanged rim. Sparse patches of brown metallic glaze on interior surface. Fabric PM 1c.
166. Large bowl. Even metallic brown interior glaze. Exterior surface and rim reduced black with a few spots of glaze. Fabric PM 1c.
167. Jar with externally thickened rim. Thin brown metallic glaze on interior. Fabric PM 1c.
168. Jar with externally thickened rim. Patchy brown metallic glaze on interior. Fabric PM 1c.
169. Jar with externally thickened squared rim. Good even dark brown metallic glaze on interior. Fabric PM 1c.
170. Jar with externally thickened rim. Thin brown metallic glaze on interior. Fabric PM1c.
171. Collar-rimmed bowl with some sooting on exterior. Even dull brown/green metallic glaze on interior surface. Fabric PM 1c.
172. Bowl with squared down-turned rim. A few spots of glaze on exterior under rim. Thin brown metallic glaze on interior. Fabric PM 1c.
173. Shallow bowl with brown green glaze on interior. Fabric PM 2a.
174. Deep bowl with externally thickened and moulded rim. Dull green interior glaze with brown speckles. Spots and splashes on rim. Fabric PM 2b.
175. Cup/small bowl. Good thick dark green glaze on interior. Exterior unglazed and burnt dark brown/grey. Fabric PM 2c.
176. Large plate with good green brown glaze on interior. Diameter 370mm. Fabric PM 3a.
177. Large plate with sparse patches of red brown glaze on interior. Diameter 360mm. Fabric PM 3a.
178. Jar/bowl with nearly all over red brown glaze with brown speckles. Bare patches are present on the exterior surface and no glaze is present on the rim. Fabric PM 3b.
179. Large bowl with brown red glaze, with sparse brown speckles, on interior surface. Fabric PM 3b.
180. Flanged bowl with all over patchy red brown glaze. Fabric PM 3b.
181. Tripod pipkin with crudely made feet. Brown red glaze, with brown speckles on interior. Exterior unglazed. Fabric PM 3b.
182. Deep bowl with dark brown red glaze, with moderate iron speckles, on interior surface. Exterior unglazed but with some horizontal ribbing. Fabric PM 3c.
183. Jar/bowl with good even tan brown glaze, with some iron speckles, on interior. Sharp edge to glaze near apex of rim. Thin splashes of glaze on exterior. Possible trace of white trailed slip externally (*i.e.*, could be PM 4a). Fabric PM 3c.

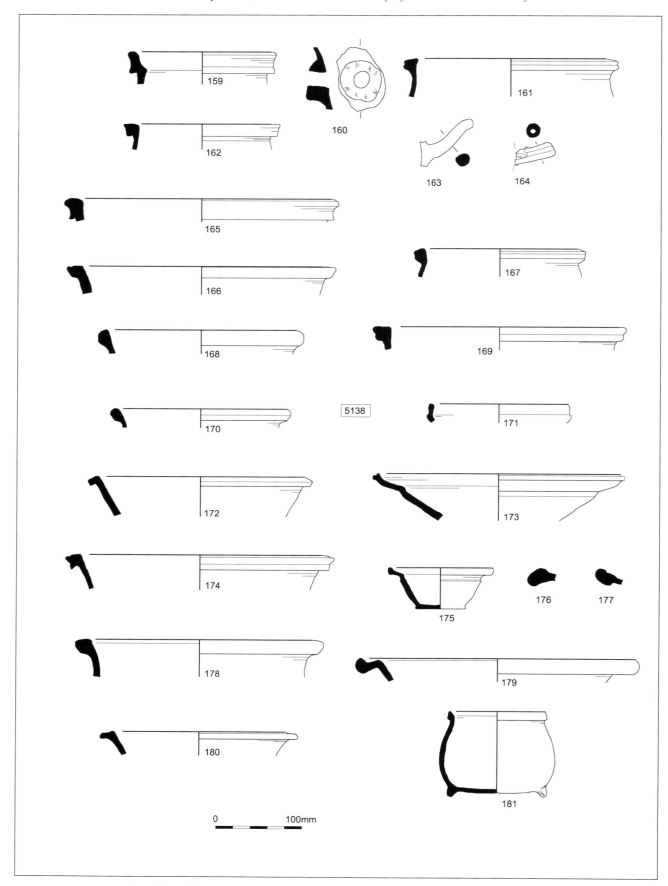

Fig. 75 Lydd Quarry: Late 17th to early 18th Century pottery (Context 5138)

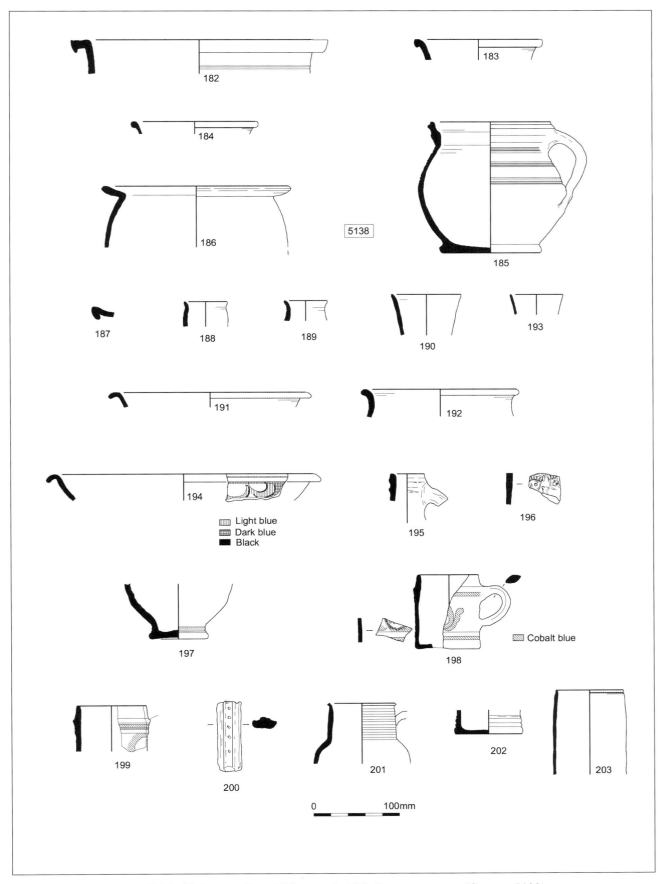

Fig. 76 Lydd Quarry: Late 17th to early 18th Century pottery (Context 5138)

184. Small jar/bowl with all over tan brown glaze with brown/iron speckles. Fabric PM 3c.

185. Handled jar/jug. Brown red internal glaze with moderate speckles. The glaze is thin and patchy near the top and sides of the interior, but thick and even toward the base. Exterior unglazed, but decorated with three bands of three incised horizontal grooves. Large thumbed indent at junction of base of handle and body. Fabric PM 3c.

186. Chamber pot with thick all over apple green glaze. Probably a Wealden product. Fabric PM 5b.

187. Plate with internal yellow glaze. Diameter 320mm. Fabric PM 5c.

188. Drug/ointment pot. Fabric PM 6a.

189. Drug/ointment pot. Fabric PM 6a.

190. Bottle/cup? with simple rim. Fabric PM 6a.

191. Bowl with simple curved rim. Fabric PM 6a.

192. Jar with simple out-turned rim. Fabric PM 6a.

193. Bottle/cup? with simple rim. Fabric PM 6b.

194. Bowl with simple curved rim. Interior decorated with light and dark blue zones, separated in places by black lines. Overall body colour is very light blue. Fabric PM 6d.

195. Frechen Bellarmine bottle with mottled dark brown iron wash under salt glaze. Fabric PM 7b.

196. Frechen Bellarmine mask (not the same vessel as No. 195). Dark iron wash under salt glaze. Fabric PM 7b.

197. Frechen Bellarmine base. Light iron wash under salt glaze. Fabric PM 7b.

198. Westerwald cobalt blue decorated mug with clear salt glaze. Two horizontal cobalt blue bands bordering incised line decoration infilled with more cobalt blue colouring. There is also part of a decorated bodysherd which may be from the front of the same vessel. This sherd is decorated with an applied medallion bordered by a wreath. Within the medallion can be seen the bottom of a 'W'(?). This is similar to examples elsewhere (Jennings 1981, No. 841) which have a crown over WR in similar medallions. Fabric PM 7c.

199. Westerwald cobalt blue decorated mug with clear salt glaze. An upper horizontal band of cobalt blue decoration is evident, and below incised line decoration surrounded by (*not* infilled by, as in the case of No. 198) cobalt blue. Cruder than No. 198. Fabric PM 7c.

200. Westerwald handle from a chamber pot with clear salt glaze and no decoration. Similar to other Westerwald chamber pot handles (Jennings 1981, No. 844). Fabric PM 7c.

201. London stoneware bulbous tavern pot. (Hilyard 1985, Cat. No. 50 – dated late 17th century). Iron wash under salt glaze. Fabric PM 8a.

202. London stoneware tankard base with exterior iron wash under salt glaze. Fabric PM 8a.

203. London stoneware tankard rim (not the same vessel as No. 202). Dark iron wash under salt glaze. Fabric PM 8a.

Denge West Quarry

The pottery assemblage consists of material from both the northern and southern parts of this quarry (2144 and 1908 sherds respectively). As the bulk of the material is unstratified it offers only limited potential for progressing the fabric series established for Lydd Quarry. However, the material is of considerable importance for establishing the onset and main periods of activity/occupation at the site and thus allowing a comparison to be made with the other quarries around Lydd.

The aims of the current report were therefore to outline as far as possible the probable date of the establishment and abandonment of the ditch system and related occupation sites, and to compare/contrast the pottery fabrics with the fabric series established for Lydd Quarry. In order to achieve these aims analysis of the Denge Quarry assemblage was undertaken at three levels. The material which was considered unstratified was simply quantified by period for each area (see below). Small groups of stratified material were spot-dated only, while larger groups of stratified material were fully quantified by fabric. All fabric codes used are from the Lydd Quarry series.

Denge West North

The northern part of the quarry produced the largest and most interesting assemblage from the site, particularly as it contained a number of stratified groups associated with both the ditch system and related occupation/activity areas. Some 984 sherds are from contexts which can assume to be reasonably 'secure'. The vast majority of these are in small assemblages, though a few larger ones are present. By far the largest is from Context 68 (Area F) which contains 460 sherds. However, the vast majority of the material from Denge West North was located during topsoil stripping and can thus be considered unstratified (1160 sherds). The chronological spread of each area's unstratified assemblage is shown in Table 26 below. It should be noted that the division between the 13th and 14th century material is not exact. The shell and sand fabric (F2b) has been placed into the 13th century category, while the majority of the sand tempered wares (*i.e.*, F3b, F3c and the F3h Rye products) have been placed into the 14th century categories. This allows easy division and, judging by the stratified groups both here and at Lydd Quarry which are dominated by F2b sherds in the 13th century, gives a rudimentary method of division. However, it does not allow for the small percentage of 13th century sand tempered wares almost certainly present in the assemblages and as such the 13th century totals are almost certainly slightly under-represented. A similar problem was encountered with the later 14th and early 15th century material, where a gradual increasing in firing temperature across this period does not allow for easy divisions between groups to be made. Despite these

Area	1200–1300	1300–1400	1400–1550	1550–1700	Post 1700	Total
Area A	195/2170g	142/878g	59/560g	-	-	396/3608g
Area B	-	34/112g	21/258g	-	-	55/370g
Area C	-	30/274g	13/184g	2/14g	-	45/472g
Area E	187/1840g	241/1716g	43/462g	2/12g	-	473/4030g
Area F	2/22g	9/64g	133/2025g	12/188g	4/20g	160/2319g
Area G	-	2/12g	7/70g	1/18g	21/210g	31/310g
Total	384/4032g	458/3056g	276/3559g	17/232g	25/230g	1160/11,109g

Table 27: (Denge West North) Number of unstratified pottery sherds by period for Areas A–G (by no. and weight)

Fabric	Number	% by number	Weight	% by weight
2b	77	78.6	694g	84.8
2d	9	9.2	32g	3.9
3b	6	6.1	38g	4.6
3c	4	4.1	48g	5.9
3i (Scarborough)	1	1.0	2g	0.2
4a	1	1.0	4g	0.5
Total	98	100	818g	99.9

Table 28: (Denge West North) Pottery from Context 9

problems it is felt the proportions of different period pottery from each area, as shown in Table 26, are still well within acceptable levels of accuracy and do give a reliable picture of the chronological span and intensity of occupation in each area.

13th century

With the exception of a very abraded Central Gaulish Samian sherd from Area G, the earliest pottery from the site was of 13th century date. Two areas of Denge West North contained significant quantities of shell and sand tempered F2b sherds in the topsoil: Areas A and E (49.2% and 39.5% of the respective assemblages by sherd count). The material includes both small and large, sometimes conjoining, sherds and is present in such proportions to suggest occupation sites, or at least concentrated activity, in or close to both areas during this period. The presence of a scattering of F2d sherds and the total absence of 12th to early 13th century flinty fabrics, suggests that most of this activity was probably within the second half of the century. The slightly flinty Fabric 1e, which is present, is thought from assemblages at Lydd Quarry to be of later 13th to early 14th century date. Undecorated F2b cooking pots and bowls predominate, as with the Lydd Quarry assemblage, though the stratified group of 13th century material (see below) shows small quantities of sand tempered wares and French imports were also present at this time. The small quantities, or absence, of 13th century pottery in all other areas suggests only limited manuring was undertaken away from the activity focus.

A few stratified assemblages of the 13th century were located during the excavations, mostly from Area A. Ditch 2 produced a combined total of 51 large unabraded sherds composed of F2b (34 sherds), F3b (11 sherds) and F4a (6 sherds), suggesting a late 13th century infilling date. Context 9 (pit fill) produced an even more secure assemblage.

The total dominance of Fabrics 2b and 2d is typical of 13th century assemblages from Lydd Quarry. The presence of low quantities of F2d, F3b, F3c and F4a suggest a probable deposition date in the second half of the century (it is possible some may be intrusive 14th century material). The F2b material is represented by a minimum of seven cooking pots and one bowl, while the F3b and F4a sherds represent a single cooking pot each, and, in the case of F3b, a single jug. The F3c and F3i Scarborough material are also from jugs. This dominance of F2b sherds is also apparent in Contexts 11, 12, 13, 19, 33, 34, 41 and 45 (all in Area A).

14th century

Considering the pottery alone, there appears to be a noticeable increase in activity at the site during the 14th century. This is almost certainly an uninterrupted progression from the 13th century activity. The presence of 14th century pottery, often in significant numbers, suggests that both occupation and manuring had intensified. Areas A and E appear to continue as occupation/activity sites (35.9% and 51% of the respective assemblages). The 14th century assemblages from Areas A and E closely resemble those found from Lydd Quarry

Fabric	Number	% by number	Weight	% by weight
1e	8	4.5	42g	4.2
2d	43	24.4	326g	32.6
3b	95	54.0	420g	42.0
3c	6	3.4	62g	6.2
3e	5	2.8	28g	2.8
4a	5	2.8	34g	3.4
4d	6	3.4	24g	2.4
3h (Rye)	6	3.4	62g	6.2
Imp 1 Saintonge	2	1.1	2g	0.2
Total	176	99.8	1000g	100

Table 29: (Denge West North) Pottery from Context 26

Site Jb (Lydd 3, Areas B and C). Dominant fabrics consist of F3b, F3c, F4a and F3h Rye-type products, as well as F4e and a few French whitewares (2 sherds from Area A and 6 sherds from Area E). The assemblage from Area E also includes six sherds from an F3i Scarborough jug. Both assemblages contain cooking pots, as well as a good selection of glazed jugs. A number of the sherds are fired to a slightly higher temperature, suggesting that a reasonable proportion of the 14th century assemblage covers the second half of the century.

Very few stratified assemblages of the 14th century were located during the excavations. Most of these are very small and only one larger, slightly unusual, group is present from Context 26 in Area A (Table 29).

The high proportions of F2d and F3b suggest this assemblage is from a time of transition between the very last of the sand and shell F2d wares and the start of the dominance by sand only tempering (F3b and c). At present it is thought this would suggest a deposition date between 1275/1300 and 1325/50. The presence of F1e sherds may hint at a date prior to 1325. However, the general small abraded size of most of the sherds within this assemblage suggest that caution is needed when using this context to refine fabric ranges.

15th to mid 16th century

Overall there is a slight decrease in the quantity of pottery from the site for this period, though occupation/activity was still clearly continuing. As with the 14th century, there is a wide spread of material (Table 27) in all areas, suggesting extensive manuring. The concentration of pottery of this period in Areas A and E has noticeably decreased (14.9% and 9.1% of the respective assemblages). The fact that the number of sherds is still above the quantity in other areas (*i.e.*, Area B and C) suggests that at least some activity was continuing into the 16th century, but at a much reduced rate. At this time however, Area F appears to have become a new occupation/activity site, with pottery of this period making up 83.1% of the unstratified assemblage (based on sherd count) from this area. Based on evidence from

Lydd Quarry it is possible this represents a migration of occupation from Areas A and E to a new site.

The ceramics of this period are represented by a mix of small to large sherds in the high-fired Transitional wares noted at Lydd Quarry. The dominant fabrics include F4e, F4f, F4h and F4j in Area A, together with a single sherd of Raeren stoneware, suggesting a predominantly 15th century date. The assemblage from Area E may be slightly later in date as, although containing many F4h sherds, harder-fired F4l, F4n and F4o sherds are also well represented. As such, it is almost certain this assemblage continues into the early part of the 16th century. The unstratified assemblage from Area F contains large unabraded sherds, suggesting they are close to their original deposition site (probably the midden – Context 68 – see below). Dominant fabrics include F4e, F4h, F4j, F4l, F4m and F4o, together with a single sherd each of Siegburg and Raeren stoneware, suggesting a later 15th to mid 16th century date. Storage jars, bowls and jugs/bunghole pitchers, some with white painted decoration, dominate the assemblage of this period.

A few stratified assemblages of this period were located during the excavations. However, by far the best is from the midden represented by Context 68 in Area F.

This group appears to be relatively free of residual material; only 25 sherds of F3b, F3c, F4a and Saintonge are certainly in this category. Only five probable intrusive sherds have been identified (Fabrics PM1d and PM3c). The remainder of the assemblage can happily be placed into a period of 1450–1550, though most could be fitted within a 1475–1525 bracket. The assemblage is dominated by F4h sherds, including one lid and at least eight jugs/pitchers. Most sherds are undecorated, though several have spots of glaze and five have white slip painted lines. The lower fired Fabric 4j is also well represented, as is the very high-fired fabric 4o, though most of the sherds from the latter fabric are probably from one bunghole pitcher. Too few diagnostic sherds are present in Context 68 to undertake an informative vessel count, however, a selection of the more diagnostic pieces is catalogued opposite and illustrated in Fig. 77.

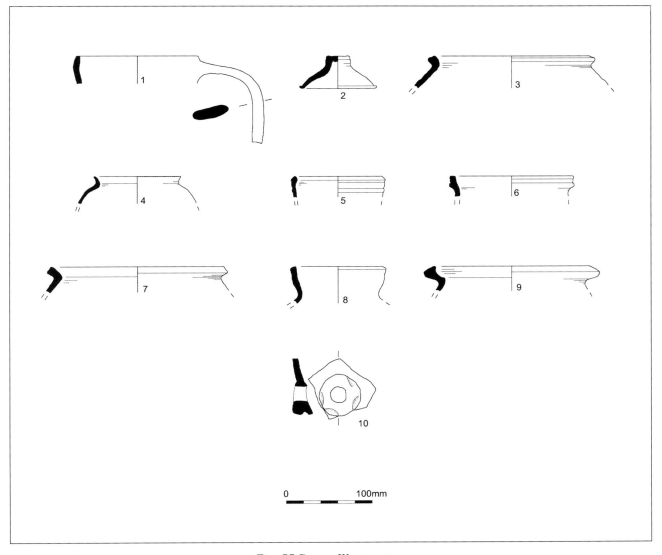

Fig. 77 Denge West: pottery

1. Large pitcher with unstabbed strap handle. Fabric 4h. Occasional spots of glaze.
2. Small lid. Fabric 4h.
3. Jar with simple squared everted rim. Fabric 4j. Occasional spots of glaze.
4. Small jar with out-turned tapered rim. Fabric 4j.
5. Jug/pitcher with slightly in-turned rim. Fabric 4j. Spots of glaze on exterior.
6. Jug/pitcher with simple collard rim. Fabric 4j.
7. Jar as No. 3. Fabric 4l.
8. Pitcher with simple rim. Unglazed. Fabric 4n. Dark blue grey core, brick red margins and dark grey surfaces.
9. Lid-seated jar. Fabric 4o. Brick red core, blue grey margins and grey brown surfaces.
10. Lightly thumbed bunghole from pitcher. Fabric 4o. Brick red core, blue grey margins with mid grey outer and dull brown inner surfaces.

Mid 16th to 17th centuries

Very little material that could be positively dated to this period was located. There is slight evidence of manuring activity in Areas C, E and G, though there is a slight concentration in Area F suggesting some activity continued into this period. This is confirmed by Context 69 (see below). Earthenwares predominate, but two Frechen bellarmine sherds are also present. None of the material would be out of place in the second half of the 16th century, suggesting occupation/activity may not have continued into the 17th century.

Only one stratified group of this period was located: Context 69, containing 56 sherds. Fabric 4h, with lesser quantities of F4n and F4o, dominates this assemblage. Of more interest is the higher number of true post-medieval earthenwares in Fabrics 4k and PM3c. There are also two Frechen stoneware sherds and a possible yellow-glazed

Fabric	Number	% by number	Weight	% by weight
3b	17	3.7	160g	3.5
3c	2	0.4	10g	0.2
4a	5	1.1	72g	1.6
Imp 1 Saintonge	1	0.2	8g	0.2
4d	9	2.0	62g	1.4
4e	13	2.8	262g	5.8
4h	215	46.7	2030g	44.8
4I	5	1.1	38g	0.8
4j	45	9.8	628g	13.8
4k	18	3.9	140g	3.1
4l	19	4.1	170g	3.7
4n	25	5.4	208g	4.6
4o	77	16.7	680g	15.0
4p	1	0.2	12g	0.3
Imp 5 Siegburg	3	0.7	18g	0.4
PM1d	2	0.4	6g	0.1
PM3c	3	0.7	32g	0.7
Total	460	99.9	4536g	100

Table 30: (Denge West North) Pottery from Context 68

Area	1200–1300	1300–1400	1400–1550	1550–1700	Post 1700
Field A	28	161	566	95	46
Field B	21	91	381	95	103
Field C	0	2	11	5	12
Field D	11	38	42	12	18
Total	60 (3.5%)	292 (16.8%)	1000 (57.5%)	207 (11.9%)	179 (10.1%)

Table 31: (Denge West South) Number of pottery sherds by period for Fields A–D

white Borderware sherd. Although this group clearly overlaps with that from Context 68, the presence of these sherds suggests it runs later and can best be given a date range covering 1525–75/1600.

Post 1700

Only low quantities of material of this date were recovered, though most was in Area G. It consists mainly of late 18th to early 19th century earthenwares and 'china'.

Denge West South

By far the majority of this assemblage can be considered totally unstratified, having been collected during the pre-extraction field-walking survey of four of the main fields in the area (Fig. 61, Fields A–D, totalling 1,738 abraded sherds). Subsequently the watching brief during extraction located two small assemblages. The first was from Area M (75 sherds), located in the northern part of Field D, which was not subjected to the field-walking survey. The second consists of a further 95 sherds located

to the north of Field A, associated with a probable pit. The former assemblage is unstratified, though the latter assemblage can be considered as partially stratified. Due to the nature of the assemblage it was decided to treat the material in a similar way to the unstratified material from Denge West North. As such, it was quantified by period for each field and re-plotted (Figs. 64 and 65) in order to gain a rough idea of the onset and duration/intensity of occupation in this area. Problems of splitting some of the pottery between periods were similar to those discussed under Denge West North (see above), but again the results are considered to be fairly accurate.

The 13th century

Very little material of this date was recovered from the four fields. That which is present is totally dominated by F2b sherds, which are usually small and abraded. No concentrations were apparent in the distribution of this material and it is likely that the pottery was deposited during manuring. The total absence of 13th century pottery in Field C is interesting. This narrow field may

Area	1200–1300	1300–1400	1400–1550	1550–1700	Post 1700
Area M	2/14g	69/890g	4/22g	-	-
North of Field A	2/20g	22/324g	71/1160g	-	-

Table 32: (Denge West South) Number of pottery sherds by period for Denge West South watching Brief

have been too wet for cultivation and was thus not subjected to manuring. This theory is strengthened by the low quantities of later pottery recovered from the same field. Whether this pottery represents manuring in the 13th century, or the last vestiges of 13th century pots being discarded in the early 14th century, is impossible to say with certainty. However, considering the presence of stratified 13th century groups from Denge West North, a 13th century date for this manuring seems more probable.

The 14th century

There is a notable increase in 14th century pottery from the four fields, though most is from Fields A and B. The quantities involved, particularly in Field A, suggest some activity/occupation other than just manuring. The dominant fabric is F4a, but F3b, F3c and F3h Rye are also common. Both cooking pots and jugs are well represented. The later, higher-fired, 14th century material tends to merge with the 15th century sherds. Within Field A the distribution of 14th century material suggests the start of activity/occupation was set back from the road (Fig. 64). The density of this material noticeably drops off across Field B and is virtually absent in Field C. The low quantities of pottery in Field D are probably the result of manuring, though some more intense activity may have been occurring to the north of the field-walked area (see Area M below).

The 15th to mid 16th century

The large quantity of pottery of this period located during the field-walking survey clearly demonstrates that definite occupation was by now established at Denge West South. Field A contained large quantities of material, again set back from the road (Fig. 64) and corresponding with spreads of ceramic building material (Fig. 65). The extensive nature of the spread suggests a large part of this field was taken up with occupation/ activity areas. A further concentration of material of this date was located in Field B, adjacent to a trackway (Figs. 64 and 65). This may represent a separate occupation site or alternatively a related activity area, perhaps associated with the stockpiling of manure and domestic waste for spreading on the fields. The remainder of the spread of pottery can be interpreted as representing manuring. The pottery of this period is similar to that from Lydd Quarry and Denge West North. It is dominated by fabrics 4d, 4h, *etc.*, with a small quantity of Raeren stoneware. Forms are limited to bunghole pitchers, jars and bowls.

The mid 16th to 17th century

Notably less material of this date was located, suggesting a sharp contraction in activity at this time, or alternatively a change in the method of rubbish disposal. Two small concentrations are notable (Fig. 65). One lies adjacent to the road in Field A, while the other corresponds to the earlier concentration in Field B. It is probable that occupation/activity continued perhaps as late as the mid 17th century. The pottery assemblage from this period is dominated by local earthenwares, but includes Frechen and Westerwald products.

Post 1700

This category covers the 18th and 19th centuries; little 20th century material was recognised. Although well represented there are no notable concentrations for this period and it is probable the scatter is the result of manuring. The pottery is again dominated by local earthenwares, although brown English stoneware, Staffordshire white salt-glazed stoneware, pearlware and transfer-printed ware are also well represented.

The Watching Brief

The assemblage from Area M (watching brief) contains 69 sherds of probable 14th century date. This accounts for 92% of the pottery assemblage collected from this point during the watching brief. The assemblage is slightly unusual in that it is dominated by F1e (x36) and F3b sherds (very few F2b/2d sherds are present). This suggests a date at the very end of the 13th or beginning of the 14th centuries, after the shell tempered wares had ceased to dominate the market, but before the sand tempered wares had fully taken their place. Securely stratified groups will be needed before the F1e sherds can be securely placed. Whatever the case, this assemblage suggests more than just manuring was occurring at this location in this period. However, the quantities involved are relatively low, suggesting no permanent domestic settlement.

The small assemblage from the north of Field A has a similar chronological spread to that located during the field-walking. This in itself suggests the context from which it came cannot be seen as secure. The 14th century material consists of F4a, F3b and F3h Rye sherds from both cooking pots and jugs; many sherds show signs of abrasion. The 15th to mid 16th century material is less abraded and consists mainly of F4h sherds. It is probable this material relates to an activity area linked to the settlement in Field A to the south.

Fabric	Number	% by number	Weight	% by weight
1a	14	14.9	138g	12.0
1h	45	47.9	608g	52.9
3a	14	14.9	224g	19.5
3a(i)	19	20.2	176g	15.3
3b	2	2.1	4g	0.3
Total	94	100	1,150g	100

Table 33: (Caldicott Farm) Pottery from Context 9

Discussion

The complete absence of 12th to early 13th flint tempered fabrics from both Denge West North and South would suggest an onset of activity at the site later than that found at Lydd Quarry. A date of perhaps around the middle of the 13th century is suggested on the current data. The quantity and unabraded condition of much of the 13th century pottery at Denge North suggests settlement was established in the second half of the century, with manuring being undertaken in the surrounding area.

Unlike Lydd Quarry, at present there does not appear to be any identifiable gap between the establishment of the field system and settlement/s and, subject to new discoveries, the two may have occurred concurrently. Although this suggests the activity pre-dated the storms of the later 13th century, it is possible it occurred afterwards but with older pottery being brought out to the new area of settlement. More work on the refining of the ceramics sequence either side of these storm events is needed to address this issue. Due to the lack of identified 'flood deposits' at the quarries around Lydd, this work will need to concentrate on assemblages from New Romney where such deposits are known.

Occupation at Denge North, Areas A and E, continued in the 14th century, with evidence of the start of at least one new occupation/activity site at Denge South. The following century appears to have seen the shift of settlement at Denge North from Areas A and E to a new location (Area F). At the same time the activity in Field A at Denge South appears to have become quite intense, suggesting a definite occupation site. A further occupation/activity area was also established in Field B. During the 16th century there appears to have been a winding down of activity. Occupation may have continued in Area F (Denge North) and Fields A and B (Denge South), albeit on a much reduced level, until the late 16th and early/mid 17th centuries respectively, when all appears to have been abandoned to periodic manuring.

The presence of large quantities of ceramics and other debris in the topsoil at the site is interesting in that it suggests the utilisation of surface middens and/or very shallow refuse pits/middens (as Context 68) during the late medieval to early post-medieval period. This lack of proper rubbish pits during this period has been noted at Lydd Quarry and suggests a change in the system of rubbish disposal.

The pottery assemblage from Denge Quarry is very similar to that of Lydd Quarry, both in the fabrics/pottery sources represented at different periods and the generally limited utilitarian nature of most of the vessels. This would tend to suggest that the Denge Quarry occupation was of similar status to that at Lydd Quarry.

Caldicott Farm

Introduction

The excavations at Caldicott Farm produced a total of 153 sherds of pottery, weighing just over 2,085g from seven different contexts. Most contexts only produced small quantities of pottery: only two contexts contain over 30 sherds. The largest group is from Context 9, which contained 94 sherds (see below).

The pottery is generally in good condition and comes from closed contexts, predominantly consisting of ditch fills. Intrusive and residual material is usually rare among the assemblages.

The ceramics from this site cover a wide chronological range. The earliest material is of late 1st to 2nd century Roman Upchurch types from Context 52. The earliest medieval pottery appears to date to the later 11th to later 12th centuries, a period not well represented in the much larger assemblages from Lydd Quarry to the south-west (Barber 1999 and 2002). There is a notable lack of shell and sand tempered wares so typical of the assemblages at Lydd Quarry, though the current site does contain small late 13th to 14th century assemblages, as well one small early 19th century (Context 3) assemblage.

The objective of the present report is to continue the work started during the study of the medieval pottery of the marsh from Lydd Quarry (see above). The pottery from Caldicott Farm has enabled some refinement to the Lydd ceramic sequence, including the identification of three new fabric groups of the 11th to 12th centuries. The specific aims of the current report included the dating of individual contexts and indeed activity at the site as a whole, together with the refinement of the fabric dating wherever possible.

The fabrics from the current site are similar to those excavated at Lydd Quarry and as such the same fabric series has been used, to which has been added the new fabrics found at Caldicott Farm (see above).

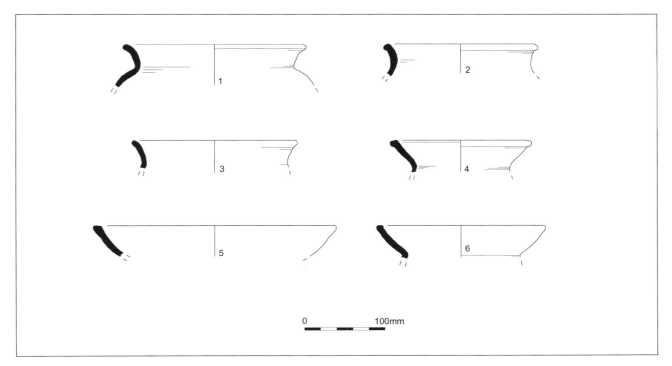

Fig. 78 Caldicott Farm pottery

Fabric	Number	% by number	Weight	% by weight
1h	28	82.4	686g	94.5
1i	3	8.8	22g	3.0
2a	2	5.9	10g	1.4
3a	1	2.9	8g	1.1
Total	34	100	726g	100

Table 34: (Caldicott Farm) Pottery from Context 86

Pottery Groups

Only two assemblages from the site were deemed appropriate for detailed fabric quantification. These contexts were selected primarily due to their early date and reasonable size. The overall aim of the selected analysis was to provide data on fabric ratios for these early groups. Detailed study of forms was not undertaken due to the limited range represented by the relatively small amount of rim-sherds. However, all main forms, where possible, are reproduced in the illustrated catalogue.

Fill 9 (Ditch 8)

This ditch is dominated by the coarse flint tempered ware F1h, although the sand-free flint tempered F1a is also well represented. The F3a sherds are similarly represented together with the new variant F3a(i). The F3b sherds are likely to be intrusive. The general unabraded nature of the sherds within this assemblage suggests that they have not been reworked and that the fabrics, with the exception of F3b, can be seen as contemporary. This is confirmed by the early cooking pot and shallow bowl rim forms.

A deposition date spanning *c*. 1075–1175 is suggested for this context.

Catalogue Nos. (Fig. 78)

1. Cooking pot with curved flaring simple rim. Fabric 1h.
2. Necked cooking pot with beaded rim. Fabric 1h.
3. Cooking pot with curved flaring simple rim. Fabric 1h.
4. Cooking pot with sharply everted flaring rim. Fabric 3a.
5. Shallow bowl with simple rim. Fabric 3a.
6. Cooking pot with sharply everted flaring rim. Fabric 3a (i).

Fill 86 (Ditch 85)

This small spur ditch is dominated by the abundant flint tempered ware (F1h), though this is somewhat misleading as most of the sherds come from a single cooking pot. The presence of the shelly F2a sherds is interesting in that it confirms the suspected early date of this rare fabric.

A deposition date spanning *c*. 1075–1175 is suggested for this context.

Discussion

The excavated pottery from the three quarries has, to date, been by far the largest group of medieval ceramics so far excavated from the Marsh. The material has enabled a glimpse into the changes in fabrics and forms through time, though there are still gaps to be filled and areas to be strengthened.

Context

The pottery has been recovered from many different kinds of contexts. The material from the ditches generally, but by no means exclusively, tends to be present in small groups, though these often tend to show the widest chronological range. Although at Lydd the earliest ditch groups are mainly of 12th century date, the majority range between the 13th and 15th centuries. Some assemblages from ditches tend to be larger, though these are virtually all late medieval in date. Virtually all assemblages from ditches have a higher degree of residuality and/or intrusiveness compared to the discrete pit assemblages.

Generally the excavated features relating to the settlements produced larger assemblages than those from the surrounding ditch system. However, at all occupation sites/activity areas no, or very little, pottery was recovered from structural features. This has meant close dating of these features has often proved problematic, however, dating to within a century has usually been possible either directly using the pottery or by using associations. The use of such small assemblages, often only represented by small bodysherds, is admittedly dangerous as the degree of residuality/intrusiveness is impossible to assess with certainty. As such, trying to understand the chronological development of internal settlement morphology has been virtually impossible, particularly with the lack of stratigraphic relationships.

Most large groups of pottery have come from a few 'midden' deposits, both at Lydd and Denge West. These dumps of material were found mainly in pits, particularly for the 13th century groups, but also appeared in the uppermost fills of gullies/ditches. Although 'purpose-dug' pits were obviously being created during the 13th and 14th centuries, any disused hole in the ground appears to have been utilised for the disposal of refuse (*i.e.*, Ditch 5091). Considering the extent to which manuring was being undertaken, it is perhaps surprising that so much refuse was discarded in dug pits, though some selection may have been undertaken between organic and inorganic materials when possible. Later, in the 15th and 16th centuries, there appears to be a slightly different pattern to rubbish disposal. No, or very few, 'purpose-dug' pits containing refuse were located, despite there being evidence for structural features. The main assemblages of pottery associated with the 15th to early 16th century activity have come mainly from infilled ditches, for example around Site L at Lydd. This change is almost certainly partly due to the fact that many of these ditches were no longer required at this time due to changes in the field system, and as such offered places for easy refuse disposal. It is also interesting to note that at Denge Quarry surface middens of this date were noted, suggesting a change in the techniques of disposal. The early 18th century group from Ditch 5137 at Lydd shows that 'opportunistic' rubbish disposal into redundant ditches was still taking place at this late date.

Chronology

The pottery from the excavated assemblages falls into one of several overlapping chronological groups which are considered briefly below.

Late 11th to early 13th centuries

Excluding the prehistoric and Romano-British material from Lydd and Caldicott Farm Quarries, the earliest pottery is of the 11th to early 12th centuries. These groups, none of which contain many sherds, are very few in number and are all confined to Caldicott Farm. The only pottery of this probable date from Lydd Quarry is the unstratified Pingsdorf sherd located at Lydd 1. The Caldicott Farm groups (Contexts 9 and 86) show that during this earliest period of activity Saxo-Norman coarse sand tempered (F3a and F3a(i)) and flint tempered (F1h and F1a) cooking pots dominate. Although some of these early fabrics are present at both Lydd and Caldicott (F1a, F3a), the latter site produced new fabrics which were not paralleled in the Lydd assemblages. This strongly suggests that the earliest Caldicott assemblages pre-date those at Lydd. As the assemblages probably relate to activity during the initial establishment, and perhaps first modification, of the ditched field system, it would appear that the ditch system excavated at Caldicott Farm was established perhaps as much as 50 to 100 years before that at Lydd Quarry. This would suggest a chronological expansion of reclamation toward the south-west. However, more early assemblages, with diagnostic forms, will be needed from this area before this hypothesis can be tested, as the close dating of the ceramics of this period is notoriously difficult.

The majority of early pottery at Lydd Quarry is best placed within the 12th century, with some groups probably extending into the early 13th century, though 12th century fabrics still usually dominate these. These groups are again always small and appear to relate to small depositions of refuse in ditches rather than any permanent occupation. The only groups of this date to survive at Lydd are those which were deposited in early ditches, which were quickly abandoned and thus not cleaned out later. As such, it is assumed these relate to either the period of initial ditch digging and/or perhaps the first pastoral use of the area. The majority of these early deposits have been removed by later maintenance of the ditch system and therefore the few left are of extreme importance in giving an indication of when reclamation began in the area. All of these early groups are dominated by the flint/flint and sand tempered cooking pots, though some groups also contain F3a coarse sand sherds, usually cooking pots or shallow bowls.

The first more permanent, perhaps seasonal, occupation/activity at Lydd is represented by Sites A, B and C. The assemblages from these are all dominated by early fabrics, including flint tempered wares (F1 variants) as well as coarse sand (F3a) and shell tempered wares (F2c and F2e), though the start of the finer sand and shell (F2b) is often in evidence, suggesting an early 13th century date. Although Site A produced a small but 'reasonable' assemblage, Site B only produced 32 sherds (Lydd 4, Context 4003), none of which were particularly diagnostic of form. As such, dating at Site B has to rely on fabrics alone. The fabric breakdown for Context 4003 is as follows: F1c – 11 sherds (110g), F1e – 6 sherds (52g) and F2e – 15 sherds (110g). A date at the beginning of the 13th century seems probable. Site C (Lydd 3, Area D) is dominated by coarse sand tempered wares (F3a) along with lesser quantities of flint tempered wares (F1 variants) and a few shell tempered sherds (F2 variants).

It is interesting to note that no pottery of this early date was recovered from Denge West Quarry, suggesting activity at this site did not begin until probably the second quarter of the 13th century.

13th to early 14th centuries

The second period, as with the first, is not represented at all of the quarries. Although the first activity at Denge West appears to relate to this period, surprisingly, no 13th century pottery was recovered from the Caldicott Farm excavations. It can only be assumed that the investigated area at this quarry was set at some distance from the associated occupation site, and extensive manuring using domestic refuse was not carried out.

Despite this, the majority of pottery from the Lydd Quarry excavations is of this period, showing it to be a time of intense occupation and activity. Sites D, E, F, G, H, I and Ja date to this period and some have produced large sealed groups of pottery (see above). The F1 flint tempered, F3a coarse sand and F2c and F2e coarse sand and shell tempered wares appear to disappear rapidly in the first quarter of the century to be replaced by the finer sand and shell tempered wares (F2b) which totally dominate the 13th century assemblages. Although fine and medium sand tempered wares (F3b and F3c) are probably always present in small quantities, they appear to become more common toward the later part of the century at the same time as finer F2d wares develop. At the same time jugs and bowls begin to become more common, though cooking pots still dominate the assemblages. These trends have been noted at Site D (Lydd 1, Area D), Site G (Lydd 5/6, Area A) and Site Ja (Lydd 3, Area B). At Site Ja (Lydd 3) the consistent presence of sand tempered wares with the shell tempered wares suggests activity

may have been toward the end of the 13th century, when the settlement at Lydd 2 appears to have been declining. It is quite possible that this later 13th century material represents activity associated with the establishment of the Lydd 3 site carried out by the occupants at Lydd 2, as chronologically the two sites appear to follow on from each other. The absence of large quantities of residual shell tempered wares in later features suggest intensive domestic occupation was never present at Site J. It would therefore appear that the main occupation site at Site H (Lydd 2) shifted to Site Jb in the first quarter of the 14th century, perhaps in an attempt to benefit from the slightly higher ground created by the shingle ridge in this area.

The pottery from Lydd Quarry is particularly interesting in that the overall assemblage contains many isolated groups, which appear to suffer very little from intrusive or residual material. This has enabled the dominance of the sand and shell tempered wares in the 13th century to be clearly demonstrated. This is extremely important when groups more prone to mixing are considered. For example, at any urban site, such as New Romney, 13th century sand and shell tempered wares may make up a significant residual element to an otherwise sand tempered dominated 14th century assemblage. The fabric ratios in such an assemblage could easily be interpreted as an equal mix of sand and shell and sand tempered products in a 13th century deposit, particularly if 14th century rim forms are not present. Although the isolated nature of many of the Lydd Quarry pits has therefore been useful, the lack of intercutting has conversely not allowed any detailed study of the chronological development of the shell and sand tempered wares throughout the 13th century.

One of the major problems with the 13th century quarry sequence is in establishing its exact end date. At present there is no way of being certain if the assemblages represent a continuous occupation through to the end of the 13th century, or into the early 14th century, or whether there is a break in the sequence brought about by the severe floods of the late 13th century. If the storms did stop occupation at the sites (and potentially disrupted production of the shell tempered wares) there may have been a gap before settlement resumed while the land was drained. This may explain the drastic change in fabric ratios seen between the 13th century F2 shell tempered dominated groups and the sand tempered dominated groups of the 14th century. If this were the case it could be suggested that the assemblages dominated by shell tempered wares predate the storms and that the sand tempered dominated assemblages represent 14th century occupation after a period of consolidation at the end of the 13th century.

Unfortunately no obvious flood deposits were located at any of the quarries to test this theory, though this could be the result of either later truncation by ploughing, or little original sedimentation due to low-energy flooding. At present the distinction between the pre and post flood pottery is not distinguishable with certainty and it is hoped that work at New Romney, where various flood deposits have been identified, will go some way to addressing this issue. However, it should be borne in mind that re-occupation of the urban context may have taken place more rapidly than in the surrounding flooded rural areas and indeed the problem of residual pre-flood pottery always remains a real danger.

14th century

There is notably less pottery of this date from the excavations at Lydd Quarry. This perhaps reflects a far smaller population in comparison to the preceding century. The main assemblages relate to the occupation site at Lydd 3 (Site Jb). Despite this, the 14th century appears to be well represented at Denge Quarry: Denge West North (Area A and E) and Denge West South (Field A). Both these areas produced large quantities of 14th century pottery, suggesting occupation may have been more intense here than in the 13th century.

The pottery groups are notable for their virtual complete absence of shell tempered (F2b and F2d) wares. Those that are present generally appear to be small and more heavily abraded residual sherds. The shell tempered wares are replaced by sand (F3b and F3c), sand and 'iron oxide' (F4a) and F3h Rye-type wares. Bowls by now are common and the presence of sooting on their exterior shows them to have been used for cooking, which would explain the relative decrease in cooking pots. Glazed jugs also become far more common and include imported material from other parts of Britain as well as the Continent.

Although the ceramic sequence at the quarries is still lacking firm anchor points, it is thought likely that the start of this phase of domestic activity was between *c.* 1300 and 1325 and spanned most of the 14th century to around 1375. Although better represented at Denge West, this period is only well represented at Lydd Quarry by Site Jb. Other than this, 14th century ceramics are only represented by isolated small groups in other parts of Lydd Quarry, though there are hints that Site G (Lydd 5/6) may have continued into the 14th century. Of interest is the fact that a number of the main ditches within the field system at Lydd appear to have been infilled at this time (*i.e.*, Ditches 5021, 5023, 5035 and 5041) and indeed ditch infilling accounts for the meagre 14th century assemblage from Caldicott Farm. If the ceramics within these ditches are not residual this suggests the beginning of field amalgamation, and thus the change in the rural society and economy, started during the 14th century.

15th to early 16th centuries

The transition from the 14th to 15th century is difficult to define using the ceramic, as there appears to have been a gradual change in the wares with higher-fired products appearing alongside the lower-fired sand tempered wares in the last quarter of the 14th century. The fact that both almost certainly coexisted leaves the dating of many contexts reliant on fabric ratios, which can easily be upset by a single rogue vessel. This period, which on the limited current evidence mainly appears to span *c.* 1375–1475/1525, covers the evolution of the high medieval fabrics and forms into the late medieval/early post-medieval Transitional wares. This change is gradual and at present its exact chronology, if indeed there is one, is not closely dated. Further work and clarification is still needed.

There are no definite groups of late 14th century pottery which can be isolated, though some surely date to this period. These are more likely to be the groups with a high Rye content, but which also contain the much higher-fired later fabrics (*i.e.*, F4d onward). However, the possibility of intrusive 'Transitional' sherds has dogged these groups. Of more certainty is the isolation of 15th to early 16th century groups; a task assisted by the presence at Lydd Quarry of closely datable leatherwork. This period is dominated by the higher-fired Transitional earthenwares with no or limited decoration and limited range of forms. The gradual increase in firing temperatures is evident throughout, though near proto stonewares coexisted with lower-fired fabrics. No high medieval fabrics and forms are present in these assemblages unless they are residual. This activity is centred on Sites L and M at Lydd Quarry, though outlying groups in ditches and other features are also present (*e.g.*, the barrel-lined well 5286 or 'sump' 5366). At Site Jb (Lydd 3, Areas B and C) the latest pottery was from a small assemblage dumped in Ditch 3150 (Fill 3151), which proved to be of the late 15th to early 16th century date. The complete absence of other pottery of this late date suggests that Site Jb did not continue in use this long and that it is probably more likely this assemblage relates to later disposal of domestic refuse in one of the partially backfilled trackway ditches. Denge West also produced a good, if largely unstratified, assemblage of this period (see above).

Post 1575/1600

No ceramic groups relating to the later 16th or early 17th centuries were recognised during the excavations, though a few isolated sherds could be of this date. All in all, very little pottery of this period was recovered and the assemblage of this period is dominated by the early 18th century group from Ditch 5137 (Fill 5138) at Lydd 5/6. This, with the exception of a very small group from the northern ditch of the southern trackway (Lydd 5/6, Ditch 5011), is an isolated assemblage and probably relates to a building depicted on Poker's map a little to the west of Area B. Small groups of 18th and 19th century pottery were recovered from all three quarries, but all relate to isolated ditch infilling episodes rather than occupation and as such too little material is present to reliably comment on.

Pottery Sources and Site Status

The majority of vessels during the 12th, and majority of the 13th, centuries consist of locally made undecorated utilitarian forms such as cooking pots and bowls with a few undecorated/unglazed jugs. Better made sand tempered glazed jugs (F3b and F3c) are present in the 13th century deposits but in negligible numbers. It is unfortunate that most of the local fabrics within the established series do not currently have a known source. This is partly due to the lack of excavated kilns of the period in the area and the fact that many production sites were producing similar fabrics at this time. The sand tempered fabrics in Group 3 are particularly difficult for sourcing. However, the petrological and chemical analysis undertaken on the F2b sherds show these difficulties are not limited to the sand tempered wares.

The dominant fabric group during the 13th century is that of the shell tempered wares (Group 2, but F2b in particular). This is reflected at a general level by considering the overall assemblages from Lydd 1 and 2. Both these assemblages were predominantly of 13th century date: at Lydd 1 the F2 fabrics combined made up nearly 80% of the assemblage by sherds count, while at Lydd 2, which is virtually an exclusively 13th century assemblage, they made up a little under 75% by sherd count. The proportions are sometimes even higher if individual contexts groups are considered singularly (see above). As noted previously (Gingell 1996 and above – F2b), similar wares were being produced at the late 12th to 13th century Potter's Corner kiln near Ashford (Grove 1952). The huge quantity of these fabrics present at Lydd suggests the Potter's Corner kiln may not be the only centre in the area producing such wares, a point confirmed by the petrological and chemical analysis. A close examination of the shell tempering indicates that, where identifiable, the shell inclusions are of cockle, although species such as *Hydrobia Ulvae*, indicative of an estuarine environment, are also present. The abundance of cockle shells at all the 13th to 14th century sites on the Marsh indicate the raw materials for the production of fabrics in Group 2 were easily at hand. This, combined with the high percentage of these wares on the Marshland sites, tends to point toward a more local 'coastal/estuarine' production site. An industry at New Romney has already been suggested (Reeves 1995). Such a location would be an obvious site as it would have access to both raw materials and transportation. The presence of shell in many of the fabrics in Group 1 suggests that these too may be of a Marshland origin and could be the precursors to the fully developed fabric Group 2 wares. Similar flint tempered wares have not been clearly described for New Romney (Willson 1987) despite similar forms being present. It is particularly interesting to note that these Group 1 wares were rare at the New Romney leper hospital site, which is known from historical sources to have begun in the late 12th century (Rigold 1964). If

New Romney, or other coastal sites, where involved with producing pottery, they would have been very susceptible to the late 13th century floods.

The forms of the local wares virtually exclusively consist of cooking pots with sagging bases and a variety of rim forms. Most of these rim forms are paralleled by Phase BB to C Shelly ware vessels from Eynsford (Rigold 1971, 157). Bowls are far less common and jugs are particularly rare in the 13th century. The proportions of vessel types from the group from Context 2400 (see above) are typical for the site. Undiagnostic bodysherds are obviously a problem with vessel identification. The local wares of Groups 1 and 2 are virtually absent of any decoration. Where present it consists simply of a few incised lines and the odd splash of clear glaze. Decoration is more common on jugs, but many undecorated jugs are also present. The amount of decoration increases through time with the increase of Group 3 and 4 fabrics in the 14th century, but this is predominantly simple external glazing on jugs. The overall assemblage from the site is one of a very limited utilitarian range of vessels from local production centres.

The dominance of 'local' fabrics (Fabrics 1, 2, 3a–c, 4 and 5) is clearly seen when the whole pottery assemblage for Lydd 2 is considered. In this assemblage, which is virtually exclusively of 13th century date, 98.4% by sherd count was in these fabrics. The imported material from Lydd 2 consisted of three sherds attributed to Rye (F3h) and Scarborough (F3i) (0.2% of overall assemblage by count) and 32 imported French sherds. The latter include 11 from a single Saintonge jug (Imp. 1), three from a 'Seine Valley' jug (Imp. 2), seven from a North French Gritty vessel (Imp. 3) and 11 from a Rouen jug (Imp. 4) (0.8% of overall assemblage by count). The remainder of the Lydd 2 assemblage consists of residual Roman sherds. The Lydd 1 assemblage is similar in that French products (Imp. 1) only made up 0.1% of the overall assemblage by sherd count (five sherds). Despite the lack of imports it should be noted that they are present from an early date as indicated by the unstratified Pingsdorf (Imp. 7) sherd from Lydd 1 and the small quantity of North French Gritty ware (Imp. 3) present in 12th century contexts.

The general lack of 13th, and to a lesser extent 14th, century imports is also apparent in the Lydd 5/6 and Denge West assemblages. At the former, only 10 sherds of imported material from outside the south-east are present (0.4% of the whole assemblage by sherd count). This would suggest low status occupation and/or limited trade networks. However, the Lydd 5/6 excavations, as well as producing French products, produced two sherds of Aardenberg-type ware jug (Contexts 5100 and 5359). Although these may in total constitute less than 40g of pottery, they demonstrate a trade link with the Low Countries. Scarborough pottery has been found at the quarries in small quantities. At Lydd 5/6 only three Scarborough sherds from a single handle were recovered from a green-glazed aquamanile. As such, it is obvious that at least some high quality vessels were getting to the 'low-status' rural sites, albeit in very small quantities. This suggests that despite their apparent low status the occupants, probably through the nearby port of New Romney, at least had access to a wide range of imported high quality goods during the 13th to 14th centuries. The fact that so few turn up at the quarry demonstrates that they were probably generally beyond the financial reach of the local rural population *and* such a population did not actually require them within their everyday lives.

The lack of Rye products in the 13th century assemblages at the quarries is surprising, as even low status settlements would have been able to afford the cooking vessels even if the jugs were seen as an extravagance. It can only be assumed that the Rye potters had not established a share of the rural market on the Marsh until the 14th century. This is possibly due to the competition of a local producer providing very cheap utilitarian wares to a rather poor populous.

During the 14th century there appears to be a radical change to the main sources supplying the excavated sites. Pottery tempered with coarse tempering agents appears to disappear rapidly in the late 13th to 14th century on the Marsh, as well as in East Sussex, though a few fabric variants continue to contain rare larger inclusions. The shell tempered wares had all but disappeared, possibly as a result of the late 13th century floods wiping out a coastal industry or, due to the potters of that industry switching to wholly sand tempered wares which had become more popular at this time. It is interesting to note that a few sherds from Site Jb have the odd shell inclusion in an otherwise sand tempered fabric. Whatever the case, sand tempered products now dominated the 14th century market. By now, a good proportion of this market was taken by the Rye industry, which had perhaps capitalised on the collapse of the shell tempered wares. This eastward expansion of the Rye market is suggested by the much higher proportion of such wares located in 14th century deposits at Broomhill Church (Gingell forthcoming), Site Jb at Lydd (Lydd 3) and Denge West.

The presence of the finely made grey sand tempered wares of 'Winchelsea Black'/Brede-type (F3e) suggest Rye was not the only East Sussex industry to exploit this gap in the market. The locally produced medium fired sand tempered wares, whether stemming from the shell tempered industry or not, may not have appeared quickly enough to keep Rye and other East Sussex products away. Although this is an attractive hypothesis, it still needs further assemblages to test whether changing wealth and status of settlement sites may be playing a role in this evolving pattern. Good groups of pottery from either town sites, such as New Romney, or the higher status rural sites (where higher quality vessels are likely to be more numerous) are needed in order to compare these sites with the low status settlements already investigated. The

present thought is that the increase in quality of pottery (including the number of glazed jugs) at Lydd and Denge West during the 14th century is due to an increase in the quality of the ceramic products, rather than an increase in social or economic status. It is interesting to note that foreign imports do not dramatically increase in the 14th century deposits. This suggests that although a trickle of imports was coming from similar sources to those noted at Lydd 1 and 2 (mainly France), they were still expensive and for the main could not be afforded/obtained by the rural low-status farmsteads so far excavated at the quarry.

The nature of the urban pottery market on the Marsh is still uncertain. It is clear that Rye products were enjoying a share of the 14th century market in New Romney, though whether they had established a toe-hold on the 13th century urban markets of the Marsh is currently uncertain. This question should be addressed when well sealed assemblages from the Marsh towns are excavated and studied: hopefully the recently excavated assemblages from New Romney will go some way toward this aim. At present published urban assemblages of size are needed from the urban sites in order to allow comparison with those excavated at the quarries. The towns would have generally been of higher status with ready access to imported goods, and it will be interesting to see the proportions of both south-eastern, other English and Continental imports compared with the more locally made products.

The source of the pottery in the 15th to early 16th centuries is problematic. The higher-fired wares which evolve throughout this period become very standardised in both fabric and form across the whole region. The decline in decoration on most vessels adds to the problem of sourcing vessels, as few workshops are currently known to have any particular decorative traits. At present it is strongly suspected that many of the vessels of this period found at Lydd (Sites Jb, L and M) and Denge West Quarries are developed Rye products, as this industry appears to have been the source of the better produced 14th century wares and there tends to be merging/inter-relationship between fabric groups of this date. Unfortunately little is currently known about the products of the 15th to 16th Rye industry and due to the possibilities of similar forms and fabrics being produced at a number of other centres, further work will be needed to source these wares with any certainty. Imports at this time are limited to the beginnings of imported German Siegburg stoneware (*i.e.*, Context 5066) and a single Merida-type vessel. This continues the trend of the preceding century where, although imports were not common, they were available to the low-status rural sites, probably via the port of New Romney or even Lydd town.

The early 18th century assemblage from Lydd 5/6 is unfortunately an isolated group at present. As such, little can be said with any certainty about the nature of pottery supply at this time. However, a few observations are worth making here. Firstly, the range of fabrics/products is wide. Although the majority of the ceramics, as would be expected, relate to probably 'local' production centres, there is a notable presence of pottery from the wider south-east region (*i.e.*, London and Borderware products), as well as from further afield English centres of production (*i.e.*, Staffordshire). To this must be added the Continental imports, most notably the Frechen stonewares, but also Beauvais products from France. It is therefore plainly apparent that by this time rural Marshland sites were easily able to acquire a wide range of coarseware and fineware products. This is undoubtedly in part due to easier communications by this date, as well as cheaper prices. To what degree it is dependent on the nature and status of the occupation cannot at present be addressed until the associated occupation sites are excavated. If, as has already been hinted, the dump of refuse in Ditch 5137 is from an inn, or a building partly serving this function, the assemblage may be atypical to what a rural domestic assemblage from the Marsh should be. The fact that the majority of the pottery in this assemblage could easily be placed in the mid 17th century, and with some pieces even earlier, is interesting. With one or two exceptions, the clay pipes, together with a small handful of pottery sherds, all clearly demonstrate a deposition date at the beginning of the 18th century. This strongly suggests that whatever the nature of the occupation there was a large proportion of 'older' vessels in use at the site in the early 18th century.

Very few comparable medieval assemblages have been excavated from the Marsh against which the sites around Lydd can be compared. No assemblages from the town of Lydd have been excavated to date, though more work has recently been done in New Romney. Rural assemblages are scarce and/or unstratified. The most extensive rural assemblages have come from field-walking (Gardiner 1994 and Reeves 1995) but do not offer reliable assemblages for comparison. Excavations along the A20270 Stockbridge to Brenzett and A259 Brookland Diversion road schemes have produced stratified medieval pottery spanning the 13th to 16th centuries (Barber 1995b and Barber 1995c), but unfortunately the groups have not been analysed due to no funds being made available for the post-excavation program. Generally the range of fabrics appears to be similar to that at the sites around Lydd. However, other fabrics, such as Beauvais slipware, are also present. The excavations at Broomhill church have only been published as an interim report (Gardiner 1988) and the final pottery report is still waiting publication. However, it is understood that the assemblage from this site, which lies some 4km to the west of Lydd Quarry, contains a high proportion of Rye material. This is probably due to the majority of the site's assemblage (Broomhill Phases 2 and 3) being predominantly of 14th century date and/or the site being closer to Rye. As such, the Broomhill assemblage would appear to correlate with the 14th century one from Lydd Quarry Site Jb (Lydd 3). It is interesting to note that the first phase at Broomhill, dated to the mid 13th century, is dominated by sand and shell wares comparable to Lydd Quarry F2b material.

The spate of excavations in recent years in New Romney has produced a number of good pottery assemblages, to complement the somewhat loosely stratified assemblage from the medieval hospital (Rigold 1964). These assemblages have been excavated to modern standards, though by their urban nature they will suffer from intrusive and residual material. At present none have been fully analysed or published yet, but should be in the near future. Perhaps the best assemblage is that from the Southlands School site (Jarrett 2002), which produced nearly 3,500 sherds of predominantly medieval (13th century) date. It would appear from studying the initial results of the ceramic assessment that, as at Lydd, the 13th century is dominated by F2b sherds (Canterbury's EM3), with the 14th century assemblages being dominated by the Rye and other sandy wares. A similar range of 'imported' material is also in evidence, including Scarborough, Saintonge, Rouen and Aardenberg-type/Low Countries products. Although the Southlands School assemblage appears to have more mixing between the sand and shell and Rye/sandy fabrics, this may be due to intrusiveness/residuality within contexts and/or Rye products enjoying some of the market in the, presumably reasonably affluent, town in the later 13th century. Similar, though smaller, assemblages have been excavated from elsewhere in the town (Blinkhorn 2001 and Linklater 2001) and when all are published should provide a good insight into the ceramics of the town.

Although much has been learnt by the analysis of the ceramics assemblage from the quarries around Lydd, there are still a number of gaps in our knowledge where future work should concentrate. Chronologically the current fabric sequence is weak for the 11th and 12th centuries, and there are insufficient feature sherds from this period to help refine dating. A similar situation is present for the majority of the 16th and 17th centuries. Although a good sequence exists for the 13th and 14th centuries, further chronological refinement is still needed. This will probably rely on stratified deposits from urban contexts, and will hopefully result in a greater confidence at differentiating pre and post 'flood' assemblages. A further research aim which needs addressing is the similarities/differences between the urban and rural assemblages of the Marsh, and indeed between the similarities/differences between the rural low status sites and the rural high status sites. Such studies should begin to shed light on the social and economic niches into which the different sites fit.

COINS, TOKENS, JETONS AND A COIN WEIGHT *by David Rudling*

Introduction

The eleven phases of excavations at Lydd Quarry yielded a total of 13 coins, 2 lead tokens and 2 jetons (reckoning counters). Of the coins, two (both from Lydd 1) are Roman and thus outside the remit of the current report. Nine of the other coins are examples of English medieval hammered silver coinage and were minted during the period from *c.* 1204 to 1603. The remaining two coins are both issues of George II and date to *c.* 1730–59. The two lead tokens probably date from the 16th to 18th centuries. The jetons comprise a 15th century English example, and a late 16th/early 17th century product from Nuremberg in Germany. Although the archaeological investigations at Denge West Quarry recovered no coins, tokens or jetons, an interesting discovery was a European coin weight for an English gold Rose Noble. All of the medieval and post-medieval items referred to above are catalogued below.

The variable use, or lack of, metal detectors during the various phases of archaeological investigations is likely to have affected the recovery of small numismatic finds. Although the total assemblage of coins and tokens is fairly small, the absence of issues which can be definitely attributed to the 17th century, and specifically the second half of this century, may indicate possible changes of use, or even abandonment, of some of the investigated areas.

The Catalogue

Coins

1. John, 1199–1216. 'Short Cross' coinage. Cut silver halfpenny. Class 5b or c, *c.* 1204–10.

   Reverse: IOHAN [ ], *i.e.*, the moneyer Iohan. The mint name is missing (N.B. several mints are possible: Canterbury, Exeter, Ipswich, Kings Lynn, Norwich or Winchester).

   Reference: North (1980, 179) 970–1.

   Lydd Quarry 5/6, Context 5175 (residual in a modern feature).

2. Henry III, 1216–72. 'Short Cross' coinage. Cut silver halfpenny. Class 7, *c.* 1217–42.

   Reverse: HEN]RI ON C[ANT, *i.e.*, the moneyer Henri of the Canterbury Mint.

   Reference: North (1980,180) 978–80.

   Lydd Quarry 5/6, Context 5010.

3. Henry III. 'Long Cross' coinage. Cut silver halfpenny. Class 3c, *c.* 1248–50.

   Reverse: HEN[RI ON LV]NDE, *i.e.*, the moneyer Henri of the London mint.

   Reference: North (1980, 182) 988.

   Lydd Quarry 5/6, Context 5024.

4. Edward I, 1272–1307. New coinage. Silver farthing of the London mint. Class I–IIIc, 1279–81. Very worn.

   Reference: North (1991, 32) 1051/1053.

   Lydd Quarry 5/6, Context 5024.

5. Edward I/II. New coinage. Silver penny of the Bury St. Edmunds mint. Class 10cf, 1301–10.

   Reference: North (1991, 32) 1040–43.

   Lydd Quarry 5/6, Context 5010.

6. Edward I/II. New coinage. Silver penny of the London mint. Class 10cf, 1301–10.

   Reference: North (1991, 32) 1040–3.

   Lydd Quarry 5/6, Context 5010.

7. Edward III, 1327–77. Pre-Treaty coinage, Series D, 1351–2. Silver halfgroat of the London mint.

   Reference: North (1991, 50) 1154.

   Lydd Quarry 5/6, Context 5281.

8. Elizabeth I, 1558–1603. Hammered coinage, second issue. Silver threepence. Dated 1580.

   Reference: North (1991, 135) 1998.

   Lydd Quarry 5/6, Context 5010.

9. Elizabeth I. Hammered coinage, third issue. Silver halfgroat. Extremely worn – mintmark illegible. Issued between 1583 and 1603.

   Reference: North (1991, 137) 2016.

   Lydd Quarry 5/6, Context 5010.

10. George II, 1727–60. Copper halfpenny. Date illegible, but possibly the coin is of the first issue *c.* 1729 and 1739.

    Lydd Quarry 2, Context 2002 (intrusive into a 13th century deposit).

11. George II. Copper farthing. Date illegible, but with a young head. Issued between 1730 and 1739.

    Lydd Quarry 5/6, Context 5309.

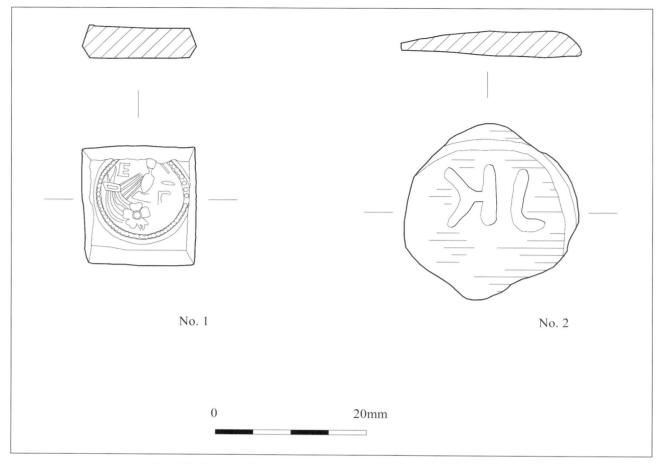

No. 1

No. 2

0   20mm

Fig. 79 Coin weight from Denge West and lead token from Lydd 7

Coin Weight (Fig. 79, No. 1)

12. A German copper-alloy weight for an English gold Rose Noble (or Ryal). Uniface 'square and tapering' type measuring 16 × 154 × 4mm.

Weight: 7.525g. 16th–18th century.

Obverse: Small facing bust of the King in the middle of a curved ship; rose beneath; a flag at the prow carries the royal cypher: a Roman E (*i.e.*, for Edward IV). The design on the right border of the die is not clear, but appears to include a capital R to the right of the King's bust (*i.e.*, for Rose Noble).

Although the first Rose Nobles (weight: 7.5g or 120 grains) were struck by Edward IV in 1465, similar coins were issued by Henry VII, Henry VIII, Mary and Elizabeth. The use of a Roman E indicates that this weight is Tudor or later (Marion Archibald, pers. comm.). German Rose Noble coin-weights were used in many 17th and 18th century coin-weight boxes (Houben 1978, 8:3). The Rose Noble had a value in 1465 of 10 shillings (*i.e.*, 120 silver pennies).

Denge West Quarry North, Area F, Context 69

Lead Tokens

13. Illegible lead token on a delicate, thin flan with some edge chips. *c.* 18mm diameter. Weight: 1.4g (*i.e.*, allowing for the edge chips, the original weight would have been in excess of 1.4g). Probably 16th or 17th century. (For a review of lead tokens of this period see Mitchiner and Skinner 1984, 1985.)

Lydd Quarry 5/6, Context 5024.

14. A uniface lead token. 20–22 mm diameter. Thickness: 3–4 mm. Weight: 8g. Crudely made and the edges show signs of seepage and are poorly finished.

Obverse: raised letters: JK, which have been erroneously cast back to front. An 18th century date is probable. (N.B., recording of this find by Luke Barber).

Lydd Quarry 7, context: Ditch recut 7026 (Fill 7027) (Fig. 79, No. 2).

Context Date (No. of contexts containing metalwork)	Iron nails	Iron objects	Copper alloy	Pewter	Lead waste	Lead fishing weights	Lead other	Total
1100–1200/25 (8 contexts)	10	7	-	-	-	-	-	18
1200–1300/25 (90 contexts)	107	63	19	1	81	88	2	361
1300/25–1400 (33 contexts)	72	14	7	1	6	9	5	114
1400–1550 (21 contexts)	97	31	20	7	18	3	-	176
Post 1550 (6 Contexts)	160	41	62	-	4	1	1	269
Uncertain (25 contexts)	33	12	10	-	9	17	1	82
Total (183 contexts)	479	168	118	9	118	119	9	1,020

Table 35: Characterization of metalwork assemblage by number from Lydd Quarry (Excavation Phases 1 to 11)

Jetons

15. English Jeton, *c*. 1344/51–1400. Latten. 30mm diameter. Weight: 11.5g.

   Obverse: Crown LE SOVDAN DE BABIL[ONE] (*i.e.*, The Soudan of Babylon – The Mohammedan King of the Romances of Chivalry), radiate Romanesque bust (likened to Postumus) right, each ray of the crown terminating in a quatrefoil; under the bust five stars of five points. Partly pierced in the centre.

   Reverse: A short cross pattée cantoned by groups of three trefoils round a pellet; an elaborate border composed of large and small quatrefoils and small trefoils, with a fructed angle enclosing a pellet opposite each end of the cross.

   Reference: Barnard (1917, 104) 53; *cf.* Mitchiner (1988, 119) 256; *cf.* Berry (1974, Plate 8: No. 2) Type 3 of Edward III and Richard II.

   Lydd Quarry 2, Unstratified

16. Nuremberg Jeton, *c*. 1586–1635. An issue from the workshop of Hans Krauwinkel II, who was a master from 1586 and who died in 1635. Brass 'rose/orb' type jeton. 22 mm diameter. Die axes: 12 o'clock. Weight: 1.27g.

   Obverse: rosette HANNS KRAVWINKEL IN N, three crowns, alternately with three lis arranged centrifugally around a central rose with 8 oval petals.

   Reverse: rosette HEIT ROTT MORGAN DOTT, Imperial orb, surmounted by a cross pattée, within a tressure with three main arches.

   Reference: Mitchiner (1988, 445) 1574–8.

   Lydd Quarry 5/6, Context 5138.

THE METALWORK *by Luke Barber*

Lydd Quarry

The excavations at Lydd Quarry produced relatively large quantities of metalwork, particularly non-ferrous items. This was due to the extensive use of metal-detectors for surveying the main areas of the site. The exceptions to this were the Phase 1 and 3 excavations, the latter being the result of overhead power lines preventing proper detector use. As a consequence the metalwork assemblages from these phases is very much poorer than those from the Phase 2 and 5/6 excavations.

The material is in variable condition. Most of the ironwork is heavily corroded, usually with thick corrosion products adhering, though the majority was identifiable to form/function without x-ray, or with only limited cleaning. The copper alloy ranges in condition from poor to very good, though only a few pieces have extensive corrosion products adhering. Similarly the lead, although coated in white corrosion, is in good condition. The pewter is more fragmentary.

A breakdown of the total assemblage from the quarry (Phases 1 to 11 – though no metalwork was found in Phases 8 and 11) can be given by showing the quantities of pieces within broad groupings by chronological phase (Table 35). It should be noted however, that this gives a rough guide only to the quantities of metalwork in use at different times, and does not take into account chronologically undiagnostic residual and intrusive material of which there is certainly some.

Although very little 12th to early 13th century material is present, the subsequent 13th century deposits produced the largest group from the site (361 pieces of metalwork from 90 different contexts). Proportionally, the quantity of metalwork in use appears to be similar for the 14th century (if the number of contexts are taken into consideration). However, there is a notable shift in emphasis with nails becoming far more common but lead objects and waste dwindling to very small numbers. It is possible some of this reduction at least is due to the limited extent of the metal detector survey at the 14th century site excavated at Lydd 3. There is a notable increase in metalwork during the 15th to early 16th centuries, again particularly amongst the ironwork. It should be noted that the Post 1550 period is 'over-represented' within Table 1, as virtually all of this period's assemblage came from one of only six contexts of this date (Lydd 5/6: Ditch 5137, Fill 5138). This particularly distorts the copper alloy assemblage as the total of 55 objects includes 44 pins or pin fragments. The late 17th to early 18th century assemblage from 5138 is also by far the largest from the Lydd Quarry excavations. This context produced 156 iron nails/nail fragments, and 36 pieces of other iron objects (including scissors, a sickle blade, a horseshoe, chain links, a spur and the large part of the rim, handle and footed base from a cast iron tripod cauldron). Context 5138 also produced 51 copper alloy objects (including buckles, furniture fittings and 44 pins) and a single piece of lead.

The aims of the metalwork report were to outline the size and extent of the assemblage, help with context dating where possible, and give an insight on the status and activities at the site in different periods. Although in many cases the metalwork confirmed the dating of the pottery, much chronologically diagnostic metalwork was obviously residual in later contexts. All the material was listed on Metalwork Record Forms (with notes, sketches and measurements) which form part of the site archive. Following this the majority of ironwork was discarded: only examples of the different types of nail and objects of particular interest were retained. All non-ferrous material has been retained.

The Iron

Nails

The 479 nails/nail fragments from the quarry are in a number of different types. Due to the relatively small size of the assemblage (particularly when the nail fragments undiagnostic of form are removed) and small numbers of contexts involved, no detailed statistical analysis has been undertaken on the occurrence of different nail types spatially or chronologically. However, Table 1 probably shows the general trend in nail use through time, even with the danger of residuality. Very few nails are present in the 12th century, though more are used during the 13th century, presumably when more settled occupation began. Most of the main structural elements in the buildings are likely to have relied totally on wooden joints (very few large 'structural' nails were recovered from the site), with the vast majority of nails only being used for secondary

fixings. It is interesting to note that no nails were found around the building at Lydd 10 (Site A) which was of an early date. After the 13th century there appears to be an increase in nail use (considering the lesser number of contexts), though the degree of residuality at this time is difficult to assess.

Although the overall nail assemblage is small, enough material is present to enable the basic types to be outlined, and it is hoped that further excavations on the Marsh may provide larger assemblages of closely dated medieval material in the future. The nail types are illustrated on Fig. 80.

Type 1a. General purpose nails. Square sectioned shank with a round flat or low-domed head. Head diameters vary between 17mm and 22mm. Overall nail lengths between 47mm and 80mm. These appear in contexts spanning the 12th to early 18th centuries.

Type 1b. As Type 1a but with square or rectangular heads. Head dimensions 10 × 10mm–20 × 20mm. Lengths up to 86mm. Located in 13th to 15th century contexts.

Type 2a. As Type 1 but a heavy duty/large variant. These nails, which would have been used for securing large structural timbers, have head diameters of 27mm to 31mm and lengths between 90mm and 126mm. Head diameter 27mm. Length 126mm. Located in 14th to 17th century contexts.

Type 2b. As Type 2a but with domed/pyramid head. Head diameters range between 17mm and 26mm. Lengths vary between 96mm and 135mm. Found in an early 18th century context at the quarry.

Type 3. Heavy studding nails (from doors, *etc.*). Large round/semi-round low domed/dished head with square sectioned shank. Head diameter 38mm, or 35 × 35mm for the sub-round/rectangular examples, with a height of between 7 and 14mm. No lengths obtained. Located in 17th century context at the quarry.

Type 4a. Large nails where shank expands to form plain square/rectangular head (similar to a farrier's nail but much larger). This type of nail is intended to be driven in flush with the surface of the wood. Head dimensions 22 × 15mm. Length 90–115mm. Located in 17th century context at the quarry.

Type 4b. As Type 4a but with head expanded so it steps out from the line of the expanding shank. Head dimensions 11 × 8mm–11 × 10mm, though one small example measures only 10 × 7mm. Lengths vary between 62 and 91mm. Located in 13th to 17th century contexts.

Type 4c. As Type 4b but larger/heavier duty.

Type 5 (Farrier's nail). Square sectioned shank which expands to form rectangular head (head dimensions 10 ×

6mm). Only one was identified from trackway ditch 5009 (Context 5010, dated 15th century). Two further farrier's nails, but with domed rectangular heads, were recovered from Lydd 2 (Contexts 2133, (Cut 2132) and 2193 (Cut 2192), both dated 13th century).

By far the largest group of nails comes from Ditch 5137 (Fill 5138), dated to between 1680 and 1720. Of the 156 nails/nail fragments in this context the following types were represented:

Nail Type	Number
1a	29
2b	5
3	1
4a	4
4b	9
4c	7
Unidentified	101

Table 36: (Context 5138) Quantification of nail types

It is quite probable that amongst the unidentified category were a number of small headless examples similar to Types 4a and 4b (*i.e.*, used for floorboards, *etc.*), however, the state of corrosion did not allow these to be positively identified.

No other individual large groups of nails are present in the assemblage, though 41 were recovered from Ditch 3150 (Fill 3151) at Lydd 3. This group consists of one Type 2a and 40 Type 1a examples and may relate to the dismantling/demolition of the adjacent structures (or remains of them) in the early 16th century. The latest nails from the quarry consist of a small assemblage from a 19th century context at Lydd 7 (Ditch fill 7024).

Unidentified Objects

A number of pieces of ironwork, although clearly not nails, were undiagnostic of form/function. Many of these pieces are simply strips or sheeting fragments, many of the former probably relating to bindings from buckets/barrels, strengthening from doors, or tyres from the wheels of farm carts. Other pieces consist of amorphous lumps, which are not even diagnostic of form: these account for most of the 12th century iron objects. However, many more diagnostic items are present and a selection of the more important ones is given below.

Household/fixings

A number of items relate to the home or household activities.

A hinge pivot from a door, window or gate was recovered from Lydd 1. Round-sectioned pivot with a rectangular-sectioned tapering shank for fixing into

wood. Context 534 (dated 13th century). (Fig. 80, No. 1).

A number of clench bolts were recovered from the quarry, though never in large quantities and always in poor condition. The badly fragmentary remains of two were located at Lydd 1 in 13th century contexts (546 and 579), while a further example from Lydd 3 (Pit 3222/Fill 3223) is dated to the 14th century. The latest dated example is from the Phase 5/6 excavations, which produced a more complete example, measuring 65mm long by 40mm wide (with a square rove 26 × 27mm) from Context 5152 (dated 15th century). Although clench bolts were used for boat construction, the low numbers at the current site, together with the site's location, suggest that most of the Lydd examples are from doors and other building components.

A number of other fittings which may have been used inside a dwelling or agricultural building were located. These include a ?door hinge from 229 (dated 13th century); brackets from 5010 (Trackway Ditch 5009) and 5012 (Trackway Ditch 5011); four chain links: (5014, Cut 5013, 15th century), (5090, Ditch 5089, 13th century), (5138, Ditch 5137 × 2, early 18th century); as well as 'U' shaped staples (5138, Ditch 5137, Fig. 80, No. 2).

A large key (see copper alloy for three further examples) with solid stem and oval bow was recovered from 5278 (13th to 14th century layer: Lydd 5/6, Area A) (Fig. 80, No. 3).

A small barrel-padlock key in round sectioned wire. Although very much smaller than those illustrated in the Museum of London Catalogue (1940, Fig. 45) and the bit is not set laterally to the shank, the general form is similar. Context 543 (dated 13th century). (Fig. 80, No. 4).

Nine fragments from a cast iron tripod cauldron with angular handles and simple feet (Fig. 80, No. 5). These items are relatively rare finds on archaeological sites, although examples are recorded from Norwich (Margeson 1993, No. 584) and Chingly Forge in Kent (Goodall in Crossley 1975). (Ditch 5137, Fill 5138).

The latest 'household' iron object from the site is a 20th century enamelled cup from 5175 (large pit 5174).

Tools

The excavations produced a few items in this category.

Although knives could be grouped under household items they have been included under the tool heading within the present report.

Small whittle-tanged knife with back and cutting blade both tapering to the tip. Similar examples have been dated to the 13th to 14th centuries in Norwich (Margeson 1993, *Fig. 93, No. 804). Lydd 1: Context 328 (12th century). (Fig. 80, No. 6).

Other whittle-tanged knife blade fragments were recovered from Lydd 2 (three fragments, all from 13th century contexts); Lydd 3 (a blade measuring 106mm long (including tang) (Cut 3362/Fill 3363, dated 13th century)) and Lydd 5/6 (a fragment from 5304, Pit 5363, dated mid 13th to early 14th century).

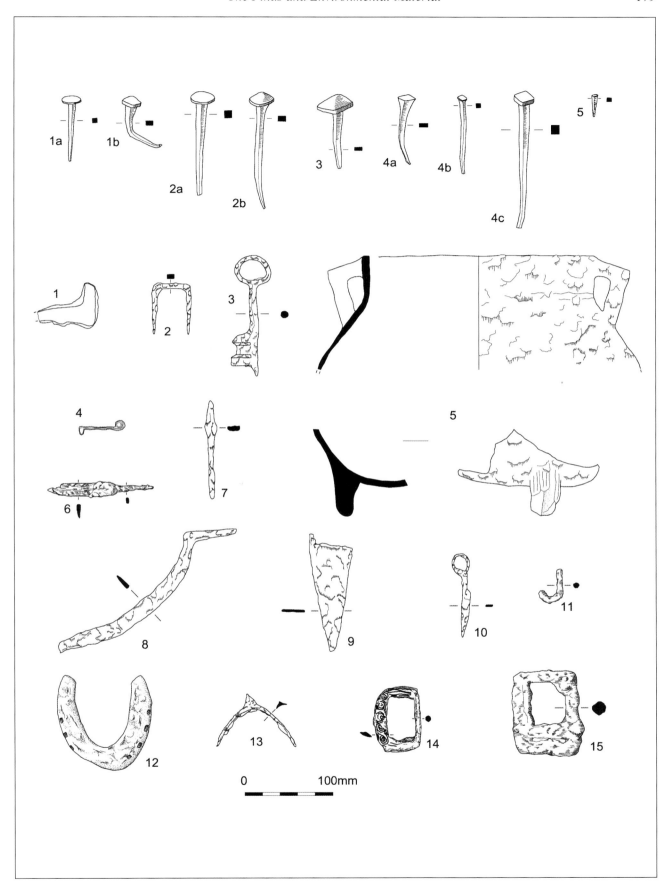

Fig. 80 Lydd Quarry: Metalwork (Iron)

A wood drill/corer bit with lanceolate terminal was located in Context 5010 (Trackway ditch 5009, dated 15th to early 16th centuries) (Fig. 80, No. 7). A similar example has been found in Norwich (Margeson 1993, 1390).

A metal sheathing, possibly from a plough, was recovered from Lydd 1 (Context 2358, Ditch 2194, dated 13th century).

Two sickle blade fragments, both from Lydd 5/6, are also present in the assemblage and may be an indication of the laborious nature of harvesting on the marsh until relatively late. One tanged example comes from Context 5287 (Cut 5286, dated late 15th to early 16th century) (Fig. 80, No. 8). The other fragment is an early 18th century example from Context 5138 (Ditch 5137) with a 24mm wide blade.

Context 5138 also contained other tools including a triangular-shaped shear blade (Fig. 80, No. 9), probably for use on sheep judging by its size, and half a pair of small scissors (Fig. 80, No. 10). Context 5138 obviously contained a mixture of domestic and agricultural material.

Surprisingly, only one fragment of fish-hook was recovered from Lydd Quarry. This came from Lydd 2 (Context 2358, Ditch 2194) and was dated to the 13th century. Unfortunately the hook is broken at both ends (Fig. 80, No. 11).

Horse equipment

A number of horseshoes are present in the assemblage, though virtually all are represented by relatively small fragments and as such are not closely datable in their own right. Fragments were recovered from Lydd 2 (11 pieces from contexts spanning the 13th to 16th centuries); Lydd 3 (two pieces from Ditch 3150/Fill 3151, dated 15th century and Ditch 3200/Fill 3320, dated 14th century) and Lydd 5/6 (Context 5012 (Trackway Ditch 5011, dated 17th century), Context 5281 (fill of Ditch 5011 in Area B, dated 17th to 18th century) and two from 5138 (Ditch 5137: dated 1680–1720).

The only complete example of a horseshoe is from Lydd 1. A small shoe with no calkins and four rectangular nail holes on each side close to outside rim of shoe was recovered from Context 319, dated on ceramics grounds to the 14th century. No exact parallels have been found, but 13th to 14th century examples of this type are known (Museum of London Cat. Fig. 36 Nos. 9, 10 and 12). Examples from Norwich however, have been shown to span the 15th to 17th centuries (Margeson 1993, Fig. 173, Nos. 1842–4). (Fig. 80, No. 12).

Only one example of a spur was located: Lydd 5/6, Context 5138 (Fig. 80, No. 13).

A small quantity of iron buckles, usually fragmentary, were located at the site. Although some or all of these could have been used for securing waist belts, they could equally have been used for horse harnesses. As such, iron buckles have been included under the horse furniture heading for the purposes of this report.

D-shaped buckle with wide flattened frame and round-sectioned pin bar. The frame is decorated with incised lines, both straight and spiralled, the latter being restricted to the front of the frame (Fig. 80, No. 14). The lines appear to be inlaid with a gold coloured metal, either gilt or, more probably, stained tinning, which is likely to be the last remains of an all over coating (Egan and Pritchard 1991, 27). Similar examples have been found in London (Egan and Pritchard 1991, Fig. 57. No. 415), however this type was extremely popular throughout the medieval and early post-medieval periods and is difficult to date closely. Lydd 1: Unstratified.

A rectangular-framed buckle (Fig. 80, No. 15) from a 13th century context at Lydd 2: Context 2141 (Cut 2140). Another probable square harness buckle was recovered from a 14th century context at Lydd 3 (Context 3320).

The Copper Alloy

A variety of copper alloy objects are present in the assemblage. These were located in contexts of all periods as well as coming from unstratified deposits, primarily associated with the southern trackway. The copper alloy artefacts include a number of intrinsically dateable pieces, although most are from dated contexts. These consist of a variety of dress accessories (buckles, broaches, *etc.*), as well as household and other items. At Lydd 5/6, these are often present in groups such as the late 17th to early 18th century assemblage from Context 5138.

Dress Accessories

This is perhaps the largest group of copper alloy objects and the material covers the medieval and post-medieval periods alike. Some of the more important pieces are catalogued below.

A probable belt chape of simple form, consisting of a pierced sheeting fragment from a 14th century context at Lydd 3: Cut 3142, Fill 3143. (Fig. 81, No. 16). Two further possible belt chapes of simple form were located in 13th century contexts at Lydd 2: Contexts 2012 (Ditch 2013) and 2135 (Ditch 2134).

An ornate tapering belt chape with pierced moulded terminal formed from a single metal sheet folded lengthways and held together by one copper alloy rivet. The upper surface is decorated with a rectilinear pattern of incised lines (Fig. 81, No. 17). This item was located in a 14th to 15th century context (Pit 3164, Fill 3165) at Lydd 3 and compares to similar examples from London which have been dated to the mid 14th to early 15th centuries (Egan and Pritchard 1991, Nos. 605–7).

Annular brooch with incised linear and dot decoration on the frame (Fig. 81, No. 18). The D-sectioned frame has broken at the constriction for the pin, which is missing. The item is from a pit fill dated to the 13th to early 14th century (Lydd 3: Pit 3016, Fill 3017) and compares

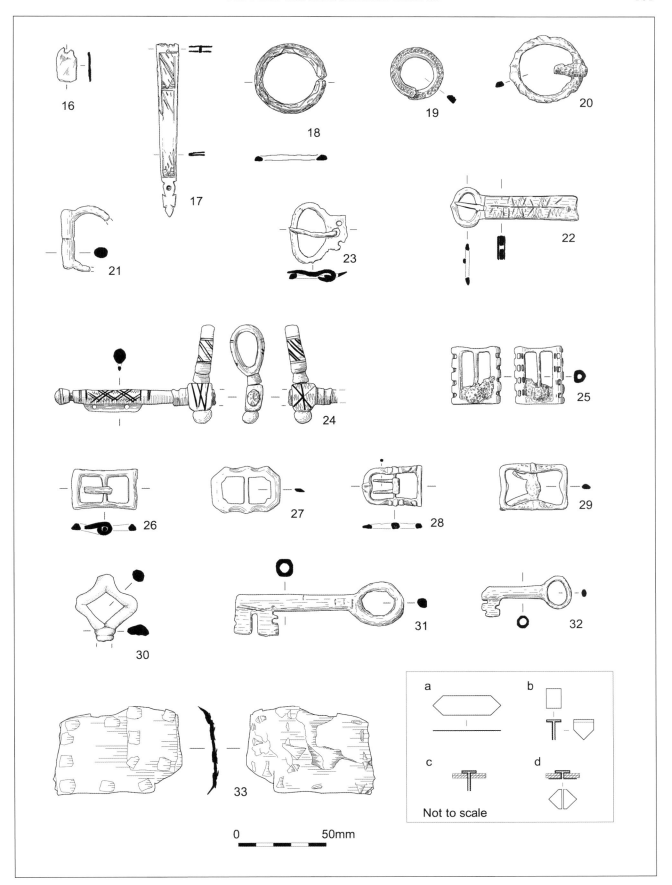

Fig. 81 Lydd Quarry: Metalwork (Non-ferrous)

closely with similar examples from London which have been dated to the later 13th to mid 14th centuries (Egan and Pritchard 1991, Nos. 1314–5 and 1318).

Annular brooch with stamped pattern of circles around frame. The frame is broken at the restriction for the pin hinge. (Fig. 81, No. 19). (Lydd 5/6: Ditch 5089, Fill 5090: dated 13th century).

Annular brooch/circular buckle with rope decoration on frame and remains of the iron pin in its original position. There is a restriction in the frame to take the pin hinge, as well as a slight pin seating on the opposite side of the frame. (Fig. 81, No. 20). (Lydd 5/6: probably residual in Ditch 5009, Fill 5010). Similar examples, though smaller, are noted from London (Egan and Pritchard 1991, Nos. 1311 and 1318).

Undecorated buckle fragment with thickened outer edge of frame with groove for pin seating. Area of pin hinge and buckle plate missing. These buckles have a wide date range, spanning the late 12th to late 14th centuries, though they are most common in the 13th century (Egan and Pritchard 1991, No. 76). (Fig. 81, No. 21). (Lydd 5/6: Residual in Ditch 5009, Fill 5010).

Buckle with two pronged spacer under folded decorated sheet buckle plate. Copper alloy pin still intact. The buckle plate is held together by a single copper alloy rivet and there are traces of leather between the folded plates and the spacer bars. The outer plate is decorated with incised zigzag line decoration. Similar buckles from London are dated to between the mid 14th and early 15th centuries (Egan and Pritchard 1991, 80). (Fig. 81, No. 22). (Lydd 5/6: Ditch 5003, Fill 5014. Dated 15th century).

Simple buckle with copper alloy pin and two circular fixing holes, possibly to secure a buckle plate, on a rectangular extension to the frame. (Fig. 81, No. 23). (Lydd 5/6: Post-hole 2509, Fill 5210. Undated – ?13th century).

Suspension loop and one arm of the suspension bar from a purse frame. Both decorated with inlaid black/niello lines, between which, on the arm, are incised zigzag lines. This type is closely paralleled in London where examples are dated to the late 15th or early 16th centuries (cf. Museum of London Type A1/A2, Plate XXXIII, No. 2). (Fig. 81, No. 24). (Lydd 5/6: residual in Ditch 5011, Fill 5012).

Bow-fronted rectangular double looped buckle with traces of iron pin and copper alloy central bar. The two long sides of the frame are formed from perforated tubes. Traces of silver plating/tinning are evident on the frame. A similar example has been dated to the 15th century (Whitehead 1996, No. 476). However, a 16th century date seems more probable for this ornate type. (Fig. 81, No. 25). (Lydd 5/6: Ditch 5043, Fill 5044. Dated late 15th to mid 16th century).

Rectangular double looped spur buckle with bevelled frame and copper alloy central bar/pin (broken). Similar examples are given quite a wide date range spanning

the mid 16th to 17th centuries (Whitehead 1996, Nos. 460–1). However, the pottery dating the current example suggests a date at the beginning of this range, if the piece is not intrusive. (Fig. 81, No. 26). (Lydd 5/6: Ditch 5043, Fill 5044 – see above).

Ditch 5137, Fill 5138 (dated to the early 18th century)
Lydd 5/6

Rectangular double looped spur buckle with ornate frame. No pin. (Fig. 81, No. 27).

Asymmetrical double looped buckle with ornate moulded frame and copper alloy double pin. 17th century. (Fig. 81, No. 28).

Two-piece rectangular ?knee buckle with traces of iron pin. The frame is internally bowed and has moulded decoration where the central bar meets it. The central bar supports the (broken) tongue and pin. Late 17th to early 18th century. (Fig. 81, No. 29).

A fragment of the frame of an elaborate 'spectacle' buckle of 17th century date, together with a 25 × 9mm single riveted belt chape, formed from folded sheeting, was also recovered from this context.

The latest dress accessories from the site consist of late 18th to 19th century plain gilt buttons (Lydd 7: Ditch fills 7024 and 7027).

Household Objects

Lozenge-shaped bow from a ?key. Key bows of this type are thought to be predominantly of the 13th to 14th centuries (Museum of London Type V. Fig. 42). A similar shaped object from London has been interpreted as a suspension loop from a 14th century brass purse bar (Egan and Pritchard 1991 Fig. 237 No. 1707). The example from Lydd is apparently broken at the start of the shank. Although the break is clean, giving the impression this may have been intentionally cast in this form, it is likely this is partly the result of the banding around the top of the shank breaking away. A small fragment of twine is present adhering to the broken face. Lydd 1: Context 151, dated 13th century. (Fig. 81, No. 30).

Large key with oval bow, hollow stem and asymmetrical bit. The stem is hollow for 55mm from the bit end. (Fig. 81, No. 31). (Lydd 5/6: Ditch 5023, Fill 5024. Dated 14th century).

Small key with nearly circular bow, hollow stem and asymmetrical bit. Probably for a chest/casket. (Fig. 81, No. 32). (in surface of natural gravel on southern trackway at Lydd 5/6).

A sheet cauldron repair. This item is of particular interest as it demonstrates the 'make do and mend' attitude shown by the inhabitants on peasant settlements of the time. The piece is a repair patch, presumably from a sheet bronze vessel such as a cauldron. The remains of the vessel sheeting is on the back of the patch, and the gash that required patching is clearly visible (Fig. 81, No. 33 – right illustration). A rectangular sheeting patch has been added over the hole on the outside of the vessel and riveted into place using 'sheet' rivets. Traces of black ?pitch are apparent between the vessel body and the sheet repair, presumably in an attempt to make the repair water-tight. The rivets are formed from narrow strips of sheeting, tapered at both ends (Fig. 81, a). These strips were folded in such a way as to resemble drawing pins when viewed side on (Fig. 81, b). Each rivet has then been inserted through a prepared punched slot which penetrates both the repair sheeting and vessel wall so the 'drawing pin-like' head sits flush with the outer surface of the repair patch (Fig. 81, c). The tapered ends of the rivets have then been folded outwards to secure the repair patch in place and the whole hammered tight (Fig. 81, d). A number of these folded back tapered ends are visible to the rear of the repair, where they appear as triangles. The first patch evidently did not work and a second, smaller patch was added using similar methods, partially overlaying the first. This cauldron was evidently a valuable item as a further patch, measuring 80 × 36mm, was recovered from the same context. This obsession with repair was not confined to Lydd in the medieval period: similar repairs to sheet vessels have been noted elsewhere, such as in Norwich (Margeson 1993, Nos. 574–7), and emphasise the throw-away society we live in today. (Lydd 5/6: Ditch 5089, Fill 5090, dated 13th century).

A number of hammered sheeting fragments were found during the excavations and it is likely that many of these are from a sheet metal vessel, or vessels, which began to replace ceramic cooking vessels toward the end of the medieval period. In addition, a number of fragments of heavier cast vessels have also been located. For example, Ditch 5009 (Fill 5010) produced two sheeting fragments, probably both from vessels, as well as a bodysherd from a cast vessel. Although the majority of material from this context is of 15th to early 16th century date, enough intrusive items are present to make it impossible to be certain whether these vessels are late medieval or, possibly, as late as the 17th century. A similar problem exists with a rim fragment from a sheet vessel in Ditch 5011 (Fill 5012), although a rim from a cast example is more securely dated to the late 15th to mid 16th century in Ditch 5043 (Fill 5044).

Some 44 pins/pin fragments were recovered from Lydd 5/6, Ditch 5137 (Fill 5138). Where discernible all have spherical heads with diameters of around 1.75mm. A number of the pins retain traces of tin-plating. Lengths are usually between 23mm and 26mm, though one is 33mm long. A very small thimble (diameter 11mm, height 14mm) with machine-punched indentations, probably dates to a similar time as the pins (Lydd 5/6: Context 5281, Ditch 5011 in Area B).

A cast tear-drop shaped draw pull, probably from a light chest of draws. Similar examples from America have been dated to between *c.* 1685 and 1720 (Noel Hume 1969, 229, No. 1). This date matches exactly that of Context 5138 at Lydd 5/6 in which the item was found (Fig. 82, No. 34).

Horse equipment

Decorative oval roundel/boss made from sheeting with central circular fixing lug. Beaded decoration on edge with concentric raised cordons around central floral motif. Probably a bridle decoration of 14th to 15th century date. A similar item has been located in Norwich (Margeson 1993, No. 579), though with a foliage rather than floral decorative motif. (Lydd 5/6: Ditch 5003, Fill 5014, dated to the 15th century). (Fig. 82, No. 35).

Other items that may relate to equestrian activity include a small rectangular decorative leather stud (measuring 10 × 5mm) from Ditch 5009 (Fill 5010) and a slightly larger example, decorated with punched dots, from Ditch 5023 (Fill 5024: dated 14th century) which measures 19 × 14mm. A further example was recovered at Lydd 2 (Context 2133, Cut 2132).

Scrap

A number of other items are included in the assemblage. Most are scrap bits of sheeting or wire, though a number are from larger unidentified objects. All are fully listed in the archive. The latest item consists of a World War II shell splinter from Context 338 at Lydd 1.

Pewter

The few pewter objects present were mainly recovered from the Lydd 5/6 area. These include a late 17th to early 18th century button (intrusive into Ditch 5009 (Fill 5010)) and three studs/tacks with low-domed circular heads (head diameters 11–12mm; overall length of tack 8mm) from Ditch 5043, Fill 5044 (dated late 15th to mid 16th century). Two badly degraded spoon fragments were also located in the same deposit. An intrusive 18th century button was located in Ditch 3006 (Fill 3007) at Lydd 3.

Lead

Some 246 pieces of lead were found during the excavations at the quarry. The lead can be divided into three main categories: cylindrical fishing weights (either rolled or unrolled); lead waste (either irregular or sheet off-cuts); and other items.

Fishing weights

Although lead fishing weights have been located during most of the phases of excavation at the quarry, the majority have come from two: those of the enclosed settlement at Lydd 2 and Area A at Lydd 5/6. As can be seen from Table 1, the vast majority of the weights,

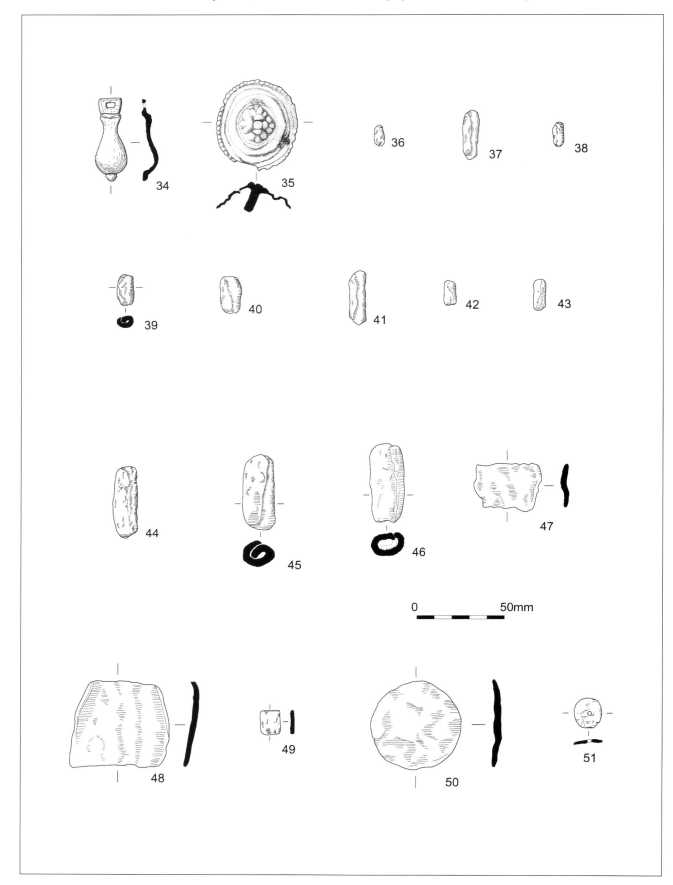

Fig. 82 Lydd Quarry: Metalwork (Non-ferrous)

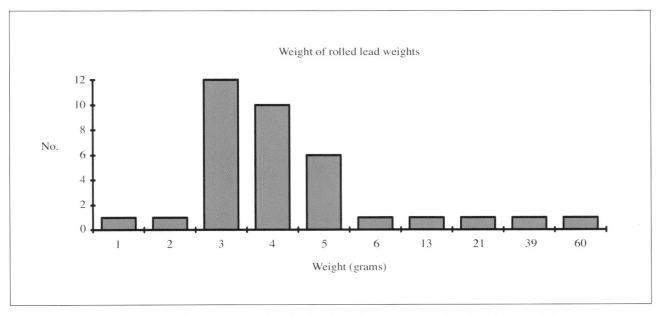

Fig. 83 Graph showing weight of rolled lead fishing weights from Lydd 2 (Site H)

as well as lead waste, are from 13th century contexts. The weights in later contexts, particularly after the 14th century, can be assumed to be residual. Weights found in contexts predating the 13th century are likely to be intrusive (indeed at Lydd 7 some were found intrusive in a Roman context). The earliest weight which is probably reliable in its context is an example (50mm long, weighing 48g) from Pit A62, Fill A63 at Lydd 10, dated late 12th to early 13th century. The weights consist of both rolled examples as well as those which have been deliberately unrolled (see below). The most detailed analysis of the weights at Lydd Quarry was undertaken on the large assemblage of 13th century weights from the Lydd 2 excavations, accounting for 64 of the lead weights, though seven of these were from 'undated' contexts. Of the 64 weights, 35 were still rolled while the remainder had been unrolled. The large assemblage from Lydd 5/6 consists of a total of 45 weights (rolled and unrolled) of which 31 are from 13th century contexts and eight are from 14th century contexts.

The fishing weights are formed from square, or rectangular, sheeting pieces being tightly rolled to form a cylinder. A narrow hole runs down the centre of the weights. Similar weights have been found in Hastings (Barber 1993b) and the type is also well known from Meare in Somerset (Steane and Foreman 1991, Fig. 12.8, Nos. 1–20). The exact way in which they functioned is uncertain, but it is probable the lead sheeting was wrapped tightly around the perimeter of a hand-thrown net used in rivers, ponds, tidal creeks or inshore coastal waters. Alternatively, the heavier examples may have been used on more static nets or on a line to sink the bait and hold it on the bottom.

The Lydd 2 assemblage was subjected to an analysis of the range in weight of the items. The results are given above in Fig. 83.

Although there is a great variety in both dimensions and weights, there are two noticeable groupings. The smaller of the weights concentrate around the 3 to 5 gram range (Fig. 83) and are by far the most common type recovered from Lydd 2 (28 examples). Examples from Contexts 2002 (Ditch 2006), 2012 (Ditch 2011), 2016, 2111 (Cut 2110) and 2135 (Ditch 2134) are shown in Fig. 82 (Nos. 36, 37, 38 and 39, 40 and 41 respectively). This type was also the most common at Lydd 5/6 (see below). Two examples are illustrated from 13th century Ditch 5324, Fill 5325 (Fig. 82 Nos. 42–3). The larger type is far less common at Lydd 2 (3 examples) and as such does not distinguish itself on Fig. 83. The larger weights are more variable and range from 21 to 60 grams (at Lydd 5/6 they reach 62 grams – see Fig. 85). Examples from this group are shown in Fig. 82 (Nos. 44 and 45, both from Context 2135, Ditch 2134 and No. 46 from Lydd 5/6 from 13th century Context 5364). It is possible that these larger weights were used to weight nets or individual lines in water where a stronger current caused the smaller weights to be less effective.

The dimensions of the weights at Lydd 2 also vary considerably. The diameter of each is recorded in the archive. This measurement is not considered a good one for comparative purposes as it is dependent on how tightly the weight has been rolled. As a general observation however, most of the smaller weights range between 5.5mm and 8mm in cross-section, while the larger fall within the 10–16mm range. The measurement of length is more useful. The bulk of the weights range in length from 12.5mm to 22.5mm (smaller types) and 32mm to 43mm (larger types).

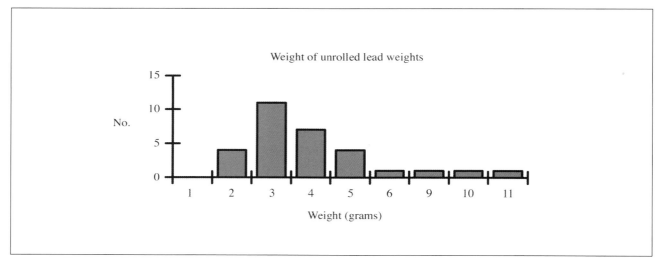

Fig. 84 Graph showing weight of unrolled lead fishing weights from Lydd 2 (Site H)

Twenty nine examples of unrolled cylindrical weights were recovered at Lydd 2. These consist of square or rectangular pieces of sheeting ranging between 1mm and 1.5mm thick. All show signs of having been rolled and as such it is assumed that all represent rolled cylindrical weights which have been removed from a line/net for re-use or for re-melting to cast new weights. The rolled examples are likely to have either deliberately or accidentally come away from rotten nets. They occur, mixed with the rolled weights, in 13th century contexts. The weights of these examples are compatible with the rolled examples (Fig. 84) with the majority falling between 3 and 5 grams. None of the larger weights were found unrolled. The dimensions of the unrolled sheeting are also a similar length to the rolled examples and range between 12mm and 28mm long. Two examples from Lydd 2 are shown in Fig. 82 (No. 47, Context 2097, Ditch 2096 and No. 48, Context 2135, Ditch 2134).

The weights, both rolled and unrolled, from the Lydd 5/6 excavations conform to the general size ranges noted for the Lydd 2 assemblage. Two main sizes are present,

with the larger having an even greater range of weight than was found at Lydd 2 (Fig. 85). The majority of the fishing weights and related waste (see below) were located in Area A (Site G) and appear to date to the 13th century.

Interestingly, only one example of a lead fishing weight was discovered at the predominantly 14th century occupation site at Lydd 3 (an unrolled example from Cut 3308 (Fill 3180) which weighs 40 grams). This stark contrast with the quantities of weights from the 13th century occupation site at Lydd 2, and indeed area A at Lydd 5/6, despite the hindered metal detector survey, suggests that fishing had stopped, or virtually stopped, by this time.

Waste lead

The scrap lead can be divided into two categories: irregular waste (totalling 36 pieces at Lydd 5/6); and sheet off-cuts (totalling 41 pieces at Lydd 5/6). A further 33 pieces, both irregular and sheeting off-cuts, were recovered from Lydd 2. Little can be said regarding the irregular waste apart from the fact that it indicates the working of the metal on the site. Better evidence comes from the sheeting fragments. These are often not diagnostic, however, several pieces of interest are present at Lydd 5/6. The form of one piece from Context 5012 shows how the molten lead was poured out onto a flat surface to form a thin sheet. The irregular nature of the edge shows the molten metal was not retained within a mould. Cut marks on this piece of waste show that the cooled sheet was subsequently cut into a rectangular sheet ready to create a rolled fishing weight. A complete sheet from 13th century Context 5364 (measuring 36 × 47mm and weighing 36g) appears to be a blank which has yet to be rolled. This is unusual as most sheet scraps have a somewhat uneven surface, suggesting they are unrolled used weights which have been cut up for recycling. This

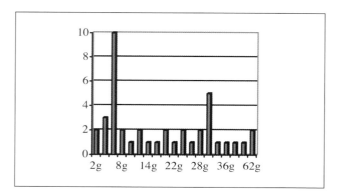

Fig. 85 Graph showing weight of rolled/unrolled lead fishing weights from Lydd 5/6 (mainly Site G) (Categories: 2, 3, 4, 8, 10, 12, 14, 18, 20, 22, 24, 26, 28, 30, 34, 36, 40, 46 and 62 grams)

fact is confirmed by the presence of part of the end of an unrolled fishing weight from Ditch 5121 (Fill 5122, dated 13th century) which exhibits a clear cut mark. Two further regular square sheet pieces were recovered from Lydd 2: one measuring 13 × 14 × 1.5mm (Context 2358); the other illustrated in Fig. 82 (No. 49, Context 2002, Ditch 2006).

The larger fishing weight assemblages

Only Lydd 2 and Lydd 5/6 produced any notable groups of fishing weights and waste: all are from 13th century contexts. The main ones are listed below.

• Context 2012: two pieces of waste, five weights (three of which unrolled)
• Context 2097: nine weights (five of which unrolled)
• Context 2135: ten pieces of waste, eleven weights (four of which unrolled)
• Context 2165: seven pieces of waste and four weights (three of which unrolled)
• Context 2358: two pieces of waste and six weights (three of which unrolled)

All of these contexts are ditch fills dated to the 13th (some possibly to the early 14th) century. With the exception of Context 2358, which is a primary fill of Ditch 2194, all the lead is from the upper fills and has been incorporated during final infilling. The quantity of leadwork on the site strongly suggests the manufacture of lead weights was being undertaken. The lack of similar quantities of leadwork at the Lydd 1 settlements cannot be seen as significant, as metal detectors were not used during these excavations (Barber 1996b).

The single largest assemblage from Lydd 5/6 Area A came from a 13th century ditch (Ditch 5089, Fill 5090) which produced 17 rolled/unrolled weights and 31 pieces of lead waste. The weights consist of seven small examples (up to 8 grams), as well as 10 medium to large examples (20 to 62 grams). The waste includes both off-cut sheeting (16 pieces) and irregular lumps (15 pieces). It seems very probable that manufacturing of weights was being undertaken at this site too.

Miscellaneous other items

Only a few pieces of lead do not fall into the above categories. One example from Lydd 2 consists of a circular disc from Context 2165 (Ditch 2164) (Fig. 82, No. 50).

Further material in this category was recovered from Lydd 5/6. This includes four 6mm diameter spheres (1g each) from 14th century Ditch 5023 (Fill 5024). One has a clear seam and the remains of a casting sprue, suggesting they were deliberately made. However, the actual function of these medieval 'shot' is uncertain. A 30mm long, 3mm wide lead strip with a number of apparent sprue of 2–3mm diameter spaced along one site

was found in Ditch 5043 (Fill 5044, dated late 15th to 16th century). Although this does not match the size of sprue noted on the sphere from 5024, this piece of lead may be evidence of the manufacture of lead pistol shot, an example of which, measuring 12mm in diameter, was located from 17th/early 18th century context 5281. The only other lead item of note consists of a small perforated disc, weighing 2g, from 13th century Ditch 5324 (Fill 5325. Fig. 82, No. 51).

Discussion

There is a notable lack of iron from the excavations, particularly structural fixtures and fittings (including nails). This absence of ironwork is not the result of poor burial conditions as, despite heavy corrosion products, even some fine ironwork had survived. Of particular interest is the absence of iron nails and other fixtures and fittings associated with the building (Site A) from Lydd 10. This suggests that either no or very little ironwork was used in its construction, or that it was dismantled and the materials recycled very thoroughly. On balance, the former suggestion is considered to be the more likely.

The material that is present does not appear to have any notable spatial concentration. Much has been recovered from the infilled ditches of the field-system, often away from the identified areas of activity. As such, the distribution of most of the recovered ironwork can be seen to be a reflection of rubbish disposal rather than reflecting the areas in which the material was used. Despite this, some nails were located within isolated features, including post-holes, and suggest the probable use within a structure. It is quite possible that timber-framed buildings were located in these areas but have left little material behind. Ironwork may have been minimal within such buildings or was re-used. Alternatively, associated spreads of maintenance and demolition waste containing ironwork may have originally formed layers above the clay subsoil which have since been truncated and dispersed by later agricultural activity. The lack of structural ironwork from the Lydd 2 occupation site would certainly support such a theory. It is equally possible that the ironwork in Areas A and B at Lydd 5/6 relates to fencing for controlling stock or delimiting areas of semi-industrial activity such as lead working.

The excavations have confirmed that the inhabitants manufactured, and presumably used, two main sizes of rolled lead fishing/net weights. Although it is probable the weights relate to net fishing, it is possible they were also used to weight lines, though the somewhat surprising virtual absence of hooks would suggest the former. However, certain types of eel fishing do not rely on hooks, instead using wool which catches the throat teeth of the fish. The presence of eel bones in the fish assemblage from the site attests their presence and it is likely they formed a widespread and relatively easily attainable food resource of the Marsh. The smaller weights, unless used

Period	No. of contexts	Nails	Objects	Total
Undated/ U/S	5	27	19	46
13th–14th century	3	3	5	8
15th–16th century	3	110	37	147
Total	11	140	61	201

Table 37: Characterisation of Denge West North Ironwork assemblage

in numbers, are unlikely to have been effective in water with a strong current. As such, these are perhaps best viewed as being used in either still or slow-moving water. The larger weights could be used in a similar situation, however, the additional weight of these would enable their use in faster running water and perhaps for inshore sea fishing. Although material associated with this activity is spread widely across the excavated area, as well as in a wide chronological range of contexts, there is a clear concentration of material around the enclosed settlement at Lydd 2 and the enclosures in Area A at Lydd 5/6. This activity was probably confined to the 13th century.

This practical ability to make, and indeed repair, objects other than lead weights is shown by the presence of small quantities of iron forging slag from the site and the determined way in which the sheet bronze cauldron from Context 5090 was patched and repatched. In such an environment it is easy to see the re-use of metal objects, particularly iron, on a regular basis, perhaps leading to less material being incorporated in the archaeological record.

The copper alloy dress accessories are a mixture of utilitarian items, expected at all levels of society, as well as a number of more 'prestigious' pieces. The latter possibly hint at the presence of more 'well-to-do' people at the site. The majority of these pieces tend to be of later medieval date and, as the purse bar and a number of the coins tend to concentrate close to the southern trackway rather than in the investigated activity areas, it is possible to suggest that many of these items were lost by higher ranking travellers passing through, or indeed, coming to monitor their tenants or to purchase agricultural produce.

The latest assemblage from the site (Ditch 5137, Fill 5138) is difficult to interpret due to the great diversity of metalwork it produced. However, this in itself shows that it did not originate from a source where repair and recycling were part of everyday life. Dress accessories such as buckles are mixed with agricultural tools and items from domestic crafts and food preparation. The related archaeological structures and deposits will need to be identified prior to the full interpretation of this deposit.

Denge West Quarry

The archaeological investigations at Denge West North produced 275 pieces of metalwork from 11 different contexts. Only very limited amounts of metalwork were located during the Denge South field-walking and subsequent watching brief, all of which can be considered unstratified. All the metalwork, from both parts of the quarry is listed in the archive. Only the assemblage from Denge North is considered in the present report.

The Iron

The assemblage is dominated by ironwork: 201 pieces from 11 contexts. The assemblage is summarised in Table 37 above.

A large proportion of the material is from topsoil in the different areas (A–K) and as such is of limited use, particularly given the difficulty of dating ironwork in its own right. However, the pottery from these topsoil assemblages suggests that most material can be considered to span the 13th to 16th centuries. The iron objects from these contexts were scanned to establish if they could shed light on activities carried out on the site during this general period. Items include three horse-shoe fragments, a key and a door hinge pivot for a wooden door frame (*i.e.*, with tapering fixing spike) (Area A). Two clench bolts, with diamond-shaped roves (Areas B and E), are also present, along with a small tanged symmetrical wedge-shaped double edged blade (blade length 68mm, tang length 25mm), possibly from a knife or small harpoon. It is interesting to note that a large proportion of the nails (Area F produced the largest unstratified assemblage: 14 examples) are of large types (Types 2a and 2b), suggesting heavy timbers were present at the site.

The stratified ironwork consists of very few 13th to 14th century pieces: three nail fragments; a tanged knife blade (Area F, Context 50); fragments of three fishing hooks (Area F, Context 50); and an unidentified object fragment (Area A).

Nail Types (as Lydd Quarry)	Type 1a	Type 1b	Type 2a	Type 2b	Type 4a	Type 4b	Uncertain
68	2	1	2	-	1	-	4
69	42	1	10	8	4	2	30

Table 38: (Denge West North) Nails in Contexts 68 and 69

Of the three 15th to 16th century contexts, only 68 and 69 (Area F) are of interest. These contexts produce a small but significant assemblage of nails.

Compared to the nails from Lydd Quarry there is a generally higher proportion of the larger types (1b, 2a and 2b) at the site, both in topsoil and stratified contexts. Some of these examples reach up to 125mm long. In addition to the nails, Contexts 68 and 69 produced 4 and 33 objects, or fragments thereof, respectively. Of interest from Context 68 are three fish hooks. One very large example (Fig. 86, No. 1) is barbed, with a spade end and must have been used for fish of considerable size. The second hook is fragmentary, but is of more usual proportions and formed from thin circular-sectioned wire (Fig. 86, No. 2). Although the point and barb (unless it was barbless) are missing, the fixing end appears to divide into two, suggesting this may have been eyed rather than spade-end. The hook appears to be non-ferrous plated (tinned). The third hook is of similar size but with the barb surviving (Fig. 86, No. 3).

Context 69 contained four horse-shoe fragments (possibly from one shoe) together with the remains of two whittle tanged knife blades and a wood drill/corer bit with lanceolate terminal. The latter piece is virtually identical to one from Lydd 5/6 (Lydd 5/6, Context 5010: Fig. 80, No. 7). Of particular interest are 11 fish hooks, or fragments thereof. A small and large example are illustrated in Fig. 86 (Nos. 4 and 5). Where discernible the hooks are all barbed with spade ends. Context 69 also contained five clench bolts with circular domed heads and diamond-shaped roves. Head diameters vary between 22mm and 30mm, with rove dimensions measuring 52 × 30mm, 46 × 28mm, 45 × 27mm, 40 × 35mm and 32 × 26mm. The thicknesses of the timbers secured (*i.e.*, the measurement between the inner surfaces of the bolt head and rove) measure 31mm, 36mm, 55mm, 55mm and 58mm. (Two examples are illustrated in Fig. 86, Nos. 6 and 7). More domestic items include a candle holder with a rectangular sectioned fixing spike/tang (Fig. 86, No. 8) and a small circular shoe/doublet buckle (Fig. 86, No. 9). One final piece of interest was located in this context: a solid cast iron sphere/shot weighing 192g with a diameter of 35/36mm. It is quite possible this is from a ship's small gun: similar sized shot in lead were recovered from the Mary Rose (Rule 1982, 164).

Non-Ferrous

In all, 73 copper alloy items were recovered. Two pieces of sheeting were from topsoil contexts with the remainder coming from Area F, Contexts 68 (3 pieces) and 69 (68 pieces), the latter including a square coin weight (see separate report above).

The assemblage from Context 68 consists of three medium sized pins with spherical heads (26–36mm long). Pins with spherical heads similarly dominate the assemblage from Context 69. These are present in three notable sizes: small (lengths 19–26mm, head diameters 1–2mm: 15 examples); medium (lengths 27–37mm, head diameters 2–3mm: 12 examples) and large (lengths 41–53mm, head diameters 3–4mm: 20 examples). In addition there is a very large pin measuring 115mm long with a 6mm diameter spherical head. Other copper alloy objects include three wire eyelets for fastening clothing and eight lace ends. A double looped rectangular framed buckle (Fig. 86, No. 10) and a handle and leg from a cast bronze tripod cooking pot are also present (Fig. 86, Nos. 11 and 12).

A single piece of lead waste was recovered from Context 69.

Discussion

The metalwork assemblage from Denge Quarry is of interest in that, despite its small size in comparison to that from Lydd Quarry, it has a proportionally high amount of material which could relate to later 15th to 16th century fishing. Although clench bolts were used to secure timbers together in doors, *etc.*, their use in boat building is well known. The fact that such a small ironwork assemblage has produced a total of seven clench bolts, together with a relatively large quantity of large nails, strongly hints that these were not solely from buildings. If this were the case more examples could be expected at Lydd Quarry. In addition, the 18 fish hooks and possible harpoon blade are more directly linked with fishing: only one hook has been identified at Lydd Quarry to date. The complete absence of rolled lead net weights at the current site is, at first appearance, odd. However, these items are notoriously difficult to locate with the naked eye as the white/grey corrosion and shape

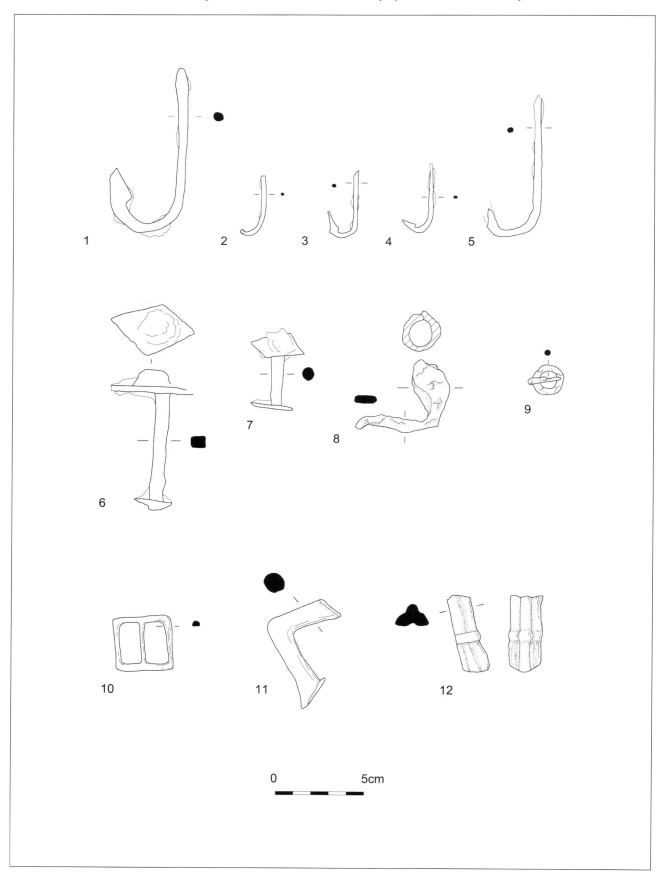

Fig 86 Denge West: metalwork

make them easily mistaken for elongated flint pebbles. This, together with the fact that the natural sub-soil at Denge Quarry was shingle, the work was undertaken as a watching brief and no metal detector survey was carried out, suggests lead net weights may have been present but were not located. However, it should be noted that a number of small non-ferrous items were recovered even without the aid of a metal detector. As such, it is possible the absence of lead weights is real, suggesting the site may have been involved with a different type of fishing to that practiced at Lydd Quarry. The Denge site may therefore have been concentrating on deep-water sea, rather than inland/inshore, fishing. It will be crucial that archaeological investigations on Denge Marsh in the future make full use of metal detector surveys.

THE METALLURGICAL REMAINS
by Luke Barber

The excavations at Lydd Quarry produced a very small assemblage of metalworking waste: 33 pieces, weighing a little under 1.5kg. Virtually all the material was recovered from hand collection, though a couple of pieces were recovered from the environmental residues. The assemblage is dominated by iron smithing slag, although a little fuel ash slag, not necessarily related to metalworking, is also present. All the material was listed for archive prior to being discarded. No concentrations of material were present but the material was represented in 13th century contexts at Lydd 1, 2 and 5/6 (*i.e.*, Context 484 contained 800g of smithing slag) and 14th century contexts at Lydd 3 and 5/6 (*i.e.*, Ditch 5021, Fill 5022). No metallurgical remains were found in later contexts. It is likely these residues are the result of small-scale 'domestic' reworking of scrap items rather than from the primary manufacture of objects. The absence of hammer-scale may simply reflect retrieval techniques in adverse conditions.

THE CERAMIC BUILDING MATERIAL *by Luke Barber*

Lydd Quarry

The excavations at Lydd Quarry produced a total of 445 pieces of ceramic building material, weighing just over 31.5kg, from around 60 individually numbered contexts. The bulk of this material came from the Lydd 5/6 excavations, which recovered 382 pieces weighing a little under 25kg. The majority of the remainder came from the Lydd 3 excavations, which accounted for a further 55 pieces, weighing a little over 6kg from 13 different contexts. The assemblage consists of brick (including 'Flemish'-type examples), roof tile, unglazed hearth tile

and glazed floor tiles. All the material is fully quantified by type, fabric and context on Post Roman Tile and Brick Record forms which are housed with the archive. With the exception of a sample of each fabric, all the material was discarded after listing for the archive.

The large proportion of the overall assemblage made up of material from Lydd 5/6 reflects the higher proportion of post 14th century contexts investigated during that stage of the excavations. Although contexts of the 14th century, as present at Lydd 3, contain ceramic building material, very few pieces are present in the earlier deposits (which dominated at Lydd 1 and 2). In order to help understand the use of new building techniques/materials by the medieval occupants of this part of the Marsh, a summary of the ceramic building material is given below. By necessity the report primarily concentrates on the material from Lydd 5/6, though that from Lydd 3 is considered where appropriate. The fabric sequences for both brick and tile were established at Lydd Quarry but have since been used, and extended by, the excavations at Denge West (see below).

Brick

Lydd 5/6 produced some 139 brick fragments, weighing just over 15kg, from 28 individual contexts. The Lydd 3 assemblage was composed of 42 pieces, weighing 4,660g, from 10 contexts. No large context groups are present: all total 15 pieces or less. Virtually all of this material is highly fragmentary and, with only three exceptions, the only obtainable dimensions were heights. At the Phase 3 excavations pieces of 'Flemish'-type brick were present in small quantities in contexts dating from the mid 14th century onwards. Only two fabric types were noted (Fabrics 1 and 2 below). The larger assemblage recovered from the 5/6 excavations includes the previously recorded fabrics and has enabled a further three to be added to the series, probably indicating the later date of many of the contexts. The fabrics are listed below. Those marked with an asterisk were only located at Denge West (see below).

Fabrics (* at Denge West only)

Fabric 1. Low-medium fired silty 'Flemish'-type brick, usually with a corky texture due to irregular voids. Inclusions consist of occasional dull red iron oxide/grog to 5mm and very rare burnt-out vegetable matter. Colour usually dull yellow to pinkish. Heights: 48–55mm. Mid 14th to mid 16th century.

Fabric 2. Low-medium fired silty 'Flemish'-type brick, usually with a corky texture due to rounded/irregular voids. Inclusions consist of occasional dull red iron oxide/grog to 7mm and white clay pellets and lenses up to 5mm. Colour usually pale dull red orange. Heights: 46mm. Widths: 96mm. 15th to mid 16th century.

Fabric 3. Very low fired powdery/silty 'Flemish'-type brick, with occasional voids. Inclusions, when present, consist of extremely rare flint pebbles to 7mm. Colour usually dull cream/yellow but occasionally orange brown. Heights: 35–51mm. 15th to mid 16th century.

Fabric 4. Medium fired silty/very fine sand with some white clay pellets and streaks, together with rare to moderate iron oxides to 4mm. Colour varies from pale purple to brick red and pale orange. Heights: 32–60mm (but most around 54mm), Widths: 82–119mm. 15th to mid 16th century.

*Fabric 4B. Low-medium fired silty/very fine sand with sparse to abundant swirls of white clay and rare to common brown/red iron oxides to 7mm. Colour usually dull orange red. 15th to mid 16th century.

Fabric 5. Medium-high fired medium sand with sparse to common black slag inclusions to 9mm and occasional white clay swirls. Colour usually dull orange red. ?16th century. Heights: 50–58mm.

*Fabric 5B. Medium-high fired medium sand with moderate to abundant black/purple slag to 12mm. Colour usually dull yellow. ?16th century.

*Fabric 5C. Low-medium fired silty very mixed fabric. Abundant white clay pellets and swirls along with red irn oxides to 7mm. Colour usually dull orange. ?16th century.

*Fabric 6. Low-medium fired silty/very fine sand with white and orange clay mix and common iron oxides to 7mm. Colour usually dull yellow orange. 15th to mid 16th century.

*Fabric 7. High fired fine sand with occasional iron slag inclusions to 6mm. Colour usually dark grey to brick red. ?later 16th to 17th century.

Discussion

The earliest brick from the site is from three 13th century contexts at Lydd 5/6, each containing a single piece (totalling 790g). This material is almost certainly intrusive into these deposits. Only one 14th century context produced brick (5024), however, the fact that it contained 12 pieces weighing just under 2.5kg (all Fabric 4) strongly suggests this material was in use at that time. This is confirmed by the Lydd 3 excavations where a number of pieces were found in contexts dating from the mid 14th century. However, it is not until the 15th to mid 16th century that brick appears to have been used in any quantity. A total of 62 pieces, weighing just over 7.5kg, from 17 different contexts are attributed to this period from Lydd 5/6. All fabrics are represented in this period (Table 39).

Fabric	Quantity (count)
1	8
2	3
3	15
4	23
5	13

Table 39: Brick – The quantity of different fabrics in 15th to mid 16th century contexts at Lydd 5/6

Despite the dramatic increase in the occurrence of brick during this period it is still only present in low quantities, suggesting that it was only used for specific tasks such as lining hearths, *etc.* The material has no obvious concentrations across the Phase 5/6 area, though a slight concentration along the trackway and in Area B could be argued for. A more obvious concentration is apparent at Lydd 3 around the hearth in Area B: Contexts 3124/3125 contained 19 pieces. The post 1550 material from Lydd 5/6 consists of 29 pieces, weighing 2.25kg, from three contexts. All five fabric types are represented, but to what degree these are residual material is impossible to be certain of. At Lydd 5/6 a further 33 pieces (just over 2kg) came from contexts of uncertain, but probably 15th to mid 16th century date.

Tile

Some 243 pieces of tile, weighing just over 9.5kg were recovered from 18 individual contexts at Lydd 5/6. The excavations in the other areas of the quarry only produced a further 17 pieces combined. Most context groups are very small, though that from Ditch 5017 (Fill 5018) is significantly larger (see below). All of this material is highly fragmentary with no complete dimensions being present. The Phase 3 excavations produced very little tile, suggesting that it was not used until the later 14th or 15th centuries at the site. The current assemblage has enabled an initial fabric series to be established for the quarry. The fabrics are listed below and include a new variant added by the work at Denge West. Two hearth tiles (56mm tick) were recovered from 14th century contexts at Lydd 3, while four green glazed floor tile fragments, and one possible ridge tile fragment, were recovered from the Lydd 5/6 area. All the remaining tile from the site appears to be from peg tiles. Fixings are predominantly square or diamond shaped, though round fixing holes are also present. Peg tile thicknesses generally range between 9mm and 12mm, while the floor tile fragments vary between 27mm and 31mm.

Fabrics (* at Denge West only)

Fabric 1a. Medium fired silty/fine sand with moderate white speckles to 1mm. Colour usually pale orange to red. Later 15th to mid 16th century.

Period	Number	Weight	No. of contexts
13th century	1	25g	1
14th century	1	130g	1
15th–mid 16th century	211	8122g	13
Post 1550	22	766g	1
Undated	8	522g	2

Table 40: Tile – The quantity of tile in different period contexts at Lydd 5/6

Fabric	Number	Weight
1a	9	322g
2	23	968g
3	81	3162g
6	26	1184g
7	2	26g

Table 41: Tile in Ditch 5017, Fill 5018 (15th to mid 16th century)

Fabric 1b. As 1a but very hard fired. Colour usually purple red often with black cores. Later 15th to mid 16th century.

Fabric 2. Medium-high fired silty/fine sand with common to abundant white clay swirls and patches. Colour usually dull orange. Later 15th to mid 16th century.

Fabric 3. Medium fired silty/fine sand with occasional small voids to 1mm but no obvious inclusions. Colour usually pale orange to dull red. Later 15th to mid 16th century.

Fabric 4. Medium fired abundant medium sand (noticeably coarse/granular to the touch) with occasional iron ore inclusions to 3mm. Only floor tiles recognised (usually with a dull green glaze). Colour usually dark brick red, sometimes with grey cores. 15th to mid 16th century.

Fabric 5. Medium fired silty/powdery fabric with no obvious inclusions. Colour usually dark grey cores and dull orange surfaces. Possibly a Roman fabric, residual in later contexts. No diagnostic pieces present.

Fabric 6. Medium fired silty/fine sand with moderate to abundant dull orange/red iron oxide pellets/plates to 7mm. Colour usually dull orange/red. Later 15th to mid 16th century.

Fabric 7. Medium fired fine to medium sand with very few inclusions. Colour ranges from grey to dull orange. Medieval.

Fabric 8. As Fabric 7 but with moderate grey/black iron oxide inclusions to 4mm. Medieval.

Fabric 9. High fired sparse fine to medium sand with noticeable sparse coarse white quartz sand inclusions. Colour varies from blue grey to brick red. 15th to mid 16th century.

*Fabric 10. Medium fired abundant fine sand (giving a notable rough/fine granular texture) with rare iron oxides and clay streaks to 4mm. Colour usually uniform brick red. ?16th century.

Discussion

The tile quantities by period for Lydd 5/6 are shown in Table 40. This clearly demonstrates the fact that it is not until the 15th to mid 16th century that the material is represented in any quantity. The 13th to 14th century material is probably intrusive.

All fabrics noted above are represented in 15th to 16th century contexts and these contexts also account for all floor tile fragments (Fabric 4). The single largest group from the site, consisting entirely of peg tile, is from Ditch 5017 (Fill 5018) which is tabulated above.

The dramatic increase in the occurrence of tile during this period suggests that at least some structures were using clay roof tiles by this time. Hearths cannot satisfactorily account for the material as none of the tiles show signs of post-manufacture burning/vitrification. However, despite the proportionally 'larger' assemblage of tile for this period there is still little at the site when absolute numbers are taken into account. A number of possibilities can be suggested for this. For example, only a few structures may have used tile roofing and/or these structures were not actually located within the investigated area. Alternatively the tile may have derived from patching roofs made of other materials. It is interesting that there is decidedly less settlement evidence in this period at the quarry when compared to say the 13th century. Area B at Lydd 5/6, and the adjacent trackway, seems to be the focus for much of the tile although, as with the brick, no striking concentrations are present. Area B may simply reflect an 'activity area' rather than a domestic occupation site and the tile may have been used to roof (or patch the roof of) a small ancillary structure. It is probable that by this time a domestic dwelling would have had a fully tiled roof and thus more tile would be expected in its immediate vicinity unless the building had been systematically recycled for its materials.

The post 1550 material from Lydd 5/6 consists of 22 pieces, weighing 776g, from one context (Ditch 5137, Fill 5138), though again the degree of residuality cannot be gauged with any accuracy. Eight pieces of tile (522g) were from contexts of uncertain date.

Denge West Quarry

The archaeological investigations at Denge West recovered a relatively large assemblage of ceramic building material. The assemblage from Denge North consists of 146 (*c*. 5.5kg) pieces of tile from 13 different contexts and 98 (just under 7kg) pieces of brick from 11 different contexts. The assemblage from Denge South consists of 1,527 pieces of ceramic building material from the field-walking (this material was not divided between tile/brick or quantified by weight prior to being discarded in 1996) and a further 17 pieces (× 6 tile, × 11 brick) from the subsequent watching brief.

The Denge South field-walking material was all unstratified, though of probable 15th to mid 16th century date. The distribution of this material is shown in Fig. 65, where it closely matches the distribution of the 1400–1550 dated pottery. Most material was from Fields A and B (A – 490 pieces, B – 865 pieces, C – 84 pieces and D – 88 pieces). The small assemblage from the watching brief is from part of Field D (Area M – × 3 brick fragments), which was not covered by the field-walking but is also unstratified. The other small watching brief assemblage, located to the north of Field A, is from a more secure context but is too small to be of any significance.

The Denge North material is dominated by the assemblages from the topsoil in the different areas (A–K). This accounts for 105 (*c*. 3.2kg) of the tile and 63 (*c*. 4.7kg) of the brick assemblages. Little can be said regarding this material except that the majority is in fabrics (see below) which have been dated elsewhere at Lydd or Denge Quarry to the 15th to mid 16th centuries. All this material has been fully listed on Brick and

Post-Roman Tile record sheets for the archive. With the exception of a sample of each fabric all the material was discarded after listing for the archive.

Several new brick and tile fabrics were identified from more secure contexts at Denge West which were noted at Lydd Quarry. These have been added onto the CBM fabric series for Lydd Quarry (see above).

Brick

Five new brick fabrics were added to the Lydd series as a result of the work at Denge West. With the exception of F2, all Lydd brick fabrics (F1, F3, F4 and F5) were present in the Denge assemblage. The earliest deposits containing brick consist of two 14th century contexts (Denge North, Area A, Contexts 13 and 26) which produced two and five fragments of F5B respectively (heights 45–50mm). Whether these are intrusive pieces (those from 26 are all from one brick) is uncertain. The remaining stratified brick comes from 15th to mid 16th century contexts, with the largest assemblage coming from Context 68. This contained 17 fragmented pieces weighing 688g (Fabrics 1, 3, 4B and 6).

Tile

With the exception of one ridge tile fragment from Area F, Context 1, all roof tile from the site, where discernible, was from peg tiles with round, square, or more commonly, diamond fixing holes. Thicknesses range between 9mm and 12mm. Only three floor tile fragments were located, two unglazed from Area G (Context 1 and Context 68: both Fabric 10) and one with green glaze (Area C, Context 1, Fabric F10). Floor tile thicknesses ranged between 31mm and 34mm.

Fabric	Number
1a	1
1b	2
2	2
3	9
6	2
10	1 (Floor)

*Table 42: (Denge West) Tile in Cut 67, Fill 68
(15th to mid 16th century)*

One new fabric (F10) was added to the Lydd series as a result of the work at Denge West. With the exception of F5, F8 and F9, all Lydd tile fabrics were present in the Denge assemblage. The earliest tile consists of a single piece of F7 (18g) from 13th century Context 9, which is probably intrusive, and two pieces (114g) from 14th century Context 26 (F1a and F7), which may be intrusive. The remaining stratified tile comes from 15th to mid 16th century contexts, with the largest assemblage coming from Context 68. This contained 17 fragmented pieces weighing 688g.

Discussion

The Denge West assemblage is limited in the information it can add to that already provided by the Lydd Quarry material. However, despite this it tends to confirm the Lydd conclusions that ceramic building material was not really used in any quantity until the 15th century in the peasant settlements around Lydd. Brick was used for specific purposes such as lining hearths and even at this time roof tile was not common. However, the quantities located in Fields A and B at Denge South strongly suggest that at least some buildings were roofed with clay tiles at this time. It is also likely that thatched roofs, some with tile patching, continued into the mid 16th century until the settlements were abandoned.

BURNT CLAY *by Luke Barber*

The excavations at Lydd Quarry recovered 1,455 pieces of burnt or fired clay, weighing just under 16.5kg, from 185 individually numbered contexts. The largest assemblages are from Lydd 1 (485 pieces weighing 5,897g from 64 contexts) and Lydd 2 (586 pieces weighing 5,232g from 67 contexts). The whole assemblage has been fully quantified on Burnt Clay Record Forms which form part of the archive.

Generally all the collected pieces are of a sandy clay burnt to varying colours, but usually an orange-red or red-orange, sometimes with cream streaks. Occasional very friable brick red pieces are present. A few pieces have voids where organic matter has burnt out of the surface, though this does not appear to be material deliberately added to the clay in most instances. Pieces are predominantly irregular, undiagnostic and featureless. Although these may be the remains of burnt daub, this is uncertain as very few diagnostic pieces with wattle marks or smoothed surfaces were present. It is equally likely that much of this material is simply derived from the natural subsoil being burnt by fires/hearths.

Daub

With the exception of Site A (Lydd 10) very little definite daub was recovered, though this may be due to the generally wet conditions at the site. A few pieces were recovered from Lydd 1. These consist of examples with flattened surfaces, one with finger-marks (Context 619), while another shows a wattle impression (Context 539). At least three pieces from Lydd 3 appear to be definite fragments of daub (Pit 3088, Fill 3217). Also of interest is the small assemblage from the late 12th to early 13th

century possible structure at Lydd 4 (Site B: Context 4003). This produced nine pieces of burnt clay, weighing 90g, at least three pieces of which exhibited smoothed faces suggesting they are daub fragments. Whether the above-mentioned daub was from building walling or ovens cannot be proven, though both are likely.

The assemblage of burnt clay from Lydd 10 is more interesting in that it is closely associated with the late 12th to early 13th century timber building (Site A). Associated contexts produced 113 pieces of silty daub weighing 2,745g. Virtually all of this material was from the fills of the post-holes (Contexts A33: 7/38g, A35: 12/114g, A37: 13/222g, A43: 10/132g, A45: 14/42g, A47: 26/306g, A51: 28/1,799g and A57: 1/7g). At least 13 of these pieces clearly show wattle marks that vary in diameter from 7mm to 14mm. The largest piece, weighing 774g, is from Context A51 (Fig. 87, No. 1). This exhibits a number of wattle marks on its interior surface and a roughly smoothed exterior surface with signs of blackening. A second smoothed side, at right angles to the first, suggests the piece bordered an aperture. The presence of all this daub in the post-holes of the building must be the result of the building's posts being removed either during repair or final demolition.

By far the majority of the daub, or indeed the burnt clay in general, came from contexts spanning the late 12th to 13th centuries. The later contexts produced only very small amounts of material, as can be seen from comparing the predominantly 13th century sites at Lydd 1 and 2 with the predominantly 14th century site at Lydd 3 (99 pieces, weighing 419g). This contrast is also shown well at Lydd 5/6 where 13th century features (mainly in Area A), accounted for 122 pieces weighing 1,316g out of a total of 163 pieces weighing 1,796g from all periods (the single largest group coming from Pit 5101 (Fill 5102 – 45 pieces weighing 514g). This reduction in the amount of burnt clay/daub in the 14th, and particularly the 15th, century is likely to be due at least in part to the apparent decrease in occupation at the site during this period. In addition it may also relate to the lessening of agricultural activities requiring heat, and/or hearths being set on brick bases rather than directly on the clay subsoil in this later period.

Other Items

With the exception of daub, very few other items were identified in the assemblage. The remains of two roughly circular low-fired loom-weights are present from Lydd 2. These have not survived well and it is possible that some of the other pieces of burnt clay may have derived from such loom-weights. Both loom-weight fragments (Fig. 87, No. 2 (Context 2129, Cut 2128) and No. 3 (Context 2165, Cut 2164) are from 13th century contexts. Part of a further example may be represented by a bun-shaped fragment from a further 13th century context (486) at Lydd 1.

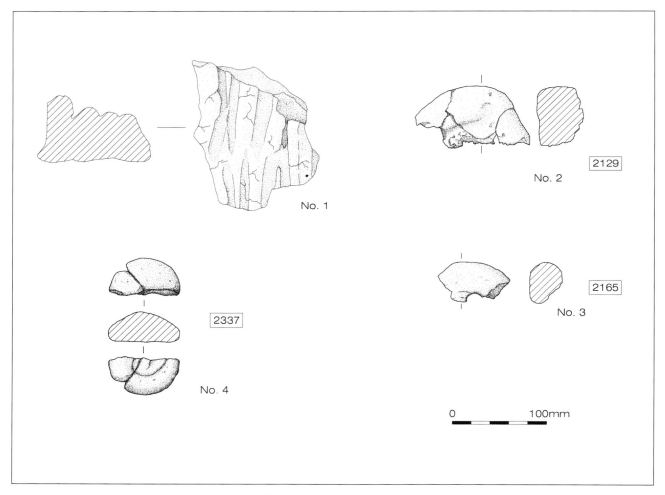

Fig. 87 Lydd Quarry: burnt/fired clay and glass

THE CLAY TOBACCO PIPES
by David Atkinson

Introduction

The excavations at Lydd Quarry produced a total of 480 clay tobacco pipe fragments from five different contexts. With the exception of five intrusive stem fragments in four different medieval contexts, all the material was excavated from Context 5138, (Ditch 5137) at Lydd 5/6.

Ditch 5137

This assemblage consists of 96 bowls/bowl fragments and 379 stem fragments.

The stem fragments, which include eight mouthpieces, are mostly thick with medium bore indicating an early 18th century date. Stems gradually became thinner with a narrow bore as the century progressed, but none of these types are present in the current assemblage.

The bowls are virtually exclusively of early 18th century type, although three earlier examples are present:

London type bowls of the late 17th century (see below). A number of the early 18th century bowls have traces of moulded initials at the base (36 examples), but quality is often poor. London products in the Queen Anne/ George I period were always of a much superior standard of finish. The pipes from Lydd are not of a very high standard of finish and appear to be country products of small-town makers. A number of the more legible early 18th century bowls, with better moulded maker's initials at the sides of the base, some surmounted by crowns, are also present. The meaning of these crowns over the initials is obscure, but they occur commonly in London from *c.* 1690 onwards and last well into the 18th century. Of the intermediate type, which appeared in the London area at this time (*c.* 1690–1710) none are present in this assemblage, though they do occur in Sussex at Hastings and Lewes, of known makers (Atkinson 1977).

Kent is a very large county, a large part of which falls in the London fringes. As such, the pipes fall into two categories: (i) those supplied by London makers in the north of the county; and (ii) the products of the various Kentish towns which appear, on present evidence, to have simply copied the prevailing London styles. These copies, particularly in the country areas, are often rather crude. Unfortunately there has been no detailed study of Kent pipes and their makers, however, it is probable that the makers in the larger towns, such as Canterbury or Dover, would have been producing pipes of superior quality, probably with moulds supplied from London. Meanwhile, the small town makers may well have had other moulds made locally (probably by blacksmiths), hence the poorer quality of the products coupled with the inferior capability of the country makers at this time reflected in the average standard of finish of most examples in the Lydd assemblage.

Makers

Note: Many of the bowls identified are partly fragmentary (initials are moulded at sides of base).

M/H: four bowls of early 18th century type, London Type 25, (Atkinson & Oswald 1969).

W/L: two bowls of London Type 25.

E/G: six bowls/pieces of early London Type 25.

E/G: twenty-one bowls/pieces with crowned E/G, early 18th century.

G/E: one bowl with crowned G/E – an error for E/G by the mould engraver.

…..: twenty-eight bowls of early 18th century type, some with poorly moulded initials (mostly probably M/H). Also number of plain bowl fragments.

…..: one bowl , milled, of London type *c.* 1670–80, no mark.

…..: one bowl of London type of *c.* 1680–90 (London examples are known stamped SA/1683).

…...: one part pipe of probable London type of *c.* 1690–1700.

Discussion

The date range of over 95% of the pipes, by their type, is early 18th century (*c.* 1710–20). There are only two earlier 'intruders', probably London made, one of *c.* 1670–80 and the other of *c.* 1680–90, and a possible third but with the upper part of the bowl missing. Although the pottery exhibits a wider chronological range of material, the clay pipes are all very close in date and suggest the assemblage was dumped over a very short period of time. No more material appears to have been added after 1720.

With the exception of the three London examples, the pipes in this assemblage appear to be of local manufacture, though at present it is not possible to identify the probable makers. None of the pipes in the assemblage are abraded by exposure on the surface and appear to have been dumped over a short period of time and rapidly covered up. Few of the pipe fragments show

signs of having been smoked very much. This deposit of pipes is very similar to the ones often found at the back of inns and taverns and it is likely this was the source of the current assemblage.

THE GLASS *by Luke Barber*

Introduction

The excavations at Lydd Quarry produced 90 pieces of glass, weighing just under 2kg, from eight different contexts. All but one piece was recovered from the Lydd 5/6 excavations. This material has been fully listed in the archive. The material is in poor to fair conditions, though all pieces exhibit at least some surface corrosion/flaking. Most contexts containing glass only did so in very small quantities. Although a little glass is present in late medieval contexts, the majority of it is probably, or in some cases certainly, intrusive. By far the majority of the assemblage is of post-medieval date.

Medieval

A single piece of glass was located in a secure 13th century context at Lydd 2 (Context 2337 in Cut 2274). This consists of part of approximately half of a bun-shaped linen smoother in black glass (Fig. 87, No. 4). Linen smoothers were used to smooth fabric after weaving in order to flatten the cloth and increase its characteristic shine. The Lydd example is similar to one from Norwich (Margesson 1993, No. 931).

Late Medieval

Five contexts dating to the 15th or early 16th centuries contained glass fragments. These accounted for 20 pieces weighing only 59g. Of these, six pieces appear to be intrusive window glass, while the remaining fragments are from vessels. Amongst the vessels are three obviously intrusive fragments from dark green wine bottles post-dating the mid 17th century (Contexts 5171, Cut 5170 and 5371, Cut 5366). The remainder of the vessels are in fine clear or light blue tinged glass. Although probably representing intrusive 16th or 17th century material, it is possible that some are of the 15th century. This is particularly the case with Cut 5170 where four vessel fragments, including a flaring turned over rim, were recovered from Fill 5171 and a further five bodysherds, some probably from the same vessel as in 5171, were recovered from Fill 5173. The vessel appears to be a flask and is similar to a type dated to the 14th or 15th centuries (Tyson 2000, 46, F3). Medieval glass is extremely rare on low-status sites (Tyson 2000, 23) and as such the Lydd material must be viewed with caution. The fact that Cut 5170 contained five definite intrusive glass fragments in its upper fill (5171), together with its proximity to Ditch 5137 (see below), suggests all the material may be intrusive. More assemblages with no intrusive material will be needed from the quarry before the presence of glass in the late medieval period can be proven.

Post-Medieval

With the exception of a single piece of glass from modern Pit 5174, and that which was intrusive into earlier contexts, all the post-medieval glass at the site comes from Ditch 5137, Fill 5138. This produced the overall largest assemblage of glass: 68 pieces weighing 1,877g. The assemblage is dominated by bottle glass of both heavy dark green wine/beer bottles (49 pieces weighing 1,730g from a minimum of six different bottles) and light blue miscellaneous bottles (seven pieces weighing 122g from a minimum of three different bottles). Three wine bottle tops/necks are present and all appear to be of types dated between 1698 and 1708 (Noel Hume 1969, 63). The light blue/clear cylindrical bottles are thin walled with high kicked bases and can be paralleled with late 17th century types found in America (Noel Hume 1969, 73, No. 8). In addition some clear and light green (two and one pieces respectively) glass is present, also probably from bottles. Other vessel types are represented by one clear and three light blue glass undiagnostic bodysherds. In addition there are five fragments of degraded window glass (8g). The total dominance of wine/beer bottles in the assemblage, together with the quantity of clay pipes recovered from the same context, suggest the material may be derived from a nearby tavern.

THE LEATHER
by Diana E. Friendship-Taylor

Introduction

Leather was only recovered from five dated contexts, relating to three features, during the Lydd 5/6 excavations. All appear to represent shoes, with a date range from the 14th to the late 18th centuries. Children's, youths' and adults' shoes are represented. Styles, where discernible, are 'standard' for their respective periods. Most of the material shows evidence for repairs, before they too wore through and the shoes were finally discarded. Apart from a cut piece in 2(d) (late 15th century), there is no evidence that any of the leather represents shoemaking or cobbling waste at any period.

Catalogue

1. Context 5123 (Sump in Ditch 5007)

Clump sole repair, broken in two, where weakened through wear at the ball of the foot, not subsequently repaired, so presumably the shoe was discarded when thoroughly worn out. It had been tunnel-stitched to a rounded toe shoe, with a slight taper, probably a lady's or youth's shoe. The toe shape suggests a date of *c.* 1490–1510, within the *c.* 1450–1550 date range of the context as suggested by the ceramics.

2. Context 5292 (Barrel-lined Pit 5286)

a) Parts of two right foot pointed toe turnshoes. The main part (broken in two at the waist) is a turnshoe sole, with edge/flesh lasting margin, with seam holes at 6–10 mm. Spacing (Fig. 88, No. 1). The lasting margin is damaged, especially on the outside edge. Estimated length: 215mm, approximately 72mm across the tread, approximately 35mm at the waist: modern size: 13 child's/1 adult's (approximately and disregarding the point). There is evidence for a clump sole repair. The inside/rear of the seat has probably been worn away. (Date: *c.* 1470s.)

b) Toe end and part of the outside of ?another sole, identical in shape, with damaged margins, but with some evidence of edge/flesh seam holes. It is difficult to interpret this as either a laminate, or a clump sole repair, as no tunnel stitch holes are apparent and it appears to have sole seam holes (Fig. 88, No. 2). (Date: *c.* 1470s.)

c) Indeterminate fragment of shoe sole margin.

d) Substantial part of the upper of a left foot, randed rounded toe (probable) turnshoe, probably of four parts, joined with butted seams (seam holes at 3mm spacing) (Fig. 88, No. 3a and b). There is a small slit at the throat, with stitch holes on the underside (flesh side) for a tongue or lining. The throat, vamp and quarters are all cut high. It is fastened at the throat by a strap, secured on the flesh side by a broad end stitched to the inside vamp (partly extant) and an iron buckle (totally mineralised), secured by a thong to the outside forepart. Part of the inside quarter has had its lasting margin cut away. There is a distinct impression of a wide rand on the main parts; a possible fragment of rand is present. Remaining lasting margin seam holes are at 8mm spacing. The rear of the quarters is missing, a corresponding part, with matching heel stiffener, being cut too low to match. Parts of another heel stiffener may belong to this or another shoe.

Delaminated fragments of sole are insufficient to indicate the sole shape, but the upper demonstrates that the toe shape is very rounded, while the waist is not as narrow as those of the 1450s–70s. Approximate sole length: 260mm: modern adult size 5/6.

The toe shape, not particularly narrow waist and the pre–1500 randed turnshoe construction, suggest a date of *c.* 1490–1500.

e) Quarter and (detached) peaked heel stiffener, from a low-cut shoe, presumably Tudor.

3. Context 5367 (Timber-lined Pit 5366)

a) Most of the insole of a child's welted shoe, made almost as a 'straight'. Estimated length: 130mm, 50mm across the tread and 35mm at the waist: approximate modern child's size 3. Edge/flesh seam holes are at 7–10mm spacing. Small medial holes were for tacking the insole to the last and there are clear impressions of

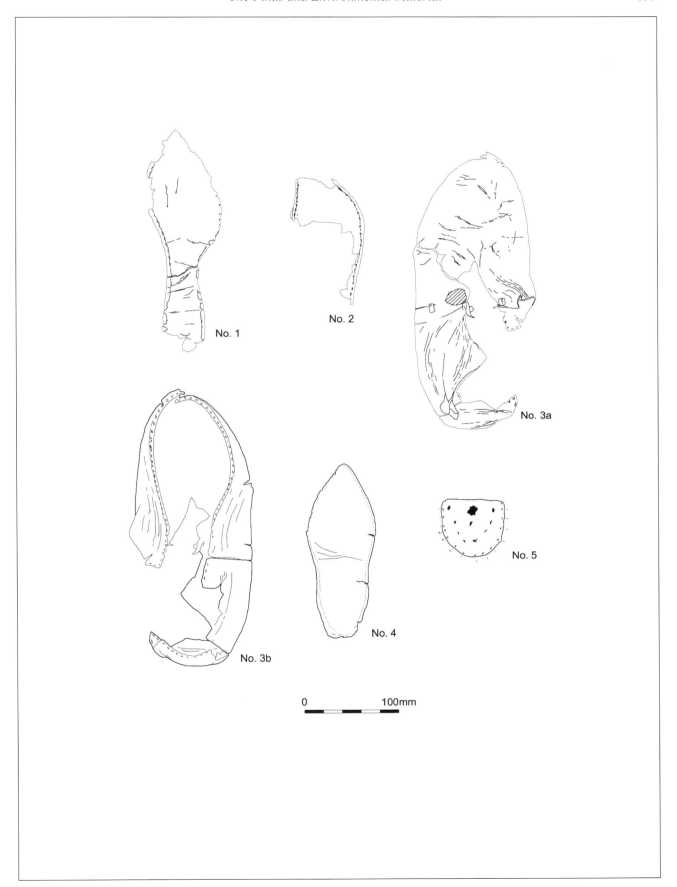

No. 1

No. 2

No. 3a

No. 3b

No. 4

No. 5

0   100mm

Fig. 88 Lydd Quarry: leather

bracing thread in the leather. There is wear at the back of the heel seat, but damage precludes deduction as to whether it was worn on the left or right foot. Small holes in the forepart may indicate repairs. Date: 16th century, possibly towards the end of the century.

b) Probable fragment of sole from a welted shoe. It probably does not belong to (a), as it appears to be too large. Grain/flesh seam holes are at 8mm spacing. It has a 'crazed', iron-stained grain surface, as 5(a). Date: indeterminate, but post–1500.

c) Two adjoining lifts of a heel from a large man's shoe, with four large wooden pegs *in situ* (though broken off), oval in section. Some of the holes may represent repairs, suggested by the number of holes and their irregularity. Smaller, marginal holes may represent primary small pegs. Date: late 18th century.

The heel lift from 5(b) (context 5370) almost certainly belongs to the same relatively flat and substantial shoe, characteristic of the late 18th century.

4. Context 5369 (Timber-lined Pit 5366)

Probable part of a turnshoe, perhaps an ankle – shoe or ankle – boot. No lasting margin survives. The top edge is cut, with the characteristic curve of the quarters. A small hole at the (presumed) centre back may be the usual perforation for hanging up the shoe. No other features are apparent. Alternatively, this could be the quarters of a 16th century shoe, but it would be cut quite high for a typical Tudor shoe.

5. Context 5370 (Timber-lined Pit 5366)

a) ?Middle sole or sole of a child's or youth's shoe, with pointed toe, made as a 'straight' (Fig. 88, No. 4). One side of the forepart is worn to the seam, suggesting that it may be the outside edge and, therefore, worn on the left foot. The heel seat is tapered to join to the (absent, estimated half an inch high) heel and shows slight wear. Estimated length: approximately 190mm (excluding pointed toe), 75mm across the tread, 56mm at the waist: modern child's size 10/11. The grain/flesh seam holes are very fine, at 2mm spacing, except on the heel seat: 1.5mm. There are bracing thread impressions on the grain side. There is an impression of a rand, widening at the waist and tapering off towards the heel seat. On the underside are traces of an oval clump sole repair, delicately attached with tunnel stitching to the ball of the foot. There is also an outline in iron corrosion products, of a displaced rectangular buckle, which may belong to this shoe, in contact with the underside during burial. Probable date: 1780s–90s.

b) Heel seat lift, almost certainly belonging with the lifts in 3(c) (context 5367). Date: late 18th century (Fig. 88, No. 5).

WORKED BONE OR ANTLER
by Ian Riddler

Only two objects of worked bone or antler were located at Lydd Quarry, both coming from Lydd 1.

Context 287 – Uppermost fill of D1, cut 288 (dated 12th century)

A fragment from a double-pointed pinbeater of bone or antler, with a circular cross-section.

Double-pointed pinbeaters are commonly thought to have been used in association with the warp-weight loom, where their principle function was to separate warp threads, although they probably served as general, utilitarian tools. It is possible that they were kept in pairs, although they were used singly (Riddler 1993). They occur in Anglo-Saxon contexts from the 5th to the 11th century, and they may have continued in use for a time beyond the Conquest. The latest examples include those from Oxford and Schleswig, of 11th or 12th century date (Jope 1958; Ulbricht and von Knocken 1984, 2–3 and Biddle 1990, 226). However, few have come from medieval contexts and where this is the case, as at Ipswich, they are thought to be residual (Riddler and Hatton forthcoming). Their gradual demise from the tenth century onwards has been related to the introduction of both the vertical two-beam loom and the horizontal loom, which effectively replaced the warp-weighted loom.

Context 617 – Fill of rubbish pit 615 in Area D, dated 13th century (Site D) (Fig. 89, No. 1)

A fragment of a bone or antler implement of rounded rectangular section with a central, axial perforation. The object is well produced with an indented area towards one end expanding to decorative faces on each narrow side. Both sides are bevelled, rounded and decorated by simple ring-and-dot motifs and combinations of diagonal and lateral lines, in order to produce animal head designs. A complete head above the indented area includes a long snout and may represent a stylised horse. Sparse traces of the repetition of this design occur on the other side of the indention, and it is possible that this represents the original midpoint of the object. At the other end the object expands to provide a further affronted head on each side, indicated by ring-and-dot motifs of diagonal lines.

The fragmentary nature of this object makes its full identification difficult. There are few direct traces of wear, although it is evident that the broad faces are undecorated, and they retain scratch marks. The indented area and the axial perforation are also of significance. The indented area may possibly have formed part of the decorative scheme, in allowing for a metal band to be secured at this point.

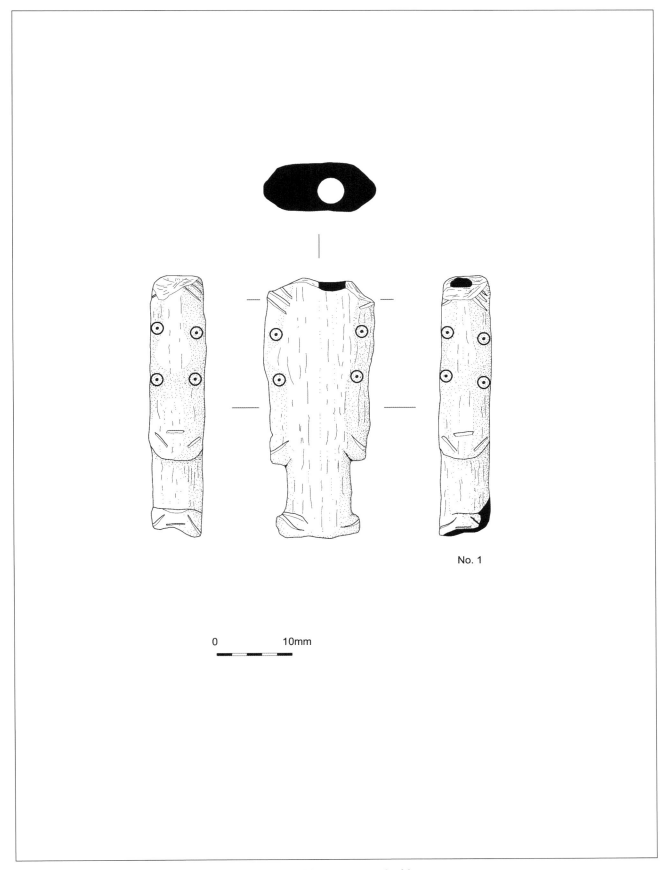

Fig. 89 Lydd Quarry: worked bone

The section and perforation of the object suggests that it may originally have formed part of an implement handle. Precise, circular, axial perforations are seen on medieval knife handles, as with several of these published recently from London and Winchester (Cowgill 1986). While these often include decoration across all sides, there is tremendous variety in their forms and decorative schemes, which could easily encompass this particular object. A small bone object of medieval date from Norwich includes zoomorphic decoration of a similar type (Williams 1988, 104 and Fig. 84.30).

GEOLOGICAL MATERIAL
by Luke Barber

Lydd Quarry

Introduction

The various phases of excavations at Lydd Quarry (Lydd 1–11) produced a combined total of 908 pieces of stone (excluding worked flint), weighing just over 179kg, from 178 different contexts. Some of this total relates to water-washed flint nodules or fire-cracked flint, though this material was not systematically collected and as a result this material, together with the chalk, is undoubtedly under-represented. The stone type series was originally established for the Lydd 1 excavations in consultation with John Cooper of the Booth Museum of Natural History, Brighton (Barber 1996c). This series was added to and upgraded in subsequent phases of excavations at both Lydd Quarry (Barber 1999b; Barber 2002c; Barber 2002d; Barber 2003b; Barber 2004c) and the sites at Denge West and Caldicott Farm (see below). The identification of stone types and provenance in the final series was re-assessed by Dr Bernard Worssam and the author in 2003 as part of the ALSF funded work prior to the amalgamation of all earlier reports on the stone from the site.

The Lydd Quarry stone analysis has identified a high number of stone types, although not all are represented in the different phases of the quarry. Three of these types were only present in Late Iron Age or Roman contexts and are not considered further in any detail. In addition four (as well as 'medieval' shale) new stone types/variants, not previously noted at Lydd quarry, were located in the assemblage from Denge West. The number of stone variants present from the overall site/s is relatively high (65 from Lydd and Denge West combined). However, many of these can be grouped together as variants of the same general type, probably simply reflecting different outcrops, or variations within one outcrop, of the same geological strata. A full list of all the rock types and their variants, along with a sample of each, forms part of the archive, though a summary is given below.

Full quantification of stone types by number and weight for each context was undertaken for all phases of work, with the information being recorded on geological record forms as part of the archive. Percentages of stone types were found to be frequently misleading due to the nature of the assemblage. Fragmentary stone, such as the lava, is over-represented by count, but a few very large boulders in other stone types tend to distort calculations by weight. As a result, although details of count and weight have been included, percentage calculations have been deliberately omitted.

The primary aims of the analysis of the geological material were to establish the main sources of exploitation of stone from the site through time and the purposes for which the stone was used. The overall assemblage is dominated by 13th century contexts, though there is a good scatter of 14th to 15th century deposits too. Earlier and later periods are less well represented, though this may reflect the density of human occupation at these times.

Being a marsh of recent creation (geologically speaking) there are no natural stone outcrops for exploitation close to the investigated sites. The only source of 'naturally' available stone would have been from the beach. As well as flint cobbles, a variety of stone types may have arrived on the beach through Longshore Drift. This material, which would have originated from the west, would be water-worn and indeed many of the pieces of stone from the site exhibit signs of such wear, as well as the burrows of sea ceatures living in the inter-tidal zone. Stone other than material in this category, including water-worn cobbles derived from east of the marsh, are assumed to have been brought to the marsh/sites by man.

The overall stone assemblage for Lydd Quarry is characterised in Table 43. The bulk of the assemblage (see below) is derived from local sources. To the east, outcrops of the Hythe and Folkestone Beds, and to the west, outcrops of the Hastings Beds, unsurprisingly appear to account for most of the stone at the site. For example, large outcrops of the Hythe and Folkestone Beds (part of the Lower Greensand series) run north-westward from the town of Hythe and would have been easily available for exploitation by marshland settlement sites. Similarly, to the west outcrops of Hastings Beds give ready access to finer sandstones. It is not possible to ascertain whether this material was brought by land or sea, however, any quarrying carried out at outcrops around Hythe and Folkestone could have been easily transported along the coast during the 12th to 14th centuries. The presence of a large number of water-worn cobbles and small boulders of Folkestone stone suggests the beach was a source of much of the material. Similar sources appear to have been exploited for the churches of the Marsh (Pearson and Potter 2002).

Summary of Stone Types
(All Lydd Phases and Denge West combined)

Lower Greensand: Folkestone stone

Medium to coarse grained (some with 2mm pebbles) calcareous glauconitic sandstones from the Folkestone formation. Although this outcrops between Sandling and Folkestone the Lydd material is more likely to be from the cliffs and foreshore at Folkestone. Fifteen variants of this general type are present. This stone group accounts for most of the querns on site. Although many other pieces are probably also from querns, a large number are from natural water-rounded cobbles/boulders. This rock group is present throughout the period of the sites' occupation.

Lower Greensand: Hythe Beds

Kentish Ragstone from the Hythe Beds. Source close to Hythe probably.

Lower Greensand or Bracklesham Beds (?) Mixon Rock from Selsey

Two variants of a fossiliferous limestone of uncertain origin.

Wealden Sandstones

Fine grained sandstones, the majority of which (12 variants) appear to be of the Hastings/Ashdown Beds. Usually a dull orange-brown colour, although there are grey and dull red examples. The stone group is used extensively for whetstones at the investigated sites, though unshaped pieces were also present. In addition five variants of Tilgate stone are present (from the Wadhurst clay in the Hastings group). The Tilgate stone is shown seperately on the tables below. Some of these are also used for whetstones. Stone from the Hastings Beds would be easily accessible on the coast and inland around Hastings and Rye. This stone group is mainly used in the 12th to 13th centuries.

Wealden Clay Ironstone

Available around Hastings and the Sussex coast. Three variants were identified.

Upper Greensand

Fine grained slighty glauconitic sandstones (three variants). Probably from Eastbourne area, however, one variant in this group may derive from Kentish Thanet sandstones. This material is shown seperately on the tables overleaf.

Flint

Both beach cobbles and nodules from the chalk are present.

Chalk

Two variants (Upper and Middle Chalk). Easily accessible at Eastbourne or Folkestone/Dover area, though much appears water-washed and could derive from the beach. There is no obvious reason why chalk would have been brought in to the sites.

Limestone?

Unknown rock type. Similar to tufa but siliceous (not calcareous). The rock, which presumably was originally a limestone, has had the calcite leached from it, leaving behind the quartz grains with many voids between. The colour is very variable (dull yellow, pink, purple). The source of this material is unknown. Only present in undated contexts.

Purbeck Limestones

Six variants were recorded, though they equate to three main variations: crushed shell limestone/Burr stone from the Swanage area; slightly shelly limestone; and fine limestone. All grinding mortars on the sites are in this stone type, which occurs from the 13th century onward.

Shale

Probably from Dorset. Although material of Roman date was found at Lydd Quarry, 'medieval' shale was only recovered at Denge West.

Slate (West Country)

Too little material is present to suggest roofs of slate at the current sites and it is likely the material came in with other material from Lydd town or New Romney.

Quartzite

Although not local geologically, quartzite pebbles would probably have been available from the beach (four variants noted). Some of these appear to have been used as whetstones from the 13th century.

Dolerite

Originally from the south-west probably, but water-washed and therefore most could have been collected from the beach (three variants noted). However, one 12th century example from Lydd 1, although water-worn, appears to be too heavy to have been transported long distances by long-shore drift. For this reason it is likely to be the result of sea-borne trade, possibly coming in with ship's ballast.

Granite

Originally from the south-west probably, but water-washed and therefore could have been collected from beach. Only from a Late Iron Age context at Lydd 9.

Upper Lias

Probably from Whitby. Only one piece is present: it contains an ammonite fossil and may have arrived with

Stone Type	12th century (13 contexts)	13th century (91 contexts)	14th century (22 contexts)	15th–mid 16th century (27 contexts)	Post 1550 (3 contexts)	Undated/ Unstrat. (22 contexts)	Total (178 contexts)
Lower Greensand: Folkestone stone	2/998g	36/32,004g	9/1,806g	7/5,538g	-	9/8,712g	63/49,058g
Lower Greensand: Hythe Beds	3/4,200g	4/7,176g	1/75g	-	-	6/3,125g	14/14,576g
Lower Greensand or Bracklesham Beds (?) Mixon Rock	-	3/8,200g	-	3/94g	-	1/1,850g	7/10,144g
Wealden Sandstones Hastings Beds fine grained sandstones	13/1,316g	79/14,620g	25/2,653g	30/15,166g	-	12/1,925g	159/35,680g
Tilgate stone	-	16/5,199g	3/7,329g	14/2,562g	-	2/1,163g	35/16,253g
Wealden Clay Ironstone	-	9/56g	-	-	-	-	9/56g
Upper Greensand/ ?Thanet sast	-	1/123g 1/2,255g	4/75g -	1/160g 4/1,290g	- 2/142g	2/10g -	8/368g 7/3,687g
Flint	-	2/1,308g	-	4,4,159g	-	151/688g	157/6,155g
Chalk	-	7/335g	2/553g	1/1,044g	10/3,000g	-	20/4,936g
Limestone?	-	-	-	-	-	3/996g	3/996g
Purbeck Limestones	-	18/11,591g	5/1,049g	1/250g	-	1/1,881g	25/14,771g
Shale	Only found in Roman contexts at Lydd Quarry						
Slate (West Country)	-	3/26g	-	-	-	1/10g	4/36g
Quartzite	-	9/1,917g	3/846g	1/342g	-	-	13/3,105g
Dolerite	2/1,416g	1/66g	-	1/5,000g	-	1/814g	5/7,296g
Granite	Only found in Roman contexts at Lydd Quarry						
Upper Lias	-	1/192g	-	-	-	-	1/192g
Coal	-	1/5g	1/5g	-	4/20g	3/25g	9/55g
German Lava Niedermendig/Mayen lava	-	325/9,393g	7/494g	11/881g	-	22/1,055g	365/11,823g
Schist/ Norweigian Ragstone	2/18g	-	1/5g	1/60g	-	-	4/83g
Total	21/7,948g	516/94,466g	61/14,890g	79/36,550g	16/3,162g	214/22,254g	908/179,270g

Table 43: Characterization of geological material assemblage (unworked and worked) for Lydd Quarry (type by period)

sea-borne trade and been kept as a curio (Lydd 1, Context 151 dated 13th century).

Coal

Probably from the east coast, though the quantities on site are so low it is suspected the medieval assemblage may be intrusive from post-medieval activities. It is interesting that coal is most common in post-medieval and undated contexts.

German Lava

Niedermendig/Mayen lava. A common find on medieval sites in Britain. All fragments, whether displaying a worked face or not, are assumed to have come from querns. As such, the material is somewhat over-represented in the worked stone assemblage.

Schist/Norweigian Ragstone

A not uncommon stone in medieval deposits, though rare at Lydd and Denge West. The few pieces from the present sites are, whether displaying a worked face or not, assumed to be from whetstones.

As the excavations at Lydd Quarry include contexts

Stone Type	12th century (7 contexts)	13th century (37 contexts)	14th century (4 contexts)	15th–mid 16th century (5 contexts)	Post 1550 (1 context)	Undated/ Unstrat. (6 contexts)	Total (60 contexts)
Lower Greensand: Folkestone stone	Q: 2/998g	Q: 11/6,014g	-	-	-	Q: 6/6,515g	19/13,527g
Lower Greensand: Hythe Beds	-	Q: 1/250g	-	-	-	-	1/250g
Wealden Sandstones Hastings Beds fine grained sandstones	W: (T1) 9/1,235g	W: (T1) 14/1,692g W: (T2) 3/3,255g roof slate 1/25g	W: (T1) 2/202g	-	-	-	29/6,409g
Tilgate stone	-	W: (T2) 3/1,165g	-	-	-	-	3/1,165g
Wealden Clay Ironstone	-	Spindle whorl 9/56g	-	-	-	-	9/56g
Upper Greensand/ ?Thanet sast	-	-	-	-	W (T1) 2/142g	-	2/142g
Purbeck Limestones	-	M: 3/10,013g	M: 2/890g	M: 1/250g	-	M: 1/1,881g	7/13,034g
Shale	Worked shale only from Roman contexts at Lydd Quarry						
Quartzite	-	W: (T3) 4/411g	-	-	-	-	4/411g
German Lava Niedermendig/Mayen lava	-	Q: 325/9,393g	Q: 7/494g	Q: 11/881g	-	Q: 22/1,055g	365/11,823g
Schist/ Norweigian Ragstone	W: 2/18g	-	W 1/5g-	W: 1/60g	-	-	4/83g
Total	13/2,251g	374/32,274g	12/1,591g	13/1,191g	2/142g	29/9,451g	443/46,900g

Table 44: Characterization of the worked stone assemblage for Lydd Quarry (type by period)
Key: Q – quern fragments; W – whetstone fragments; M – mortar fragments, (T1–3) – whetstone type

from a wide chronological spread, the quantities of the different stone groups have been divided into one of several periods. This data is shown in Table 43 opposite. Stone from unstratified or undated contexts is considered most likely to belong to the 13th to 15th centuries.

12th century

The 13 contexts of this period contained only 21 pieces of stone weighing just under 8kg. Folkestone stone and Kentish Rag (Hythe Beds) are present, the former being used for querns. In addition fine grained Hastings Beds sandstones account for a fair proportion of the assemblage, often being used for whetstones. As such, sources to the east and west were being exploited at this early date. In addition imported Schist whetstone fragments are present as well as a little Dolerite, the latter possibly coming in with ship's ballast.

13th century

This period produced the majority of the overall assemblage from the site: 516 pieces (just under 94.5kg) from 91 contexts. Virtually the full range of stone types is

present and in much larger quantities, suggesting this was the period when stone was utilised at Lydd on a moderate to relatively large scale. Folkestone stone is again used for querns (though not in the same stone variant as the earlier querns) as well as appearing as water-washed cobbles. Kentish Rag is also present, some apparently used for querns as well. Other Kentish stone includes some possible Thanet sandstone, though none is worked. To the west of the Marsh, Hastings Beds sandstones were still being exploited, again primarily for whetstones (including some new stone variants), and scatters of Upper Greensand and possibly Mixon Rock suggest coastal contact much further west, as does the presence of Purbeck limestones and slate. The presence of the west country slate is interesting in that this roofing material is associated with wealthy buildings, usually close to a port where the material could easily be brought in by sea. The few scraps present at the quarry do not indicate the use of such material for roofing here. However, they suggest geological material was possibly being acquired from sources in Lydd and/or New Romney, such as ship's ballast, and small fragments of imported stone were incorporated into the collected material prior to its transportation back to the farmsteads. It is during this period that German lava querns are first encountered at the quarry.

14th century

Only 61 pieces of stone (just under 15kg) from 22 different contexts are present for this period. Although the main difference in quantities would initially appear to be purely the result of less activity on the site, there is still an apparent reduction in the quantity of stone in use. Whatever the case, a similar range of stone sources is still represented, though the degree of residuality is difficult to ascertain. Worked stone, particularly querns and whetstones, in this period is notably lacking.

15th to mid 16th century

The 27 contexts of this period produced 79 pieces of stone weighing just over 36.5kg. This material exhibits a similar range of stone types to those noted in earlier contexts, suggesting the exploitation of similar natural resources. However, it is felt this may be a misleading picture as a large part of the assemblage from this period came from infilled ditches which also contained, judging by the ceramics and metalwork, a reasonable proportion of residual material. This suggestion is reinforced when contexts of this period containing little residual ceramics are considered. For example, Ditch 5043, Fill 5044 only contained one piece (158g) of Wealden sandstone, and Pits 5081 and 5083 (Fills 5082 and 5084 respectively) also contain one piece of stone each (both Wealden/ Hastings Beds sandstones). If much of the material in the contexts of this period is residual, it would explain the apparent close correlation of the stone types across time. It is equally possible that the stone brought to the site in earlier centuries was adequate for the smaller late medieval population, who simply recycled the material and thus had little need of bringing large quantities of new material to the site. More late medieval contexts, with demonstrably no, or very low quantities of, residual material will be needed prior to any firm conclusions being made regarding exploitation in this late period.

Post 1550

Only very little material is present for this period. It is dominated by chalk and coal, though one ?Thanet sandstone whetstone is also present.

Worked Stone

The worked stone assemblage from Lydd quarry is characterised in Table 44 (previous page) and discussed by type below.

Querns

Unfortunately, virtually all the quern fragments from the quarry are small, and although they are all from rotary hand querns it is impossible to tell whether upper or lower stones are represented. Although no measurable diameters are present, stone thickness ranged between 45 and 58mm. Six of the fragments are from unstratified/ undated contexts, however, they are likely to be of medieval date as they are similar in both form and stone type to the stratified material. Folkestone stone appears to be the most commonly used stone for querns during the 13th century. The earliest querns are also of this stone group and appear in 12th to early 13th century deposits. These consist of two small pieces from Lydd 5/6 (Context 5158: 998g), both in a Folkestone stone variant not used in the 13th century. The stones have a thickness of about 30mm, though are too small to measure diameter. The presence of a rectangular socket for an inserted wooden turning handle on one of the stones suggests upper stones are represented. The majority of Folkestone stone querns (11 confirmed pieces) are from 13th century deposits where five variants of the stone type appear to be used. One quern, again from a 13th century context, is in Kentish Rag, showing the exploitation of the Hythe as well as the Folkestone Beds. No large groups are present, the largest being at Lydd 2 where Context 2400 produced four quern fragments from four different querns.

The site produced a large quantity of German lava fragments (365 pieces weighing just under 12kg). Unfortunately the vast majority of these pieces are small and undiagnostic of form, though they are undoubtedly from querns. As such, all pieces of lava have been included in the worked stone table. However, as a result the ratio of Folkestone stone to German lava querns cannot be relied upon, as only definite quern fragments were included on this table for the Folkestone stone due to the presence of unworked water-washed boulders. The lava querns appear for the first time in 13th century contexts, but are only present in small quantities later, by which time most pieces may be residual (a single large piece from a 14th to early 15th century context at Lydd 3 suggests some usage later). A large proportion of the lava fragments were from the excavation of the settlement site at Lydd 2 (248 pieces weighing 7,352g from 18 different contexts). Although most pieces were amorphous lumps, a few larger pieces retained the original surfaces. A study of these shows that the range of thickness of the stones was between 28mm and 45mm, with most falling around 35mm. However, a piece from Lydd 3 (Context 3151) is 53mm thick: a larger sample of measurable fragments (only seven measurable pieces were present in the Lydd 2 & 3 assemblages) may alter these preliminary observations. No pieces of lava quern were large enough to estimate stone diameter or distinguish whether they were upper or lower stones.

Whetstones

Forty whetstone fragments are present representing three main types (Types 1–3). Virtually all are of fine grained Hastings Beds sandstones (Ashdown Beds sandstone being the most common, but Tilgate stone also being used), though a few other types are present as well (namely, quartzite, ?Thanet sandstone and Schist). The whetstones in general appear to have been discarded with domestic refuse, and few conjoining pieces were located. The largest groups include Lydd 2 Context 2358 with four fragments and 2193 with three fragments (none of which conjoined).

Type 1

This is by far the most common type (represented by 27 pieces) and consists of square-sectioned or rectangular-sectioned tapering whetstones. The fragments vary considerably in size, particularly in cross-sectional dimensions. This is partly due to the presence of variable sized whetstones, as well as fragments coming from different sections of the same tapering stone. Unfortunately, no complete examples were found. Most do not show signs of grooving from point-sharpening, but usually all four faces of the stones are uniformly worn smooth from blade sharpening. The rock type used in the manufacture of these stones (and those of Type 2) nearly all fall within the Hastings Beds sandstone group of fine sandstones, although a number of minor variants are present. This rock type was specifically brought in for use as whetstones. A few unshaped fragments of this sandstone are present from the site, suggesting that some whetstones may have been manufactured on site: Context 579 contained a piece weighing 1443g. The lack of small pieces of this stone would suggest that if this were done it was not on a regular basis, and that most whetstones were brought in ready-made. Most of the whetstones are from 12th to 13th century contexts. The earliest Type 1 whetstone (Ashdown Beds) is from Lydd 5/6 (Pit 5158, Fill 5159, dated 12th century). This example has one point sharpening groove along one of its widest sides. Three conjoining pieces of a Type 1 whetstone were recovered from Context 4003 (dated early 13th century). Only one Type 1 stone is present in post 13th century contexts, but it is impossible to clarify whether this is residual or not.

One whetstone from the site is similar to the Type 1 stones but is notably more rounded in section. This was recovered from the Lydd 5/6 excavations where it was recovered from a late 17th to early 18th century context.

Type 2

Only six examples, all in 13th century contexts, of this type are present, although they are of the same stone group as the Type 1 whetstones. The type consists of larger blocks worn smooth on the upper face, some with evidence of deliberate shaping of the block. If these are deliberately made whetstones (as opposed to simply utilising a large chunk of suitable stone) they are stationary examples against which the object would be moved rather than the stone itself. Two Type 2 whetstones (Ashdown Beds) were recovered from Lydd 5/6: Context 5118 (Cut 5117. Weighing 2,115g) and Context 5325 (Ditch 5324. Weighing 40g).

Type 3

These are perhaps the most problematic of the whetstones because they are simply water-rounded pebbles which could have been collected from the beach for use as whetstones or for any other function. Because they are already water-rounded and hard (all being of quartzite), definite signs of wear and sharpening grooves are absent. A few examples of water-worn quartzite are present with marine worm encrustations attached. These were presumably brought from the beach but were never used for sharpening as such activity would have removed the burrows. All of these whetstones are from 13th century contexts.

Schist/Norweigen Ragstone

Only four pieces of these whetstones were uncovered at Lydd: two (18g) from a 12th to early 13th century context (Lydd 10, Pit A62), one (5g) from a 14th century context (Lydd 3, Context 3193) and one (60g) from a 15th to early 16th century context (Lydd 5/6, Ditch 5009, Fill 5010). All conform to the usual form of elongated, slightly irregular, though smooth, stones. No complete examples are present. These imported whetstones are frequently encountered at medieval sites in England and it is surprising that only four pieces have been found from Lydd to date.

Whetstone catalogue (Fig. 90, overleaf).
(All in Hastings Beds sandstone unless otherwise stated)

1. Roughly rectangular-sectioned tapering whetstone. Cross-section measures between 20 × 24mm–41 × 44mm. Type 1. Scoring on end face. Context 188 (13th century).

2. Tapering rectangular-sectioned whetstone fragment. Cross-section measures between 30 × 16mm–18 × 9mm. Two point-sharpening grooves on one face and a further groove on adjacent face. Type 1. Context 271 (12th to mid 13th century).

3. Whetstone fragment with irregular profile. One point-sharpening groove. Type 1. Context 227. (12th to early 13th century).

4. Large square-sectioned whetstone fragment. Tapering from cross-section of 58 × 63mm–54 × 55mm. Point-sharpening grooves apparent on all four faces. Type 1. Context 328. (12th to early 13th century).

5. Sharply tapering, rectangular-sectioned whetstone fragment with faint grooving on one face. Type 1. Context 539. (late 13th to 14th century).

6. Square-sectioned whetstone fragment with original tapering for terminal. Type 1. Surviving length 67mm. One shallow point sharpening groove apparent. Context 2358. (13th century).

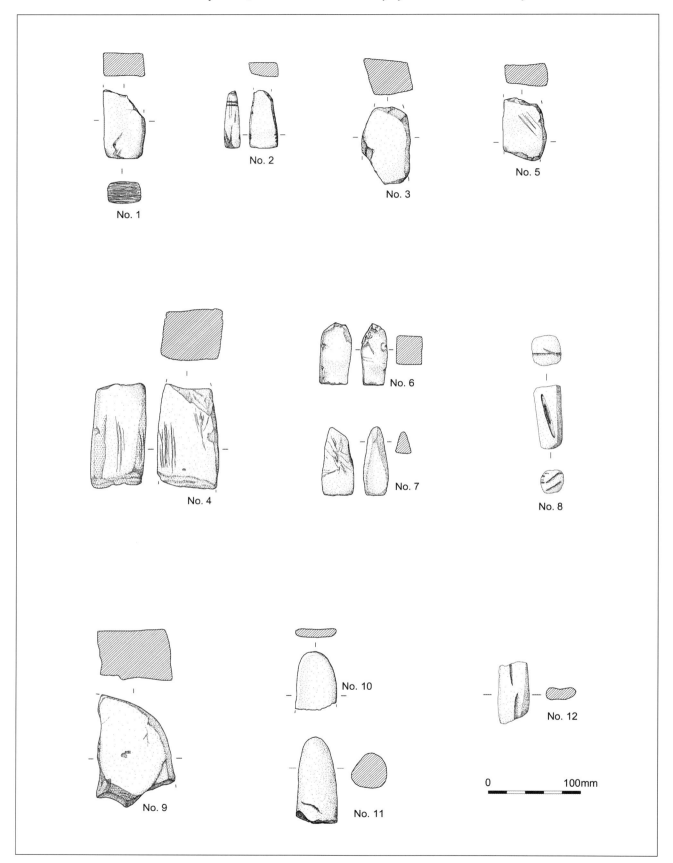

Fig. 90 Lydd Quarry: geological material (whetstones)

7. Roughly rectangular-sectioned tapering whetstone fragment. Type 1. This stone has been subjected to heavy wear on opposed faces creating a wedge-shaped stone. One shallow point sharpening groove apparent. Surviving length 76mm. Context 2358. (13th century).

8. Tapering whetstone fragment with sub-square section similar to, but not the same as, the Type 1 stones. The stone is represented by two pieces in fine ?Thanet sandstone (142g). Interestingly, this example not only has a point sharpening groove along the face of one of its original sides and several on its original end face, it also has evidence of point sharpening on its broken edge. Context 5138 (Ditch 5137: late 17th to early 18th century).

9. Whetstone with irregular underside and curved smoothed side. Type 2. Context 238. (13th century).

10. Flattened quartzite pebble ?whetstone. Type 3. Context 152. (13th century).

11. Elongated round-sectioned ?quartzite pebble whetstone. Type 3. Context 2193. (late 12th to 13th century).

12. Fragment from an elongated whetstone with evidence of point sharpening grooving in Schist/Norwegian Ragstone. Ditch 5009 (Fill 5010, dated 15th to early 16th century).

Mortars

All the mortar fragments from Lydd Quarry are in one of two types of Purbeck limestone. Two fragments were recovered from Lydd 1. One is of a simple common form (532 – 13th century) which can be paralleled at Colchester (Crummy 1980, Fig. 43). Unfortunately no lugs remain and only part of the rim and side wall are present. The exterior is pecked and there is limited wear on the interior. The other mortar fragment from Lydd 1 is of a more unusual type (Fig. 91, No. 13). This piece, which was unfortunately unstratified, is of a fossiliferous Purbeck limestone (Burr stone). The surviving fragment consists of a squared base from which the mortar walls rise. The squared base would not only give the mortar stability but also provide a fairly long-lasting grinding base. A further four fragments, from at least three different mortars, were recovered at Lydd 3. These consist of a plain rim fragment with a wall thickness of 33mm but indeterminate diameter (Context 3017 – 13th century); part of a base with a diameter of around 240mm (Context 3318 – 14th century) and part of a plain rim (wall thickness 38mm) with the remains of a plain rectangular-sectioned lug (55mm wide). This plain type of mortar is closely paralleled at Seaford (Barber 1995d, Fig. 14, Nos. 16–17). The remaining mortar fragment from Lydd

3 (Context 3324 – 14th century) consists of the remains of a lug with round cross-section (35mm) with small square-sectioned vertical rib running down its apex.

A large part (approximately 2/3rds, weighing 9,500g) of a further mortar in Purbeck limestone was located in Fill 5359 at Lydd 5/6 (dated 13th century). The mortar is similar to that from Lydd 1 (No. 13) in that it has a solid square base from which springs the body of the circular vessel (Fig. 91, No. 14). At the front is a prominent grooved pouring spout, situated over one corner of the square base. To the sides are two perforated triangular/diamond-sectioned lug handles (only one of which is complete). The back of the vessel is missing, however, the corner of the square base opposite the spout does not suggest there was a third lug similar to the other two at this point. As such, the vessel probably only had two handles, or possibly a simple small unperforated rear lug. The upper interior surfaces of the vessel show clear pecking marks while the exterior has been finished with linear tooling. The interior exhibits signs of wear, particularly around the base, adjacent to the junction with the vessel walls. The circular worn depression at this point in the base suggests a pestle with a grinding end some 40mm across. Despite the wear there is no obvious reason for the break. Mortars with perforated lugs are far less common than those with simple solid lugs more frequently found at the quarry (Barber 1996c). However, similar examples have been found in Southampton (Platt and Coleman-Smith 1975, 310, No. 2214) and Northolt Manor (Dunning 1961, No. 4, dated to the early 14th century). However, mortars with pierced lugs, particularly of triangular/diamond-section are more common amongst French mortars (Dunning 1977).

Other

Only one other worked piece of stone is present: the remains of a clay ironstone turned spindle whorl (Fig. 91, No. 15) from 13th century Context 5064 (Cut 5063). The surviving nine fragments weigh 56 grams, but the full weight and dimensions are uncertain. A single piece of Wealden sandstone roofing slate, as well as a little west country slate, are probably derived from more affluent buildings in Lydd or New Romney.

Caldicott Farm

The excavations at Caldicott Farm only produced five pieces of stone (2,366g) from three different contexts. The earliest (86) dates to the 11th to 12th centuries but contains only weathered quartzite slabs. A 14th century context (46) produced a single Type 1 whetstone in Hastings Beds (Ashdown Sand) sandstone and Context 3 (dated 19th century) produced a single small piece of coal.

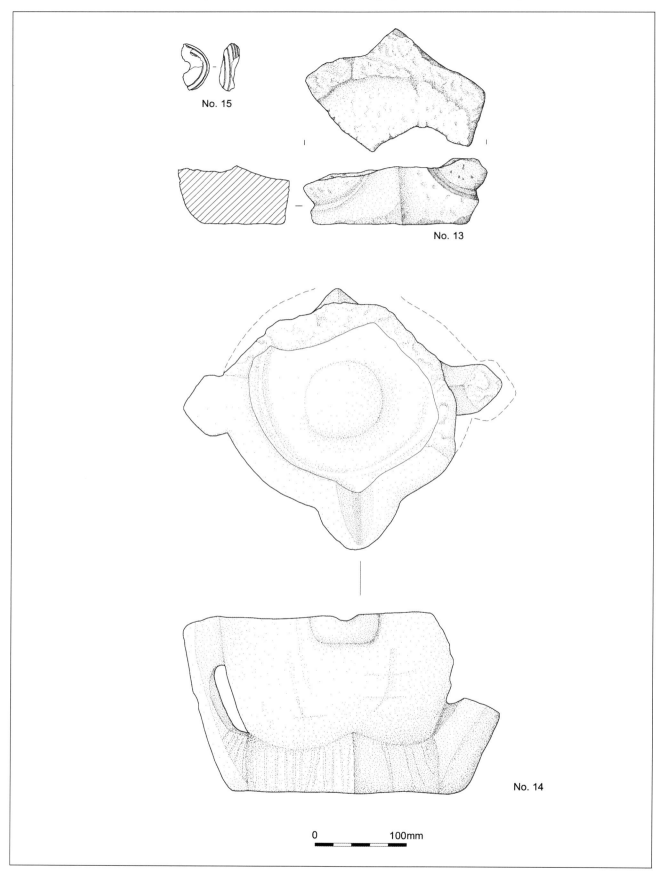

Fig. 91 Lydd Quarry: geological material (other)

Denge West Quarry

The investigations at Denge West North quarry produced an assemblage of 45 pieces of stone, weighing a little over 10.2kg, from 12 different contexts. Although a small quantity of stone was also collected from the Denge West South field-walking and watching brief, the majority of the material was discarded in the field after counting. As such, this material is not further considered here. All the material from Denge North has been fully recorded on Geological Material record forms which are housed with the archive.

The Denge North assemblage includes 18 of the stone types/variants already identified at Lydd Quarry. However, four new types/variants were also present. These consist of three new variants of Purbeck Limestone and one of Wealden ironstone. Unfortunately, with the exception of the ironstone variant from Context 9 (dated to the 13th century), all these new types are from the topsoil and thus not closely datable.

The unstratified assemblage at Denge North consists of 24 pieces (just over 6.3kg). Due to the wide date range of material in these topsoil contexts, as indicated by the pottery, little can be learnt from this material except for a few general observations. It is interesting to note that the stone types are similar to those noted at Lydd Quarry, suggesting a similar source of exploitation. It is also notable that many of the stones show extensive signs of water-rounding and have obviously been collected from the beach. These examples include both Folkestone stone, Hastings sandstones and quartzite cobbles. Worked pieces from this unstratified group include fragments from a Type 1 whetstone in Hastings Beds sandstone (Area B. 104g), a fragment of schist whetstone with section measuring 27 × 22mm (Area C. 122g) and part of a 39mm wide rim from a mortar (358g) in Purbeck limestone (Area B). This material is similar to the objects from Lydd Quarry.

The stratified assemblage includes material of 13th century (6 pieces weighing 798g from three contexts) and 14th century (5 pieces weighing 1,418g from one context) date. The material includes Folkestone stone, Hastings Beds fine sandstones (including Tilgate stone) and quartzite. Although no definite worked pieces are present, a quartzite pebble (36g) from Ditch 2 may have been utilised as a Type 3 whetstone.

Two stratified assemblages of later 15th to 16th century date are present (Contexts 68 and 69). These both produced five pieces of stone each (435g and 1,032g respectively). The material includes a predominance of Folkestone stone but Hastings Beds sandstones and quartzite are again present. The only worked pieces of stone consist of a fragment of 36mm thick lava quern (324g) and part of a shale bead (< 1g), both from Context 68. The bead has a diameter of 13mm with a 2mm diameter central hole. The surviving height is 8mm, though it is suspected that the bead is biconical in profile and is therefore likely to have originally measured 16mm

in height. Unfortunately, both these contexts contain at least some residual 13th to 14th century material and as with many of the contexts at Lydd Quarry the integrity of the stone sample must remain uncertain for this later period.

Conclusions

The medieval occupation at the investigated sites appears to have utilised geological resources to a great extent, particularly considering the lack of stone available on the marsh itself (excluding flint). Most of this is likely to have come from fairly local outcrops situated to the east and west of the marsh. Outcrops in the Hythe/Folkestone and Hastings/Rye areas appear to have been most exploited, stone probably being brought in via the port of New Romney or Lydd, either 'intentionally', as in the case of the querns and whetstones, or 'unintentionally' as ballast (Pearson and Potter 2002). Although the worked stone would have been put to use for grinding foodstuffs and sharpening, the majority of the stone may simply have been collected to create floors, paths or sill walls.

Although there appears to be an increase in ceramics from the west (*i.e.*, Rye) during the 14th and 15th centuries at Lydd Quarry this is not reflected by the geological material from this, or the Denge West site. No noticeable shift in the source of exploitation of this material through time is apparent from the excavated data: both east and west were exploited, though by weight more appears to have come from the east.

The 12th century exploitation appears to mainly involve the utilisation of stone objects, principally whetstones, from the Hastings area, though the quern material was acquired from Folkestone. The presence of two fragments of quernstone in a 12th century context at Lydd 5/6 is interesting in that it suggests some crop processing may have been occurring at this early date. Although this early grinding could relate to food preparation for gangs of early workers establishing the ditch system, it could also be argued that it may represent the processing of crops grown on the site at an earlier date than previously thought. More contexts of this period are needed to clarify exactly what activities were being undertaken. On a general level however, the low numbers of querns and the relatively high proportion of whetstones at this early date point toward a more pastoral economy. Whetstones could easily have been used by shepherds for sharpening shears.

Stone exploitation on the sites appears to have really begun on a large scale during the 13th century, presumably as a result of the establishment of more permanent occupation associated with extensive arable cultivation. Stone from east and west was again used but on a much larger scale, both worked and unworked. The presence of a relatively high proportion of water-worn stones suggests much of the material was derived from secondary sources such as rivers or, more likely, the beach. However, these water-worn boulders/cobbles often include Lower Greensand (Folkestone and Hythe Beds) and other stone variants which have their outcropping source to the east of the Marsh. As it is considered unlikely this material naturally travelled against the direction of Longshore Drift, it is probable they were brought in from the Hythe/Folkestone area, possibly as ship's ballast, and after dumping were collected for use by the rural inhabitants. It is probable the stone was used to create floors, paths and drystone sill walls in an attempt to keep structural timbers out of the damp ground. The fact that no obvious concentrations of stones have been noted is best explained by the recycling of material in the late medieval period and the truncation and dispersal of virtually all medieval occupation layers by late post-medieval/modern ploughing. More imported stone is apparent, most notably the German lava, but also the Purbeck limestones. Other stone may simply have been brought to the site unintentionally with other material, or simply as curios.

Stone use, and the shift in its supply, in the later periods at the investigated sites are difficult to comment on with certainty due to both the reduction in the amount of contexts involved and the danger of residual material. However, it would appear that although useage went down, possibly as the result of a decreasing population, the general types in use were the same as those during the 13th century. One point of interest is that although some lava quern fragments are present in later contexts none in Folkestone stone are present. Although the dramatic decrease in quern fragments between the 13th and 14th/15th centuries at Lydd Quarry may simply be the result of the smaller sample for the later period it may reflect the increasing importance of pastoral agriculture in the area. However, there is also a drastic decline in whetstones in the same period (only one 14th century example being found at Lydd 3, which could itself be residual). A larger assemblage of 14th to mid 16th century stone from contexts free of residual material will be needed before detailed comparisons can be made.

THE ANIMAL BONE *by Lucy Sibun*

Lydd Quarry

Introduction

All phases of excavation at Lydd Quarry produced animal bone and this totalled 4907 fragments. These were recovered from contexts dating from the Roman to post-medieval periods. This report concentrates on the large mammal assemblage from the medieval period only (12th to 16th centuries). Many of the phases of excavations at the quarries produced very small assemblages. As a consequence, most analysis work was undertaken on the larger, and usually better sealed, assemblages from Lydd

Quarry Phases 1, 2, 3 and 5/6. However, all material was scanned and significant observations relating to the other smaller assemblages have been considered where relevant.

Methods

The large mammal bone assemblage was recovered mainly by hand collection (100% of excavated deposits), though some material was recovered from the residues of the environmental samples. Full quantification of the material was undertaken. Wherever possible bone fragments were identified to species and the skeletal element represented. The resulting data produced NISP (Number of Identified Specimen) and MNE (Minimum Number of Elements) counts. The NISP totals include all skeletal elements such as skull fragments, ribs and vertebrae. However, for the purposes of this report, multiple cranial or rib fragments from the same context, which are deemed uninformative, have been counted as one. To assist with the MNE calculations, and in an attempt to avoid the distortion caused by differing fragmentation rates, the elements were recorded according to the part and proportion of the bone present. The MNI (Minimum Number of Individuals) was calculated from the most common element according to the MNE, by taking sides into consideration. No attempt was made to differentiate between sheep and goat or horse and donkey. Undiagnostic fragments categorised as cattle size or sheep size, have been included in the percentages of identifiable bone.

Epiphyseal fusion was recorded and subsequently interpreted using data provided by Silver (1969). Dental wear was recorded using Grant's system (1982). Dental eruption was calculated using data from Silver (1969), and Levine (1982). Schmid (1972) was used to sex pig canines. Where measurements were possible these were undertaken using methods outlined by Von Den Driesch (1976). Each fragment was then studied for signs of butchery, burning, gnawing and pathology.

The Assemblage

The final, securely dated and re-quantified assemblage comprises 1767 fragments. The preservation of the bone was generally good but the assemblage was found to be fragmentary, with few complete bones surviving. There is little evidence for weathering processes on the bone, suggesting that it was not left on the surface long before deposition. However, evidence for carnivorous gnawing indicates that some of the bone material was accessible. The fragmentary nature of the assemblage has unfortunately limited the availability of ageing, sexing and metrical data. As a result, all calculations have produced small totals for MNE and MNI, and this should be borne in mind when considering the interpretation based upon them.

This assemblage has been divided into phases of occupation: 12th century; late 12th to early 13th century;

NISP	Butchery	Gnawing	Burnt
1767	277	85	43
	15.4	4.7	2.4

Table 45: Percentages of butchered, gnawed and burnt bone fragments

Animal Type	12th century	12th/13th century	13th century	14th century	15th/16th century	Total
Cattle	74(4)	90(3)	199(6)	53(3)	240(10)	656
Sheep/goat	58(3)	58(4)	241(8)	68(5)	173(9)	598
Pig	35(3)	19(2)	125(4)	81(3)	93(5)	353
Horse	12(2)	5(2)	38(3)	10(2)	14(2)	79
Dog	1(1)	5(1)	34(2)	1(1)	4(1)	45
Cat	-	-	13(1)		20(2)	33
Deer	-	-	2(1)	-	1(1)	3
Total	180	177	652	213	545	1767

Table 46: Lydd Quarry – Quantification of assemblage by phase
(Data are presented in terms of NISP with MNI in brackets)

Animal Type	12th century	12th–13th century	13th century	14th century	15th–16th century
Cattle	44(4)	54(3)	35(6)	26(3)	48(10)
Sheep/Goat	35(3)	35(4)	43(8)	34(5)	34(9)
Pig	21(3)	11(2)	22(4)	40(3)	18(5)

Table 47: Percentages of main food species by century (based on NISP)

13th century; 14th century; 15th/16th centuries. The majority of the bone was recovered from a few large pits and deliberately filled ditches. In addition to this were a number of other pits, post-holes and ditches which contained much smaller quantities of bone forming the remainder of the assemblage.

The following taxa were identified: cattle (*Bos taurus*); sheep/goat (*Ovicaprid*); pig (*Sus scrofa*); horse (*Equus caballus*); red deer (*Cervus elaphus*); dog (*Canis familiaris*); cat (*Felis domesticus*). The assemblage has been quantified in Table 46 (above middle).

As the table indicates, the largest number of fragments was recovered from the 13th and 15th/16th century phases, with significantly fewer recovered from the 12th, 12th/13th and 14th centuries.

Cattle, sheep/goat (sheep from here forward) and pig

Table 47 (above bottom) shows the relative percentages of the three main domesticate species by phase in terms of NISP with MNI in parenthesis.

Cattle comprise the largest percentage of the assemblage in the 12th and early 13th centuries, with sheep and pig forming the next largest respectively. However, the MNI calculations indicate that sheep may be better represented than the NISP figures indicate. The relative and increasing significance of sheep is shown by the MNI calculations for the 13th, 14th and 15th/16th centuries. The 15th/16th centuries show a marked increase in the quantity of all species.

Bone Type	Cattle	Sheep	Pig
Mandible	7	5	5
Scapula	2	-	-
Humerus	7	2	2
Radius	2	3	-
Ulna	1	1	-
Pelvis	1	1	2
Femur	2	3	1
Tibia	4	4	-
Calcaneum	1	-	-
Metapodial	4	5	2
Phalanx I	2	-	-

Table 48: MNE (MNI in brackets) 12th century

Bone Type	Cattle	Sheep	Pig
Mandible	5	3	2
Scapula	1	2	2
Humerus	6	3	5
Radius	2	1	1
Ulna	2	-	1
Pelvis	1	2	2
Femur	2	3	1
Tibia	-	8	-
Calcaneum	1	1	-
Metapodial	5	5	-
Phalanx I	3	1	-

Table 49: MNE (MNI in brackets) 12th/13th century

Bone Type	Cattle	Sheep	Pig
Mandible	9	15	8
Scapula	9	11	6
Humerus	4	7	8
Radius	5	8	1
Ulna	1	1	1
Pelvis	1	3	1
Femur	4	1	3
Tibia	8	15	7
Calcaneum	3	3	1
Metapodial	6	13	-
Phalanx I	13	8	-

Table 50: MNE (MNI in brackets) 13th century

Bone Type	Cattle	Sheep	Pig
Mandible	1	1	6
Scapula	2	2	6
Humerus	3	1	3
Radius	2	7	5
Ulna	3	2	-
Pelvis	2	-	-
Femur	4	1	1
Tibia	2	5	
Calcaneum	1	1	1
Metapodial	1	5	5
Phalanx I	-	3	5

Table 51: MNE (MNI in brackets) 14th century

Bone Type	Cattle	Sheep	Pig
Mandible	5	16	9
Scapula	10	5	3
Humerus	12	8	3
Radius	10	7	4
Ulna	4	1	4
Pelvis	11	3	2
Femur	16	7	2
Tibia	12	13	6
Calcaneum	9	2	2
Metapodial	9	7	-
Phalanx I	9	2	1

Table 52: MNE (MNI in brackets) 15th to 16th centuries

Body Part Data

The MNE for the main domesticate species through time has been calculated for a selection of elements and the resulting tables can be found opposite and above (Tables 48 to 52). The data shown indicate the MNE.

Cattle

In all phases of occupation both mature and immature individuals are present and represented by all parts of the skeleton, the main meat joints and skeletal extremities. The most abundant elements in the 12th and early 13th centuries seem to have been the extremities, but this pattern appears to change with the relative quantity of meat joints increasing significantly by the 15th/16th centuries. These later centuries also see a slightly increased proportion of immature individuals in the assemblage.

The evidence for cattle butchery suggests little change throughout the medieval period and all parts of both mature and immature individuals are affected. However, the evidence suggests a slight increase in the proportion of immature bone fragments showing evidence for butchery in the 15th/16th centuries. There is evidence of shallow cuts to the extremities suggesting skinning and the primary stages of butchery, split vertebrae and cuts and chops to long-bones conducive with splitting and jointing the carcass.

Age (years)	CATTLE				
	C12th	C12th–13th	C13th	C14th	C15th/16th
<2	-	-	1	-	1
2+	-	-	5	-	1
Total	-	-	6	-	2

Table 53: Dental eruption (cattle)

Age (years)	SHEEP					PIG				
	C12th	C12th–13th	C13th	C14th	C15th/16th	C12th	C12th–13th	C13th	C14th	C15th/16th
0–1.5	-	1	3	-	8	-	-	3	2	7
1.5+	4	2	12	1	8	2	1	0	0	2
Total	4	3	15	1	16	2	1	3	2	9

Table 54: Dental eruption (sheep/pig)

MOLAR WEAR SCORE (Grant system, 1982)		
Cattle (1 mandible)	Sheep/goat (8 mandibles)	Pig (7 mandibles)
23	30–33	15
	35	17
	36–41	20
	36–41	20
	39	20
	39	21
	41	27
	42	

Table 55: Dental wear (15th to 16th century)

Sheep

There are no distinct patterns visible in the sheep assemblage, either through the centuries or with regard to the body parts represented. Both mature and immature individuals are present but mature bone fragments are more numerous in all phases. Butchery evidence is sparse in all phases but perhaps even more so from the 14th century onwards. The limited evidence almost exclusively affects mature individuals and includes shallow cuts to ribs and long-bones, as well as a single split vertebrae.

Pig

There is very little body part data available for pig but all parts of the skeleton are represented and both mature and immature individuals are present. Butchery evidence for pig is very sparse and more frequently involves immature bone fragments. The evidence is limited to shallow cuts or chops to ribs, long-bones and vertebrae.

Ageing Data

Dental eruption and wear was recorded for the main domesticate species. It was only possible to provide an approximate age for 8 cattle, 40 sheep and 17 pig mandibles, but the results are summarised here.

Dental eruption

Unfortunately, the limited data for cattle does not permit any meaningful interpretation of results (Table 53). The evidence from the forty sheep mandibles (Table 54) demonstrates the dominance of mature individuals in the assemblage, but in the 15th/16th century the proportion of immature individuals has increased to 50%. The limited data available for pig shows a dominance of immature individuals, particularly in the later phases of occupation.

Dental Wear

Due to a lack of evidence from earlier centuries, only dental wear from the 15th/16th century has been tabulated below. The data further illustrates the dominance of older sheep and younger pig in the assemblage.

Epiphyseal fusion

The ageing data from epiphyseal fusion is tabulated on the following pages (Tables 56 to 70) and a summary follows. The quantities involved are very small and as a result the reliability of any interpretations based upon the data must be questioned. For this reason some general observations have been made without significant interpretations of the results.

Age	Type	Fused	Unfused	Total	% Fused
7–18 months	scapula	2	0	2	
	p. radius	0	1	1	
	d. humerus	4	3	7	
	phalanx 1	2	0	2	
	Total	8	4	12	66%
2–3 years	d. tibia	1	1	2	
	d. metapodia				
	Total	1	1	2	50
3.5–4 years	p. ulna	1	0	1	
	p. humerus	1	0	1	
	p. femur				
	d. femur				
	d. radius	1	1	2	
	p. tibia	1	0	1	
	calcaneum				
	Total	4	1	5	80%

Table 56: Epiphyseal fusion (12th century cattle)

Age	Type	Fused	Unfused	Total	% Fused
6–16 months	scapula				
	p. radius	1	0	1	
	d. humerus	2	0	2	
	phalanx 1				
	Total	3	0	3	100%
18–28 months	d. tibia	3	2	5	
	d. metapodia				
	Total	3	2	5	60%
2.5–3.5 years	p. ulna	1	0	1	
	p. humerus				
	p. femur				
	d. femur				
	d. radius	0	1	1	
	p. tibia	0	2	2	
	calcaneum	1	3	4	25%
	Total	2	6	8	25%

Table 57: Epiphyseal fusion (12th century sheep)

Age	Type	Fused	Unfused	Total	% Fused
1 year	scapula				
	p. radius				
	d. humerus				
	Total				
2 years	d. tibia				
	d. metapodia				
	Total				
3–3.5 years	p. ulna				
	p. humerus	0	1	1	
	p. femur				
	d. femur	0	1	1	
	d. radius				
	p. tibia				
	calcaneum				
	Total	0	2	2	0%

Table 58: Epiphyseal fusion (12th century pig)

Age	Type	Fused	Unfused	Total	% Fused
7–18 months	scapula	1	0	1	
	p. radius	2	0	2	
	d. humerus4	4	0	4	
	phalanx 1	2	0	2	
	Total	9	0	9	100%
2–3 years	d. tibia				
	d. metapodia				
	Total				
3.5–4 years	p. ulna	2	0	2	
	p. humerus	1	0	1	
	p. femur	0	1	1	
	d. femur				
	d. radius	1	0	1	
	p. tibia				
	calcaneum	1	0	1	
	Total	5	1	6	83%

Table 59: Epiphyseal fusion (late 12th to early 13th century cattle)

Age	Type	Fused	Unfused	Total	% Fused
6–16 months	scapula	2	0	2	
	p. radius	1	0	1	
	d. humerus	1	0	1	
	phalanx 1				
	Total	4	0	4	100%
18–28 months	d. tibia	1	3	4	
	d. metapodia	0	1	1	
	Total	1	4	5	20%
2.5–3.5 years	p. ulna				
	p. humerus				
	p. femur	1	1	2	
	d. femur	0	1	1	
	d. radius	1	0	1	
	p. tibia	1	1	2	
	calcaneum	1	0	1	
	Total	4	3	7	57%

Table 60: Epiphyseal fusion (late 12th to early 13th century sheep)

Age	Type	Fused	Unfused	Total	% Fused
1 year	scapula	2	0	2	
	p. radius				
	d. humerus	1	1	2	
	Total	3	1	4	75%
2 years	d. tibia				
	d. metapodia				
	Total				
3–3.5 years	p. ulna	0	1	1	
	p. humerus				
	p. femur	0	1	1	
	d. femur				
	d. radius				
	p. tibia				
	calcaneum				
	Total	0	2	2	0%

Table 61: Epiphyseal fusion (late 12th to early 13th century pig)

Age	Type	Fused	Unfused	Total	% Fused
7–18 months	scapula	4	1	5	
	p. radius	3	0	3	
	d. humerus	1	0	1	
	phalanx 1	10	0	10	
	Total	18	1	19	95%
2–3 years	d. tibia	1	2	3	
	d. metapodia	1	2	3	
	Total	2	4	6	33%
3.5–4 years	p. ulna	1	0	1	
	p. humerus	1	0	1	
	p. femur	1	1	2	
	d. femur	0	1	1	
	d. radius	2	1	3	
	p. tibia	2	0	2	
	calcaneum	1	1	2	
	Total	8	4	12	66%

Table 62: Epiphyseal fusion (13th century cattle)

Age	Type	Fused	Unfused	Total	% Fused
6–16 months	scapula	5	1	6	
	p. radius	1	0	1	
	d. humerus	3	0	3	
	phalanx 1	4	1	5	
	Total	13	2	15	86%
18–28 months	d. tibia	2	4	6	
	d. metapodia	7	1	8	
	Total	9	5	14	64%
2.5–3.5 years	p. ulna				
	p. humerus	0	1	1	
	p. femur	0	1	1	
	d. femur				
	d. radius	1	2	3	
	p. tibia	1	0	1	
	calcaneum	0	2	2	
	Total	2	6	8	25%

Table 63: Epiphyseal fusion (13th century sheep)

Age	Type	Fused	Unfused	Total	% Fused
1 year	scapula	2	3	5	
	p. radius				
	d. humerus	4	2	6	
	Total	6	5	11	54%
2 years	d. tibia				
	d. metapodia				
	Total				
3–3.5 years	p. ulna				
	p. humerus				
	p. femur	0	1	1	
	d. femur	0	1	1	
	d. radius				
	p. tibia	1	2	3	
	calcaneum				
	Total	1	4	5	20%

Table 64: Epiphyseal fusion (13th century pig)

Age	Type	Fused	Unfused	Total	% Fused
7–18 months	scapula p. radius d. humerus phalanx 1	2 2 2	0 0 0	2 2 2	
	Total	6	0	6	100%
2–3 years	d. tibia d. metapodia	1	0	1	
	Total	1	0	1	100%
3.5–4 years	p. ulna p. humerus p. femur d. femur d. radius p. tibia	1 0 1	1 1 3	2 1 4	
	calcaneum	0	1	1	
	Total	2	6	8	25%

Table 65: Epiphyseal fusion (14th century cattle)

Age	Type	Fused	Unfused	Total	% Fused
6–16 months	scapula p. radius d. humerus phalanx 1	 1 2	 0 0	 1 2	
	Total	3	0	3	100%
18–28 months	d. tibia d. metapodia	1	0	1	
	Total	1	0	1	100%
2.5–3.5 years	p. ulna p. humerus p. femur d. femur d. radius p. tibia calcaneum	1	1	2	
	Total	1	1	2	50%

Table 66: Epiphyseal fusion (14th century sheep)

Age	Type	Fused	Unfused	Total	% Fused
1 year	scapula p. radius d. humerus	2 0 2	4 2 0	6 2 2	
	Total	4	6	8	50%
2 years	d. tibia d. metapodia				
	Total				
3–3.5 years	p. ulna p. humerus p. femur d. femur d. radius p. tibia calcaneum	 0 1 1	 2 0 0	 2 1 1	
	Total	2	2	4	50%

Table 67: Epiphyseal fusion (14th century pig)

Age	Type	Fused	Unfused	Total	% Fused
7–18 months	scapula	4	0	4	
	p. radius	8	0	8	
	d. humerus	6	1	7	
	phalanx 1	1	0	1	
	Total	19	1	20	95%
2–3 years	d. tibia	4	5	9	
	d. metapodia	4	1	5	
	Total	8	6	14	57%
3.5–4 years	p. ulna	2	0	2	
	p. humerus	1	1	2	
	p. femur	4	4	8	
	d. femur	2	2	4	
	d. radius	1	4	5	
	p. tibia	1	0	1	
	calcaneum	2	6	8	
	Total	13	17	30	43%

Table 68: Epiphyseal fusion (15th to 16th century cattle)

Age	Type	Fused	Unfused	Total	% Fused
6–16 months	scapula	5	0	5	
	p. radius	4	1	5	
	d. humerus	6	0	6	
	phalanx 1	0	1	1	
	Total	15	2	17	88%
18–28 months	d. tibia	1	2	3	
	d. metapodia	1	2	3	3
	Total	2	4	6	33%
2.5–3.5 years	p. ulna				
	p. humerus				
	p. femur				
	d. femur	2	1	3	
	d. radius	1	2	3	
	p. tibia	1	0	1	
	calcaneum	1	1	2	
	Total	5	4	9	56%

Table 69: Epiphyseal fusion (15th to 16th century sheep)

Age	Type	Fused	Unfused	Total	% Fused
1 year	scapula	2	0	2	
	p. radius	2	0	2	
	d. humerus	2	0	2	
	Total	6	0	6	100%
2 years	d. tibia	3	1	4	
	d. metapodia				
	Total	3	1	4	75%
3–3.5 years	p. ulna	0	2	2	
	p. humerus				
	p. femur	0	1	1	
	d. femur	0			
	d. radius	0	2	2	
	p. tibia				
	calcaneum	2	0	2	
	Total	2	5	7	29%

Table 70: Epiphyseal fusion (15th to 16th century pig)

Cattle

During the 12th and 13th centuries the majority of cattle appear to have reached maturity (3–4 years). This may suggest that they were used primarily for milk production or to work the land rather than as a meat resource. From the 13th century onwards there appears to be a trend towards culling at an earlier age, with an increased number of immature individuals in the assemblage and fewer reaching maturity. This may reflect a change in emphasis from milk to meat production.

Sheep

Unfortunately the 12th, 12th/13th and 14th centuries did not produce enough data to merit consideration. The dental evidence for the 13th century suggests that the majority of sheep were aged at least 18 months. The epiphyseal fusion data indicates that the majority of sheep were being culled before the age of 3 years. This contradicts the general trend noted in the entire assemblage for a greater proportion of mature individuals in all periods. It may be that there was a change in practice in the 13th century, with increased meat production. However, it could also be an unreliable figure, resulting from the small data set available. By the 15th/16th century the numbers of both mature and immature individuals has increased, though the latter more so, suggesting that both meat and wool may have been increasing in importance.

Pig

The data available for pig is very limited and as a result only evidence from the 13th to 15th/16th centuries has been considered. It would seem that in the 13th and 14th centuries approximately 50% of individuals were reaching the age of 1 year. In the 15th/16th century this has risen to 100% with progressively fewer reaching 2 and 3 years. This suggests a meat source with prime age for meat production of between 1 and 3 years.

Metrical data

Unfortunately, very few fragment measurements were possible as a result of the fragmentary nature of the assemblage. Those possible are outlined below.

Cattle

A single fragment from a 15th century context (5010) was available for withers height estimation. This was a radius providing an estimate of approximately 1.19m.

Sheep

Two measurements were available for the estimation of withers heights, a radius (Context 5152) and a talus (Context 5123), both from the 15th century.

Withers estimate from radius – 0.55m
　　　　　　　　　　talus – 0.59m

Horse

A total of 79 horse bone fragments were identified in the assemblage, but this small number did provide an MNI calculation of at least 2 in all phases of occupation. In the 12th and 12th/13th centuries only skeletal extremities are present, but these provide evidence for at least two individuals older than, and one less than, 18 months. Skeletal extremities predominate the 13th century assemblage, but fragments of tibia and scapula are also present. In the 14th century, horse are represented by long-bone fragments and the extremities. The only possible measurements were the distal breadth (69.4mm) and the distal depth (39.4mm) of a tibia (Context 5024). Dental wear provides an age estimate of 7–8 years for one individual (Context 5024). The 15th century produced fourteen fragments. These included longbones, metapodials, tarsals and a loose tooth. The tooth provided an age estimate of approximately 13 years (Context 5024). A single metatarsal (Context 5010) provided a lateral length measurement of 254mm, giving a withers height estimate of 1.35m. A fragment of talus from the 15th century appears to have been sliced through (Context 5044).

Dog

The assemblage contained 45 fragments of dog and the majority of these (34) were recovered from the 13th century assemblage. However, at least one individual is represented in each phase. In the 12th/13th century a radius provides a greatest length measurement of 145.5mm (Context 197). The large quantity of dog bone fragments in the 13th century can be explained by the presence of a complete, adult, female skeleton (Context 575). Greatest femoral length measurements of 142.4mm and 144.3mm were recorded for this individual. The left metatarsals IV and V appear foreshortened and new bone formation mid-shaft suggests a fracture (Wood 1996). The presence of carnivorous gnawing on approximately 5% of bone fragments is a further indication that dog was present in all phases of occupation.

Cat

Thirty-three bone fragments represent cat. The 13th century fragments, largely comprising the fore and hind limbs, may represent the deliberate burial of an adult cat (Context 593). Fragments from the 15th/16th century represent at least two adult individuals. These include long-bones, cranial fragments and vertebrae.

Deer

Three fragments of deer were identified. The 13th century produced two fragments of red deer; an incomplete metacarpal and a juvenile radius (Context 5063). A single tibia fragment recovered from the 15th century represented roe deer (Context 5044). Unfortunately, these fragments did not provide any additional information.

Pathology

In addition to the dog (Context 575) discussed above, cattle, pig and horse bone fragments display pathological changes. Osteo-arthritis is most common, occurring in five cattle phalanges and an ulna from the 12th to 14th centuries (Contexts 202, 225, 327, 328, 484) and 12th and 13th century horse metacarpals (Contexts 275, 268). 12th and 13th century contexts (173, 178, 194, 221, 275, 357/361, 435) also produced humerus fragments from two cattle and one pig displaying ossified haematomas, eburnation on mandibular condyles of two cattle and gum disease on a pig mandible. In the 15th century (Contexts 5084, 5044) the results of localised infection were visible in a cattle ulna and pig radius as well as eburnation in a horse acetabulum.

Denge West Quarry

The animal bone assemblage from Denge West comprises 278 fragments weighing 2,519g. This material was recovered from 15 separate contexts. Eight of these were unstratified or undated and have therefore not been studied in detail. Of the remaining seven, five date approximately to the 13th century (Area A, Contexts 9, 12, 13, 26 and 41). Area F, Contexts 68 and 69, date to the late 15th to 16th centuries. The assemblage is highly fragmentary but the fragments themselves are in a good state of preservation.

The identified 13th century assemblage comprises 17 fragments with cattle, sheep/goat, and pig being present. Cattle are represented by long bone fragments, ribs and phalanges. Longbone fragments, ribs and a scapula represent sheep/goat, and only longbone fragments of pig were present. The calculated minimum number of individuals (MNI) for each species is one. No metrical or ageing data was available.

The 15th to 16th century assemblage comprises 82 identified fragments. Cattle, sheep/goat, pig, dog and chicken were all present. A further three fragments of unidentified bird and five fish vertebrae were also noted. 33 fragments including longbone fragments, ribs, and dentition represented cattle. A single rib fragment shows evidence for butchery. A MNI of two was calculated. 32 longbone fragments, ribs, maxillary and mandibular fragments provide a MNI calculation of one sheep/goat. Dentition indicates the presence of a juvenile animal. A single rib shows signs of butchery. Pig are represented by 11 fragments which include longbones, cranial fragments, and dentition. The MNI calculation for pig is two and dental eruption suggests the presence of a juvenile animal. No metrical data was available. Single fragments represent dog and chicken.

The excavations also produced three unstratified human cranial fragments of uncertain age. Full reports can be found in the archive. All three bones were almost complete and in a good state of preservation. An isolated frontal bone has been identified as juvenile or young adult. If the remains are adult the characteristics suggest a female individual. Mild *Cribia orbitalia* was noted in the orbits. One further individual was represented by two parietal bones. The size of the bones would suggest an adult individual, but there is no evidence for fusion along any cranial sutures.

Discussion

The evidence from the excavated assemblages indicates that cattle, sheep and pig were all farmed throughout the medieval period. It would appear that during the earliest phases of occupation (the 12th and 13th centuries) cattle and sheep were being kept as much for their secondary products (milk and wool) as for meat. Meat appears to have come from older cattle and sheep as well as pig. Historical data supports the archaeological evidence and suggests that pig played a supplementary role in the farming regime (Sweetinburgh, this volume). Whilst it is possible that the prevalence of older cattle may reflect their use as working animals, documentary sources would suggest that this work was as, if not more, likely to have been undertaken by horse (Sweetinburgh, this volume, Mate 1990).

Historical records indicate that the established mixed farming regime was changing through the medieval period with increasing emphasis placed on livestock and pasture. The archaeological record highlights the 13th and 15th/16th century as the most productive phases, but general trends can be seen through the 13th, 14th and 15th centuries. In the 13th and 14th centuries there is a general increase in cattle but particularly in immature individuals, suggesting that the importance of meat as a commodity was increasing. From the limited data available it would appear that sheep were still valued primarily for wool.

The documented changes in farming practice are more evident by the mid 16th century when "...the balance had changed profoundly towards livestock production." (Sweetinburgh, this volume). This change does appear to be mirrored in the archaeological record. The 15th/16th century assemblage demonstrates a general increase in both cattle and sheep production. Cattle appear to have been increasingly important as a meat resource, with a larger quantity of immature individuals present and a correspondingly large quantity of butchery evidence on immature bones. The archaeological evidence would suggest that sheep were still valued primarily for wool rather than meat. However, despite the increasing quantity of mature individuals and the decrease in butchery evidence, an increased quantity of sheep killed at a younger age is also suggested. As sheep production in general was increasing it appears that younger meat was becoming a more viable option. The preference for sheep over cattle indicated by the historical record is not as apparent in the archaeological data. Pig remain a constant throughout the medieval period with little change evident.

An attempt was made to compare the 13th century assemblages from three separate 'occupation' sites, excavated as Lydd 1 (Site D), 2 (Site H) and 5/6 (Site G). Unfortunately, the Site G assemblage is not large enough for comparison. There are no obvious differences in the remaining two assemblages, except perhaps that Site H contained a much larger proportion of skeletal extremities than Site D, which contained more upper and lower limb bones and a greater quantity of butchery evidence.

OTHER VERTEBRATE REMAINS
by Deborah Jaques

Introduction

Excavations of the different areas at Lydd Quarry have produced small quantities of fish, bird, small mammal and amphibian bones (Table 71). These were recovered, mainly from sieved sediment samples, but additionally by hand-collection, from 33 deposits across the site. The latter included ditch, pit and cut fills and were primarily of medieval and early post-medieval date. Spot dates provided by the pottery allowed the material to be assigned to several general date groups. The identified vertebrate remains represent five of these groups: 12th century, 13th century, 14th century, 15th century and 18th century.

Methods

Recovery of the bone was by hand-collection and by sieving. Bone from the samples was sorted from the 1mm residue. The amount of sediment per sample processed ranged from 5 litres to 30 litres.

The remains detailed by this report were recovered from several areas of the site and were reported upon individually at the time of excavation. These earlier reports on the fish, small mammal, amphibian and bird remains did not record fragment counts but merely the presence of different species or species groups within a particular deposit. In Table 71, an asterisk shows the presence of a particular species, together with, in some cases, an actual amount. The numerical data refer to material from one particular area of the site, that known as 'Lydd 5/6'.

Notes on Identification

Geese and ducks were recorded within the assemblage, but identification to particular species was not always possible. Different species of geese cannot be distinguished on the basis of morphological characteristics, but the size of the bones can narrow the identification down to large or small geese. The overlap in size between the grey geese (*i.e.*, pink-footed, white-fronted, grey-lag) makes further identification problematic; bones from domestic geese, however, tend to be larger than all the wild species. Identification of the various duck species can also be problematic. At Lydd, the larger bones, identified as *Anser* sp., are likely to represent domestic individuals, whilst the smaller goose bones are comparable in size to those of barnacle geese (*Branta leucopsis* (Bechstein)).

Results

12th century

Remains of birds and fish were generally rather scarce from deposits of this date. Chicken was the only bird present, and was represented by quite small individuals.

One of the earliest deposits, Context 5159, produced several large fish vertebrae, which, although damaged by fresh breakage, were identified as possible cod remains. Comparison of the vertebrae with modern reference specimens of known size suggested that these bones represented an individual that was over a metre in length. Additionally, the remains of herring and thornback ray were also identified.

13th century

Deposits of this date produced bones belonging to several small mammals, including mole, bank vole and wood/yellow-necked mouse. Their remains, particularly those identified as mole, may represent intrusive elements, possibly of modern origin, as all are active burrowers. The single rabbit bone identified is also unlikely to be ancient. Amphibian remains were also noted.

Chicken remains were again present, together with two fragments identified as probable barnacle goose. These are likely to represent wild birds which had been snared or netted.

A similar range of fish species was identified from the 13th century deposits as was found in the earlier 12th century features. Additionally, eel, hake, whiting and flatfish bones were recorded. Flatfish remains were mainly recovered from a single pitfill; none, however, represented characteristic skeletal elements which could advance their identification beyond family level.

14th century

Three deposits of 14th century date produced a small quantity of fish bones. Eel and flatfish bones, including turbot, were identified. No small mammal or bird bones were recovered.

Species		C12th	C13th	C14th	C15th	C18th	Total
Talpa europaeus L.	mole	-	*	-	-	-	*
Oryctolagus cuniculus (L.)	rabbit	-	1	-	-	-	1
Murine/microtine	mouse/vole	-	1*	-	-	-	1
Clethrionomys glareolus (Schreber)	bank vole	-	*	-	-	-	*
Apodemus sylvaticus (L.) *A. flavicollis* (Melchior)	wood/yellow-necked mouse	-	*	-	-	-	*
Anser sp.	goose	-	-	-	1	1	2
cf. Branta leucopsis (Bechstein)	?barnacle goose	-	2	-	-	-	2
Anas sp.	duck	-	-	-	-	2	2
Anas crecca L.	teal	-	-	-	1	-	1
Gallus f. domestic	chicken	*	*	-	13	-	13*
Charadriformes	waders	-	-	-	1	-	1
Passerine	small perching bird	-	-	-	1	-	1
Unidentified bird				-	3	-	3
Raja clavata L.	thornback ray	*	*	-	-	-	*
Clupea harengus L.	herring	*	*	-	-	-	*
Anguilla anguilla (L.)	eel	-	4*	*	5*	1	10*
Gadidae	cod family	1 *	1*	-	*	-	2*
Merlangius merlangus (L.)	whiting	-	2	-	-	-	2
Gadus morhua L.	cod	*	-	-	-	-	*
cf. Gadus morhua L.	?cod	5	-	-	-	-	5
Merluccius merluccius (L.)	hake	-	*	-	-	-	*
cf. Trigla lucerna L.	?tub gurnard	-	-	-	*	-	*
Gasterosteidae	stickleback	-	-	-	-	6	6
Scophthalmus maximus (L.)	turbot	-	-	*	-	-	*
Pleuronectidae	flat fish	-	14*	*	1*	-	15*
Unidentified fish		*	46*	*	7*	-	53*
Amphibian	frog/toad	-	-	-	2	6	8
Rana temporaria L.	frog	-	*	-	-	-	*
Unidentified		-	6	-	15	-	21
Total		6*	77*	*	50*	16	149*

Table 71: Small mammal, fish and bird remains recovered from Lydd Quarry

15th century

The small assemblage recovered from 15th century deposits included bird and fish remains, together with several amphibian fragments. Bones of goose and chicken (mainly the part skeleton of a chick) were identified, whilst single fragments of teal, a small sparrow-sized bird and a wader (neither of the latter could be identified to species) were also noted. Fish bones were not numerous, and although some were unidentifiable, eel, gadid and flatfish remains were recorded. An additional record was that of ?tub gurnard.

18th century

Two deposits of this date produced bone. There is some uncertainty concerning the dating of the vertebrate remains from Context 5370 (fill of a cut). Pottery within this fill dates to the 16th century, while leather fragments suggest a later 18th century date. The bones were few and could be from either period. Several amphibian fragments (representing a single individual), an eel vertebra and some stickleback bones were recovered from this deposit, whilst material from the other deposit, Context 5138, included duck and goose bones.

Skeletal element representation

Where records were available, most skeletal elements for birds were wing (radius, ulna and carpometacarpus) or lower limb (tarsometatarsus) bones. These may be elements removed prior to cooking. Fish remains were typically of rather varied preservation, and were mainly vertebrae or unidentified spines and finrays. Other skeletal elements, from the head for example, were generally extensively fragmented. For some species such as flatfish, skeletal element representation indicated that all parts of these fish were present. The stickleback fragments recovered were mainly the most robust, elements, *e.g.*, cranium fragments and scutes (boney plates).

Discussion

On the basis of bones recovered from the samples, and the small number of hand-collected fragments, both bird and fish remains were scarce within the deposits at Lydd and they appear to have formed only a minor component of the diet of the medieval and early post-medieval inhabitants. However, some caution is needed in interpretation, as although preservation of small bone was generally good the sampling of features was not as rigorous as might be expected on a more recent excavation.

The avian bones identified were mainly from domestic birds, with juvenile chicken remains suggesting that hens were kept and bred within the vicinity. The presence of wild geese and ducks provide limited evidence of wild fowling and hint at the utilisation of the vast expanses of wetland and marsh nearby, although the duck remains are from a possible 18th context and may be domestic.

The small mammal and amphibian remains may represent individuals that had fallen into the pits and ditches and been unable to get out. Given that most rodents are burrowers, the possibility of their being intrusive must be borne in mind, especially as their remains were not recovered from primary deposits.

Although few fish fragments were recovered, some comments can be made regarding the identified remains.

Large fish, such as that represented by the cod remains from one 12th century deposit (Context 5159) and hake (Context 2358), were generally caught in deep water using hooks attached to long lines (Enghoff 2000), and were typically processed for storage. The latter involved gutting and often decapitation, prior to salting, drying or smoking. This resulted in the disposal of certain elements, including the head and, occasionally, some or all of the precaudal vertebrae. The cod precaudal vertebrae recovered from Context 5159, could represent fresh fish or waste from the processing of fish. From the 11th century onwards marine taxa such as cod became increasingly important (Barrett *et al.* 1999; Enghoff 2000; Locker 2001) and the extensive trade in salt fish (also known as stockfish) has been well-documented (Locker *op. cit.*).

The other gadid represented (the whiting) is an inshore fish and, together with the gurnard and the flatfish, was probably caught locally. Some flatfish (*e.g.*, flounders, *Platichthys flesus* L.) can also be found in estuarine and fresh waters. These and eels were most likely caught using nets or traps and suggest the exploitation of inland water courses and creeks.

Herring and thornback ray, recovered from 12th and 13th century deposits, are typically recorded from sites of medieval date; herring, in particular, being a staple of the medieval diet. These fish clearly formed a major part of the diet of the monks at Battle Abbey, East Sussex (Locker 1985). The monks probably acquired their fish from ports such as Winchelsea, Rye, Hastings and Pevensey, which were frequented by the herring fleet. At Dover, excavations revealed evidence for a fishermen's quarter, dating to the medieval period (CBA 1997). Numerous fish bones were recovered, of which herring were particularly abundant. At Dungeness documentary evidence from the 14th century suggests that the promontory was the location of a number of fishermen's huts which were occupied on a seasonal basis (Gardiner 1996). Fishermen from Dungeness were known to work the East Coast fisheries (Gardiner *op. cit.*), so supplies of fish should have been readily available to the inhabitants at Lydd.

The only flatfish remains identified to species represented turbot (*Scophthalmus maximus* (L.)), a fish that was considered a delicacy because of its flavour and the quality of its flesh. These fish are found in relatively shallow water and could be caught from the shore using lines or shoreline traps. They were certainly of some importance in the medieval and post-medieval period as a survey in the 16th century indicated. This suggested that the Lord of Burgh on Sands (in Cumbria) had a right to the "royal and principal fishes, namely whales, sturgeons, porpoises, seals, turbots and such like" (Salzman 1923).

Sticklebacks are today considered inedible and were probably caught inadvertently whilst netting or trapping eels. However, a 19th century English translation of a late medieval Flemish book on wildfowling and fishing (Boekske 1872) suggests that sticklebacks were eaten in the past and that one of the best times to eat them was just before they spawned. Whether this was also common practice in this country in the medieval period and later is difficult to determine.

Despite the paucity of evidence from the vertebrate remains for the exploitation of the local wetlands, many lead fishing weights were recovered from the site (Barber 1998 and this volume). These were almost certainly being made on site and their size suggested that they were probably weights for nets used for fishing on inland creeks and watercourses. Additionally, the remains of a possible fish trap were found close by at Denge West Quarry (Priestley-Bell and Gardiner 1994 and this volume). These clearly suggest that fishing was undertaken in the vicinity.

The small size of the vertebrate assemblages may be a consequence of the recovery techniques, *i.e.*, no systematic sampling programme was implemented during excavation. Many small fish species are characteristic of inshore and inland fisheries and their remains are unlikely to be recovered by hand-collection. Additionally, both fish and bird remains are generally recovered from deposits associated with their storage, preparation or consumption, *e.g.*, kitchen areas, drains, cesspits *etc.* Their absence from the bone assemblage may be because these types of deposits were not encountered or sampled. The nature of the site, therefore, and the economic activities undertaken, is, on the basis of the vertebrate remains, still ambiguous. Fish remains, from similar medieval rural settlements at Shapwick, Somerset, were also rare despite an extensive programme of sieving and sampling. Here it was interpreted as restriction of access to wetland resources by wealthy landowners and ecclesiastical institutions (Jaques 2002).

The dearth of fish from rural sites, despite their close proximity to a wealth of resources, as seen at Lydd, may be a 'real' trend, but supply of fish and trading networks to rural settlements cannot be understood until the absence of evidence can confidently be confirmed as evidence of absence. Little further can be said regarding the importance of fish in the economy at Lydd until a realistic interpretative framework has been constructed.

THE INSECT REMAINS
by Harry Kenward

Introduction

One of the environmental samples, from the waterlogged fill (Context 5370) of cut 5366, produced an assemblage of insect remains. Pottery gave a spot-date of 1425–1500 for this fill, but leatherwork suggested a later date (18th century). The insect remains were picked from the washover and residue of a bulk sample. Five litres of sediment had been processed, using 1mm mesh. Fossils were submitted loose and dry, and were often distorted as a result; they were transferred to industrial methylated spirits for identification.

Bulk-sieving is not the best way of recovering insect remains, the standard method being sieving to 300 microns and paraffin flotation (Kenward *et al.*, 1980). Initial inspection showed that the insect assemblage from Cut 5366 was strongly skewed towards larger forms, so that interpretation was inevitably limited. In view of this, the doubts about dating and possible residuality, and project constraints, no attempt was made to make difficult, time-consuming identifications, and semi-quantitative recording was used (see Kenward 1992). The taxa noted are listed in Table 72.

These remains are clearly a 'pitfall trap' assemblage, even allowing for the effects of non-standard processing. The presence of a range of larger ground beetles (*Carabus* to *Amara* in Table 72) is very typical of such groups, although the rarity of larger *Staphylinidae* is a little unusual. Almost all smaller species have been lost (they must have been present initially), either during sieving or because they are very difficult to see while sorting dry residues. The only very small species recovered was the *Corticaria*.

DIPTERA
Diptera sp. (puparium)

COLEOPTERA
Carabus ?granulatus Linnaeus
Dyschirius sp.
Clivina fossor (Linnaeus)
Trechus obtusus Erichson or *quadristriatus* (Schrank)
Pterostichus ?cupreus (Linnaeus)
Pterostichus madidus (Fabricius) (several)
Pterostichus melanarius (Illiger) (many)
Calathus fuscipes (Goeze)
Calathus sp. (>1)
Agonum marginatum (Linnaeus)
Amara spp. (>1)
Helophorus grandis Illiger or *aquaticus* (Linnaeus)
Histeridae sp?p. (>1)
Xantholinus linearis (Olivier) or *longiventris* Heer
Philonthus sp.
Tachinus signatus Gravenhorst
Aphodius ?prodromus (Brahm) (>1)
Aphodius sp. (>1)
Onthophagus sp.
Anobium punctatum (Degeer)
Cantharis sp.
Elateridea sp.
Corticaria sp.
Apion sp.
Otiorhynchus sp.
Sitona spp. (several)
Hypera nigrirostris (Fabricius)
Hypera punctata (Fabricius)
Mecinus ?pyraster (Herbst)

HYMENOPTERA
Formicidae sp.

Table 72: Insect remains from Cut 366, Lydd Quarry. 'Several' and 'many' are used in the semi-quantitative sense defined by Kenward (1992)

Spot Date	Period Grouping
1100–1175; 1125–1200/1225	C12th
1175–1225/1250	Late C12th/early C13th (lC12th/eC13th)
1200–1275; 1225–1300/1325	C13th
1250–1350; 1275–1350; 1300–1375; 1325–1400	C14th
1350–1450; 1375–1475, 1400–1500/1525	C15th
1450–1550; 1475–1575	C16th

Table 73: The relationship between spot-dates from pottery and period groupings used in this report

Discussion

Reconstruction of the surroundings can only be tentative in view of the recovery method used. The ground beetles are broadly typical of areas disturbed by human activity, including occupation sites where disturbance is not excessive. The single water beetle (*Helophorus aquaticus* (L.) or H. *grandis* Illiger) is very migratory and abundant in 'background fauna' (*sensu* Kenward 1975), and the cut was probably not suitable for the development of an aquatic fauna. Some plants appear to have been present in the surroundings (assuming – and on the basis of work at many other sites (Kenward and Hall 1997) this is an assumption to be made cautiously – that there is no evidence for the importation of materials such as hay which may have contained plant feeders). *Sitona* species are common on vetches, clovers and their allies, and the two *Hypera* are associated with the same group of plants. *Mecinus pyraster* (Herbst) is a plantain (*Plantago* spp.) feeder. There is almost no evidence for accumulations of decaying matter of the type typical of occupation sites, either *in situ* or nearby. The species present which are associated with rotting matter might have been attracted to dead insects in the cut, or be 'background fauna' derived from elsewhere. The *Aphodius* and *Onthophagus* dung beetles may have been similarly attracted or entered accidentally, but perhaps hint at dung nearby (although the numbers are not large enough to indicate the presence of abundant livestock). There is no 'house fauna' community (*sensu* Kenward and Hall 1995; Carrott and Kenward 2001) typical of house or stable floors, even allowing for the loss of small species. The single *Anobium punctatum* (Degeer) (woodworm beetle) may have come from fairly old structural timber of any kind, possibly from the timber-lining.

One possibility which arises in view of the apparently restricted fauna is that this was primarily a well, kept clean in use, and only used for dumping at its last, short-lived, abandonment stage.

The insects provide a weak piece of evidence for a late date, in that *Pterostichus madidus* Fabricius) is numerous. There are very few fossil records of this large and distinctive black ground beetle, which is now extremely common in large areas of Britain and usually (though not exclusively) found around areas strongly modified by humans. No records were made by Hall and Kenward (1990) or Kenward and Hall (1995), for example, although hundreds of archaeological samples were analysed for insect remains. The reason for the paucity of records is unclear, but it appears to have undergone a significant change in abundance: its distinctive fossils cannot often have been overlooked. It may only recently have adapted to a synanthropic way of life, although it certainly occurs in natural habitats, where it may be common (*e.g.*, Judas *et al.*, 2002). Conceivably it originated outside its present known range, but there is no evidence for this. Certainly, if it was as abundant in the past as it is now, it would be expected to be a frequent component of archaeological assemblages.

THE MARINE MOLLUSCS
by Elizabeth M. Somerville

Introduction

The Lydd Quarry site has produced a great number of marine molluscs, particularly cockles (*Cerastoderma edule*). This report brings together the material which has been separately described after three of the phases of work at the site (Lydd 1, Lydd 3, and Lydd 5/6) together with previously undescribed material from the Lydd 2 excavations and the small assemblage from Denge West Quarry. The main results from the latter site are also included at the end of this report as a separate section. The major difference between this and previous reports is that period groupings have been consolidated to an agreed set, as shown in Table 73, and this also gives a finer subdivision to the temporal groupings than that used previously. This revision to groupings has also included some changes in the spot-dates assigned to contexts. The combination of these two revisions means that any preliminary conclusions drawn in previous reports about changes in the marine molluscs over time must be discarded.

In addition, there was a small amount of 18th century material.

The majority of the shell came from three periods in the middle of this time range (13th century, 14th century and 15th century) and the analysis will concentrate on these periods in terms of comparison with other sites. Much of

Period		Species					
		Oyster	Cockle	Mussel	Whelk	Winkle	*Acanthocardia*
C12th	MNI	5	4	7	2	0	3
	Weight (gms)	119.2	16.1	8.5	32.2	0	19.9
lC12th/eC13th	MNI	10	12	173	9	0	1
	Weight (gms)	218.8	57.4	2545	124.8	0	5.8
C13th	MNI	283	2968	108	162	3	8
	Weight (gms)	8699.4	9581.4	527.6	2730.3	4.8	46.2
C14th	MNI	76	223	14	7	6	2
	Weight (gms)	3630.4	1135.2	29.8	48.3	11.7	27.7
C15th	MNI	109	214	105	2	141	1
	Weight (gms)	3291.8	897.6	79.5	31.9	288.8	3.6
C16th	MNI	42	12	0	9	0	1
	Weight (gms)	2311.7	55.8	0	82.6	0	4.2
C18th	MNI	5	0	0	0	0	0
	Weight (gms)	460.7	0	0	0	0	0
nd	MNI	16	416	17	25	0	0
	Weight (gms)	784	1366.9	69.7	421	0	0

Table 74: MNI and weight of shell by period for common species

the shell from Lydd comes from average to small molluscs which, especially in the case of the conspicuously small cockles, may indicate over-exploitation of this resource.

Methods

All whole shells were identified to species (Fish & Fish 1989). Partial shells and fragments were identified as far as possible. All identified shell was weighed. Fragments smaller than approx 1sq. cm were discarded. Gastropods were counted as being either complete, a partial shell with an apex or a fragment. Bivalves were counted as whole right/left valves; right/left umbos or fragments. Umbos which could not be sided were noted separately. These counts were used for the calculation of the minimum number of individuals (MNI) which was done for each context. For bivalves the greater of the two numbers for the sided valves plus umbos was taken, plus half (rounded down) of any unsided umbos. For gastropods, the MNI was the sum of whole shells plus apices. Where

Period	Oyster – wet meat weight (gm)	Cockle – cooked meat weight (gm)
C12th	37.5	6.92
lC12th/eC13th	75.0	20.76
C13th	2122.5	5134.6
C14th	570	385.8
C15th	817.5	370.2
C16th	315	20.8
C18th	37.5	0
nd	120	719.7

Table 75: Meat weight for oysters and cockles

the species was only represented by fragments and/or a single unsided umbo, then an MNI of 1 was given.

The maximum length (from umbo to opposite margin) and width (orthogonal to length) were measured for bivalves, and the maximum height (from apex to the bottom of the last whorl or to the end of the siphon if present) and width (orthogonal to this) were measured for gastropods. Whole oyster shells were also scored for a number of other characteristics including age and the extent to which the surface of the shell bore the marks of infestation by one or more of the polychaete worm species *Polydora ciliata*, *P. hoplura* and the burrowing sponge *Cliona celata*.

Results

Species Present

Six of the species identified were recorded in the majority of periods – these were oyster (*Ostrea edulis*), cockle (*Cerastoderma edule*), mussel (*Mytilus edulis*), one of the *Acanthocardia* species, most probably the spiny cockle (*Acanthocardia echinata*) but the diagnostic shell sculpture was too worn for this to be more than a tentative identification, whelk (*Buccinum undatum*) and winkle (*Littorina littorea*). Table 74 (previous page) shows the MNI and total shell weight for these species by the period groupings. The 16th century data for oyster included material from both Lydd and Denge West, but the other shells recorded in the 16th century period were only found at Denge West.

In addition there were two fragments of Scallop species: one, Queen Scallop (*Aequipecten opercularis*) from a 15th century context; and one, probably *Pecten maximus* from a 16th century context, plus single specimens of

limpet (*Patella vulgaris*) from a 13th century context and a second winkle species (*L. saxatalis*) from a 15th century context. Three specimens of Scrobicularia plana were found in undated but probably medieval ditch deposits. All except L. saxatalis are considered edible (Mâitre–Allain 1991).

Meat Weight

The MNIs were used to calculate meat weights for the cockles and for oysters, following the methods used by Winder (1980). It should be noted, however, that many of the cockles from this site are rather small, so the meat weight given here is likely to be an over-estimate (Table 75 above).

Taphonomy and Depositional Practise

Across the site at Lydd there is an extensive network of ditches, many of which appear to have remained open throughout the medieval period. Comparison of the shell material from ditches with that from pits can be used to address some simple questions about depositional practise, on the working hypothesis that material is deliberately deposited in pits, but arrives in ditches by a variety of routes, mostly incidental to the distribution of the material around the site, but also possibly including some deliberate deposition as individual ditches went out of use as drainage channels.

The contexts included in this analysis are not evenly distributed through time and, obviously, they are not of uniform volume. Nonetheless, there do appear to be some possibly interesting differences in patterning in the data summaries in Table 76 opposite. The cockles are more likely to be deposited in pits than in ditches, whereas the oyster and whelks are distributed more evenly between

Feature	Oyster	Cockle	Mussel	*Acanthocardia*	Whelks	Winkle (*L. littorea*)
Ditches	174 (32.8)	565 (16.5)	72 (17.6)	8 (50)	66 (34.6)	137 (91.3)
Pits	208 (39.3)	2682 (78.1)	38 (9.3)	1 (6.3)	58 (30.4)	10 (6.7)
Site Total	530	3433	407	16	191	150

Table 76: The distribution of the common species, given as MNIs and, in brackets, as a percentage of the total for each species, from contexts securely identified as pits and ditches.
Data given as site totals only includes dated contexts.

Feature	Whole valves and whole shells	Part shells – umbos and apices	Shell fragments
Ditches	832 (1194.6)	764 (432.5)	1343 (1311.8)
Pits	4457 (4094.4)	1151 (1482.5)	4465 (4496.2)

Table 77: The pattern of breakage of shell in dated ditches and pits for the common species, together with the expected values of shell remains in brackets.

these two contexts. Mussels are found less frequently in either of these situations than elsewhere (post-holes, layers, spreads and cuts). The winkles came almost entirely from one context (3151), which happened to be a ditch.

As well as possible differences in species distribution, the pattern of breakage was examined across the two different types of context. This is shown in Table 77 above.

A χ-squared test shows this distribution to be non-random ($\chi^2 = 471.26$, df = 2, p<.001), and inspection of the values in Table 5 shows that this comes from there being fewer whole shell and more part shell in ditches, and more whole shell and less part shell in pits. Thus the shell in ditches is, as might be anticipated, more broken than the shell in the pits, but not by being more fragmented.

Analysis of Individual Species

Only species which produced more than 50 whole shells from at least one period are considered here: namely oysters, cockles, whelks and winkles. Although there were high numbers of mussels in terms of MNI (see Table 74), the number of whole shells was small, as is commonly the case with this species. As detailed below, this part of the analysis was affected by some changes in

methodology which had occurred during the time while the various phases of Lydd have been excavated and processed. In addition, the concentration of material in the 13th century contexts makes statistical comparison across periods somewhat dubious. Although the discussion here is limited as described, the data for all measurements on whole shell is in the archive as an Excel workbook.

Oysters

Oysters were found in all time periods, with the highest representation, in terms of MNI, in the 13th century and 15th century contexts. However, as shown in Table 78, the 15th century contexts contain proportionally fewer whole shells, and this probably reflects the derivation of 110 of the total 191 umbos from a single ditch context (3151). The uneven distribution of whole shell makes it problematic to undertake more than a description of the characteristics of the shell from each period, and this approach is followed below. Thus, although the length of the valves appears to be increasing through time, the 15th century and later samples are much smaller than the 13th century and 14th century samples, making any overall statistical comparison of doubtful value. A t-test on just the 13th century and 14th century data found no significant difference between them (t=-1.6, df = 76, n.s.).

Period	Whole valves	Average length (cm)	Umbos	Fragments	MNI
C12th	2	7.05	3	0	5
lC12th/eC13th	0	-	7	11	10
C13th	68	7.44	312	244	283
C14th	33	7.97	74	89	76
C15th	9	7.33	191	191	109
C16th	16	8.02	56	23	42
C18th	5	9.54	1	6	5
Total	134		644	564	530

Table 78: The distribution of oyster shell through the time periods, with the MNI as given in Table 74 for information. (No distinction is made here between right and left valves or umbos. The average length of whole valves is from right and left valves combined).

Period	Distorted valves	Smooth valves	Distorted umbos	Smooth umbos
C12th	1 (50)	1 (50)	Not available	Not available
lC12th/eC13th	No whole valves	No whole valves	0 (0)	4 (100)
C13th	19 (27.9)	49 (72.1)	8 (11.3)	63 (88.7)
C14th	5 (14.3)	30 (85.7)	2 (6.9)	27 (93.1)
C15th	4 (44.4)	5 (55.6)	36 (42.9)	48 (57.1)
C16th	8 (50)	8 (50)	19 (47.5)	21 (52.5)
C18th	1 (20)	4 (80)	Not available	Not available

Table 79: The amount of distortion seen on oyster shells and on umbos. For comparison, percentage values are given in brackets. N.B. umbo data was not collected for Lydd 1 nor for the sole umbo from the 18th century deposits.

*Fig. 92 shows the changes in the distribution of valve length for right and left valves combined. Hardly surprisingly, the largest sample (13th century) is the closest to a normal distribution, but this could also indicate unselective harvesting, with considerable numbers being taken from the lower size groups. This practice of the harvest including relatively small oysters continues through the 14th and 15th century data, although it is notable that no oysters smaller than 6cm are found in the 16th century sample.

Plotting growth of oysters can give additional information about growing conditions. *Fig. 93 shows this as a scatter plot where the estimated age, counted from growth lines at the umbo, is plotted against the length of the shell.

The plots for the different periods are clearly all superimposed, implying that the oysters were growing at similar rates. There is an apparent decrease in the number of older oysters with time, but this is confounded with sample size.

The characteristics of the shell of oysters can also be used to give information about growing conditions. For all whole oysters, data was collected on how distorted the shell was. With the exception of Lydd 1, this data was also collected for oyster umbos. The results are given above in Table 79.

Period	Whole valves			Umbos		
	ph	pc	cc	ph	pc	cc
C12th	0/2	2/2	0/2	No data	No data	No data
lC12th/eC13th	-	-	-	yes	yes	yes
C13th	1/68	18/68	10/68	yes	yes	yes
C14th	1/35	5/35	6/35	yes	yes	yes
C15th	0/9	6/9	0/9	yes	yes	yes
C16th	0/16	11/16	1/16	no	yes	yes
C18th	0/5	0/5	2/5	No data	No data	No data

Table 80: Data on the main infesting species P. hoplura (ph), P. ciliata (pc) and C. celata (cc) for whole valves and for umbos. This is recorded simply as presence (yes) and absence (no) for the umbos, but for the whole valves it is given as prevalence, i.e., the number of valves infested by that species/total number of valves.

Period	0– no infestation	1– infestation present	2– up to 1/3 area of shell affected	3– 1/3–2/3 area of shell affected	4– shell severely affected – "rottenback"
C12th	-	2	-	-	-
C13th	39	15	2	6	3
C14th	24	6	1	1	2
C15th	3	4	1	1	-
C16th	5	3	6	2	-
C18th	3	1	-	1	-

Table 81: The degree of infestation on whole valves, given as the number of shells in each category

There is a consistent trend in the data from both the umbos and the whole valves which shows that the proportion of distorted valves rises in the 15th and 16th century oysters as compared to the 13th and 14th century oysters. Unfortunately, too many of the expected values are below 5 for a χ-squared test to be valid for this data.

The final set of information which can be extracted from the data on oysters is the infesting species and the amount of infestation. The former can be derived, although less reliably, from umbos as well as whole valves and the results of this inspection are given in Table 80 (above top) for the main infesting species found in oysters from the south-east of England, namely *P. hoplura*, *P. ciliata* and *C. celata*. In addition, there were occasional instances of calcareous worms (probably *Pomotoceros triqueter*), sand tubes (from one of the sabellid worms, probably *Sabella pavonina*), and bryozoa. As before, umbos from Lydd 1 are not included in these results.

The data from whole valves and umbos is broadly consistent, although the larger numbers of umbos often record the presence of the two rarer species (*P. hoplura* and *C. celata*) when these are absent from the whole valves.

The degree of infestation was scored for the whole valves on a 5 point scale from 0 (no infestation) to 4 ('rotten-back'). With the exception of the 16th century data, the majority of valves which showed infestation were scored as category 1, *i.e.*, very light infestation.

Period	Whole valves	Average length (cm)	Number of valves <2.3cm	Umbos	Fragments	MNI
C12th	4	2.5	1	1	1	4
lC12th/eC13th	5	2.76	0	8	50	12
C13th	4890 (2402 LHS)	2.20	1600	837	3457	2968
C14th	204	2.40	82	182	1302	223
C15th	156	2.40	55	236	685	214
C16th	18	2.57	0	3	7	12
Total	5277			1267	5502	3433

Table 82: The distribution of cockles through the time periods, with the MNI as given in Table 74 for information

Period	Whole shells	Mean height (cm)	Apices	Fragments	MNI
C12th	1	6.3	0	1	2
lC12th/eC13th	0	-	3	28	9
C13th	87	6.0	67	137	162
C14th	1	5.4	5	3	7
C15th	1	6.5	1	3	2
C16th	4	5.6	5	2	9
Total	94		81	174	191

Table 83: The distribution of whelks through the time periods, with the MNI as given in Table 74 for information.

Cockles

Cockles were extremely numerous in some of the Lydd contexts and this led to differences in recording and analysing practice in different phases of the project. For the second and third phases, all whole valves were measured and are included in the analysis described here. For Lydd 5/6, all whole valves were recorded but only left valves were measured. Because Lydd 5/6 provided the vast majority of cockles for the 13th century period, only left valves have been included in the metric analysis here. For all other periods, both right and left valves are included. Counts of numbers of valves and MNI values are derived from all recorded shell.

There appears to be a decrease and then an increase in the size of the cockles, although the very uneven distribution makes it difficult to analyse this trend statistically. The modern cockle fisheries in the Burry Inlet, South Wales, had a bye-law passed in 1959 which forbade the removal of cockles smaller that 2.3cm (Hancock & Urquhart 1966), and the number of valves from Lydd which fall below this modern cut-off point are also given in Table 82 (above top).

*Fig. 94 compares the distribution of length classes for the 13th, 14th and 15th century, with data necessarily being shown as percentages. What is notable here is that none of these distributions are normal and whereas the

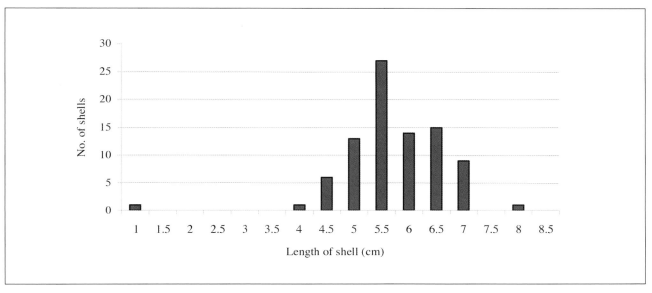

Fig. 95 13th century whelks (length)

Period	Whole shells	Mean length (cm)	Apices	Fragments	MNI
C13th	1	1.4	1	1	3
C14th	3	2.1	3	0	6
C15th	69	2.1	72	13	141
Total	73		76	14	150

Table 84: The distribution of winkles (L. littorea) through the time periods,
with the MNI as given in Table 74 for information

13th and 15th century data have a single peak, the 14th century data looks as if it may be bimodal.

Whelks

Whelks were the most widely distributed gastropod species although, as Table 83 (opposite) shows, they were concentrated in the 13th century deposits. The small 16th century sample comes from the Denge West location. It is impossible on this basis to say whether there is any trend over time.

The distribution of shell length for the 13th century data is shown above (Fig. 95). The single very small shell may have been an apex measured in error, or it may have been a juvenile specimen.

Winkles

Although there were a few specimens in other periods, as shown in Table 84 above, the majority of winkles came not just from a single period (15th century) but from a single context (3151) which is described as ditch fill.

The distribution of lengths is shown in Fig. 96 overleaf. This appears to show a tendency to harvesting of winkles which are between 2.0 and 2.5cm in height, although there is quite a tail to the distribution of smaller shells.

Discussion

Species Present

Although the presence of marine molluscs has often been noted from sites in south-east England, it is only relatively recently that the characteristics of the assemblages, particularly those from Sussex, have been reported in any detail. In general, the main species found at Lydd have also been found in East Sussex at Lewes, at the Friary site (Somerville 1996), the Priory (Somerville 1997) and at St Nicholas Hospital (Somerville forthcoming), and in the town of Pevensey (Dulley 1967; Somerville, unpublished

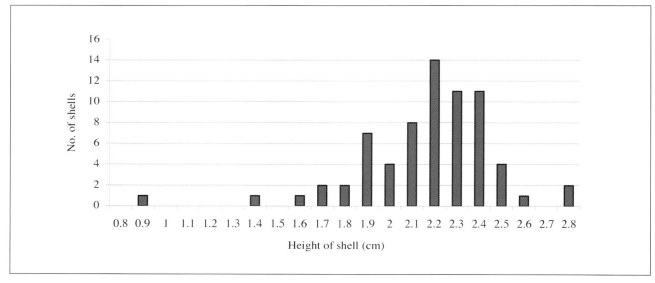

Fig. 96 15th century winkles from 3151 (height)

data) as well as the castle (Somerville, unpublished data). However, cockles are only found in quantity at Lydd and Pevensey, and the numbers of whelks and winkles found is very variable.

The marine molluscs from Lydd Quarry are all common in the English Channel. The virtual absence of Limpets, and the rarity of winkles except for one context, indicate that the occupants of the site did not have regular access to rocky shores. With the exception of *Acanthocardia* all of the species can be collected from the shore at low tide, although whelks can also be caught in pots and oysters may be dredged. The presence of the *Acanthocardia* shells may indicate dredging for oysters with these being taken as well. Alternatively, the empty shells may simply have been collected from the shore. The calculations for meat weight for the two commonest species (Table 75) shows clearly that marine molluscs made only a small contribution to the diet. These calculations also show clearly that harvesting cockles, especially small ones, as at Lydd, is a fairly labour-intensive means of adding protein to the diet.

Taphonomy and Depositional Practice

There does appear to be some partitioning of shell between the ditches and pits at Lydd, although the variation in number of contexts and their volume makes this a difficult process to tease out in terms of behaviour. It is possible that the apparently selective discard of cockle shells into pits was a result of the sheer numbers which were being processed, resulting in disposal into pits rather than into the general rubbish around the site which eventually ended up in ditches. However, the only evidence for assuming that material which was finally deposited in ditches was subject to more movement around the site is the breakage pattern, and that does not bear evidence

of any more extensive fragmentation but simply greater breakage of the shell into still recognisably large units (umbos and apices).

Individual Species

Oysters

Oysters have been found at all the medieval sites studied by the author in East Sussex, as well as at Lydd, which gives a basis for comparison of the size of the harvested shells. At Lewes Friary (Somerville 1996) the mode for right valve length was 7–8.9cm, and at St Nicholas Hospital (Somerville forthcoming) average right valve lengths were between 7.7 and 8.2cm for the medieval material. From Pevensey town (Somerville, unpublished data) the earliest group (11th/12th century to 12th/13th century) had an average right valve length of 6.8cm, rising to 7.9cm in the 13th to 13th/14th century group and dropping back to 6.9cm in the 14th to 14th/15th century group. The medieval material from Pevensey castle (Somerville, unpublished data) gave values for left valves of 6.9cm (early medieval, up to 12th century) and 7.2–7.4cm (medieval to 15th century), and for right valves of 6.8cm for the earlier phases and 6.3–6.6cm for the later phases. At Lydd the average length of valves (both sides combined) ranges between 7.3 and 8.0cm for the medieval material. Winder (1992) gives a general average for "medieval" (11th to 16th century) oysters of 7.5cm for left and 6.4cm for right valves. Modern farmed oysters would be expected to reach these dimensions at between 3 and 6 years of age (Walne 1974). Thus the Lydd oysters are generally comparable to the medieval assemblages from Sussex and, like all of this material, appear to be at or slightly above the average size for medieval oysters.

In terms of infesting, adhering and encrusting species, the oysters from Lydd are similar to those from Lewes in terms of the low number of epifaunal species, which contrasts with the oysters from Pevensey, both town and castle. However, in terms of the proportions of the common infesting species, the material from Lydd is comparable to that from Pevensey in that *P. ciliata* is the commonest species, whereas in the material from Lewes *C. celata* was the most common. The Lydd material had a lower proportion of distorted shell and very little adhering shell, which is a marked contrast to the material from Pevensey. Overall, the characteristics of the oysters from Lydd are consistent with a population coming from relatively shallow water, as indicated by the dominance of *P. ciliata* over *P. hoplura* (Cole 1956; Smith 1987). The majority of shells are undistorted, indicating good growing conditions, and the lack of adhering shell implies management of the beds rather than the exploitation of a wild reef-forming population. However, the presence of small shell, especially in the larger 13th century sample, could imply that the harvesting was relatively indiscriminate and the presence throughout of old shells is not consistent with an intensively managed population.

Cockles

Lydd is remarkable amongst this group of Sussex medieval sites for the vast quantities of cockles. The only other site to produce any amount of cockles was Pevensey Castle. The sizes are very similar to those for the Pevensey Castle material, although the conspicuously small cockles less than 2.0cm length, which are quite numerous in both the 13th and 14th century material from Lydd, are largely absent from Pevensey. For both these sites, the small average size throughout the medieval period is puzzling, especially since the modern cockle fisheries in the Burry Inlet, South Wales, had a bye-law passed in 1959 which forbade the removal of cockles smaller that 2.3cm (Hancock & Urquhart 1966). Since the Welsh bye-law was set on the basis of investigations intended to maintain a viable cockle industry, it would appear that the cockles harvested from both Lydd and Pevensey were in danger of being over-exploited by modern standards. However, the continuation of exploitation of cockles at Lydd from the 13th to 15th centuries either means that there were sufficient cockle beds that over-exploitation and exhaustion did not affect the overall harvest, or it means that conditions in the medieval period were such that the cockles were breeding at a smaller size.

Whelks

Whelks are only found in abundance in the 13th century contexts and their average height of 6.0cm compares well to a modern sample from Shoreham of 6.2cm (Nicholson & Evans 1997), although it is somewhat smaller than a modern commercial sample from Pevensey bay of 6.5mm (Bonnell pers. comm.). Some of the smaller Lydd whelks would not have been sexually mature (Kideys *et*

al., 1993) and this implies that, like the cockle fishery, there may have been some danger of over-exploitation. The virtual disappearance of the whelks from the later deposits is, however, unlikely to be due to this because Pevensey has a persistent presence of much smaller (4.7–4.9cm in height) whelks throughout the medieval period.

Winkles

Winkles were not found in any abundance at Lydd, apart from what may be a single instance of importation of the species in the 15th century, which ended in the shells being discarded in a ditch (Context 3151). The size of these winkles falls between those found at Pevensey Town in the 13th and 13th/14th century contexts (where the mean shell height was only 1.8cm), and the 2.3cm mean shell height of the winkles from the early medieval phases of Pevensey Castle.

Scrobicula plana

Although only three complete shells, *i.e.*, paired valves of *Scrobicula plana*, were found at Lydd, this species is worth commenting on since it may give direct information about the environment at Lydd. The shells all came from context 5054 (Ditch 5053) which has no pottery for dating, but is thought to have been infilled, like most other ditches, by early post-medieval times. This species lives deep in thick estuarine mud (Fish & Fish 1989), a somewhat different environment to that of the other marine molluscs, although just possibly overlapping with *Cerastoderma edule*. This species is edible (Maître–Allain 1991) although it is also possible, given that these were found as paired valves, that these shells may be true ecofacts indicating that the ditch was open to marine influence.

Concluding Remarks

Bringing together the reports on the marine molluscs from Lydd, shows clearly how sampling across a complex site can affect interpretation. In previous reports much was made of the small size of the marine molluscs from Lydd, but once all the data is collated and placed in a single consistent temporal framework, this feature of the assemblage can be seen to be most obvious for the cockles, and to be most striking for this species in the 13th century period where it appears in greatest abundance, though their small size suggests they were over-exploited. It is not possible to be certain if the cockles were cultivated. However, considering the large tracts of suitable habitat off the coast in this area, cultivation may not have been necessary. Despite this apparent over-exploitation the species does not disappear from the site until the 16th century, which implies either that alternative sources for the cockles were found, or that modern practices of harvest are rather conservative compared to those of the medieval period. It is also possible that the growing conditions for the cockles were such that they matured at

Species	Total Weight of shell (grams)	MNI
Oyster (*Ostrea edulis*)	2044.4	34
Whelk (*Buccinum undatum*)	82.6	9
Cockle (*Cerastoderma edule*)	55.8	12
Rough/Spiny Cockle (*Acanthocardia* spp.)	4.2	1
Scallop (*cf. Pecten maximus*)	3.0	1

Table 85: Denge West: Species of shell found (total weight of shell for each species and the MNI)

a smaller size. However, the climatic trend through this period is from warmer in the 13th century to colder in the 14th and 15th centuries (Lamb 1995), which does not fit very well with an observed upward trend in size.

The oysters found at Lydd also include specimens which would be considered too small for exploitation in a modern fishery, although they are well within the range described by Winder (1992) as average for the medieval period, and are also comparable to the size of oysters from the medieval sites in Lewes and Pevensey examined by the author. According to Cole (1956), modern farmed flat oysters were harvested at 5 years of age, when they would have reached about 8cm in length (Walne 1974). Oysters of the size of the lower end of the distribution (6cm and smaller) found at Lydd are considerably less fecund than older oysters (Walne 1974), an important consideration for long-term exploitation of a wild population, but possibly not so relevant here as the shell characteristics are consistent with a farmed population.

Denge West Quarry

The shell sample from this site is too small to draw any firm conclusions from, and the material has already been considered alongside the much larger assemblage from Lydd Quarry above. However, a summary of the stratified shell from Denge West is included here, due both to the site's different geographical location and because this data allows a fuller insight into the contribution this site has made in the above overview. Only two contexts were examined, both of 15th/16th century date. Both contexts came from a midden deposit. The methodology of study was as described above. Whole oyster shells were scored for distortion of the shell, age and extent to which the surface bore the marks of infestation by one or more of the infesting and epifaunal species listed below.

1. *Polydora ciliata* (polychaete worm)
2. *Polydora hoplura* (polychaete worm)
3. *Cliona celata* (a burrowing sponge)
4. Calcareous worm-tube (probably *Pomotoceros triqueter*)
5. Sandtubes (probably from sabellid worms)
6. *Bryozoa* spp.
7. Barnacles (shell, baseplate or marks therof)

In addition notes were made of the presence of drillholes in shells, indicating attack by predatory gastropods and whether the shells showed signs of having had nail-holes punched through them.

Species Represented

Bivalves identified from the site were oyster (*Ostrea edulis*), cockle (*Cerastoderma edule*), either the spiny or rough cockle (*Acanthocardia* sp.) and part of a scallop shell, probably *Pecten maximus*. The only gastropod present was whelk (*Buccinum undatum*).

Oysters dominate this small assemblage, which otherwise contains no species not found at Lydd Quarry.

Analysis of Individual Species

Oysters

There were rather few whole oyster valves (6 left and 8 right). The mean length was 8.1cm, well above the average of 6.4cm given by Winder (1992) for shells from the 11th to 16th century. Although about half the shells were rated as 'distorted', this was never extreme and only one whole shell had adhering shell indicating growth in reef conditions. 71% of the shells showed some infestation, primarily with *Polydora ciliata*. The data from umbos gave a similar picture, although about a third of the left umbos had adhering shell. *P. ciliata* was the most common infesting species, with a few shells showing evidence of *Cliona celata*. One right umbo showed evidence of re-use by people in the form of a square nail-hole (*cf.*, Holden 1963). With one exception, the oysters which could be aged appeared to have been harvested no older than 6 years, which would be consistent with a farmed population, although a similar pattern could come from organised harvesting of a wild bed. The size of the shells is comparable with modern growth rates (Walne 1974). From the dominance of *P. ciliata* as the infesting organism, it is likely that the bed or beds were under shallow water (Cole 1956; Smith 1987).

Whelks

The mean length is 5.6cm, which is small, between 5 and 10% less than a modern assemblage from the Sussex Coast. However, with only 4 individuals, the sample is too small for any great significance to be placed on this finding, although it is consistent with data from other phases at Lydd.

Cockles

There were 18 whole valves and the mean length, combining both right and left valves, was 2.6cm, which is slightly larger than those found in some of the phases of the Lydd excavations.

THE VEGETATION AND ENVIRONMENT OF THE MEDIEVAL AND LATER PERIODS; POLLEN AND WOOD ANALYSIS
by Rob Scaife and Sophie Seel
with contributions by Rowena Gale and Louise Bashford

Introduction to the Pollen, Charcoal and Wood Analysis

An extensive sampling strategy for environmental materials was adopted at the Lydd sites. This comprised bulk sampling for seeds (see P. Hinton below) and charcoal, and the targeted sampling of a number of ditch sections for pollen analysis. The principal aims of these investigations were to establish the palaeoenvironment and palaeoecology of the site in relation to the medieval human activity in this region of the marsh. This section deals with the water-logged wood and charcoal from the Lydd 2, 3 and 5/6 excavations, and pollen data obtained from Lydd 1 and 2, Ditches 7 (Section 5) and 2011 (S20), the latter which was cut into earlier (early historic period) peat. It was anticipated that these data sources might provide background information on the general vegetation environment of the medieval period, plus data concerning woodland management, woodland species selection and local resource exploitation. It was anticipated that this might be correlated with the existing palaeoenvironmental framework for the Romney Marsh, however, few data dealing with this period are available.

Some Notes on the Taphonomy of the Pollen and Charcoal Samples

One of the principal aims of this study was to characterise vegetation habitats and especially the nature of land-use of the adjacent fields. There have been few such agricultural landscape studies undertaken using pollen analysis, and there are few published data relating to the taphonomic problems involved in the interpretation of such pollen data. Dimbleby (1988) has, however, highlighted some of the problems associated with pollen from ditch contexts. Studies have been previously carried out for Romano-British sites by Tinsley and Smith (1974) at Fortress Dike, Yorkshire, and by Dickson *et al.* (1979) for the Roman fort ditch at Bearsden, Scotland. More recent studies include those of Robinson (1983) studying an

Iron Age ditched enclosure at Shiels near Glasgow, for a Romano-British agricultural ditch/depression at Haddon, Cambridgeshire (Scaife 1994) and from a multi-period site at West Deeping, Cambs. (Rackham and Scaife in press).

Whilst charcoal and wood are frequently recovered form archaeological site contexts, similar taphonomic problems also exist, since the majority of contexts are clearly the result of human activity, *i.e.*, pits, post-holes and hearths and, as such, should be treated with caution when attempting environmental reconstruction. Perhaps most useful for reconstruction are the ditch features, from which the taxa present are less likely to be the sole result of human activity. However, species growing in ditches are likely to differ from those of the vegetation growing in the wider environment and this is attested in the Lydd assemblage.

Pollen Analysis *by Rob Scaife*

Pollen analysis was carried out on excavated sections from Lydd 1 and Lydd 2. The former (Lydd 1) comprised ditch sediments of late 12th and 13th century date and a Romano-British palaeosol (not reported here). The latter (Lydd 2) comprised a medieval ditch cut into an earlier organic peat deposit. Although the analysis was only carried out to an assessment level, some useful data has been obtained. This study was undertaken to ascertain whether sub-fossil pollen and spores are present in the archaeological contexts and, if so, their potential for reconstructing the past environmental history of the area. Aspects of particular relevance and consideration were the character/nature of local land use and the possibility of marine influences. Such data, if present, might be correlated with work previously undertaken on the marsh.

The Pollen: Methodology and Data

Samples from the ditch fills were of inorganic, minerogenic character and rigorous pollen extraction procedures were required. The character of the sediments also suggested poor pollen preserving conditions. The peats, however, posed no problem having remained wet. Extraction procedures followed those outlined by Moore *et al.* (1991). Samples of 2ml volume were decalcified with 10% HCL and deflocculated with 8% KOH. Coarse debris was removed through sieving at 150m and clay by micro-mesh (10m). Remaining silica was digested with 40% hydrofluoric acid. Erdtman's acetolysis was carried out for removal of cellulose. The concentrated pollen and spores were stained with safranin and mounted in glycerol jelly. Pollen was identified and counted with an Olympus biological research microscope with phase contrast facility at magnifications of 400× and 1000×. These extraction techniques were successful and a preliminary pollen diagram has been constructed for the

Species	Context		
	199	202	222
Trees/Shrubs			
Betula	1	-	5
Pinus	1	2	10
Quercus	7	7	11
Alnus	6	2	20
Tilia	-	-	1
Corylus avellana type	2	-	9
Salix	1	-	-
Herbs			
Ranunculus type	-	-	1
Sinapis type	15	3	22
Chenopodium type	-	3	27
Polygonum sp.	-	-	-
Fabaceae indet.	-	-	1
Lotus type	-	-	1
Rosaceae indet.	-	-	1
Rumex	-	-	1
Plantago maritima type	-	-	1
Scrophulariacae	-	-	1
Convolvulaceae	-	-	1
Bidens type	-	-	-
Anthemis type	-	-	1
Aster type	-	1	-
Lactucoideae	43	56	21
Poaceae	23	15	51
Cereal type	-	1	4
Unidentified	-	8	5
Marsh			
cf. Sparganium type	-	-	
Cyperaceae	-	-	5
Spores			
Osmunda regalis	15	8	22
Pteridium aquilinum	3	7	1
Dryopteris type	17	19	94
Polypodium vulgare	-	-	3
Sphagnum	1	1	10
Pre-Quaternary	18	9	15

Table 86: Pollen data for Ditch 7, Lydd 1 (Cut 198), Section 5; Fills 199, 202, 222

ditch section using *Tilia* and *Tilia* Graph. Pollen data is calculated as a percentage of total pollen and spores as a percentage of total pollen plus spores. The pollen taxonomy in general follows that of Moore and Webb (1978), modified according to Bennett *et al.* (1994) for pollen types and Stace (1991) for plant descriptions. These procedures were carried out in the Palaeoecology Laboratory of the Department of Geography, University of Southampton.

The data is presented here in table form for Ditch 7 (Cut 198, Fills 222, 209 and 199) (Table 86 above) and in a standard pollen diagram from Ditch 2011 (Fig. 97 opposite). With the exception of the lower peat in Ditch 2011, which is thought to be of Iron Age to Romano-British date, all other samples are of 12th and 13th century date, and thus provide information on the site and its near regional environment.

Ditch 7; (Cut 198), Section S5; Fills 222, 209 and 199 (See Fig. 23, S5)

Four samples were examined from medieval Ditch 7, which contained identifiable pollen in sufficient quantities to enable pollen counts of between 100 and 200 grains (plus spores) to be made. A total of 31 identifiable taxa was recorded (Table 86). These comprised largely herbs but with trees, shrubs, marsh and spore categories. It is noted, however, that in contexts 199 and 209 pollen was less well preserved and the higher relative values of some taxa, such as the *Lactucoideae* (*Asteraceae*; dandelion type) and monolete spores of *Dryopteris* type, indicate that some differential preservation in favour of types with more robust exines has occurred. Context 222, at the base of the ditch, has better preserved pollen.

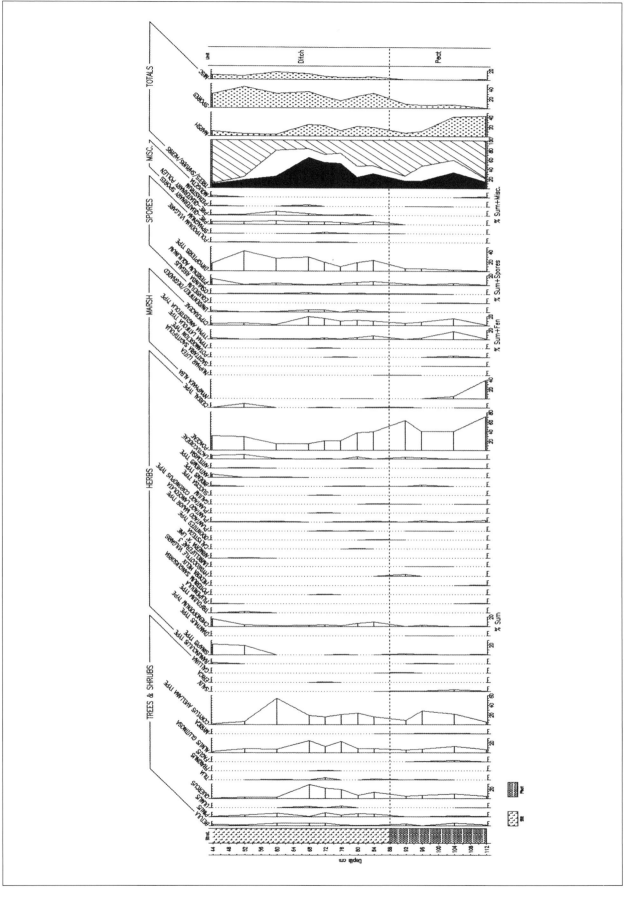

Fig. 97 Pollen Diagram for Ditch 2011 (Lydd 2)

The Inferred Vegetation

Although 'spot' samples cannot provide a temporal perspective, the sequence of samples here span the medieval, late 12th to early/mid 13th century and some interpretations can be made. The lower sample (222) contains slightly higher arboreal pollen values and greater herbs diversity. *Brassicaceae* (*Sinapis* type), *Chenopodiaceae* and *Poaceae* are dominant, but markedly lesser values of *Lactucoideae* than the above two contexts. *Lactucoideae* increase markedly in Contexts 199 and 202 and this may be due to poorer pollen preserving conditions in the upper levels of the ditch fill. This also equates with a reduction in pollen taxonomic diversity. Spores of *Pteridium aquilinum*, *Dryopteris* type and *Polypodium vulgare* are present. Marsh plants include *Cyperaceae*, *Sphagnum* and *Osmunda regalis*.

Overall, an open grassland environment is indicated with a possible salt-marsh or shingle halophytic component represented by the relatively high vales of *Brassicaceae*, *Sinapis* type and *Chenopodiaceae*, although these may also have derived from arable habitats for which there is some minor indication. The sporadic arboreal pollen is likely to be from growth in areas away from the marsh, but which is under-represented because of dominance of the local vegetation in the pollen rain. One of the aims of the study was to examine for evidence of human activity in the pollen record. Obviously the presence of the archaeological features sampled implies local human activity. However, the pollen evidence is less conclusive. Whilst cereal cultivation is tentatively suggested, it is possible that the cereal pollen comes from the wild, possibly halophytic taxa. The pollen spectra do, however, indicate that the region was one of open herbaceous grassland, and it is likely that pastoralism was being practiced. These data are comparable with the upper section of Ditch 11 (see below). From the small number of samples examined it is not possible to analyze the changes in regional woodland.

Ditch 2011 (Fills 2012, 2022, 2042 and underlying natural deposits)

A number of medieval features were cut into earlier, underlying late prehistoric or early historic peat and mineral sediments. The archaeological features include Ditch 2011 (Figs. 16 and 24, S20) and Cut 2098/2219 (Fig. 16); the latter provided the longest stratigraphical sequence available. The two deepest sections were sampled for pollen with, however, only one of the sequences being studied. Ditch 2011 was chosen for pollen analysis because it provided a stratigraphical sequence through the basal grey (?marine clay), *c.* 30cm of late prehistoric fen peat and the overlying ditch/fill feature of 12th to 13th century date. However, it should be recognised that the upper peat layers will have been removed by the digging of the medieval ditch. Sequential pollen samples at 2cm and 4cm intervals were taken directly from the open faces of the archaeological sections. Because of the dryness of

the ground due to the exceptional summer, it was not possible to obtain complete monolith tray sections. A total of 12 sub-samples were examined for their pollen content. These span the lower and highly organic peat which pre-dates the archaeological features and the fills of the ditch.

A total of 55 taxa was recorded from the 12 levels analysed and the results plotted (Fig. 97). Preservation, as expected, was excellent in the lower fen peat (112–88cm) but poor in the minerogenic ditch fills. However, it was possible to obtain preliminary pollen counts of 100 grains excluding definite marsh taxa and spores of ferns, moss spores of *Sphagnum* and derived pre-Quaternary palynomorphs. There are thus two essentially contrasting pollen preserving environments which are characterised as follows:

The lower peat sequence: (112–88cm). Although the peat sequences were not the principle subject of this study, it is useful that they provide some idea of the earlier, on-site environment. Samples were taken vertically down through the ditch profile and into the underlying peat, hence the upper peat levels are not represented in this study. The characteristics of the pollen assemblages, however, confirm the late-prehistoric age suspected for this unit. Pollen content was extremely high with taxa recovered attributable to the local environment of deposition and to pollen influx from the local region. The 'on-site' (autochthonous) pollen component comprises *Typha angustifolia*/*Sparganium* type and *Typha latifolia* (bur reed and reed mace), *Cyperaceae* (sedges) and high basal values of *Nymphaea* (white water lily). Other marsh and aquatic taxa are present in smaller numbers including *Nuphar* (yellow water lily), *Sagittaria* (arrow-head) and *Potamogeton* (pond weed). *Gramineae* (*Poaceae*; grasses) are the dominant herb category and at least some of these may derive from the on-site vegetation. This assemblage of aquatic and fen marsh taxa suggests that the peat was deposited in a shallow water fen with fringing reed swamp. *Alnus* (alder) pollen is present with values to 15%, which is regarded as too low to indicate local alder growth and has been included in the tree pollen category. *Salix* (also represented in the tree/shrub category) is, however, a small pollen producer and may have been present locally on drier areas on, or fringing, the fen.

Non-marsh taxa are dominated by tree and shrub pollen, including *Corylus avellana* type (principally hazel but may also include undifferentiated sweet gale) and *Quercus* (oak). *Betula* (birch) is also consistent. There are sporadic occurrences of *Pinus* (pine; long distant component), *Ulmus* (elm) and *Tilia* (lime) and *Fagus* (beech). The latter taxa are very substantially under-represented in pollen spectra and may thus have formed local tree growth along with oak-hazel woodland. The pollen sum is relatively small and therefore the herbaceous diversity is also restricted. There is, however, evidence of agricultural activity with some cereal pollen present, indicating at least some arable agriculture. The large percentages of *Gramineae* (*Poaceae*) and occurrence of *Plantago lanceolata* (ribwort plantain) also suggest a local pastoral habitat(s).

Dating of this peat has not yet been carried out but the virtual absence of *Tilia* suggests that the peat is of very late prehistoric or, most probably, early historic age; post-dating the lime decline (which generally occurred during the later Bronze Age period) at *c.* 1000 BC. This is further substantiated from stratigraphical pollen work carried out on Romney Marsh which has shown that the final date for peat accumulation was during the Romano-British period (Dr A. Long pers. comm.)

The medieval ditch fills: (88–44cm). Although pollen was present, preservation was generally poorer than the underlying peat, especially at the top of the sequence. This is manifested in the higher percentages/numbers of taxa with robust pollen walls (exines); for example, *Sinapis* type (charlocks), *Taraxacum* type (dandelion types) and fern spores of *Pteridium aquilinum* (bracken) and monolete *Dryopteris* type (typical fern types). However, data have been obtained from which environmental interpretation can be made. *Quercus* (oak), *Alnus* (alder) and *Corylus avellana* (hazel) are the dominant tree types with some *Betula* (birch), *Pinus* (pine of long distance origin) and sporadic *Tilia* (lime) and *Fraxinus* (ash). The relative abundance of these tree and shrub types, and the fact that pollen input into this ditch is likely to be of very local origin (see section 2 above), indicate that woodland was possibly local from regions of the marsh. This would include drier areas where oak, hazel and birch may have been able to grow and may have been managed for coppice, although this cannot be established from the pollen analysis alone. Occasional occurrences of elm and especially lime will have derived from areas outside of the marsh with well drained soils. However, further pollen data are required to confirm this.

The depositional environment of the ditch is unclear and this may affect the pollen taphonomy; whether the fills occurred rapidly and deliberately or through longer periods of natural sedimentation. Definite pollen horizonation in the fills do, however, suggest infilling over a longer period of time. In the ditch pollen spectra, there are consistent levels of *Cyperaceae* (sedges) in the lower fills along with *Typha angustifolia/Sparganium* and *Typha latifolia* and occasional *Potamogeton* type (probably common pond weed) and *Nyphaea alba* (white water lily). These show, perhaps, that the ditch was at least wet and possibly even with standing water. Alder (*Alnus glutinosa*) pollen is present in the lower ditch fill and, whilst the values are not great enough to suggest on or near site fen-carr woodland, it is probable that alder was growing along the banks of rivers/streams and drainage ditches.

There are distinct changes at 60–68cm with a clear reduction in tree and shrub pollen and expansion of herbs in the upper ditch profile. Values of birch (*Betula*),

elm (*Ulmus*), oak (*Quercus*) and possibly lime (*Tilia*) decline. In response, there is a sharp increase in hazel (*Corylus avellana*) and subsequently an expansion of herbs including cereal. Although only a single level of hazel expansion, it might be postulated that reduction in woodland (through clearance?) may have resulted in expansion of hazel scrub. Alternatively, this may have been from the establishment of new fields with hedgerows. This is, however, very tenuous, and additional pollen data is required. It does appear, however, that there was a significant reduction in the remaining early medieval woodland, a fact which is also suggested from the analysis of charcoals (see Seel section (below) which shows similar changes between the 13th and 14th centuries.

Overall, herbs are dominant with *Poaceae* (grasses) most important with only small numbers of arable agricultural types (also described from the underlying peat) including cereal type pollen and possibly *Brassicaceae* (*Sinapis* type). The overall importance of grasses (with ribwort plantain and other taxa) perhaps suggests a largely pasture habitat but with possible cereal cultivation and certainly use of cereals on-site. Of interest in the upper levels (52–44cm) are the relatively high percentages of *Chenopodium* type (goosefoots, oraches, glassworts), *Sinapis* (*Brassica* types) type and a single occurrence of *Armeria* (thrift) which may be indications of nearby marine influences on the vegetation.

The Water-logged Wood and Charcoal
by Sophie Seel with Rowena Gale, Luke Barber and Louise Bashford

Methodology

All charcoal samples were passed through 4mm and 1mm sieves respectively, and bagged ready for analysis. Material passing through the 1mm sieve was considered too small to be of use and therefore dismissed from further analysis but retained for future reference. Following sieving it was apparent that there was more charcoal than was manageable to identify within the time limits, thus the following sub-sampling strategy was employed. From samples with less than 20 charcoal pieces over 4mm all 4mm fragments were analyzed. The majority of samples contained 20+ 4mm fragments, and 20 fragments were randomly handpicked for analysis. In addition, 10 fragments of 1mm size were randomly selected from all samples and analysed in order to reduce the possibility of taphonomic factors determining species visibility. The procedure for charcoal identification was as follows. Each fragment was pressure fractured using a razor blade to provide surfaces in the transverse, radial longitudinal and tangential longitudinal planes, mounted in plasticine on a microscope slide and examined under a bi-focal epi-illuminating microscope at magnifications up to 400×. With regard to the waterlogged wood remains, all wood was analysed due to the relatively small quantity of remains. The wood was sectioned using a razor blade in the above-mentioned three planes and mounted on a microscope slide using distilled water and a cover slip. The sections were then examined under a high power binocular microscope at magnifications up to 400×. Identification to the lowest taxonomic level possible was made according to the anatomical characteristics described in Schweingruber (1990). Occasional reference was made to modern reference charcoal for confirmation of identification. Binominal names are given only where one member of the genus is native to the British flora. Botanical nomenclature follows that of Stace (1991).

1200–1300 (Lydd 2)

The majority of the excavated contexts are clearly the result of human activity, *i.e.*, pits, post-holes and hearths and, as such, should be treated with caution when attempting any environmental reconstruction. Perhaps most useful for any such reconstruction are the ditch features, from which the taxa present are less likely to be the sole result of human activity. Species growing in ditches are, however, likely to differ from those of the vegetation growing in the wider environment. This is clearly attested in the wood assemblages from Lydd where *Alnus glutinosa* (alder) has been found in ditches of 14th century date (see below).

The wood charcoal attributed to the 13th century (largely from the Lydd 2 excavations) represents a relatively diverse assemblage in terms of species (Table 87). Twelve taxa have been identified from this period, which broadly represent both open, mixed deciduous woodland and wetland tree and shrub species. Woodland consisted of structurally differentiated vegetation types depending on ecological factors such as edaphic, topographical and hydrological variation. It is not generally possible to identify such community types from a charcoal assemblage. However, the location of Lydd on Romney marsh indicates that such vegetation differentiation would have been locally important. The wood from sites excavated to date do appear to indicate the existence of both wetland vegetation local to the site, and the presence of species of drier land which were possibly growing at some distance from the site itself.

The most abundant taxon for this period (from Lydd 2) is *Quercus* sp. Although both native British oaks are indistinguishable anatomically, the preference of *Quercus robur* (pendunculate oak) for the heavier clay soils of southern Britain (Godwin 1975) suggests that this species, rather than *Q. petraea* (sessile oak), is represented in the Lydd charcoal. The complex taphonomic factors involved in charcoal formation and preservation urge caution in assuming a direct relationship between fragment numbers and species abundance in the palaeo-environment. However, the ecological preferences of all the species represented in the

Lydd 2 assemblage, combined with the types of medieval woodland management evidenced in documentary sources, suggests that the abundance of *Quercus* here represents a real dominance in the environment both on and around the marsh. By 1350 pressure on the English woodlands had reached a maximum, and the majority of medieval woodlands were managed (Rackham 1993). The dominance of *Quercus* therefore, does not indicate undisturbed, mature woodland at Lydd, but is more likely to have derived from a managed habitat.

Second in abundance in the assemblage is *Corylus avellana* (hazel) suggesting the possible existence of coppice-with-standards in managed woodland possibly near to the site. Oak-hazel copse was a favoured combination in the medieval landscape and it appears likely that at least some of the charcoal derived from this type of woodland environment.

Fagus sylvatica (beech) and *Carpinus betulus* (hornbeam) are present and indicate the existence of dryland species near the site. *Fagus* requires well-drained soils and would almost certainly not have been growing on the water-logged soils of the marsh. In addition, Beech (*Fagus*) is a shade-bearing tree, under which many of the above species do not grow in association. Although *Carpinus* tolerates deep, moist soils it will also not tolerate water-logging (Christy 1924) and the two species, therefore, indicate exploitation of off-site woodland from areas with well-drained soils. However, *Carpinus* and *Fagus* do not grow in woodland together and probably formed two distinct vegetation types. *Fagus* may have formed almost pure stands, around the margins of which the more light-demanding species such as *Prunus*, *Corylus* and *Betula* may have grown. The *Carpinus* could have derived from a *Quercus-Carpinus* copse off-site, or from relatively open, mixed woodland in which *Quercus*, *Ulmus* (elm), *Corylus* and *Prunus* would have flourished.

The heavily cultivated nature of the English landscape during the medieval period resulted in much of the land being divided up through hedging. Many of the species identified from this period (12th to 13th century) will grow in hedges which, during this period, were coppiced and exploited for timber. It is possible that all the species above, apart from *Fagus*, may have constituted hedge vegetation. *Carpinus* is a common component of hedges in association with *Quercus*, *Prunus* and the *Maloideae* (*e.g.*, hawthorn). Given the plant macro-fossil assessment for this phase indicating field conditions, the presence of hedge vegetation near the site is highly probable.

Aside from the existence of dryland, and possibly managed woodland, the charcoal assemblages also demonstrate the existence of wetland vegetation growing local to the site and on the Marsh itself. The presence of *Betula* (birch), and *Salicaceae* (willows and poplars) are likely to be part of the drier fen vegetation on the Marsh. Often common on such drier areas of fen are *Quercus robur*, *Corylus avellana* and *Prunus* sp. (blackthorn and/or wild cherry) and at least some of the above trees from which the Lydd 2 charcoal of this period may have been gathered from the wetland vegetation local to the site. The absence of *Alnus* charcoal is surprising for this period in the assemblage (although not in later ones; *e.g.*, Context 2027) given the marsh environment of the area. *Alnus* is normally ubiquitous in such areas and its scarcity suggests that it was not growing in pure stands at the site itself. Pure *Alnus* stands may have grown on the wetter areas of the marsh, with individual alder trees colonising the ditch areas of the site some distance from the parent population. The pollen data (Scaife above) similarly suggest that carr woodland was not prevalent at this time.

With regards to wood species selection and utilisation, the ambiguous function of pit features is problematic and probably varied spatially and temporally across the site(s). The two post-holes from this period (Contexts 2251 and 2199) yielded charcoal which is overwhelmingly weighted towards *Quercus*. This clearly suggests the selection of this species for structural purposes. Apart from this example, most species are fairly well distributed throughout contexts, with the exception of wetland species dominating the ditch features. Little may therefore be said of species selection during this period.

In general the assemblage for the 13th century represents the wetland species growing on the marsh itself and their human exploitation. Also indicated is the character and exploitation of woodland further afield, as demonstrated by species which are intolerant of the waterlogged conditions of the Marsh.

1300 to 1500 (Lydd 3)

The 14th to 15th century is represented largely by the charcoal and waterlogged assemblages from the Lydd 3 excavations (see Table 88 overleaf). The small quantity of 15th century charcoal from the Lydd 5/6 excavations is of little use in that most that was identifiable to species was of oak. Overall, the wood material from Lydd 3 shows a slight shift in species representation to those of the 13th century. *Quercus* remained the dominant taxa in terms of fragment abundance, and undoubtedly still formed an important component of the utilised woodland. Interestingly, however, hazel (*Corylus avellana*) disappears from the assemblage to be replaced by *Acer campestre* (Field maple) as the second most abundant taxon represented. Also present (although in small quantities) is *Fraxinus excelsior* (ash). In general, there is an increase of the more light-demanding species in this phase. In particular, *Prunus* spp. (blackthorn and/or wild cherry) and *Acer* require light for establishment and growth and will flourish given such conditions. This may indicate the regeneration of previously cleared land on the drier areas of the site resulting in an increase of the light-demanding/pioneer species. Alternatively, the species favoured for coppice may have shifted

from *Corylus* to *Acer*. *Acer* coppices well and was a component of medieval woodlands along with *Fraxinus* and *Quercus*.

Perhaps most interesting from this period is the absence of *Carpinus* and greatly decreased values of *Fagus* in comparison to the 13th century assemblage. Since it is suggested that these species may represent the exploitation of areas off the marsh, their absence from this phase possibly indicates the cessation of off-site woodland exploitation. Interestingly, the dates from most of the contexts in this phase fall around those for the Black Death of 1348, and the enormous effect this event had on socio-economic organisation may in part explain the absence of off-site flora. If the occupants were less able or prepared to travel afar for wood resources, this would explain the absence of hornbeam and beech in the charcoal record for this and the later phases. Alternatively, their absence may indicate a real change in the environment, in which conditions were getting wetter, thus creating intolerable conditions for dryland species. The dates do in fact also coincide with those for the Little Ice Age which may have increased groundwater, rendering conditions unfavourable for these species. The nature and effects of this cooler period have not, however, been established and the absence of two species from a relatively small charcoal assemblage cannot be used with any certainty as evidence for climatic deterioration. Indeed, the apparent shift in species presence or absence during this phase may well be a product of taphonomic distortions rather than indicative of a real change in the palaeo-environment and/or human exploitation of that environment. Additionally, the charcoal record for this phase is smaller than that for the previous period, a fact which may in itself explain the apparent disappearance of these species from the palaeo-environment.

The presence of *Alnus glutinosa* (alder in Ditches 2026 (a waterlogged piece only), 3150 and Pit 3088) and *Salicaceae* (willow in various contexts) from this period demonstrate the existence of woodland vegetation on drier areas of the marsh and along the ditches as discussed above for the earlier period.

Overall, the charcoal from the 14th to early 15th centuries represents open woodland with pioneer species of regeneration present such as *Fraxinus* and *Acer*. It is possible that previously cleared and cultivated land had become largely neglected during the Black Death. This may have resulted in the secondary regeneration of certain species. Alternatively, coppicing regimes may have changed, shifting from a preference of hazel (*Corylus*) to one of oak-ash-field maple (*Quercus-Fraxinus-Acer*) coppice. Evidence of wetland flora is still documented from the ditch contexts with willow and incoming alder. There are indications that human exploitation of the vegetation was more local during this phase and all the species identified would have been found growing local to the site itself.

Context	2103	2105	2107	2113	2133	2199	2251	2220	2304	2313	2315	2335	2358	2367	3057	3217
Feature	2102	2104	2106	2112	2132	2198	2198	2219	21206	2104	2140	2336	2194	2106	(Cut 3056)	3088
Description	Pit	Pit	Pit	Pit	Ditch	Pit/PH	Pit/PH	Ditch	Pit	Hearth	Pit	Ditch	Ditch	Pit	Pit	Pit
Date/Period	1200–1275	1200–1300	1275–1300	1200–1275	1225–1300	1200–1275	1200–1275	1200–1274	1200–1275	1200–1300	1200–1300	1200–1275	1200–1300	1200–1275	1200–1300	1225–1325
Site (Lydd)	2	2	2	2	2	2	2	2	2	2	2	2	2	2	3	3
Ulmus sp.														2		
Fagus sylvatica		13	2					6	2			1	1	1		4
Quercus sp.	16	1	13	15	21	17	5	2	8	9	12	19	18	8		4
Betula sp.	8	2								1			5			
Alnus glutinosa														13		
Carpinus betulus		1		15												
Corylus avellana	4	3				5		1	5	7	4					
Salicaceae			4										1			2
Prunus sp.		1	8								2	3				
Maloideae											3					
Acer campestre															9	
Unidentified	2	1	3		3	6		17	11	6	9	7	4	5	13	2
Total	30	22	30	30	30	28	5	26	26	23	30	30	30	30	22	12

Table 87: (Charcoal) 13th century contexts from Lydd Quarry

Context	3336	3341	3349	3350	3259	3330	3089	3105	3111	3117	3151	3237
Feature	3074	3200	3348	3348	3074	3200	3088	3104	3110	3116	3150	3088
Description	Pit	Ditch	Pit	Pit	Pit	Ditch	Pit	Pit	Post Hole	Fill	Ditch	Pit
Date/Period	1350–1450	1250–1325	1375–1475	1375–1475	1350–1450	1325–1425	1250–1350	1350–1450	1350–1450	1300–1400	1425–1525	1350–1450
Site (Lydd)	3	3	3	3	3	3	3	3	3	3	3	3
Ulmus sp.			2	1								
Fagus sylvatica											1	4
Quercus sp.	5	1	5	2	1		1	12	3	4	20	4
Betula sp.											4	
Alnus glutinosa											4	9
Fraxinus Excelsior						1						1
Salicaceae		1			1				1			2
Prunus sp.												7
Maloideae												
Acer campestre									1		1	4
Unidentified									1			1
Total	5	2	7	3	2	1	1	12	7	4	30	30

Table 88: (Charcoal) 14th to 15th century contexts from Lydd Quarry

Context No.	Feature	Date	Timber No.	Species	Description
3336	Pit 3074 Primary fill	1350–1450	A	*Quercus* sp. ×2 (oak)	Plank fragments, one which has a dowel hole and tooling marks from adze?
3336	Pit 3074 Primary fill	1350–1450	3	*Quercus* sp. ×1	No sign of working
3336	Pit 3074 Primary fill	1350–1450	5	*Quercus* sp. ×1	No sign of working
3336	Pit 3074 Primary fill	1350–1450	6	*Quercus* sp. ×1	No sign of working
3341	Ditch 3200 Primary fill	1250–1325	7	*Salicaccae* ×1 (willow)	Wooden stake
3341	Ditch 3200 Primary fill	1250–1325	8	*Quercus* sp. ×1	Wooden radially split stake
3349	Sump 3348 Above 3350	1375–1475	9	*Quercus* sp. ×1	Plank with mortise
3349	Sump 3348 Above 3350	1375–1475	10	*Quercus* sp. ×1	Stake
3349	Sump 3348 Above 3350	1375–1475	11	*Quercus* sp. ×1	Circular-sectioned pole
3349	Sump 3348 Above 3350	1375–1475	12	*Ulmus* sp. ×1 (elm)	No sign of working
3349	Sump 3348 Above 3350	1375–1475	-	*Quercus* sp. ×2 *Ulmus* sp. ×1	No sign of working
3259	Pit 3074 Above 3336	1350–1450	-	*Quercus* sp. ×2 *Salicaccae* ×1 *Alnus* ×1 (alder)	*Quercus*: stake *Alnus*: fragments from a lathe-turned bowl
3330	Ditch 3200 Above 3341	1325–1425	-	*Salicaccae* ×1	No signs of working
3350	Sump 3348 Below 3349	1375–1475	-	*Quercus* sp. ×2 *Ulmus* sp. ×1	No sign of working

Table 89: Summary of Waterlogged Wood (Lydd 3: Site Jb – 14th to 15th century)

The Wooden Artefacts and Wood Utilisation (Lydd 3 and 5/6) from the Period AD1400–1600

Although a small quantity of waterlogged wood was recovered from the excavations at Lydd 3 (Site Jb) the majority of it did not exhibit clear signs of working. However, the assemblage, which is primarily of mid 14th to 15th century date, included part of a wooden bowl (Fig. 98, No. 1), some planks and a few stakes (Table 89 above). The majority of the evidence for woodworking comes from the Lydd 5/6 excavations. These provided a moderate sized assemblage, predominantly of the 15th to early/mid 16th centuries. Wood demonstrating evidence of human working was recovered from nine waterlogged contexts (Contexts 5124, 5129, 5138, 5291, 5292, 5329, 5330, 5367, 5376). All of these contexts derive from only five features; Ditches 5007, 5025 and 5137, and Pits 5286 and 5366. Pit 5286 contained the remains of a barrel and a wooden bowl (Fig. 98, No. 2), and Pit 5366 was lined with wooden planks *in situ*. The material is summarised in Table 90 overleaf.

Palaeoenvironmental reconstruction for this period from such selected woods is not feasible, although information can be gained on species selection for industrial purposes. Only five taxa were identified from this period, all of which are indicative of wetland and open woodland. The restricted species diversity is most likely to be a product of small sample size, rather than indicative of an environmental change. Unfortunately, two samples from contexts 5369 and 5370 provided no identifiable wood due to its uncharred and/or dried-out waterlogged status. Given this small database, little more can be inferred but that wetland species such as *Alnus* and *Salicaceae* with the associated *Fraxinus* and *Corylus* were apparently still available for exploitation at the site. As in previous phases they probably formed the local vegetation of the area, and it is this local resource use that appears apparent in the Lydd 5/6 assemblage.

Despite the minimal palaeoenvironmental data available from this period, there is evidence for species selection in the form of the worked wood. The qualities of oak for structural timbers are well known and the majority of planks and barrel staves (from the Lydd 5/6 excavations) are constructed from this wood. Where usage required flexibility, *i.e.*, withy and the barrel hoops, the supple wood of *Fraxinus* appears to have been selected. As in earlier phases, it is possible that the wood for these

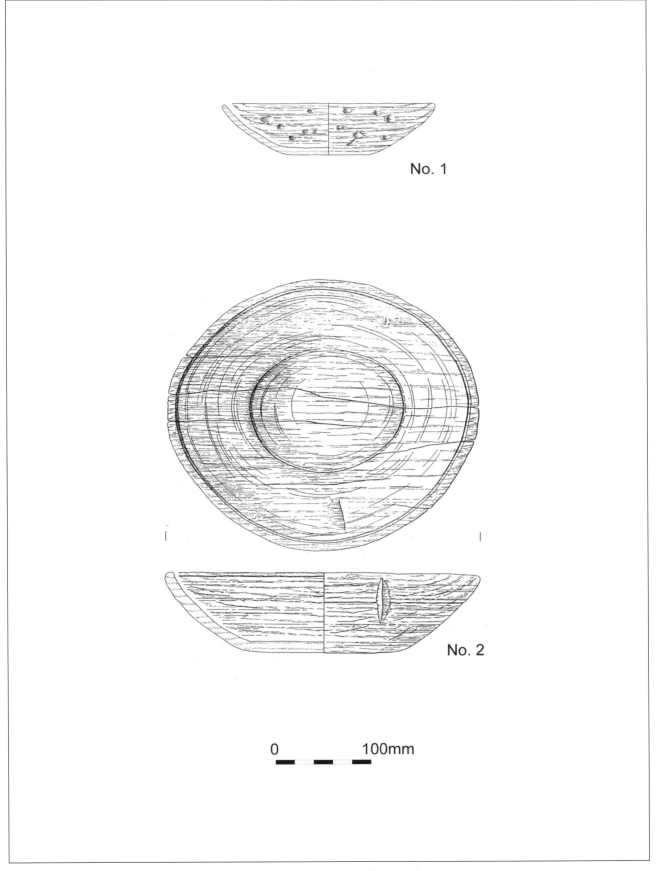

No. 1

No. 2

0   100mm

Fig. 98 Lydd Quarry: wooden artefacts

Context No.	Feature	Date	Timber No.	Species	Description
5124	Sump in Ditch 5007	1425–1525?	3	*Fraxinus excelsior* ×3 (ash)	Nine roundwood withies and a circular piece (×3 sampled)
5123	Sump in Ditch 5007	1425–1525	2	*Fraxinus excelsior* ×3 *Salicaccae* ×1 (willow)	Twigs and timber (unworked)
5026	Ditch 5025	1375–1475	1	*Quercus* sp.	Irregular (unworked)
5129	Ditch 5025	1375–1475?	12	*Corylus avellna* ×4 (hazel) *Quercus* sp. ×1 (oak)	Five stakes. One radially split with triangular section and surviving bark. Point trimmed. Adze/axe marks. Four roundwood with bark (diameters 23–58mm) and points sharpened by cutting two or three faces with axe. Max. surviving length 380mm.
5138	Ditch 5137	1680–1720	4	*Quercus* sp.	Radially split plank with scoop on one side. Adze marks.
5292	Pit 5286 (barrel-lined)	1475–1525	5	*Alnus* (alder)	Lathe-turned wooden bowl in three pieces.
5292	Pit 5286	1475–1525	6	Unidentified	Pieces of bark associated with Timber 7.
5292	Pit 5286	1475–1525	7	*Fraxinus excelsior*	×40 pieces of split roundwood withies from barrel. 25 × 12mm in section X8 with 3mm diameter nail holes (one with 15mm diameter iron stain from nail head).
5292	Pit 5286	1475–1525	8	Unidentified	Twisted wood/twine associated with barrel.
5292	Pit 5286	1475–1525	10	*Corylus avellna* ×3	Twigs/stems with 8mm diameter and bark surviving (unworked). Max. 220mm long.
5291	Pit 5286	1450–1500?	9	*Quercus* sp.	Barrel staves ×22. Split. Nail holes at end of three, one with withie impressions. 105–115mm wide, 8mm thick. Surviving lengths up to 340mm.
5329	Pit 5286	1450–1500?	16	*Fraxinus excelsior*	Outer hoop of barrel (in 21 fragments, 2 of which have nail holes at T13).
5330	Pit 5286	1450–1500?	13	*Fraxinus excelsior*	Inner hoop of barrel. Evidence of three nail holes. D-sectioned.
5367	Pit 5366 (plank-lined)	timber 1450–1500 but deposited C18th?	15	*Quercus* sp.	Plank with 4mm diameter nail hole at one end (surviving plank dimensions 195 × 98mm) and split piece of roundwood with no bark.
5376	Pit 5366	1450–1500	11	*Quercus* sp.	65mm thick sawn plank fragment (up to 910mm surviving) with 4 dowel holes (dowel hole diameters 30–38mm), one still containing dowel.
5376	Pit 5366	1450–1500	11 and 14	*Quercus* sp.	Dowels from structure. T14 complete: cylindrical measuring 64mm long × 28mm in diameter.

Table 90: Summary of Waterlogged Wood (Lydd 5/6: various – 15th to 18th centuries)

artefacts derived from a managed woodland, consisting of *Quercus*, *Fraxinus* and *Corylus* copse. Alternatively, all the timber could have been collected from the relatively marshy vegetation growing local to the site itself. This, however, remains unclear.

The wooden items have been worked using a variety of carpentry methods, including lathe-turning, splitting, sawing, and drilling, with some of the wood showing signs of having been nailed together to form vessels

or structures. Several of the timbers were sharpened to form stakes, but the majority of the timbers found were associated with the barrel in Pit 5286 and the plank-lined pit (5366). The lack of mortises and rebates leads to the conclusion that none of the timbers recovered were re-used from a building or other structure. The wooden bowl from Pit 5286 (Context 5292) is a simple lathe-turned vessel (Fig. 98, No. 2). There are two gouges out of the wall of the bowl, one internally and one externally.

These appear to have been deliberately cut with a blade, probably a small axe. It is possible they were intended to help grip the bowl when it was full.

The Changing Medieval Habitat

Throughout the phases of occupation at Lydd, two major vegetation types are indicated, although broad gradations between these types is to be expected. The presence of *Alnus*, *Betula* and *Salicaceae* indicate the classic arboreal vegetation of wetland marsh areas. Also to be expected within the drier areas of this woodland are the trees and shrubs *Corylus*, *Fraxinus*, *Quercus*, *Ulmus* and *Prunus* spp. It appears that *Quercus* was the dominant species throughout occupation, probably due to both its ability to grow on deep fen peat and in open, mixed woodland, and its selection within the medieval landscape for copse-with-standards. The presence of all the above species indicate exploitation of the local vegetation for fuel-wood and structural purposes. Oak (*Quercus*) and hazel (*Corylus avellana*) wood and charcoal and the pollen of these taxa suggest that documentary evidence (Rackham 1993) for managed woodland in the medieval age is correct for this region. This especially attested for the period 1200 to 1300 from charcoal from the pits and ditches excavated at Lydd 2 (Site H).

The presence of both *Fagus* and *Carpinus* suggest the exploitation of woodland off the marsh. *Fagus* may have grown in almost pure stands with *Carpinus*, *Quercus*, *Corylus*, *Acer*, *Fraxinus* and *Prunus* growing at the woodland edges where the heavy shade of *Fagus* was reduced. The absence of the two dryland species at Lydd 3 may indicate restricted exploitation ranges, possibly due to the effects of the Black Death on the population. Certainly with the disappearance of these shade-bearing trees, an increase in light-demanding species is evidenced, suggesting secondary regeneration of previously cleared areas. Also important, when considering the types of woodland outside the wetland vegetation, is the presence of a managed landscape. This would greatly effect the structure and composition of trees available in the area and almost certainly any woodland off the marsh would have been exposed to management practices. This may well explain the presence/abundance of species recovered from Lydd, many of which are classic components of copse. The evidence for species selection of *Quercus* and *Fraxinus* indicates a knowledge of timber properties and it is difficult to conceive of this knowledge not being present in conjunction with relatively sophisticated management practices.

Furthermore, the managed landscape evident during the medieval age also provided many plant refuges such as hedges. The majority of the species recovered from Lydd are common to hedge flora and will not necessarily be found in woodland. Since both the pollen and macrofossil evidence from Lydd suggest the existence of agricultural practices, it is likely that hedges were a feature of the local landscape. Many of the dryland species found at Lydd may well have been cut from hedged vegetation rather than woodland.

The character of the wetland marsh vegetation has been seen from two sources. Wood of alder (*Alnus glutinosa*) and charcoal of *Salicaceae* (willow but possibly include poplar) and possibly birch (*Betula*) may indicate fen woodland vegetation. However, pollen data suggest that at least in some local areas, alder carr woodland was not a dominant constituent; it is more likely that trees were growing along the edges of drainage ditches and river banks. Areas of drier fen woodland have been suggested from the charcoal analysis and it is likely that this is the case, although taphonomic problems of both pollen and wood/charcoal makes this difficult to prove. Both the pollen and the wood used in domestic contexts such as the oak for posts (as in Post-hole 2198) may have been transported from drier areas of woodland marginal to the marsh.

Both the pollen and wood/charcoal analyses are commensurate in showing a range of other less well represented tree taxa. This under-representation results from the poor pollen representation, less overall growth/ abundance in the landscape and differential selection of timber/wood for domestic uses. Thus, we see evidence of beech and ash and possibly evidence of hedgerows with hornbeam, *Prunus* and *Maloides* (*e.g.*, hawthorn) being typical. As with all such records, arguments remain tenuous since it is again not possible to differentiate whether pollen and wood of these taxa come from woodland/copses or from established hedgerows.

Conclusions

Lydd is interesting for its clear evidence of both wetland and dryland woodland exploitation. The study has proven that pollen is present in the ditch contexts and has provided some of the first data pertaining to the historic period. Generally, the very local wetland vegetation appears to have been exploited at the site. However, there is some evidence for exploitation of resources off the Marsh. The pollen and charcoal/wood studies presented here demonstrate some conformity, suggesting the presence of oak and hazel in the landscape which was most probably managed woodland. A moderate range of other tree and shrub taxa have also been recorded which derive from the marsh and areas outside of the wetland zone, which may indicate the presence of hedgerows and woodland copses. These are evidenced by their pollen production and dispersal, and from their selected use by the human communities occupying the Lydd settlement.

It has been assumed that these drainage ditches silted up through time and thus the pollen was contemporaneous with the occupation of the site. In fact, both the pollen and wood analyses seem to show a phase of woodland clearance and possible extension of agriculture from the 14th century. The work on this period of medieval occupation is, however, at an early stage. If further work were to be undertaken, more detailed pollen counts from a range of different features and contexts would be desirable to elucidate in more detail the character of the vegetation communities which were growing on and near the site. Clearly any additional excavations would also provide further quantities of charred and water-logged wood and seeds, the study of which would increase our knowledge of the medieval environment, agricultural practices and species utilisation.

PLANT MACROFOSSILS
by Pat Hinton

Methods

Soil samples were processed by the excavators; those from the first phase by wet-sieving but all subsequently by on-site flotation, and the floated results passed to the writer as 'flots'. The exception was from Context 2220, which was processed by the writer by bucket flotation and repeated washing over. For all but the samples from the first phase minimum sieve mesh was 0.5mm Charred material was dried but waterlogged material was kept wet.

Preliminary sorting and most identification was by binocular zoom microscope at (usually) 7× to 40× magnification, but for some species, *e.g.*, sedges, 160× magnification with compound microscope was used for surface details. Identification was aided by reference to standard publications and modern comparative material. Smaller samples were searched in entirety, but in several cases very large amounts of charred material were sub-sampled and totals of the most numerous seeds estimated. The remaining fractions of these samples were scanned to check for any additional species.

The majority of the preserved plant parts are seeds, and this term is used loosely to include caryopses, achenes, fruits, *etc.*, unless noted otherwise. Vernacular names are used in the text with scientific names given only at first mention. The majority of seeds may be identified to generic level but many, particularly when preservation is imperfect, cannot be securely identified to species. Uncertain identifications are recorded as 'cf'. Nomenclature and order of wild plants in the tables accords with Stace 1997.

For wheat the naming system agreed at a specialists' workshop (Hillman *et al.*, 1996) is followed. All those in these samples appear to be free-threshing wheats and the great majority of grains show typical features of hexaploid species and all are recorded as *Triticum aestivum* L. group. Any possibility of other species is noted when applicable. All samples include indeterminate fragmented cereals.

All larger amounts of barley grains include some of the axially askew grains which indicate a 6-row variety (*Hordeum vulgare* L.) but the 2-row variety (*Hordeum distichon* L.) now more commonly cultivated, cannot be excluded. Only rarely are there any rachis parts sufficiently intact to be helpful and, although morphologically distinct, Stace (1997) suggests both should be amalgamated as con-varieties of *Hordeum vulgare* L.

Cultivated and wild species of oats cannot be differentiated in the absence of diagnostic chaff parts and these are therefore listed as *Avena* sp. For both barley and oats further details are described where necessary.

Of the cultivated species of leguminous plants, small broad or field beans (*Vicia faba*) are readily identifiable, given reasonable preservation, by the size, more or less oblong shape and the position of the hilum. The globose seeds of peas (*Pisum sativum*) and vetches (*Vicia sativa*) are more difficult to distinguish. When in good condition the characteristic oval hilum of peas and the linear or wedge-shaped hilum of vetches are definitive, but in the majority of cases the seeds have lost the testa, many have split into two cotyledons or smaller fragments and the hilum cannot be discerned.

In the condition in which the seeds are commonly found it is almost impossible to distinguish cultivated common vetch (*V. sativa* ssp. *sativa*) from the native *V. sativa* ssp. nigra) from which it was derived. The hilum of the cultivated species is slightly longer and as the legume (pod) contains more seeds they can sometimes appear slightly compressed, but the effects of charring may disguise this. All are therefore listed as *V. sativa* s.l. Other vetches and vetchlings are plants of grassy or other open places, including arable, and these are recorded as *Vicia/Lathyrus* spp. The small hairy and smooth tares (*Vicia hirsuta* and *V. tetrasperma*) were troublesome weeds but were also reaped for fodder or ploughed in for their soil-enhancing properties. All legumes are therefore grouped together in the tables.

Results

Almost all seeds were preserved by charring and whether used for human or animal consumption indicate human intervention. Seeds preserved by the anoxia of waterlogged conditions are valuable as illustrations of surrounding vegetation and some may reflect human usage. Other uncharred seeds, when found in dry deposits, are questionable; their usually partially degraded condition suggests they are not recent contaminants and it is likely that in appropriate surroundings survival for a few centuries is possible. Means of preservation are shown in the tables of results.

The results are presented in chronological order with cereals described first, followed by legumes and other cultivated plants.

Site		Caldicott Farm, Lydd			Lydd Quarry
Date/Period		11th–12th century	12th century		1125–1225
Feature		Ditch CFL 8			Ditch 1
Context		CFL 9	CFL 86	CFL 46	287
Sample volume (litres)		6	5	5	6
Cereals					
Triticum aestivum group	bread wheat	2	2	109	37
Secale cereale L.	rye				2(1)
Hordeum vulgare L.	hulled barley	2		1	52
Avena sp.	oats	1(1)	1	1	9
Avena/Bromus sp.	oats or brome				6
Cerealia indet.– grains & frags. (ml.)	indeterminate cereals	<0.5	<0.5	1.0	0.5
Legumes					
Vicia sativa s.l.	common vetch	1			
Vicia/Lathyrus sp.	vetch or vetchling	1	>3	c.8	
Plants of arable, ruderal or grassland					
Persicaria lapathifolia (L.) Gray	pale persicaria	1			
Polygonum arenastrum/aviculare	knotgrass				1
Festuca sp.	fescues				1
Plants of damp or wet-land					
Eleocharis palustris/uniglumis	common or slender spike-rush			1	
Schoenoplectus lacustris (L.) Palla	common club-rush			1	
Carex sp.	sedge			1	
Plants of wood, hedge or scrub					
Corylus avellana L.	hazel				1
Unidentified seeds				2	

Table 91: 12th to early 13th century contexts (Key: ( ) = uncertain)

12th to early 13th Century (Table 91)

The earliest charred cereal remains from the medieval occupation of the Quarry site came from one sample from Ditch 1 (Contexts 287), which dated between 1125 and 1225. It contained grains of wheat, barley and oats, and one also included rye.

All the wheat grains are identified as free-threshing species, loosely referred to as bread wheat (*Triticum aestivum* group), but the sample also contains a few shorter (less than *c.* 4.0mm) blunt-ended plump grains. These are comparable to the grains of a compact variety of wheat with shorter rachis internodes. Barley appears to slightly outnumber wheat, but oats occur only in small numbers. Almost no wild plant seeds were recovered from this early sample.

Late 12th to early 13th Century (Tables 92a, 92b, 92c)

Slightly later (1175–1250), in a post-hole in Lydd 2 (Context 2355) and a pit fill in Lydd 10 (Context A64) were the same cereals, beans and common vetch. The two vetch seeds (Context 2355) are small (<3.0mm) and may have been the native ssp. *nigra*, a plant of grassland,

Feature	Post-hole	Pit 2102	Pit 2104		Pit 2106			Pit 2112	Pit 2140		Pit 2170
Date/Period	1175–1250	1200–1275	1200–1275/1300					1200–1275	1200–1300		1200–1275
Context	2355	2103	2105	2313	2107	2304	2367	2113	2141	2315	2177
Sample volume (litres)	11	30	30	30	30	30	30	30	30	30	20
Cereals											
Triticum aestivum group — bread wheat grains	18	66	63	58	46	31	19	42	24	50	123
bread wheat rachis frags.									1		
Secale cereale L. — rye		2		1		(1)					5(4)
Hordeum cf. *vulgare* — hulled barley grains	60	95	76	104	42	28	45	108	44	41	253
hulled barley rachis frags.								(1)	3		
Avena sp. — oat	4	79	25	37	59	45	20	122	80	101	159
Cerealia indet. — indeterminate cereal grains and frags. (vol. ml.)	1.5	2.5	2.0	1.5	1.5	0.5	1.5	1.5	1.5	2.0	25
Legumes											
Pisum sativum L. — pea			(1)			1	1			3	
cf. *Lens culinaris* L. — lentil										1	
Vicia faba L. — broad bean	1	5	2	3(1)	2	1	1	2	1		
Vicia sativa s.l. — common vetch	2	1	1	5(3)	5	15	4	1(1)	5	4(2)	1
V. hirsuta (L.) Gray — hairy tare			1		1	11	4			18	3
V. tetrasperma (L.) Schreb. — smooth tare		4	4						6	1	
V. hirsuta/tetrasperma — hairy or smooth tare		3	3	1(1)	1(3)		1	5	6	5	5
Vicia/Lathyrus sp. — vetch or vetchling			4		18						9
Medicago lupulina L. — black medick		1	3		12	10	2	4	1		
Trifolium repens L. — white clover		10		1		6		9	3	7	
T. pratense L. — red clover		3		2		6	3	2	3	2	2
Trifolium sp. — indeterminate clover		15	5		11(5)	4	8	5	3	34	6
Fibre Plant											
Linum usitatissimum L. — flax/linseed		1	1(2)								
Plants of arable, ruderal or grassland											
Ranunculus acris/repens/bulbosus — meadow, creeping or bulbous buttercup		2(1)		1	2		1		4	5	
Papaver rhoeas/dubium — common or long-headed poppy		1									
Fumaria sp. — fumitory						1					
Urtica dioica L. — common nettle		1	1								
Chenopodium cf. *polyspermum/rubrum* — small-seeded goosefoot		15	6			3		23	7	7	22
Chenopodium album L. — fat-hen		4			1(1)	5	2(2)	24	4	3	25
Atriplex prostrata/patula — spear-leaved or common orache	2			2	2	6	6	14	8	15	10

Stellaria media/neglecta	common or greater chickweed	3		2	1		5	9		1
Stellaria graminea L.	lesser stitchwort			1		2	2			
Cerastium cf. *fontanum*	common mouse-ear	1		1						1
Persicaria maculosa Gray	redshank				4	2			4	
Persicaria lapathifolia (L.) Gray	pale persicaria	4(4)		1(1)	1	1		2	4	5
Polygonum arenastrum/aviculare	knotgrass	2	1			1	2	1	2	
cf. *Fallopia convolvulus*	black bindweed			1						
Rumex acetosella L.	sheep's sorrel		1			1			2	1
Rumex sp.	dock	7	1	4(2)	2	2	32	5	3	5
Brassica sp.	cabbage, turnip, rape, *etc.*		1	2				3	2	1
Raphanus raphanistrum	wild radish pod sections		1	1	2	1			1	2
Solanum nigrum L.	black nightshade			2	1					
Lamium cf. *purpureum*	red dead-nettle		1							
Plantago lanceolata L.	ribwort plantain								1	1
Euphrasia/Odontites	eyebright or bartsia	2		1			2	3	3	5
Galium aparine L.	cleavers	1		1						1
Cirsium arvense (L.) Scop.	creeping thistle		1							
Anthemis cotula L.	stinking chamomile	26	1	41	12	16	77	36	52	32
Tripleurospermum inodorum L. Schultz. Bip	scentless mayweed		5	1	2		3	3	3	6
Asteraceae	daisy family seed / daisy family capitula	2		2			1	2	2	2
Lolium sp.	rye-grasses					1	1			1
Festuca sp.	fescues	2	1			3		7		2
Lolium/Festuca	rye-grass or fescue						3			
Cynosurus cristatus L.	crested dog's tail	1								
Poa annua L.	annual meadow-grass	5		5(10)	2	3	1	5	10	3
Alopecurus/Phleum	foxtail or cat's tail				2			2	3	
Bromus cf. *secalinus.*	rye-brome	7	14	10	6(1)	5	5	9(4)	4	4
Danthonia decumbens (L.) DC	heath-grass			3(1)						1
Molinia caerulea (L.) Moench	purple moor-grass							2		
Poaceae indet.	unidentified grasses	31	10	6	10	5	2	22		8

Table 92a: Late 12th to 13th century contexts
Key: ( ) = identification uncertain " = uncharred

Continued on page 256

		Post-hole	Pit 2102	Pit 2104		Pit 2106			Pit 2112	Pit 2140		Pit 2170
Feature				1200–1275/1300								
Date/Period		1175–1250	1200–1275						1200–1275	1200–1300		1200–1275
Context		2355	2103	2105	2313	2107	2304	2367	2113	2141	2315	2177
Sample volume (litres)		11	30	30	30	30	30	30	30	30	30	20
Plants of damp or wet ground												
Ranunculus flammula L.	lesser spearwort		1						1			1
Lychnis flos-cuculi L.	ragged robin						1					
Pedicularis palustris L.	marsh lousewort					1						
Eleocharis palustris/uniglumis	common or slender spike-rush		6			1	2	2	20	4	21	30
Bolboschoenus maritimus (L.) Palla	sea club-rush											3
Schoenoplectus lacustris (L.) Palla	common club-rush		2			3			2	1(1)	2	6(2)
Carex otrubae	false fox-sedge				1				1			
C. cf. acutiformis	lesser pond-sedge	1				3			24			2
C. pseudocyperus	cyperus sedge								6			
C. nigra	common sedge							1	1			
Carex sp.	sedge	1				1	12	7	4	1	16	10
Plants of open water (aquatics)												
Potomageton sp.	pondweed									1		
Lemna sp.	duckweed	5 ᵘ	9 ᵘ			3 ᵘ	1 ᵘ	1 ᵘ	2 ᵘ			2 ᵘ
Plants of wood, hedge or scrub												
Rubus fruticosus agg.	blackberry									1 ᵘ		
Cornus sanguinea L.	dog-wood						1					
Miscellaneous												
Cennococcum geophilum Fr.	fungus sclerotia	5	10			15			c.50			

Table 92a: Late 12th to 13th century contexts
Key: ( ) = identification uncertain ᵘ = uncharred

Feature		Posthole 2160	Cut 2170	Cut 2194	Ditch 2132	Ditch 2132	Ditch 2219	Ditch 2285	Ditch 2336	Ditch 2399	Ditch 2399	Ditch 2164	Hearth 2066
Date/Period		1200–1275	1200–1300	1200–1275/1300	1225–1275/1300	1200–1275	1200–1275	1225–1300	1200–1275	?	1200–1275	?	1200–1300
Context		2161	2171	2358	2133	2262	2220	2286	2335	2401	2402	Pot 2406	2067
Sample volume (litres)		30	25	30	30	30	10	30	30	3	8		5
Cereals													
Triticum aestivum group	bread wheat grains	9	12	57	7	5	15	7	24	13	2	24	15
	bread wheat rachis frags.						2					1	
Secale cereale L.	rye		1(2)	(2)						1			
Hordeum cf. *vulgare*	hulled barley grains	24	21	75	51	28	11	14	12	11	16	89(1)	28
	hulled barley rachis frags.		1(2)	1(2)	1		3			2(1)			
Avena sp.	oat grains	4	6	26	7(1)	8	22	5	5	47	10	20	22
	oat floret bases						1						
	oat awn frags.						1						
Cerealia indet.	indeterminate cereal grains and frags. (vol. ml.)	1.0	0.5	0.5	<0.5	<0.5	<0.5	<0.5	0.5	1.0	<0.5	1.0	1.0
Legumes													
Pisum sativum L.	pea			1									
Vicia faba L.	broad bean	1		2		4							
Vicia sativa s.l.	common vetch	1	3	9	4		3	2	5	2			5
V. hirsuta (L.) Gray	hairy tare												2
V. tetrasperma (L.) Schreb	smooth tare			1		1	3						
V. hirsuta/tetrasperma	hairy or smooth tare			3		2	3			2		2	
cf. *Lotus corniculatus*	bird's foot-trefoil						11						
Medicago lupulina L.	black medick			5				2	2	2		2	1
Trifolium repens L.	white clover				4	2		2	1				
T. pratense L.	red clover				1								
Trifolium sp.	indeterminate clover	1		5	5	2		2	2	4	2		
Plants of arable, ruderal or grassland													
Ranunculus acris/ repens/bulbosus	meadow, creeping or bulbous buttercup	1			1		3						
R. sardous Crantz	hairy buttercup									1			
Urtica dioica L.	common nettle				1		5 [u]						
Fumaria sp.	fumitory				1								
Chenopodium polyspermum/rubrum	many-seeded or red goosefoot	3	2	10	1	2	20	4	1	1		1	

Table 92b: 13th century contexts

Key: ( ) = identification uncertain "u" *= uncharred*

Continued on page 258

Feature		Posthole 2160	Cut 2170	Cut 2194	Ditch 2132	Ditch 2132	Ditch 2219	Ditch 2285	Ditch 2336	Ditch 2399	Ditch 2399	Ditch 2164	Hearth 2066
Date/Period		1200–1275	1200–1300	1200–1275/1300	1225–1275/1300	1200–1275	1200–1275	1225–1300	1200–1275	?	1200–1275	?	1200–1300
Context		2161	2171	2358	2133	2262	2220	2286	2335	2401	2402	Pot 2406	2067
Sample volume (litres)		30	25	30	30	30	10	30	30	3	8		5
Plants of arable, ruderal or grassland													
Chenopodium album L.	fat-hen			9	4	4	2	1			2		1(1)
Atriplex prostrata/patula	spear-leaved or common orache			6			3					2	4
Stellaria media/neglecta	common or greater chickweed	3	1				2		2				
Cerastium cf. fontanum	common mouse-ear	1	1										
Persicaria maculosa Gray	redshank								1				
Persicaria lapathifolia (L.) Gray	pale persicaria			2		2(1)	1						
Polygonum arenastrum/aviculare	knotgrass					2							
Rumex acetosella L.	sheep's sorrel			1									
Rumex cf. *rispus*	curled dock			10									
Rumex sp.	dock	2						2					
Brassica sp.	cabbage, turnip, rape, *etc.*					2	7				1		
Raphanus raphanistrum	wild radish pod sections				1		1				1		
Aethusa cynapium L.	fool's parsley						2^{u}						
Solanum nigrum L.	black nightshade				4				1^{u}				
Lamium cf. *purpureum*	red dead-nettle				1		1	1					
Euphrasia/Odontites	eyebright or bartsia	1	4						1	1			
Galium aparine L.	cleavers							1					
Cirsium arvense (L.) Scop.	creeping thistle						1						
Anthemis cotula L.	stinking chamomile	4	10	1			6	2	5		1(1)	1	4
Tripleurospermum inodorum L. Schultz. Bip.	scentless mayweed		1	1									
Poa annua L.	annual meadow-grass	2			3		4				1		2
Festuca/Lolium sp.	fescue or rye grass		2					1					
Bromus cf. *secalinus*	rye-brome		1(1)	2		2	2	1	1		1	2(1)	
Danthonia decumbens (L.) DC	heath-grass												3(1)
Poaceae indet.	unidentified grasses	1		7			5		3	7	1		
Plants of damp or wet ground													
Ranunculus flammula L.	lesser spearwort								1				
Pedicularis palustris L.	marsh lousewort						19^{u}						

Species	Common name										
Oenanthe aquatica (L.) Poir	fine-leaved water-dropwort					2 u					2
Apium graveolens L.	wild celery			1		9 u					
Alisma plantago-aquatica L.	water plantain					3					
Triglochin maritimum L.	sea arrowgrass					3					
Juncus cf. *effusus*	soft-rush					18					
Eleocharis palustris/uniglumis	common or slender spike-rush	5	1	7	3	11	2	3	4	1	2
Bolboschoenus maritimus (L.) Palla	sea club-rush			2			1		1		
Schoenoplectus lacustris (L.) Palla	common club-rush	3		11	2	3		1	1		1
Carex otrubae	false fox-sedge			2		2	1				1
C. ovalis	oval sedge			(1)							
C. cf. *acutiformis*	lesser pond-sedge			2		2		2			1
C. cf. *pseudocyperus*	cyperus sedge			4							1
C. nigra	common sedge	2		4		3	3				
Carex sp.	sedge	2		21	7	2	3	1			4
Plants of open water (aquatics)											
Chara sp.	stonewort oogonia					1 u					
Ranunculaceae sub-g. *Batrachium*	water-crowfoot					1 u					
Potomageton sp.	pondweed					5 u					
Lemna sp.	duckweed			1 u		c.250 u		34 u			
Plants of wood, hedge or scrub											
Ilex aquifolium L.	holly			1			1				
Rubus fruticosus agg.	blackberry					5 u		2			
Sambucus nigra L.	elder			1		2 u	1 u				
Miscellaneous											
Cenococcum geophilum Fr.	fungus sclerotia	3		4	2			10			22
Daphnia spp.	water flea ephippia				27						
Bryozoa	moss animal statoblasts				17						

Table 92b: 13th century contexts

Key: ( ) = identification uncertain   u = uncharred

	Feature	Pit 554	Pit 556		Ditch 9	Ditch 10	Pit 3206	Pit 5363	Bldg. 7032	Pit A62	Ditch A78
	Date/Period	1225–1300	1200–1275		?	1200–1300	1225–1300	1250–1325	Late 12th–mid 13th century	Late 12th–early 13th century	Mid–Late 13th century
	Context	578	565	567	223	197	3207	5304	7032	A64	A79
	Sample volume (litres)	5.5	4.5	4.5	4.5	4	15	26	10	10	16
Cereals											
Triticum aestivum group	bread wheat	11(1)	4	27		1	3	51		22	40
Secale cereale L.	rye			1	1						
Hordeum vulgare	hulled 6-row barley grains	9(1)	1	53	4	5(2)	1	42	2	49	25
Avena sp.	oat	1	1	2			1	29		7	19
Avena/Bromus sp.	oat or brome			2							
Cerealia indet.	indeterminate cereal grains & frags. (vol. ml.)	1.0	<0.5	1.0	<0.5	<0.5	<0.5	0.5		1.5	1.0
Legumes											
Pisum sativum L.	pea	1									
Vicia faba L.	broad bean				(1)					1	
Vicia sativa s.l.	common vetch		1					12		4	2
Vicia/Lathyrus spp.	vetch or vetchling			6(5)				8		7	2
V. hirsuta (L.) Gray	hairy tare										
Trifolium repens L.	white clover									5	2
T. pratense L.	red clover									5	
Trifolium sp.	indeterminate clover									3	4
Plants of arable, ruderal or grassland											
Ranunculus acris/repens/bulbosus	meadow, creeping or bulbous buttercup								1	3	1
R. sardous Crantz	hairy buttercup									1	
Chenopodium polyspermum/rubrum	many-seeded or red goosefoot							2		1	1
Chenopodium album L.	fat-hen			2(3)				2		2	
Atriplex prostrata/patula	spear-leaved or common orache			1					1	4	1
Stellaria medis/neglecta	common or greater chickweed									3	1
Stellaria graminea L.	lesser stitchwort										1
Persicaria maculosa Gray	redshank									1	1
Persicaria lapathifolia (L.) Gray	pale persicaria									4	

Scientific name	Common name					
Fallopia convolvulus (L.) A. Löve	black-bindweed	1	1			
Rumex crispus L.	curled dock		1			1
Rumex sp.	dock	1				1
Anthemis cotula L.	stinking chamomile	8		2		1
Bromus cf. *secalinus*	rye-brome				3	
Bromus sp.	brome	2	1			
Molinia caerulea (L.) Moench	purple moor-grass		3			
Poaceae indet.	unidentified grasses		36	3		
Plants of damp or wet ground						
Montia fontana L.	blinks		1			
Persicaria hydropiper (L.) Spach	water-pepper		2			
Hydrocotyle vulgaris L.	marsh pennywort		2			
Juncus cf. *effusus*	soft-rush capsules		98			
Bolboschoenus maritimus (Asch.) Palla	sea club-rush		2		1	
Schoenoplectus lacustris (L.) Palla	common club-rush	7	5	3		
Eleocharis palustris/uniglumis	common or slender spike-rush		234			
Carex otrubae	false fox-sedge		7			
C. ovalis	oval sedge	1	3			
C. pseudocyperus	cyperus sedge		8			
C. cf. *panicea*	carnation sedge		5			
Carex sp.	sedge		135			
Eleocharis/Carex sp.	spike rush or sedge		27			
Glyceria cf. *fluitans*	floating sweet-grass		2			
cf. *Claviceps purpurea*	ergot		1			
Plants of wood, hedge or scrub						
Corylus avellana L.	hazel nut shell frags.			1		
Prunus spinosa	blackthorn fruit stone			1		
Miscellaneous						
Cenococcum geophilum Fr.	fungus sclerotia		15			
Unidentified seeds			30			

Table 92c:: 13th century contexts

Key: ( ) = identification uncertain " = uncharred

sandy soils, dunes and shingle, but possibly they were cultivated. Vetches are known to have been grown as fodder crops from at least the 12th century in south-east England, and probably earlier (Currie 1988).

A few seeds of arable or ruderal weeds are present in these samples. The sedges (*Carex* spp.) in Context 2355 suggest damper ground, and uncharred seeds of duckweed (*Lemna* sp.) must mean standing water at some time.

In Context A64 (Table 92c) unusually well-preserved charred wild plant seeds outnumbered those of crop plants; some are of plants of disturbed ground or other open places, but the majority are of muddy or wet grassland and pond or ditch margins. Spike rushes (*Eleocharis* spp.), sedges and grasses (*Poaceae*) are the most numerous. Of particular interest are almost a hundred immature seed capsules of rushes (*Juncus* sp.), which, if dehiscent would release more than 8,000 seeds (Salisbury, 1961 estimates an average of *c.* 82 seeds per capsule). A few capsules are intact, and in others part of the wall is abraded and the seeds can be seen in the three locules. Capsule shapes vary, particularly at the apex, which may reflect different stages of ripeness, but it is possible that more than one species is represented. Breaking a capsule failed to separate the closely packed seeds, but occasionally in damaged capsules the side of a seed is exposed and it is possible, with higher magnification, to glimpse the surface cell pattern which suggests that most, if not all, are the common soft rush (*Juncus effusus* group). The almost mature condition of the capsules indicates that the stems were cut and burned in mid-summer.

One charred item *c.* 9mm in length, 1.0mm to 2.0mm in diameter, slightly curved and with dense black internal texture, has been identified as a *sclerotium*, probably of ergot (*Claviceps purpurea*). Ergot is a parasitic fungus of cereals and grasses which develops in place of the normal grain.

13th Century (Tables 92a, b, c)

The greatest number of samples (the majority of *c.* 30 litres of soil) came from this period. Because data have come from so many contexts Table 92 is presented in three parts. In Tables 92a and 92b are listed results from one area (Lydd 2), while Table 92c includes results from 13th century deposits from other parts of the site. The pit fills, presumably deliberate depositions, produced greater numbers of charred seeds than those from ditches and minor features.

Cereals

Wheat is present in 30 of the 32 sampled contexts of this period and in all cases the grains suggest free-threshing species and, as before, are listed as *Triticum aestivum* group. Only two contexts (2401 and 2406) contained fragments of chaff and these confirm a hexaploid free-threshing species.

Barley was found in all contexts but with fragments of rachis only in seven, two of which indicate a 6-row form. A few asymmetric lateral grains were seen in most of the larger assemblages.

Oats were present in 29 of the 32 contexts of this period, but only one essential floret base was found (in ditch context 2220) and this had the typical disarticulation scar of a cultivated species (*Avena sativa* or *A. strigosa*). Oat grains, when occurring in large numbers or forming a significant proportion of the total cereals (as in several pit contexts here), are almost certainly mainly cultivars, but it is very likely that wild oat species (*Avena fatua* or *ludoviciana*) were present as weeds of crops.

Rye (*Secale cereale*) was found, only as a very minor presence in six samples and uncertainly in two others. In the latter they could not be safely distinguished from poorly preserved attenuated wheat grains.

All samples included varying amounts of indeterminate fragmentary cereal grains, sometimes recognisable only by their characteristic vacuolated texture.

Legumes

Peas were present in seven of the 13th century samples and field beans in 17, always fewer than cereal grains. Vetches and similar seeds occur in almost all samples, but only a minority were sufficiently complete to measure. It is likely that those of *c.* 3.0mm to 4.0mm diameter include both grassland plants and those cultivated for fodder. Small seeds of *c.* 2mm diameter are probably of hairy or smooth tare.

One seed was thought to be lentil (*Lens culinaris*); the putative identification was made on its typical bi-convex lenticular shape and marginal hilum, but no further similar seeds were found.

Flax or linseed (*Linum usitatissimum*) seeds were found in two pit contexts. (2103 and 2105).

Wild Plants

There is a wide range of wild plant seeds, often only in low numbers. Some are very characteristic weeds of arable fields, such as stinking chamomile (*Anthemis cotula*), now very rarely found, and wild radish (*Raphanus raphanistrum*), both typical of heavy soils.

Others are more indicative of grassland and may occur in a number of soil types but some, *e.g.*, lesser spearwort (*Ranunculus flammula*), ragged robin (*Lychnis floscuculi*), marsh lousewort (*Pedicularis palustris*), spike rushes (*Eleocharis* spp.), purple moor grass (*Molinia caerulea*) and heath grass (*Danthonia decumbens*) are more typical of damper parts. The sedges, not all of which have been identified, may grow in damp grassy places, pond or ditch sides.

Some plants indicate very much wetter conditions; the pondweeds (*Potamogeton* spp.) and duckweeds (*Lemna* spp.) are aquatics which grow in gently flowing or still water. Some of these seeds are not charred and, although their contemporaneity can be questioned, taken with the other charred wetland seeds they are not out of place. Common and sea club-rush (*Schoenoplectus lacustris* and *Bolboschoenus maritimus*) are plants of shallow ponds or dykes, sometimes growing in proximity, but the latter more commonly in brackish conditions near the coast.

A few seeds of holly (*Ilex aquifolium*), blackberry (*Rubus fruticosus*), elder (*Sambucus nigra*) and dogwood (*Cornus sanguinea*) suggest nearby woodland or scrub.

14th Century (Table 93)

Five samples of varying sizes are included in Table 93 (overleaf) as falling within the 14th century, although Context 3225 (dated 1275–1350) and Context 3237 (dated 1350–1425) just overlap with the preceding and succeeding centuries. (These two were both from Area B; the other three from Area C.)

Cereals

In Area B (Context 3225) wheat and barley occur in almost equal volume with the very few oats possibly only of weed status. Wheat was the major constituent from a spread in the same Area (Context 3237) and in the three pit samples from Area C (Contexts 3325, 3318 and 3328), which contained many more cereals. As before, the wheat grains are all apparently free-threshing species, but some variations in overall shape were noted. The majority of the better-preserved grains have an almost square form with rounded back and steep scutellum, and some have a slight hump behind the scutellum. There are others which are slightly longer, with a more ridged back, but these are often heavily charred and possibly distorted. There are also many intermediate forms.

The only sample to produce fragments of wheat rachis nodes, *i.e.*, the most robust parts of the spikes, was Context 3318. Of eight fragments one suggests a hexaploid wheat, but three show signs of swellings immediately below the glume insertions, only fragments of which remain, and in one of these three there remains sufficient length of internode to show that there are no longitudinal striations on the abaxial surface such as can usually be seen in hexaploid species. Four other node fragments are too damaged to be helpful. These various features suggest that several varieties of wheat were being grown, and there is a possibility that free-threshing tetraploid species (*Triticum durum*/*T. turgidum*) may have been among them, although three very poorly preserved rachis fragments are far from proof.

Barley, apart from the earlier Context 3225, formed a smaller proportion of the total cereals and a few of the rachis fragments from Context 3325 confirm the presence of 6-row barley. Oats were more prominent than before and in such numbers most probably represent cultivation. Unfortunately no diagnostic chaff parts were found for specific identification.

Rye was found in four contexts but only as a very minor proportion, although it may well have been unrecognised among the smaller and more distorted wheats.

Legumes

Peas, field beans and vetches are present in all five, with more in the four pit samples, but always in lesser proportions to cereals. In these the beans were readily identifiable. Not all of the peas and vetches could be satisfactorily distinguished and the two are listed together in the Table. They may well have grown together.

Wild Plants

Some of the seeds found with the larger cereal deposits are typical arable weeds, for example, corn cockle (*Agrostemma githago*), black bindweed (*Fallopia convolvulus*), cleavers (*Galium aparine*) and stinking chamomile. Other identified plants are more likely to appear in grassland or other open areas. *Sclerotia* of *Cenococcum geophilum* are frequently associated with grasses.

Spike rushes and common club-rushes indicate marshy ground and the probable pond sedge (*Carex cf. riparia*) and water plantain (*Alisma plantago-aquatica*) illustrate shallow water or muddy pond edges. Sea club-rush suggests brackish conditions.

Uncharred seeds of the fresh-water aquatic plants water crowfoot (*Ranunculus* subg. *Batrachium*) and duckweed (*Lemna* sp.) demonstrate a time when the deposit was under water and may have entered the contexts at a later time of inundation or through drainage from elsewhere. *Oogonia* (female reproductive organs) of stoneworts (*Chara* spp.), a form of green algae found uncharred in Context 3225, are aquatics of various depths of fresh or brackish water.

15th Century (Table 94)

The seeds in one of the 15th century samples were preserved by charring, but in three they have survived with only minor changes owing to the restriction of oxygen in wet conditions. Two other samples were dry but the uncharred plant contents again indicate a period of wetness.

Cereals in the charred sample (Context 3125) (fewer than in earlier periods) included small amounts of wheat, barley, oats and rye. A few peas and one bean are the only cultivated legumes and the wild plants included only one small hairy or smooth tare. The very few other charred seeds suggest grass or waste with rushes indicating moisture. Several uncharred oogonia of stoneworts again suggest a time under water.

The waterlogged samples (Contexts 3259, 3349 and 3350) are comprised almost entirely of uncharred seeds preserved by the wet conditions. They include many of the common ruderal or grassland plants found charred in other samples, and also damp ground species such as rushes and sedges, water-side or shallow water plants

Feature		Pit 3224	Pit 3339	Pit 3317		Spread 3237
Date/Period		1275–1350	1300–1400	1325–1400		1350–1425
Context		3225	3325	3318	3329	3237
Sample volume (litres)		40	21	21	10	10
Cereals						
Triticum aestivum group	bread wheat grains bread wheat rachis frags.	132	c.3,500	c.600 1(4)	c.750	144
cf. T. turgidum/durum	*cf.* rivet or macaroni wheat rachis frags.			(3)		
Secale cereale L.	rye		4	2	4	2
Hordeum vulgare	hulled barley grains hulled barley rachis frags.	140	235 16	47	43	18
Avena sp.	oat grains	3	273	69	68	4
Avena/Bromus sp.	oat or brome	2	21	16	4	1
Cerealia indet.	indeterminate cereal grains & frags. (vol. ml.) indeterminate cereal culm nodes & frags. (vol. ml.)	1.0	c.5.0 8	2.0 6	2.0	1.5
Legumes						
Pisum sativum L. (including *V. sativa*)	pea	c.20	c.90	c.24	40	12
Vicia faba L.	broad or field bean	5	c.15	4	5	2
V. sativa s.l.	common vetch	9		11	17	13
Vicia/Lathyrus spp.	vetch or vetchling	3		12		
V. hirsuta (L.) Gray	hairy tare		1	2		
V. tetrasperma (L.) Schreb	smooth tare			6		
V. hirsuta/tetrasperma	hairy or smooth tare	2	1	3	2	
Trifolium sp.	clover	3				
Trifolium/Medicago sp.	clover or medick	2			2	2
Plants of arable, ruderal or grassland						
Ranunculus acris/repens/bulbosus	meadow, creeping or bulbous buttercup	2	2			
Fumaria sp.	fumitory	1		6		
Urtica dioica L.	common nettle			1	1	
U. urens L.	small nettle				1	
Chenopodium polyspermum/rubrum	many-seeded or red goosefoot	9	2		1	2
Chenopodium album L.	fat-hen	10	3	1	4	
Atriplex prostrata/patula	spear-leaved or common orache		1	4	1	2
Stellaria medis/neglecta	common or greater chickweed		2	3	1	
Stellaria graminea L.	lesser stitchwort	7				
Agrostemma githago L.	corncockle				2	
Silene sp.	campion					1
Persicaria lapathifolia (L.) Gray	pale persicaria			1		
Polygonum arenastrum/aviculare	knotgrass	1				
Fallopia convolvulus (L.) A. Löve	black-bindweed	1			1	
Rumex obtusifolius L.	broad-leaved dock					
Rumex sp.	dock	3	7	3	4	
Brassica cf. nigra (L.) Koch	black mustard	2		5		1
Potentilla sp.	cinquefoil			1		
Aphanes arvensis L.	parsley-piert	1				
Solanum dulcamara L.	bittersweet			1 [u]		
Plantago lanceolata L.	ribwort plantain				2	
Galium aparine L.	cleavers		15	1	3	1
Cirsium vulgare (Savi) Ten.	spear thistle				1	
Cirsium/Carduus	thistles			4	5	

Feature		Pit 3224	Pit 3339	Pit 3317		Spread 3237
Date/Period		1275–1350	1300–1400	1325–1400		1350–1425
Context		3225	3325	3318	3329	3237
Sample volume (litres)		40	21	21	10	10
Plants of arable, ruderal or grassland						
Anthemis cotula L.	stinking chamomile	1	4	26	28	
Tripleurospermum inodorum L. Schultz. Bip.	scentless mayweed			3		
Senecio vulgaris L.	groundsel				3	
cf. Lolium perenne	rye-grass				1	
Festuca sp.	fescue	1				
Poa annua L.	annual meadow-grass	2		2	1	
Bromus cf. secalinus	rye-brome	5		2	4	1
Poaceae indet.	unidentified grasses		1			
Plants of damp or wet ground						
Mentha aquatica/arvensis	water or field mint		2			
Alisma plantago-aquatica L.	water plantain			1 ᵘ		
Eleocharis palustris/uniglumis	common or slender spike-rush				1	
Bolboschoenus maritimus (Asch) Palla	sea club-rush		2			
Schoenoplectus lacustris (L.) Palla	common club-rush		5	1		
Carex otrubae/ovalis	false fox or oval sedge			1		
C. cf. riparia	greater pond-sedge			5		
Carex sp.	sedge			2	1	1
Plants of open water (aquatics)						
Chara sp.	stonewort oogonia	14 ᵘ	2 ᵘ			
Ranunculaceae sub-g. *Batrachium*	water-crowfoot			3 ᵘ		
Lemna sp.	duckweed			5 ᵘ		
Plants of wood, hedge or scrub						
Tree buds		1			5	
Thorns/Prickles			7			
Miscellaneous						
Cenococcum geophilum Fr.	fungus sclerotia	2	8	2	3	

Table 93: 14th century contexts
Key: ( ) = identification uncertain ᵘ *= uncharred*

such as hemlock (*Conium maculatum*), fine-leaved water-dropwort (*Oenanthe aquatica*) and club-rushes, together with aquatics such as water crowfoot and duckweed.

Context 3259 also included a charred pea or vetch, and Contexts 3349 and 3350 contained single charred grains of rye and barley and a bean; illustrations of the scatter of charred material commonly found near human activity.

Samples from two contexts from Cut 5366, although dry, also produced many uncharred remains. Context 5370 is the lower of the two and the flot and residue contained fragments of wood, twigs, moss and a large number of seeds preserved by waterlogging. The majority of the seeds reflect the immediate environment of fields, grass, ditches or scrub. Wet conditions are demonstrated by seeds of aquatic plants, water flea egg cases and caddis fly larva cases. Context 5369, lying above 5370, contained less wood but more large (probably reed) stem fragments and a large number of burdock (*Arctium lappa*) seeds. Seed taxa are similar but proportions vary between the two levels. Both included aquatic flora such as water crowfoot, but with duckweed in the higher level and water flea and caddis fly parts in the lower level.

Feature		Cut 3124	Pit 3074	Well/Sump 3348		Cut 5366	
Date/Period		1375–1475	1350–1450	1375–1475		?	1425–1500
Context		3125	3259	3349	3350	5369	5370
Sample volume (litres)		30	17	10	10	20	5
Preservation (C = Charred / W = Waterlogged)		C	W	W	W	?W	?W
Cereals							
Triticum aestivum group	bread wheat	31					2 ᶜ
Secale cereale L.	rye		1 ᶜ				
Hordeum vulgare L.	hulled barley	3			1 ᶜ		
Avena sp.	oat	1					1 ᶜ
Cerealia indet.	indeterminate cereal grains & frags. (vol. ml.)	1.0					
Legumes							
Pisum sativum L.	pea	3					
Pisum sativum/Vicia sativa	pea or common vetch		1 ᶜ				
Vicia faba L.	broad bean	2			1 ᶜ		
V. hirsuta/tetrasperma	hairy or smooth tare seeds	1	7				
	hairy or smooth tare pod frags.		3				
Onobrychis viciifolia L.	sainfoin					4	7
Medicago lupulina L.	black medick		1 ᶜ	1 ᶜ			4
Medicago/Trifolium	medick or clover	11					
Fibre Plants							
Cannabis sativa L.	hemp					1	c. 3
Plants of arable, ruderal or grassland							
Pteridium aquilinum (L.) Kuhn	bracken		1				
Ranunculus acris/ repens/bulbosus	meadow, creeping or bulbous buttercup		2	1	13	32	104
Urtica dioica L.	common nettle		c.80	84	124	42	6
Urtica urens L.	small nettle					10	2
Chenopodium polyspermum/rubrum	many-seeded or red goosefoot			6	7	12	17
Chenopodium album L.	fat hen	1	7	11	21	16	34
Atriplex prostrata/patula	spear-leaved or common orache	1	7	11	20	2	14
Stellaria media/neglecta	common or greater chickweed			7	14	2	
Stellaria graminea L.	lesser stitchwort					2	7
Agrostemma githago L.	corncockle				2		
Silene sp.	campion				1	1	
Polygonum arenastrum/aviculare	knotgrass		7	2	5	12	249
Fallopia convolvulus (L.) A. Löve	black-bindweed	1	2				
Rumex cf. crispus L.	curled dock		6	6	4		
Rumex cf. conglomeratus Murray	clustered dock		33				
Rumex cf. obtusifolius L.	broad-leaved dock		13	8	c.50		1
Rumex sp.	dock	1	26	6	77		2
Malva sylvestris L.	common mallow		5				
Brassica cf. nigra (L.) Koch	black mustard		4	5	1	29	5
Brassica sp.	cabbage, turnip, rape, *etc.*					13	
Raphanus raphanistrum	wild radish pod sections					1	1
Primula/Anagallis	primrose or pimpernel		2				
Potentilla sp.	cinquefoil					1	
Anthriscus sylvestris (L.) Hoffm.	cow parsley		4				
Pastinaca sativa/ Heracleum sphondylium sp.	parsnip or hogweed		2		1		
Torilis japonica (Houtt) DC	upright hedge-parsley		7		11		
Hyoscyamus niger L.	henbane					5	2
Solanum dulcamara L.	bittersweet		5	1	18		3

Feature		Cut 3124	Pit 3074	Well/Sump 3348		Cut 5366	
Date/Period		1375–1475	1350–1450	1375–1475		?	1425–1500
Context		3125	3259	3349	3350	5369	5370
Sample volume (litres)		30	17	10	10	20	5
Preservation (C = Charred / W = Waterlogged)		C	W	W	W	?W	?W
Plants of arable, ruderal or grassland							
Lamium cf. purpureum	red dead-nettle		15	76	30	9	1
Mentha arvensis/aquatica	field or water mint	1					
Plantago lanceolata L.	ribwort plantain	1					
Galium aparine L.	cleavers		1				
Cirsium arvense (L.) Scop.	creeping thistle		12		4	5	
C. vulgare (Savi) Ten.	spear thistle		24		15		
Cirsium/Carduus	thistles		10			4	11
Lapsana communis L.	nipplewort		3		9		
Anthemis cotula L.	stinking chamomile				1 c	1	
Picris echioides L.	bristly ox-tongue		11			3	
Sonchus arvensis L.	perennial sow-thistle		20	10	9		
Sonchus asper (L.) Hill	prickly sow-thistle		29	15	7	1	
Asteraceae	daisy family seed		5				
	daisy family capitulum	1					
Plants of damp or wet ground							
Musci sp.	mosses stem fragments					2	c.20
Ranunculus flammula L.	lesser spearwort			4			
Lychnis flos-cuculi L.	ragged robin						4
Persicaria hydropiper (L.) Spach	water-pepper			3			
Oenanthe aquatica (L.) Poir	fine-leaved water-dropwort		1	1	2		
Conium maculatum L.	hemlock		12	9	51	52	2
Apium graveolens L.	wild celery		4		8		
Alisma plantago-aquatica L.	water plantain			25	14		
Pedicularis palustris L.	marsh lousewort		1				
Bidens tripartita L.	trifid bur-marigold		3				
Juncus cf. effusus	soft-rush	1	4		3		
Eleocharis palustris/uniglumis	common or slender spike-rush						3
Bolboschoenus maritimus (L.) Palla	sea club-rush		9				
Schoenoplectus lacustris (L.) Palla	common club-rush		2		1		2
Carex ovalis Gooden	oval sedge					3	7
C. otrubae/ovalis	false fox or oval sedge		6	3	9		
C. hirta/riparia	hairy or greater pond-sedge					1	3
C. cf. riparia	greater pond-sedge		1	3	1		
Carex sp.	sedge		49	4	5	4	2
Plants of open water (aquatics)							
Chara sp.	stonewort oogonia	28 u			3		
Ranunculaceae sub-g. *Batrachium*	water-crowfoot		c.240	181	103	21	452
Potomageton sp.	pondweed				1		
Lemna sp.	duckweed		c.300	8	51	19	
Plants of wood, hedge or scrub							
Pteridium aquilinum Kuhn	bracken pinnule		1				
Rubus fruticosus agg.	blackberry		27	9	15		
Sambucus nigra L.	elder		1				
Arctium lappa L.	greater burdock		5	2	6	73	1
Tree buds		1	5	5	12		18
Miscellaneous							
Daphnia spp.	water fleas ephippia		c.10	4	40		22
Trichoptera	Caddis fly larva cases						5
Cennococcum geophilum Fr.	fungus sclerotia	10					

Table 94: 15th century contexts
Key: U = *uncharred;* C = *charred*

Feature		Ditch 3150	Ditch 507	Cut 5286	Ditch 5137
Date/Period		1425–1525		1475–1525	1700–1720
Context		3151	5123	5292	5138
Sample volume (litres)		180	20	5	23
Preservation (C = charred / W = waterlogged)		C	C	W	W
Cereals					
Triticum spelta	spelt spikelet forks		2		
T. aestivum group	bread wheat grains	c.26,000	c.8,000	5 [C]	
	bread wheat rachis frags.		35		
Secale cereale L.	rye	24	?3		
Hordeum vulgare	hulled barley grains	c.1,650	2,500	1 [C]	
	hulled barley rachis frags.	4	15		
Avena sp.	oat	c.200	c.650	1 [C]	
Avena/Bromus sp.	oat or brome	c.20			
Cerealia indet.	indeterminate cereal grains & frags. (vol. ml.)	c.18.0	c.5.0		
Legumes					
Pisum sativum L.	pea		57		
Vicia sativa s. l.	common vetch		c.30	1 [C]	
Pisum sativum/Vicia sativa	pea or vetch	c.960			
Vicia faba L.	broad bean	c.100	47		
V. tetrasperma (L.) Schreb	smooth tare	3	5		
V. hirsuta/tetrasperma	hairy or smooth tare	16	20		
Onobrychis viciifolia L.	sainfoin				1
Trifolium sp.	indeterminate clover	3	2		
Fibre Plant					
Cannabis sativa L.	hemp		1		
Plants of arable, ruderal or grassland					
Ranunculus acris/repens/bulbosus	buttercups	3	2		8
Urtica dioica L.	common nettle			8	15
U. urens L.	small nettle			1	
Chenopodium polyspermum/rubrum	many-seeded or red goosefoot	3	c.30	1	10
Chenopodium album L.	fat-hen	16	c.50	14	12
Atriplex prostrata/patula	spear-leaved or common orache	2	c.20		10
Stellaria media/neglecta	common or greater chickweed	10		10	3
Stellaria graminea L.	lesser stitchwort	2			
Agrostemma githago L.	corn cockle	94	2		
Polygonum arenastrum/aviculare	knotgrass		4	2 + 1 [C]	2
Fallopia convolvulus (L.) A. Löve	black-bindweed	16			
Rumex obtusifolius L.	broad-leaved dock seed & perianth	1			
Rumex sp.	dock	20	17		11
Brassica sp.	cabbage, turnip, rape, *etc.*	4	4		13
Raphanus raphanistrum L.	wild radish fruit sections		1	2	
Torilis japonica (Houtt) DC	upright hedge-parsley		1		
Solanum dulcamara L.	bittersweet				3
Lamium cf. purpureum	red dead-nettle				5
Plantago lanceolata L.	ribwort plantain		1		
Galium aparine L.	cleavers	2	4		
Cirsium/Carduus sp.	thistles		2		2
Anthemis cotula L.	stinking mayweed	2	6		
Tripleurospermum inodorum L. Schultz. Bip.	scentless mayweed	1	3		
Sonchus asper (L.) Hill	prickly sow-thistle			1	1
Asteraceae	daisy family	3			
Poa annua L.	annual meadow grass	5			

Feature		Ditch 3150	Ditch 507	Cut 5286	Ditch 5137
Date/Period		1425–1525		1475–1525	1700–1720
Context		3151	5123	5292	5138
Sample volume (litres)		180	20	5	23
Preservation (C = charred / W = waterlogged)		C	C	W	W
Plants of arable, ruderal or grassland					
Bromus cf. secalinus	rye-brome	6			
Bromus sp.	brome		2	2 [C]	
Poaceae indet.	unidentified grasses	22	12	3	3
Plants of damp or wet ground					
Apium graveolens L.	wild celery		2		
Juncus cf. effusus	soft-rush	4			
Eleocharis palustris/uniglumis	common or slender spike-rush	14	17		3
Bolboschoenus maritimus (L.) Palla	sea club-rush	10			
Schoenoplectus lacustris (L.) Palla	common club-rush	11	2		56
Schoenoplectus cf. tabernaemontani	grey club-rush				3
Carex ovalis Gooden	oval sedge				2
Carex sp.	sedge	4	5		1
Plants of open water (aquatics)					
Chara sp.	stonewort oogonia	8 [U]			
Lemna sp.	duckweed	5 [U]		2	
Plants of wood, hedge or scrub					
Pteridium aquilinum L.	bracken pinnules	2			
Rubus fruticosus agg.	blackberry				1
Prunus domestica ssp. *insititia*	wild plum fruit stone			2	1
Rosa sp.	thorn				1
Sambucus nigra L.	elder			2	
Arctium lappa L.	greater burdock	2			75

Table 95: 15th to early 16th century and early 18th century contexts
Key: [U] *= uncharred;* [C] *= charred*

As in other waterlogged contexts there are few seeds of cultivated plants other than two charred wheat grains and an oat, but an exception here is hemp (*Cannabis sativa*), represented by five half nutlets and therefore at least three seeds in Context 5370 and one in 5369. These have split apart and the embryo seedlings are missing, suggesting natural ripening.

There are no seeds of cultivated legumes but notable inclusions are seven pods of sainfoin (*Onobrychis viciifolia*) in Context 5370 and four in Context 5369. These are small (3.0mm to 3.3mm), dried and empty but the external surface of the pods retains the distinctive hooks and reticulation. They are very much smaller (even allowing for shrinkage and degradation) than modern cultivated forms and it is most likely that they are wild species. A dwarf form, assumed to be native, grows today in calcareous grassland and has been recorded (Preston, Pearman & Dines, 2002) in southern parts of Britain, including east Kent. It could be that the wild sainfoin was at least noted and utilised as forage.

15th to early 16th Century (Table 95)

Two charred samples (Contexts 3151 and 5123 (both 1425–1525) produced the greatest volume of charred cereal grains, pulses and wild plant seeds.

Context 3151 was an exceptionally large bulk sample (*c.* 180 litres) which produced *c.* 1.30 litres of flot. This was passed through a stack of sieves (7.0mm to 0.25mm), larger charcoal was returned to the excavators and sub-samples taken from the remaining charred material retained in the various fractions, *i.e.*, about a quarter of >2mm., one-eighth from the 1.5mm and 1.0mm and one-sixteenth from the large amount of fine charred material retained on the 0.5mm sieve. Seeds in the sub-samples were counted and totals estimated but all was then briefly scanned to seek for additional species.

Of a total of almost 28,000 recognisable cereal grains, wheat (with an estimated *c.* 26,000 grains) was very much the dominant cereal. Barley grains make up about 6% of the total and oats only about 0.7%. Rye, as in other samples, was only a very minor presence. There was, however, an estimated volume of *c.* 18ml of unidentifiable cereal fragments included in the large mass of finer charcoal.

There were also a large number of legumes, of which about a hundred were beans and almost ten times as many peas and/or vetches. There were far fewer smaller seeded *Vicia* sp. such as tares.

Other wild plant seeds were proportionately less in this sample with a few common arable weeds and slightly more grassland plants, with spike rushes and club-rushes indicating wetter areas.

Context 5123, a much smaller bulk sample, also produced a large amount of flot, *i.e.*, *c.* 1,150ml, which was sub-sampled as above and totals estimated. The cereal grains are heavily charred, few are entirely complete but many could be identified to genus even if only part of the grain survives. However, there is at least an equal volume of fragments that cannot be identified any more closely than as cereal. From a small sub-sample (*c.* one sixteenth) 605 grains were sufficiently well preserved to study and comprised 400 (66%) wheat, 163 (27%) barley, and 42 (7%) oats. Rye was possibly present but not safely distinguished from the wheat.

Wheat grains ranged in size from 3.8mm to 5.2mm, with the majority *c.* 4.0mm in length, but the length to breadth ratio varied. Some of the shorter grains with a steep radicle depression could be described as club wheat type, but may be less well-developed grains. All appear to be free-threshing bread wheats and this is confirmed by several parts of the rachis or main stem of the ear, some with three or four nodes. The linking internodes have the curved sides, widest just below the glume insertions, and show striations characteristic of hexaploid wheats. None showed the straighter sides and typical bulge below the glumes of free-threshing tetraploid wheats.

Unexpected were two spikelet forks, *i.e.*, rachis nodes each retaining the bases of two glumes. These very characteristic rachis parts can be confidently identified as spelt (*Triticum spelta*), a glume wheat, but further searching failed to find more. Although identification of a wheat species from the grain is unreliable it could be that markings discovered on the sides of two slightly slimmer grains are impressions made by tightly enclosing glumes.

The barley grains are in a similar state of preservation as the wheat and many are damaged but most appear to have the angular features of hulled barley and show a slight twist to the axis suggestive of lateral grains of a six-row variety. Two rachis fragments, however, have the longer internodes of a lax-eared barley. Oat grains were the least numerous and no floret parts which could determine whether these were cultivated or wild oat species were seen. The possibility of rye is only suggested by one or two rather thin grains with very sloping radicle areas, but these could well be poorly preserved or immature wheats.

Fragments of cereal straw and smaller grass-like stems on which the more robust nodes have survived formed a large proportion of the charred material.

Seeds of other cultivated plants occur more rarely and the entire sample was searched for them. Pulses are represented by small broad beans, peas and a series of vetches, but possibly not all of the latter are cultivated species. The peas, identifiable when the hilum could be seen, are 4.1mm to 4.9mm in diameter, but this size range may include common vetch. Other smaller vetch seeds may include wild species and weeds such as tares.

One other charred crop plant seed is hemp, unfortunately in poor condition, but the identification is backed up by the presence of better preserved uncharred seeds in two 15th century waterlogged samples.

Wild plants, as in other deposits, include weeds of arable land probably gathered with crops and ruderal or grassland plants, some typical of damp to wet areas.

Context 5292 (1475–1525) came from the base of a wooden barrel in Cut 5286 and produced a few charred seeds including wheat, barley, oats and several common arable weeds. There were also several small amorphous lumps which do not have the texture of cereals but are likely to be other burned organic material.

The major part of the flot consists of uncharred woody fragments among which are uncharred seeds more typical of grassland, with two of elder and two fruit stones of wild plum, both scrub or hedgerow plants. Two seeds of duckweed indicate a period of standing water.

Early 18th Century (Table 95)

Context 5138 (1700–20)

No cereals or legumes, except a fragment of a sainfoin pod, were found in this sample of ditch fill. The seeds and fragments of wood and bark are not charred but their dry, shrivelled condition indicates that they are certainly not recent. Seeds generally are fewer than in waterlogged samples, but there are larger numbers of club-rush and greater burdock seeds. Although not apparently waterlogged, it is possible that fluctuating levels of dampness have retarded decay for 300 years. This is the latest sample from the Lydd Quarry.

Caldicott Farm (Table 91)

From Caldicott Farm three samples from Ditch 8 were examined. Two contexts (9 and 86) are of 11th to 12th century date and thus pre-date the earliest of the Lydd Quarry samples. The third (Context 46) is dated as 12th century.

The few charred cereals in the earlier two samples are poorly preserved and fragmentary, but two grains of bread wheat type were identifiable in each. Barley was found in one and oats in both.

In the later sample (Context 46) more than a hundred

grains of wheat were identifiable, but only one each of barley and oats.

All three samples included a few small vetch or vetchling seeds, all with an approximate diameter of less than 3.0 mm, but with no hila visible to aid identification. These, with the other very few charred seeds, may be of field or grassland plants, with a sedge, spike rush and a common club-rush indicating damp ground, but there is the possibility of small cultivated vetches

Discussion

Cereals and legumes were the major crops throughout and the results show some indications of changes in their relative importance. Comparisons can be misleading because many factors such as preservation, recovery and, in the case of charred remains, the circumstances of burning affect what is actually recovered; the numbers of identified seeds in a deposit do not necessarily reflect what was grown. Nevertheless the plant remains recovered during excavation are material evidence which can be compared with the documentary records, which come mainly from the accounts of monastic and manorial land owners. If documentary evidence existed for those of the peasantry and tenants of small plots it would no doubt be very different, but the land and the care necessary to produce good harvests is common to both.

There are early records of grazing on the marsh and by Domesday some land was under cultivation (Sweetinburgh, this vol.). The earliest (12th century) sample from Lydd Quarry produced cereals only in small numbers, but wheat, barley, oats and rye were all present, which, with the 11th to 12th century vetches from Caldicott Farm, are indications of established mixed farming (Table 91).

More written sources of information are available from the 13th century onwards, showing the continuance of mixed farming on the surrounding marshland (Gross and Butcher 1995, Sweetinburgh, this vol.), and there are detailed accounts of agricultural regimes in England generally from the mid 13th to the mid 15th centuries (Campbell 2000).

The analysed samples from the 13th century provide a picture of agricultural activity particularly from Lydd 2 where most of the samples were taken, but with glimpses from other parts of the site. (Tables 92a, b, c). The same cereals were present but barley and oats slightly outnumber wheat in most of the contexts. On Canterbury Cathedral's reclaimed marshland oats were generally the first crop to be sown as the land dried and the high water table ensured that they continued to be grown (Campbell 2000). There are more beans, peas and vetches, reflecting an increase in legumes generally, all indicating a mixed farming regime to provide food for humans and animals. Oxen and horses worked on the land and horses were becoming more commonly used for cart haulage (Campbell 2000).

In the 14th century deposits wheat was the major cereal, but barley was present in all and there were more oats. Beans, peas and vetches were much more prominent and, with the oats, again parallel the steadily increasing use of horses for the transport of produce.

Wheat accounts for most of the few grains in the one charred sample from the 15th century and also is clearly the dominant cereal in the two very rich deposits of charred remains from the 15th to 16th century ditch deposits. Beans, peas and vetches were present in all three, in similar proportions to earlier finds.

These two ditch deposits of cereal grains, legumes and a lesser number of wild plant seeds must represent dumps of burned material from one or several sources. If they were from single sources they might represent cleaned crops. Possibly they reflect the changes in regime shown in records of this time, when arable farming was giving way to increased use of the marshes for livestock pasture (Sweetinburgh, this vol.). Cereals and legumes could well have been grown for market.

All the wheat grains recovered from these excavations indicate free-threshing bread wheats and although variations in grain morphology were seen, the only indications of other species are the dubious chaff fragments of rivet wheat from a 14th century pit and the more definite identification of spelt in a 15th to early 16th century ditch.

There are early historical references to rivet, by Fitzherbert in 1523 and Tusser in 1573 who refers to 'red rivet and whight' (Grigson 1984), but grains and diagnostic rachis parts have been found in archaeological deposits dating from at least the 12th century in southern and midland England (Moffett 1991). The presence of rivet at this site, however, is very far from certain.

More substantial is the evidence of spelt. Only a few possible grains were found, but the two spikelet forks are unmistakable. Spelt was the major wheat of the later prehistoric and Roman periods, but became replaced by bread wheat from which the grains were more freely shed at threshing. Appearances of spelt in late Saxon and medieval contexts are infrequent, but sufficient for its status to be questioned – has it survived as a weed in later crops; are the grains and fragments disturbed and re-deposited remnants from earlier periods (spelt was found in samples from Romano-British occupation at this site); or was spelt selected as an alternative wheat? It is a useful wheat, makes good bread and tolerates cold and wet conditions.

Wheat, for which the alluvial soils were ideal, was grown primarily for bread, or mixed with other cereals, peas or beans for pottages. On poorer soils it was sometimes grown with rye as maslin as a cheaper alternative, but little rye has been found at this site.

Barley and oats, grown separately or together as dredge, were occasionally used in pottage but mainly provided food for draught animals. Barley may have been for brewing, but no sprouted grains were found to suggest malting. Oats did well on reclaimed marshland but were increasingly replaced by legumes.

Although legumes are usually found less frequently than cereals, probably because their treatment and usage was less likely to lead to charring, they have long been a valued crop. Pulses such as peas and beans are useful human food, but vetches were used (except in times of hardship) only as fodder. They have been found from prehistoric times onwards.

Documentary evidence for sowing suggests that the farmers of the lands around Lydd were among the subsequent pioneer growers of vetches. Currie (1988) gives accounts of vetch seed purchases in Kent in the first decade of the 13th century, implying that they were cultivated well before then, and also suggests on linguistic grounds that seeds came from across the Channel. Campbell (1988) suggests Kent as the "prime candidate for the initial locus" of vetch cultivation, since the crop was grown in greater quantities there and the county was well placed for continental provenance. Their value as soil improvers (by nitrogen fixation) had long been appreciated, but increasingly they were grown to feed working animals.

There are few historical records of lentils, which were grown probably in small plots. They were found in 12th century deposits near Oxford (Greig 1992), which makes more tantalising the one doubtful 13th century seed from this site.

Seeds of flax in two 13th century pits and of hemp in a 15th century cut and 15th to early 16th century ditch deposit, point to two other minor crops used in the production of fibres for linen, canvas, ropes and halters. These plants were grown extensively on peasant holdings, rarely on demesnes and then usually confined to gardens (Campbell 2000). The flax plant produces edible seeds (linseed) and evidence for their consumption is found in waterlogged deposits such as cesspits, but flax was grown principally for the production of linen thread.

Hemp fibres were used in Britain probably as early as the Bronze Age (Ryder 1999) and the plant is known as a garden crop since at least 1304 (Thirsk 1997). The purchase of three and-a-half bushels of seed in 1319–20 by Battle Abbey (Sweetinburgh, this volume), however, suggests cultivation on a larger scale, although it could have been distributed to individual tenants (one bushel = 35,238 litres). Later, in 1532, a government statute required a quarter acre in every sixty acres of arable land to be sown with flax or hemp. (Thirsk 1997).

Hemp is dioecious, *i.e.*, it has male and female flowers on separate plants, but incorrectly the seed-bearing plant has commonly been called the male plant. This contradiction is presumably because the female plant's coarser fibres (it was left longer for the seeds to mature) was used by male workers for ropes, halters, canvas, *etc.*, and the finer fibres of the male plant (gathered after pollination) provided the housewife with textiles ('hempen home-spun').

The evidence here is only of the female plant. If used for its fibre, and canvas was produced locally, the plants would have been uprooted and then left in water to soften the stems for retting to separate the fibres. The oil-containing seeds could have been stripped off before steeping and after treatment fed to stock (Stephens 1855). Flax stems require similar treatment. Tusser (*c.* 1580) advised pulling hemp and beating out the seeds as part of 'September's husbandrie'. Both plants do well in alluvial soils so appropriate conditions for growing and processing would have been available locally.

Hay may also be regarded as a crop, but is less easily recognised, although many of the deposits include seeds of grassland plants. Some, such as buttercups and clovers, are typical of hay meadows (which may have been the source of the sainfoin) and marsh hay could be the explanation of the many damp ground seeds in a 13th century pit (Context A64).

This deposit contained a large number of the seeds of rushes, spike-rushes, sedges and damp grassland plants, outweighing the number of cereals and arable weeds. These might have been included if gathered for domestic or other usage such as flooring, animal litter, turf or thatching, although very few stem fragments were included with the charcoal in the flot. The seeds of low-growing plants such as blinks (*Montia fontana*) and marsh pennywort (*Hydrocotyle vulgaris*), which flower and set seeds at ground level, would have been missed in normal cutting but could have been included with cut turf.

An alternative explanation is that the seeds in this deposit, including the low-growing blinks and marsh pennywort, came from the dung of grazing or hay-fed animals. Seeds and small plant parts can survive in fair condition in horse dung, but in cattle and sheep they are more damaged by the slower digestive process.

The context is a single assemblage, but if not burned *in situ* was deposited as debris from a fire which may have burned unwanted material from several sources, including crop processing, domestic or other waste. Alternatively, the entire deposit may have been derived from animal care. Cereals, weeds, beans, vetches, hay and litter were all necessary to maintain working animals.

A fuller picture of the background vegetation is given by the seeds preserved in waterlogged deposits (Tables 94 and 95). Many of the plants indicate lush grassland, no doubt maintained by the high water table, seasonal flooding or more major inundation. Aquatic plants such as water crowfoot are frequent in flowing streams, while others such as duckweed and pondweed grow in or nearby standing water of ponds or ditches. Water fleas (*Daphnia*) and the moss-animals (*Bryozoa*) indicate fresh water. A few plants (sea club-rush, wild celery, and some charophyte species) suggest brackish waters, but no true halophytes were detected.

Conclusion

There is no question that the common cereals (wheat, barley, oats and rye) were all cultivated, but there are gaps in the record which might be filled by further archaeological work. The presence here of two wheat species (rivet and spelt) is very questionable but further samples of cereal remains from this part of England might elucidate the problem.

Beans, peas and common vetches are well represented, particularly from the later contexts, but solid evidence from earlier periods might throw more light on the earliest cultivation of vetches.

Sainfoin, (and clover and lucerne) were first sown in the 1620s–30s and in the later 17th century sainfoin was grown on chalky soils in Kent (Thirsk 2000). The few seeds found here in 15th century contexts (and a fragment in an early 18th century ditch fill) are most likely native wild plants, but could have been gathered, with clover, as forage. However, south-east England,

and particularly Kent, was to the fore with earlier fodder crop introductions from across the Channel and further research would be worthwhile.

Flax and hemp were extensively grown and there are numerous records, mainly from East Anglia, another pioneering area (Campbell 2000). These crops were grown and later became particularly prominent in parts of Somerset, Dorset and Sussex where soils and climate were appropriate. Conditions on Romney Marsh during the time of the occupation of the Lydd Quarry site would have been suitable, but there are very few seeds to confirm this.

In summary, the site has produced much useful evidence about farming and the natural environment over several centuries, but more material evidence is needed. Fragments such as cereal chaff, essential for specific identification, may often not survive but further sampling, with particular attention to the recovery of very fine charred material, may help to fill out the picture and its changes over time.

4

Discussion

by Luke Barber and Mark Gardiner

The excavations at the sites around Lydd have provided a huge amount of data on various aspects of medieval life on the Marsh. In order to try to tie most, though not all, of this data together into a coherent overview, they have been organised into different periods with various research themes discussed under each. The way in which so many aspects of data inter-relate makes it impossible to avoid some repetition, for example, using the same piece of evidence to strengthen hypotheses on different topics. It has been considered desirable to present a chronological model for the development of the investigated areas, rather than to discuss the sites under the original three main academic research aims. The latter are discussed under each period. A wider overview of the excavated sites in relation to other wetlands and medieval rural settlement studies more generally is given in the next section.

PERIOD 1: THE PIONEER PHASE: ESTABLISHING THE FIELD SYSTEM (UP TO THE EARLY 13TH CENTURY)
(*Fig. 28)

Reclamation

Research undertaken on Romney and Walland Marsh over the last decade has established that the earliest medieval settlement occurred in the north-east; the area of Romney Marsh proper (Eddison 2000, 65). That part of the marshland seems to have been thoroughly settled by the time of the Domesday survey in the late 11th century and very probably before, but it is also likely that much of the south-east of the marsh, the area around Lydd, was also exploited from an early date. The shingle of the Dungeness formation, although of limited value for agriculture, provided higher land on which communities could settle and exploit the surrounding wetlands. The early charters for the Lydd area, which date from the 8th century onwards, have been discussed by Ward (1931) and Brooks (1988), and are summarised by Sweetinburgh above. They suggest that land around Lydd had been divided up into territories (Fig. 99 overleaf). The boundary of the kingdoms of Kent and Sussex was clearly identified, and lay broadly, perhaps even exactly,

in the same position as the county boundary recorded in the 19th century. The division was also established between the king's estate, which formed the core of the later manor of Denge, and the archbishop of Canterbury's estate at Lydd which came to be part of the manor of Aldington. The boundary between the two is mentioned in a charter purportedly of 774, but with possibly later bounds of the 10th century (BCS, 214; S. No. 111). That charter shows that the estate of Lydd was bounded on the north-east by the sea, to the south by the estate of Denge and to the north-west by *bleccing*.

It is instructive to compare the bounds of the estate with those of Lydd recorded in 1556 (CKS, LY/ZM1). The boundary between the two lordships of Lydd and that of Denge ran along the Dengemarsh Sewer. The sinuous line of the sewer suggests that in origin it was a natural salt marsh channel formed behind the shingle barrier, and in the 8th (or 10th) century it must have been a major feature in the landscape. The north-west boundary of the manor lay towards an embankment known in the mid 16th century as Pigwell Wall, and so lay about 500 metres east of Bletching Fleet (see Gardiner above). It seems that the boundaries of the manor were not substantially different in the 16th century from those at the time of the grant. The land given was confined very largely to the shingle underlying the town of Lydd, the marshes to the south and the shingle to the south-east, including the 'lows' of South Brooks and part of the Wicks. It did not extend for any distance into the marsh to the north-west: the 16th century boundary ran parallel to, and a few hundred metres north-west of, the road from Jury's Gap to Lydd. The marsh beyond to the north-west was either not worth claiming, or lay in another lordship.

The evidence of the surviving pre-Conquest charters is likely to be correct in reflecting a real difference between the occupied land around Lydd, for which there are two charters, and the rest of Walland Marsh which appears to have been little used (Brooks 1988). Present understanding of the early geography of the marsh suggests that a major tidal channel ran to the north and north-west of Lydd. This inlet owed its width to tidal flow from the sea into the salt marshes behind the shingle barrier beach. The Soil Survey recognised two courses

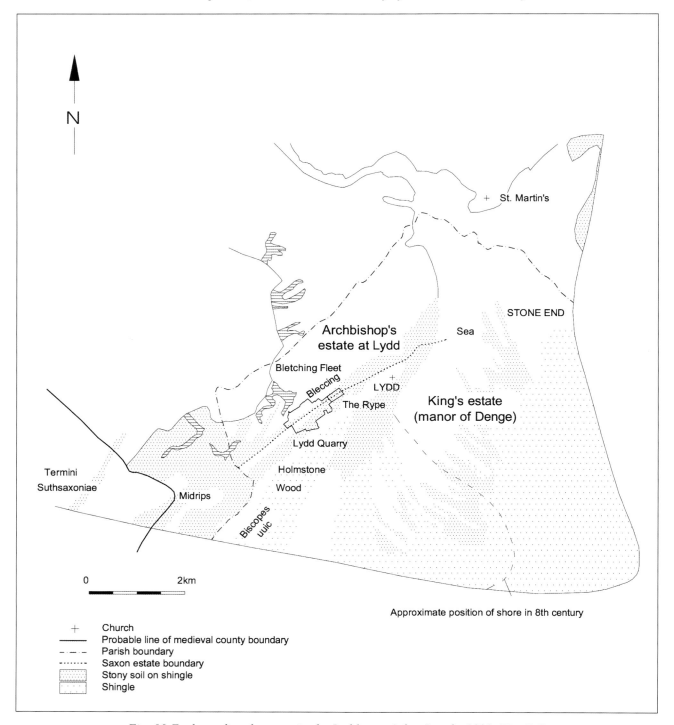

Fig. 99 Early medieval estates in the Lydd area (after Brooks 1988, Fig. 8.6)

associated with the channel. Trunk Creek (Ridge) No. 1, as Green (1968, 41) called it, had a mouth near Kemp's Hill, but seems to have been blocked by the finger of shingle which now carries the road from Lydd to Isles Bridge (Fig. 100 opposite). Trunk Creek (Ridge) No. 2 (hereafter TC2) ran to the north and had a mouth nearer Old Romney. The land between the two creeks was known as Midley, the 'middle island'. At some point, possibly in

the 12th century, TC2 began to silt up. It was evidently this change which allowed land to be reclaimed to the north of Lydd and, from at least the first decade of the 13th century, on a large scale further to the south-west in the Broomhill area. This is discussed further below.

It has been argued elsewhere that the earliest use of the marshland in the area which has been termed the 'Archbishops' Innings' was for the grazing of animals

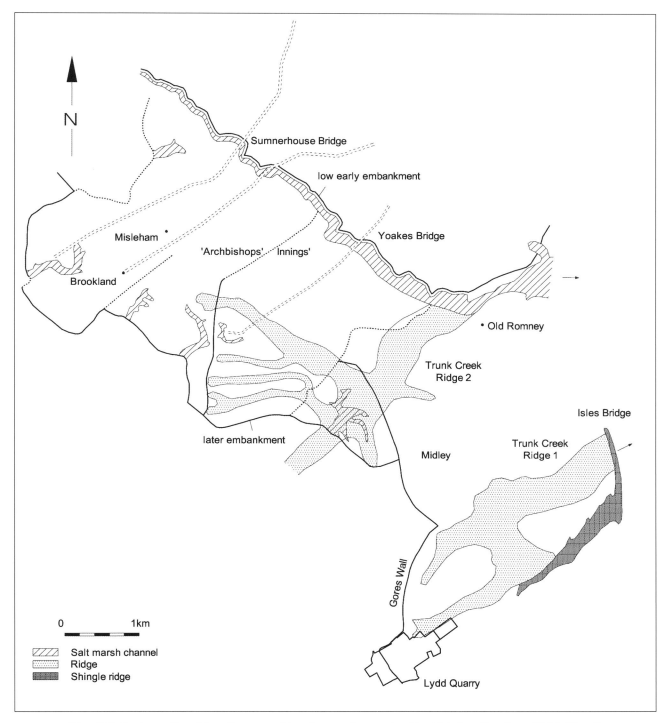

Fig. 100 Early medieval landforms and landuse to the north of Lydd (after Gardiner 2005, Fig. 7)

on unenclosed salt marsh (Gardiner 2005) (Fig. 100). A series of roads run south-westwards over the creek, named by Allen (1999a), perhaps incorrectly, the *Rumensea*, and into marsh beyond. These roads have been compared to similar trackways which survived into the 19th century on the unenclosed marshland at Warham in Norfolk. These roads appear to originate at a time when the creek was still a significant feature, since they cross away from the mouth, evidently in positions which were easier to ford or bridge. A 9th century charter mentions an estate at Misleham (BCS 408; S No. 1623), but it is improbable that this was enclosed at such an early date. It is more likely to be referring to an area of unenclosed pasture.

The situation in Denge Marsh to the south-east of Lydd was rather different. The developing ness was moving eastwards with the result that spits or 'tails' of shingle were deposited to the north in the area of Denge Marsh on top of inter-tidal mud flats (Plater and Long 1995, 17–20). The chronology of the shingle emplacement has become clearer as a result of radiocarbon determinations and historical evidence, allowing the development of Denge Marsh to be better understood (Fig. 101 opposite).

The organic materials used for radiocarbon dating do not provide dates for the emplacement of the shingle: they are taken from various organic material and we need to consider their relationship to coastal processes. The lower peat deposits sampled from Wickmaryholm Pit must date from after the period of shingle deposition when freshwater vegetation developed within a naturally occurring pool. The shingle was therefore deposited *before* the date of 357 BC to AD 213 (all dates quoted at two sigma, cal. years; Long and Hughes 1995). The samples from Manor Farm, Denge Marsh comprised shells within a silty sand which accumulated in the back barrier environment. Therefore, the shingle must have been laid down *before* the period AD 640–850 (Plater *et al.* 2002). The relationship of the whale bones found at the Denge West North quarry to the foreshore development is less certain. They were recovered by dragline from sandy silts from beneath the gravel and must therefore predate it. These provided dates with outer limits of AD 840–1043 (Gardiner *et al.* 1998). The shingle must have been laid down *after* that date.

These figures suggest that the shingle was being laid down very rapidly in the early medieval period, allowing the rapid accumulation of back barrier sediments. Similar conclusions were reached by Plater *et al.* (2002) who also noted that tidal deposition rates in back-barrier environments in the order of 1 metre per year are attested elsewhere. The conditions which allowed the Denge Marsh to be utilised for grazing may have developed very fast during the second half of the first millennium AD.

The later history of the back barrier landscape is dependent upon documentary sources of which the most important is the survey in the Bilsington chartulary. It indicates that in the time of Henry I (1100–35) the manor of Bilsington drew rents of 60*s.* 8*d.* from its lands at Lydd, as well as rent from salt-making and a render of herring (Neilson 1928, 206). Part of the lands of Bilsington lay to the west of the shingle ridge carrying the Lydd to Isles Bridge road. However, the 132 acres lying there cannot account for all of the very substantial rents: the rent per acre would have been too great. The remainder must have lain to the east of the road, on the north edge of Denge Marsh. We know that the archbishop of Canterbury's lands in Lydd were divided from those of the priory of Bilsington on the east of the road by an embankment called Green Wall, which is readily recognisable (CKS, LY/ZM1; Fig. 101). Vollans (1995) has considered the geography of the land described in the survey of 1381 of

Bilsington Priory, but it is difficult to be certain, either of the area, or of the precise location of the land paying rent in *temp.* Henry I. However, we must assume that by the early 12th century the shingle ridges must have already been emplaced to the south-east of the farm of Belgar to allow land behind to be drained and at rent.

It has been suggested above that the Dengemarsh Sewer marks the remnant of a major back-barrier channel with its mouth to the north-east. The reclamation of this area seems to have proceeded in three stages through the construction of bridging embankments (terminology from Allen 1997, 16–17) to span the gap between the shingle underlying Lydd and that of the Dungeness formation. The first two embankments have not hitherto been recognised, but they are mentioned in the 1556 Lydd rental and survey (EKA, Ly/Fac 1). The earliest embankment may be that called Dane John or Lamberts Wall. It cannot be certainly located, though it ran between Dengemarsh Road, and the Dengemarsh Sewer and, presumably, to the finger of shingle beyond. It carried a lane in the 16th century and is therefore tentatively identified here with a double-ditched trackway running south-west from Lydd towards a finger of shingle (Fig. 101). This embankment may, however, have been constructed not to prevent flooding from the ingress of tidal water through the marsh to the north-east, but to stop water from the occasional sea floods percolating through the shingle from the south.

The second embankment can be identified with greater certainty. In the 16th century Dungeness Road was called 'Hett Wall Way', implying that it ran upon an embankment. It is very significant that the former course of the road had a marked bend (now straightened) at Cockerells Bridge, exactly at the point at which it crossed the Dengemarsh Sewer. Such deviations in alignment are commonly found at the points at which walls cross marsh creeks. Creeks were the most difficult of terrain on which to construct earthen embankments and were usually crossed at rights angles to the channel as near the head as possible. The road alignment is thus likely to be the product of engineering considerations in the construction of the underlying embankment. The third stage of reclamation was marked by the construction of the Green Wall which has already been mentioned. None of the dates of these embankments is known.

We can therefore envisage the site of Lydd around the year 1000 surrounded by salt or brackish marsh to the north-west towards TC2 and to the south-east in Denge Marsh. The marsh would have been dissected by deep channels and tidal creeks, such as that at Bletching and Denge Sewer. Salt extraction may have taken place behind the coastal barrier beach, and salt-making mounds have been recorded near Belgar (Vollans 1995). Fishing is likely to have been practised from around this time or shortly after from a base on the lee or eastern side of Dungeness (Gardiner 1996). It was for here that earl Godwin sailed in 1052 from Flanders to collect boats to support his reinstatement in England (*Anglo Saxon*

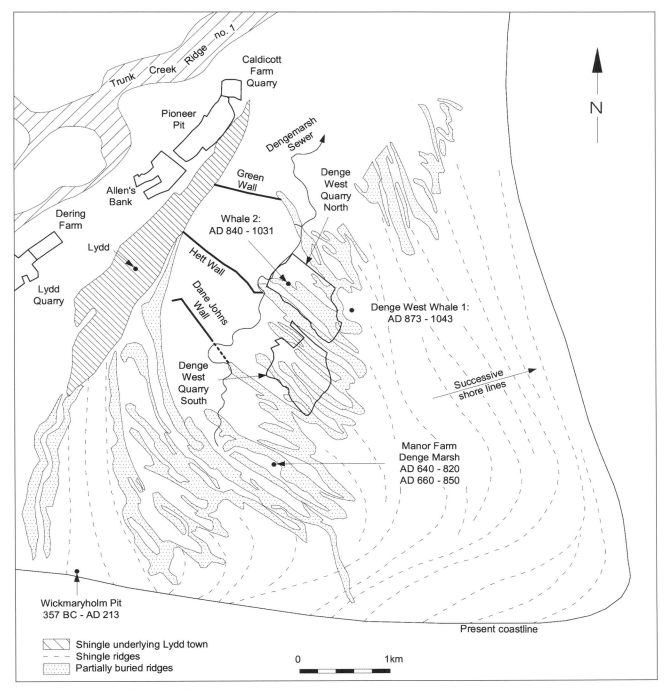

Fig. 101 The development of the Dungeness foreland and associated innings

Chronicle, s.a.). The church at Lydd was constructed around this time or earlier, and the inhabitants of the settlement could look to the north-east where the town of New Romney was developing (Jackson and Fletcher 1959; Jackson *et al.* 1968; Gardiner 2000b). New Romney was certainly a town by the late 11th century when it had 85 burgesses and had been the landing place of some of the boats separated from William the Conqueror's invasion fleet (*Gesta Guillelmi of William of Poitiers* ii, c 27).

It would be wrong to think that Lydd occupied an isolated position. The barrier beach which protected the south part of Walland Marsh provided access to the Lydd area from the west. That route was described in the early 13th century as a king's highway, and it is probable that the medieval track, like the present coastal road, turned north-eastwards to run along the edge of the exposed shingle of the Dungeness formation and so provided access to Lydd from that direction (British

Library, Egerton Ch. 383). The routes to Lydd from the north and north-east would have involved crossing to New Romney or passing over the marsh by roads. Lydd church occupied a nodal position on the road network at the junction of routes from all directions. The marshes around Lydd may have been used for hunting, fishing and fowling and the vegetated marshes may have been grazed, an aspect considered further below. It may have had a pattern of utilisation similar to that seen during the Romano-British period (Cunliffe 1988).

It appears that the earliest material from the three main quarry sites is that from Caldicott Farm, where ceramics suggest a possible 11th or early 12th century start for the ditch system, though a slightly earlier date is possible. The earliest ditches at Caldicott Farm appear to be situated on, and aligned with, the south-west to north-east orientated shingle ridge closest to the road. The extensive excavations at Lydd Quarry to the south-west, have demonstrated that the establishment of the ditch system here, based on the evidence of ceramics, was probably during the 12th century. Unfortunately, too few diagnostic ceramic assemblages were present to establish a precise date within this century, though it is notably later than that at Caldicott Farm and could belong to the early to middle part of the century. However, some caution is needed. The exact relationship of the early pottery to the ditch system at Lydd is not always clear. A number of the groups are in ditches, an unlikely place perhaps for the actual ditch diggers to dispose of their refuse considering the effort used to dig the very same ditches. It could therefore be argued that this 'mid to late' 12th century pottery is refuse from seasonal domestic occupation associated with livestock, within the already established field system. If that were the case, then the initial excavation of the ditch system could date to the early part of the 12th century, or even the end of the 11th century. Equally, the Caldicott Farm ditches could be pushed back by 50 years or so. It is unfortunate that the area investigated at Caldicott Farm was not larger as this may have allowed the location of early occupation sites. Whether any such sites existed in the Pioneer Pit immediately to the south-west will never be certainly known, though the evidence from Allen's Bank suggests a lack of activity in this area.

Evidence for field systems between Caldicott Farm, and Dering Farm and Lydd Quarry is unfortunately sparse, despite previous archaeological work and analysis of aerial photographs. No medieval remains were located at the Pioneer Pit immediately to the south of Caldicott Farm. This may be due to the working methods employed at this quarry which were not conducive to the collection of archaeological data, although a similar absence of medieval material is suggested by the preliminary works at the proposed Allen's Bank quarry. At this site, the study of aerial photographs, geophysical survey and trial trenching have failed to locate traces of any medieval field system or occupation within the extant field

boundaries, despite the location of yet another Roman site. The trenched area was admittedly small, but even so the total absence of medieval finds is of some note. Although further more extensive excavation will be needed to test the preliminary results of the evaluation, these works, together with the study of aerial photographs recently undertaken, suggests this area may not have been subjected to the creation of a formal field system as seen at Caldicott Farm and Lydd Quarry during the medieval period. This suggestion is further strengthened by a number of the historic maps which show much of the Pioneer Pit and Allen's Bank sites as one large, slightly meandering tract of land (field drawing for the first-edition OS, *c.* 1800–5, Fig. 4). The presence of the Roman sites in this area is due to them being sited on the edge of a large tidal lagoon which was situated to the north of Lydd at this time. As such, it is quite possible this area may still have been too wet, or considered too difficult, for reclamation during the medieval period. The current evidence suggests that the inning of this area did not progress across from Caldicott Farm to Lydd Quarry as one simple south-westerly advance but leap-frogged an area not considered suitable for some reason. This area may have, in part, been used for rough pasture which may explain the presence of the apparent stock enclosures in the area, though the date of these features has still not been resolved.

More detailed work has been possible on the field system at Lydd Quarry. The presence of elements of a 12th century ditch system to the south-west of Gores (later Burnthouse) Wall requires some explanation, although we need to consider the wider context to understand the sequence of events here. Examination of the 6-inch maps made in the late 19th century shows very clearly that Gores Wall was laid out across the field system, not only in the area of Lydd Quarry, but also to the north-east. The field boundaries there continue across the line of the wall and it is probable they were established before the Gores Wall was constructed (Fig. 102 opposite). This, however, presents considerable problems for interpretation. Gores Wall is not a late addition to the pattern of embankments. It adjoins the Midley Wall and is butted by, and therefore pre-dates, Tore Wall: it is an integral, and indeed fundamental, element in the system of embankments in this part of the marsh. An interpretation requires an examination of the sequence of events to the north of TC2.

That area on the south-west side of the Rhee Wall has been known by historians as the 'Archbishops' Innings' since they were given that name by Elliott (1862). He suggested that they were enclosed by the archbishops of Canterbury whose names they were thought to bear – Thomas (1162–70), Baldwin (1184–90), Boniface (1241–70) and Peckham (1279–92). More recently, this attribution has been challenged, since it has been argued that Baldwin's Wall and Baldwin's Sewer derive their names not from the archbishop, but from Baldwin

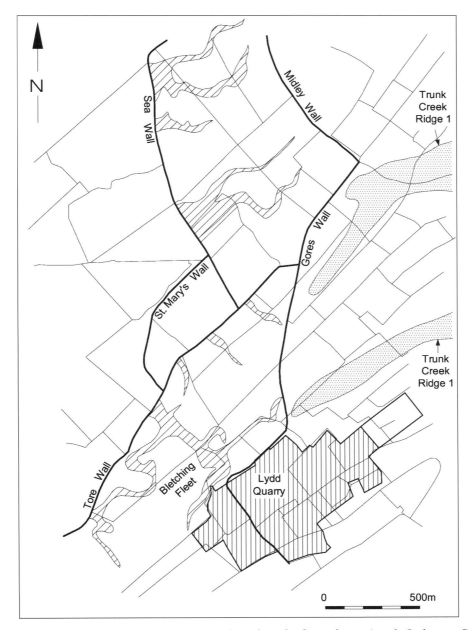

Fig. 102 Gores Wall in its landscape setting. (Plan based on the first edition 6 inch Ordnance Survey Map)

Scadeway who, in *c.* 1160, was granted as much land at Misleham as he could enclose from the sea (Eddison 1983, 56–7; Brooks 1988, 100–1). The field pattern would in that case date to the mid or late 12th century when the land was being ditched and drained. Moreover, it has been noted that the embankment associated with Baldwin's Sewer, apparently associated with the grant of land to Baldwin Scadeway, has its bank on the north-east or landward side. This is a most improbable position for an embankment to be constructed since the sewer lay on its seaward face (Eddison and Draper 1997, 84). Furthermore, Eddison (1983, 57) has noted that in a number of places the lines of the field boundaries appear

to have continued across the embankment defining the Archbishops' Innings, as if it too was a secondary feature.

It is generally assumed in the study of marshlands that the first act in utilising the land was the construction of the embankment to prevent the ingress of water and allow the land within to be divided up and drained. However, land could certainly be used as pasture without enclosing it. The excavations at Lydd, and landscape evidence elsewhere from this area of the marsh, have indicated that the land was divided into parcels before embankments were constructed. The walls were only built later as need arose. Either the likelihood of flooding was remote, or the land was used as pasture and the consequences of flooding were unimportant. However, during the course of the 12th century, the incidence of flooding may have increased or the farming regime may have changed, presumably to arable which was less tolerant of water-logging. At this stage a series of embankments were constructed, probably in a rather piecemeal manner judging by their irregular morphology. It is not certain whether these embankments had sides which extended laterally towards a channel identified by the Soil Survey and called by Allen (1999a), perhaps incorrectly (Eddison 2003, 129), the *Rumenesea*. Indeed, there appears to have been no embankment to prevent water entering the 'Archbishops' Innings' from that side, so evidently it was not a problem (*cf.* Allen 1996; Allen 2002). Perhaps as curious is the fact that no embankment has been detected to prevent water from flowing up the TC2 from the direction of Old Romney. However, the straight road to the south-west of the Rhee Wall, which was adopted as the boundary of the Liberty of Old Romney, might indicate the line of a possible wall.

The dating of the construction of Gores Wall is uncertain. Documentary sources suggest it is most likely to have been built in the 11th or 12th centuries. The archaeological evidence is ambiguous. If the mid to late 12th century ceramics relate to the initial establishment of the ditch system, and this system originally ran to the south-west of Gores Wall, then the wall must post-date the ceramics. Alternatively, if these ceramics represent refuse by shepherds and herdsmen, then the construction of the ditch system can easily be pushed back to the beginning of the 12th century. If this were the case, then the Gores Wall is likely to have been constructed in the first half of the 12th century. The construction date for Tore Wall, to the north-west of Gores Wall, is currently thought to belong to the 12th or early 13th centuries from *documentary* evidence (Sweetinburgh, above; see also below). Taking the *archaeological* evidence as a whole, it is considered more likely that this was constructed in the early to middle part of the 13th century, after consolidation and settlement of the area enclosed by Gores/Burnthouse Wall. The location and excavation of any field system ditches, or indeed occupation or activity areas, between Gores and Tore Walls should help prove its chronology. Similarly, any stratified medieval finds to the west of, or incorporated into or under, Gores/Burnthouse Wall will be of extreme importance.

It is interesting to note that part of Gores Wall adjacent to Site F had been removed prior to the beginning of quarry works at the site, but after 1908, according to the historic maps (Fig. 9). Topsoil stripping of this area revealed two parallel ditches which may have represented a third trackway running roughly parallel to those excavated to the south. The wall and putative track alignment follow, at least in part, another shingle ridge. The trackway may have been replaced by an embankment at this point to minimise the loss of farmland in its construction. However, as this part of the site was preserved *in situ*, none of the features was excavated. It is therefore impossible to be certain whether this was a trackway and indeed its original date. Some 13th to 14th century pottery was collected from the surface of one of the ditches suggesting a later date, but Gores Wall could not have been constructed as late as this. It is probable the pottery was deposited during a period of repairs to the wall, probably during the 14th century, or alternatively is totally residual in the ditches. If the latter is the case, these ditches may be nothing more than early 20th century boundary features put in to control stock movement when the wall was breached here after 1908. Further excavation work on this area in the future may answer these questions.

The excavations, together with historical sources, have enabled the processes associated with the creation of the field system to be fairly well understood, at least on this part of Walland Marsh. The field systems of the area were laid out in relation to the natural topography and, as such, their orientation was dictated to be the north-east to south-west trending shingle ridges, at least in the areas at Lydd and Caldicott Farm Quarries. Access would have been gained along the ridge tops along unmarked access-ways which had probably been utilised since prehistoric times. From these higher ridges, ditches would have been laid out and excavated at right angles to the ridge orientation. These ditches were primarily cut through the finer grained sediments in the troughs between the ridges where drainage would have been the worst. Some of these ditches ran across the ridges, presumably not for drainage but to mark property boundaries and to control the movement of stock. Where extant natural sinuous creeks were present they appear to have been utilised and incorporated into the system, with differing degrees of modification. This practice has been seen at a number of places at Lydd Quarry, particularly at Lydd 1. Where no existing channels were present (which seems to have been the case for the majority of the area), straight ditches were established from the outset. Such planning and regularity over relatively large tracts of land demonstrate that this was not a piecemeal undertaking by individuals but an organised venture, probably by lords with the involvement of their peasants.

The Period 1 reclamation is best viewed as a 'pioneering' period concerned with laying the foundation for the subsequent Period 2 subdivision and refinement of drainage. This is apparent from the marsh creeks which were initially incorporated into the pattern of drains. They were found particularly on the west and north-west side of the site nearest to the major creek, Bletching Fleet. Within a few years of establishing the extensive system of drainage, it is probable that the land would have been suitably improved to allow more intense usage grazing. The more intense use of the new land for such purposes may explain why towards the end of this period the first activity areas appear (Sites A–C) which relate to temporary occupation, storage or shelter for animal husbandry. The small quantity of domestic waste associated suggests any human occupation was short-term or seasonal. Some archaeological evidence, particularly the quern stones and seeds, from the excavations suggest it is quite possible that by the end of the 12th century (or beginning of the 13th century) some arable cultivation was already occurring on the newly won area, but it is unlikely that this would have been practical before the construction of Gores Wall.

Settlement

The three excavated sites belonging to Period 1 (Sites A–C) all appear to date to the latter part of the 12th or early 13th centuries. They are likely to have been established after the initial ditch system, but before the onset of permanent settlement in Period 2. Exactly how long these sites lasted is uncertain, but the ceramics suggest they did not continue for long into the 13th century and all were disused by the middle of the century at the very latest. Site A is undoubtedly the most substantial, and probably long-lived, of these and represents the only clear building plan from any of the quarries. The building on that site was constructed on a slightly elevated band of shingle. It was constructed using earth-fast posts, the normal building method in the first half of the 13th century.

The function of Site A is important to our understanding of this period. The various possibilities have been outlined above. The building may have had an agricultural function, though whether it was used for sheltering animals, storing their fodder or crops, or both is uncertain. Alternatively, it may have been a domestic building, though the archaeobotanical evidence suggests that livestock were kept nearby. The presence of only a single rubbish pit is not surprising: indeed, it is more surprising that there was a pit at all, since the usual practice in the countryside was to collect waste in a midden and then spread it upon arable fields, though many of the Period 2 sites contain rubbish pits. Unfortunately, the evidence for the function of the building is not decisive. In either case, the roof would probably have been of straw or reed thatch, or less probably of shingles, and the timber walls infilled with wattle and daub. The small quantity of domestic refuse suggests that at least some cooking or eating occurred at this site.

The remaining two sites of this period at Lydd Quarry (B and C) are more enigmatic. Site B may represent the worn floor of a shepherd's hut, the superstructure of which would probably be very light and leave little or no trace. A similar structure was present at Caldicott Farm but was very small for a shepherd's hut. The best parallels for such structures are the shielings or *hafod* buildings found in various areas of Britain. The dating of these buildings is often difficult because of the absence of pottery or other datable finds, but they were generally small and poorly constructed. Such buildings have been recorded on Dartmoor (Beresford 1979, 111–12), Bodmin Moor (Herring 1996, 38–9), Westmorland (Ramm 1970), the Brecon Beacons (Ward 1997), the Isle of Man (Gelling 1962–3) and in the Antrim uplands in Ireland (Williams 1984), amongst other places. Although most such sites are known from the upland areas of Britain and Ireland, a possible shepherd's sunken hut of 8th to 10th century date has been recorded from the South Downs (Drewett *et al.* 1986; Gardiner 2003, 154) and comparable building of probably more recent date from the Cotswolds (O'Neil 1967, 27). It is also instructive to compare the building in Area B with 'lookers'' or shepherds' huts dating from the late 18th and 19th centuries found on Walland and Romney Marsh. These buildings were constructed to house tools and might be used for overnight accommodation at busy times of the year when the shepherd needed to stay close to the sheep, particularly during lambing (Reeves and Eve 1998). All of these buildings provide possible parallels in either form or function for the building at Site B at Lydd Quarry and less certainly that at Caldicott Farm. We can conclude that the Site B building was slightly built and was too small for accommodation for a long period. It is likely that it served as a shelter at certain times of year, probably related to the care of livestock.

The position of the three sites of this period may be significant. Sites A and B are set in the fields, whereas Site C is situated adjacent to the southern principal trackway or droveway across the area. The system of ditches at Lydd Quarry Site C has no certain function, though it is probably related to stock control and care. If Site C does indeed represent a medieval sheepfold of sorts, then its position adjacent to the track would facilitate driving animals into and out of the enclosures. However, all three sites have small quantities of domestic waste suggesting that whatever activities took place here, people were also eating at these locations.

There is no evidence of activity at Denge West Quarry during the 12th and very first part of the 13th century. This is, perhaps, surprising given the chronology of the development of the barrier shingle discussed above.

Economy and Trade

Most of the archaeologically attested activity in this period was related to the establishment of the main elements of the ditch system. This work was probably undertaken alongside grazing herds or flocks and the exploitation of natural marshland resources, activities which had been occurring for many years previous. At least some of these animals were being eaten on site, though the numbers of bones are small and they may relate to meat brought in as food from occupation sites within or close to Lydd town. The chicken and fish bones recovered from these early deposits may have had a similar origin. Little can be said of economy and trade as there is little refuse relating certainly to occupation. However, it should be noted that even at this early date there is some French pottery present.

By the end of this period it is probable that the first arable cultivation was under way. This is suggested by the presence of limited amounts of cereals at this time (Site A), as well as the occasional quern stone fragment. Exactly where at the site crops were being grown is uncertain, though it was probably confined to small areas with the best drainage. The presence of much damp grassland at this time is still suggested by the archaeobotanical remains, though some of the grass may have been involved with hay production.

PERIOD 2: CONSOLIDATION AND SETTLEMENT (EARLY AND MID 13TH CENTURY) (*Fig. 29)

Reclamation

After the construction of embankments in the early 13th century, the field system was consolidated, and in places rationalised, by the insertion of various new ditches and, occasionally, the backfilling of selected earlier ones. Whether this happened in one planned scheme of works, or as a series of small improvements is difficult to determine. The creation of a number of small square or rectangular fields, often under 0.4 hectare (1 acre) in extent, suggests they may have been intended primarily for arable agriculture. Similar sized fields have been noted elsewhere on the Marsh (Reeves 1996, 7; 1997, 65). The small fields each separated by ditches would have been both well drained and suitable for intensive cultivation. Most of the smaller fields at Lydd were situated between the northern and southern trackways in this period (*Fig. 29), suggesting this may have been the focus of arable activity. The area was divided into long narrow plots in a fairly regular pattern. If the phasing of the ditch system is correct, then the fields were not laid out at a single time, but evolved through the sub-division of the larger fields of Period 1. Long parallel ditches, typically set about 25m apart, are now known from a number of marshlands. A relict system has been identified at East Guldeford (Gardiner 2002, 113) and one pre-dating the late 13th century flooding recorded near Broomhill (Gardiner and Hartwell 2006). A system probably dated to the medieval period has been recognised from the Huntspill-Mark area of the Somerset Levels (Rippon 1997, 210–12). There are, however, differences between these field patterns, and it is notable, in particular, that the Lydd Quarry ditches are much shorter than those elsewhere.

The sinuous ditches found in Lydd 1 in the first period were filled in. These formed from salt marsh creeks, probably part of the system associated with Bletching Fleet which lay to the north-west. During the second period these creeks were straightened to allow the creation of a more regular field pattern.

The land to the north and south of the closely ditched area was divided into larger fields, typically up to 1 hectare. These were relatively unchanged from the previous period and may continue to have been used for grazing livestock. The different field patterns may be related to the micro-relief within the area examined. A band of buried shingle, named by Spencer *et al.* (1998, Fig. 2.3) Ridge 1, runs through the excavated area of Lydd Quarry in a east-north-east to west-south-west orientation. Differential autocompaction of the fine-grained sediments (Allen 1999b) overlying the shingle leads to slight differences in elevation at ground level which were exploited by the medieval communities. The drier areas on, and to the north of, the shingle ridge were used for arable, while those to the south, overlying the area described as the Scotney Marsh Trough (Spencer *et al.* 1998, Fig. 2.3) where the shingle has a lower elevation, were used for pasture.

At about the same time, in the early to mid 13th century, the first evidence of reclamation and occupation at Denge West Quarry appears. This area, which is divided by more prominent shingle banks, must have been very poor land, even in comparison with the marshland around the area of Lydd Quarry. The absence of fine-grained sediments over much of the area would not have been conducive to pastoralism, but even more inhibiting for cultivation. The ceramic dating at the site suggests the somewhat fragmented ditch system detected here was established at about the same time. The earliest infilling of the Denge West ditches, where tested by excavation, appears to relate to the later 13th century, suggesting some at least may have been initially established in the early part of that century. Denge West did not produce any clearly 12th century material, suggesting that little activity, for either reclamation or occupation, occurred within the investigated areas at this time.

We can set the expansion of reclamation in the excavated areas within the wider context of events elsewhere on Walland Marsh. The early decades of the 13th century were a period of enormous activity in the area, with numerous references in documentary sources to the construction of embankments and the drainage of new lands. The planning of these embankments was a critical matter. The aim of the engineers was to enclose the largest area for the least labour. Embankments constructed too far out beyond vegetated marsh on the mud flats were difficult to construct and liable to be removed by floodwaters; those which did not enclose a sufficient area were uneconomic. It has already been noted that the engineers were faced with particular problems when constructing the embankments over large creeks, since the ground there was unstable and liable to compaction, and consequently required considerable quantities of fill to provide a secure base. The land occupied by creeks (or 'fleets' as they were known once they had been cut off by the embankment) was low-lying and of little value for agriculture. The engineers therefore attempted to align the embankment to cross the creeks as near to the head as possible where they were narrower or, if possible, to avoid the creeks entirely. There may have also been other considerations. The marshland may

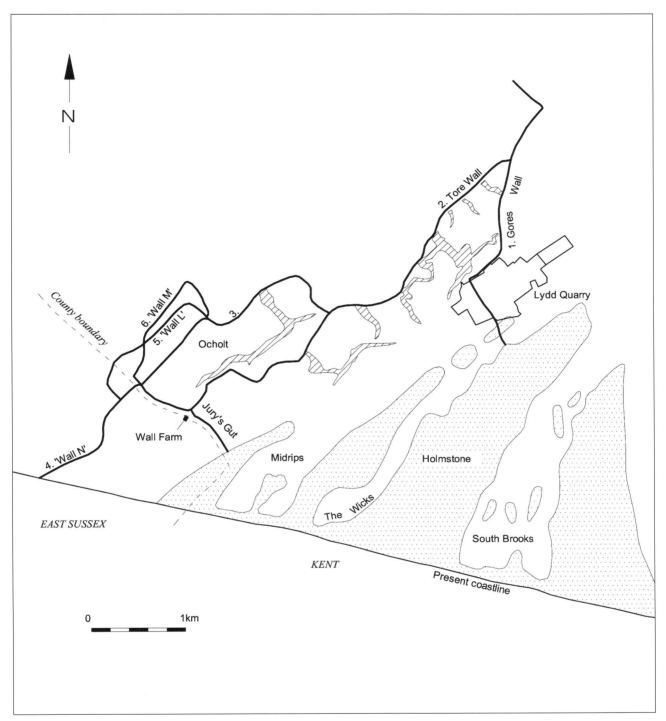

Fig. 103 Sequence of reclamation in the Lydd Quarry area

have already been divided between separate lordships before enclosure, perhaps using a simple ditch or plough furrow, or a line of stakes, as at Huttoft in Lincolnshire (Owen 1996, No. 40). In that case, embankments did not establish the boundaries of the lordship; they followed those already defined.

It is possible to trace the sequence of enclosure to the south-west of Lydd Quarry. The first embankment

here was Tore Wall, which sprang from Gores Wall and therefore was later than it (Fig. 103 above). It ran parallel to the shingle exposure, was 4km long and enclosed an area of approximately 350 hectares (850 acres). It may have built upon slightly raised land overlying buried shingle ridges, but the line of the wall in detail was determined by the presence of a series of creeks which drained north-westwards towards the Wainway. These may be clearly identified on Green's soil map, and the wall generally turns inwards at each point where it intersected a creek to cross it as far from its mouth as possible. Tore Wall turns south-eastwards at the site of Wall Farm to return to the shingle exposure. The corner of the enclosure was probably chamfered to increase the strength of the embankment and make it less liable to erosion in flood conditions.

Kestner (1975, 402–3) has shown that the construction of an embankment in a salt marsh hastens the deposition of sediment beyond its outside face, so that each wall prepares the way for the subsequent enclosure. The construction of the Tore Wall with consequential silting in the salt marsh beyond, together with the deposition of sediment which was in any case taking place within TC2, allowed a second area to be enclosed (Fig. 103, No. 3). This was roughly parallel to the first and, although smaller in area, may have been more problematic in construction because it cut across a particular deep fleet at Oakhill (*Ocholt*). Enclosure continued south of the county boundary with the construction of what has been called Wall N. The sequence of the subsequent embankments, Walls L and M, will be discussed elsewhere (Gardiner and Hartwell 2006) and it is sufficient to note here that they represent successive enclosures. Wall L was breached by tidal water coming from the west and was replaced by a less ambitious structure, Wall M, which again seems to have been aligned upon the county boundary.

It is not possible to identify any of these enclosures with the activity recorded in documentary sources, with one exception (see Gardiner 1988, Fig. 10.1 for a diagrammatic reconstruction of the documentary evidence). This is the prior of Christchurch Canterbury's lands at *Ocholt*, an area known in the 15th and 16th centuries (when it had reverted to salt marsh) as 'Prior's Salts' (Bodleian MS, KeS/13; Canterbury Cathedral Library (CCL), MA 25, ff. 157v, 162a). Clarissa, daughter of Robert de Gestling and wife of Robert de Auberville, quitclaimed any rights she had in this land to the Priory during the priorate of John (1222 to *c*. 1238). It is apparent from the charter that she is releasing rights she might have inherited from her father, as these are distinguished from the land enclosed by her husband in Broomhill (CCL, Charta Antiqua A117). The land released to Christchurch Priory was apparently part of that which her grandfather, John de Gestling, had enclosed in the marsh. He also had land in a marsh called *Grikes* in Broomhill (Lincoln's Inn Library, Hale MS 87, ff. 50–2) and in the *Terrae Perjuratae*, a name remembered in Jury's Gut. We can therefore identify the land enclosed by Wall N with the land of John de Gestling, probably in the early part of the 13th century. The construction of Tore Wall must have preceded that and Gores Wall must be earlier still.

Settlement

Permanent farmsteads and associated activity areas were established from about the second quarter of the century and continued through at least until the storms at the end of the century. Perhaps one of the key problems in interpreting the settlement pattern in this and subsequent periods is the difficulties in identifying site function. The absence of good structural evidence at the occupation sites poses a number of problems. If a proper settlement occupied more or less permanently leaves no structural traces, as for example at Lydd Quarry Site D, how is it to be differentiated from an 'activity area' without permanent occupation? It is suggested that Site E at Lydd 1 was a small enclosure for the collection and storage of manure and domestic rubbish prior to dispersal on to the fields. The difference between this and Site D lies only in its location within the field system and the number of pits at each site, rather than the presence of domestic rubbish. If there is such a problem in identifying the nature of such sites from excavation, the difficulty will obviously become more acute when interpreting surface scatters of material found in field-walking. The density of occupation sites thus revealed, particularly from slight variation in surface material (Reeves 1995, 80), needs to be treated with caution.

Despite these problems at Lydd Quarry, 13th century settlement appears to have included at least two definite occupation sites (Sites D and H), one probable occupation site/activity area (Site G) and four associated activity areas (E, F, I and Ja). These sites can be divided up into two main groups: three sites are located to the north of the northern trackway (D, E and F) while the remainder are set between the northern and southern trackways (*Fig. 29). The domestic settlement at Site D is characterised by numerous pits, other features and dense concentration of domestic waste. Unfortunately, little can be said regarding the settlement's internal morphology, though it seems likely that the associated building was situated in the western part of the site and almost certainly used sill-beam construction, either on low drystone walls or post-pads, set directly on the ground surface. Rubbish disposal appears to have been concentrated in the eastern part of the site. This site is set adjacent to the northern trackway to afford easy access. To the north, well away from the trackway, are the other two sites. Of these, Site E was the most extensively investigated. Although consisting of an enclosure associated with significant quantities of domestic waste, this site did not have the density of 'domestic' features noted at Site D. This, combined with the fact that it is set out in the fields away from the track, suggests an agricultural activity area, perhaps associated with manuring. The collection of dung into heaps for drying before manuring is attested by the Christ

Church Priory records of the later 13th century (Gross and Butcher 1995, 110). Similarly, Site F was set at some distance from the track, had few features and produced little domestic waste. Although more cleaning and excavation at this site may have revealed more, on the current evidence this is thought to represent an activity, possibly associated with later 13th century repairs to Gores Wall, rather than an occupation site. Both Sites E and F could be 'satellite' sites of Site D.

There were four sites of this general period between the northern and southern trackways. Site H is perhaps the best preserved domestic site at Lydd Quarry in that something of its internal morphology of the croft can be deduced, despite the limited remains. It is notable that the site is situated, like Site D, adjacent to a trackway and contains a high concentration of 'domestic' features and refuse. The site, set within its enclosure, at least initially, appears to have been quite well organised into functional zones. The area of the probable house is marked by the total absence of cut features. This sterile area suggests a structure measuring about 10 × 5m. A ground-plan of these dimensions would be in keeping with the smaller medieval houses, such as that of Rype Cottage, Lydd, thought to have been the most common house type in the rural areas of the marsh (Pearson 1995, 95–6). The absence of cut features for this putative structure suggests the construction also utilised sill-beams rather than earth-fast posts. The sill beams may have been set on low drystone walls, which might account for some of the stone brought to the site. Similar construction was noted in New Romney (Willson 1987), though this was obviously in an urban context. The absence of a central hearth may be the result of ground reduction by ploughing. This suggestion is supported by the evidence from the unploughed old pasture areas of the marsh where settlement sites often appear as actual mounds (Reeves 1996, 9). If such sites were ploughed level, as at Lydd, serious truncation of the features is bound to occur. Building materials are likely to have been similar to those used at Site A with a thatched roof and rushes used on the floor. An access path to the south had been kept clear of features, though to the east of it was an area of pits, presumably for domestic refuse in the main. The southern part of the enclosure may have been used, at least in part, for securing livestock, perhaps from theft during the night and to allow their dung to be collected or to help with lambing at certain times of the year. The organisation of this site seems to have become less structured over time and the infilling of the enclosure ditch allowed the settlement to begin to expand and refuse to be deposited in a wider area. Although this site was certainly in use throughout the 13th century, its precise abandonment date is hard to be certain of. The ceramics suggest a mainly 13th century date, though a few pieces could, but not necessarily have to, stretch into the early 14th century. All in all it is quite possible this site was abandoned at or immediately after the floods of the late 13th century, though at present this cannot be proven.

Two satellite activity areas appear to have been associated with Site H. To the east lay a small area of activity, possibly representing the site of an ancillary structure (Site I), while to the south-west an area of activity appears to have revolved around the junction of a subsidiary track with the principal southern track or droveway (Site Ja). The fact that this latter site is adjacent to the main track, but does not contain large quantities of 'domestic' features and refuse, suggests it may be primarily concerned with stock control.

The remaining site between the northern and southern principle tracks is Site G. This is a difficult site to characterise and, falling between Sites D and H, appears to be somewhat independent of them. It is interesting to note that like Site Ja it is located next to the junction of a subsidiary track and one of the main (this time the northern) principal tracks. This, particularly when considered alongside the evidence for the small enclosures at the site, strongly suggests it was related to stock control. However, the size of this 'activity' area is considerably larger than any of the others and there is ample evidence to suggest some domestic occupation. The presence of a possible building at this site suggests shelter was afforded to some of the livestock and/or farm-hands. The fact that domestic refuse appears to increase toward the latter part of the period suggests that by this date some full-time, or at least temporary, domestic activity was occurring here. It is possible the site represents a 'communal' sheepfold for a number of the farmsteads in the area.

The overall picture of the settlement pattern at Lydd Quarry during this period suggests a relatively dense period of occupation, though once a division between domestic sites and activity areas is made, occupation is spread more evenly across the area. It seems likely that each farmstead had outlying satellite sites relating to everyday agricultural tasks, though it is interesting that, with the occasional exception of the 'odd' pit, no sites, whether domestic or 'activity', were situated to the south of the southern trackway during this period. The settlement density for this period suggested by Anne Reeves (1997, 87) for other areas was one settlement for every six hectares (15 acres). The results from Lydd are in line with this, if Site G is considered a settlement, though as previously pointed out, the criteria for the identification of settlement sites from surface scatters of pottery alone needs careful consideration.

It is difficult to evaluate this figure. Peasants with 15 acres or half a virgate would have made a bare living in the 13th century, according to Dyer's calculations, but many had considerably less land (Dyer 1989, 117, 119).

However, if we compare the figure of 15 acres ascertained by excavation and fieldwork, with those recorded in rentals and surveys covering Denge Marsh in the early 15th century, there is a considerable disparity (Gardiner 1998, 134). By the opening of the 15th century, when the population had probably dropped considerably from its peak around 1300, comparatively few peasants (less than 20%) would have had as much land as 15 acres. However, a number of peasants in the Lydd area may have been living within the town, while farming the area in the surrounding countryside (Gardiner 1998, 139). The number of houses found in excavation in the vicinity of the town would not therefore be representative of the whole marsh. We also need to remember that farming may have been simply one strand in the economy of such peasants: trading and fishing may have also been important.

The ceramic evidence from Denge West Quarry, unlike Lydd Quarry, does not suggest a gap between the establishment of the field system and permanent occupation, although such a period of consolidation may have been short-lived and thus not detectable in the ceramics. Why the area was occupied so quickly after the start of the 'reclamation' works is uncertain, but it could relate to pressure on the land not allowing people to wait for the land to be properly consolidated prior to settling. Another possibility is that the ditches were created by seasonal fishermen who, by the time of the 13th century, were looking to supplement their income by adopting agriculture. Such people may have had earlier seasonal occupation sites closer to the sea and outside the investigated area.

At Denge West North one possible occupation site (Area A) and one possible occupation/activity site (Area E) belong to this period. The closeness of these two sites would certainly suggest that both are not for permanent occupation. The presence of low scatters of 13th century ceramics in a number of other areas, including Denge West South fields, strongly suggests manuring was also occurring at this time: Area E could represent a similar type of site to Site E at Lydd 1. Unfortunately, too little of the Denge West occupation sites were investigated to be able to comment on the settlement morphology. However, the location of post-holes at Denge West North, albeit few in number, is interesting. This, together with Site A at Lydd 10, strongly suggests that ground-set post construction was utilised where ground conditions were better drained on the shingle. In the lower areas, with finer sediments, sole-plates are more likely to have been employed, resting either on the ground surface or on low sill walls.

Strangely, in this period of intense activity at Lydd and Denge West Quarries, no activity, including finds assemblages, was noted at Caldicott Farm, though this may be due to the relatively small area investigated.

Economy and Trade

Little woodland was present on the Marsh and most timber appears to have been brought in, probably by water, from the Weald to the north where managed woodland was common (Sweetinburgh, above). The charcoal and pollen data from the excavations would agree with this on the whole in that dryland, as well as wetland, habitats are indicated by the species present. However, the same data suggest the possibility of some local woodland on the marsh itself, though more data would be needed to prove this. On the marsh historical sources indicate that thorn was grown and managed quite extensively and indeed this material was noted in the charcoal assemblage, albeit in small quantities. The resultant material was not only used in the construction of sea defences, but would have also been useful for creating barriers and windbreak shelters for livestock, as well as providing kindling for fires. Although it is impossible to prove from the current archaeological data, it is tempting to speculate on the utilisation of thorn. The small enclosures excavated at Lydd 5/6 could have been small plantations. In addition, thorn hedges at the edges of fields should be considered, as the excavated drainage ditches, even accounting for truncation through ploughing and the fact that they would probably have been water-filled, are too shallow to provide a stock-proof barrier. Further measures, either using hedges or hurdles, are likely to have been needed. Any trace of disturbance from roots may have been removed by ploughing, particularly if the thorn hedge had been planted on the excavated upcast banks from the drainage ditches. The evidence from the pollen and charcoal reinforces the suggestion that hedges were present in the landscape, and these may have accommodated several tree species as well as scrub-like plants. The only fence line found so far was at Lydd 2 (Figs. 16 and 42) which ran parallel to Ditch 2098/2134. The reason this boundary was marked both with a ditch and fence is uncertain. The fence line was not traced beyond the junction of Ditches 2098 and 2011 (Fig. 16), however, there was slight evidence to suggest the fence may have turned to follow the line of Ditch 2011. Both the post-holes and Ditch 2098/2134 appear to be of 13th to 14th century date, although the upper fills of the ditch were not deposited until the 15th to early 16th centuries. It is probable due to this being a more important boundary, possibly between two land ownerships, which warranted marking with an above-ground barrier as well as a ditch.

Documentary sources show that much of the Marsh lay in the lordship of ecclesiastical bodies in the 13th century. There were substantial demesnes at Cheney to the west of the sites investigated (held by archbishop of Canterbury: *Cal Inq. Misc.*, 6, no. 319) and at Denge to the south (held by Battle Abbey). The greater part of the land was not cultivated directly by lords, but held by tenants. Unlike land in the Weald, which was often held in consolidated blocks, the land in the area examined here appears to have been divided between a number of places. The *c.* 1432 rental of Denge manor implies that the pieces of land were often in the same area, if not contiguous, a pattern which seems to have been typical of Kent more generally (PRO, E315/56; Baker 1965, 157–8).

The documentary records for the ecclesiastical houses show a mixed farming regime during the 13th to early 14th centuries, with considerable numbers of sheep (Sweetinburgh, above; Gardiner 1998, 133). We do not know whether peasants adopted a similar regime of mixed agriculture during this period, but the evidence from Lydd Quarry seems to bear this suggestion out. The differing size of fields implies that they were used for different purposes. Cattle and sheep figure in both the documentary sources and the excavated bone assemblages, though most herds and flocks of peasants would have been small (Sweetinburgh, above). Sheep appear more common in the 13th century, but the bone assemblages are too small to allow firm conclusions to be drawn. The dominance of mature animals in this period might suggest milk products and wool were perhaps more important than meat, a point well attested from the documentary sources (Gross and Butcher 1995, 113). However, it was common practice to fatten ageing animals, either for sale at the market or for consumption at the farmer's table, and it is probably the bones of these animals which are appearing in the archaeological record. A policy of maximising wool production has been detected on a number of large estates in the later 13th and early 14th centuries (Biddick 1989, 46, 112; Page 2003, 154; *cf.* Stone 2003). Pigs were always present along with horses, the latter probably being used for traction. Areas of wet grassland, indicated by the seed remains, would undoubtedly have still been close by and provided good pastoral land for the herds and flocks.

Arable cultivation was dominated by cereals, particularly wheat, barley and oats, though lesser quantities of legumes and vetches were also grown. The proportion of these crops which was used for animal fodder is uncertain, however, it is probable that at least the oats and vetches were produced for this purpose and hay was also produced in certain fields (Gross and Butcher 1995, 113). Some crops, such as the flax and hemp, though only present in small quantities, suggest some farmers may have been growing small amounts of crops for sale, a fact also attested by the historical sources. However, some of the flax and hemp may have been retted on the farms and the remains of a glass linen-smoother (Site H), a bone pin-beater and three loom-weights (Site H) hint at domestic cloth production. Strangely, there are the remains of only one spindle whorl from the quarry.

The economy, or perhaps more correctly the diet, of the Lydd Quarry settlements appears to have been supplemented by fishing, and probably fowling. The quantity of lead net weights demonstrates that these were both being made and used at Lydd Quarry at this time, particularly at Site H. It is likely that the majority were used on inland rivers, streams or ponds or tidal creeks, rather than in the open sea. This suggestion is supported by the presence of flatfish and eels in the bone assemblage. Both these species could have been caught by nets in local tidal creeks and inlets, and indeed the Denge manor accounts of 1374–5 record receipts of 20*s.* from eels caught in the Brooks (PRO, SC6/889/25). However, some of the larger net weights would have coped with inshore waters so this possibility cannot be ruled out. The small fish assemblage shows a mixture of salt and freshwater species at this time, though what was caught by the inhabitants and what brought from other fishermen cannot be proven. It is suspected at Lydd Quarry that although never of great importance, the inhabitants supplemented their diet by fishing the local creeks, but probably bought deep sea fish, such as cod, from more specialist fisherman who probably used hooks and line for the larger specimens. The absence of rolled net weights at Denge West Quarry, where large hooks were more prolific, suggests this settlement was more involved with such sea fishing, though it should be noted no metal detector was used at this latter site. The huge quantities of shellfish, particularly cockles, may have been gathered directly from the shore or purchased at market.

The economic base of the 13th century settlements at Denge West is difficult to establish without more detailed excavation and further environmental sampling. However, based on the current evidence, it seems likely that they relied more heavily on the exploitation of marine resources, particularly fishing, with the mixed agriculture on the poor soils of the area providing a supplementary income.

The pottery from 13th century contexts shows a dominance of locally produced wares. The site drew from sources largely eastwards and north-eastwards, around New Romney and Hythe or Folkestone. These sources supplied the largest share of ceramics and the introduced stone, including Lower Greensand rotary querns. A little material was coming along the coast from the west, most notably whetstones probably from the Rye or Hastings area, though coastal trade in general appears important. Despite the dominance of local material, continental produce was imported in small quantities, probably through the port of New Romney, though some may have come in through Lydd's own small harbour at Dungeness in this, or the following century. This material includes German lava querns as well as some French pottery. In addition, a little Scarborough pottery may be of this date (rather than the 14th century). The latter could easily have been brought back on an *ad hoc* basis by local fishermen who are known to have worked the East Coast ports, including Scarborough, during the summer and autumn months (Gardiner 1996). The presence of the Lias ammonite fossil is almost certainly from the same source.

PERIOD 3A: START OF THE DECLINE (LATE 13TH TO 14TH CENTURY) (*Fig. 30)

The Field System

Direct archaeological evidence for the late 13th century storms is notably absent at the investigated sites around Lydd, despite postulated storm deposits having being found in New Romney (Linklater 2001, Oxford Arch. Unit 2001 and Jarrett 2002). A number of explanations may be offered. It is possible that any flood deposits were shallow and have subsequently been ploughed away. However, elements of such deposits, particularly if they were derived from a high-energy event, should have survived in at least some of the negative features which may have been open at the time. Another explanation could be that the breaches in the shingle barrier may have been sufficiently distant from the sites at Lydd Quarry to allow for indirect flooding, which did not so much destroy but saturate by raising the watertable or impeding the drainage of surface water. Silting from such flooding would be difficult to differentiate from normal silting in water-filled negative features.

The land to the north-west of the Tore Wall is notably higher, suggesting that the floodwaters, and the consequent deposits, were limited by this embankment (Jill Eddison pers. comm.). That conclusion is reinforced by survey work nearer Broomhill which has shown clear evidence of the breaching of Walls L, M and N (Gardiner and Hartwell 2006). Though the survey work has not examined the area enclosed around the lands of the manor of Scotney, this does not appear to have been flooded. The documentary record confirms this impression. The accounts of the manor of Scotney and *Ocholt* in 1361–3 show maintenance works on the embankments at Great and Little *Ocholt* (Bodleian MS, dd All Souls C183/51a). If that land had been flooded in 1288, it had certainly been recovered by the mid 14th century. Inquiries made in 1350/51 and 1363 are consistent in the picture of the flooded area (Sweetinburgh, above). The boundary between the flooded area of salt marsh and the reclaimed lands to the south ran from *Ocholt* along the Tore Wall (also called in the documents 'All Saints Wall' or 'All Hallows Wall') and St Mary's Wall to Midley's land (ESRO RYE 57/4, ff. 131–2; Bodleian MS, dd All Souls C184/1). We can observe from field evidence that flooding had also taken place at Midley House, where Green (1968, 27) noted that the embankment had been breached and is now much wider due to a repair constructed across

the fleet. That breach must have allowed water to flow to the north-west and south-east where there were similar breaches in other walls to the north-west and south-east marked now by 'horseshoe' repairs (Fig. 104 opposite).

Horseshoe-shaped deviations in the line of an embankment are a certain indication of the location of former breaches. The in-rushing of water through a narrow breach in an embankment produces a deep scour hole. The repaired embankment cannot be readily constructed across such deep pits and instead is built on either the seaward or landward side. This produces a horse-shoe deviation from the line of the wall to avoid the position of the scour hole.

It is clear then that the effects of the floods to the land of Lydd Quarry were considerable. Though the Tore Wall probably stopped the main surge from the north-west, the land at Lydd Quarry may have been covered by water from seepage through the shingle to the south or up the Wicks, where there is a horseshoe repair in the Lower Wick Wall. Circumstantial evidence from the possible short break in the ceramic sequence from Lydd might suggest some interruption to activity, though the ceramic series cannot be used to provide such a close date range for deposition of deposits.

Settlement

During extensive field-walking programmes on Romney Marsh proper it was noticed that there was a notable decrease in the density of sites of the 14th century, compared with those of the preceding century (Reeves 1995, 89). The reason for this downward turn in settlement cannot be proven beyond doubt at present, however, it is probable that the area lost some of its population as a result of the late 13th century storms which, even if not flooding the actual excavation sites, would have had a considerable impact on the marsh's economy. However, it is possible to exaggerate the impact of the flooding. There was considerable investment in the period after 1288 to recover land which had been lost to the sea, as Gross and Butcher (1995) have shown in their study of the Christchurch Priory manors of Ebony and Agney. At Winchelsea too, money was spent on trying to protect an area of marshland between 1337 and 1341, although that was ultimately unsuccessful (Gardiner 2002, 102). Work to recover the north-west corner of Walland Marsh seems to have been under way in the 1390s (Gardiner 202. 104). However, the reality was that these works only touched upon some of the areas which had reverted to salt marsh.

The impact of the Great Famine of 1315–17 and Black Death would have accentuated these problems. It is little wonder depopulation became extensive in certain parts (*cf.* Mate 1991a). Coastal districts were also threatened by French raids in the periods 1338–42, 1360 and 1377–80. Although the destruction of major coastal ports is well attested, even minor places, sometimes a considerable distance inland, were also raided. For example, the market centre of Appledore (Kent) was raided in 1380,

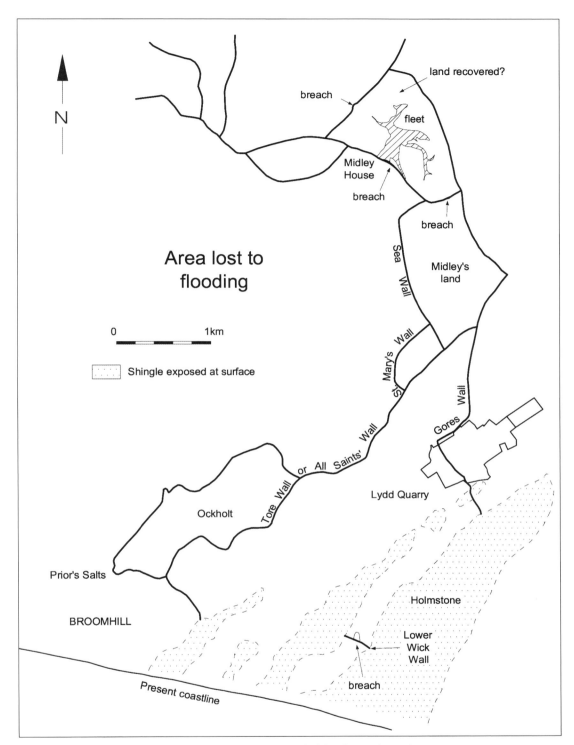

Fig. 104 Map showing area flooded by the early 14th century

the shops and bridge burnt and hay destroyed, and in 1403 the French ventured as far as Selmeston (Sussex), some 10kms from the coast (Mate 1984, 350; Anon. 1863, 213). Whether Lydd suffered directly at the hands of the French is not apparent, but the fear of raids must have had a destabilising effect. Hostilities across the Channel also made fishing difficult (Dulley 1969, 41). The fishermen of New Romney and Lydd concluded an agreement in the early 15th century with the French from settlements on the opposite side of the Channel to pay ransoms if boats and their crews from either side were captured (EKA, LY/CPz1).

A progressive depopulation is suggested at Lydd Quarry where only one occupation site (Jb) of this period was located. Site Jb straddled the southern principal track or droveway. Its northern part lay just to the east of the activity area Ja, which may have been one of the reasons for the establishment of Jb here. It is possible Site Jb represents a migration of Site H westwards, a suggestion that would certainly be supported by the ceramics. Why this shift happened cannot be proven, however, it is quite possible Site H was abandoned after the late 13th century storms and Site Jb established as its new site, possibly in the early 14th century after a period of consolidation. Unfortunately, the ceramics cannot be independently dated closely enough to distinguish between pre- and post-flood activity. However, it is interesting to note the dramatic change from shell-tempered wares of the 13th century at Site H to sand-tempered wares of the 14th century at Site Jb. Although this change is rapid elsewhere in Kent (J. Cotter, pers. comm.), at Lydd it is so notable that it is tempting to speculate that the shell-dominated assemblages of the 13th century are pre-flood but there was a break in the occupation, though not necessarily utilisation, after. As such, assemblages from the end of the 13th century, when there could expect to be a transitional period between shell and sand, are absent. When occupation began again in the 14th century, after a period of consolidation, the shell-tempered wares were virtually gone. Although an interesting and alluring theory, the current knowledge of ceramics on the Marsh still cannot be relied upon to prove or disprove such a suggestion. Further work on assemblages from New Romney may go some way to redressing this shortcoming in the future.

The fact that Site Jb straddled the trackway, ensured it made the most of the slightly higher ground of the low shingle ridge along which the track ran. The majority of the highest ground, averaging 2.8m to 2.9m OD, was to the south of the track and this is where the domestic buildings were situated. The height difference between the sites is small: at Site H the average elevation by the 'domestic building' was 2.5m to 2.6m OD. However, this extra height probably counted for considerably better drainage as well as peace of mind. It is interesting to note the use of shingle 'floors' in the two postulated buildings at Site Jb, presumably another sign of an increased awareness of drainage problems. A similar possible 'floor' was noted at Dering Farm (Trench B) which, although not possible to date closely, may also be of 14th century date. The northern part of Site Jb, to the north of the track, is also on higher ground (up to 3m OD) but this drops away to the north and west into the area of Site Ja. Again there appears to be a suggestion of zonation within this site, though it is not completely clear. A working area, with hearth, lay to the north of the track, while the domestic buildings lay to the south, around which were situated a number of pits containing refuse. As with the 13th century settlements, an out-

lying 'satellite' area of activity (Site K) appears to have been related to Site Jb. This area was set adjacent to the subsidiary trackway, which ran north from the western edge of Site Jb. Although the function of Site K can only be guessed at, its position, morphology and lack of finds would suggest possibly a shelter for livestock.

Two possible interpretations have been suggested for the main building at Site Jb, but the suggestion that it was a single building of two parts marked by gravel floors separated by a cross-entry is the more probable. The southern wall of the building appears to be marked by the 'Pits' 3156, 3160 and the Slot 3318, which may have contained stone underpinning, presumably robbed out at the time of abandonment. The other walls presumably coincided with the edge of the gravel giving a building measuring approximately 13.5 × 6m internally. This was apparently a structure of three or four bays. The position of the hall to the east is indicated by the hearth marked by the depression 3327 with much charcoal in the fill (*Fig. 48, S112). The service end, which is unusually large in relationship to the size of the building, would therefore have lain to the west. The building faced northwards to the track and may have had an ancillary building to the rear and slightly further east. If the identification of 3348 as a cess-pit is correct, it would also have occupied a suitable position away from the house and closer to the chamber than the service end.

We can compare this building with the evidence from the demesne leases of the All Souls manors, particularly the buildings at Scotney Court, and also with those recorded in the accounts of Denge manor. The leases cover the middle of the 15th century, while the accounts survive particularly for the later 14th century. The buildings on the All Souls estate were all timber-framed with daubed panels and were constructed on sill walls. Stone for the sills was not readily available locally and in 1459–60 some 16 loads of stone were brought from New Romney to underpin the new barn and house (Bodleian MS, dd All Souls C 323). Timber was bought in to make new bridge and to construct, or more probably repair, a barn at Gogyhall, and build a new barn at Newland which lay to the north of the site of Lydd Quarry (Bodleian MS, dd All Souls C 268.216, 323). Lathes and withies were bought on numerous occasions for roofing. All this tends to suggest that wood and timber were not readily available on the demesnes of the All Souls manors. The Denge accounts give a similar impression. In 1367–8 timber was brought down river from Bodiam to 'Lydd Bridge' and in 1373–4 oak was brought overland to Winchelsea and thence by water to *le Trenche* (PRO, SC6/889/22, /24). The roofs of the buildings on the All Souls estate were covered variously with shingles, straw, reeds and rushes. Reeds were both bought and cut on the manor at Scotney Court. One hundred 'bakke stones' were bought in 1459–60 for 8*d*. when work was being done on the manor house and kitchen (Bodleian MS, dd All Souls C 323). These were too few for building any structure, but would have been suitable for the floors of hearths. It is not clear whether these 'bakke stones' were hearth tiles or 'Flemish'-type bricks.

The evidence from excavations confirms the picture suggested by the records of work at Scotney Court. Tiles and 'Flemish'-type bricks begin to occur only towards the latter part of the 14th century, but they become far more numerous during the 15th century. Despite this, these materials only ever appear to have been used at the excavated sites for limited specific tasks, such as lining hearths. There is no evidence that any roofs were tiled in their entirety or that bricks were used in wall construction at any of the excavated sites. Roofs continued to be thatched into the 15th century.

The pattern of settlement at Denge West, based on the current evidence, differs from that of Lydd Quarry in the 14th century in that there appears to be no notable downturn in activity. Indeed the reverse could be argued: at Denge North, Areas A and E appear to continue in use and at Denge South a new occupation/activity site appears in Field A, with an enclosure further to the north. The exact reason for this pattern is uncertain, however, it may be due to a number of different factors. The area may have avoided inundation in the late 13th century or have been drained rapidly after any such flooding. Alternatively, the fact that the settlements at Denge were on a slightly different economic footing, and thus less reliant on agriculture compared to those at Lydd Quarry, may have allowed them to see through the events without much disruption. Whatever the case, settlement at Denge West appears to have developed through the 14th century.

Economy and Trade

Although the mixed agricultural regime of the 13th century almost certainly continued throughout most of the 14th century, the apparent decline in population would have meant labour-intensive arable cultivation would have probably been harder to maintain in all areas. As a result, the demographic decline would have been instrumental, or at least complimentary, to the beginning of the documented increase in pastoralism in the second half of the century. No obvious change is apparent in the animal bone assemblage for this period, though the small size of the assemblage precludes conclusions to be drawn with certainty. However, it is impossible to distinguish assemblages from before and after the mid 14th century on the current evidence. As this is the crucial period when the agricultural regime may have been modified due to demographic factors, little can be said at present on the changes, if any, at this point. It should be noted that the excavated seeds suggest the continuation of arable cultivation, though there is a notable drop in the number of excavated quern fragments, suggesting more of the arable harvest may have been destined for animal rather than human consumption. The evidence from the

pollen and charcoal hints at a decrease in the exploitation of dryland woodland during this period. This, together with the slight signs of regeneration in these woods, may also be the result of a smaller population.

At Lydd Quarry there is a drastic decrease in the rolled net weights in 14th century contexts, suggesting fishing had declined sharply and did not supplement the Site Jb diet to any great extent. This may be in part due to the smaller number of contexts of this period excavated, however, it may mean the smaller population during this period had to use most of its time on the 'specialising' economic base. Despite this, eel and flatfish remain in the excavated assemblages. At Denge West the type of fishing appears to have been of a different type from the start – utilising hook/line in saltwater. Although there are few reliable sealed contexts of this date, there is little reason to believe that fishing was scaled down at this site.

Imported pottery appears to have increased during the 14th century, possibly because late 13th century storms severely reduced a local pottery industry. Material from off the marsh, such as that from Rye, took a large share of the market, and Scarborough, French and Low Countries pottery, although not common, appear more frequently than in the preceding century. Despite this increase in the range of pottery, the excavated settlements can still be regarded as peasant farmsteads: the increase in quality of the pottery represents the greater availability of finer products rather than any increase in fortunes of the occupants.

Access by land to markets was limited for the occupants of the sites examined here. Within Romney Marsh, there were markets at New Romney, Lydd and Brookland. Competition between them is reflected in a writ *temp*. Richard II sought by the former to shut down the latter two on the grounds that they were unlicensed (CKS, NR/FAc2, f. 53). There was an unlicensed market at Dungeness, but it is probable that the main, and perhaps the only, item of trade there was fish. (Sweetinburgh above; PRO, SC6/1107/10). A further market about which little is known was held at Eastbridge (*Quo Warrante*, 360). There were a number of other trading centres in the upland surrounding the marsh (Mate 1996; McLain 1997) which included the towns of Winchelsea, Rye, Tenterden and Hythe, but also much smaller places: Rolvenden (PRO, SC6/Hen VIII/1757), Smallhythe (ESRO, NOR 15/106), Appledore (*Cal. Charter Rolls 1341–1417*, 157; CCL, Register C, f. 249v.) and Warehorne (*Cal. Charter Rolls 1257–1300*, 85; *Cal. Charter Rolls 1257–1300*, 233). Simple measurement of the proximity of markets may give a false impression. On Romney Marsh, as on other wetlands, water transport was often as important as movement by land. Boats on the inland waterways and along the River Rother provide a rapid means of access to the Weald, and other areas of the Marsh were widely used for the movement of both goods and people (Gardiner 2007). From the fishing base at Dungeness, there was ready access to ports in Kent and Sussex. Places nearer to landing sites may have been more significant for those living around Lydd than inland markets and commercial centres inaccessible by water.

PERIOD 3B: CONTINUING DECLINE (15TH TO MID 16TH CENTURY)
(*Fig. 30)

The Field System

The archaeological evidence from Lydd Quarry suggests that, although the infilling of drainage ditches to form larger fields probably began during the 14th century, the process accelerated during the 15th to early 16th centuries. The period was marked by a continuing decline in settlement, and the change in the field pattern was a response to the growth of pastoral farming increasingly dominated by sheep grazing. Peasants on the marsh, like those elsewhere in England, found there were ready profits to be made by raising stock for meat and wool. Moreover, in the south-east there was a ready market for that meat for the armies fighting in France, and also for the English garrison at Calais (Mate 1987, 524). However, it is a simplification to concentrate solely on pastoral farming, for at Lydd there is evidence for the continuing production of cereals, and a number of the fields remained relatively small and suited to arable cultivation.

Conditions on the marsh were often difficult for farmers. Brandon (1969, 82–93) has shown how the production of cereals was dependent upon weather conditions during the growing season in his study of the Barnhorne estate to the west of Hastings. Similar problems seem to have affected land on the marsh during the heavy rains in the late 1420s and 1430s, for the surface water would have been difficult to drain from the flat land (Mate 1991b, 126). Documentary sources have shown that, at least in the areas of Scotney and Denge, considerable expense was incurred on the drainage ditches and also constructing or strengthening sea defences (Sweetinburgh, above; PRO, SC6/1262/13/4). However, evidence from Lydd Quarry would suggest that this expenditure was probably not concerned with digging new ditches, but infilling some existing examples while cleaning out and enlarging others to establish a proper rectilinear system of larger fields. The resultant pattern at Lydd appears to have survived virtually intact until the 20th century quarrying.

Settlement

Documentary sources demonstrate that this was a period of significant change on the marsh. In the last twenty years of the 15th century a considerable number of smaller holdings (most were below 5 acres) were engrossed to make larger farms (Gardiner 1998, 136–7). Draper (1998) has investigated the emergence of some of the individuals

who were engrossing lands. She follows Dyer (1981) and sees the farming out (or leasing) of demesnes as one of the means which allowed the yeoman farmers to emerge. The social tensions created by predatory engrossers of land have been investigated by Dimmock (2001), who has shown how there was considerable conflict within the town of Lydd between the emerging larger farmers and other parties. The implications of these changes for the settlement pattern have not been entirely worked out. It is clear that, as properties were engrossed, the surplus houses were allowed to fall into disrepair or were demolished. However, new houses may have been constructed at the same time in the centre of the consolidated farms.

The other significant development, which we presume to have taken place in the later 15th or early 16th centuries, was the increasing incidence of leasing. Early modern historians are aware that tenants paying quit-rents were frequently not farming the lands themselves, but were letting it to others: the owners and occupiers were different people. Hipkin (1998) has shown that this was the case on Romney Marsh by the later 16th century. Medieval historians presume that generally those who paid the rent were working the land. The transition between the two patterns may have been marked by a change in settlement pattern. Large landholders ceased to occupy a house amidst their lands, but could live elsewhere and draw rent from them. It was the abandonment of the larger farm complexes that was vexing the burgesses of Lydd in the 1570s and 1580s, when the views of frankpledge record that the farms at Scotney, Belgar, Jacks Court, Sir Anthony Mayne's house in Dengemarsh and many others were ruinous (EKA, JQs 1, f. 53 ff.). The same change has been recorded at Newland where a hall house present in the late 15th century had gone by the 1560s when the family moved to Canterbury (Draper 1998, 121).

At Lydd Quarry there have been no definite domestic occupation sites excavated for this period so far, though Site La (Lydd 5/6) may have seen some at least temporary domestic activity. The last few pieces of refuse dumped in the trackway ditches at Site Jb may be of this date, but are probably derived from the opportunistic dumping of refuse along the track from other sites rather than relating necessarily to occupation at Jb. This phenomena is apparent elsewhere at the quarry where outlying dumps of refuse were tipped into the tops of some of the drainage ditches as part of the process of infilling and changing the field system. The majority of this activity is concentrated in the south-western half of the Lydd 5/6 area where three 'activity areas' were located: Sites La, Lb and M. These sites are generally not associated with high quantities of domestic refuse, with the exception of Site Lb, which is a grouping of otherwise isolated pits, including a possible well. Site La may well relate to a looker's hut and compound; its position adjacent to the southern track would facilitate the movement of animals. It is interesting to note that a later sheepfold was established immediately to the south of Site La from at least the 1870s, though it may have been there from an earlier date.

The presence of all these activity areas suggests they are satellite sites to a domestic occupation site, which would also be the source of the domestic waste found here and elsewhere across the excavated area. At present the former building known to have stood to the west of the Lydd 5/6 area is the prime candidate (see below). Although cartographic evidence for this building survives from the later 16th century, it is considered likely, judging from the archaeological finds in the vicinity, that the building was established at some point during the 15th century.

As with the previous century, settlement at Denge West appears to have continued unhindered into the 15th century, though it has left little structural evidence. At least two notable concentrations of finds, one from Denge South (field-walking only) and one from Denge North, hint at two domestic sites, though the nature of that to the south is untested by excavation. It is not until the end of the 15th (or beginning of the 16th) century that a decline at Denge West is noticed, a fact that correlates well with the documentary sources. This is again in contrast to the evidence from Lydd Quarry which suggests a continuing decline, at least in population/settlement density, throughout this period. At Denge North activity in Areas A and E appear to wind down and shift to Area F where a new occupation site is situated. At Denge South the occupation in Field A and the enclosure to the north-west intensifies, judging by the increase in ceramics, and a new area of activity begins in Field B. This increase in activity, particularly when contrasted with that at Lydd Quarry, demonstrates that the Denge sites were different. It is almost certain that this is the result of a different economy.

Economy and Trade

Documentary sources suggest that towards the end of this period sheep farming dominated the economy, though some arable cultivation was still taking place. This was not a new phenomena but the end point of a trend begun in the middle of the 14th century, though as noted above, it is difficult to identify archaeologically. Although generally there is a notable decrease in the archaeological evidence for arable cultivation, the excavated data shows this not to be a consistent pattern. The largest cereal assemblages come from some of the contexts of this period, though admittedly these may be the result of abnormal dumping episodes or unusual specific events. Whatever the case, arable cultivation was still clearly continuing in areas, even though pastoralism may have been on the increase. As with the 14th century, the extent to which the arable crops were used for fodder cannot be proven, though it is probable a good proportion were.

The bone assemblage for this period shows that, despite the continuing presence of cattle, there was an increase in sheep. It should be noted, however, that this increase is slight and not as dramatic as some historical sources might suggest. This may be a reflection between the grazing of livestock, and the consumption which is reflected in the archaeological record. The increase in the butchery of younger animals hints at the increase in importance of meat production over wool/milk in this later period. However, larger bone assemblages will be needed from other rural parts of the marsh in order to test this suggestion.

Fishing at Denge West continued and, indeed, it is this period which has provided the best evidence of this trade from the site. The partially excavated occupation site at Denge North (Area F) almost certainly did not rely on agriculture, particularly arable, for survival. Artefactual evidence from this site strongly suggests that fishing was of importance to this settlement and the site would have been fairly well situated to exploit these resources. The size of the hooks recovered, together with the presence of clench bolts and numerous large nails, suggests line fishing from clinker-built boats for large fish, both in inshore and offshore waters. It is probable the boats associated with this community were launched on the sheltered eastern beach of the shingle ness with the associated occupation site, as represented at Denge Quarry, set further inland (Gardiner 1996). It is therefore possible that the excavated sites at Denge Quarry initially had a mixed economy of fishing and, to a lesser extent, pastoralism, with some limited arable cultivation occurring as the ditch system began to make certain areas possible to work. It is a great shame that no suitable contexts for environmental sampling were uncovered.

The activity at Lydd Quarry by this time does not show any evidence of fishing. The lack of lead fishing weights which had been so common in the 13th century, as well as the notable decrease in shell, suggests that the Lydd communities did not have easy access to, or more probably were not particularly concerned with, these resources. The Lydd Quarry economic base at this time would therefore appear to be totally concentrating, or specialising, on one type of agriculture to create a living.

The pottery recovered from the excavations at all sites of this period show the typical shift to well-fired utilitarian vessels with little or no decoration, which are common throughout the south-east at this time. These vessels are present at both high and low status sites and do not allow differentiation between the two, particularly with small assemblages. Imports are also more limited at this time and the few German stoneware sherds from the excavated sites, although showing continental trade, are typical of this period. However, the presence of certain types of metalwork, such as keys and the purse frame from around the southern trackway, suggest that some of the settlement may have been of a higher status. It is quite possible this material relates to the settlement alluded to above (Site N), situated just to the west of the Lydd 5/6 area. If this were the case it is tempting to suggest this new settlement was owned by a farmer involved with amalgamating earlier plots to create a more extensive specialist agricultural regime.

PERIOD 4: THE POST-MEDIEVAL PERIOD (MID 16TH CENTURY ONWARDS) (*Fig. 31)

The Field System

Very few ditches appear to have been infilled between the 16th and 20th centuries. Those that were, appear to have been infilled during the late 19th and 20th centuries as a result of changing agricultural economy and technology. During the earlier part of this period it is probable that some further drainage works were carried out in more marginal areas which may not have been touched by the medieval system. Such areas probably include the land to the west of Gores/Burnthouse Wall as well as the central area to the south of the southern track. Fields in these areas appear to have been quite large from the outset and are thus considered to be of post-medieval date. After this there appears to be a lull and the system stayed largely static. As such, the extant field system prior to gravel extraction was virtually identical to that of the mid 16th century.

Settlement

No sites of this period were excavated at Lydd Quarry. However, the presence of the late 17th to early 18th century finds assemblage in Ditch 5137 (Site N) clearly demonstrates an occupation site close-by. This is almost certainly the same as the substantial building depicted on late 16th century maps, as well as Poker's map of 1617,

and recorded in the 1552 survey (Gardiner, above). It is possible that this prestigious building has its origins in the 15th century. The finds suggest that the building continued in use, perhaps being used in part as a tavern, up until at least the 18th century. If Hasted was using up-to-date information for his map, a building appears to survive at the site until the 1790s and the adjacent Wall is still shown as Gores Wall. At some point after this it seems probable the building was burnt down. This appears to have happened before 1812 when cartographic sources show Gores Wall had been re-named to Burnthouse Wall.

At Denge West there is a marked decline in activity during this period, with perhaps the last occupation lingering on in Area F and Field B into the late 16th or early 17th centuries. Beyond this, only Boulderwall Farm continued in use with all other areas simply receiving refuse from light manuring. Quite why the activity decreased at Denge West is uncertain, considering that it survived the earlier problems. The change is almost certainly economic and it is perhaps possible that the increase of the Rye fishing industry at this time, coupled with the final silting of New Romney's harbour, meant even fishing no longer offered a guaranteed living.

Economy and Trade

There is currently too little excavated data from the present sites to address seriously the exact nature of the economy at this time, though ample historical sources cover this topic. The few environmental samples of this period are interesting in that they now show virtually no arable cultivation, though more would be needed to prove this. It is more than likely that during this period pastoralism, heavily weighted on sheep, was the dominant economy. Such farming was undoubtedly undertaken in enlarged fields inherited from the 16th century amalgamations which did not change radically until the recent past.

5

The Wider Context

by Mark Gardiner

The work described in this volume represents one of the larger medieval settlement projects undertaken in recent years. The purpose of the concluding section is to assess the wider implications of the work in the Lydd area and to set the results in the context of current understanding and recent approaches. This section begins by reflecting upon the approaches adopted in the study of medieval settlement in England and the methods used here. Secondly, it considers the results of the work specifically in relationship to other studies of wetlands. Thirdly, the results of the work at Lydd are set in the broader context of our changing understanding of later medieval settlement in Britain more generally. The possibilities and research aims for future work on Walland Marsh are considered in the final part.

ARCHAEOLOGY OF LANDSCAPES

The study of medieval rural settlement since the Second World War has taken two main directions. The first was site-based excavation and this effectively began with the work at Wharram Percy in 1953. In the following 25 years, there were excavations at Wharram and the other key sites of Goltho (Lincolnshire), Gomeldon (Wiltshire), Grenstein (Norfolk), Hangleton (Sussex), Houndtor (Devon), Riplingham (East Yorkshire) and Seacourt (Oxfordshire) to identify evidence of the farmstead – the house and its associated farm buildings – and record the history of the village. The work was largely focussed on deserted medieval villages, since these had conspicuous remains which were threatened, generally by the expansion of arable farming or, less commonly, by building. The role of John Hurst, after his appointment to the Inspectorate of Ancient Monuments, in channelling money through the Medieval Settlement Research Group was crucial in ensuring the excavation of these sites (Dyer 2002). By the end of the 1970s, however, the policy of excavation was being replaced by a greater emphasis on preservation. The Ancient Monuments and Areas Act of 1979 gave increased protection to scheduled sites, which included many deserted medieval villages. As the legislation became effective, planning practice evolved during the 1980s so that development was only permitted on sites which were perceived as having lesser importance. Consequently, there were fewer large-scale excavations of medieval settlements.

During the 1960s and 1970s, there was an increasing awareness that the excavated area needed to be set in the broader context, not only of the total area of the toft, but also the larger settlement and even the wider landscape. Landscape archaeology began to play a progressively more important role through the well-established methods of earthwork recording and aerial photography, but also through the growing use of field-walking and the reconstruction of the parishes using cartographic and documentary sources. This formed the second direction in the study of medieval settlements. The concept of the medieval landscape as an object of research had evolved from the work of Hoskins (1955) and Beresford (1957). They had shown how many features of the medieval landscape could still be identified on the ground. The fieldwork element was further developed by the study of earthworks in surveys undertaken by the Royal Commission on Historic Monuments of England, particularly in Cambridgeshire, Dorset and Northamptonshire. One of the earliest surveys which combined a study of the landscape with selected excavation took place at Overton Down (Wilts.) and developed out of initial work there by the RCHME (Fowler 2000). The fieldwork at West Whelpington, which came to a conclusion in 1976, was typical of the growing awareness of the wider landscape. West Whelpington is one of the most completely excavated English medieval settlements. The site had been threatened by the expansion of a quarry. However, even with the methods adopted and a prolonged campaign of work which extended from 1958, it was not possible to record more than a fraction of the village and the excavations had, therefore, to concentrate very largely on the houses themselves. Some areas on the green in the centre of the village were stripped, revealing the sites of cottages, and areas to the rear of the crofts were also dug. The final stage of fieldwork was a study of the earthworks, including ridge and furrow, in the parish and of the standing buildings, allowing the excavation to be placed in context (Evans and Jarrett 1987; Evans *et al.*

1988). A somewhat similar approach informed the later years of the Wharram Percy excavations. The adoption of a landscape approach led to field-walking and the study of earthworks throughout the whole parish. There was, therefore, by the mid and later 1970s, a growing awareness of the need to study both the settlement and also the surrounding landscape (Beresford and Hurst 1990, 85–100).

Excavation work up to about 1980 had been marked by threats to very large areas of medieval remains. As these remains were protected more thoroughly and construction work was directed away from known sites, the opportunities for digging medieval settlements on a large scale were reduced. The emphasis shifted to locating less evident remains through survey work undertaken at an early stage in the planning process, and this itself helped to engender a wider understanding of the diversity of remains of medieval date in the countryside. The study extended to include fields, woodland, hedges and waste, as well as the buildings, such as mills and barns. The survey of West Yorkshire published in 1981 showed how combined documentary and fieldwork study could recover evidence for these elements (Faull and Moorhouse 1981). The approach was reflected in the journal, *Landscape History*, established about the same time, and in another Yorkshire initiative, the study of boundaries (Patourel *et al.* 1993). A consequence of the study of landscapes was a growing interest in areas where there were no villages. Areas of dispersed settlement found outside the 'village belt' in the north-west of England and the south-east became a new subject for analysis (Austin 1989; Taylor 1983).

The Shapwick parish project was one of the first field studies which sought to examine medieval settlement and started with the wider landscape. It began with extensive field-walking and continued with a programme of test-pitting among the houses of the existing village and a study of standing buildings (Aston and Gerrard 1999). The approach and results from Shapwick had a strong influence upon the direction of the Whittlewood project set up in 2000 to examine a very large block of land lying across the boundary of the 'village belt' or Central Province, and including an area of more dispersed settlement to the south. There was no attempt to excavate sites or settlements at Whittlewood, but the project sought to identify the changing location of the settlements through test-pitting.

Rural settlement studies since 1980 have increasingly adopted an approach of limited excavation driven by specific development threats, or excavation and other fieldwork set within a wider study of the landscape. The work in the Lydd area described above seems distinctively at variance with these approaches: it was not a limited excavation, but nor did it set out to be a landscape project. There were, however, important differences between the landscape studies mentioned above and the work at Lydd. Shapwick and Whittlewood were university-based research projects; the work at Lydd took place in the context of contract archaeology. It was driven by the need to record remains before their destruction by quarrying. The refinements of research aims were subordinate to the demands of excavation within a period limited by the time and the finance which might reasonably be demanded of the quarry operators. To that extent, it more closely resembled the large-scale excavations of the 1960s. However, unlike the work of the 1960s, the excavated areas were set in a much broader context by stripping large areas under archaeological direction and surveying all remains to provide a record of a large tract of landscape. Stripping such enormous areas would have been beyond the budget of most projects, but was undertaken as part of the site works in advance of quarrying. The archaeological methods employed sought to reconcile the practical requirements of planning control and the commercial constraints of the quarry operators, with the current approaches and thinking in medieval settlement studies.

Quarrying provided a unique opportunity to investigate a landscape in a manner which is very rarely possible. The evolving methodology of excavation has been outlined above. It is possible, in retrospect, to identify approaches which might have been used and work which might usefully have been undertaken. For example, it is apparent with hindsight that a study of documentary sources and aerial photographs at an earlier stage might have informed excavation strategy. However, in some respects the work, particularly at Lydd Quarry, was experimental and the possibilities revealed by large-scale topsoil stripping could not be anticipated. The work was also particularly unusual in its application to a medieval wetland landscape. Previous work in such areas had used the techniques of landscape analysis variously combined with aerial photography, geophysical survey, field-walking and limited excavation. Each method provides a limited insight into the character of the archaeology. Aerial photography and geophysical survey can identify the presence of a ditch, but cannot date it, nor can they reveal its stratigraphic relationship with another ditch. In the work described here it has been possible to strip large areas and to excavate selectively complete blocks of landscape. That has provided a view of the development of marshland no other approach could provide.

The contrast in approach is most clearly indicated by comparing the results of the survey work and sample excavation at Denge West, or the trenching at Dering Farm with the work at Lydd Quarry. Although the information from Denge West and Dering Farm is useful, it does not provide the understanding of the development of a landscape which was possible at Lydd Quarry where large areas were stripped and more extensive excavation took place. The result is that the study of Lydd Quarry, in particular, has revealed a new perspective on the occupation and utilisation of marshland.

WETLAND ARCHAEOLOGY AND LYDD

Wetland archaeology has emerged in recent years as a distinct branch within the wider study of the past. It has established a distinctive identity, both because organic remains survive in a remarkable state of preservation, and also because the environment poses particular problems for the archaeologist. Wetlands offer unique potential for study in another respect. They allow the examination of settlement formation in areas which had not been occupied in the immediately preceding centuries. The medieval wetland landscapes owed little or nothing to their Roman and prehistoric predecessors. They were usually founded on sediment which had been laid down in the early and mid 1st millennium during a period of marine transgression (Rippon 1997, 138–51). The landscapes created were therefore a direct reflection of the cultures which created them, not a response to their predecessors. If prior settlement was less significant in the formation of marsh landscapes, environment was correspondingly more important. The discussion above has shown that at Lydd the land-use and settlement pattern were very substantially a response to the different conditions of the land. We can, therefore, contrast wetlands and drylands. In summary, one could say that in the first the environment was the most important factor; and in the second the earlier landscapes were often more significant.

The work at Lydd and Denge has thrown into relief some of the prevailing ideas of wetland usage. It has been widely assumed that the most important stage in the development of the wetland landscape was the construction of embankments which allowed the land to be ditched and drained. Although the exploitation of marshland prior to embankment has been discussed, little evidence has been brought forward to show the character of the landscape in that state. The work at Lydd has revealed more clearly than before that marshes could be intensively utilised, even though they remained unembanked. This archaeological work can be supplemented by a recent study of Warham Marsh on the north coast of Norfolk, which has identified a similar landscape of a salt marsh divided into fields with a pattern of droveways, which was evidently not embanked against tidal water. Warham Marsh was utilised in that manner in the early 19th century, though the pattern may be medieval in origin (Gardiner 2005). It is now apparent that embankments were constructed for a number of reasons. They were built to allow the land to be converted to arable, as a defence against increasing incidence of flooding, or to reclaim marshland which had otherwise been little exploited. Earlier work has tended to emphasise only the last of these.

A further result of the present work, and no less important, has been the evidence that the pattern of fields, separated by ditches, was not fixed and unaltered. The earliest maps depict a pattern which has only a distant resemblance to the medieval arrangement. On the other hand, the fields recorded on 16th century maps made for All Souls College, or in the 16th century surveys (Gardiner, above) show that they changed little between 1600 and 1939. Earlier work on wetland landscapes had tended to suggest that they might be analysed as a series of zones, each the product of a different period of reclamation (*e.g.*, Rippon 1996, 42–5; Rippon 2002, 90–2). It has been assumed that the field pattern of each enclosure had been effectively brought into existence at the moment of reclamation by the construction of drainage ditches and had been preserved with little change. If this were correct, then wetlands would provide a unique chance to study field patterns of medieval date. It is now apparent that marsh landscapes were very much more dynamic than we had realised. Furthermore, flooding has been suggested as another force in effecting landscape change (Gardiner 2002). The work at Lydd demonstrates that, even when flooding was not a factor, there may have been social and economic reasons for re-modelling field patterns on marshlands, as in drier environments.

Wetland landscapes are sometimes seen as a direct response to the economics of agriculture. That interpretation was first established by Postan and Duby. Postan (1975, 20–9) stressed the importance of the growing population and the need to take in new lands in order to feed it. The expansion on to marshlands was therefore part of a wider movement into 'marginal' areas, such as woods, moors and heaths. Duby (1968, 65–87) placed this expansion in a European-wide context and included the colonisation of the former Slav areas of Germany and eastern Europe. Postan's model of marginality has been criticised in a number of recent works (Bailey 1989, 1–25; Dyer 1989). Rippon (2000, 260–3) has recast the use of coastal wetlands in terms of environments with potential which might be utilised in various ways and placed these within the context of developing estate structures. This represents a useful, more developed version of the economic approaches to the exploitation of wetlands presented by Postan and Duby. None of these approaches places the social context at the heart of the analysis. Communities might have chosen to utilise the wetlands at any time. Indeed, once we realise that it was not necessary to invest the considerable time and labour in the work of embanking before utilising the marsh, then it becomes more surprising that it was not exploited on a large scale before the 12th century. Instead of these models, we can formulate an alternative perspective which sees the use of marshland as the outcome of changing perception of the environment.

It is not possible or appropriate here to discuss in detail the changing perceptions of wetlands, though it is necessary to outline these in brief. Marshland in the early medieval period was consistently associated with remoteness and places forsaken by God. The best known expression of this is in the 8th century life of St Guthlac, a soldier who gave up warfare and went to live an eremetic life at Crowland in the Fens. There, on an island, he was tormented by demons, but continued to live for many years (*Life of St Guthlac*). Much the same views of wetlands are expressed in *Beowulf* (l. 102–4), where the fens and moors are described as the dwelling place of the demon, Grendel. Somewhat later, the marshes of Somerset are described in Asser's *Life of Alfred* (c. 53), as the refuge of Alfred and the remnants of his army. Here the learned king retires from fighting and is described as living a 'restless life in great distress', with little to eat, except that which he could obtain by raids on the Vikings. However, Alfred established a fort at an inaccessible island at Athelney which he used as a base to attack the Vikings. Later in Alfred's reign Athelney was established as a monastery (*ibid.*, c. 55, 92) Much the same impression of desolation of the marshes during Alfred's time is given in the *Vita S. Neoti*, probably written in the late 10th century. The historicity of these stories is less important than the use of the environment in the story. The *topos* of a sainted figure suffering on an island refuge in the marshes was well established in the early medieval period. The marshes were places which provided a haven for both monks and refugees remote from society.

This was, however, more than just a literary *topos*. The perceived isolation of the marshes made them attractive to the religious reformers of the 10th century. New monasteries were established on marshland sites at, for example, Ramsey, Thorney and Muchelney, and the already established houses of Glastonbury and Athelney, in Somerset, and Ely, Peterborough and Crowland in the Fens were reformed to ensure that they followed strict monastic rule. The aim of the 10th century reformation was to revert to a rigour of religious practice and ensure a separation of the church from worldly matters (Knowles 1950, 31–56). The isolated location of the wetlands provided a suitable context for these stricter religious communities. William of Malmesbury may exaggerate the situation when he describes women visitors being received at Thorney as if they were monsters, but it does emphasise the continuing isolation and austerity of the monastic house (*De Gestis Ponitificum*, 327). The continuing inaccessibility of Ely made it attractive to Hereward in the late 11th century in his struggle against the Norman invaders. After the island was taken, the Normans are thought to have constructed the Aldreth causeway as a means of access. Nevertheless, Ely remained attractive as a remote site providing a stronghold for Nigel, bishop of Ely and subsequently for Geoffrey de Mandeville in their battle against King Stephen's armies during the period of the Anarchy (*VCH Cambridgeshire and Ely* 2, 381–8).

During the course of the 12th century a new theme emerged in writing about marshlands. This emphasised the value of the products of the wetlands. Hugh Candidus, a monk of Peterborough Abbey writing about the middle of the century, reflects this perspective very clearly. While the marsh was uninhabitable except in a few areas of higher ground, he notes, it was very valuable for its hay and thatch, and contained many birds and fish (*Chronicle of Hugh Candidus*, 4–5). The marshes around Thorney are described by William of Malmesbury as a smooth plain on which trees for timber grow and grasses flourish (*De Gestis Pontificum Anglorum*, 326). This view also emerges in the pages of Domesday Book which, while it treats marshland in an inconsistent and often uninformative manner, shows the value of such areas for pasture, eels and other fish (Darby 1977, 157–61, 352–3). It was not until the 13th century that accounts of the work of bringing the marshes under cultivation begin to appear. The theme of the transformation of desolate places into farmed lands was, of course, a favourite one among monastic chroniclers, and was employed as much by those whose estates were on the dry uplands, as those on the marsh. Matthew Paris in the middle of the 13th century contrasted the horrors of the fen in the midst of which St Guthlac had dwelt, with the arable and meadow lands which were now found there (*Chronica Maiora* v, 570). Standing between these 12th and 13th century views of the marshes is the description of the fen around Ramsey made in *c.* 1170, which admits that it is covered with alders, reeds and bulrushes, but says that the land has been brought under the plough (*Chronicon Abbatia Rameseiensis*, 8). This nicely reflects the shifting perceptions of the wetlands.

The purpose in summarising these descriptions of marsh is not to suggest that any one of them is necessarily accurate, but to argue that they reflect the way wetlands were regarded and which influenced their utilisation. There was, in particular, a shift from emphasising the natural products (the rushes, wood, fish and birds) and the pasture of the marsh to the chroniclers of the 13th century who stressed the transformation of the wetland. In contrast to the neo-Malthusian view emphasised by Postan which stressed economic forces, we can see that there was a change in perception of wetlands. This developing view encouraged first the settlement of the area and the exploitation of its resources, and subsequently the transformation of its character through the drainage of land for arable. Each stage can be identified in the Lydd area. The construction of the church at Lydd on an 'island' site on the shingle amidst the marsh at some uncertain, but pre-Conquest, date may be compared to the foundation of monastic sites elsewhere. There is no evidence that Lydd was a minster church, but it was a Christian presence within a desolate place. The utilisation of the marshes for pasture is reflected in the shepherds' huts at Lydd Quarry and less certainly at Caldicott Farm, and in the ditched fields which preceded embankment. Finally, the construction of the walls marked the shift to conditions suitable for arable agriculture. The excavation work described above is unique in allowing these changes to be identified through archaeology.

Neo-Malthusian views have dominated thinking about

the occupation of wetlands, but they have also played a part in the interpretation of the depopulation of the same areas. The corollary of the rising population which encouraged the settlement of marginal areas was that, as the population dropped in the late 14th and 15th centuries, there was a retreat from these places. Wetlands, which required high investment to maintain the water courses and sea defences, would be abandoned in favour of other environments. It is certainly true that there were problems on wetlands (Rippon 2001). The crisis on Walland Marsh began with the widespread flooding of the area in the late 13th century, and although there was considerable investment in maintaining embankments and trying to recover some land which had been lost, the greater part of the inundated lands were to remain unenclosed for the next 200 years (Gardiner 2002). We should be careful to distinguish problems resulting from a climatic downturn from those consequent on a falling population. Documentary research suggests that the last few decades of the 15th century saw a rapid decline in population on the marsh, but that was precisely the period when there was considerable investment in strengthening defences on the west side of Walland Marsh and constructing new embankments (Gardiner 1998). Instead of the neo-Malthusian view, we might suggest that this was the period when a new perception of the marsh was emerging. The possibility of operating the land as a vast sheep ranch was gaining ground, and this encouraged the construction of embankments of the late 15th and 16th centuries by the investors, including Sir Edward Guldeford and Richard Smith (Eddison 2000, 116).

An understanding of the social factors operating on marsh landscapes also requires that we consider the groups which were instrumental in their creation and change. We know relatively little of the communities and individuals who, in the 12th century, began constructing embankments, but it is notable that the monastic houses and major lords, who were active in this work in the 13th century, do not seem to have played a leading role earlier. The Men of Misleham and the Men of Broomhill, as well as Ellis of Rye, were some of those important in the reclamation of Walland Marsh (Tatton–Brown 1988, 106; Gardiner 1988, 117), and further afield, in the Fens, individuals such as Conan of Holbeach played a significant role (Hallam 1965, 10, 15–16). Such communities and individuals operated without a clear legal structure for managing or regulating these reclamations, except for a developing body of customary law. Their work appears to have often been *ad hoc*, so that lengths of embankment were built separately and subsequently joined together. More detailed study in the Fens and in Walland Marsh is necessary to examine this further, but it explains the otherwise very odd pattern of early embankments. The right-angle turn of Gores Wall at the point it reaches Midley Wall (Fig. 102) seems to be best interpreted as the work of at least two separate groups, rather than the outcome of a single project. Equally, the defensive embankments around the 'Archbishops' Innings' should probably be viewed in the same light. It also raises the question as to whether some embankments may initially have been incomplete. They may have been constructed with open ends, perhaps only extending across creeks (*cf.* Allen 1997, 16–17).

The individualistic construction of embankments was not a successful method of operating in the longer term. Large-scale schemes of enclosure became more common in the early 13th century, as monastic houses increasingly played a more important role in reclamation; they had the capital and organisational structure to manage them. At the same time a system of regulation emerged, which required individuals to maintain their embankments for the benefit of all. Subsequently, bailiffs and jurats were empowered to collect scots from all landowners to clear ditches and maintain walls (Neilson 1928). The jurats of Romney Marsh, who in 1252 were granted a charter to maintain the marsh, appear to have been operating before that date (*Cal Close Rolls 1251–3*, 153). These changes are reflected in the landscape which they created. Embankments and fields planned on a large scale were fundamentally different from the irregular line of walls of the 'Archbishops' Innings' and the fields behind it. The linkage of landscape form to the structure of the communities creating them remains, however, an under-developed aspect of the study of marshlands.

MEDIEVAL SETTLEMENT STUDIES AND LYDD

Three research themes were outlined in the introduction: the reclamation and evolution of the landscape; medieval settlement patterns; and the rural economy and exploitation of natural resources. The wider implications of the first of these has been already examined; it remains to consider the other two. We have already seen that the work at Lydd was unlike other contemporary surveys in its methods, and exceptional in exposing large areas of landscape. The method of working only allowed the identification of negative features, *ie.*, remains cut into the underlying subsoil. We have a thorough record of pits and ditches, but little evidence for any upstanding remains, including most of the buildings. This is, in part, a reflection of a landscape which had been ploughed flat before excavation began, although the potentialities of the topsoil might have been explored (see below).

It was always going to be difficult to say a great deal about medieval settlement sites when so little remained of them. The excavations do, however, allow us to say something about the plans of some of the farmsteads. The position of the buildings can only be identified in most cases from the absence of other features, but the post-holes of the structure at Site A and the gravel floor of the building at Site Jb at Lydd Quarry are exceptions. The structure of Site A has been discussed above, although the character and function of the building is still uncertain.

Site Jb is also open to different interpretations. For the purpose of the present discussion, it is assumed that the building on Site A may have been a house and the two gravel areas on Site Jb were the floors of a house. The plan of the toft, but not of the buildings at Site H, is also sufficiently clear to allow its study.

The plans of peasant tofts have been sorted by Astill (1988, 41–3) into four regions. Lydd lies in an unclassified area just beyond his Region 2. Instead of using Astill's regional classification, the plans of the tofts may be examined employing a simple distinction between peasant farms which had a street-front plan and those with a courtyard plan. The former had the main building situated on or close to the street, which limited access to the farmyard behind. In the latter plan the buildings were situated around a courtyard and the house was set at the back overlooking the yard, though not necessarily facing the entrance. Site A is a good example of the street-front plan, since although there is no apparent street, the house (assuming it to be one) is close to, and faces, the entrance which lies between the two ditches (Fig. 32, A19 and A67). The building restricts access to the area, behind which was enclosed by the substantial ditch A78. Site Jb had a similar arrangement. The house faced the ditched trackway to the north, and ancillary buildings were set to the rear. Site H has a courtyard plan with the house, which was presumably set at the north side of the plot overlooking the area in front. In this case the courtyard is created by ditches and is not different in essence from the plan of Croft E at Barton Blount (Derbyshire) where the toft was surround by banks (Beresford 1975, Fig. 6).

The plans of farmsteads at Lydd can be set into the wider context of sites elsewhere in late medieval England. Unlike the toft and croft arrangement commonly found in the north of England, the farmsteads at Lydd were very compact. Site H did not have a large area for outbuildings, barns, ricks or gardens, which are assumed to have filled peasant tofts elsewhere (Astill 1988, 54–61). The interior area of the toft at Site H measured 25 × 11m (a total of 275 sq. m), which is much smaller than the croft at Grenstein (Norfolk) which was 2025 sq. m (Wade–Martins 1980, Fig. 57) or Goltho (Lincolnshire) Croft E, measuring 675 sq. m (Beresford 1975, Fig. 7), but is comparable with Barton Blount (Derbyshire) Croft E with an area of 285 sq. m (Beresford 1975, Fig. 6). There was clearly little space at Lydd Site H to store agricultural produce, which must have been kept within the farmhouse or outside in a small rick. Lydd Site A had a toft area of 500 sq. m. The 'house' was constructed in a more open landscape, in which one might imagine there was less pressure on space. We cannot at this stage say whether these small tofts were the result of regional variation which Astill (1988) has identified, or the agricultural economy, or a reflection of the low social status of the occupants.

A further aspect of the settlement pattern at Lydd, which has not been considered so far, is the distribution of the farmsteads within the landscape. It hardly needs to be said that the settlement pattern revealed in excavations at Lydd and Denge is dispersed rather than nucleated. Dispersed settlement is found over much of south-east England, particularly the Weald and the North and South Downs, as well as the marshlands. Yet there were nucleated medieval villages within all these areas, including, close to the sites of excavations, the market settlement at Lydd. The early history and development of Lydd is uncertain, but it has been shown that the villages in the Weald developed at a late date, mostly in the second half of the 13th or in the 14th century as centres of commerce. Some of these developed spontaneously as trading places close to churches, but others were planned, apparently after the potential for commerce had become apparent (Gardiner 1997). It is possible that Lydd may have had a similar origin, for the market-place lay at the entrance to the churchyard, which was itself flanked on the south-west and south-east sides by a line of narrow buildings (Gardiner 1998, Fig. 8.4). Whether these buildings had been constructed upon part of the former churchyard, or by taking a little land from the highway, is uncertain. The opportunities for attracting customers from congregations attending church services were commonly recognised in late medieval England, even though from the early 13th century sabbatarians sought to ensure that markets were not held on Sundays and to prevent trading within the churchyard itself (Britnell 1981, 212; Dymond 1999, 472–5). However, their efforts were not always very successful and in 1368 Archbishop Stephen Langham had to order the cessation of a Sunday market at Minster in Sheppey, where the noise was so loud that it prevented the congregation from hearing mass (*Registrum Simonis Langham*, 193–4).

We have already noted above that Reeves (1995, 90) has shown that late medieval settlements on Romney Marsh proper were typically situated along the edges of lanes and trackways. This was no less true for medieval sites in the area examined in excavation and is also reflected in the reconstruction of the 1552 survey (above) and on the Poker's map. In those parts of England where the farmsteads were situated rather closer together than they were on the marsh, a string of buildings set out along a road is sometimes known to medieval archaeologists as an 'interrupted row'. Clearly, there was an evident benefit in siting farmsteads beside the road, although this was not the only pattern found in areas of dispersed settlement. Buildings might cluster in hamlets, as they often did in south-west England, or be sited around the edge of commonland which is found in East Anglia. However, the roadside location of medieval buildings in Romney and Walland marshes may be due to the lines chosen for these routes. They often ran along on slightly higher or better drained ground – a feature which is very apparent at Lydd Quarry.

The final question which post-excavation work sought to address was that of the economy of the rural settlements. It is arguable that the results from this have been the least successful of the three research aims. The reasons for this are not specific to the excavation at Lydd, but are common to late medieval archaeology. Account rolls from the 13th and 14th centuries provide detail about the acreage sown, the rate of sowing and the yields. The archaeological data are much less informative. There is poorer chronological resolution and they are less abundant and detailed about the extent to which a particular crop was grown. But there is the further problem of an under-development of the methodology for interpreting archaeological evidence. The discussion of the evidence from Lydd (above) reflects considerable uncertainties in determining whether animal bones were indicative of production, consumption or both. For example, sheep may be raised for their wool, but eaten as mutton towards the end of their life. Their bones reflect both production and consumption. Many animals will leave little archaeozoological evidence, at least on rural sites, because they will have been destined for the market and consumed elsewhere. The extent of market production is unclear. While the archaeological evidence from rural sites tends to suggest that peasants were consuming animals raised on the farm, the historical sources emphasise the importance of the market as a source of meat (Albarella 1999, 872). A slightly different problem relates to the bones of fish. Salt-water fish must have been caught away from the sites examined, but often we cannot be sure in coastal areas, such as Lydd, whether the fish were caught by the occupants of the excavated settlement or were caught by others and purchased in the market.

Animal bones, therefore, provide a very uncertain reflection of production, but can they provide a guide to consumption? Is it possible to assume that all the bones found on the site were from animals that had been eaten? We can probably ignore the bones of certain animals which are unlikely to have been consumed for practical or other reasons. Dogs and cats were rarely eaten for cultural reasons, and the English distrust of hippophagy appears to be of long-standing: horses were valued as working animals, not for their meat. Even though bones with butchery marks are likely to have provided meat for consumption, they were not necessarily eaten by humans. Some may have been fed to dogs, for example (Wilson and Edwards 1993). Equally, we cannot assume that all bones, even from pigs, sheep and cattle, represent animals that were eaten. Presentments in borough records of the sale of rotten meat and fish suggest that some flesh was considered unfit for consumption. There was a greater tolerance for consuming diseased animals than at present, but even so, some stock may have been rejected.

There is a considerable disparity between the proportions of cattle and sheep reflected in the archaeological and historical records. Albarella (1999, 869) has considered this problem and noted that some of the difference may be accounted for by the poor collection of sheep bones. Sheep were very prone to disease and dead animals may have been buried in fields rather than on the settlement.

Finally, he reminds us that account rolls are a record of demesne stock, rather than the animals of the peasants who were likely to have a smaller proportion of sheep. All these are pertinent considerations when we attempt to look at the economy of rural settlements and seek evidence for the changing importance of horn and corn.

One of the more significant results which did emerge from the archaeological work related to the practice of fishing. The importance of fishing to coastal communities has only recently been recognised using documentary sources (Fox 2001). The work at Lydd and Denge on fishing weights and hooks has provided an entirely new and very informative approach to the subject. The distinction made in the report between the lighter weights used for inland slow-moving water and the heavier weights used for inshore fishing is significant. The discovery of the means of fishing (weights, hooks and boat roves) gives a useful indicator of this element of the economy. These artefacts provide the means to identify individual farmsteads from which fishing was practised, and in this case can combine it with documentary evidence for the fishing base at Dungeness (Gardiner 1996). A wider picture for the prevalence of fishing will only emerge when more sites are excavated, or metal-detected, but the approach to be used has been established here.

THE RESEARCH AGENDA FOR THE FUTURE

The work discussed here is the latest stage in research on the development of the medieval landscape of Romney and Walland Marsh. When, in 1983, the Romney Marsh Research Group (later Trust) began work, there was little knowledge of the archaeology of the area. The work undertaken around Lydd, together with the studies of Anne Reeves (1995; 1997) in the north-east of Romney Marsh, and surveys undertaken in the Broomhill area, have effectively transformed the understanding of the development of the landscape. Our knowledge of Romney and Walland Marsh in the medieval period has changed from almost total ignorance to a situation now when it is among the best studied regions in south-east England. It is clear from the report above that there are a number of problems in interpreting the archaeological evidence, and it is useful here to consider the future research agenda, both in terms of specific and general problems, and the methods which might be used.

The methods employed in the work at the Lydd area have gradually developed as work has continued. It is possible, in retrospect, to identify a number of aspects which required greater attention. The most apparent problem is the failure to undertake sufficient study of the environmental evidence. The potential of the area for studies of beetles, pollen and plant macrofossils has been demonstrated above, but there is the strong impression that none of the areas have contributed all they might have done. The opportunities for involving specialists on site as the archaeology is revealed is often limited, particularly as it requires negotiation with the planning authorities and developers. However, the survival of waterlogged and semi-waterlogged contexts provides immense potential to allow some of the outstanding questions of environment to be addressed. Wet-sieving of selected contexts to recover smaller bones has also shown considerable potential and this should also be given priority in future work.

The possibility should be investigated of incorporating into the archaeological study some of the sedimentological approaches which have been used on the earlier Holocene deposits. Questions about the origin and date of the fine-grained sediments found above the prehistoric and Roman deposits and below the medieval remains need to be addressed. The issue of the extent of late medieval flooding and any deposits from such events also needs to be addressed. This work will need to go alongside a greater level of recording of the variation in the subsoil deposits revealed on removing the ploughsoil. The position of the underlying shingle has been variably recorded in the different phases of stripping, and a more consistent approach is necessary and will help understand settlement/landscape morphology at a number of levels. It has also been possible to identify the position of palaeo-creeks in some areas. These features appear to have been of fundamental importance in determining the medieval landscape and need to be investigated more systematically.

Some of the environmental methods suggested here will also provide greater information on the economy of settlements. The problems of identifying this has been mentioned. It is apparent that metal-detectors must be used in future work, since these have played a major part in the recovery of fishing weights and hooks, and hence added to our understanding of this aspect of the economy. Fishing weights have not figured very prominently in archaeological studies of rural sites, but they have been shown here to provide a key to an aspect of the economy which is, on the whole, not well covered by documentary sources (*cf.* Fox 2001; Steane and Foreman 1991; Lucas 1998).

The refinement of simple excavation techniques is also necessary to address some other outstanding issues. One of the questions which has been raised in discussion is the use of ditch sections to date features. The ditches were re-cut on numerous occasions and it was rarely possible to match the contexts found in one length of ditch with those in another. It is not clear why this was the case. It would be useful to excavate some longer lengths of ditch to address the question of the lateral extent and variability of fills. We cannot interpret individual sections until we understand the nature of the sample. Equally, we

need to know how the pottery is arriving in the ditch. It may have been incorporated into the topsoil through manuring and have been washed in as the ditch silted up. The ditch fills would, therefore, incorporate a high degree of residual material. Alternatively, the pottery may be dumped directly into the ditch. Farmers on the marsh today still use the ditches as convenient places for disposing of rubbish, even though they will have to clean out the same ditches at some future date. We might wish to consider whether dumping took place near settlement sites. These problems can be addressed through more detailed excavation and analysis, which may include three-dimensional recording of selected sections, sherd re-fitting and the study of abrasion.

At Lydd Quarry the archaeological investigation began at the subsoil after the removal of the ploughsoil. The topsoil is widely recognised as an archaeological resource in itself. Many, perhaps even the majority, of the artefactual remains from a site are found in the ploughsoil. Field-walking and metal-detecting should take place, at least in sample areas, to allow the results to be compared with those discovered after stripping. This will also allow the closer integration of the methods used in landscape surveys elsewhere with the methods used at Lydd Quarry.

The above has provided a simple 'shopping list' of work which might take place in future phases of work on the quarry area. It would be possible to extend the list by adding further work to be done in the surrounding fields. More extensive field-walking, the study of aerial photographs over a wider area and the sectioning of embankments would all help to place the excavated area in context, but cannot be envisaged in the immediate future or with developer funding. At this stage we do need to ask a fundamental question: though we may need to refine the picture, have the major questions been answered? Has a large enough area of landscape been stripped to address the main issues for, at least the medieval period? The historical evidence suggests that the remaining area with planning permission for quarrying to the south-west is likely to lie in the demesne of the manor of Scotney. Fewer buildings are likely to be found, for the lord's barns and farmhouse will have stood near the present Scotney Court Farm. The archaeology here will be different, but no less interesting. The possibility of excavating a demesne landscape presents interesting possibilities, especially since it may be possible to link it with documentary sources. It will also be interesting to examine further the early stages of the marsh landscape. The results to be found in future excavations at Lydd Quarry may be both as unexpected and informative as those uncovered in the work described here.

Bibliography

Documentary sources

Alfred the Great: Asser's Life of King Alfred and Other Contemporary Sources, eds. S. Keynes and M. Lapidge (1983). Harmondsworth.

Beowulf: A Student Edition, ed. G. Jack (1994). Oxford.

The Chronicle of Hugh Candidus: a Monk of Peterborough, ed. W.T. Mellows (1949). London.

Chronica Maiora, Matthaei Parisiensis, Monachi Sancti Albani, ed. H.R. Luard (Rolls ser. 57, 1872–83), seven vols. London.

Chronicon Abbatia Rameseiensis, ed. W.D. Macray (Rolls ser. 83, 1886). London.

Felix's Life of Saint Guthlac, ed. B. Colgrave (1956). Cambridge.

De Gestis Ponitificum, William of Malmesbury, ed. N.E.S.A. Hamilton (Rolls ser. 52, 1870). London.

The Gesta Guillelmi of William of Poitiers, eds. R.H.C. Davis and M. Chibnall (1998). Oxford.

Registrum Simonis Langham (Canterbury and York Society 53 (1956)), ed. A.C. Wood

BCS   Birch, W de G. 1885–93. *Cartularium Saxonicum* London.

S.   Sawyer, P.H., 1968. *Anglo-Saxon Charters: An Annotated List and Bibliography*. London.

Alberella, U., 1999. The mystery of husbandry: medieval animals and the problem of integrating historical and archaeological evidence, *Antiquity* 73, 867–75.

Allen, J.R.L., 1996. The sequence of early land-claims on the Walland and Romney Marshes, south Britain: a preliminary hypothesis and some implications, *Proceedings of the Geologists' Association* 107, 271–80.

Allen, J.R.L., 1997. The geo-archaeology of land-claim in coastal wetlands: a sketch from Britain and the north-west European Atlantic-North Sea coasts, *Archaeological Journal* 154, 1–54.

Allen, J.R.L., 1999a. The Rumensea Wall and the early settlement landscape of Romney Marsh (Kent), *Landscape History* 21, 5–18.

Allen, J.R.L., 1999b. Geological impacts on coastal wetland landscapes: some general effects of sediment autocompaction in the Holocene of northwest Europe. *The Holocene* 9, 1–12.

Allen, J.R.L., 2002. 'The Rumensea Wall, Romney and Walland Marshes: a commentary', in A. Long, S. Hipkin and H. Clarke (eds.), *Romney Marsh: Coastal and Landscape Change through the Ages*, 101–20. Oxford.

Anonymous, 1863. Proofs of age of Sussex families: Selwyne, *Sussex Archaeological Collections* 15, 211–14.

Astill, G.G., 1988. 'Rural settlement: the toft and the croft', in G. Astill and A. Grant (eds.), *The Countryside of Medieval England*, 36–61. Oxford.

Aston, M. and Gerrard, C., 1999. Unique, traditional and charming: the Shapwick project, Somerset, *Antiquaries Journal* 79, 1–58.

Atkinson, D., 1977. *Sussex Clay Tobacco Pipes and the Pipemakers*. Eastbourne.

Atkinson, D.R. and Oswald, A., 1969. London Clay Tobacco Pipes, *Journal of the British Archaeological Association* 3 ser., 32, 171–227.

Austin, D., 1989. 'The excavation of dispersed settlement in medieval Britain', in M. Aston, D. Austin and C. Dyer (eds.), *The Rural Settlements of Medieval England*, 231–46. Oxford.

Bailey, M., 1989. *A Marginal Economy?: East Anglian Breckland in the Later Middle Ages*. Cambridge.

Baker, A.R.H., 1965. Some Fields and Farms in Medieval Kent, *Archaeologia Cantiana* 80, 152–74.

Barber, L., 1993a. 'The Pottery', in D. Rudling, L. Barber and D. Martin, Excavations at the Phoenix Brewery Site, Hastings, 1988, *Sussex Archaeological Collections* 131, 88–95.

Barber, L., 1993b. 'The Metalwork', in D. Rudling and L. Barber, Excavations at the Phoenix Brewery Site, Hastings, 1988, *Sussex Archaeological Collections* 131, 98–100.

Barber, L., 1995a. A259 Brookland Diversion, Kent: An Archaeological Evaluation, *South Eastern Archaeological Services (SEAS) Unpub. Rep. Project* 191.

Barber, L., 1995b. A259 Brookland Diversion, Kent: An Archaeological Watching Brief, Post-excavation assessment and proposals for future work. *SEAS Unpub. Rep. Project* 191.

Barber, L., 1995c. 'The pottery', in G. Priestley-Bell, A Post Excavation Assessment for Archaeological Works on the A2070 Stockbridge to Brenzett Road Improvement Scheme, Kent, *SEAS Unpub. Rep. Project* 410.

Barber, L., 1995d. 'Geological Material', in M. Gardiner, Aspects of the History and Archaeology of Medieval Seaford, *Sussex Archaeological Collections* 133, 206–7.

Barber, L., 1996a. 'The Romano-British pottery', in I. Greig and M. Gardiner, The Excavation of Medieval Occupation Sites, a Medieval Field System and a pre-Medieval Land Surface at Lydd, Kent, *SEAS Unpub. Rep. Project* 59, 16–25.

Barber, L., 1996b. 'Metalwork', in I. Greig and M. Gardiner, The Excavation of Medieval Occupation Sites, a Medieval Field System and a pre-Medieval Land Surface at Lydd, Kent, *SEAS Unpub. Rep. Project* 59, 57–8.

Barber, L., 1996c. 'Geological Material', in I. Greig and M. Gardiner, The Excavation of Medieval Occupation Sites, a Medieval Field System and a pre-Medieval Land Surface at Lydd, Kent, *SEAS Unpub. Rep. Project* 59, 48–54.

Barber, L., 1998a. An Early Romano-British Salt-Working Site At Scotney Court, *Archaeologia Cantiana* 118, 327–54.

Barber, L., 1998b. 'Medieval Rural Settlement and Economy at Lydd: Preliminary Results from the Excavations at Lydd Quarry', in J. Eddison, M. Gardiner and A. Long (eds.), 1998, 89–108.

Barber, L., 1999a. 'The Pottery', in G. Priestley-Bell, The Excavation of an Enclosed Medieval Occupation Site, Ditch System and Trackway at Lydd Quarry (Stage 2), *Archaeology South-East (ASE) Archive Report* 250, 11–30.

Barber, L., 1999b. 'Geological Material', in G. Priestley-Bell The Excavation of an Enclosed Medieval Occupation Site, a Medieval Ditch System and Trackway at Lydd Quarry (Stage 2), *ASE Archive Report* 250, 35–40.

Barber, L., 2002a. Medieval Adaptation, Settlement and Economy of a Coastal Wetland: The Evidence from around Lydd, Romney Marsh, Kent: A Project Design and Costing for the synthesis and publication of excavations at Lydd Quarry and other related sites, *ASE Unpub. Report* P26.

Barber, L., 2002b. 'The Pottery', in G. Priestley-Bell, The Excavation of Ditch Systems, Trackways and Settlement Sites at Lydd Quarry (Stage 3), *ASE Archive Report* 354, 8–35.

Barber, L., 2002c. 'Geological Material', in G. Priestley-Bell, The Excavation of Ditch Systems, Trackways and Settlement Sites at Lydd Quarry (Stage 3), *ASE Archive Report* 354, 37–41.

Barber, L., 2002d. 'Miscellaneous Material', in G. Priestley-Bell, The Excavation of Prehistoric, Romano-British and Medieval Remains at Lydd Quarry (Stage 4), *ASE Archive Report* 455, 18.

Barber, L., 2003a. 'The Pottery', in G. Priestley-Bell, The Excavation of Medieval Occupation Sites, Medieval Ditch Systems and Trackways at Lydd Quarry (Stage 5/6), *ASE Archive Report* 517, 12–54.

Barber, L., 2003b. 'Geological Material', in G. Priestley-Bell, The Excavation of Medieval Occupation Sites, Medieval Ditch Systems and Trackways at Lydd Quarry (Stage 5/6), *ASE Archive Report* 517, 71–6.

Barber, L., 2004a. 'The Pottery', in G. Priestley-Bell, 2004a, 22–26.

Barber, L., 2004b. 'The Pottery', in G. Priestley-Bell, 2004b.

Barber, L., 2004c. 'Geological Material', in G. Priestley-Bell, 2004a, 35–6.

Barnard, F.P., 1917. *The Casting-Counter and the Counting-Board.* Oxford.

Barrett, J.H., Nicholson, R.A. and Cerón-Carrasco, R., 1999. Archaeo-ichthyological evidence for long-term socioeconomic trends in northern Scotland: 3500 BC to AD 1500, *Journal of Archaeological Science* 26, 353–88.

Barton, K., 1979. *Medieval Sussex Pottery.* Chichester.

Beck, D., 1995. 'Drainage of Romney Marsh and maintenance of the Dymchurch Wall in the early 17th century', in J. Eddison (ed.), *Romney Marsh: The Debatable Ground*, 164–8. Oxford.

Beck, D., 2004. Can't see the wood for the trees?, *Romney Marsh Irregular* 23, 19–21.

Bendall, S., 1995. Enquire 'When the Same Platte Was Made and by Whome and to What Intent': Sixteenth-Century Maps of Romney Marsh, *Imago Mundi (The International Journal for the History of Cartography)* 47, 36.

Bennett, K.D., Whittington, G. and Edwards, K.J., 1994. Recent plant nomenclatural changes and pollen morphology in the British Isles, *Quaternary Newsletter* 73, 1–6.

Beresford, G., 1975. The Medieval Clay-Land Villages: Excavations at Goltho and Barton Blount, *Society for Medieval Archaeology, Monograph* 6. London.

Beresford, G., 1979. Three deserted medieval settlements on Dartmoor: a report on the late E. Marie Minter's excavations, *Medieval Archaeology* 23, 98–158.

Beresford, M.W., 1957. *History on the Ground: Six Studies in Maps and Landscapes.* London.

Beresford, M.W. and Hurst, J.G., 1990. *Wharram Percy Deserted Medieval Village.* London.

Berry, G., 1974. *Medieval English Jetons.* London.

Biddick, K., 1989. *The Other Economy: Pastoral Husbandry on a Medieval Estate.* Oxford.

Biddle, M., 1990. Object and Economy in Medieval Winchester, *Winchester Studies* 7. Oxford.

Blinkhorn, P., 2001. 'Pottery Assessment', in Oxford Archaeological Unit 'land to the rear of the Old School House, Church Lane, New Romney, Kent' Client Report.

Blythe, K., 1998. A Report on the Pottery from the Excavation of Brett's Lydd Quarry, Kent, *Unpublished Dissertation, University College London, Institute of Archaeology.*

Blythe, K., 1999. A Medieval Zoomorphic Handle from Brett's Lydd Quarry in Kent, *Unpublished Archive Report.*

Boekske, K., 1872. *A literal translation into English of the earliest known book on fowling and fishing written originally in Flemish and printed at Antwerp in the year 1492.* London.

Brandon, P.F., 1971. Agriculture and the effects of floods and weather at Barnhorne, Sussex, during the Late Middle Ages, *Sussex Archaeological Collections* 109, 69–93.

Bridbury, A., 1955. *England and the Salt Trade in the Later Middle Ages.* Oxford.

Britnell, R.H., 1981. The proliferation of markets in England, 1200–1349, *Economic History Review* 2nd ser., 34, 209–21.

Brooks, N., 1988. 'Romney Marsh in the early Middle Ages', in J. Eddison and C. Green (eds.), 1988, 90–104.

Butcher, A.F., 2000. Peasant use of cannabis in the early fourteenth century, *paper given at the University of Kent.*

Butcher, A.F. and Gross, A., 1991. The History of Romney Marsh *c.* 1150–1350 – A Pilot Study: *c.* 1275–1300, *end of award report.*

Campbell, B.M., 1988. The diffusion of vetches in medieval England, *Economic History Review* 2nd ser., 41, 193–208.

Campbell, B. M., 2000. *English Seigniorial Agriculture 1250–1450.* Cambridge.

Carrott, J. and Kenward, H., 2001. Species associations among insect remains from urban archaeological deposits and their significance in reconstructing the past human environment, *Journal of Archaeological Science* 28, 887–905.

Clarke, R., 2003. A Medieval Moated Site and Windmill: Excavations at Boreham Airfield, Essex 1996, *East Anglian Archaeology, Occasional Paper* 11. Chelmsford.

Cole, H.A., 1956. *Oyster Cultivation in Britain: A Manual of Current Practice.* London.

Cotter, J., 2002. Medieval Shelly Wares in Kent: a summary of recent research, *Canterbury's Archaeology 1999–2000*, 56–60.

Council for British Archaeology, 1997. Medieval fisherman's quarter found in Dover, *British Archaeology* 22.

Cowgill, J., 1986. *Knives and Scabbards, Medieval Finds from Excavations in London* 1. London.

Cristy, M., 1924. Biological Flora of the British Isles, *Carpinus betulus L., Journal of Ecology.*

Cross, R., 1997. Archaeology at West Hythe: Excavations in October 1996, *The Romney Marsh Irregular* 12, 6–7.

Crummy, N., 1988. The Post-Roman small finds from excavations in Colchester 1971–85, *Colchester Archaeological Report* 5. Colchester.

Cullen, P., 1997. Place-Names of the Lathes of St Augustine and Shipway, Kent, *PhD thesis, University of Sussex.*

Cunliffe, B., 1988. 'Romney Marsh in the Roman Period', in J. Eddison and C. Green (eds.), 1988, 83–7.

Currie, C.R., 1988. Early vetches in medieval England: a note, *Economic History Review*, 2nd ser., 41, 114–16.

Darby, H.C., 1977. *Domesday England*. Cambridge.

Dickson, J.H., Dickson, C. and Breeze, D.J., 1979. Flour bread in a Roman military ditch at Bearsden, Scotland, *Antiquity* 53, 47–51.

Dimbleby, G.W., 1988. *The Palynology of Archaeological Sites*. London.

Dimmock, S., 1998. Class and the Social Transformation of a Late Medieval Small Town: Lydd *c.* 1450–1550, *PhD thesis, University of Kent at Canterbury.*

Dimmock, S., 2001. English small towns and the emergence of capitalist relations, *c.* 1450–1550, *Urban History* 28, 5–24.

Dixon, M., 1992. Economy and Society in Dover, 1509–1640, *PhD thesis, University of Kent at Canterbury.*

Draper, G., 1997. The Leasing of the Demesnes and the Farmers of Romney Marsh in the Later Middle Ages, *MA dissertation, University of Kent at Canterbury.*

Draper, G., 1998. 'The farmers of Canterbury Cathedral Priory and All Souls College on Romney Marsh *c.* 1443–1545', in J. Eddison, M. Gardiner and A. Long (eds.), *Romney Marsh: Environmental Change and Human Occupation in a Coastal Lowland*, 109–28. Oxford.

Drewett, P.L., Holgate, B., Foster, S. and Ellerby, H., 1986. The excavation of a Saxon sunken building at North Marden, West Sussex, 1982, *Sussex Archaeological Collections* 124, 109–18.

Driesch, A. v.d. 1969. A guide to the measurement of animal bones from archaeological sites, *Peabody Museum Bulletin* 1.

Du Boulay, F.R.H., 1966. *The Lordship of Canterbury.* London.

Duby, G., 1968. *Rural Economy and Country Life in the Medieval West*. London.

Dulley, A.J.F., 1967. Excavations at Pevensey, Sussex 1962–6, *Medieval Archaeology* 11, 209–32.

Dulley, A.J.F., 1969. The early history of the Rye fishing industry, *Sussex Archaeological Collections* 107, 36–64.

Dunning, G., 1961. 'Stone Mortars', in J. Hurst, The Kitchen Area of Northolt Manor, Middlesex, *Medieval Archaeology* 5, 279–84.

Dunning, G., 1977. 'Mortars', in H. Clarke and A. Carter, Excavations in King's Lynn 1963–70, *Society of Medieval Archaeology Monograph Series* 7, 320–47.

Dyer, C.C., 1981 'Were there any capitalists in fifteenth-century England?', in J. Kermode (ed.), *Enterprise and Individuals in Fifteenth-Century England*, 1–24. Stroud.

Dyer, C.C., 1989. 'The retreat from marginal land: the growth and decline of medieval rural settlements', in M. Aston, D. Austin and C. Dyer (eds.), *The Rural Settlements of Medieval England*, 45–57. Oxford.

Dyer, C.C., 2002. Obituary – John Hurst, *Annual Report of the Medieval Settlement Research Group* 17, 5–6.

Dymond, D., 1999. God's disputed acre, *Journal of Ecclesiastical History* 50, 464–97.

Eddison, J., 1983. The reclamation of Romney Marsh: some aspects reconsidered, *Archaeologia Cantiana* 99, 47–58.

Eddison, J., 1992a. A Report on the Archaeological Implications of Proposed Sand and Gravel Extraction at Denge West, Lydd, Kent, *Unpub. Romney Marsh Research Trust (RMRT) Report.*

Eddison, J., 1992b. A Report on the Archaeological Implications of an area North of Brookland, Kent, *RMRT Report.*

Eddison, J., (ed.), 1995. Romney Marsh: The Debatable Ground, *Oxford University Committee for Archaeology, Monograph* 41. Oxford.

Eddison, J., 2000. *Romney Marsh. Survival on a Frontier.* Stroud.

Eddison, J., 2003. 'The purpose, construction and operation of a 13th century watercourse: the Rhee, Romney Marsh, Kent', in A. Long, S. Hipkin and H. Clarke (eds.), Romney Marsh: Coastal and Landscape Change through the Ages, *Oxford University Committee for Archaeology Monograph* 56, 127–39. Oxford.

Eddison, J. and Draper, G., 1997. A landscape of medieval reclamation: Walland Marsh, Kent, *Landscape History* 19, 75–88.

Eddison, J. and Green, C., (eds.), 1988. Romney Marsh: Evolution, Occupation, Reclamation, *Oxford University Committee for Archaeology, Monograph* 24. Oxford.

Eddison, J., Gardiner, M. and Long, A., (eds.), 1998. Romney Marsh: Environmental Change and Human Occupation in a Coastal Lowland, *Oxford University Committee for Archaeology, Monograph* 46. Oxford.

Egan, G. and Pritchard, F., 1991. *Dress Accessories c. 1150–1450, Medieval Finds from Excavation in London 3.* London.

Elks, S., 1987. Lydd 1540–1644: a demographic study, *MA thesis, University of Kent at Canterbury.*

Elliot, J., 1862. Views reported in T. Lewin, *The Invasion of Britain by Julius Caesar* (2nd edition). London.

Enghoff, I. B., 2000. Fishing in the southern North Sea region from 1st to 16th century AD: evidence from fish bones, *Archaeofauna* 9, 59–132.

Evans, J.H., 1953. Archaeological horizons in the north Kent marshes, *Archaeologia Cantiana* 64, 103–46.

Evans, R., 1997. The properties of All Souls College in Romney Marsh: the rent rolls to 1506, *unpublished.*

Evans, D.G. and Jarrett, M.G., 1987. The deserted village of West Whelpington, Northumberland: third report, part 1, *Archaeologia Aeliana* 5th ser., 15, 199–308.

Evans, D.G, Jarrett, M.G. and Wrathmell, S., 1988. The deserted village of West Whelpington, Northumberland: third report, part 2, *Archaeologia Aeliana* 5th ser., 16, 139–92.

Everitt, A., 1986. *Continuity and Colonization: the Evolution of Kentish Settlement*. Leicester.

Farmer, D.H., 1978. *The Oxford Dictionary of Saints*. Oxford.

Farmer, P. G., 1979. *An Introduction to Scarborough Ware and a Re-assessment of Knight Jugs*. Hove.

Faull, M.L. and Moorhouse, S.A., 1981. *West Yorkshire: an Archaeological Survey to AD 1500*. Wakefield.

Finn, A. (ed.), 1911. *Records of Lydd*. Ashford.

Fish, J.D. & Fish, S., 1989. *A Student's Guide to the Seashore.* London.

Fowler, P.J., 2000. *A Landscape Plotted and Pieced: Landscape History and Local Archaeology in Fyfield and Overton, Wiltshire*. London.

Fox, H.S.A., 2001. *The Evolution of the Fishing Village: Landscape and Society Along the South Devon Coast, 1086–1550*. Leicester.

Gardiner, M., 1988. 'Medieval Settlement and Society in the Broomhill area and Excavations at Broomhill Church', in J. Eddison and C. Green (eds.), 1988, 112–27.

Gardiner, M., 1992. Sample Excavations at Dering Farm, Lydd, Kent: A Preliminary Report, *Field Archaeology Unit Archive Report*, March 1992.

Gardiner, M., 1994. Old Romney: An Examination of the evidence for a Lost Saxo-Norman Port, *Archaelogia Cantiana* 114, 329–45.

Gardiner, M., 1995a. A Pre-Extraction Survey of Denge West (South) Gravel Quarry, Lydd, *SEAS Unpub. Rep. Project* 53.

Gardiner, M., 1995b. The Priory, Queens Road, Lydd: Archaeological watching brief, *SEAS Unpub. Report* 312.

Gardiner, M., 1995c. 'Medieval farming and flooding in the Brede valley', in J. Eddison (ed.), *Romney Marsh: The Debatable Ground*, 127–37. Oxford.

Gardiner, M., 1996. A seasonal fisherman's settlement at Dungeness, Kent, *Medieval Settlement Research Group Annual Report* 11, 18–20.

Gardiner, M., 1997. Trade, rural industry and the origins of villages: some evidence from south-east England, *Rural Settlements in Medieval Europe, Papers of the Medieval Europe Brugge 1997 Conference* 6, 63–73. Belgium.

Gardiner, M., 1998. 'Settlement change on Walland Marsh, 1400–1550', in J. Eddison, M. Gardiner and A. Long (eds.), *Romney Marsh: Environmental Change and Human Occupation in a Coastal Lowland*, 129–45. Oxford.

Gardiner, M., 2000a. Vernacular buildings and the development of the later medieval domestic plan in England, *Medieval Archaeology* 44, 159–79.

Gardiner, M., 2000b. Shipping and trade between England and the Continent during the eleventh century, *Anglo-Norman Studies* 22, 71–93.

Gardiner, M., 2002. 'The late medieval 'antediluvian' landscape of Walland Marsh', in A. Long, S. Hipkin and H. Clarke (eds.), *Romney Marsh: Coastal and Landscape Change through the Ages*, 101–20. Oxford.

Gardiner, M., 2003. 'Economy and landscape change in post-Roman and early medieval Sussex, 450–1175', in D. Rudling (ed.), *The Archaeology of Sussex to AD 2000*, 151–60. King's Lynn.

Gardiner, M., 2005. Archaeological evidence for the exploitation, reclamation and flooding of salt marshes, *Ruralia V: Water Use and Management in Europe*, 73–83. Prague.

Gardiner, M., 2007. 'Hythes, small ports and other landing places in later medieval England', in J. Blair (ed.), *Water Transport and Management in Medieval England*, 85–109. Oxford.

Gardiner, M. and Hartwell, B., 2006. Landscapes of failure: the archaeology of flooded wetlands at Titchwell and Thornham (Norfolk), and Broomhill (East Sussex), *Journal of Wetland Archaeology* 6, 137–60.

Gardiner, M., MacPherson-Grant, N. and Riddler, I., 2001. Continental Trade and Non-Urban Ports in Mid-Anglo-Saxon England: Excavations at Sandtun, West Hythe, Kent, *Archaeological Journal* 158, 161–290.

Gardiner, M., Stewart, J. and Priestley-Bell, G., 1998. Anglo-Saxon Whale Exploitation: Some Evidence From Dengemarsh, Lydd, Kent, *Medieval Archaeology* 42, 96–101.

Gardiner, M. and Murray, E.V., in preparation. *Timber Buildings in England and Wales, 900–1200.*

Gelling, P.S., 1962–3. Medieval shielings in the Isle of Man, *Medieval Archaeology* 6–7, 156–72.

Gibson, A., 2002. 'The Bronze Age Pottery', in G. Priestley-Bell, The Excavation of prehistoric, Roman and medieval deposits at Lydd Quarry (Stage 4), *ASE Archive Report* 455, 5–7.

Gingell, T., 1996. 'The Medieval Pottery', in I. Greig and M. Gardiner, The Excavation of Medieval Occupation Sites, a Medieval Field System and a pre-Medieval Land Surface at Lydd, Kent, *SEAS Unpub. Archive Rep.* 59, 25–32.

Gingell, T., forthcoming. 'The Pottery', in M. Gardiner, *Excavations at Broomhill.*

Goodall, I., 1975. 'The Metalwork', in D. Crossley, *The Bewl Valley Ironworks, Kent, c. 1300–1730*, 59–89. London.

Goodwin, H., 1975. *The History of the British Flora* (2nd edition). Cambridge.

Grant, A., 1982. 'The use of tooth wear as a guide to the age of domestic ungulates', in B. Wilson, C. Grigson and S. Payne, (eds.), Ageing and Sexing Animals from Archaeological Sites, *BAR Brit Series* 109, 91–108. Oxford.

Greatorex, C., 1993. An Archaeological Watching Brief at the Rhee Wall, Brenzett, Kent, *SEAS Unpub. Rep. Project* 1993/56.

Greatorex, C., 1994. A2070 Stockbridge-Brenzett Road Improvement, A Summary of the Archaeological Field Evaluation, Stage Two, *SEAS Unpub. Rep. Project* 1994/57.

Green, C., 1988. 'Palaeography of marine inlets in the Romney Marsh area', in J. Eddison and C. Green (eds.), 1988, 77–82.

Green, R., 1968. Soils of Romney Marsh, *Soil Survey of Great Britain, Bulletin* 4. Harpenden.

Greig, I., 1992a. A2070 Stockbridge-Brenzett Road Improvement: Field-walking Survey, *SEAS Unpub. Rep. Project* 1991/56.

Greig, I., 1992b. A2070 Stockbridge-Brenzett Road Improvement: Trial Trenching Report (First Stage), *SEAS Unpub. Rep. Project* 1992/67.

Greig, I., 1992c. A2070 Stockbridge to South Ashford Road Archaeological Watching Brief, *SEAS Unpub. Rep. Project* 1992/39 (part ii).

Greig, I. and Gardiner, M., 1996. The Excavation of Medieval Occupation Sites, a Medieval Field System and a pre-Medieval Land Surface at Lydd, Kent, *SEAS Unpub. Archive Rep.* 59.

Greig, J., 1992. 'Plant Resources', in A. Grenville and A. Grant (eds.), *The Countryside of Medieval England*, 109–27. Oxford.

Griffin, N., 1999. An Archaeological Watching Brief at the RSPB Nature Reserve, Boulderwall Farm, Dungeness, *ASE Unpub. Rep. Project* 1017.

Griffin, N., 2002. An Archaeological Watching Brief at Harden Road, Lydd, *ASE Unpub. Rep. Project* 140.

Grigson, G., 1984. *Five Hundred Points of Good Husbandry. Thomas Tusser 1580 edn.* Oxford.

Gross, A. and Butcher, A., 1995. 'Adaptation and investment in the age of great storms: agricultural policy on the manors of the principal lords of the Romney Marshes and the marshland fringe *c.* 1250–1320', in J. Eddison (ed.), 1995, 107–17.

Grove, L., 1952. A 13th century Kiln site at Ashford, *Archaeologia Cantiana* 65, 174–93.

GSB Prospection, 1998. Allens Bank, Lydd, *Unpub. Client Report for John Samuels Archaeological Consultants, Report* 98/132.

Hall, A.R. and Kenward, H.K., 1990. Environmental evidence from the Colonia: General Accident and Rougier Street, *The Archaeology of York* 14 (6), 289–434 + Plates II–IX + Fiche 2–11. London.

Hallam, H.E., 1965. *Settlement and Society: A Study of the Early Agrarian History of South Lincolnshire.* Cambridge.

Hancock, D. and Urquhart, A., 1966. The fisheries for cockles in the Burry Inlet, South Wales, *Fisheries Investigations Series* 2, 25 (3).

Hasted, E., 1799. *The History and Topographical Survey of the County of Kent*, vol. 8 (Canterbury 1799, reprinted 1972).

Herring, P., 1996. 'Transhumance in medieval Cornwall', in H.S.A. Fox (ed.), *Seasonal Settlement* (Vaughan Paper 39), 35–44. Leicester.

Hildyard, R., 1985. Browne Muggs: English Brown Stoneware. *Victoria & Albert Museum Ceramic Series.* London.

Hillman, G.C., Mason, S., de Moulins, D. and Nesbitt, M., 1995. Identification of archaeological remains of wheat: the 1992 London workshop, *Circaea, The Journal for Environmental Archaeology* 12 (2) (1996), 195–209.

Hipkin, S., 1998. 'The structure of land occupation in the Level of Romney Marsh during the late 16th and early 17th centuries', in J. Eddison, M. Gardiner and A. Long (eds.), 1998, 147–63.

Holden, E., 1963. Excavations at the deserted Medieval village of Hangleton, Part 1, *Sussex Archaeological Collections* 101, 54–181.

Hoskins, W.G., 1955. *The Making of the English Landscape.* London.

Houben, G., 1978 *European Coin-Weights for English Coins.* Holland.

Hurst, J., Neal, D. and Van Beuningen, H., 1986. Pottery Produced and Traded in North-West Europe 1350–1650, *Rotterdam Papers* VI. Rotterdam.

Jackson, E. and Fletcher, E., 1959. The pre-Conquest basilica at Lydd, *Journal of the British Archaeological Association* 22, 41–52

Jackson, E., Dudley, C. and Fletcher, E., 1968. Excavations at the Lydd basilica, 1966, *Journal of the British Archaeological Association* 31, 19–26.

Jaques, D., 2002. Technical report: Fish remains from 17 sites excavated around Shapwick, Somerset, *PRS* 2002/50.

Jarrett, C., 2002. An Assessment of Archaeological Excavations on the Site of Southlands School, Fairfield Road, New Romney, Kent, *Pre-Construct Archaeology Unpub. Report.* July.

Jennings, S., 1981. Eighteen Centuries of Pottery from Norwich, *East Anglian Archaeology* 13. Norwich.

John Samuels Consultants, 1999. An Archaeological Evaluation at Allens Bank, Lydd, Kent, *Unpub. Client Report JSAC* 447/99/001.

Jope, E.M., 1958. The Clarendon Hotel, Oxford. Part 1. The Site, *Oxoniensia* 23, 1–83.

Judas, M., Dornieden, K. and Strothmann, U., 2002. Distribution patterns of carabid beetle species at the landscape level, *Journal of Biogeography* 29, 491–508.

Kent County Council 2003. *Kent Historic Towns Survey.*

Kenward, H.K., 1975. Pitfalls in the environmental interpretation of insect death assemblages, *Journal of Archaeological Science* 2, 85–94.

Kenward, H.K., 1992 for 1991. Rapid recording of archaeological insect remains – a reconsideration, *Circaea, the Journal of the Association for Environmental Archaeology* 9, 81–8.

Kenward, H.K. and Hall, A.R., 1995. Biological evidence from Anglo-Scandinavian deposits at 16–22 Coppergate, *The Archaeology of York* 14 (7), 435–797 + xxii + loose figures. York.

Kenward, H.K. and Hall, A.R., 1997. Enhancing bioarchaeological interpretation using indicator groups: stable manure as a paradigm, *Journal of Archaeological Science* 24, 663–73.

Kenward, H.K., Hall, A.R. and Jones, A.K.G., 1980. A tested set of techniques for the extraction of plant and animal macrofossils from waterlogged archaeological deposits, *Science and Archaeology* 22, 3–15.

Kestner, F.J.T., 1975. The loose-boundary regime of the Wash, *Geographical Journal* 141, 388–414.

Kideys, A.E., Nash, R.D.M. and Hartnoll, R.G., 1993. Reproductive cycle and energetic cost of reproduction of the neogastropod *Buccinum undatum* in the Irish Sea, *J. Mar. Biol. Ass. U.K.* 73, 391–403.

Kowaleski, M., 2000. The expansion of the south-western fisheries in late medieval England, *Economic History Review* 53, 429–54.

Knowles, D., 1950. *The Monastic Order in England.* Cambridge.

Lamb, H.H., 1995. *Climate, History and the Modern World* (2nd edition). London.

Leenhardt, M., 1983. 'Pottery used in the Chateau de Caen from the 12th to 14th century', in P. Davey and R. Hodges (eds.), *Ceramics and Trade*, 55–62. Sheffield.

Levine, M., 1982. 'The use of crown height measurements and eruption-wear sequences to age horse teeth', in B. Wilson, C. Grigson and S. Payne (eds.), Ageing and Sexing Animals from Archaeological Sites, *BAR Brit Series* 109, 91–108. Oxford.

Linklater, A., 2001. An Interim Report of an Archaeological Excavation at the rear of Prospect House, Fairfield Road, New Romney, Kent, *Canterbury Archaeological Trust Client Report*, July.

Locker, A., 1985. 'Animal and plant remains', in J.N. Hare, Battle Abbey. The Eastern Range and the Excavations of 1978–80, 183–9, *Historic Buildings and Monuments Commission for England*, London.

Locker, A., 2001. The role of stored fish in England 900–1750 AD: the evidence from historical and archaeological data, *PhD thesis, University of Southampton.*

London Museum, 1940. *Medieval Catalogue.* London.

Long, A. J. and Hughes, P.D.M., 1995. Mid and late Holocene evolution of the Dungeness foreland, UK, *Marine Geology* 124, 253–71.

Long, A., Waller, M., Hughes, P. and Spencer, C., 1998. 'The Holocene Depositional History of Romney Marsh Proper', in J. Eddison, M. Gardiner and A. Long (eds.), 1998, 45–63.

Luard, H.R. (ed.), 1880. *Matthaei Parisiensis, Chronica Majora*, vol. 5. London.

Lucas, G., 1998. A medieval fishery on Whittlesea Mere, Cambridgeshire, *Medieval Archaeology* 42, 19–44.

Lyne, M., 1999. 'The Pottery', in L. Barber, The excavation of Land adjacent to the Old Farmhouse, Pevensey, East Sussex, 1994, *Sussex Archaeological Collections* 137, 105–13.

Lyne, M., 2002. 'Late Iron Age, Roman and Medieval Pottery', in G. Priestley-Bell, 2002b.

Lyne, M., 2004. 'The Romano-British Pottery', in G. Priestley-Bell, 2004a.

McLain, B.A., 1997. Factors in market establishment in medieval England: the evidence from Kent 1086–1350, *Archaeologia Cantiana* 117, 83–104.

Maître-Allain, T., 1991. *La Vie en Bord de Mer.* France.

Major, A., 1981. *A New Dictionary of Kent Dialect.* Rainham.

Margeson, S., 1993. Norwich Households: The Medieval and Post-Medieval Finds from Norwich Survey Excavations 1971–8, *East Anglian Archaeology Report* 58. Norwich.

Mate, M., 1984. Agrarian economy after the Black Death: the manors of Canterbury cathedral priory 1348–91, *Economic History Review*, 2nd ser., 37, 341–54.

Mate, M., 1987. Pastoral farming in south-east England in the fifteenth century, *Economic History Review*, 2nd ser., 40, 523–36.

Mate, M., 1990. 'Farming Practice and Techniques: Kent and Sussex', in E. Miller (ed.), *The Agrarian History of England and Wales III: 1348–1500*, 268–85. Cambridge.

Mate, M., 1991a. 'The agrarian economy of south-east England before the Black Death: depressed or buoyant?', in B.M.S. Campbell (ed.), *Before the Black Death: Studies in the 'Crisis' of the Early Fourteenth Century*, 79–109. Manchester.

Mate, M., 1991b. 'Occupation of the land: Kent and Sussex', in E. Miller (ed.), *Agricultural History of England and Wales III: 1348–1500*, 119–36. Cambridge.

Mate, M., 1996. The rise and fall of markets in south-east England, *Canadian Journal of History* 31, 59–86.

Middleton-Stewart, J., 1996. 'Down to the sea in ships: decline and fall on the Suffolk coast', in C. Rawcliffe, R. Virgoe and R. Wilson (eds.), *Counties and Communities: essays on East Anglian history*, 69–83. Norwich.

Mitchiner, M., 1988. *Jetons, Medalets & Tokens, Volume 1: The Medieval Period and Nuremberg*. London.

Mitchiner, M. and Skinner, A., 1984. English Tokens, c. 1200–1425, *The British Numismatic Journal* 1983, 53, 29–77.

Mitchiner, M. and Skinner, A., 1985. English Tokens, c. 1425–1672, *The British Numismatic Journal* 1984, 54, 86–163.

Moffett, L., 1991. 'The archaeobotanical evidence for free-threshing tetraploid wheat in Britain', in Palaeoethnobotany and Archaeology. International Work-Group for Palaeoethnobotany 8th Symposium, Nitra-Nové, Vozokany, 1989. *Acta Interdisciplinaria Archaeologica* VII, 233–43.

Moore, P.D. and Webb, J.A., 1978. *An illustrated guide to pollen analysis*. London.

Moore, P.D., Webb, J.A. and Collinson, M.E., 1991. *Pollen analysis* (2nd edition). Oxford.

Morgan, P. (ed.), 1983. *Domesday Book, Kent*. Chichester.

Murray, K.M.E. (ed.), 1945. *Register of Daniel Rough: common clerk of Romney 1353–80*. Kent Records, Ashford.

Needham, S., 1988. 'A Group of Early Bronze Age Axes from Lydd', in J. Eddison and C. Green (eds.), 1988, 77–82.

Neilson, N. (ed.), 1928. The Cartulary and Terrier of the Priory of Bilsington, Kent, *British Academy Records of the Social and Economic History of England and Wales* 7. London.

Nicholson, G.C. and Evans, S.M., 1997. Anthropogenic impacts on the stocks of the common whelk *Buccinum undatum* (L.), *Marine Environmental Research* 44, 305–14.

Noel Hume, I., 1969. (reprinted 1991). *A Guide to the Artefacts of Colonial America*. New York.

North, J.J., 1980. *English Hammered Coinage, Volume 1, Early Anglo-Saxon to Henry III, c. 600–1272* (2nd edition). London.

North, J.J., 1991. *English Hammered Coinage, Volume 2, Edward I to Charles II, 1272–1662* (3rd edition). London.

O'Neil, H.E., 1967. Bevan's Quarry round barrow, Temple Guiting, Gloucestershire, 1964, *Transactions of the Bristol and Gloucestershire Archaeological Society* 86, 16–41.

Owen, A.E.B., 1996. The Medieval Lindsey Marsh: Select Documents, *Lincoln Record Society* 85. Woodbridge.

Oxford Archaeology Unit, 2001. Land to the rear of the Old School House, Church Lane, New Romney, Kent, *Unpub. Report* F7234, February.

Page, M., 2003. The technology of medieval sheep farming: some evidence from Crawley, Hampshire, 1208–1349, *Agricultural History Review* 51, 137–54.

Patourel, H.E.J. le, Long, M.H. and Pickles, M.F., (eds.), 1993. *Yorkshire Boundaries*. Leeds.

Pearce, J., 1992. *Post-medieval Pottery in London, 1500–1700; Vol 1: Borderware*. London.

Pearce, J.E. and Vince, A., 1988. A dated Type-Series of London Medieval Pottery Part 4: Surrey Whitewares, *LAMAS Special Paper* 10. London.

Pearson, A. and Potter, J., 2002. Church building fabrics on Romney Marsh and the Marshland fringe: a geological perspective, *Landscape History* 24, 89–110.

Pearson, S., 1995. 'The medieval houses of the Marsh: the missing evidence', in J. Eddison (ed.), 1995, 92–8.

Pearson, S., Barnwell, P. S. and Adams, A.T., 1994. *A Gazetteer of Medieval houses in Kent*. London.

Peterken, G.F. and Hubbard, J.C.E., 1972. The shingle vegetation of southern England: the holly wood on Holmstone Beach, Dungeness, *Journal of Ecology* 60, 547–72.

Philp, B. and Willson, J., 1984. Roman Salt-working site at Scotney Court, Lydd, *Kent Archaeological Review* 68, 156–61.

Place, C., 1993a. A259(T) New Romney Bypass Archaeological Field Evaluation, *SEAS Unpub. Rep. Project* 1992/58.

Place, C., 1993b. A259(T) St Mary's Bay & Dymchurch Bypass Archaeological Field Evaluation, *SEAS Unpub. Rep. Project* 1992/58.

Place, C., 1994. A259, New Romney and St. Mary's Bay/Dymchurch Bypass. The Archaeological Evidence, *SEAS Unpub. Rep. Project* 1994/45.

Plater, A., 1993 (revised 1995). The Sediments of Denge Marsh: a study of shingle and marsh interdependance during the late Holocene. *Dept. Geography, University of Liverpool.*

Plater A. and Long. A., 1995. 'The morphology and evolution of Denge Beach', in J. Eddison (ed.), 1995, 8–36.

Plater, A., Stupples, P., Roberts, H. and Owen, C., 2002. 'The evidence for late Holocene foreland progradation and rapid tidal sedimentation from the barrier and marsh sediments of Romney Marsh and Dungeness: a geomorphological perspective', in A. Long, S. Hipkin and H. Clarke (eds.), *Romney Marsh: Coastal and Landscape Change through the Ages*, 40–57. Oxford.

Platt, C. and Coleman-Smith, R., 1975. *Excavations in Medieval Southampton 1953–69. Vol 2: The Finds*. Leicester.

Postan, M.M., 1975. *The Medieval Economy and Society: An Economic History of England in the Middle Ages.* Harmondsworth.

Prendergast, M., 1974. Limpsfield medieval coarseware: a descriptive analysis, *Surrey Archaeology Collections* 70, 57–77.

Preston, C.D., Pearman, D.A. and Dines, T.D., 2002. *New Atlas of the British & Irish Flora*. Oxford.

Priestley-Bell, G., 1994. An interim Report on Archaeological Remains revealed during Gravel Extraction at Denge West, Lydd, Kent, *SEAS Unpub. Rep. Project* 1994/53.

Priestley-Bell, G., 1995. A Post Excavation Assessment for Archaeological Works on the A2070 Stockbridge to Brenzett Road Improvement Scheme, Kent, *SEAS Unpub. Rep. Project* 410.

Priestley-Bell, G., 1998. An Archaeological Watching Brief at Denge West South Quarry, Lydd, Kent, *ASE Unpub. Rep. Project* 595.

Priestley-Bell, G., 1999. The Excavation of an Enclosed Medieval Occupation Site, Ditch System and Trackway at Lydd Quarry (Stage 2), *ASE Archive Report* 250.

Priestley-Bell, G., 2002a. The Excavation of Ditch Systems, Trackways and Settlement Sites at Lydd Quarry (Stage 3), *ASE Archive Report* 354.

Priestley-Bell, G., 2002b. The Excavation of Prehistoric, Romano-British and Medieval Remains at Lydd Quarry (Stage 4), *ASE Archive Report* 455.

Priestley-Bell, G., 2003. The Excavation of Medieval Occupation Sites, Medieval Ditch System and Trackways at Lydd Quarry (Stage 5/6), *ASE Archive Report* 517.

Priestley-Bell, G., 2004a. The Excavation of Prehistoric and Medieval Remains at Lydd Quarry (Stages 7 to 11), *ASE Archive Report* 611/793/926/1008/1160.

Priestley-Bell, G., 2004b. Excavations at Caldicott farm Quarry, Lydd, *ASE Archive Report* 809.

Priestley-Bell, G., in prep. A Late Iron Age and early Roman Salt-working site at Lydd Quarry (Stages 12–14), *ASE Archive Report*.

Priestley-Bell, G. and Gardiner, M., 1994. An interim Statement on the Results of the Watching Brief at Denge West North Quarry (Phases 1–5), Lydd, Kent, *SEAS Unpub. Rep. Project* 1994/53.

Rackham, O., 1993. *Trees and Woodland in the British Landscape. The Complete History of Britain's Trees, Woods and Hedgerows*. London.

Rackham, J. and Scaife, R.G., (in press). The environmental remains from excavations at West Deeping.

Ramm, H.G., 1970. *Shielings and Bastles*. London

Reeves, A., 1995. 'Romney Marsh: the Field-walking Evidence', in J. Eddison (ed.), 1995, 78–91.

Reeves, A., 1996. Reclamation and Cultivation: Further earthworks survey on Romney Marsh, *Unpub. Rep.*

Reeves, A., 1997. Earthworks Survey, Romney Marsh, *Archaeologia Cantiana* 116, 61–92.

Reeves, A., 2004. The testimony of trees, *Romney Marsh Irregular* 24, 21–4.

Reeves, A. and Eve, D., 1998. 'Sheep-keeping and looker's huts on Romney Marsh', in J. Eddison, M. Gardiner and A. Long (eds.), 1998, 191–207.

Riddler, I.D., 1993. 'Saxon Worked Bone', in R. J. Williams (ed.), *Pennyland and Hartigans: two Iron Age and Saxon Sites in Milton Keynes, Monograph* 4, 107–19. Aylesbury.

Riddler, I.D. and Hatton, S., forthcoming. *Objects and Waste of Bone and Antler from Ipswich Excavations, 1974–94*.

Rigold, S.E., 1964. Two Kentish Hospitals Re-examined: S. Mary, Ospringe and SS. Stephen and Thomas, New Romney, *Archaeologia Cantiana* 79, 31–69.

Rigold, S.E., 1971. Eynsford Castle, *Archaeologia Cantiana* 86, 109–71.

Rippon, S., 1996. The Gwent Levels: The Exploitation of a Wetland Landscape, *CBA Research Rep.* 105. York.

Rippon, S., 1997. *The Severn Estuary: Landscape Evolution and Wetland Reclamation*. London.

Rippon, S., 2000. *The Transformation of Coastal Wetlands: Exploitation and Management of Marshland Landscapes*. Oxford.

Rippon, S., 2001. Adaptation to a changing environment: the response of marshland communities to the late medieval 'crisis', *Journal of Wetland Archaeology* 1, 15–39.

Rippon, S., 2002. 'Romney Marsh: evolution of the historic landscape and its wider setting', in A. Long, S. Hipkin and H. Clarke (eds.), *Romney Marsh: Coastal and Landscape Change through the Ages*, 84–100. Oxford.

Robinson, D., 1983. 'Pollen and plant macrofossil analysis of deposits from the Iron Age ditched enclosure at Shiles, Govan, Glasgow', in M. Jones (ed.), Integrating Subsistence Economy, *BAR International Ser.* 181, 123–34. Oxford.

Rule, M., 1982. Reprinted/revised 1983. *The Mary Rose*. Leicester.

Ryder, M.L., 1999. Probable Fibres from Hemp (*Cannabis sativa* L.) in Bronze Age Scotland. *Environmental Archaeology* 4, 93–5.

Salisbury, E.J., 1961. *Weeds and Aliens*. London.

Salzman, L.F., 1923. *English Industries of the Middle Ages*. Oxford.

Salzman, L.F., (ed.), 1948. *Victoria County History of Cambridgeshire and Ely* 2. Oxford.

Sawyer, P.H., 1968. *Anglo-Saxon Charters: an annotated list and bibliography*. London.

Scaife, R.G., 1994. 'The plant remains', in French, C.A.I., The archaeology along the A605 Elton-Haddon Bypass, Cambridgeshire, *Fenland Archaeological Trust Monograph* 2, 154–67. Cambridge.

Scargill-Bird, S.R. (ed.), 1887. Custumals of Battle Abbey, *Camden Society, New Series*, vol. 41.

Schmid, E., 1972. *Atlas of Animal Bones*. London.

Scweingruber, F., 1990. *Microscopic Wood Anatomy* (3rd edition). Birmensdorf.

Searle, E., 1974. *Lordship and Community: Battle Abbey and its banlieu 1066–1538*. Toronto.

Searle, E., 1980. *The Chronicle of Battle Abbey*. Oxford.

Silver, I.A., 1969. 'The Ageing of Domestic Animals', in D. Brothwell, E. Higgs and G. Clark, (eds.), *Science in Archaeology* (2nd edition), 283–302. London.

Smith, P.S., 1987. 'Marine mollusca' 170–2, in T. Rook, The Roman villa site at Dicket Mead, *Herts. Arch.* 9, 79–175.

Smith, R.A.L., 1943. *Canterbury Cathedral Priory*. Cambridge.

Smith, R.A.L., 1969. *Canterbury Cathedral Priory: a Study in Monastic Administration*. Cambridge.

Somerville, E.M., 1996. 'Marine Molluscs', in M. Gardiner, M. Russell and D. Gregory, Excavations at Lewes Friary 1985–6 and 1988–9, *Sussex Archaeological Collections* 134, 71–123.

Somerville, E.M., 1997. 'Marine Shells', in M. Lyne, Lewes Priory: excavations by Richard Lewis 1969–82, 167–70, *Lewes Priory Trust*. Lewes.

Somerville, E.M., forthcoming. 'The Shell', in L. Barber and L. Sibun, *Excavations at St Nicholas' Hospital, Lewes, East Sussex*.

Spencer, C., Plater, A. and Long, A., 1998. 'Holocene barrier estuary evolution: the sedimentary record of the Walland Marsh region', in J. Eddison, M. Gardiner and A. Long (eds.), 1998, 13–29.

Stace, C., 1991. *New Flora of the British Isles*. Cambridge.

Stace, C., 1997. *New Flora of the British Isles* (2nd edition). Cambridge.

Stephens, H., 1855. *The Book of the Farm*. Edinburgh.

Steane, J.M. and Foreman, M., 1991. 'The archaeology of medieval fishing tackle', in G.L. Good, R.H. Jones and M.W. Ponsford (eds.), Waterfront Archaeology: Proceedings of the Third international Conference, *CBA Research Report* 74, 88–101. London.

Stevens, S., 1996. Fieldwalking at Denge West South, Lydd, Kent, *SEAS Unpub. Rep. Project* 372.

Stone, D., 2003. The productivity and management of sheep in late medieval England, *Agricultural History Review* 51, 1–22.

Stubbs, W. (ed.), 1880. *The Historical Works of Gervase of Canterbury*, vol. 2. London.

Sweetinburgh, S., 2000. The cellarer and the cheese: dairying on the manor of Agney, *c*. 1280–1350, *Romney Marsh Irregular* 15, 6–9.

Sweetinburgh, S., 2002. 'Land holding and the land market in a 15th century peasant community', in A. Long, S. Hipkin and H. Clarke (eds.), *Romney Marsh: Coastal and Landscape Change through the Ages*, 140–56. Oxford.

Sweetinburgh, S., forthcoming. 'Hooks, nets and boats: sharing the catch in Kentish fishing communities', in A.F. Butcher (ed.), *Strategies of Inheritance in Late Medieval Kent.*

Tatton-Brown, T., 1988. 'The topography of the Walland Marsh area between the eleventh and thirteenth centuries', in J. Eddison and C. Green (eds.), 1988, 105–11.

Taylor, C.C., 1983. *Village and Farmstead: a History of Rural Settlement in England.* London.

Thirsk, J., 1997. *Alternative Agriculture, A History from the Black Death to the Present Day.* Oxford.

Tinsley, H.M. and Smith, R.T., 1974. Ecological investigations at a Romano-British earthwork in the Yorkshire Pennines, *Yorkshire Archaeological Journal* 46, 23–33.

Tooley, M., 1995. 'Romney Marsh: the debatable ground', in J. Eddison (ed.), 1995, 1–7.

Trice Martin, C., 1877. *Catalogue of the Archives in the Muniment Room of All Souls' College.* London.

Tyson, R., 2000. *Medieval Glass Vessels found in England c. AD 1200–1500*, CBA Research Report 121. York.

Ulbricht, I., Die Verarbeitung von Knochen, I., 1984. Geweth und Horn im mittelalterlichen Scheleswig, Ausgrabungen in Schleswig, *Berichte und Studien* 3, taf 95, 2–3.

Vince, A., 2003. Characterisation Studies of some Medieval Pottery from Lydd Quarry, Kent, *Unpub. Archive Report for ASE* (AVAC Report 2003/106).

Vince, A. and Jenner, A., 1991. 'The Saxon and Early Medieval Pottery of London', in A. Vince (ed.), Aspects of Saxo-Norman London: 2. Finds and Environmental Evidence, *LAMAS Special Paper* 12, 19–119. London.

Vollens, E., 1995. 'Medieval salt-making and the inning of tidal marshes at Belgar, Lydd', in J. Eddison (ed.), 1995, 118–26.

Wade-Martins, P., 1980. Fieldwork and Excavation on Village Sites in Launditch Hundred, Norfolk, *East Anglian Archaeology* 10. Dereham.

Wallenberg, J.K., 1934. *The Place-Names of Kent.* Uppsala.

Waller, M., Burrin, P. and Marlow, A., 1988. 'Flandrian Sedimentation and palaeoenvironments in Pett Level, the Brede and lower Rother valleys and Walland Marsh', in J. Eddison and C. Green (eds.), 1988, 3–29.

Walne, P., 1974. *The Culture of Bivalve Molluscs: 50 Years Experience at Conwy, West Byfleet.*

Ward, A., 1997. 'Transhumance and settlement in the Welsh uplands: a view from the Black Mountain', in N. Edwards (ed.), Landscape and Settlement in Medieval Wales, *Oxbow Monograph* 81, 97–111. Oxford.

Ward, G., 1931. Saxon Lydd, *Archaeologia Cantiana* 43, 29–37.

Ward, G., 1936. The Wilmington Charter of A.D. 700, *Archaeologia Cantiana* 48, 11–28.

Williams, B.B., 1984. Excavations at Ballyutoag, County Antrim, *Ulster Journal of Archaeology* 47, 37–49.

Williams, V., 1988. 'Bone, Antler and Ivory Objects', in B. Ayers, Excavations at St. Martin-at-Palace-Plain, Norwich, 1981, *East Anglian Archaeology* 37, 100–7. Dereham.

Willson, J., 1987. Medieval Buildings Discovered at New Romney, *Kent Archaeological Review* 89, 198–212.

Wilson, B. and Edwards, P., 1993. Butchery of horse and dog at Witney Palace, Oxfordshire, and the knackering and feeding of meat to hounds during the post-medieval period, *Post-Medieval Archaeology* 27, 43–56.

Whitehead, R., 1996. *Buckles 1250–1800.* Chelmsford.

Winder, J., 1980. 'The marine mollusca', in P. Holdsworth, *Excavations at Melbourne Street Southampton 1971–6*, 121–7, CBA Research Report 33. London.

Winder, J., 1992. A Study of the Variation in Oyster Shells from Archaeological Sites and a Discussion of Oyster Exploitation, *PhD thesis, Southampton University.*

Wood, W., 1996. 'The Animal Bone', in I. Greig and M. Gardiner, 1996, 32–37.

Zell, M.L., 1994. *Industry in the Countryside: Wealden society in the sixteenth century.* Cambridge.

Index

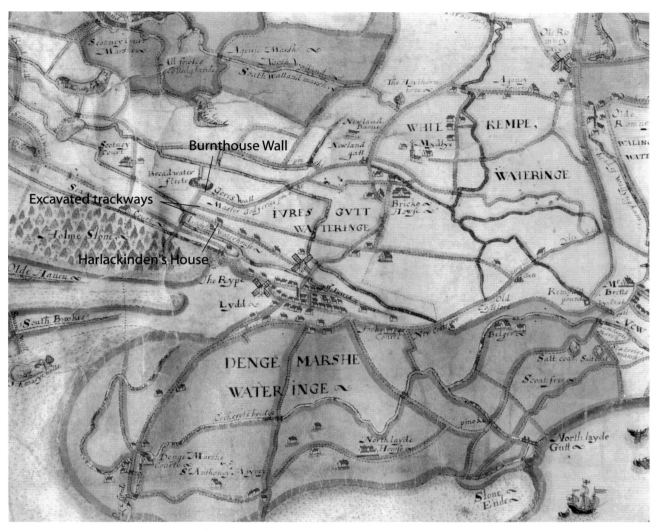

Burnthouse Wall

Excavated trackways

Harlackinden's House

Fig. 3 Reproduction of part of Poker's map showing excavated area at Lydd Quarry (north to top of page) (see the converging trackways to the south of Gores Wall). (© Maidstone Museum)

Fig. 8 Topsoil stripping at Lydd 1. (Ian Greig © UCLFAU)

Fig. 11 Aerial photograph of Lydd 1 after topsoil stripping (from the south, looking north-east) (photo taken by the late Graham Alleyne). (© UCLFAU)

Fig. 12 Aerial photograph of Lydd 1 after topsoil stripping (from west, looking east) (photo taken by the late Graham Alleyne). (© UCLFAU)

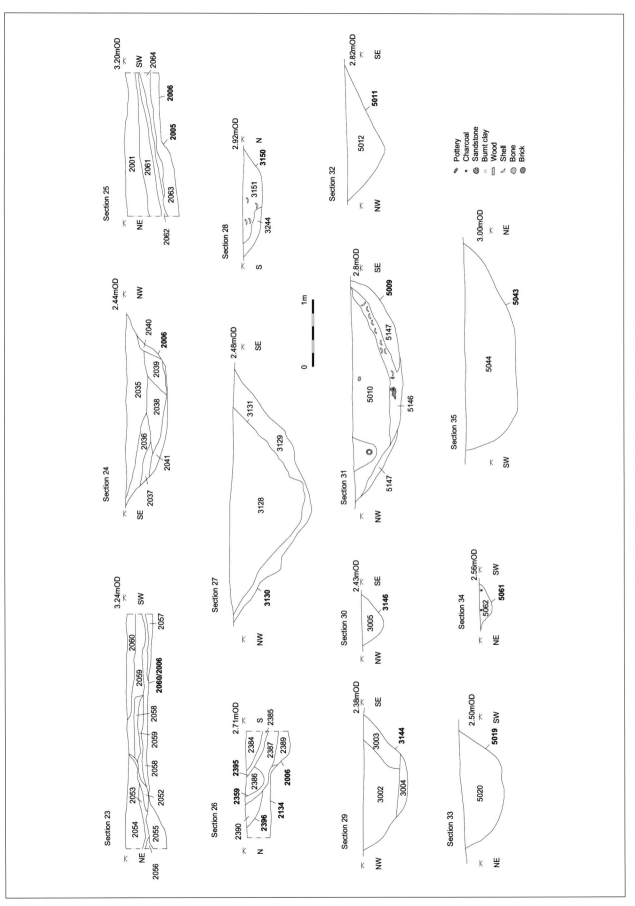

Fig. 25 Lydd Quarry, Ditch System: Sections 23–35

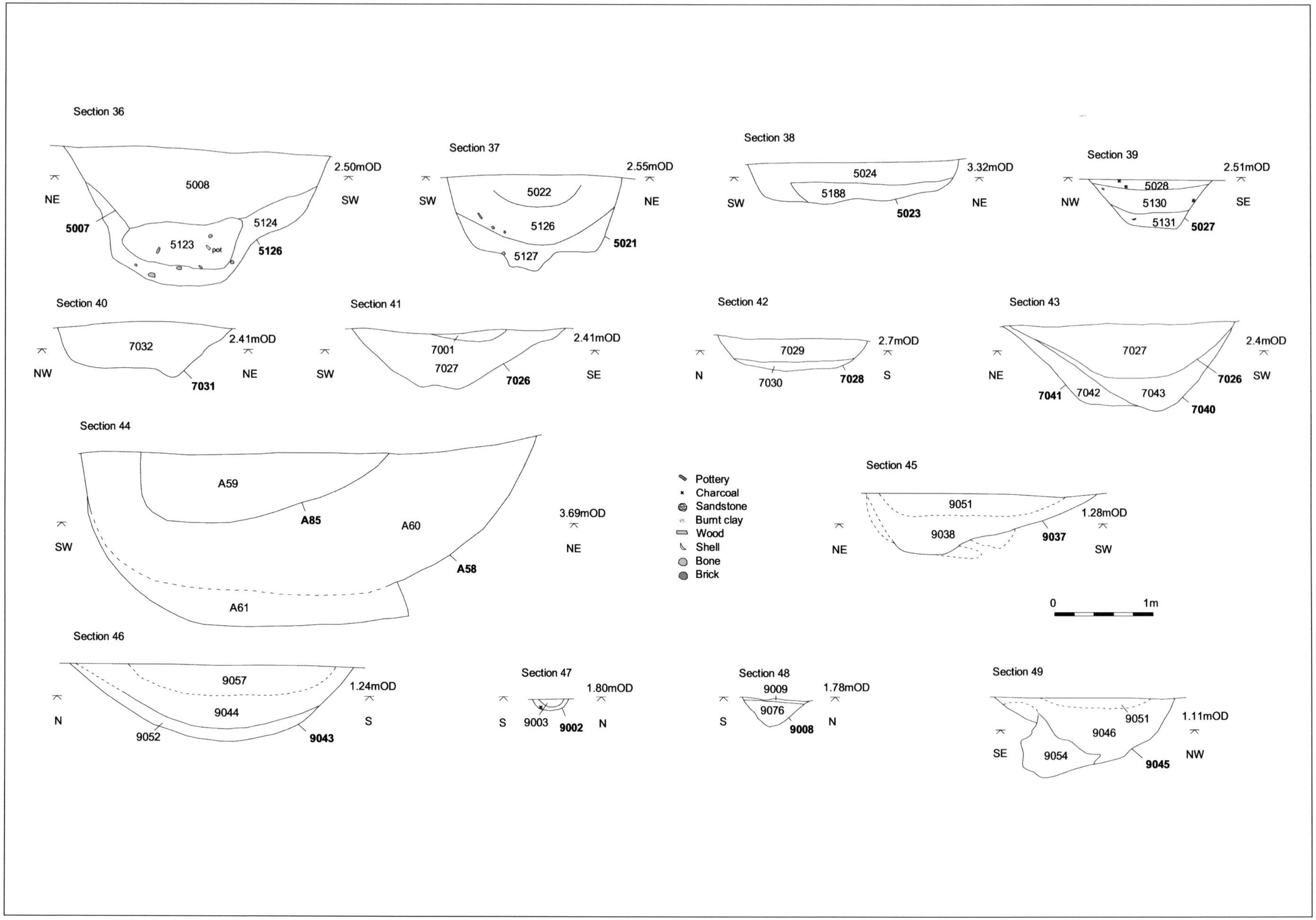

Fig. 26 Lydd Quarry, Ditch System: Sections 36–49

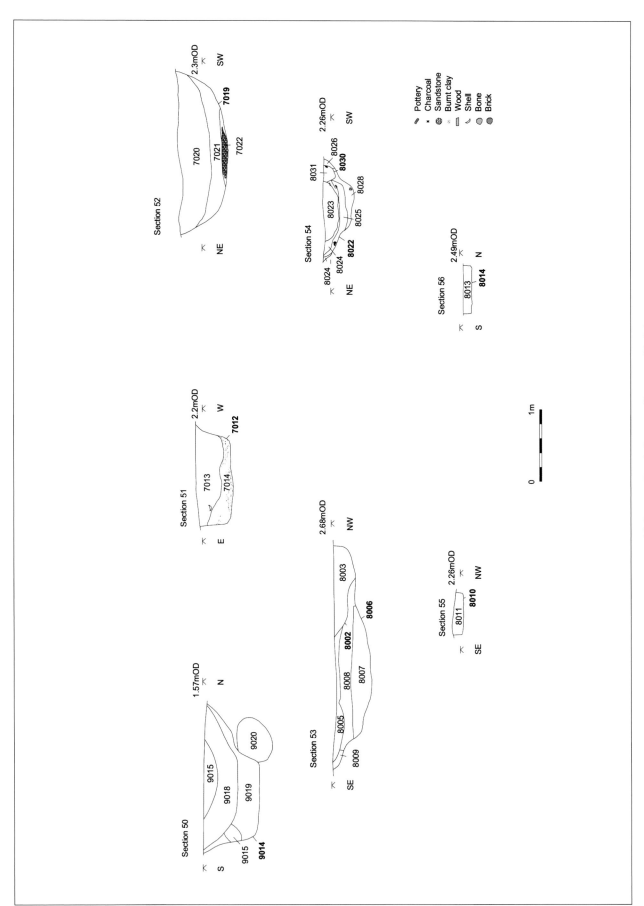

Fig. 27 Lydd Quarry, Ditch System: Sections 50–56

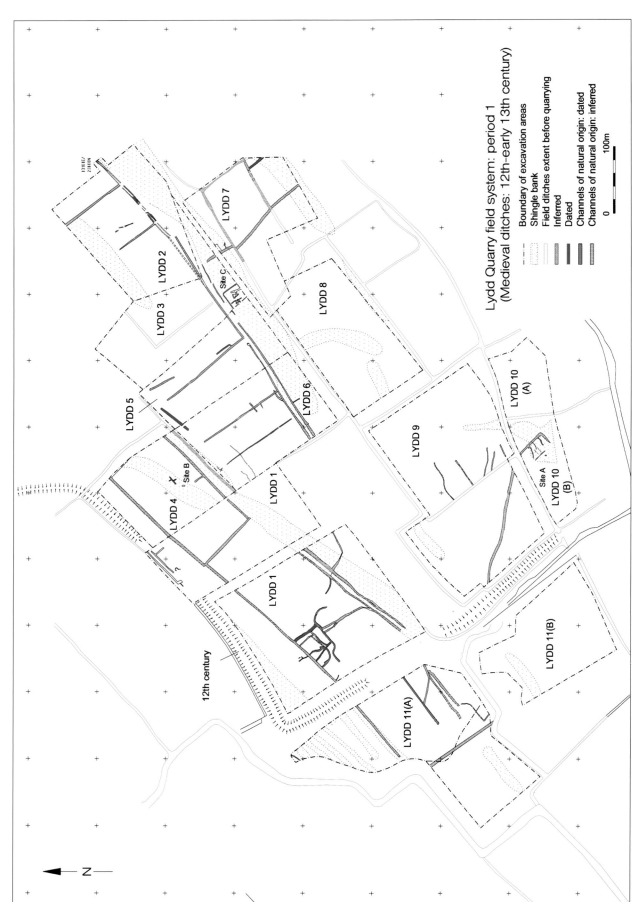

Lydd Quarry field system: period 1
(Medieval ditches: 12th–early 13th century)

Boundary of excavation areas
Shingle bank
Field ditches extent before quarrying
Inferred
Dated
Channels of natural origin: dated
Channels of natural origin: inferred

0   100m

LYDD 2

LYDD 3

LYDD 5

LYDD 4

LYDD 1

LYDD 1

12th century

LYDD 11(A)

LYDD 11(B)

LYDD 7

Site C

LYDD 8

LYDD 6

LYDD 9

LYDD 10
(A)

Site A
LYDD 10
(B)

Site B

N

Fig. 28 Lydd Quarry, Field System Phasing: 12th to early 13th century

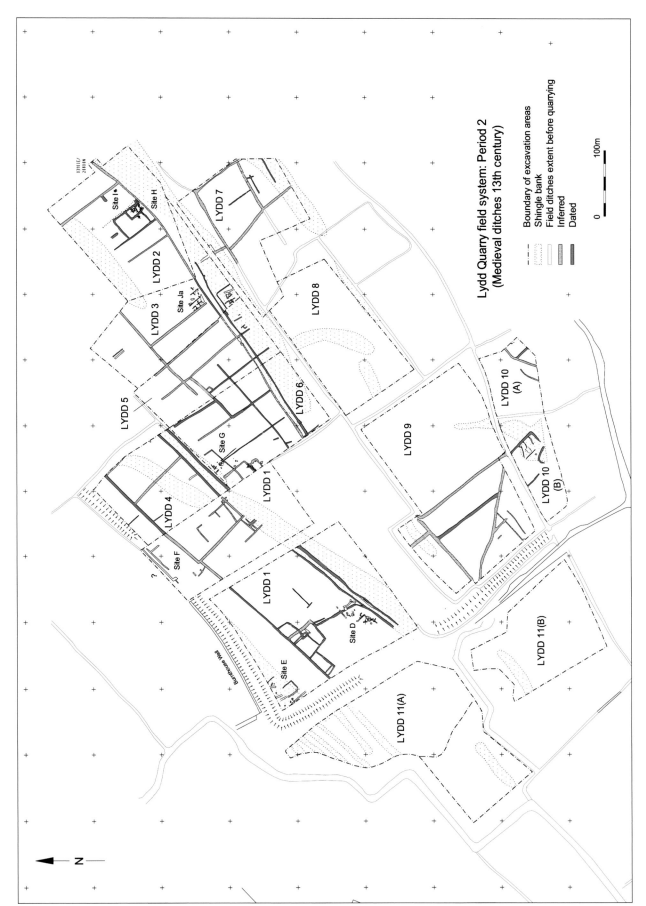

Lydd Quarry field system: Period 2
(Medieval ditches 13th century)

Boundary of excavation areas
Shingle bank
Field ditches extent before quarrying
Inferred
Dated

0   100m

Site I •
Site H
Site Ja
Site G
Site F
Site E
Site D

Barnhouse Wall

LYDD 1
LYDD 2
LYDD 3
LYDD 4
LYDD 5
LYDD 6
LYDD 7
LYDD 8
LYDD 9
LYDD 10 (A)
LYDD 10 (B)
LYDD 11(A)
LYDD 11(B)

N

Fig. 29 Lydd Quarry, Field System Phasing: 13th century

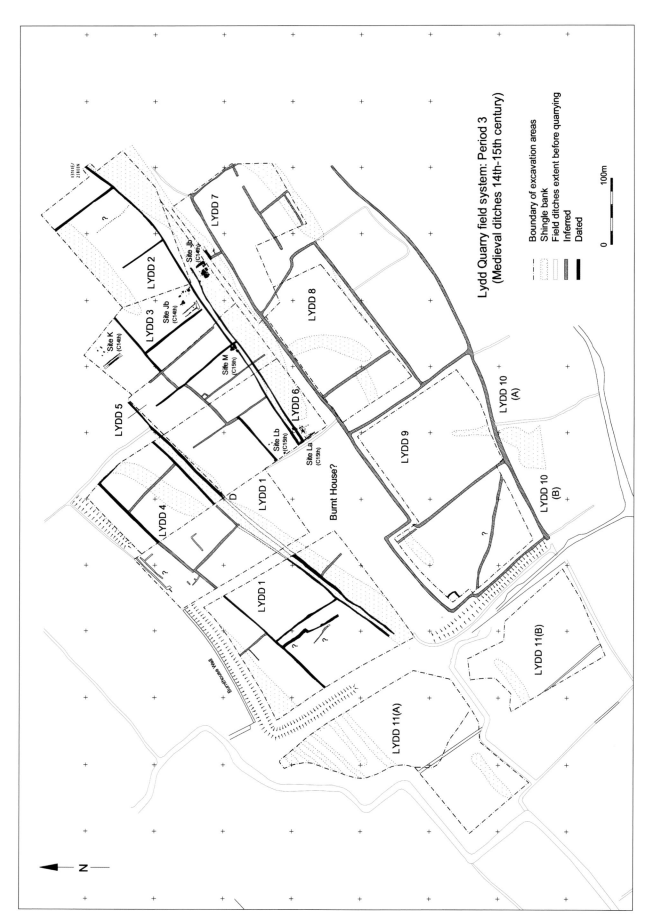

Lydd Quarry field system: Period 3
(Medieval ditches 14th–15th century)

LYDD 7

LYDD 2

LYDD 3

Site Jb
(C14th)

Site K
(C14th)

Site Jb
(C14th)

Site M
(C15th)

LYDD 8

LYDD 5

LYDD 6

Site Lb
(C15th)

Site La
(C15th)

Burnt House?

LYDD 4

LYDD 1

D

LYDD 9

LYDD 10
(A)

LYDD 10
(B)

Burnthouse Wall

LYDD 1

LYDD 11(A)

LYDD 11(B)

N

Boundary of excavation areas

Shingle bank

Field ditches extent before quarrying

Inferred

Dated

0   100m

Fig. 30 Lydd Quarry, Field System Phasing: 14th to 15th century

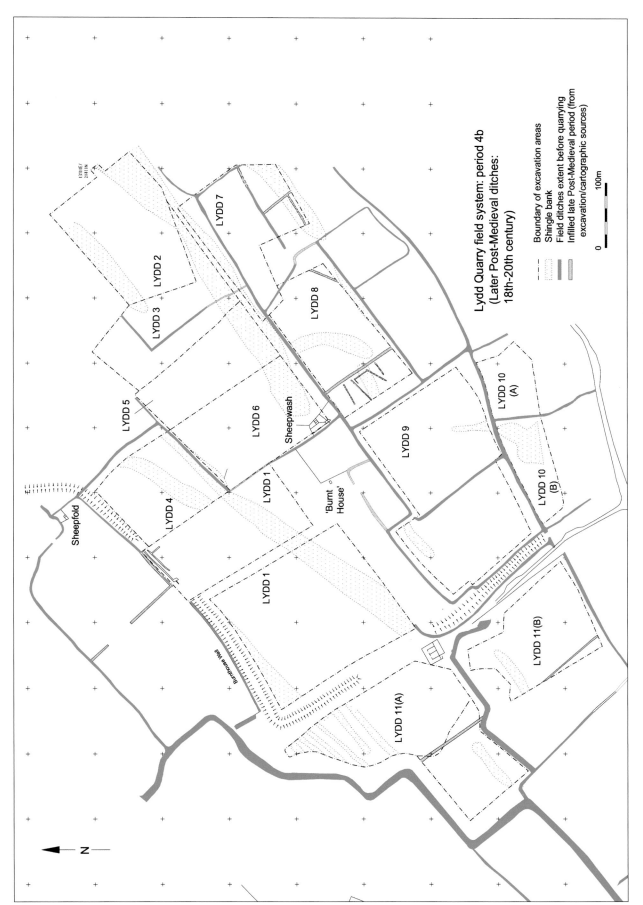

Fig. 31 Lydd Quarry, Field System Phasing: Later Post-medieval

Lydd Quarry field system: period 4b
(Later Post-Medieval ditches:
18th–20th century)

— · — Boundary of excavation areas
Shingle bank
Field ditches extent before quarrying
Infilled late Post-Medieval period (from
excavation/cartographic sources)

0 ____ 100m

LYDD 7
LYDD 2
LYDD 3
LYDD 8
LYDD 5
LYDD 6
Sheepwash
LYDD 1
LYDD 4
LYDD 10 (A)
LYDD 9
LYDD 10 (B)
'Burnt House'
Sheepfold
Burnthouse Wall
LYDD 1
LYDD 11(A)
LYDD 11(B)

N

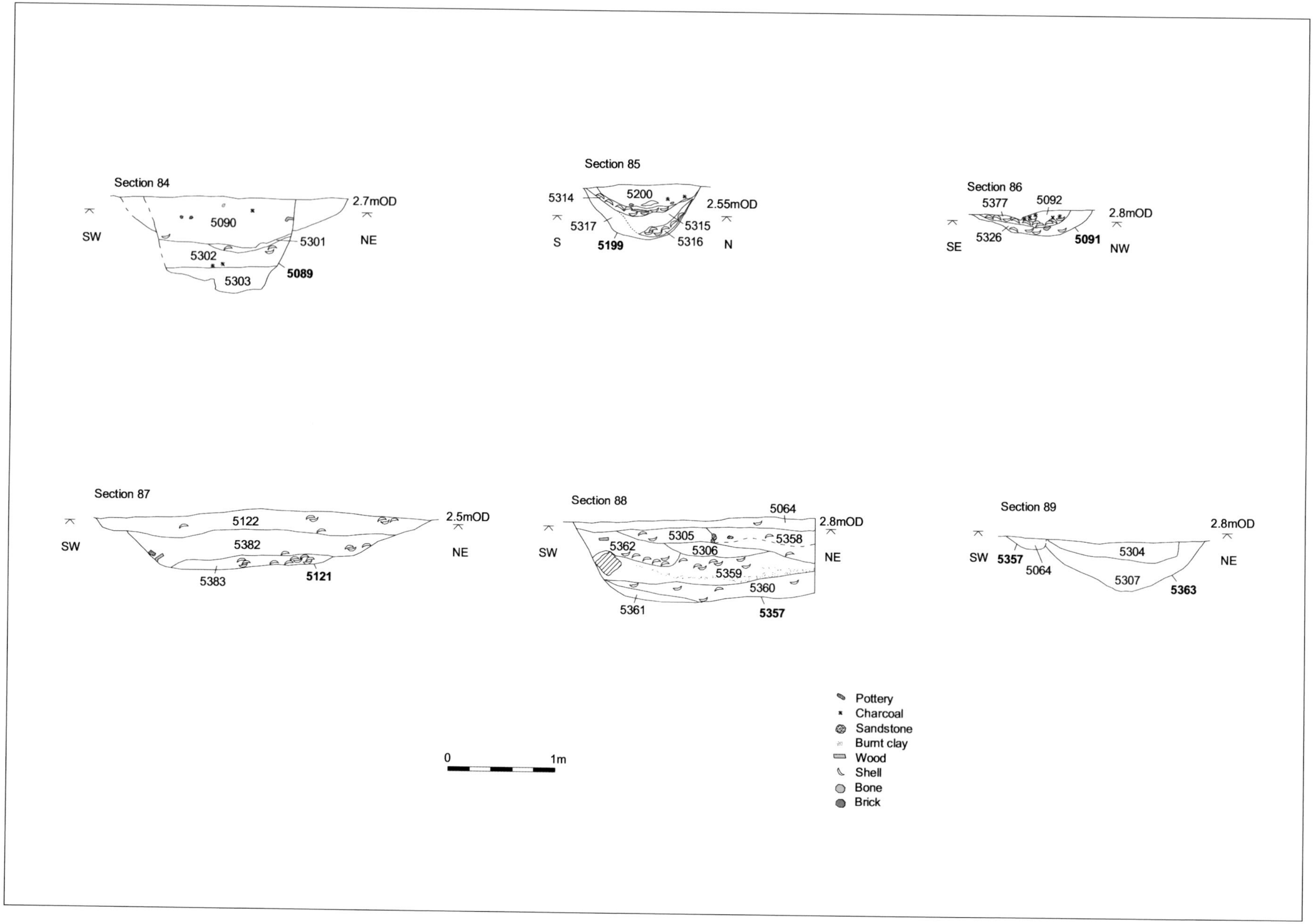

Fig. 40 Lydd Quarry, Site G: Sections 84–89

Legend:
- Pottery
- Charcoal
- Sandstone
- Burnt clay
- Wood
- Shell
- Bone
- Brick

Section 84
SW / NE
2.7mOD
5301
5089
5090
5302
5303

Section 85
S / N
2.55mOD
5314
5200
5315
5316
5317
5199

Section 86
SE / NW
2.8mOD
5377
5092
5326
5091

Section 87
SW / NE
2.5mOD
5122
5382
5121
5383

Section 88
SW / NE
2.8mOD
5064
5358
5360
5357
5359
5305
5306
5362
5361

Section 89
SW / NE
2.8mOD
5304
5307
5363
5357
5064

0   1m

Fig. 41 Lydd 5/6 shell midden Pit 5115. (Jennifer Sawyer © UCLFAU)

*Fig. 44 Reconstruction drawing of Site H in the 13th century from the south, looking north
(Casper Johnson © UCLFAU)*

Fig. 47 Lydd Quarry, Site Jb gravel floor being extracted, looking south
(Greg Priestley-Bell © UCLFAU)

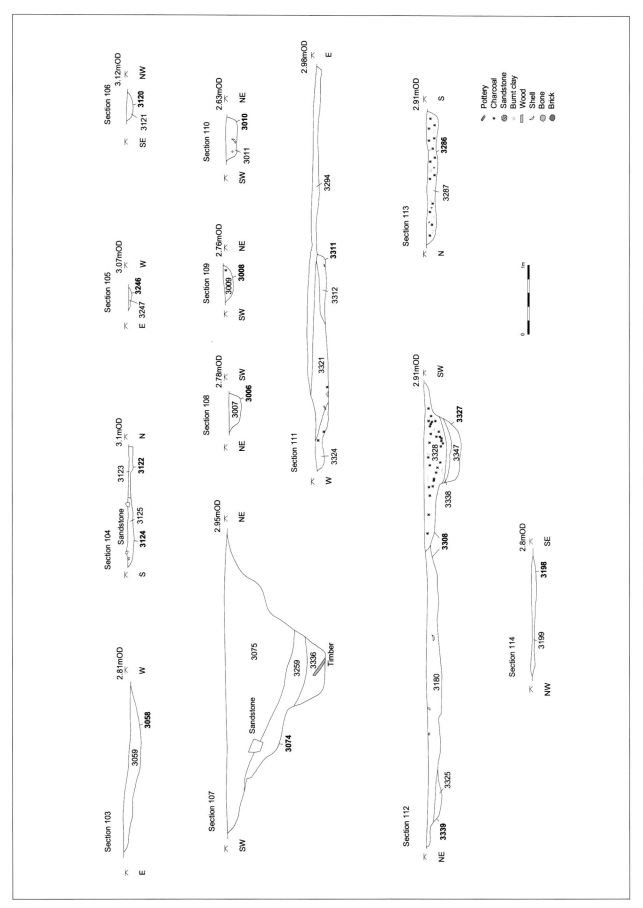

Fig. 48 Lydd Quarry, Sites Ja and Jb: Sections 103–114

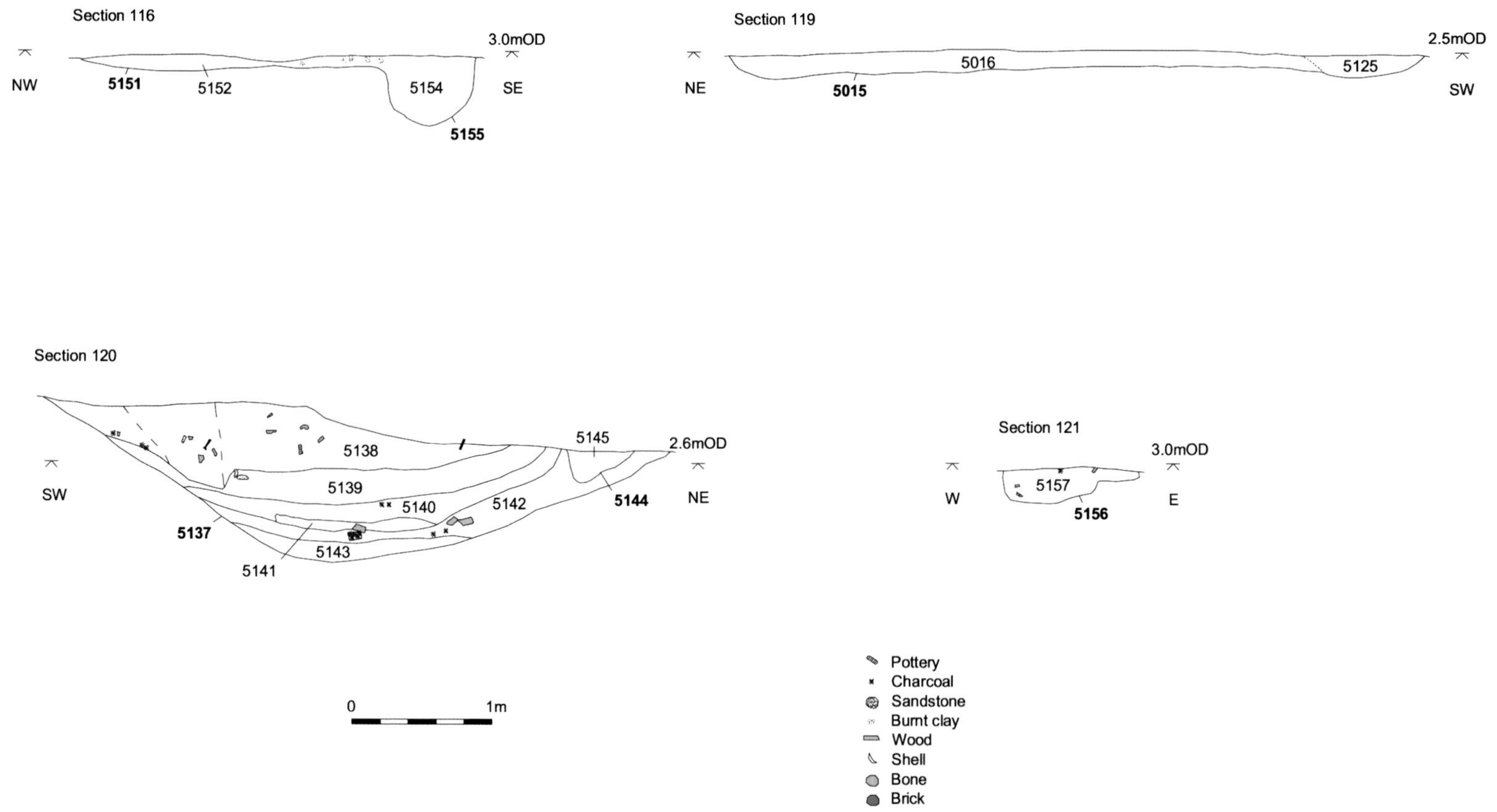

Fig. 54 Lydd Quarry, Sites La and M: Sections 116 and 119–121

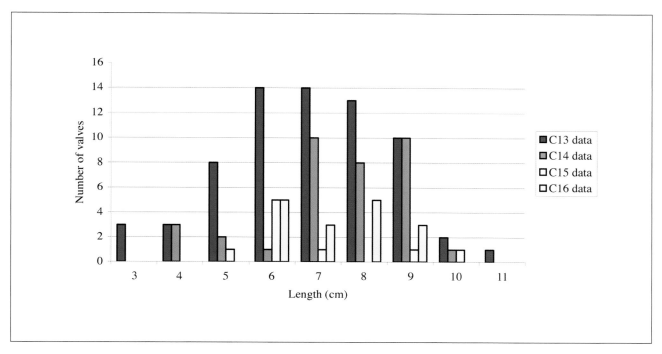

Fig. 92 Graph showing length of oyster valves

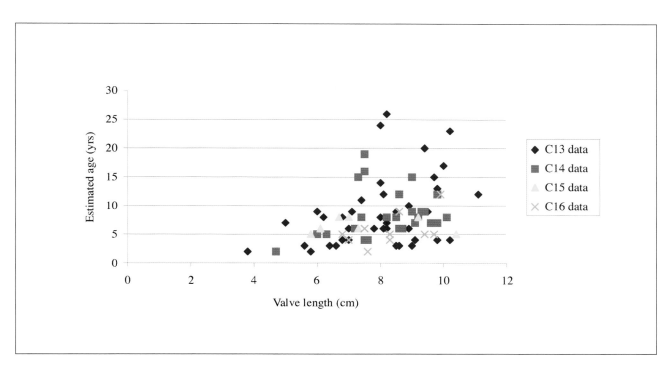

Fig. 93 Scatter plot of age: valve length for oysters

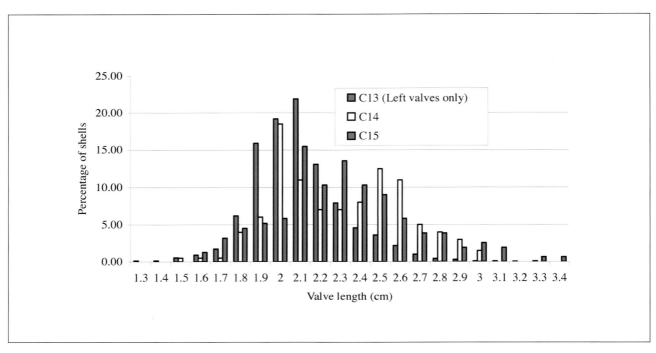

Fig. 94 Graph showing cockle valve length